Dedications

To the memory of my parents, Glenn and Rosemary Austin, my first teachers. – *Julie Anderson*

A ma mère, trop tôt disparue, et à mon père. – *Hervé Franceschi*

Preface

The Purpose of this Book and Its Audience

Java 5 Illuminated covers all of the material required for the successful completion of an introductory course in Java. While the focus is on presenting the material required for the Computer Science I (CS1) curriculum, students enrolled in Information Systems, Information Technology, or self-directed study courses will find the book useful, as well. It has been written to provide introductory computer science students with a comprehensive overview of the fundamentals of programming with Java. In addition, the book presents other optional topics of interest, including graphical user interfaces (GUI), data structures, file input and output, and applets.

Throughout the book, we have attempted to take an "active learning" approach to presenting the material. Instead of merely presenting the concepts to students in a one-sided, rote manner, we have asked them to take an active role in their understanding of the language through the use of numerous interactive examples, exercises, and projects.

Coverage and Approach

Our approach is to teach Object-Oriented Programming in a progressive manner. We start in Chapter 1 by presenting an overview of object-oriented programming. In Chapter 3, we delve a little deeper into the concepts of classes and objects and introduce the student to many of the useful classes in the Java Class Library. Our emphasis at this point is on using classes; we teach the student how to read APIs in order to determine how to instantiate objects and call methods of the classes. In Chapter 7, we move on to designing user-defined classes, and in Chapter 10, we present inheritance, polymorphism, and interfaces. Throughout the book, we present concepts in an object-oriented context.

Throughout the book, we emphasize good software engineering practices, focusing on designing and writing correct, maintainable programs. As such, we discuss pseudocode, testing techniques, design tradeoffs, and other software engineering tips.

We teach the student basic programming techniques, such as accumulation, counting, calculating an average, finding maximum and minimum values, using flag and toggle variables, and basic searching and sorting algorithms. In doing so, we emphasize the patterns inherent in programming. Concepts are taught first, followed by fully implemented examples with source code. We promote Java standards, conventions, and methodologies.

This book supports the important new features of the latest version of Sun Microsystems' Java, 5.0. The Scanner class is used to simplify user input from the keyboard. The new *enum* functionality is presented as a user-defined data type in Chapter 7. Autoboxing and unboxing concepts are introduced in Chapter 3 with the Java wrapper classes, and are demonstrated with parameterized types and the enhanced *for* loop in the Chapter 9 coverage of ArrayLists.

Learning Features

Recognizing today's students' growing interest in animation and visualization, we distribute techniques for producing graphical output and animation throughout the book, starting in Chapter 4 with applets. An example using either animation or graphical output is included in most chapters. Instructors who are not interested in incorporating graphics into their curriculum can simply skip these sections. In addition, some of our examples are small games, which we find motivational for students.

In each chapter, we include one or two Programming Activities, which are designed to provide visual feedback to the students so that they can assess the correctness of their code. In most Programming Activities, we provide a framework, usually with a graphical user interface, to which the student adds code to complete the application. The student should be able to finish the Programming Activity in about 15 to 20 minutes; thus, these activities can be used in the classroom to reinforce the topics just presented. Each Programming Activity also includes several discussion questions that test the student's understanding of the concepts the activity illustrates. The Programming Activities are also appropriate for a closed or open laboratory environment. In short, this book can be used in a traditional lecture environment, a computer-equipped classroom, or a lab environment.

In addition, we supplement each chapter with a browser-based module that animates sample code, illustrating visually the assignment of variable values, evaluation of conditions, and flow of control.

Java 5 Illuminated provides the instructor and students with an extensive variety of end-of-chapter material: multiple-choice questions, examples that ask the student to predict the output of prewritten code or to fill in missing code, debugging activities, short exercises, programming projects, technical writing assignments, and a higher-difficulty group project.

Chapter-by-Chapter Overview

The chapters are logically organized from simple to more difficult topics, while incorporating Object Orientation as needed, taking into account the specifics of the Java language. Here is a brief summary of the topics covered in each chapter:

Chapter 1: Introduction to Programming and the Java Language

We introduce the student to the concept of programming, first covering computer hardware and operating systems, and following with a brief evolution of programming languages, including an introduction to object-oriented programming. We explain programming basics and pseudocode as a program design technique. The student writes, compiles, and debugs their first program using an integrated development environment.

Chapter 2: Programming Building Blocks—Java Basics

In this chapter, we concentrate on working with variables and constants of primitive data types and composing arithmetic expressions. We illustrate the differences between integer and floating-point calculations and introduce operator precedence.

Chapter 3: Object-Oriented Programming, Part 1: Using Classes

Chapter 3 introduces classes from the user, or client, standpoint and discusses the benefits of encapsulation and code reuse. The student learns how to instantiate objects and call methods. We also demonstrate useful Java classes for console input and output, dialog boxes, formatting output, performing mathematical calculations, and generating random numbers.

Chapter 4: Introduction to Applets and Graphics

Chapter 4 presents several methods of the Graphics class that can be used to create graphical output by drawing shapes and text. The windowing graphics coordinate system is explained and using color is also explored. We demonstrate these graphics methods in applets because an applet window provides an easy-to-use palette for drawing. Instructors wishing to postpone or skip Graphics coverage altogether can use as little or as much of this chapter as they desire.

Chapter 5: Flow of Control, Part 1: Selection

Various forms of the *if*, *if/else*, and *if/else if* statement are presented, along with the appropriate situations in which to use each form. We also demonstrate nested *if/else* statements and testing techniques. As part of our object-oriented programming coverage, we teach the importance of comparing objects using the *equals* method. This chapter also covers the conditional operator and the *switch* statement.

Chapter 6: Flow of Control, Part 2: Looping

This is probably the most important chapter in the book. We have found that looping and repetition are the most difficult basic programming concepts for the average student to grasp. We try to ease the student's understanding of looping techniques by presenting patterns to follow in coding basic algorithms: accumulation, counting, calculating an average, and finding minimum and maximum values. We present a motivational and engaging example of repetition in the animation of a ball rolling across the screen. Looping is further explored as a tool for validation of input values. We concentrate on using the *while* loop for event-controlled and sentinel-controlled repetition, and the *for* loop for count-controlled looping. A large section focuses on constructing loop conditions, which is often a challenging task for the student. Sections are also provided on testing techniques for *while* loops and for *for* loops. In this chapter, we also introduce reading data from a text file using the *Scanner* class.

Chapter 7: Object-Oriented Programming, Part 2: User-Defined Classes

In this chapter, we teach the student to write classes, as well as client applications that use the instantiated objects and call methods of the class. We present class design techniques and standard patterns for writing constructors, mutators and accessors, and the *toString, equals,* and other user-defined methods. We also explain how and when to use the keywords *this* and *static. Enum* is also covered as a user-defined class type. Finally, we teach the student how to use Javadoc and how to create a package.

Chapter 8: Single-Dimensional Arrays

This chapter begins with the declaration, instantiation, and initialization of single-dimensional arrays. From there, the student learns to perform the basic programming techniques (accumulation, counting, calculating an average, and finding maximum and minimum values) on array elements. We also cover arrays as instance variables of a class, and demonstrate maintaining encapsulation while accepting arrays as method parameters. Basic searching and sorting algorithms are also presented, including sequential and binary searches and selection and bubble sorts.

Chapter 9: Multidimensional Arrays and the *ArrayList* Class

We focus in this chapter on two-dimensional array processing, including techniques for processing all the elements in the entire array, or the elements in a specific column or row. We also demonstrate the extra processing needed to handle arrays with rows of different lengths. A bar chart of the data in each row of the array is also demonstrated. In addition, we extrapolate the concepts from two-dimensional arrays to discuss multidimensional arrays.

We present the *ArrayList* class as an expandable array and demonstrate Java 5's enhanced *for* loop, as well as autoboxing and unboxing.

Chapter 10: Object-Oriented Programming, Part 3: Inheritance, Polymorphism, and Interfaces

Continuing our object-oriented programming coverage, we discuss the important concepts and benefits of inheritance and the design of class hierarchies, including abstract classes. We cover inherited members of a class, constructing objects of a subclass, adding specialization to a subclass, overriding inherited methods, and calling methods of the superclass. We discuss the tradeoffs of declaring members as *protected* versus *private*. We demonstrate polymorphism with a graphical example, and introduce the student to interfaces, which are used extensively in Graphical User Interfaces. (See Chapter 12.)

Chapter 11: Exceptions and Input/Output Operations

Recognizing that building robust applications requires error handling, we present exception handling as a tool for validating user input and recovering from errors at run time. We demonstrate handling predefined exceptions and writing user-defined exceptions.

With this knowledge, the student is ready to perform file input and output operations. We demonstrate reading and writing *Strings* and primitive data types to text files, and reading and writing objects directly to files. The *StringTokenizer* class is also presented for parsing input from structured text files.

Chapter 12: Graphical User Interfaces

This chapter introduces the student to event-driven programming, and writing event handlers for text fields, buttons, radio buttons, checkboxes, lists, combo boxes, and mouse activities. We also demonstrate panels and several layout managers for organizing GUI components as well as how to nest components.

Chapter 13: Recursion

Recursion is presented as a design technique, reducing the size of a problem until an easy-to-solve problem is reached. We demonstrate recursive methods with one base case and with multiple base cases, and with and without return values. Specific examples provided include computing the factorial of a number, finding the greatest common divisor, performing a binary search, determining if a phrase is a palindrome, calculating combinations, solving the Towers of Hanoi problem, and performing animation. The benefits and trade-offs of recursion versus iteration are also discussed.

Chapter 14: An Introduction to Data Structures

Throughout this chapter, we use a user-defined, nongeneric *Player* class to present the concepts and implementations of various types of linked lists, stacks, and queues. The elements stored in a linked list, stack, or queue are *Players*. Thus, our approach is object-oriented without being too abstract. We cover many types and uses of a linked list: a singly linked list, a linked list as a stack, a linked list as a queue, a doubly linked list, a sorted linked list, and a recursively defined linked list. Arrays as stacks and circular arrays as queues are also covered in great detail.

Pedagogy

Concepts are always taught first, followed by complete, executable examples illustrating these concepts. Most examples demonstrate real-life applications so that the student can understand the need for the concept at hand. The example code is colored to better illustrate the syntax of the code and to reflect the use of colors in today's IDE tools, as shown in this example from Chapter 3:

```
1  /*  A demonstration of reading from the console using Scanner
2      Anderson, Franceschi
3  */
4
5  import java.util.Scanner;
6
7  public class DataInput
8  {
9    public static void main( String [ ] args )
10   {
11       Scanner scan = new Scanner( System.in );
12
13       System.out.print( "Enter your first name > " );
14       String firstName = scan.next( );
15       System.out.println( "Your name is " + firstName );
16
17       System.out.print( "\nEnter your age as an integer > " );
18       int age = scan.nextInt( );
19       System.out.println( "Your age is " + age );
20
21       System.out.print( "\nEnter your GPA > " );
22       float gpa = scan.nextFloat( );
23       System.out.println( "Your GPA is " + gpa );
24   }
25 }
```

EXAMPLE 3.18   Reading from the Console using *Scanner*

Tables and figures are used to illustrate or summarize the concept at hand, such as these from Chapters 6 and 7:

Figure 6.1

Flow of Control of a *while* Loop

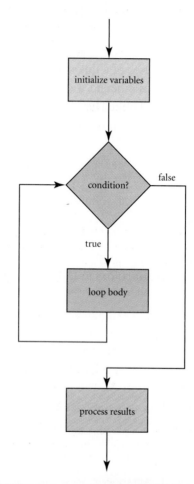

TABLE 7.1 Access Modifiers	
Access Modifier	**Class or member can be referenced by . . .**
public	methods of the same class, as well as methods of other classes
private	methods of the same class only
protected	methods in the same class, as well as methods of subclasses and methods in classes in the same package
no modifier (package access)	methods in the same package only

In each chapter, we emphasize good design concepts using "Software Engineering Tips," such as the one to the right from Chapter 7.

We also provide "Common Error Traps," such as the one to the right from Chapter 5, to alert students against common syntax and logic errors.

In each chapter, "active learning" programming activities reinforce concepts with enjoyable, hands-on projects that provide visual feedback to the students. These activities can be done in lab-type classrooms or can be assigned as projects. A header for a Programming Activity looks like this:

SOFTWARE ENGINEERING TIP

Define instance variables of a class as *private* so that only methods of the class will be able to set or change their values.

COMMON ERROR TRAP

Be sure that both operands of the logical AND and logical OR operators are *boolean* expressions. Expressions such as this: x < y && z, with x, y, and z being numeric types, are illegal. Instead, use the expression:

x < y && x < z

6.9   Programming Activity 1: Using *while* Loops

In this activity, you will work with a sentinel-controlled *while* loop, performing this activity:

Write a *while* loop to process the contents of a grocery cart and calculate the total price of the items. It is important to understand that, in this example, we do not know how many items are in the cart.

Supplementing each chapter, we provide a browser-based module (developed in Director and implemented as Shockwave animation) on the CD-ROM, which illustrates the execution of code that implements the concepts taught in the chapter. Each movie animates a brief code sample, one line at a time, and is controlled by the user via a "Next Step" button. These modules can be beneficial for students who learn best with visual aids, graphs, illustrations, and at their own pace outside the classroom. The modules are announced in each chapter using a special icon as in the sample below.

CODE IN ACTION

In the Chapter 6 folder on the CD-ROM included with this book, you will find a Shockwave movie showing a step-by-step illustration of a *for* loop. Just double-click on *Loops.html* to start the movie.

Graphics Coverage

Graphics are distributed throughout the book, and are used to engage the student and reinforce the chapter concepts. The Graphics coordinate system, methods for drawing shapes and text, and color concepts are presented with simple applets in Chapter 4. Animation using loops is demonstrated in Chapter 6, while drawing a bull's-eye target illustrates both looping and using a toggle variable. Classes for displayable objects are presented in Chapter 7; drawing a bar chart of array data is illustrated in Chapters 8 and 9; and polymorphism is demonstrated using a Tortoise and Hare Race in Chapter 10; GUIs are covered in Chapter 12; and animation using recursion is demonstrated in Chapter 13. The two figures below illustrate graphical examples from Chapters 7 and 8.

Figure 7.10

The *AstronautClient2* Window

Figure 8.15

The *cellBills* Array as a Bar Chart

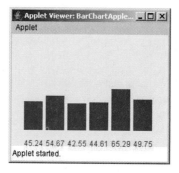

End-of-Chapter Exercises and Problems

A large collection of exercises and problems is proposed at the end of each chapter. Short and small exercises cover programming from a variety of angles: multiple choice concept questions, reading and understanding code segments, filling in some code, correcting errors, and interpreting compiler error messages to diagnose application bugs. Many programming projects are proposed with an emphasis on writing *classes,* not just a *program.* A more challenging group project is proposed in each chapter, allowing students to work as a group and develop communications skills, in accordance with recommendations from accreditation organizations. Small, essay-type questions are also proposed to enable students to acquire proficiency in technical writing and communication.

CD-ROM Accompanying this Book

Included in the CD-ROM accompanying this book are:

- Programming Activity framework code
- Full example code from each chapter
- Browser-based modules with visual step-by-step demonstrations of code execution
- The following Integrated Development Environments:
    - jGRASP
    - JCreator from Xinox Software
    - BlueJ
    - Borland JBuilder Foundation X
- TextPad
- The Java 2 Standard Edition version 5.0 SDK

Appendices

The appendices include the following:

- Java reserved words and keywords
- Operator precedence

- Unicode character set

- Representing negative numbers

- Representing floating point numbers

- Java classes and APIs presented in this book

- Answers to selected exercises

Instructor Materials

These materials are available to instructors on the Jones and Bartlett website (http://computerscience.jbpub.com/j5i), and include

- Programming activity solution code (for instructors only)

- Answers to many end-of-chapter exercises

- PowerPoint slides for each chapter

Contacting the Authors

We have checked and rechecked the many technical details in this book. Despite our best efforts, however, we realize that some errors may have been missed. If you discover a technical error in the book, please contact us at jaanderson@capitol-college.edu or hfranceschi@capitol-college.edu. We will post any corrections on the book's website: http://computerscience. jbpub.com/j5i.

Acknowledgments

We would like to acknowledge the contributions of many partners, colleagues, and family members to this book.

First and foremost, we would like to thank our Publisher, Jones and Bartlett. Stephen Solomon, Acquisition Editor, worked closely with us on developing the book concept and guided us through the 18 months of writing and production. We want to express appreciation to Amy Rose, Director of Production, for her publishing expertise and patience with missed deadlines, and to Caroline Senay, who supported us first as an editorial assistant, then later as a production assistant. We also want to thank Kristin Ohlin, Adam Alboyadjian, and Jeremy Castonguay, who oversaw the redesign and deployment of the movies; and Mike and Sigrid Wile of Northeast Compositors, who performed all the comp work on the book and carefully colored the code samples.

Second, we extend our thanks to the reviewers: Robert Burton, Brigham Young University; Barbara Guillott, Louisiana State University; James Brzowski, University of Massachusetts, Lowell; Paul Tymann, Rochester Institute of Technology; Daniel Joyce, Villanova University; Paolo Bucci, The Ohio State University; Gian Mario Basani, DePaul University; and Hans Peter Bischof, Rensselaer Polytechnic Institute. We have taken your thoughtful comments to heart and the book is better for them.

Julie Anderson would also like to acknowledge the pedagogical insight of Richard Rasala and Viera Proulx of Northeastern University. In a workshop they presented during Julie's first year of teaching, Richard and Viera introduced her to the possibilities and motivational benefits of graphics programming.

We both want to recognize Jon Dornback, who, while a student at Capitol College, wrote the visualization of linked lists, which we use as Programming Activity 2 in Chapter 14. Thanks also to all our colleagues who were supportive of our efforts, especially Pat Smit, former Academic Dean of Capitol College, and Earl Gottsman.

I am extremely grateful for the help extended by many family members. My father, Glenn Austin, proofread many of the early chapters. My son, Brian Anderson, contributed his graphic expertise and suggestions on usability to the examples and Programming Activities. My daughter-in-law, Silvia Eckert, reviewed the early chapters from a student's perspective. I also thank my mother-in-law, Virginia Anderson, for cooking so many dinners while I wrote. And of course, much gratitude goes to my loving husband, Tom, for his support and encouragement.

—Julie Anderson

I also recognize the support of my family. In particular, my brother, Paul, provided feedback on our sample chapter and the movies, and his wife Kristin gave her support and provided advice as to our relationship with the publisher.

—Hervé Franceschi

Contents

CHAPTER 1

Introduction to Programming and the Java Language

CHAPTER CONTENTS

Introduction

Computer applications touch almost every aspect of our lives. They run automated teller machines, the grocery store's checkout register, the appointment calendar at your doctor's office, airport kiosks for flight check-in, a restaurant's meal-ordering system, and online auctions, just to name a few. On your personal computer, you may run a word processor, virus detection software, a spreadsheet, computer games, and an image processing system.

Someone, usually a team of programmers, wrote those applications. If you're reading this book, you're probably curious about what's involved in writing applications, and you would like to write a few yourself. Perhaps you have an idea for the world's next great application or computer game.

In this book, we'll cover the basics of writing applications. Specifically, we'll use the Java programming language. Keep in mind, however, that becoming a good programmer requires more than mastering the rules, or **syntax**, of a programming language. You also must master basic programming techniques. These are established methods for performing common programming operations, such as calculating a total, finding an average, or arranging a group of items in order.

You also must master good software engineering principles, so that you design code that is readable, easily maintained, and reusable. By readable, we mean that someone else should be able to read your program and figure out what it does and how it does it. Writing readable code is especially important for programmers who want to advance in their careers, because it allows someone else to take over the maintenance of your program while you move on to bigger and better responsibilities. Ease of maintenance is also an important aspect of programming, because the specifications for any program are continually changing. How many programs can you name that have had only one version? Not many. Well-designed code allows you and others to incorporate prewritten and pretested modules into your program, thus reducing the time to develop a program and yielding code that is more robust and has fewer bugs. One useful feature of the Java programming language is the large supply of prewritten code that you are free to use in your programs.

Programming is an exciting activity. It's very satisfying to decompose a complex task into computer instructions and watch your program come alive. It can be frustrating, however, when your program either doesn't run at all or produces the wrong output.

Writing correct programs is critical. Someone's life or life savings may depend on the correctness of your program. Reusing code helps in developing correct programs, but you must also master effective testing techniques to verify that the output of your program is correct.

In this book, we'll concentrate not only on the syntax of the Java language, but also on basic programming techniques, good software engineering principles, and effective testing techniques.

Before you can write programs, however, it's important to understand the platform on which your program will run. A platform refers to the computer hardware and the operating system. Your program will use the hardware for inputting data, for performing calculations, and for outputting results. The operating system will start your program running and will provide your program with essential resources, such as memory; and services, such as reading and writing files.

1.1 Basic Computer Concepts

1.1.1 Hardware

As shown in Figure 1.1, a computer typically includes the following components:

- a CPU, or central processing unit, which executes the instructions of a program

- a memory unit, which holds the instructions and data of a program while it is executing

- a hard disk, used to store programs and data so that they can be loaded into memory and accessed by the CPU

- a keyboard and mouse, used for input of data

- a monitor, used to display output from a program

- other accessories (not shown) such as a graphics card, a DVD/CD-ROM drive, a modem, and a LAN card.

Figure 1.1

**A Typical Design of a
Personal Computer**

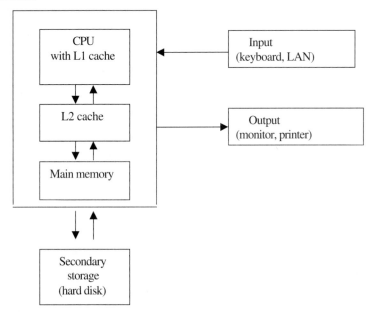

For example, if you were to go to a computer store in search of the latest personal computer, you might be shown a computer with this set of specifications:

- a 3.4-GHz Intel Pentium 4 Processor
- 1 MB of L2 cache memory
- 1 GB of RAM (Random Access Memory)
- a 200-GB hard disk

In the typical PC above, the Intel Pentium 4 Processor is the CPU. Other processors used as CPUs in desktop computers and servers include the Sun Microsystems SPARC, the Hewlett-Packard HP-RISC processor, and the IBM PowerPC G5 processor.

CPUs consist of an Arithmetic Logic Unit (ALU) [also called an Integer Unit (IU)], which performs basic integer arithmetic and logical operations; a Floating Point Unit (FPU), which performs floating-point arithmetic; a set of hardware registers for holding data and memory addresses; and other supporting hardware, including a control unit to sequence the instructions. Each CPU comes with its own set of instructions, which are the operations that it can perform. The instructions typically invoke arithmetic and logic operations, move data from one location to another, and change the flow of the program (that is, determine which instruction is to be executed next).

The first step in executing a program is loading it into memory. The CPU then fetches the program instructions from memory one at a time and executes them. A program consists of many instructions. An Instruction Pointer register (also called a Program Counter) keeps track of the current instruction being executed.

The speed of a CPU is related to its clock cycle, typically rated in MHz (Megahertz) or even GHz (Gigahertz); at the time of this edition, a high-end CPU speed would be rated at 3.4 GHz. It takes one clock cycle for a processor to fetch an instruction from memory, decode an instruction, or execute it. Current RISC processors feature pipelining, which allows the CPU to process several instructions at once, so that while one instruction is executing, the processor can decode the next instruction, and fetch the next instruction after that. This greatly improves performance of applications.

A CPU rated at 500 MHz is capable of executing 500 million instructions per second. That translates into executing one instruction every two 10^{-9} seconds (or two nanoseconds).

A CPU rated at 2 GHz is capable of executing 2 billion instructions per second. That translates into executing one instruction every 0.5 10^{-9} seconds (or half a nanosecond).

Memory or storage devices, such as L2 cache, memory, or hard disk, are typically rated in terms of their capacity, expressed in bytes. A byte is eight binary digits, or bits. A single bit's value is 0 or 1. Depending on the type of memory or storage device, the capacity will be stated in Kilobytes, Megabytes, or Gigabytes. The sizes of these units are shown in Table 1.1.

TABLE 1.1   Memory Units and Their Sizes

Memory Unit	Size
KB, or Kbytes, or Kilobytes	About 1,000 bytes (exactly 2^{10} or 1,024 bytes)
MB, or Mbytes, or Megabytes	About 1 million bytes (exactly 2^{20} or 1,048,576 bytes)
GB, or Gbytes, or Gigabytes	About 1 billion bytes (exactly 2^{30} or 1,073,741,824 bytes)

For the CPU to execute at its rated speed, however, instructions and data must be available to the CPU at that speed as well. Instructions and data come directly from the L1 cache, which is memory directly located on the CPU chip. Since L1 cache is located on the CPU chip, it runs at the same speed as the CPU. However, L1 cache typically is small, for example, 32 Kbytes, and eventually the CPU will need to process more instructions and data than can be held in the L1 cache at one time. At that point, the CPU typically brings data from what is called the L2 cache, which is located on separate memory chips connected to the CPU. A typical speed for the L2 cache would be 10 nanoseconds access time, and this will considerably slow down the rate at which the CPU can execute instructions. L2 cache size today is typically 256 Kbytes or 512 Kbytes, and again, the CPU will eventually need more space for instructions and data than the L2 cache can hold at one time. At that point, the CPU will bring data and instructions from main memory, also located outside, but connected to, the CPU chip. This will slow down the CPU even more, because main memory typically has an access time of about 50 nanoseconds. Main memory, though, is significantly larger in size than the L1 and L2 caches, typically anywhere between 128 and 512 Mbytes. When the CPU runs out of space again, it will have to get its data from the hard disk, which is typically between 20 and 80 Gbytes in size, but with an access time in the milliseconds range.

As you can see from these numbers, a considerable amount of speed is lost when the CPU goes from main memory to disk, which is why having sufficient memory is very important for the overall performance of applications.

Another factor that should be taken into consideration is cost per Kilobyte. Typically the cost per Kilobyte decreases significantly stepping down from L1 cache to hard disk, so high performance is often traded for low price.

Main memory (also called RAM) uses DRAM, or Dynamic Random Access Memory technology, which maintains data only when power is applied to the memory and needs to be refreshed regularly in order to retain data. L1 and L2 cache use SRAM, or Static Random Access Memory technology, which also needs power but does not need to be refreshed in order to retain data. Memory capacities are typically stated in powers of 2. For instance, 256 Kbytes of memory is 2^{18} bytes, or 262,144 bytes.

Memory chips contain cells, each cell containing a bit, which can store either a 0 or a 1. Cells can be accessed individually or as a group of typically

TABLE 1.2   A Comparison of Memory Types

Device	Location	Type	Speed	Capacity (MB)	Cost/KB
L1 cache	On-chip	SRAM	Very fast	Very small	Very high
L2 cache	Off-chip	SRAM	Fast	Small	High
Memory	Off-chip	DRAM	Moderate	Moderate	Moderate
Hard disk	Separate	Disk media	Slow	Large	Small

4, 8, or 16 cells. For instance, a 32-Kbit RAM chip organized as 8K $\times$ 4 is composed of exactly 2^{13}, or 8,192 units, each unit containing four cells. This RAM chip will have four data output pins (or lines) and 13 access pins (or lines), enabling access to all 8,192 cells because each access pin can have a value of 0 or 1. Table 1.2 compares the features of various memory types.

1.1.2   Operating Systems

An operating system (OS) is a software program that

- controls the peripheral devices (for instance, it manages the file system)

- supports multitasking, by scheduling multiple programs to execute during the same interval

- allocates memory to each program, so that there is no conflict among the memory of any programs running at the same time

- prevents the user from damaging the system. For instance, it prevents user programs from overwriting the OS or another program's memory

The operating system loads, or **boots**, when the computer system is turned on and is intended to run as long as the computer is running.

Examples of operating systems are MacOS for the Macintosh computers, Microsoft Windows, Unix, and Linux. Windows has evolved from a single-user, single-task DOS operating system to the multiuser, multitasking Windows 2000. Unix and Linux, on the other hand, were designed from the beginning to be multiuser, multitasking operating systems.

1.1.3   Application Software

Application software consists of the programs written to perform specific tasks. These programs are run by the operating system, or as is typically said, they are run "on top of" the operating system. Examples of applications are word processors, such as Microsoft Word or Corel WordPerfect; spreadsheets, such as Microsoft Excel; database management systems, such as Oracle or Microsoft SQL Server; Internet browsers, such as Netscape and Microsoft Internet Explorer; and most of the programs you will write during your study of Computer Science.

1.1.4   Computer Networks and the Internet

Computer Networks

Computer networks connect two or more computers. A common network used by many corporations and universities is a LAN, or Local Area Network. A typical LAN connects several computers that are geographically close to one another, often in the same building, and allows them to share resources, such as a printer, a database, or a file system. In a LAN, most user computers are called **clients**, and one (or more) of them acts as a **server**. The server controls access to resources on the network and can supply services to the clients, such as answering database requests, storing and serving files, or managing e-mail.

The Internet

The Internet is a network of networks, connecting millions of computers around the world. The Internet evolved from ARPANET, a 1969 U.S. military research project whose goal was to design a method for computers to communicate. Most computers on the Internet are clients, typically requesting resources, such as Web pages, through an Internet browser. These resources are provided by Web servers, which store Web pages and respond to these requests.

For example, when you, acting as a client, type *www.yahoo.com/index.html* into your Web browser, you are requesting a resource. Here that resource is a Web page (*index.html*), from the Web server located at *www.yahoo.com*. That request will make its way to the server with the help of routers—special computers that find a path through the Internet networks from your computer to the correct destination.

Every machine on the Internet has a unique ID, called its IP address (IP stands for Internet Protocol). A computer can have a static IP address, which is dedicated to that machine, or a dynamic IP address, which is assigned to the computer when it connects to the Internet. An IP address is made up of four octets, whose values in decimal notation are between 0 and 255. For instance, 58.203.151.103 could represent such an IP address. In binary notation, this IP address is 111010.11001011.10010111.1100111. Later in this chapter, we will learn how to convert a decimal number, such as 103, to its binary equivalent, 1100111.

Most people are familiar with URL (Uniform Resource Locator) addresses that look like *www.yahoo.com*. URLs are actually Internet domain names. Domain name resolution servers, which implement the Domain Name System (DNS), convert domain names to IP addresses, so that Internet users don't need to know the IP addresses of Web sites they want to visit. The World Wide Web Consortium (W3C), an international group developing standards for Internet access, prefers the term Uniform Resource Identifier (URI) rather than URL, because URI covers future Internet addressing schemes.

Skill Practice
with these end-of-chapter questions

1.7.1   Multiple Choice Exercises

Questions 1, 2, 3, 4

1.7.3   General Questions

Questions 21, 22, 23

1.7.4   Technical Writing

Questions 31, 32, 33

1.2   Practice Activity: Displaying System Configuration

We have explored hardware and operating systems in general. Now, let's discover some information about the hardware and operating system on your computer. Depending on whether you're using a Windows operating system or a Linux operating system, follow the appropriate directions below to display the operating system's name, the CPU type, how much memory the computer has, and your home directory (for Unix/Linux users).

1.2.1   Displaying Windows Configuration Information

To display system configuration information on a Windows computer, run *msinfo32.exe* from the command line. From the *Start* menu, select *Run* and type *msinfo32* into the text box. You will get a display similar to the one below, although the information displayed varies, depending on the version of Windows you are running.

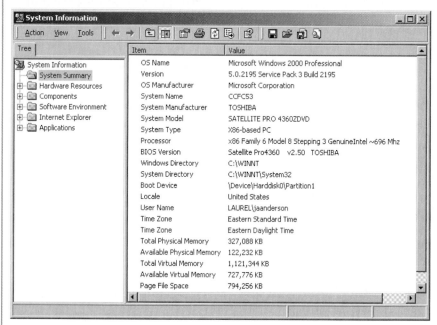

As you can see, this computer is running Windows 2000 Professional, version 5.0.2195. The CPU is an Intel Pentium III processor running at 696 MHz, and the computer has 327,088 KB of memory, 122 KB of which is not being used at the time of the display.

1.2.2   Displaying Unix/Linux Configuration Information

1. To retrieve the name of the operating system, at the $ prompt, type echo $OSTYPE.

```
$ echo $OSTYPE
linux-gnu
```

This tells you that the machine is running the GNU version of the Linux operating system.

2. To retrieve the name of your home directory, at the prompt, type
   `echo $HOME`.

   ```
   $ echo $HOME
   /home/username
   ```

3. To retrieve information about your computer's main memory, at the
   prompt, type `cat /proc/meminfo`. This will display the contents of the
   file *meminfo* in the *proc* directory.

   ```
   $ cat /proc/meminfo
           total:      used:     free:    shared:  buffers: cached:
   Mem:   131158016 120090624 11067392 17285120 13152256 91246592
   Swap: 271425536 3055616    268369920
   MemTotal:      128084 kB
   MemFree:        10808 kB
   MemShared:      16880 kB
   Buffers:        12844 kB
   Cached:         89108 kB
   SwapTotal:     265064 kB
   SwapFree:      262080 kB
   ```

   From this display, we see that the computer has 128 Mbytes of memory, 10 Mbytes of which is not being used at the time of the display.
   Other types of memory are also shown here, but discussion of these
   types of memory is beyond the scope of this course.

4. To retrieve information on your computer's CPU, type `cat`
   `/proc/cpuinfo`. This will display the contents of the file *cpuinfo* in the
   proc directory.

   ```
   $ cat /proc/cpuinfo
   processor       : 0
   vendor_id       : GenuineIntel
   cpu family      : 6
   model           : 1
   model name      : Pentium Pro
   stepping        : 7
   cpu MHz         : 199.459
   cache size      : 256 KB
   fdiv_bug        : no
   ```

```
hlt_bug          : no
sep_bug          : no
f00f_bug         : no
coma_bug         : no
fpu              : yes
fpu_exception    : yes
cpuid level      : 2
wp               : yes
flags            : fpu vme de pse tsc msr pae mce cx8 sep mtrr pge
                   mca cmov
bogomips         : 397.31
```

From this display, we see that the computer's CPU is an Intel Pentium Pro, running at 200 MHz. Again, discussion of the other information displayed is beyond the scope of this course.

DISCUSSION QUESTIONS ❓

1. Compare the system information on several computers. Is it the same or different from computer to computer? Explain why the information is the same or different.

2. In the sample display for Windows 2000, the computer has 327 KB of memory, but only 122 KB of memory is available. Why do you think some memory is not available?

3. Compare your computer to the ones on the previous pages shown here. Which do you think would have better performance? Explain your answer.

1.3   Data Representation

1.3.1   Binary Numbers

As mentioned earlier, a CPU understands only binary numbers, whose digits consist of either 0 or 1. All data is stored in a computer's memory as binary digits. A bit holds one binary digit. A byte holds eight binary digits.

Binary numbers are expressed in the base 2 system, because there are only 2 values in that system, 0 and 1. By contrast, most people are used to the decimal, or base 10, system, which uses the values 0 through 9.

There are other number systems, such as the octal, or base 8, system, which uses the digits from 0 to 7, and the hexadecimal, or base 16, system, which uses the digits 0 to 9 and the letters A to F.

As we know it in the decimal system, the number 359 is composed of three digits:

3, representing the hundreds, or 10^2

5, representing the tens, or 10^1

9, representing the ones, or 10^0

Therefore, we can write 359 as

$359 = 3*10^2 + 5*10^1 + 9*10^0$

Thus, the decimal number 359 is written as a linear combination of powers of 10 with coefficients from the base 10 alphabet, that is the digits from 0 to 9. Similarly, the binary number 11011 is written as a linear combination of powers of 2 with coefficients from the base 2 alphabet, that is, the digits 0 and 1.

For example, the binary number 11011 can be written as

$11011 = 1*2^4 + 1*2^3 + 0*2^2 + 1*2^1 + 1*2^0$

Table 1.3 lists the binary equivalents for the decimal numbers 0 through 8, while Table 1.4 lists the decimal equivalents of the first 15 powers of 2.

TABLE 1.3   Binary Equivalents of Decimal Numbers 0 Through 8

Decimal	Binary
0	0000
1	0001
2	0010
3	0011
4	0100
5	0101
6	0110
7	0111
8	1000

TABLE 1.4   Powers of 2 and Their Decimal Equivalents

2^{14}	2^{13}	2^{12}	2^{11}	2^{10}	2^9	2^8	2^7	2^6	2^5	2^4	2^3	2^2	2^1	2^0
16,384	8,192	4,096	2,048	1,024	512	256	128	64	32	16	8	4	2	1

Note that in Table 1.3, as we count in increments of 1, the last digit alternates between 0 and 1. In fact, we can see that for even numbers, the last digit is always 0 and for odd numbers, the last digit is always 1.

Because computers store numbers as binary, and people recognize numbers as decimal values, conversion between the decimal and binary number systems often takes place inside a computer.

Let's try a few conversions. To convert a binary number to a decimal number, multiply each digit in the binary number by $2^{position-1}$, counting the rightmost position as position 1 and moving left through the binary number. Then add the products together.

Using this method, let's calculate the equivalent of the binary number 11010 in our decimal system.

```
11010 = 1*2⁴ + 1*2³ + 0*2² + 1*2¹ + 0*2⁰
      = 16  +  8  +  0  +  2  +  0
      = 26
```

Now let's examine how to convert a decimal number to a binary number. Let's convert the decimal number 359 into its binary number equivalent. As we can see from the way we rewrote 11011, a binary number can be written as a sum of powers of 2 with coefficients 0 and 1.

The strategy to decompose a decimal number into a sum of powers of 2 is simple: first find the largest power of 2 that is smaller than or equal to the decimal number, subtract that number from the decimal number, then do the same with the remainder, and so on, until you reach 0.

The largest power of 2 that is smaller than 359 is 256 or 2^8 (the next larger power of 2 would be 512, which is larger than 359). Subtracting 256 from 359 gives us 103 ($359 - 256 = 103$), so we now have

```
359 = 2⁸*1 + 103
```

Now we apply the same procedure to 103. The largest power of 2 that is smaller than 103 is 64 or 2^6. That means that there is no factor for 2^7, so that digit's value is 0. Subtracting 64 from 103 gives us 39.

Now we have

```
359 = 2⁸*1 + 2⁷*0 + 2⁶*1 + 39
```

Repeating the procedure for 39, we find that the largest power of 2 smaller than 39 is 32 or 2^5. Subtracting 32 from 39 gives us 7.

So we now have

```
359 = 2⁸*1 + 2⁷*0 + 2⁶*1 + 2⁵*1 + 7
```

Repeating the procedure for 7, the largest power of 2 smaller than 7 is 2^2, or 4. That means that there are no factors for 2^4 or 2^3, so the value for each of those digits is 0. Subtracting 4 from 7 gives us 3, so we have

```
359 = 2⁸*1 + 2⁷*0 + 2⁶*1 + 2⁵*1 + 2⁴*0 + 2³*0 + 2²*1 + 3
```

Repeating the procedure for 3, the largest power of 2 smaller than 3 is 2 or 2^1 and we have:

```
359 = 2⁸*1 + 2⁷*0 + 2⁶*1 + 2⁵*1 + 2⁴*0 + 2³*0 + 2²*1 + 2¹*1 + 1
```

1 is a power of 2; it is 2^0, so we finally have

```
359 = 2⁸*1 + 2⁷*0 + 2⁶*1 + 2⁵*1 + 2⁴*0 + 2³*0 + 2²*1 + 2¹*1 + 2⁰*1
```

Removing the power of 2 multipliers, 359 can be represented in the binary system as

```
359 = 2⁸*1 + 2⁷*0 + 2⁶*1 + 2⁵*1 + 2⁴*0 + 2³*0 + 2²*1 + 2¹*1 + 2⁰*1
    =   1     0     1     1     0     0     1     1     1
```

or

```
1 0110 0111
```

CODE IN ACTION

In the Chapter 1 folder on the CD-ROM included with this book, you will find a Shockwave movie showing a step-by-step illustration of how to convert between decimal and binary numbers. Just double-click on *NumberFormatConversion.html* to start the movie.

In a computer program, we will use both positive and negative numbers. Appendix D explains how negative numbers, such as −34, are represented in the binary system. In a computer program, we also use floating-point numbers, such as 3.75. Appendix E explains how floating-point numbers are represented using the binary system.

1.3.2   Using Hexadecimal Numbers to Represent Binary Numbers

As you can see, binary numbers can become rather long. With only two possible values, 0 and 1, it takes 16 binary digits to represent the decimal value +32,768. For that reason, the hexadecimal, or base 16, system is often used as a shorthand representation of binary numbers. The hexadecimal system uses 16 digits: 0 to 9 and A to F. The letters A to F represent the values 10, 11, 12, 13, 14, and 15.

The maximum value that can be represented in four binary digits is $2^4 - 1$, or 15. The maximum value of a hexadecimal digit is also 15, which is represented by the letter F. So you can reduce the size of a binary number by using hexadecimal digits to represent each group of four binary digits.

Table 1.5 displays the hexadecimal digits along with their binary equivalents.

To represent the following binary number in hexadecimal, you simply substitute the appropriate hex digit for each set of four binary digits.

```
0001 1010 1111 1001 1011 0011 1011 1110
  1    A    F    9    B    3    B    E
```

TABLE 1.5   Hexadecimal Digits and Equivalent Binary Values

Hex Digit	Binary Value
0	0000
1	0001
2	0010
3	0011
4	0100
5	0101
6	0110
7	0111
8	1000
9	1001
A	1010
B	1011
C	1100
D	1101
E	1110
F	1111

Here's an interesting sequence of hexadecimal numbers. The first 32 bits of every Java applet are:

`1100 1010 1111 1110 1011 1010 1011 1110`

Translated into hexadecimal, that binary number becomes:

`CAFE BABE`

1.3.3 Representing Characters with the Unicode Character Set

Java represents characters using the Unicode Worldwide Character Standard, or simply Unicode. Each Unicode character is represented as 16 bits, or two bytes. This means that the Unicode character set can encode 65,536 characters.

The Unicode character set was developed by the Unicode Consortium, which consists of computer manufacturers, software vendors, the governments of several nations, and others. The consortium's goal was to support an international character set, including the printable characters on the standard QWERTY keyboard, as well as international characters such as é or λ.

Many programming languages store characters using the ASCII (American Standard Code for Information Interchange) character set, which uses 7 bits to encode each character, and thus, can represent only 128 characters. For compatibility with the ASCII character set, the first 128 characters in the Unicode character set are the same as the ASCII character set.

Table 1.6 shows a few examples of Unicode characters and their decimal equivalents.

For more information on the Unicode character set, see Appendix C or visit the Unicode Consortium's Web site at *http://www.Unicode.org*.

Skill Practice
with these end-of-chapter questions

1.7.1   Multiple Choice Exercises

Questions 5, 6, 7, 8

1.7.2   Converting Numbers

Questions 15, 16, 17, 18, 19, 20

1.7.3   General Questions

Questions 24, 25, 26

TABLE 1.6   Selected Unicode Characters and Their Decimal Equivalents

Unicode Character	Decimal Value
NUL, the null character (a nonprintable character)	0
*	42
1	49
2	50
A	65
B	66
a	97
b	98
}	125
delete (a nonprintable character)	127

1.4   Programming Languages

1.4.1   High- and Low-Level Languages

Programming languages can be categorized into three types:

- machine language
- assembly language
- high-level language

In the early days of computing, programmers often used machine language or assembly language. Machine language uses binary codes, or strings of 0s and 1s, to execute the instruction set of the CPU and to refer to memory addresses. This method of programming is extremely challenging and time consuming. Also, the code written in machine language is not portable to other computer architectures. Machine language's early popularity can be attributed largely to the fact that programmers had no other choices. However, programmers rarely use machine language today.

Assembly languages are one step above machine language, using symbolic names for memory addresses and mnemonics for processor instructions,

for example: *BEQ* (branch if equal), *SW* (store), or *LW* (load). An Assembler program converts the code to machine language before it is executed. Like machine language, assembly languages are also CPU-dependent and are not portable among computers with different processors (for instance, between Intel and SPARC). Assembly language is easier to write than machine language, but still requires a significant effort, and thus is usually used only when the program requires features, such as direct hardware access, that are not supported by a high-level language.

High-level languages, such as Fortran, Pascal, Perl, C, C++, and Java, are closer to the English language than they are to machine language, making them a lot easier to use for software development and more portable among CPU architectures. For this reason, programmers have embraced high-level languages for more and more applications.

Characteristics of high-level languages, such as Java, are

- The languages are highly symbolic. Programmers write instructions using keywords and special characters and use symbolic names for data.

- The languages are somewhat portable (some more portable than others) among different CPUs.

- The languages can be specialized, for instance:
  - C, C++, and Java are used for general-purpose applications.
  - Perl is used for Internet applications.
  - Fortran is used for scientific applications.
  - COBOL is used for business applications and reports.
  - Lisp and Prolog are used for artificial intelligence applications.

High-level languages are compiled, interpreted, or a combination of both. A program written in a compiled language, such as C or C++, is converted by a compiler into machine code, then the machine code is executed.

By contrast, a program written using an interpreted language, such as Perl, is read and converted to machine code, line by line, at execution time. Typically, a program written in an interpreted language will run more slowly than its equivalent written in a compiled language.

Java uses a combination of a compiler and an interpreter. A Java program is first compiled into processor-independent byte codes, then the byte code file is interpreted at run time by software called the Java Virtual Machine (JVM).

1.4.2   An Introduction to Object-Oriented Programming

Initial high-level languages, such as Fortran or Pascal, were procedural. Typically, programmers wrote task-specific code in separate procedures, or functions, and called these procedures from other sections of the program in order to perform various tasks. The program's data was generally shared among the procedures.

In the mid-1970s, the first object-oriented programming language, Smalltalk, was introduced, enabling programmers to write code with a different approach. Whereas procedures or functions dealt mainly with basic data types such as integers, real numbers, or single characters, Smalltalk provided the programmer with a new tool: classes and objects of those classes.

A class enables the programmer to encapsulate data and the functions needed to manipulate that data into one package. A class essentially defines a template, or model, from which objects are created. Creating an object is called **instantiation**. Thus, objects are created—instantiated—according to the design of the class.

A class could represent something in real life, such as a person. The class could have various attributes such as, in the example of a "person" class, a first name, a last name, and an age. The class would also provide code, called **methods**, that allow the creator of the object to set and retrieve the values of the attributes.

One big advantage to object-oriented programming is that well-written classes can be reused by new programs, thereby reducing future development time.

Smalltalk was somewhat successful, but had a major deficiency: its syntax was unlike any syntax already known by most programmers. Most programmers who knew C, were attracted by the object-oriented features of Smalltalk, but were reluctant to use it because its syntax was so different from C's syntax. C++ added object-oriented features to C, but also added complexity.

Meanwhile, the Internet was growing by leaps and bounds and gaining popularity daily. Web developers used HTML to develop Web pages and soon felt the need to incorporate programming features not only on the server side, but also directly on the client side. Fortunately, Java appeared on the scene.

1.4.3   The Java Language

On May 23, 1995, Sun Microsystems introduced Java, originally named Oak, as a free, object-oriented language targeted at embedded applications for consumer devices. A Java Virtual Machine was incorporated immediately into Netscape Navigator, and as the Internet grew, small Java programs, known as applets, began to appear on Web pages in increasing numbers. Java syntax is basically identical (with some minor exceptions) to that of C++, and soon programmers all over the world started to realize the benefits of using Java. Those benefits include

- syntax identical to that of C++, except that Java eliminates some of C++'s more complex features

- object orientation

- Internet-related features, such as applets, which are run by the browser, and servlets, which are run by the Web server

- an extensive library of classes that can be reused readily, including Swing classes for providing a Graphical User Interface and Java Database Connectivity (JDBC) for communicating with a database

- portability among every platform that supports a Java Virtual Machine

- built-in networking

As we mentioned earlier, a Java program is first compiled into processor-independent byte codes, then the byte codes are interpreted at run time by the Java Virtual Machine (JVM). As its name implies, the JVM simulates a virtual processor with its own instruction set, registers, and instruction pointer. Thus, to run a Java program, you only need a JVM. Fortunately, JVMs are available on every major computing platform.

Because Java programs are interpreted at run time, they typically run more slowly than their C++ counterparts. However, many platforms provide Java compilers that convert source code directly to machine code. This results in greater execution speed, but with an accompanying loss of portability. Just-in-Time (JIT) compilers are also available. These JITs compile code at run time so that subsequent execution of the same code runs much faster.

Java programs can be written as applets, servlets, or applications.

Java applets are small programs designed to add interactivity to a Web page. Applets are launched by an Internet browser; they cannot run stand-alone. As the user requests a Web page that uses an applet, the applet is downloaded to the user's computer and run by the JVM in the browser. Due to browser incompatibilities, limitations imposed by security features, and slow download times, however, applets have fallen out of favor.

Java servlets are invoked by the Web server and run on the server, without being downloaded to the client. Typically, servlets dynamically generate Web content by reading and writing to a database using JDBC.

Java applications run standalone on a client computer. In this book, we will write a few applets, but mainly we will write Java applications.

Sun Microsystems provides a valuable Web site (*www.java.sun.com*) which has information on using the prewritten classes, a tutorial on Java, and many more resources for the Java programmer. We will refer you to that site often in this book.

1.5   An Introduction to Programming

1.5.1   Programming Basics

In many ways, programming is like solving a puzzle. You have a task to perform and you know the operations that a computer can perform (input, calculations, comparisons, rearranging of items, and output). As a programmer, your job is to decompose a task into individual, ordered steps of inputting, calculating, comparing, rearranging, and outputting.

For example, suppose your task is to find the sum of two numbers. First, your program needs to read (input) the numbers into the computer. Next, your program needs to add the two numbers together (calculate). Finally, your program needs to write (output) the sum.

Notice that this program consists of steps, called **instructions**, which are performed in order ("First," "Next," "Finally"). Performing operations in order, one after another, is called **sequential processing**.

The order in which instructions are executed by the computer is critical in programming. You can't calculate the sum of two numbers before you have read the two numbers, and you can't output a sum before you have calculated it. Programming, therefore, requires the programmer to specify the ordering of instructions, which is called the **flow of control** of the program. There are four different ways that the flow of control can progress through a program: sequential execution, method call, selection, and looping. We've just seen sequential execution, and we'll discuss the other types of flow of control in the next section.

Because getting the flow of control correct is essential to getting a program to produce correct output, programmers use a tool called **pseudocode** (pronounced *sue dough code*) to help them design the flow of control before writing the code.

1.5.2 Program Design with Pseudocode

Pseudocode, from *pseudo*, which means "appearing like," is a method for expressing a program's order of instructions in English language, rather than a programming language. In this way, the programmer can concentrate on designing a program without also being bogged down in the syntax of the particular programming language.

The pseudocode for calculating the sum of two numbers would look like Example 1.1:

```
read first number
read second number
set total to (first number + second number)
output total
```

EXAMPLE 1.1   Pseudocode for Summing Two Numbers

Fortunately, the rules for writing pseudocode are not rigid. Essentially, you can use any wording that works for you.

Let's look at another example. Suppose your program needs to calculate the square root of an integer. The instructions for calculating a square root are rather complex; fortunately, Java provides prewritten code that computes the square root of any integer. The prewritten code is called a **method**, and your program can execute that code by **calling the method**. As part of the method call, you tell the method which integer's square root you want to calculate. This is called **passing an argument to the method**. When the method finishes executing its instructions, control is passed back to your program just after the method call. Another way of looking at method calls is to consider what happens when you're reading a book and find a word you don't understand. You mark your place in the book and look up the word in a dictionary. When you're finished looking up the word, you go back to the book and continue reading.

Example 1.2 shows the pseudocode for calculating the square root of an integer.

```
read an integer
call the square root method, passing the integer
output the square root of the integer
```

EXAMPLE 1.2   Using a Method Call to Calculate a Square Root

The order of operations is still input, calculate, and output, but we're calling a method to perform the calculation for us.

Now suppose your task is to determine whether a number is positive or negative. First, your program should input the number into the computer. Next, you need to determine whether the number is positive or negative. You know that numbers greater than or equal to 0 are positive and numbers less than 0 are negative, so your program should compare the number to 0. Finally, your program should write a message indicating whether the number is positive or negative.

Like Examples 1.1 and 1.2, the operations are input, calculate, and output, in that order. However, depending on whether the number is positive or negative, your program should write a different message. If the number is greater than or equal to 0, the program should write a message that the number is positive, but if the number is less than 0, the program should write a message that the number is negative. Code used to handle this situation is called **selection**; the program selects which code to execute based on the value of the data.

The pseudocode for this program could be written as that shown in Example 1.3.

```
read a number
if the number is greater than or equal to 0
   write "Number is positive."
else
   write "Number is negative."
```

EXAMPLE 1.3   Using Selection

Notice the indentation for the code that will be selected based on the comparison of the number with 0. Programmers use indentation to make it easier to see the flow of control of the program.

Now let's get a little more complicated. Suppose your program needs to find the sum of a group of numbers. This is called **accumulating**. To accomplish this, we can take the same approach as if we were adding a group of numbers using a calculator. We start with a total of 0 and add each number, one at a time, to the running total. When we have no more numbers to add, the running total is the total of all the numbers.

Translating this into pseudocode, we get the code shown in Example 1.4.

```
set total to 0
read a number
while there was a number to read, repeat next two instructions
  add number to total
  read the next number
write total
```

EXAMPLE 1.4   Accumulating a Total

The indented code will be repeated for each number read until there are no more numbers. This repeated execution of the same code is called **looping**, or **iteration**, and is used extensively in programming whenever the same processing needs to be performed on each item in a set.

Accumulating a total and determining whether a number is positive or negative are just two of many commonly performed operations. In programming, you will often perform tasks for which there are standard methods of processing, called **algorithms**. For example, the algorithm for accumulation is to set a total to 0, use looping to add each item to the total, then output the total. More generally, you can think of an algorithm as a strategy to solve a problem. Earlier in the chapter, we used an algorithm to convert a decimal number to its binary representation.

Other common programming tasks are counting items, calculating an average, sorting items into order, and finding the minimum and maximum values. In this book, you will learn the standard algorithms for performing these common operations. Once you learn these algorithms, your programming job will become easier. When you recognize that a program requires these tasks, you can simply plug in the appropriate algorithm with some minor modifications.

Programming, in large part, is simply reducing a complex task to a set of subtasks that can be implemented by combining standard algorithms that use sequential processing, method calls, selection, and looping.

SOFTWARE ENGINEERING TIP

Looking for patterns will help you determine the appropriate algorithms for your programs.

The most difficult part of programming, however, is recognizing which algorithms to apply to the problem at hand. This requires analytical skills and the ability to see patterns. Throughout this book, we will point out common patterns wherever possible.

1.5.3   Developing a Java Application

Writing a Java application consists of several steps: writing the code, compiling the code, and executing the application. Java source code is stored in a text file with the extension *.java*. Compiling the code creates one or more *.class* files, which contain processor-independent byte codes. The Java Virtual Machine (JVM) translates the byte codes into machine-level instructions for the processor on which the Java application is running. Thus, if a Java application is running on an Intel Pentium 4 processor, the JVM translates the byte codes into the Pentium 4's instruction set.

Sun provides a Java Software Development Toolkit (SDK) on its Web site (*www.java.sun.com*), which is downloadable free of charge. The SDK contains a compiler, JVM, and an applet viewer, which is a minimal browser. In addition, the SDK contains a broad range of prewritten Java classes that programmers can use in their Java applications.

If you are downloading and installing Java yourself, be sure to follow the directions on the Sun Microsystems Web site, including the directions for setting the path for *javac,* the Java compiler. You need to set the path correctly so that you can run the Java compiler from any directory on your computer.

To develop an application using the SDK, write the source code using any text editor, such as Notepad, Wordpad, or the vi editor. To compile the code, invoke the compiler from the command line:

```
javac ClassName.java
```

where *ClassName.java* is the name of the source file.

If your program, written in the file *ClassName.java*, compiles correctly, a new file, *ClassName.class*, will be created in your current directory.

To run the application, you invoke the JVM from the command line:

```
java ClassName
```

Typically, programmers use an Integrated Development Environment (IDE) to develop applications. An IDE consists of a program editor, a compiler, and a run-time environment, integrated via a Graphical User Interface. The advantage to using an IDE is that errors in the Java code that are found by the compiler or the Java Virtual Machine can be linked directly to the program editor at the line in the source file that caused the error. Additionally, the Graphical User Interface enables the programmer to switch among the editor, compiler, and execution of the program without launching separate applications.

Skill Practice
with these end-of-chapter questions

1.7.1   Multiple Choice Exercises

Questions 9, 10, 11, 12, 13, 14

1.7.3   General Questions

Questions 27, 28, 29, 30

1.7.4   Technical Writing

Question 34

1.5.4   Programming Activity 1: Writing a First Java Application

Let's create our first Java program. This program prints the message, "Programming is not a spectator sport!" on the screen.

For Windows users, we provide specific instructions on using a simple IDE, TextPad, from Helios Software Solutions. If you are using an operating system other than Windows, you may want to select another IDE or invoke the *javac* compiler and run your programs from the command line as described in the previous section.

Start by launching TextPad. You'll see a blank document window. This is where you will write the code for the program.

Before we type any code, however, let's name the document. We do this by saving the document as *FirstProgram.java*. Be sure to capitalize the F and the P and keep the other letters lowercase. Java is case-sensitive, so Java considers *firstprogram.java* or even *Firstprogram.java* to be a different name. After saving the document, notice that the file name *FirstProgram.java* is now displayed in the left window.

Keeping case sensitivity in mind, type in the program shown in Example 1.5.

```
1 // First program in Java
2 // Anderson, Franceschi
3
4 public class FirstProgram
5 {
6    public static void main( String [ ] args )
7    {
8       System.out.println( "Programming is not a spectator sport!" );
9
10      System.exit( 0 );
11   }
12 }
```

EXAMPLE 1.5   A First Program in Java

At this point, we ask that you just type the program as you see it here, except for the line numbers, which are not part of the program. Line numbers are displayed in this example to allow easy reference to a particular line in the code. We'll explain a little about the program now; additional details will become clear as the semester progresses.

The first two lines, which start with two forward slashes, are comments. They will not be compiled or executed; they are simply information for the programmer and are used to increase the readability of the program.

Line 4 defines the class name as *FirstProgram*. Notice that the class name must be spelled exactly the same way—including capitalization—as the file name, *FirstProgram.java*.

COMMON ERROR TRAP

Java is case-sensitive. The class name and the file name must match exactly, including capitalization.

The curly braces in lines 5 and 12 mark the beginning and ending of the *FirstProgram* class, and the curly braces in lines 7 and 11 mark the beginning and ending of *main*. Every Java application must define a class and a *main* method. Execution of a Java application always begins with the code inside *main*. So when this application begins, it will execute line 8, which writes the message "*Programming is not a spectator sport!*" to the system console. Next, it executes line 10, *System.exit(0)*, which exits the program. Including this line is optional; if you omit this line, the application will exit normally.

As you type the program, notice that TextPad automatically colors your text. Comments are displayed in green and *String* literals ("*Programming is not a spectator sport!*") are displayed in a blue-green. Java class names (*String*, *System*) and Java keywords (*public*, *class*, *static*)—which are reserved for specific uses in Java—are displayed in blue. Curly braces, brackets, and parentheses, which have syntactical meaning in Java, are displayed in red. Your IDE may use different colors. If you are running from the command line using Notepad (in Windows) or vi (in Unix) as your source code editor, your text will simply be black and white.

When you have completed typing the code in Example 1.5, compile the code. Using TextPad, select *Compile Java* from the *Tools* menu to compile the code. You don't need to save the changes to the file; the compiler will do that automatically. While the compiler is running, the Command Results window is displayed. If everything is typed exactly right, the compiler will create a *FirstProgram.class* file, which contains the byte codes for the program.

If you got a clean compile with no errors, congratulations! You're ready to execute the application. Otherwise, check your program to make sure that you have entered it exactly as it is written above.

To execute the application using TextPad, from the *Tools* menu, select *Run Java Application*. This will invoke the Java Virtual Machine and pass it the *FirstProgram.class* file created by the compiler. If all is well, you will see the message, *Programming is not a spectator sport!*, displayed on the **Java console**, which is the text window that opens automatically. Figure 1.2 shows the correct output of the program.

Figure 1.2

Output from Example 1.5

Debugging Techniques

If the compiler found syntax errors in the code, these are called **compiler errors**, not because the compiler caused them, but because the compiler found them. When the compiler detects errors in the code, it writes diagnostic information about the errors in the Command Results window.

For example, try typing *println* with a capital P (as *Println*), and recompiling. The compiler displays the following message in the Command Results window:

```
C:\JavaPrograms\FirstProgram.java:8: cannot resolve symbol
symbol  : method Println  (java.lang.String)
location: class java.io.PrintStream
    System.out.Println( "Programming is not a spectator sport!" );
                ^
1 error
```

The first line identifies the file name that contains the Java source code, as well as the line number in the source code where the error occurred. In this case, the error occurred on line 8. The second line identifies the symbol *Println* as being the cause of the error. As further help, the location information in the third and fourth lines display line 8 from the source code, using a caret (^) to point to *Println*. All these messages point you to line 8, especially emphasizing the spelling of *Println*. If you're using TextPad, double-clicking on the first line in the Command Results window transfers you to the source code window with your cursor positioned on line 8 so you can correct the error.

Many times, the compiler will find more than one error in the source code. When that happens, don't panic. Often, a single problem, such as a missing semicolon or curly brace, can cause multiple compiler errors.

For example, after correcting the error above, try deleting the left curly brace in line 7, then recompiling. The compiler reports four errors:

```
C:\JavaPrograms\FirstProgram.java:7: ';' expected
^
C:\JavaPrograms\ FirstProgram.java:10: <identifier> expected
       System.exit( 0 );
            ^
```

```
C:\JavaPrograms\ FirstProgram.java:12: 'class' or 'interface' expected
}
^
C:\JavaPrograms\ FirstProgram.java:12: 'class' or 'interface' expected
}
^
4 errors
```

It is sometimes easier to fix one error at a time and recompile after each fix, because the first fix might eliminate many of the reported errors.

When all the compiler errors are corrected, you're ready to execute the program. From the *Tools* menu, select *Run Java Application.*

It is possible to get a clean bill of health from the compiler, yet the program still won't run. To demonstrate this, try eliminating the brackets in line 6 after the word *String.* If you then compile the program, no errors are reported. But when you try to run the program, you get a **run-time error.**

Instead of *Programming is not a spectator sport!,* the following message is displayed on the Java console:

```
Exception in thread "main" java.lang.NoSuchMethodError: main
```

When you see this error, it typically means that the *main* method header (line 6) was not typed correctly.

Thus, we've seen that two types of errors can occur while you are developing a Java program: compiler errors, which are usually caused by language syntax errors or misspellings, and run-time errors, which are often caused by problems using the prewritten classes. Run-time errors can also be caused by exceptions that the JVM detects as it is running, such as an attempt to divide by zero.

Testing Techniques

Once your program compiles cleanly and executes without run-time errors, you may be tempted to conclude that your job is finished. Far from it—you must also verify the results, or output, of the program.

In the sample program, it's difficult to get incorrect results—other than misspelling the message or omitting the spaces between the words. But

Software Engineering Tip

Because one syntax error can cause multiple compiler errors, correct only the obvious errors and recompile after each correction.

TABLE 1.7   Types of Program Errors and Their Causes

Type of Error	Usual Causes
Compiler errors	Incorrect language syntax or misspellings
Run-time errors	Incorrect use of classes
Logic errors	Incorrect program design or incorrect implementation of the design

any nontrivial program should be tested thoroughly before declaring it production-ready.

To test a program, consider all the possible inputs and the corresponding correct outputs. It often isn't feasible to test every possible input, so programmers usually test **boundary conditions**, which are the values that sit on the boundaries of producing different output for a program.

For example, to test the code that determines whether an integer is negative or nonnegative, you would feed the program -1 and 0. These are the boundaries of negative and nonnegative integers. In other words, the boundary between negative and nonnegative integers is between -1 and 0.

When a program does not produce the correct output, we say the program contains **logic errors**. By testing your program thoroughly, you can discover and correct most logic errors. Table 1.7 shows types of program errors and their usual causes.

We'll talk more about testing techniques throughout the book.

DISCUSSION QUESTIONS ❓

1. In the Debugging Techniques section, we saw that making one typo could generate several compiler errors. Why do you think that happens?

2. Explain why testing boundary conditions is an efficient way to verify a program's correctness.

3. Did any errors occur while you were developing the first application? If so, explain whether they were compiler or run-time errors and what you did to fix them.

1.6 Chapter Summary

- Basic components of a computer include the CPU, memory, a hard disk, keyboard, monitor, and mouse.

- Each type of CPU has its own set of instructions for performing arithmetic and logical operations, moving data, and changing the order of execution of instructions.

- An operating system controls peripheral devices, supports multi-tasking, allocates memory to programs, and prevents the user from damaging the system.

- Computer networks link two or more computers so that they can share resources, such as files or printers.

- The Internet connects millions of computers around the world. Web servers deliver Web pages to clients running Internet browsers.

- Binary numbers are composed of 0s and 1s. A bit holds one binary digit. A byte holds eight binary digits.

- To convert a binary number to a decimal number, multiply each digit in the binary number by $2^{position-1}$, counting the rightmost position as position 1 and moving left through the number. Then add the products together.

- To convert a decimal number into a binary number, first find the largest power of 2 that is smaller than or equal to the decimal number, subtract that number from the decimal number, then do the same with the remainder, and so on, until you reach 0.

- Hexadecimal digits can be used to represent groups of four binary digits.

- The Unicode character set, which Java uses, can encode up to 65,536 characters using 16 bits per character.

- Machine language and assembly language are early forms of programming languages that require the programmer to write to the CPU's instruction set. Because this low-level programming is time consuming, difficult, and the programs are not portable to other

CHAPTER SUMMARY

CPU architectures, machine language and assembly language are rarely used.

- High-level languages are highly symbolic and somewhat portable. They can be compiled, interpreted, or as in the case of Java, converted to byte codes, which are interpreted at run time.

- A good program is readable, easily maintained, and reusable.

- Object-oriented programming uses classes to encapsulate data and the functions needed to manipulate that data. Objects are instantiated according to the class design. An advantage to object-oriented programming is reuse of the classes.

- Programs use a combination of sequential processing, method calls, selection, and iteration to control the order of execution of instructions. Performing operations in order, one after another, is called sequential processing. Temporarily executing other code, then returning, is called a method call. Selecting which code to execute based on the value of data is called selection. Repeating the same code on each item in a group of values is called iteration, or looping.

- Pseudocode allows a programmer to design a program without worrying about the syntax of the language.

- In programming, you will often perform tasks for which there are standard methods of processing, called algorithms. For example, accumulating is a common programming operation that finds the sum of a group of numbers.

- Programming, in large part, is reducing a complex task to a set of subtasks that can be implemented by combining standard algorithms that use sequential processing, selection, and looping.

- Java source code is stored in a text file with an extension of *.java*. Compiling the code produces one or more *.class* files.

- An Integrated Development Environment (IDE) consists of a program editor, a compiler, and a run-time environment, integrated via a Graphical User Interface.

- Compiler errors are detected by the compiler and are usually caused by incorrect Java syntax or misspellings. Run-time errors are detected by the Java Virtual Machine and are usually caused by exceptions or incorrect use of classes. Logic errors occur during program execution and are caused by incorrect program design.

1.7   Exercises, Problems, and Projects

1.7.1   Multiple Choice Exercises

1. Which one of these is not an operating system?

   - ❏ Linux
   - ❏ Java
   - ❏ Windows
   - ❏ Unix

2. Which one of these is not an application?

   - ❏ Word
   - ❏ Internet Explorer
   - ❏ Linux
   - ❏ Excel

3. How many bits are in three bytes?

   - ❏ 3
   - ❏ 8
   - ❏ 24
   - ❏ 0

4. In a network, the computers providing services to the other computers are called

   - ❏ clients
   - ❏ servers
   - ❏ laptops

5. A binary number ending with a 0
   - ❏ is even
   - ❏ is odd
   - ❏ cannot tell

6. A binary number ending with a 1
   - ❏ is even
   - ❏ is odd
   - ❏ cannot tell

7. A binary number ending with two 0s
   - ❏ is a multiple of 4
   - ❏ is not a multiple of 4
   - ❏ cannot tell

8. Using four bits, the largest positive binary number we can represent is 1111
   - ❏ true
   - ❏ false

9. Which one of these is not a programming language?
   - ❏ C++
   - ❏ Java
   - ❏ Windows
   - ❏ Fortran

10. Which one of these is not an object-oriented programming language?
   - ❏ C
   - ❏ Java
   - ❏ C++
   - ❏ Smalltalk

11. What is the file extension for a Java source code file?
   - ❏ .java
   - ❏ .exe
   - ❏ .class

12. What is the file extension of a compiled Java program?

 ❏ .java

 ❏ .exe

 ❏ .class

13. In order to compile a program named *Hello.java,* what do you type at the command line?

 ❏ java Hello

 ❏ java Hello.java

 ❏ javac Hello

 ❏ javac Hello.java

14. You have successfully compiled *Hello.java* into *Hello.class.* What do you type at the command line in order to run the application?

 ❏ java Hello.class

 ❏ java Hello

 ❏ javac Hello

 ❏ javac Hello.class

1.7.2   Converting Numbers

15. Convert the decimal number 67 into binary.

16. Convert the decimal number 1,564 into binary.

17. Convert the binary number 0001 0101 into decimal.

18. Convert the binary number 1101 0101 0101 into decimal.

19. Convert the binary number 0001 0101 into hexadecimal.

20. Convert the hexadecimal number D8F into binary.

1.7.3   General Questions

21. A RAM chip is organized as $\times$ 8 memory, i.e., each unit contains 8 bits, or a byte. There are 7 address pins on the chip. How many bytes does that memory chip contain?

22. If a CPU is rated at 750 MHz, how many instructions per second can the CPU execute?

23. If a CPU can execute 100 million instructions per second, what is the rating of the CPU in MHz?

24. Suppose we are using binary encoding to represent colors. For example, a black-and-white color system has only two colors and therefore needs only 1 bit to encode the color system as follows:

Bit	Color
0	black
1	white

    With 2 bits, we can encode four colors as follows:

Bit pattern	Color
00	black
01	red
10	blue
11	white

    With 5 bits, how many colors can we encode?

    With n bits (n being a positive integer), how many colors can we encode? (Express your answer as a function of n.)

25. In HTML, a color can be coded in the following hexadecimal notation: #*rrggbb* where

    rr represents the amount of red in the color

    gg represents the amount of green in the color

    bb represents the amount of blue in the color

    rr, *gg*, and *bb* vary between 00 and FF in hexadecimal notation, i.e., 0 and 255 in decimal equivalent notation. Give the decimal values of the red, green, and blue values in the color #33AB12.

26. RGB is a color system representing colors: R stands for red, G for green, and B for blue. A color can be coded as *rgb* where *r* is a number between 0 and 255 representing how much red there is in the color; *g* is a number between 0 and 255 representing how much green there is in the color, and *b* is a number between 0 and 255 representing how

much blue there is in the color. The color grey is created by using the same value for *r*, *g*, and *b*. How many shades of grey are there?

27. List three benefits of the Java programming language.

28. What is the name of the Java compiler?

29. Write the pseudocode for a program that finds the product of two numbers.

30. Write the pseudocode for a program that finds the sums of the numbers input that are greater than or equal to 10 and the numbers input that are less than 10.

1.7.4   Technical Writing

31. List the benefits of having a Local Area Network vs. standalone computer systems.

32. For one day, keep a diary of the computer applications that you use. Also note any features of the applications that you think should be improved or any features you'd like to see added.

33. You are looking at two computers with the following specifications, everything else being equal:

PC # 1	PC # 2
2.4-GHz CPU	2-GHz CPU
256 KB L2 cache	256 KB L2 cache
128 MB RAM	512 MB RAM
60-GB Hard drive	60-GB Hard drive
$999	$999

Which PC would you buy? Explain the reasoning behind your selection.

34. Go to the Sun Microsystems Java site (*http://java.sun.com*). Explain what resources are available there for someone who wants to learn Java.

1.7.5   Group Project (for a group of 1, 2, or 3 students)

35. In the octal system, numbers are represented using digits from 0 to 7; a 0 is placed in front of the octal number to indicate that the octal

system is being used. For instance, here are some examples of the equivalent of some octal numbers in the decimal system:

Octal	Decimal
000	0
001	1
007	7
010	8
011	9

In the hexadecimal system, numbers are represented using digits from 0 to 9 and letters A to F; 0x is placed in front of the hexadecimal number to indicate that the hexadecimal system is being used. For instance, here are some examples of the decimal equivalents of some hexadecimal numbers:

Hexadecimal	Decimal
0x0	0
0x1	1
0x9	9
0xA	10
0xB	11
0xF	15
0x10	16
0x11	17
0x1C	28

1. Convert 0xC3E (in hexadecimal notation) into an octal number.

2. Convert 0377 (in octal notation) into a hexadecimal number.

3. Discuss how, in general, you would convert a hexadecimal number into an octal number and an octal number into a hexadecimal number.

CHAPTER 2

Programming Building Blocks— Java Basics

CHAPTER CONTENTS

Introduction

If you boil it down to the basics, a program has two elements: instructions and data. The instructions tell the CPU what to do with the data.

The data may be different in each execution of the program, but the instructions stay the same. In a word processor, the words (data) are different from document to document, but the operation (instructions) of the word processor remains the same. When a line becomes full, for example, the word processor automatically wraps to the next line. It doesn't matter which words are on the line, only that the line is full. When you select a word and change the font to bold, it doesn't matter which word you select, it will become bold.

In Chapter 1, we discussed the types of operations that the computer can perform: input, calculation, comparisons of data and subsequent changes to the flow of control, data movement, and output. The Java language provides a syntax for expressing instructions using keywords, operators, and punctuation. In this chapter, we'll look at basic Java syntax for keyboard input, performing calculations, data movement, and output.

The Java language also provides a syntax for describing a program's data using keywords, symbolic names, and data types. The data used by a program can come from a variety of sources. The user can enter data from the keyboard, as happens when you type a new document into a word processor. The program can read the data from a file, as happens when you load an existing document into the word processor. Or the program can generate the data itself, as happens when a computer card game deals hands. Finally, some data is already known, for example, the number of hours in a day is 24, the number of days in December is 31, and the value of pi is 3.14159. This type of data is constant. In this chapter, we'll discuss how to define the data to be used in the program, how to perform calculations on that data, and how to output program results to the screen.

2.1   Java Application Structure

Every Java program consists of at least one class. It is impossible to write a Java program that doesn't use classes. As we said in Chapter 1, classes describe a logical entity that has data as well as methods (the instructions) to manipulate that data. An object is a physical instantiation of the class that contains specific data. We'll begin to cover classes in detail in the next chapter. For now, we'll just say that your source code should take the form of the shell code in Example 2.1.

```
 1 /*  An application shell
 2     Anderson, Franceschi
 3 */
 4 public class ShellApplication
 5 {
 6    public static void main( String [ ] args ) //required
 7    {
 8       // write your code here
 9    }
10 }
```

EXAMPLE 2.1   A Shell for a Java Application

In Example 2.1, the numbers to the left of each line are not part of the program code; they are included here for your convenience. In TextPad, you can display line numbers by selecting *Line Numbers* from the *View* menu.

From application to application, the name of the class, *ShellApplication*, will change, because you will want to name your class something meaningful that reflects its function. Each Java source code file must have the same name as the class name with a *.java* extension. In this case, the source file must be *ShellApplication.java*. Whatever name you select for a class must comply with the Java syntax for identifiers.

Java **identifiers** are symbolic names that you assign to classes, methods, and data. Identifiers must start with a **Java letter** and may contain any combination of letters and digits, but no spaces. A Java letter is any character in the range *a–z* or *A–Z*, the underscore (_), or the dollar sign ($), as well as many Unicode characters that are used as letters in other languages. Digits are any character between 0 and 9. The length of an identifier is essentially unlimited. Identifier names are case-sensitive, so *Number1* and *number1* are considered to be different identifiers.

In addition, none of Java's **reserved words** can be used as identifiers. These reserved words, which are listed in Appendix A, consist of keywords used in Java instructions, as well as three special data values: *true*, *false*, and *null*. Given that Java identifiers are case-sensitive, note that it is legal to use *True* or *TRUE* as identifiers, but *true* is not a legal variable name. Table 2.1 lists the rules for creating Java identifiers.

The shell code in Example 2.1 uses three identifiers: *ShellApplication*, *main*, and *args*. The remainder of Example 2.1 consists of comments, Java keywords, and required punctuation.

TABLE 2.1   Rules for Creating Identifiers

Java Identifiers
▪ Must start with a Java letter (*A–Z, a–z, _, $*, or many Unicode characters)
▪ Can contain an almost unlimited number of letters and/or digits (0–9)
▪ Cannot contain spaces
▪ Are case-sensitive
▪ Cannot be a Java reserved word

The basic building block of a Java program is the **statement**. A statement is terminated with a semicolon and can span several lines.

Any amount of **white space** is permitted between identifiers, Java keywords, operands, operators, and literals. White space characters are the space, tab, newline, and carriage return. Liberal use of white space makes your program more readable. It is good programming style to surround identifiers, operands, and operators with spaces and to skip lines between logical sections of the program.

A **block**, which consists of 0, 1, or more statements, starts with a left curly brace ({) and ends with a right curly brace (}). Blocks are required for class and method definitions and can be used anywhere else in the program that a statement is legal. Example 2.1 has two blocks: the class definition (lines 5 through 10) and the *main* method definition (lines 7 through 9). As you can see, nesting blocks within blocks is perfectly legal. The *main* block is nested completely within the class definition block.

SOFTWARE ENGINEERING TIP

Liberal use of white space makes your program more readable. It is good programming style to surround identifiers, operands, and operators with spaces and to skip lines between logical sections of the program.

Comments document the operation of the program and are notes to yourself and to other programmers who read your code. Comments are not compiled and can be coded in two ways. **Block comments** can span several lines; they begin with a forward slash-asterisk (/*) and end with an asterisk-forward slash (*/). Everything between the /* and */ is ignored by the compiler. Note that there are no spaces between the asterisk and forward slash. Lines 1–3 in Example 2.1 are block comments and illustrate the good software engineering practice of providing at the beginning of your source code a few comments that identify yourself as the author and briefly describe what the program does.

The second way to include comments in your code is to precede the comment with two forward slashes (//). There are no spaces between the forward slashes. The compiler ignores everything from the two forward slashes to the end of the line. In Example 2.1, the compiler ignores all of line 8, but only the part of line 6 after the two forward slashes.

SOFTWARE ENGINEERING TIP

Include a block comment at the beginning of each source file that identifies the author of the program and briefly describes the function of the program.

2.2 Data Types, Variables, and Constants

For the data in your program, you need to assign a symbolic name (an identifier) that you will use to refer to that data item. You must also specify to the compiler the data type. Java supports eight **primitive data types**: *byte*, *short*, *int*, *long*, *float*, *double*, *char*, and *boolean*. They are called primitive data types because they are not classes.

The data type you specify tells the compiler how much memory to allocate and the format in which to store the data. For example, if you specify that a data item is an *int*, then the compiler will allocate four bytes of memory for it and store its value as a 32-bit signed binary number. If, however, you specify that a data item is a double-precision floating-point number, then the compiler will allocate 8 bytes of memory and store its value as an IEEE 754 floating-point number.

Once you declare a data type for a data item, the compiler will monitor your use of that data item. If you attempt to perform operations that are not allowed for that type or are not compatible with that type, the compiler will generate an error. Because the Java compiler monitors the operations on each data item, Java is called a **strongly typed language**.

Take care in selecting identifiers for your programs. The identifiers should be meaningful and should reflect the data that will be stored in a variable, the concept encapsulated by a class, or the function of a method. For example, the identifier *age* clearly indicates that the variable will hold the age of a person. When you select meaningful variable names, the logic of your program is more easily understood, and you are less likely to introduce errors. Sometimes, it may be necessary to create a long identifier in order to clearly indicate its use, for example, *numberOfStudentsWhoPassedCS1*. Although the length of identifiers is essentially unlimited, avoid creating extremely long identifiers because they are more cumbersome to use. Also, the longer the identifier, the more likely you are to make typos when entering the identifier into your program. Finally, although it is legal to use identifiers, such as *TRUE*, which differ from Java keywords only in case, it isn't a good idea because they easily can be confused with Java keywords, making the program logic less clear.

2.2.1 Declaring Variables

Every variable must be given a name and a data type before it can be used. This is called **declaring a variable**. The data item is called a **variable** if its value can be changed during the program's execution, or if its value can be different from one execution of the program to another. A variable is like a box that can hold one item at a time. You can put an item in the box and later replace that item with a different item, but the box remains the same. Similarly, a variable can hold one data value at a time. You can change the data value it holds, but at any time, a variable has one value.

The syntax for declaring a variable is:

```
dataType identifier; // this declares one variable
```

or

```
dataType identifier1, identifier2, ...; // this declares multiple
                                        // variables of the same
                                        // data type
```

Note that a comma follows each identifier in the list except the last identifier, which is followed by a semicolon.

By convention, the identifiers for variable names start with a lowercase letter. If the variable name consists of more than one word, then each word after the first should begin with a capital letter. For example, these identifiers are conventional Java variable names: *number1*, *highScore*, *booksToRead*, *ageInYears*, and *xAxis*. Underscores conventionally are not used in variable names; they are reserved for the identifiers of constants, as we shall discuss later in the chapter. Similarly, do not use dollar signs to begin variable names. The dollar sign is reserved for the first letter of programmatically generated variable names; that is, variable names generated by software, not people. Although this may sound arbitrary now, the value of following these conventions will become clearer as you gain more experience in Java and your programs become more complex.

2.2.2   Integer Data Types

An integer data type is one that evaluates to a positive or negative whole number. Java provides four integer data types, *int*, *short*, *long*, and *byte*.

The *int*, *short*, *long*, and *byte* types differ in the number of bytes of memory allocated to store each type, and therefore, the maximum and minimum values that can be stored in a variable of that type. All of Java's integer types are signed, meaning that they can be positive or negative; the high-order, or leftmost, bit is reserved for the sign.

Table 2.2 summarizes the integer data types, their sizes in memory, and their maximum and minimum values.

In most applications, the *int* type will be sufficient for your needs, since it can store positive and negative numbers up into the 2 million range. The *short* and *byte* data types typically are used only when memory space is critical, and the *long* data type is needed only for data values larger than 2 million.

Let's look at some examples of integer variable declarations. Note that the variable names clearly indicate the data that the variables will hold.

```
int testGrade;
int numPlayers, highScore, diceRoll;
short xCoordinate, yCoordinate;
long cityPopulation;
byte ageInYears;
```

TABLE 2.2   Integer Data Types

Integer Data Type	Size in Bytes	Minimum Value	Maximum Value
byte	1	−128	127
short	2	−32,768	32,767
int	4	−2,147,483,648	2,147,483,647
long	8	−9,223,372,036,854,775,808	9,223,372,036,854,775,807

2.2.3   Floating-Point Data Types

Floating-point data types store numbers with fractional parts. Java supports two floating-point data types: the single-precision *float* and the double-precision *double*.

REFERENCE POINT

Floating-point numbers are stored using the IEEE 754 standard, which is discussed in Appendix E.

The two types differ in the amount of memory allocated and the size of the number that can be represented. The single-precision type (*float*) is stored in 32 bits, while the double-precision type (*double*) is stored in 64 bits. *Floats* and *doubles* can be positive or negative.

Table 2.3 summarizes Java's floating-point data types, their sizes in memory, and their maximum and minimum values.

Because of its greater precision, the *double* data type is usually preferred over the *float* data type. However, for calculations not requiring such precision, *floats* are often used because they require less memory.

Although integers can be stored as *doubles* or *floats*, it isn't advisable to do so because floating-point numbers require more processing time for calculations.

Let's look at a few examples of floating-point variable declarations:

```
float salesTax;
double interestRate;
double paycheck, sumSalaries;
```

2.2.4   Character Data Type

REFERENCE POINT

The encoding of ASCII and Unicode characters is discussed in Appendix C.

The *char* data type stores one Unicode character. Because Unicode characters are encoded as unsigned numbers using 16 bits, a *char* variable is stored in two bytes of memory.

Table 2.4 shows the size of the *char* data type, as well as the minimum and maximum values. The maximum value is the character whose encoding is equal to the unsigned hexadecimal number *FFFF*. At this time, no Unicode character has been assigned the encoding of *FFFF*.

TABLE 2.3   Floating-point Data Types

Floating-point Data Type	Size in Bytes	Minimum Value	Maximum Value
float	4	1.4E-45	3.4028235E38
double	8	4.9E-324	1.7976931348623157E308

TABLE 2.4   The Character Data Type

Character Data Type	Size in Bytes	Minimum Value	Maximum Value
char	2	The character encoded as *0000*, the *null* character	The character encoded as *FFFF*, currently unused

Obviously, since the *char* data type can store only a single character, such as a
K, a *char* variable is not useful for storing names, titles, or other text data. For
text data, Java provides a *String* class, which we'll discuss later in this chapter.

Here are a few declarations of *char* variables:

```
char finalGrade;
char middleInitial;
char newline, tab, doubleQuotes;
```

2.2.5   Boolean Data Type

The *boolean* data type can store only two values, which are expressed using
the Java reserved words *true* and *false*, as shown in Table 2.5.

Booleans are typically used for decision making and for controlling the
order of execution of a program.

Here are a few declarations of *boolean* variables:

```
boolean isEmpty;
boolean passed, failed;
```

2.2.6   Initial Values and Literals

When you declare a variable, you can also assign an initial value to the data.
To do that, use the **assignment operator** (=) with the following syntax:

```
dataType variableName = initialValue;
```

TABLE 2.5   The *boolean* Data Type

boolean Data Type	Possible Values
boolean	true
	false

COMMON ERROR TRAP

Although Unicode characters occupy two bytes in memory, they still represent a single character. Therefore, the literal must also represent only one character.

COMMON ERROR TRAP

Commas, dollar signs, and percent signs (%) cannot be used in integer or floating-point literals.

or

```
dataType variable1 = initialValue1, variable2 = initialValue2;
```

Notice that assignment is right to left. The initial value is assigned to the variable.

One way to specify the initial value is by using a **literal value**. In the following statement, the value *100* is an *int* literal value, which is assigned to the variable *testGrade*.

```
int testGrade = 100;
```

Table 2.6 summarizes the legal characters in literals for all primitive data types.

TABLE 2.6   Literal Formats for Java Data Types

Data Type	Literal Format
int, short, byte	Optional initial sign (+ or −) followed by digits 0–9 in any combination. A literal in this format is an *int* literal; however, an *int* literal may be assigned to a *byte* or *short* variable if the literal is a legal value for the assigned data type.
long	Optional initial sign (+ or −) followed by digits 0–9 in any combination, terminated with an *L* or *l*. It's preferable to use the capital *L*, because the lowercase *l* can be confused with the number *1*.
float	Optional initial sign (+ or −) followed by a floating-point number in fixed or scientific format, terminated by an *F* or *f*.
double	Optional initial sign (+ or −) followed by a floating-point number in fixed or scientific format.
char	▪ Any printable character enclosed in single quotes. ▪ A decimal value from 0–65,535. ▪ '\m', where \m is an escape sequence. For example, '\n' represents a newline, and '\t' represents a tab character.
boolean	*true* or *false*

Notice in Table 2.6 under the literal format for *char*, that \n and \t can be used to format output. We'll discuss these and other escape sequences in the next section of this chapter.

Example 2.2 shows a complete program illustrating variable declarations, specifying a literal for the initial value of each.

```
1   /* Variables Class
2      Anderson, Franceschi
3   */
4
5   public class Variables
6   {
7    public static void main( String [ ] args )
8    {
9      // This example shows how to declare and initialize variables
10
11     int testGrade = 100;
12     long cityPopulation = 425612340L;
13     byte ageInYears = 19;
14
15     float  salesTax = .05F;
16     double interestRate = 0.725;
17     double avogadroNumber = +6.022E23;
18     // avogadroNumber is represented in scientific notation;
19     //    its value is 6.022 x 10 to the power 23
20
21     char finalGrade = 'A';
22     boolean isEmpty = true;
23
24     System.out.println( "testGrade is " + testGrade );
25     System.out.println( "cityPopulation is " + cityPopulation );
26     System.out.println( "ageInYears is " + ageInYears );
27     System.out.println( "salesTax is " + salesTax );
28     System.out.println( "interestRate is " + interestRate );
29     System.out.println( "avogadroNumber is " + avogadroNumber );
30     System.out.println( "finalGrade is " + finalGrade );
31     System.out.println( "isEmpty is " + isEmpty );
32    }
33  }
```

EXAMPLE 2.2   Declaring and Initializing Variables

Line 9 shows a single-line comment. Line 17 declares a *double* variable named *avogadroNumber* and initializes it with its value in scientific notation. The Avogadro number represents the number of elementary particles in one mole of any substance.

Figure 2.1 shows the output of Example 2.2.

Another way to specify an initial value for a variable is to assign the variable the value of another variable, using this syntax:

```
dataType variable2 = variable1;
```

Two things need to be true for this assignment to work:

- *variable1* needs to be declared and assigned a value before this statement appears in the source code.

- *variable1* and *variable2* need to be compatible data types; in other words, the precision of *variable1* must be lower than or equal to that of *variable2*.

For example, in these statements:

```
boolean isPassingGrade = true;
boolean isPromoted = isPassingGrade;
```

isPassingGrade is given an initial value of *true*. Then *isPromoted* is assigned the value already given to *isPassingGrade*. Thus, *isPromoted* is also assigned the initial value *true*. If *isPassingGrade* were assigned the initial value *false*, then *isPromoted* would also be assigned the initial value *false*.

Figure 2.1

Output of Example 2.2

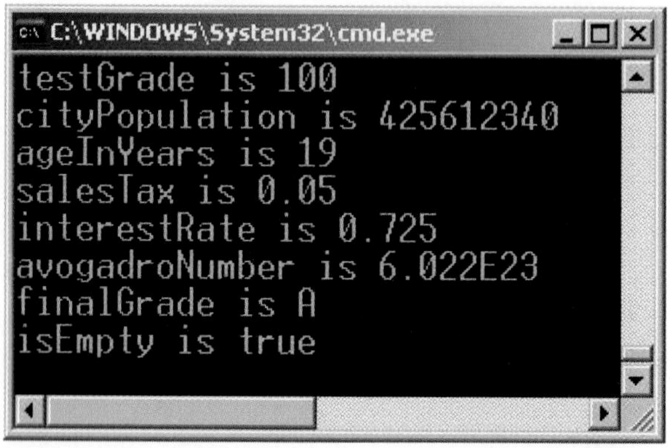

And in these statements:

```
float salesTax = .05f;
double taxRate = salesTax;
```

the initial value of .05 is assigned to *taxRate*. It's legal to assign a *float* value to a *double*, because all values that can be stored as *floats* are also valid *double* values. However, these statements are *not* valid:

```
double taxRate = .05;
float salesTax = taxRate; // invalid; float is lower precision
```

Even though *.05* is a valid *float* value, the compiler will generate a "possible loss of precision" error.

Similarly, you can assign a lower-precision integer value to a higher-precision integer variable.

Table 2.7 summarizes compatible data types; a variable or literal of any type in the right column can be assigned to a variable of the data type in the left column.

Variables need to be declared before they can be used in your program, but be careful to declare each variable only once; that is, specify the data type of the variable only the first time that variable is used in the program. If you attempt to declare a variable that has already been declared, as in the following statements:

```
double twoCents;
double twoCents = 2; // incorrect, second declaration of twoCents
```

TABLE 2.7   Valid Data Types for Assignment

Data Type	Compatible Data Types
byte	byte
short	byte, short
int	byte, short, int, char
long	byte, short, int, char, long
float	byte, short, int, char, long, float
double	byte, short, int, char, long, float, double
boolean	boolean
char	char

COMMON ERROR TRAP

Declare each variable only once, the first time the variable is used. After the variable has been declared, its data type cannot be changed.

you will receive a compiler error similar to the following:

```
twoCents is already defined
```

Similarly, once you have declared a variable, you cannot change its data type. Thus, these statements:

```
double cashInHand;
int cashInHand; // incorrect, data type cannot be changed
```

will generate a compiler error similar to the following:

```
cashInHand is already defined
```

CODE IN ACTION

In the Chapter 2 folder on the CD-ROM included with this book, you will find a Shockwave movie showing a step-by-step illustration of how to convert between decimal and binary numbers. Just double-click on *DataTypesAndArithmetic.html* to start the movie.

2.2.7   String Literals and Escape Sequences

In addition to literals for all the primitive data types, Java also supports *String* literals. *Strings* are objects in Java, and we will discuss them in greater depth in Chapter 3.

A **String** literal is sequence of characters enclosed by double quotes. One set of quotes "opens" the *String* literal and the second set of quotes "closes" the literal. For example, these are all *String* literals:

```
"Hello"
"Hello world"
"The value of x is "
```

We used a *String* literal in our first program in Chapter 1 in this statement:

```
System.out.println( "Programming is not a spectator sport!" );
```

We also used *String* literals in output statements in Example 2.2 to label the data that we printed:

```
System.out.println( "testGrade is " + testGrade );
```

The + operator is the **String concatenation operator**. Among other uses, the concatenation operator allows us to print primitive data types along with *Strings*. We'll discuss the concatenation operator in more detail in Chapter 3.

String literals cannot extend over more than one line. If the compiler finds a newline character in the middle of your *String* literal, it will generate a compiler error. For example, the following statement is not valid:

```
System.out.println( "Never pass a water fountain
        without taking a drink." );
```

In fact, that statement will generate several compiler errors:

```
C:\StringTest.java:9: unclosed string literal
     System.out.println( "Never pass a water fountain
                         ^

C:\StringTest.java:10: unclosed string literal
         without taking a drink." );
                                  ^

C:\StringTest.java:11: ')' expected
^
```

If you have a long *String* to print, break it into several strings and use the concatenation operator. This statement is a correction of the invalid statement above:

```
System.out.println( "Never pass a water fountain,"
                + " without taking a drink." );
```

Another common programming error is omitting the closing quotes. Be sure that all open quotes have matching closing quotes on the same line.

Now that we know that quotes open and close *String* literals, how can we define a literal that includes quotes? This statement

```
System.out.println( "She said, "Java is fun"" ); // illegal quotes
                                                  // within literal
```

generates this compiler error:

```
C: \StringTest.java:24: ')' expected
System.out.println( "She said, "Java is fun."" ); // illegal quotes
                                ^
```

COMMON ERROR TRAP

All open quotes for a *String* literal should be matched with a set of closing quotes, and the closing quotes must appear before the line ends.

And since *String* literals can't extend over two lines, how can we create a *String* literal that includes a newline character? Java solves these problems by providing a set of escape sequences that can be used to include a special character within *String* and *char* literals. The escape sequences \n, \t, \b, \r, and \f are nonprintable characters. Table 2.8 lists the Java escape sequences.

In Example 2.3, we show how escape sequences can be used in *Strings*.

```
1  /*  Literals Class
2       Anderson, Franceschi
3  */
4
5  public class Literals
6  {
7    public static void main( String [ ] args )
8    {
9      System.out.println( "One potato\nTwo potatoes\n" );
10     System.out.println( "\tTabs can make the output easier to read" );
11     System.out.println( "She said, \"Java is fun\"" );
12   }
13 }
```

EXAMPLE 2.3   Using Escape Sequences

Figure 2.2 shows the output of Example 2.3. Line 9 shows how \n causes the remainder of the literal to be printed on the next line. The tab character, \t,

TABLE 2.8   Java Escape Sequences

Character	Escape Sequence
newline	\n
tab	\t
double quotes	\"
single quote	\'
backslash	\\
backspace	\b
carriage return	\r
form feed	\f

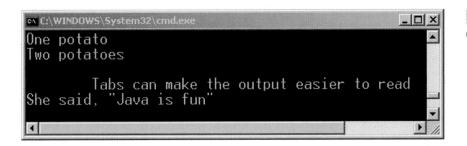

Figure 2.2
Output of Example 2.3

used in line 10, will cause the literal that follows it to be indented one tab stop when output. Line 11 outputs a sentence with embedded double quotes; the embedded double quotes are printed with the escape sequence \".

2.2.8   Constants

Sometimes you know the value of a data item, and you know that its value will not (and should not) change during program execution, nor is it likely to change from one execution of the program to another. In this case, it is a good software engineering practice to define that data item as a **constant.**

Defining constants uses the same syntax as declaring variables, except that the data type is preceded by the keyword *final*.

```
final dataType constantIdentifier = assignedValue;
```

Assigning a value is optional when the constant is defined, but you must assign a value before the constant is used in the program. Also, once the constant has been assigned a value, its value cannot be changed (reassigned) later in the program. Any attempt by your program to change the value of a constant will generate the following compiler error:

```
cannot assign a value to final variable
```

Think of this as a service of the compiler in preventing your program from unintentionally corrupting its data.

By convention, *constantIdentifier* consists of all capital letters, and embedded words are separated by an underscore. This makes constants stand out in the code and easy to identify as constants. Also, constants are usually defined at the top of a program where their values can be seen easily.

Example 2.4 shows how to use constants in a program.

```
1 /* Constants Class
2    Anderson, Franceschi
3 */
4
5 public class Constants
6 {
7   public static void main( String [ ] args )
8   {
9     final char ZORRO = 'Z';
10    final double PI = 3.14159;
11    final int DAYS_IN_LEAP_YEAR = 366, DAYS_IN_NON_LEAP_YEAR = 365;
12
13    System.out.println( "The value of constant ZORRO is " + ZORRO );
14    System.out.println( "The value of constant PI is " + PI );
15    System.out.println( "The number of days in a leap year is "
16                           + DAYS_IN_LEAP_YEAR );
17    System.out.println( "The number of days in a non-leap year is "
18                           + DAYS_IN_NON_LEAP_YEAR );
19
20    // PI = 3.14;
21    // The statement above would generate a compiler error
22    // You cannot change the value of a constant
23  }
24 }
```

EXAMPLE 2.4   Using Constants

SOFTWARE ENGINEERING TIP

Use all capital letters for a constant's identifier; separate words with an underscore (_). Declare constants at the top of the program so their value can be seen easily.

SOFTWARE ENGINEERING TIP

Declare as a constant any data that should not change during program execution. The compiler will then flag any attempts by your program to change the value of the constant, thus preventing any unintentional corruption of the data.

Lines 9, 10, and 11 define four constants. On line 11, note that both *DAYS_IN_LEAP_YEAR* and *DAYS_IN_NON_LEAP_YEAR* are constants. You don't need to repeat the keyword *final* to define two (or more) constants of the same data types. Lines 13 to 18 output the values of the four constants. If line 20 were not commented out, it would generate a compiler error because once a constant is assigned a value, its value cannot be changed. Figure 2.3 shows the output of Example 2.4.

Constants can make your code more readable: PI is more meaningful than 3.14159 when used inside an arithmetic expression. Another advantage of using constants is to keep programmers from making logic errors: Let's say we set a constant to a particular value and it is used at various places

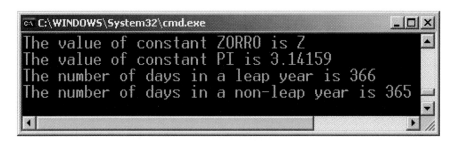

Figure 2.3
Output of Example 2.4

throughout the code (for instance, a constant representing a tax rate); we then discover that the value of that constant needs to be changed. All we have to do is make the change in one place, most likely at the beginning of the code. If we had to change the value at many places throughout the code, that could very well result in logic errors or typos.

Skill Practice
with these end-of-chapter questions

2.7.1   Multiple Choice

Questions 1, 2

2.7.2   Reading and Understanding Code

Questions 4, 5, 6

2.7.3   Fill in the Code

Questions 23, 24, 25, 26

2.7.4   Identifying Errors in Code

Questions 33, 34, 38, 39

2.7.5   Debugging Area

Questions 40, 41

2.7.6   Write a Short Program

Question 46

2.7.8   Technical Writing

Question 52

2.3   Programming Activity 1: Exploring Data Types

For Programming Activity 1, let's explore the Java data types by finding and printing their maximum and minimum values.

Open the *ShellApplication.java* source code shown in Example 2.1. You will find this file on the CD-ROM accompanying this book.

Replace the class name, *ShellApplication*, with the name *DataTypeValues*. Since this is now the name of our class, save the source file as the name *DataTypeValues.java*. Also replace the comment in the first line with a description of what this application will do: "Java data types and their values," and add your name to the second line. Your source file should look like Example 2.5

```
 1 /*  Java data types and their values
 2      your name here
 3 */
 4 public class DataTypeValues
 5 {
 6   public static void main( String [ ] args ) // required
 7   {
 8     // write your code here
 9   }
10 }
```

EXAMPLE 2.5   *DataTypeValues*, Version 1

The maximum and minimum values for the numeric data types are available for use in our program as the Java predefined constants shown in Table 2.9.

Let's start by declaring two variables of the *byte* data type. We'll assign one variable the minimum value and the other variable the maximum value. Include these declarations following the comment:

```
// write your code here
```

```
byte minByte = Byte.MIN_VALUE, maxByte = Byte.MAX_VALUE;
```

Following the declarations, type these lines to print the minimum and maximum byte values.

```
System.out.println( "The minimum byte value is " + minByte );
System.out.println( "The maximum byte value is " + maxByte );
```

In these statements, we're using *String* literals (the words enclosed in quotes) and the *String* concatenation operator (+) to join the *String* literals to the

COMMON ERROR TRAP

Forgetting to add a blank space to the end of a *String* literal before concatenating a value makes the output more difficult to read.

TABLE 2.9   Predefined Constants for Minimum and Maximum Values

Data Type	Minimum Value	Maximum Value
Integers		
byte	Byte.MIN_VALUE	Byte.MAX_VALUE
short	Short.MIN_VALUE	Short.MAX_VALUE
int	Integer.MIN_VALUE	Integer.MAX_VALUE
long	Long.MIN_VALUE	Long.MAX_VALUE
Floating Point		
float	Float.MIN_VALUE	Float.MAX_VALUE
double	Double.MIN_VALUE	Double.MAX_VALUE

value of the variables. Note that the last character in each *String* literal is a space. If you omit the space, the minimum and maximum values will begin immediately after the "is," which makes the output more difficult to read.

Compile the program and run it. Your output should look like Figure 2.4.

To print the *short* minimum and maximum values, declare two *short* variables:

```
short minShort = Short.MIN_VALUE, maxShort = Short.MAX_VALUE;
```

and include these two statements to print the values:

```
System.out.println( "The minimum short value is " + minShort );
System.out.println( "The maximum short value is " + maxShort );
```

At this point, your program should look like Example 2.6.

SOFTWARE ENGINEERING TIP

Developing and testing your programs in steps makes it easier to find and fix errors.

Figure 2.4

Minimum and Maximum *byte* Values

```
1 /*  Java data types and their values
2     your name here
3 */
4 public class DataTypeValues
5 {
6   public static void main( String [ ] args ) // required
7   {
8     // write your code here
9     byte maxByte = Byte.MAX_VALUE, minByte = Byte.MIN_VALUE;
10    System.out.println( "The minimum byte value is " + minByte );
11    System.out.println( "The maximum byte value is " + maxByte );
12
13    short maxShort = Short.MAX_VALUE, minShort = Short.MIN_VALUE;
14    System.out.println( "The minimum short value is " + minShort );
15    System.out.println( "The maximum short value is " + maxShort );
16  }
17 }
```

EXAMPLE 2.6   *DataTypeValues*, Version 2

Compile and run the program and check your output. If your output is correct, define two variables for each remaining numeric data type and follow the pattern to print the minimum and maximum values for each numeric data type. You can even copy and paste these statements, changing the data type as appropriate. Compile and run the program after adding each data type to your program. When you are finished, your output should look like Figure 2.5.

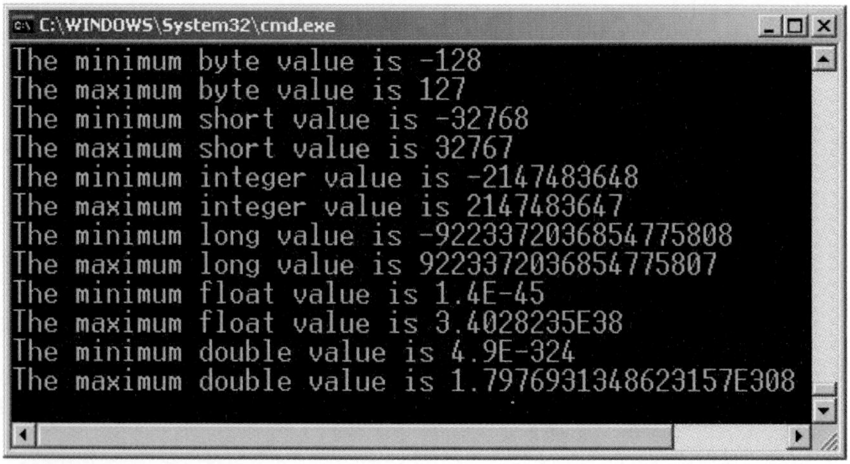

Figure 2.5

Minimum and Maximum Data Type Values

```
The minimum byte value is -128
The maximum byte value is 127
The minimum short value is -32768
The maximum short value is 32767
The minimum integer value is -2147483648
The maximum integer value is 2147483647
The minimum long value is -9223372036854775808
The maximum long value is 9223372036854775807
The minimum float value is 1.4E-45
The maximum float value is 3.4028235E38
The minimum double value is 4.9E-324
The maximum double value is 1.7976931348623157E308
```

1. What are the advantages of having different data types?

2. Why do you think it's important to be able to find the maximum and minimum values of each data type?

2.4 Expressions and Arithmetic Operators

2.4.1 The Assignment Operator and Expressions

In the previous section, we mentioned using the assignment operator to assign initial values to variables and constants. Now let's look at the assignment operator in more detail.

The syntax for the assignment operator is:

```
target = expression;
```

An expression consists of operators and operands that evaluate to a single value. The value of the expression is then assigned to *target*, which must be a variable or constant having a data type compatible with the value of the expression.

If *target* is a variable, the value of the expression replaces any previous value the variable was holding. For example, let's look at these instructions:

```
int numberOfPlayers = 10; // numberOfPlayers value is 10
numberOfPlayers = 8;      // numberOfPlayers value is now 8
```

The first instruction declares an *int* named *numberOfPlayers*. This allocates four bytes in memory to a variable named *numberOfPlayers* and stores the value 10 in that variable. Then, the second statement changes the value stored in the variable *numberOfPlayers* to 8. The previous value, 10, is discarded.

An expression can be a single variable name or a literal of any type, in which case, the value of the expression is simply the value of the variable or the literal. For example, in these statements,

```
int legalAge = 18;
int voterAge = legalAge;
```

the literal *18* is an expression. Its value is *18*, which is assigned to the variable *legalAge*. Then, in the second statement, *legalAge* is an expression, whose value is *18*. Thus the value *18* is assigned to *voterAge*. So after these statements have been executed, both *legalAge* and *voterAge* will have the value *18*.

One restriction, however, is that an assignment expression cannot include another variable unless that variable has been defined previously. The definition of the *height* variable, below, is **invalid,** because it refers to *weight*, which is not defined until the next line.

```
int height = weight * 2; // invalid reference
int weight;
```

The compiler flags this error as an

```
illegal forward reference
```

An expression can be quite complex, consisting of multiple variables, constants, literals, and operators. Before we can look at examples of more complex expressions, however, we need to discuss the *arithmetic operators*.

2.4.2 Arithmetic Operators

Java's arithmetic operators are used for performing calculations on numeric data. The operators are shown in Table 2.10.

All these operators take two operands; thus, they are called **binary operators**.

TABLE 2.10   Arithmetic Operators

Operator	Operation
+	addition
−	subtraction
*	multiplication
/	division
%	modulus (remainder after division)

Example 2.7 shows how these operators can be used in a program.

```
1 /* SimpleOperators Class
2    Anderson, Franceschi
3 */
4
5 public class SimpleOperators
6 {
7    public static void main( String [ ] args )
8    {
9      int a = 6;
10     int b = 2;
11     int result;
12
13     result = a + b;
14     System.out.println( a + " + " + b + " is " + result );
15
16     result = a - b;
17     System.out.println( a + " - " + b + " is " + result );
18
19     result = a * b;
20     System.out.println( a + " * " + b + " is " + result );
21   }
22 }
```

EXAMPLE 2.7   Using Arithmetic Operators

Lines 9 and 10 declare and initialize two *int* variables. Line 13 adds them and assigns the result to the variable *result*, which was declared at line 11; thus, the value of the expression *a + b* is assigned to *result*, which is then output at line 14. Lines 16 and 17, as well as lines 19 and 20, do the same with the subtraction and multiplication operators (− and *). Figure 2.6 shows the output when Example 2.7 is executed.

SOFTWARE ENGINEERING TIP

For readable code, insert a space between operators and operands.

Figure 2.6
Using Arithmetic Operators

2.4.3   Operator Precedence

The statements in Example 2.7 perform simple calculations, but what if you want to calculate how much money you have in coins? Let's say you have two quarters, three dimes, and two nickels. To calculate the value of these coins in pennies, you might use this expression:

```
int pennies = 2 * 25 + 3 * 10 + 2 * 5;
```

In which order should the computer do the calculation? If the value of the expression were calculated left to right, then the result would be

```
= 2 * 25 + 3 * 10 + 2 * 5
=   50   + 3 * 10 + 2 * 5
=       53   * 10 + 2 * 5
=           530   + 2 * 5
=                 532 * 5
=                     2660
```

Clearly, 2,660 pennies is not the right answer. To calculate the correct number of pennies, the multiplications should be performed first, then the additions. This, in fact, is the order in which Java will calculate the expression above.

The Java compiler follows a set of rules called **operator precedence** to determine the order in which the operations should be performed.

Table 2.11 provides the order of precedence of the operators we've discussed so far. The operators in the first row—parentheses—are evaluated first, then the operators in the second row (*, /, %), and so on with the operators in each row. When two or more operators on the same level appear in the same expression, the order of evaluation is left to right, except for the assignment operator, which is evaluated right to left.

TABLE 2.11   Operator Precedence

Operator Hierarchy	Order of Same-Statement Evaluation	Operation
()	left to right	parentheses for explicit grouping
*, /, %	left to right	multiplication, division, modulus
+, −	left to right	addition, subtraction
=	right to left	assignment

As we introduce more operators, we'll add them to the Order of Precedence chart. The complete chart is provided in Appendix B.

Using Table 2.11 as a guide, let's recalculate the number of pennies:

```
int pennies = 2 * 25 + 3 * 10 + 2 * 5;
            =  50   +   30  +  10
            =  90
```

As you can see, *90* is the correct number of pennies in two quarters, three dimes, and two nickels.

We also could have used parentheses to clearly display the order of calculation. For example,

```
int pennies = (2 * 25) + (3 * 10) + (2 * 5);
            =  50    +   30   +   10
            =  90
```

The result is the same, 90 pennies.

It sometimes helps to use parentheses to clarify the order of calculations, but parentheses are essential when your desired order of evaluation is different from the rules of operator precedence. For example, to calculate the value of this formula:

$$\frac{x}{2y}$$

you could write this code:

```
double result = x / 2 * y;
```

This would generate incorrect results because, according to the rules of precedence, *x/2* would be calculated first, then the result of that division would be multiplied by *y*. In algebraic terms, the statement above is equivalent to

$$\frac{x}{2} * y$$

To code the original formula correctly, you need to use parentheses to force the multiplication to occur before the division:

```
double result = x / ( 2 * y );
```

2.4.4 Integer Division and Modulus

Division with two integer operands is performed in the Arithmetic Logic Unit (ALU), which can calculate only an integer result. Any fractional part is truncated; no rounding is performed. The remainder after division is available, however, as an integer, by taking the modulus (%) of the two integer operands. Thus, in Java, the integer division (/) operator will calculate the quotient of the division, whereas the modulus (%) operator will calculate the remainder of the division.

```
 1 /* DivisionAndModulus Class
 2    Anderson, Franceschi
 3 */
 4
 5 public class DivisionAndModulus
 6 {
 7   public static void main( String [ ] args )
 8   {
 9     final int PENNIES_PER_QUARTER = 25;
10     int pennies = 113;
11
12     int quarters = pennies / PENNIES_PER_QUARTER;
13     System.out.println( "There are " + quarters + " quarters in "
14             + pennies + " pennies" );
15
16     int penniesLeftOver = pennies % PENNIES_PER_QUARTER;
17     System.out.println( "There are " + penniesLeftOver
18             + " pennies left over" );
19
20     final double MONTHS_PER_YEAR = 12;
21     double annualSalary = 50000.0;
22
23     double monthlySalary = annualSalary / MONTHS_PER_YEAR;
24     System.out.println( "The monthly salary is " + monthlySalary );
25   }
26 }
```

EXAMPLE 2.8   How Integer Division and Modulus Work

In Example 2.8, we have 113 pennies and we want to convert those pennies into quarters. We can find the number of quarters by dividing 113 by 25. The *int* variable *pennies* is assigned the value 113 at line 10. At line 12, the variable *quarters* is assigned the result of the integer division of *pennies* by the constant *PENNIES_PER_QUARTER*. Since the quotient of the division of 113 by 25 is 4, *quarters* will be assigned 4. At line 16, we use the modulus operator to assign to the variable *penniesLeftOver* the remainder of the division of *pennies* by *PENNIES_PER_QUARTER*. Since the remainder of the division of 113 by 25 is 13, 13 will be assigned to *penniesLeftOver*. Notice that integer division and modulus are independent calculations. You can perform a division without also calculating the modulus, and you can calculate the modulus without performing the division.

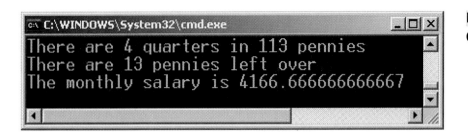

Figure 2.7
Output of Example 2.8

At line 23, we divide a *double* by a *double;* therefore, a floating-point division will be performed by the floating-point unit (FPU), and the result will be assigned to the variable *monthlySalary.* Figure 2.7 shows the output of the program.

The modulus is actually a useful operator. As you will see later in this book, it can be used to determine whether a number is even or odd, to control the number of data items that are written per line, to determine if one number is a factor of another, and for many other uses.

CODE IN ACTION

To see arithmetic operators used in a program, look for the Shockwave movie in the Chapter 2 directory of the CD-ROM accompanying this book. Double-click on the *DataTypesAndArithmetic.html* file to start the movie.

Skill Practice
with these end-of-chapter questions

2.7.2 Reading and Understanding Code

Questions 7, 8, 9, 10, 11, 12, 13

2.7.3 Fill in the Code

Questions 27, 29, 32

2.7.4 Identifying Errors in Code

Question 35

2.7.6 Write a Short Program

Question 44

2.4.5   Division by Zero

As you might expect, Java does not allow integer division by 0. If you include this statement in your program:

```
int result = 4 / 0;
```

the code will compile without errors, but at run time, when this statement is executed, the JVM will generate an exception and print an error message on the Java console:

```
Exception in thread "main" java.lang.ArithmeticException: / by zero
```

In most cases, this stops the program. In Chapter 11, we'll show you how to handle the exception so that you can write a message to the user and continue running the program.

In contrast, floating-point division by zero does not generate an exception. If the dividend is non-zero, the answer is *Infinity*. If both the dividend and divisor are zero, the answer is *NaN*, which stands for "Not a Number."

Example 2.9 illustrates the three cases of dividing by zero. As we can see on the output shown in Figure 2.8, line 16 of Example 2.9 never executes. The exception is generated at line 15 and the program halts execution.

```
 1 /* DivisionByZero Class
 2    Anderson, Franceschi
 3 */
 4
 5 public class DivisionByZero
 6 {
 7   public static void main( String [ ] args )
 8   {
 9     double result1 = 4.3 / 0.0;
10     System.out.println( "The value of result1 is " + result1 );
11
12     double result2 = 0.0 / 0.0;
13     System.out.println( "The value of result2 is " + result2 );
14
15     int result3 = 4 / 0;
16     System.out.println( "The value of result3 is " + result3 );
17   }
18 }
```

EXAMPLE 2.9   Results of Division by Zero

Figure 2.8
Dividing by Zero

Although floating-point division by zero doesn't bring your program to a halt, it doesn't provide useful results either. It's a good practice to avoid dividing by zero in the first place. We'll give you tools to do that in Chapter 5.

2.4.6   Mixed-Type Arithmetic and Type Casting

So far, we've used a single data type in the expressions we've evaluated. But life isn't always like that. Calculations often involve data of different primitive types.

When calculations of mixed types are performed, lower-precision operands are converted, or **promoted**, to the type of the operand that has the higher precision.

The promotions are performed using the *first* of these rules that fits the situation:

1. If either operand is a *double*, the other operand is converted to a *double*.

2. If either operand is a *float*, the other operand is converted to a *float*.

3. If either operand is a *long*, the other operand is converted to a *long*.

4. If either operand is an *int*, the other operand is promoted to an *int*.

5. If neither operand is a *double*, *float*, *long*, or an *int*, both operands are promoted to *int*.

Table 2.12 summarizes these rules of promotion.

This arithmetic promotion of operands is called **implicit type casting** because the compiler performs the promotions automatically, without our specifying that the conversions should be made. Note that the data type of any promoted variable is not permanently changed; its type remains the same after the calculation has been performed.

TABLE 2.12   Rules of Operand Promotion

Data Type of One Operand	Data Type of Other Operand	Promotion of Other Operand	Data Type of Result
double	char, byte, short, int, long, float	double	double
float	char, byte, short, int, long	float	float
long	char, byte, short, int	long	long
int	char, byte, short	int	int
short	char, byte	Both operands are promoted to int	int
byte	char	Both operands are promoted to int	int

Table 2.12 shows many rules, but essentially, any arithmetic expression involving integers and floating-point numbers will evaluate to a floating-point number.

Lines 9 to 12 of Example 2.10 illustrate the rules of promotion. At line 11, the expression *PI * radius * radius* is a mixed-type expression. This expression will be evaluated left to right, evaluating the mixed-type expression *PI * radius* first. *PI* is a *double* and *radius* is an *int*. Therefore, *radius* is promoted to a *double* (4.0) and the result of *PI * radius* is a *double* (12.56636). Then, the next calculation (*12.56636 * radius*) also involves a mixed-type expression, so *radius* is again promoted to a *double* (4.0). The final result, 50.26544, is a *double* and is assigned to *area*. Figure 2.9 shows the output of the complete program.

Sometimes, it's useful to instruct the compiler specifically to convert the type of a variable. In this case, you use **explicit type casting**, which uses this syntax:

```
(dataType) ( expression )
```

The expression will be converted, or type cast, to the data type specified. The parentheses around *expression* are needed only when the expression consists of a calculation that you want to be performed before the type casting.

Type casting is useful in calculating an average. Example 2.10 shows how to calculate your average test grade. Your test scores are 94, 86, 88, and 97, making the combined total score 365. We expect the average to be 91.25.

```
 1 /*  MixedDataTypes Class
 2      Anderson, Franceschi
 3 */
 4
 5 public class MixedDataTypes
 6 {
 7   public static void main( String [ ] args )
 8   {
 9       final double PI = 3.14159;
10       int radius = 4;
11       double area = PI * radius * radius;
12       System.out.println( "The area is " + area );
13
14       int total = 365, count = 4;
15       double average = total / count;
16       System.out.println( "\nPerforming integer division, "
17                           + "then implicit typecasting" );
18       System.out.println( "The average test score is " + average );
19       // 91.0 INCORRECT ANSWER!
20
21       average = ( double ) ( total / count );
22       System.out.println( "\nPerforming integer division, "
23                           +  "then explicit typecasting" );
24       System.out.println( "The average test score is " + average );
25       // 91.0 INCORRECT ANSWER!
26
27       average = ( double ) total / count;
28       System.out.println( "\nTypecast one variable to double, "
29                           +  "then perform division" );
30       System.out.println( "The average test score is " + average );
31       // 91.25 CORRECT ANSWER
32   }
33 }
```

EXAMPLE 2.10   Mixed Data Type Arithmetic

Line 15 first attempts to calculate the average, but results in a wrong answer because both *total* and *count* are integers. So integer division is

Figure 2.9
Output of Example 2.10

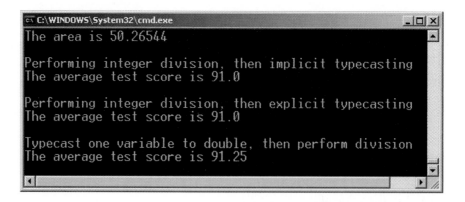

performed, which truncates any remainder. Thus, the result of *total / count* is 91. Then 91 is assigned to *average*, which is a *double*, so 91 becomes 91.0.

Line 21 is a second attempt to calculate the average; again, this code does not work correctly because the parentheses force the division to be performed before the type casting. Thus, because *total* and *count* are both integers, integer division is performed again. The quotient, *91*, is then cast to a *double*, *91.0*, and that *double* value is assigned to *average*.

At line 27, we correct this problem by casting only one of the operands to a *double*. This forces the other operand to be promoted to a *double*. Then floating-point division is performed, which retains the remainder. It doesn't matter whether we cast *total* or *count* to a *double*. Casting either to a *double* forces the division to be a floating-point division.

Figure 2.9 shows the output of the complete program.

CODE IN ACTION

To see the calculation of an average, look for the Shockwave movie in the Chapter 2 directory of the CD-ROM accompanying this book. Double-click on the *DataTypesAndArithmetic.html* file to start the movie.

2.4.7 Shortcut Operators

A common operation in programming is adding 1 to a number (**incrementing**) or subtracting 1 from a number (**decrementing**). For example, if you were counting how many data items the user entered, every time you read another data item, you would add 1 to a count variable.

Because incrementing or decrementing a value is so common in programming, Java provides shortcut operators to do this: ++ and −−. (Note that there are no spaces between the two plus and minus signs.) The statement

```
count++;
```

adds 1 to the value of *count*, and the statement

```
count--;
```

subtracts 1 from the value of *count*. Thus,

```
count++;
```

is equivalent to

```
count = count + 1;
```

and

```
count--;
```

is equivalent to

```
count = count - 1;
```

Both of these operators have **prefix** and **postfix** versions. The prefix versions precede the variable name (++a or −−a) whereas the postfix versions follow the variable name (a++ or a−−). Both increment or decrement the variable. If they are used as a single, atomic statement (as in the statements above), there is no difference between the two versions. So

```
a++;
```

is functionally equivalent to

```
++a;
```

and

```
a--;
```

is functionally equivalent to

```
--a;
```

However, if they are used inside a more complex expression, then they differ as follows. The prefix versions increment or decrement the variable first, then the new value of the variable is used in evaluating the expression. The postfix versions increment or decrement the variable after the old value of the variable is used in the expression.

Example 2.11 illustrates this difference.

```
1 /* ShortcutOperators Class
2    Anderson, Franceschi
3 */
4
5 public class ShortcutOperators
6 {
7   public static void main( String [ ] args )
8   {
9     int a = 6;
10    int b = 2;
11
12    System.out.println( "At the beginning, a is " + a );
13    System.out.println( "Increment a with prefix notation: " + ++a );
14    System.out.println( "In the end, a is " + a );
15
16    System.out.println( "\nAt the beginning, b is " + b );
17    System.out.println( "Increment b with postfix notation: " + b++ );
18    System.out.println( "In the end, b is " + b );
19  }
20 }
```

EXAMPLE 2.11   Prefix and Postfix Increment Operators

Lines 9 and 10 declare and initialize two *int* variables, *a* and *b*, to 6 and 2, respectively. In order to illustrate the effect of both the prefix and postfix increment operators, we output their original values at lines 12 and 16. At line 13, we use the prefix increment operator to increment *a* inside an output statement; *a* is incremented before the output statement is executed, resulting in the output statement using the value 7 for *a*. At line 17, we use the postfix increment operator to increment *b* inside an output statement; *b* is incremented after the output statement is executed, resulting in the output statement using the value 2 for *b*. Lines 14 and 18 simply output the values of *a* and *b* after the prefix and postfix operators were used at lines 13 and 17. Figure 2.10 shows the output of this example.

Another set of shortcut operators simplify common calculations that change a single value. For example, the statement

```
a = a + 2: // add 2 to a
```

can be simplified as

```
a += 2; // add 2 to a
```

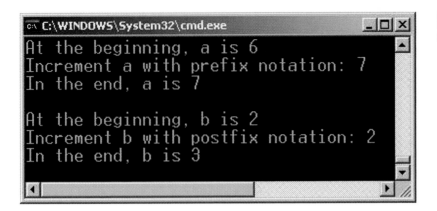

Figure 2.10
Output of Example 2.11

The value added to the target variable can be a variable name or a larger expression.

The shortcut addition operator (+=) is a single operator; there are no spaces between the + and the =. Also, be careful not to reverse the order of the operators. For example, in the following statement, the operators are reversed, so the compiler interprets the statement as "assign a positive 2 to a."

```
a =+ 2 ; // Incorrect! Assigns a positive 2 to a
```

Java provides shortcut operators for each of the basic arithmetic operations: addition, subtraction, multiplication, division, and modulus. These operators are especially useful in performing repetitive calculations and in converting values from one scale to another. For example, to convert feet to inches, we multiply the number of feet by 12. So we can use the *= shortcut operator:

```
int length = 3; // length in feet
length *= 12;   // length converted to inches
```

Converting from one scale to another is a common operation in programming. For example, earlier in the chapter we converted quarters, dimes, and nickels to pennies. You might also need to convert hours to seconds, feet to square feet, or Fahrenheit temperatures to Celsius.

Table 2.13 summarizes the shortcut operators and gives an example for each operator.

COMMON ERROR TRAP

No spaces are allowed between the arithmetic operator (+) and the equal sign. Note also that the sequence is +=, not =+.

TABLE 2.13   Shortcut Operators

Shortcut Operator	Example	Result
++	a++; or ++a;	add 1 to *a*
−−	a−−; or −−a;	subtract 1 from *a*
+=	a += 3;	add 3 to *a*
−=	a −=10;	subtract 10 from *a*
*=	a *= 4;	multiply *a* by 4
/=	a /= 7;	divide *a* by 7
%=	a %= 10;	mod *a* by 10

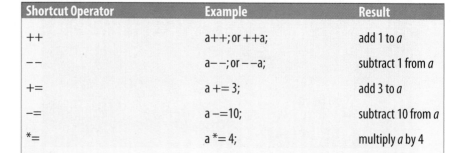

SOFTWARE ENGINEERING TIP

Learn the shortcut operators because Java programmers use them, and you will be able to read and understand their code.

Table 2.14 shows where the shortcut operators fit into the order of operator precedence.

Skill Practice
with these end-of-chapter questions

2.7.1   Multiple Choice Exercises

   Question 3

2.7.2   Reading and Understanding Code

   Questions 14, 15, 16, 17, 18, 19, 20, 21, 22

2.7.3   Fill in the Code

   Questions 28, 30, 31

2.7.4   Identifying Errors in Code

   Questions 36, 37

2.7.5   Debugging Area

   Questions 42, 43

2.7.6   Write a Short Program

   Question 45

2.7.8   Technical Writing

   Question 51

TABLE 2.14 Order of Operator Precedence

Operator Hierarchy	Order of Same-Statement Evaluation	Operation
( )	left to right	parentheses for explicit grouping
++, --	**right to left**	**shortcut postincrement**
++, --	**right to left**	**shortcut preincrement**
*, /, %	left to right	multiplication, division, modulus
+, -	left to right	addition or *String* concatenation, subtraction
=, +=, -=, *=, /=, %=	right to left	assignment operator and **shortcut assignment operators**

2.5 Programming Activity 2: Exercising the Arithmetic Operators

In this Programming Activity, you will write a program that calculates the sum, difference, product, quotient, and modulus of two integers.

Open the *ShellApplication.java* source code shown in Example 2.1. You will find this file on the CD-ROM accompanying this book.

Replace the class name, *ShellApplication*, with the name *ArithmeticOperations*. Since this is now the name of our class, save the source file as the name *ArithmeticOperations.java*. Also replace the comment in line 1 with a description of what this application will do: "Exercising the Arithmetic Operators," and add your name. Your source file should look like Example 2.12.

```
1 /* Exercising the Arithmetic Operators
2    your name here
3 */
4
5 public class ArithmeticOperations
6 {
7    public static void main( String [ ] args ) // required
8    {
9       // write your code here
10   }
11 }
```

EXAMPLE 2.12 *ArithmeticOperations*, Version 1

After the comment

```
// write your code here
```

declare two integer variables, *number1* and *number2*, and assign them the initial values 10 and 3, respectively.

```
int number1 = 10, number2 = 3;
```

Let's start by printing the values of the variables:

```
System.out.println( "number1 is " + number1 );
System.out.println( "number2 is " + number2 );
```

Then define variables to hold the sum, difference, product, quotient, and modulus of these two numbers. Because these variables will hold the results of integer calculations, they should also be declared as *ints*. The variables don't need initial values, however, because we will assign values as we perform the calculations.

```
int sum, difference, product, quotient, modulus;
```

Now calculate the value of each variable and print the result. For example, here's the code for computing and printing the sum.

```
sum = number1 + number2;
System.out.println( "The sum is " + sum );
```

Remember to insert a space before the second quotation marks. Compile, run, and test your results. Then do the same for the remainder of the arithmetic operators. When you are finished, your output should look like Figure 2.11.

DISCUSSION QUESTIONS ?

1. Explain how the division operator and the modulus operator perform complementary functions for integer division.

2. What happens if you omit the space at the end of the *String* literal in the *System.out.println* statements?

Figure 2.11

Output from
ArithmeticOperations

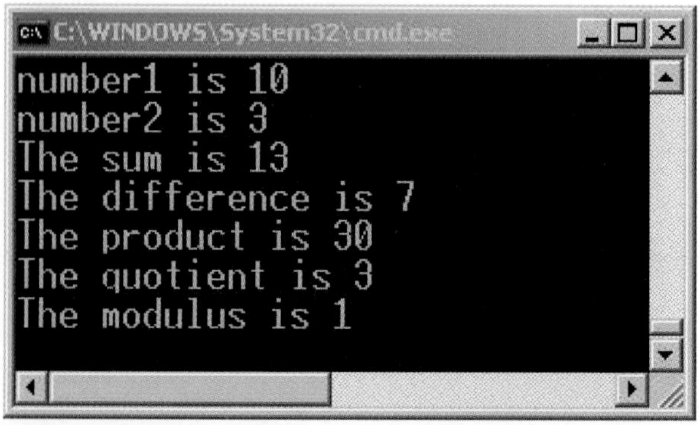

```
number1 is 10
number2 is 3
The sum is 13
The difference is 7
The product is 30
The quotient is 3
The modulus is 1
```

2.6   Chapter Summary

- Java programs consist of at least one class.

- Identifiers are symbolic names for classes, methods, and data. Identifiers should start with a letter and may contain any combination of letters and digits, but no spaces. The length of an identifier is essentially unlimited. Identifier names are case-sensitive.

- Java's reserved words cannot be used as identifiers.

- The basic building block of a Java program is the statement. A statement is terminated with a semicolon and can span several lines.

- Any amount of white space is permitted between identifiers, Java keywords, operands, operators, and literals. White space characters are the space, tab, newline, and carriage return.

- A block, which consists of 0, 1, or more statements, starts with a left curly brace and ends with a right curly brace. Blocks can be used anywhere in the program that a statement is legal.

- Comments are ignored by the compiler. Block comments are delineated by /* and */. Line comments start with // and continue to the end of the line.

- Java supports eight primitive data types: *double, float, long, int, short, byte, char*, and *boolean*.

- Variables must be declared before they are used. Declaring a variable is specifying the data item's identifier and data type. The syntax for declaring a variable is: `dataType identifier1, identifier2, ...;`

- Begin variable names with a lowercase letter. If the variable name consists of more than one word, begin each word after the first with a capital letter. Do not put spaces between words.

- An integer data type is one that evaluates to a positive or negative whole number. Java recognizes four integer data types: *int, short, long*, and *byte*.

- Floating-point data types store numbers with fractional parts. Java supports two floating-point data types: the single-precision type *float*, and the double-precision type *double*.

- The *char* data type stores one Unicode character. Because Unicode characters are encoded as unsigned numbers using 16 bits, a *char* variable is stored in two bytes of memory.

- The *boolean* data type can store only two values, which are expressed using the Java reserved words *true* and *false*.

- The assignment operator (=) is used to give a value to a variable.

- To assign an initial value to a variable, use this syntax when declaring the variable:

```
dataType variable1 = initialValue1;
```

- Literals can be used to assign initial values or to reassign the value of a variable.

- Constants are data items whose value, once assigned, cannot be changed. Data items that you know should not change throughout the execution of a program should be declared as a constant, using this syntax:

```
final dataType constantIdentifier = initialValue;
```

- Constant identifiers, by convention, are composed of all capital letters with underscores separating words.

- An expression consists of operators and operands that evaluate to a single value.

- The value of an expression can be assigned to a variable or constant, which must be a data type compatible with the value of the expression and cannot be a constant that has been assigned a value already.

- Java provides binary operators for addition, subtraction, multiplication, division, and modulus.

- Calculation of the value of expressions follows the rules of operator precedence.

- Integer division truncates any fractional part of the quotient.

- When an arithmetic operator is invoked with operands that are of different primitive types, the compiler temporarily converts, or promotes, one or both of the operands.

- An expression or a variable can be temporarily cast to a different data type using this syntax:

  (dataType) (expression)

- Shortcut operators ++ and −− simplify incrementing or decrementing a value by 1. The prefix versions precede the variable name and increment or decrement the variable, then use its new value in evaluation of the expression. The postfix versions follow the variable name and increment or decrement the variable after using the old value in the expression.

- Java provides shortcut operators for each of the basic arithmetic operations: addition, subtraction, multiplication, division, and modulus.

2.7 Exercises, Problems, and Projects

2.7.1 Multiple Choice Exercises

1. What is the valid way to declare an integer variable named *a*? (Check all that apply.)

   ❏ int a;

   ❏ a int;

   ❏ integer a;

2. Which of the following identifiers are valid?

   ❏ a

   ❏ sales

   ❏ sales&profit

   ❏ int

   ❏ inter

   ❏ doubleSales

   ❏ TAX_RATE

   ❏ 1stLetterChar

   ❏ char

3. Given three declared and initialized *int* variables *a*, *b*, and *c*, which of the following statements are valid?

☐ `a = b;`

☐ `a = 67;`

☐ `b = 8.7;`

☐ `a + b = 8;`

☐ `a * b = 12;`

☐ `c = a - b;`

☐ `c = a / 2.3;`

☐ `boolean t = a;`

☐ `a /= 4;`

☐ `a += c;`

2.7.2 Reading and Understanding Code

4. What is the output of this code sequence?

```
double a = 12.5;
System.out.println( a );
```

5. What is the output of this code sequence?

```
int a = 6;
System.out.println( a );
```

6. What is the output of this code sequence?

```
float a = 13f;
System.out.println( a );
```

7. What is the output of this code sequence?

```
double a = 13 / 5;
System.out.println( a );
```

8. What is the output of this code sequence?

```
int a = 13 / 5;
System.out.println( a );
```

9. What is the output of this code sequence?

```
int a = 13 % 5;
System.out.println( a );
```

10. What is the output of this code sequence?

```
int a = 12 / 6 * 2;
System.out.println( a );
```

11. What is the output of this code sequence?

```
int a = 12 / ( 6 * 2 );
System.out.println( a );
```

12. What is the output of this code sequence?

```
int a = 4 + 6 / 2;
System.out.println( a );
```

13. What is the output of this code sequence?

```
int a = ( 4 + 6 ) / 2;
System.out.println( a );
```

14. What is the output of this code sequence?

```
double a = 12.0 / 5;
System.out.println( a );
```

15. What is the output of this code sequence?

```
int a = (int) 12.0 / 5;
System.out.println( a );
```

16. What is the output of this code sequence?

```
double a = (double) ( 12 ) / 5;
System.out.println( a );
```

17. What is the output of this code sequence?

```
double a = (double) ( 12 / 5 );
System.out.println( a );
```

18. What is the output of this code sequence?

```
int a = 5;
a++;
System.out.println( a );
```

19. What is the output of this code sequence?

```
int a = 5;
System.out.println( a-- );
```

20. What is the output of this code sequence?

```
int a = 5;
System.out.println( --a );
```

21. What is the output of this code sequence?

```
int a = 5;
a += 2;
System.out.println( a );
```

22. What is the output of this code sequence?

```
int a = 5;
a /= 6;
System.out.println( a );
```

2.7.3   Fill in the Code

23. Write the code to declare a *float* variable named *a* and assign *a* the value 34.2.

```
// your code goes here
```

24. Write the code to assign the value 10 to an *int* variable named *a*.

```
int a;
// your code goes here
```

25. Write the code to declare a *boolean* variable named *a* and assign *a* the value *false*.

```
// your code goes here
```

26. Write the code to declare a *char* variable named *a* and assign *a* the character B.

```
// your code goes here
```

27. Write the code to calculate the total of three *int* variables *a*, *b*, and *c* and print the result.

```
int a = 3;
int b = 5;
int c = 8;

// your code goes here
```

28. Write the code to calculate the average of two *int* variables *a* and *b* and print the result. The average should be printed as a floating-point number.

```
int a = 3;
int b = 5;

// your code goes here
```

29. Write the code to calculate and print the remainder of the division of two *int* variables with the values 10 and 3 (the value printed will be 1).

```
int a = 10;
int b = 3;

// your code goes here
```

30. This code increases the value of a variable *a* by 1, using the shortcut increment operator.

```
int a = 7;

// your code goes here
```

31. This code multiplies the value of a variable *a* by 3, using a shortcut operator.

```
int a = 7;

// your code goes here
```

32. Assume that we already have declared and initialized two *int* variables, *a* and *b*. Convert the following sentences to legal Java expressions and statements.

❑ b equals a plus 3 minus 7

❑ b equals a times 4

❑ a equals b times b

❑ a equals b times 3 times 5

❑ b equals the quotient of the division of a by 2

❑ b equals the remainder of the division of a by 3

2.7.4 Identifying Errors in Code

33. Where is the error in this code sequence?

```
int a = 3.3;
```

34. Where is the error in this code sequence?

```
double a = 45.2;
float b = a;
```

35. Where is the error in this code sequence?

```
int a = 7.5 % 3;
```

36. What would happen when this code sequence is compiled and executed?

```
int a = 5 / 0;
```

37. Where is the error in this code sequence?

```
int a = 5;
a - = 4;
```

38. Is there an error in this code sequence? Explain.

```
char c = 67;
```

39. Is there an error in this code sequence? Explain.

```
boolean a = 1;
```

2.7.5   Debugging Area—Using Messages from the Compiler and the JVM

40. You coded the following on line 8 of class *Test.java*:

```
int a = 26.4;
```

When you compile, you get the following message:

```
Test.java:8: possible loss of precision
found : double
required: int
  int a = 26.4;
          ^

1 error
```

Explain what the problem is and how to fix it.

41. You coded the following on line 8 of class *Test.java*:

```
int a = 3
```

When you compile, you get the following message :

```
Test.java:9: ';' expected.
^
1 error
```

Explain what the problem is and how to fix it.

42. You coded the following in class *Test.java*:

```
int a = 32;
int b = 10;
double c = a / b;
System.out.println( "The value of c is " + c );
```

The code compiles properly and runs, but the result is not what you expected. The output is

```
The value of c is 3.0
```

You expected the value of *c* to be 3.2. Explain what the problem is and how to fix it.

43. You coded the following in class *Test.java*:

```
int a = 5;
a =+ 3;
System.out.println( "The value of a is " + a );
```

The code compiles properly and runs, but the result is not what you expected. The output is

```
The value of a is 3
```

You expected the value of *a* to be 8. Explain what the problem is and how to fix it.

2.7.6 Write a Short Program

44. Write a program that calculates and outputs the square of each integer from 1 to 9.

45. Write a program that calculates and outputs the average of integers 1, 7, 9, and 34.

46. Write a program that outputs the following:

```
****
```

2.7.7 Programming Projects

47. Write a program that prints the letter X composed of asterisks (*). Your output should look like this:

```
*    *
 *  *
  *
 *  *
*    *
```

48. Write a program that converts 10, 50, and 100 kilograms to pounds (1 lb = .454 kg).

49. Write a program that converts 2, 5, and 10 inches to millimeters (1 inch = 25.4 mm).

50. Write a program to compute and output the perimeter and the area of a circle having a radius of 3.2 inches.

2.7.8 Technical Writing

51. Some programmers like to write code that is as compact as possible, for instance, using the increment (or decrement) operator in the

middle of another statement. Typically, these programmers document their programs with very few comments. Discuss whether this is a good idea, keeping in mind that a program "lives" through a certain period of time.

52. Compare the following data types for integer numbers: *int*, *short*, and *long*. Discuss their representation in binary, how much space they take in memory, and the purpose of having these data types available to programmers.

CHAPTER 3

Object-Oriented Programming, Part 1: Using Classes

CHAPTER CONTENTS

Introduction

Writing computer programs that use classes and objects is called **object-oriented programming**, or **OOP**. Every Java program consists of at least one class.

In this chapter, we'll introduce object-oriented programming as a way to use classes that have already been written. Classes provide services to the program. These services might include writing a message to the program's user, popping up a dialog box, performing some mathematical calculations, formatting numbers, drawing shapes in a window, or many other basic tasks that add a more professional look to even simple programs. The program that uses a class is called the **client** of the class.

One benefit of using a prewritten class is that we don't need to write the code ourselves; it already has been written and tested for us. This means that we can write our programs more quickly. In other words, we shorten the development time of the program. Using prewritten and pretested classes provides other benefits as well, including more reliable programs with fewer errors.

In Chapter 7, we'll show you how to write your own classes. For now, we'll explore how using prewritten classes can add functionality to our programs.

3.1   Class Basics and Benefits

In Java, classes are composed of data and operations—or functions—that operate on the data. Objects of a class are created using the class as a template, or guide. Think of the class as a generic description, and an object as a specific item of that class. Or you can think of a class as a cookie cutter; the objects of that class are the cookies made with the cookie cutter. For example, a *Student* class might have the following data: name, year, and grade point average. All students have these three data items. We can create an object of the *Student* class by specifying an identifier for the object, for example, *student1*, along with a name, year, and grade point average for a particular student, for example, *Maria Gonzales*, *Sophomore*, 3.5. The identifier of the object is called the **object reference**. Creating an object of a class is called **instantiating an object**, and the object is called an **instance of the class**. Many objects can be instantiated from one class. There can be many instances of the *Student* class, that is, many *Student* objects can be instantiated from the *Student* class. For example, we could create a second object of the *Student* class, *student2*, with its data as *Mike Smith, Junior*, 3.0.

The data associated with an object of a class are called **instance variables**, or **fields**, and can be variables and constants of any primitive data type (*byte, short, int, long, float, double, char,* and *boolean*), or they can be objects of other classes.

The operations for a class, called **methods**, set the values of the data, retrieve the current values of the data, and perform other class-related functions on the data. For example, the *Student* class would provide methods to set the values of the name, year, and grade point average; retrieve the current values of the name, year, and grade point average; and perhaps promote a student to the next year. Invoking a method on an object is called **calling the method**. With a few exceptions, only class methods can directly access or change the instance variables of an object. Other objects must call the methods to set or retrieve the values of the instance variables. Together, the fields and methods of a class are called its **members**.

In essence, a class is a new data type, which is created by combining items of Java primitive data types and objects of other classes. Just as the primitive data types can be manipulated using arithmetic operators (+, −, *, /, and %), objects can be manipulated by calling class methods.

We like to think of classes as similar to M&M™ candies: a protective outer coating around a soft center. Because the methods to operate on the data are included in the class, they provide a protective coating around the data inside. In a well-designed class, only the class methods can change the data. No other methods can directly access the data. We say that the data is *private* to the class. In other words, the class **encapsulates** the data and the methods that operate on that data. The benefit from this encapsulation is that the class methods ensure that only valid values are assigned to an object. For example, the method to set the grade point average would allow values only between 0.0 and 4.0.

Let's look at another example of a class. The *Date* class, written by the authors, has the instance variables *month, day,* and *year*. An object of this class, *independenceDay*, could be instantiated with data values of *7, 4,* and *1776*. Another object of that class, *examDay*, might be instantiated with the values *12, 4,* and *2006*. Methods of the *Date* class ensure that only valid values are set for the month, day, and year. For example, the class methods would not allow us to set a date with a value of January 32. Other class methods might be provided to increment the date to the next day or to print the date in *mm/dd/yyyy* format.

SOFTWARE ENGINEERING TIP

By convention, class names in Java start with a capital letter. Method names, instance variables, and object names start with a lowercase letter. In all of these names, embedded words begin with a capital letter.

Notice that the class names we used, *Student* and *Date*, begin with a capital letter, and the object names, *student1*, *independenceDay*, and *examDay*, start with a lowercase letter. By convention, class names start with a capital letter. Object names, instance variables, and method names conventionally start with a lowercase letter. Internal words start with a capital letter in class names, object names, variables, and methods.

There are many benefits to using classes in a program. Some of the most important benefits include reusability (not only in the current program but also in other programs), encapsulation, and reliability.

A well-written class can be reused in many programs. For example, a *Date* class could be used in a calendar program, an appointment-scheduling program, an online shopping program, and many more applications that rely on dates. Reusing code is much faster than writing and testing new code. As an added bonus, reusing a tested and debugged class in another program makes the program more reliable.

Encapsulation of a class's data and methods helps to isolate operations on the data. This makes it easier to track the source of a bug. For example, when a bug is discovered in an object of the *Student* class, then you know to look for the problem in the methods of the *Student* class, because no other code in your program can directly change the data in a *Student* object.

You do not need to know the implementation details of a class in order to use it in your program. Does the *Date* class store the date in memory as three integers, *month*, *day*, and *year*? Or is the date stored as the number of milliseconds since 1980? The beauty of object orientation is that we don't need to know the implementation of the class; all we need to know is the class **application programming interface (API)**, that is, how to instantiate objects and how to call the class methods.

The benefits of using classes are clear. We will leave the details of creating our own classes until Chapter 7. In the meantime, let's explore how to use classes that are already written.

3.2 Creating Objects Using Constructors

A class describes a generic template for creating, or instantiating, objects. In fact, an object must be instantiated before it can be used. To understand how to instantiate an object of a class and how to call methods of the class, you must know the API of a class, which the creators of the class make public. Table 3.1 shows the API of the *Date* class, written by the authors of this textbook.

Instantiating an object consists of defining an object reference—which will hold the address of the object in memory—and calling a special method of the class called a **constructor**, which has the same name as the class. The job of the constructor is to assign initial values to the data of the class.

Example 3.1 illustrates how to instantiate objects of the *Date* class.

```
 1 /*  A Demonstration of Using Constructors
 2      Anderson, Franceschi
 3 */
 4
 5 public class Constructors
 6 {
 7    public static void main( String [ ] args )
 8    {
 9      Date independenceDay;
10      independenceDay = new Date( 7, 4, 1776 );
11
12      Date graduationDate = new Date( 5, 15, 2008 );
13
14      Date defaultDate = new Date( );
15    }
16 }
```

EXAMPLE 3.1   Demonstrating Constructors

Declaring an object reference is very much like declaring a variable of a primitive type; you specify the data type and an identifier. For example, to declare an integer variable named *number1*, you provide the data type (*int*) and the identifier (*number1*), as follows:

```
int number1;
```

TABLE 3.1   The *Date* Class API

Date Class Constructor Summary
`Date( )`
allocates a *Date* object with initial default values of 1, 1, 2000.
`Date( int mm, int dd, int yy )`
allocates a *Date* object with the initial values of *mm*, *dd*, and *yy*.

Date Class Method Summary	
Return value	**Method name and argument list**
`int`	`getMonth( )` returns the value of *month*.
`int`	`getDay( )` returns the value of *day*.
`int`	`getYear( )` returns the value of *year*.
`void`	`setMonth( int mm )` sets the *month* to *mm*; if *mm* is invalid, sets *month* to 1.
`void`	`setDay( int dd )` sets the *day* to *dd*; if *dd* is invalid, sets *day* to 1.
`void`	`setYear( int yy )` sets the *year* to *yy*.
`String`	`toString( )` returns the value of the date in the form: *month/day/year*.
`boolean`	`equals( Date obj )` compares the date to another *Date* object.

One notable difference in declaring an object reference is that its data type is a class, not a primitive data type. Here is the syntax for declaring an object reference:

```
ClassName objectReference1, objectReference2, ...;
```

In Example 3.1, lines 9, 12, and 14 declare object references for a *Date* object. *Date*, the class name, is the data type, and *independenceDay*, *graduationDate*, and *defaultDate* are the object references.

Object references can refer to **any** object of its class. For example, *Date* object references can point to any *Date* object, but a *Date* object reference cannot point to objects of other classes, such as a *Student* object.

Once an object reference has been declared, you instantiate the object using the following syntax:

```
objectReference = new ClassName( argument list );
```

This calls a constructor of the class to initialize the data. The **argument list** consists of a comma-separated list of initial data values to assign to the object. Classes often provide multiple constructors with different argument lists. Depending on which constructor you call, you can accept default values for the data or specify initial values for the data. When you instantiate an object, your argument list—that is, the number of arguments and their data types—must match one of the constructors' argument lists.

As shown in Table 3.1, the *Date* class has two constructors. The first constructor, *Date( )*, is called the **default constructor**, because its **argument list is empty**. This constructor assigns default values to all data in the object. Thus, in line 14 of Example 3.1, which uses the default constructor, the data for the *independenceDay* object is set to the default values for the *Date* class, which are *1*, *1*, and *2000*.

We see from Table 3.1 that the second constructor for the *Date* class, *Date(int mm, int dd, int yy)*, takes three arguments, all of which should evaluate to integer values. The first argument is the value for the month, the second argument is the value for the day, and the third argument is the value for the year.

Lines 10 and 12 of Example 3.1 instantiate *Date* objects using the second constructor. In line 10, the argument list tells the constructor to give the value *7* to the month, *4* to the day, and *1776* to the year. In line 12, the argument list tells the constructor to give the value *5* to the month, *15* to the day, and *2008* to the year. Note that no data types are given in the argument list, only the initial values for the data. The data types of the arguments are specified in the API so that the client of the class knows what data types the constructor is expecting for its arguments.

Lines 12 and 14 also illustrate that you can combine the declaration of the object reference and instantiation of the object in a single statement.

When an object is instantiated, the JVM allocates memory to the new object and assigns that memory location to its object reference. Figure 3.1 shows the three objects instantiated in Example 3.1.

 COMMON ERROR TRAP

Do not forget to instantiate all objects that your program needs. Objects must be instantiated before they can be used.

It's important to understand that an object reference and the object data are different: The object reference represents the memory location, and the object data are the data stored at that memory location. Notice in Figure 3.1 that the object references, *independenceDay*, *graduationDate*, and *defaultDate*, point to the locations of the object data.

3.3 Calling Methods

Once an object is instantiated, we can use the object by calling its methods. As we mentioned earlier, the authors of classes publish their API so that their clients know what methods are available and how to call those methods.

Figure 3.2 illustrates how calling a class method alters the flow of control in your program. When this program starts running, the JVM executes instruction 1, then instruction 2, then it encounters a method call. At that point, the JVM **transfers control to the method** and starts executing instructions in the method. When the method finishes executing, the JVM transfers control back to the program immediately after the point the method was called and continues executing instructions in the program.

A class API consists of the class method names, their return values, and their argument lists. The argument list for a method indicates the order and number of arguments to send to the method, along with the data type of each argument. Each item in the argument list consists of a data type and a name. The arguments can be literals, constants, variables, or any expression that evaluates to the data type specified in the API of the method. For example, the API in Table 3.1 shows that the *setMonth* method takes one argument, which must evaluate to an integer value.

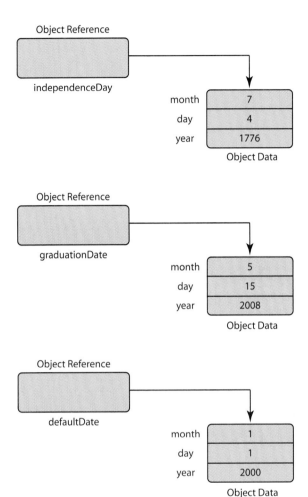

Figure 3.1

Three *Date* Objects after Instantiation

A method may or may not return a value, as indicated by a data type, class type, or the keyword **void** in front of the method name. If the method returns a value, then the data type or class type of its **return value** will precede the method's name. For instance, in Table 3.1, the *getDay* method returns an integer value. The call to a **value-returning method** will be used in an expression. When the method finishes executing, its return value will replace the method call in the expression. If the keyword *void* precedes the method name, the method does not return a value. Because methods with a *void* return type have no value, they cannot be used in an expression;

Figure 3.2
Flow of Control of a
Method Call

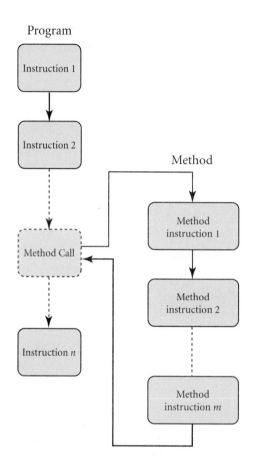

instead, a method call to a method with a *void* return type is a complete statement. In Table 3.1, the *setYear* method is a *void* method.

Another keyword you will see preceding the method call in an API is *public*. This keyword means that any client of the class can call this method. If the keyword *private* precedes the method name, only other methods of that class can call that method. Although we will not formally include the *public* keyword in the API, all the methods we discuss in this chapter are *public*.

To call a method for an object of a class, we use the **dot notation**, as follows:

```
objectReference.methodName( arg1, arg2, arg3, . . . )
```

The object reference is followed immediately by a **dot** (a period), which is followed immediately by the method name. (Later in the chapter, when we call *static* methods, we will substitute the class name for the object reference.) The arguments for the method are enclosed in parentheses.

Let's look again at the methods of the *Date* class. The first three methods in the *Date* class API take an empty argument list and return an *int*; thus, those methods have a return value of type *int*. You can call these methods in any expression in your program where you could use an *int*. The value of the first method, *getMonth( )*, is the value of the month in the object. Similarly, the value of *getDay( )* is the value of the day in the object, and the value of *getYear( )* is the value of the year. These "get" methods are formally called **accessor methods**; they enable clients to access the value of the instance variables of an object.

The next three methods in the *Date* class API take one argument of type *int* and do not return a value, which is indicated by the keyword *void*. These methods are called in standalone statements. The first method, *setMonth (int mm)*, changes the value of the month in the object to the value of the method's argument, *mm*. Similarly, *setDay(int dd)* changes the value of the day in the object, and *setYear(int yy)* changes the value of the year in the object to the value of the method's argument. These "set" methods are formally called **mutator methods**; they enable a client to change the value of the instance variables of an object.

Example 3.2 illustrates how to use some of the methods of the *Date* class. Line 10 calls the *getMonth* method for the *independenceDay* object. When line 10 is executed, control transfers to the *getMonth* method. When the *getMonth* method finishes executing, the value it returns (7) replaces the method call in the statement. The statement then effectively becomes:

```
int independenceMonth = 7;
```

In lines 15–16, we print the value of the day in the *graduationDate* object. Again, control transfers to the *getDay* method, then its return value (15) replaces the method call. So the statement effectively becomes:

```
System.out.println( "The current day for graduation is "
                    + 15 );
```

Line 18 calls the *setDay* method, which is used to change the value of the day for an object. The *setDay* method takes one *int* argument and has a *void* return value. Line 18 is a complete statement, because the method call to a

COMMON ERROR TRAP

When calling a method that takes no arguments, remember to include the empty parentheses after the method's name. The parentheses are required even if there are no arguments.

COMMON ERROR TRAP

When calling a method, include only values or expressions in your argument list. Including data types in your argument list will cause a compiler error.

Figure 3.3

Output of Example 3.2

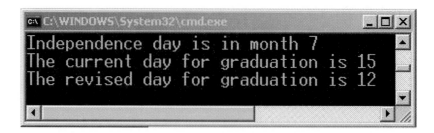

method with a *void* return value is a complete statement. The method changes the value of the day in the *graduationDate* object, which we illustrate in lines 19–20 by printing the new value as shown in Figure 3.3.

```
 1 /*  A demonstration of calling methods
 2      Anderson, Franceschi
 3 */
 4
 5 public class Methods
 6 {
 7   public static void main( String [ ] args )
 8   {
 9     Date independenceDay = new Date( 7, 4, 1776 );
10     int independenceMonth = independenceDay.getMonth( );
11     System.out.println( "Independence day is in month "
12                         + independenceMonth );
13
14     Date graduationDate = new Date( 5, 15, 2008 );
15     System.out.println( "The current day for graduation is "
16                         + graduationDate.getDay( ) );
17
18     graduationDate.setDay( 12 );
19     System.out.println( "The revised day for graduation is "
20                         + graduationDate.getDay( ) );
21   }
22 }
```

EXAMPLE 3.2   Calling Methods

For now, we'll postpone discussion of the last two methods in the class API, *toString* and *equals*, except to say that their functions, respectively, are to convert the object data to a printable format and to compare the object data to another object's data. All classes provide these methods.

Skill Practice
with these end-of-chapter questions

3.10.1 Multiple Choice Exercises

Questions 2, 3, 4, 5, 9, 10

3.10.8 Technical Writing

Questions 69, 70

3.4 Using Object References

As we have mentioned, an object reference points to the data of an object. The object reference and the object data are distinct entities. Any object can have more than one object reference pointing to it, or an object can have no object references pointing to it.

In Example 3.3, two *Date* object references, *hireDate* and *promotionDate*, are declared and their objects are instantiated at lines 9 and 14. Lines 10–12 and 15–18 output the respective data member values of *hireDate* and *promotionDate*. Then, line 20 uses the assignment operator to copy the object reference *hireDate* to the object reference *promotionDate*. After line 20, both object references have the same value and therefore point to the location of the same object, as shown in Figure 3.4. The second object, with values (9, 28, 2004), no longer has an object reference pointing to it and is now marked for **garbage collection**. The **garbage collector**, which is part of the Java Virtual Machine, releases the memory allocated to objects that no

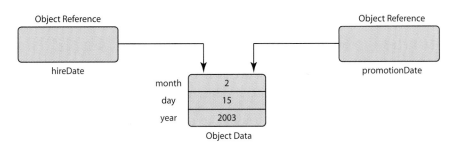

month	2
day	15
year	2003

Object Data

Figure 3.4
Two Object References Pointing to the Same Object

longer have an object reference pointing to them. Lines 23–25 and 26–29 output the respective data member values of *hireDate* and *promotionDate* again. These are now identical, as shown in Figure 3.5.

```
1 /*  A demonstration of object reference assignment
2      Anderson, Franceschi
3 */
4
5 public class ObjectReferenceAssignment
6 {
7    public static void main( String [ ] args )
8    {
9       Date hireDate = new Date( 2, 15, 2003 );
10      System.out.println( "hireDate is " + hireDate.getMonth( )
11                          + "/" + hireDate.getDay( )
12                          + "/" + hireDate.getYear( ) );
13
14      Date promotionDate = new Date( 9, 28, 2004 );
15      System.out.println( "promotionDate is "
16                          + promotionDate.getMonth( )
17                          + "/" + promotionDate.getDay( )
18                          + "/" + promotionDate.getYear( ) );
19
20      promotionDate = hireDate;
21      System.out.println( "\nAfter assigning hireDate "
22                          + "to promotionDate:" );
23      System.out.println( "hireDate is " + hireDate.getMonth( )
24                          + "/" + hireDate.getDay( )
25                          + "/" + hireDate.getYear( ) );
26      System.out.println( "promotionDate is "
27                          + promotionDate.getMonth( )
28                          + "/" + promotionDate.getDay( )
29                          + "/" + promotionDate.getYear( ) );
30   }
31 }
```

EXAMPLE 3.3   **Demonstrating Object Reference Assignments**

When an object reference is first declared, but has not yet been assigned to an object, its value is a special literal value, **null**.

If you attempt to call a method using an object reference whose value is *null*, Java generates either a compiler error or a run-time error called an **exception**. The exception is a *NullPointerException* and results in a series of messages printed on the Java console indicating where in the program the

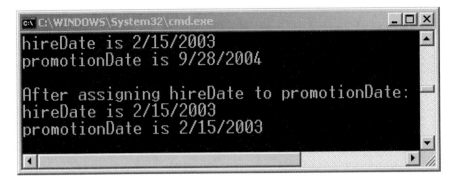

Figure 3.5
Output of Example 3.3

Figure 3.6
Compiler error from Example 3.4

null object reference was used. Line 10 of Example 3.4 will generate a compiler error, as shown in Figure 3.6, because *aDate* has not been instantiated.

```
1  /*  A demonstration of trying to use a null object reference
2      Anderson, Franceschi
3  */
4
5  public class NullReference
6  {
7    public static void main( String [ ] args )
8    {
9      Date aDate;
10     aDate.setMonth( 5 );
11   }
12 }
```

EXAMPLE 3.4 Attempting to Use a *null* Object Reference

There is no way in Java to explicitly delete an object. One way to indicate to the garbage collector that your program is finished with an object is to set its object reference to *null*. Obviously, once an object reference has the value *null*, it can no longer be used to call methods.

Example 3.5 shows a *NullPointerException* being generated at run time. Line 9 instantiates the *independenceDay* object, and lines 10–11 print the

 **COMMON ERROR TRAP**

Using a *null* object reference to call a method will generate either a compiler error or a *NullPointerException* at run time. Be sure to instantiate an object before attempting to use the object reference.

Figure 3.7

Output of Example 3.5

```
The month of independenceDay is 7
Exception in thread "main" java.lang.NullPointerException
        at NullReference2.main(NullReference2.java:15)
```

month. Line 13 assigns *null* to the object reference and lines 15–16 attempt to print the month again. As Figure 3.7 shows, a *NullPointerException* is generated. Notice that the console message indicates the name of the application class (*NullReference2*), the method *main*, and the line number *15*, where the exception occurred. The JVM often prints additional lines in the message, depending on where in your program the error occurred.

```
 1 /*  A demonstration of trying to use a null object reference
 2      Anderson, Franceschi
 3 */
 4
 5 public class NullReference2
 6 {
 7   public static void main( String [ ] args )
 8   {
 9       Date independenceDay = new Date( 7, 4, 1776 );
10       System.out.println( "The month of independenceDay is "
11                           + independenceDay.getMonth( ) );
12
13       independenceDay = null;  // set object reference to null
14       // attempt to use object reference
15       System.out.println( "The month of independenceDay is "
16                           + independenceDay.getMonth( ) );
17   }
18 }
```

EXAMPLE 3.5   Another Attempt to Use a *null* Object Reference

Figure 3.8 shows the *independenceDay* object reference and object data after setting the object reference to *null*.

Figure 3.8

The *independenceDay* Object Reference Set to *null*

Object Reference

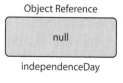

null

independenceDay

Object Data

month	7
day	4
year	1776

3.5 Programming Activity 1: Calling Methods

Let's put this all together with a sample program that uses a *Date* object. In this Programming Activity, we'll use a program that displays the values of the object data as you instantiate the object and call the methods of the class.

In the Chapter 3 Programming Activity 1 folder on the CD-ROM accompanying this book, you will find three source files: *Date.java*, *DateClient. java*, and *Pause.java*. Copy all the *.java* and *.class* files to a directory on your computer. Note that all files should be in the same directory.

Open the *DateClient.java* source file. You'll notice that the class already contains some source code. Your job is to fill in the blanks. Search for five asterisks in a row (*****). This will position you to the places in the source code where you will add your code. This section of code is shown in Figure 3.9.

Notice that line 15 is a declaration of a *Date* object reference, *dateObj*. You will use this object reference for instantiating an object and for calling the methods of the *Date* class.

In the source file, you should see eight commented lines that instruct you to instantiate the object or call a method. You will also notice that there are seven lines that look like this:

```
// animate( "message" );
```

These lines are calls to an *animate* method in this class that displays the object reference and the object data after you have executed your code. The *message* is a *String* literal that describes what action your code just took. The *animate* method will display the message, as well as the object data. Note that when you call a method in the same class, you don't use an object reference and dot notation.

To complete the Programming Activity, write the requested code on the line between the numbered instruction and the *animate* method call. Then **uncomment** (remove the two slashes from) the *animate* method call.

For example, after you've written the code for the first instruction, lines 22 through 25 should look like this. The line you write is shown in bold below.

```
/* 1. Instantiate a dateObj using empty argument list */

dateObj = new Date( );
animate( "Instantiated dateObj - empty argument list" );
```

Compile and run the code and you will see a window that looks like the one in Figure 3.10.

Figure 3.9

Partial Listing of
DateClient.java

```
13    int animationPause = 3; // 3 seconds between animations
14
15    Date dateObj; // declare Date object reference
16
17    public void workWithDates( )
18    {
19      animate( "dateObj reference declared" );
20
21      /***** Add your code here *****/
22      /**** 1. Instantiate dateObj using an empty argument list  */
23
24
25      //animate( "Instantiated dateObj - empty argument list" );
26
27      /***** 2. Set the month to the month you were born */
28
29
30      //animate( "Set month to birth month" );
31
32      /***** 3. Set the day to the day of the month you were born */
33
34
35      //animate( "Set day to birth day" );
36
37      /***** 4. Set the year to the year you were born */
38
39
40      //animate( "Set year to birth year" );
41
42      /***** 5. Set the day to 32, an illegal value */
43
44
45      //animate( "Set day to 32" );
46
47      /***** 6. Set the month to 13, an illegal value */
48
49
50      //animate( "Set month to 13" );
51
52      /***** 7. Assign the value null to dateObj */
53
54
55      //animate( "Set object reference to null" );
56
57
```

```
58    /***** 8. Attempt to set the month to 1 */
59
60   }
```

As you can see, the *dateObj* reference points to the *Date* object, and the *month*, *day*, and *year* instance variables have been assigned default values.

Write the code for the remaining seven instructions, compiling and running the program after completing each task. The program will display the changes you make to the object data.

The pause between animations is set by default to three seconds. To change the pause time, change the value assigned to *animationPause* on line 13 to the number of seconds you would like to pause between animations.

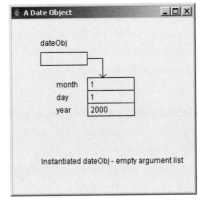

Figure 3.10
Programming Activity 1 Output

? DISCUSSION QUESTIONS

1. After instructions 5 and 6 have executed, why do the day and month values get set to 1?

2. At the end of the execution of the program, a *NullPointerException* is generated. Which statement in the program causes this error? Explain why.

3.6   Calling *Static* Methods and Using *Static* Class Variables

Classes can also define **static methods** that can be called without instantiating an object. These are also called **class methods**. The API of these methods has the keyword *static* before the return type:

```
static dataType methodName( arg1, arg2, . . . )
```

One reason a class may define *static* methods is to provide some quick, one-time functionality without requiring the client to instantiate an object. For example, dialog boxes typically pop up only once in a program. Creating an object for a dialog box, when it is used only once, is a waste of memory and processor time. We'll see later in this chapter how it's possible to create dialog boxes and to perform mathematical calculations without creating an object.

Class, or *static*, methods are invoked using the class name, as in the following syntax:

```
ClassName.staticMethodName( argumentList );
```

For example, in this statement:

```
absValue = Math.abs( someNumber );
```

The class name is *Math*, and the *static* method is *abs*, which returns the absolute value of the argument (*someNumber*). We use the class name rather than an object reference, because *static* methods can be used without instantiating an object. Later in this chapter, we will explore some *static* methods of the *Math* class in greater detail.

Because *static* methods can be called without an object being instantiated, *static* methods cannot access the instance variables of the class (since instance variables are object data which exist only after an object has been instantiated). *Static* methods can access **static data**, however, and classes often declare *static* data to be used with *static* methods. *Static* data belong to the class, rather than to a particular object, or instance, of the class.

A common use of *static* class variables is to define constants for commonly used values or for parameters for the *static* class methods. For example, as we'll discuss in Chapter 4, the *Color* class provides *static* constants that can be assigned to a *Color* object reference.

Like *static* methods, *static* constants are also accessed using the class name and dot operator, as in this syntax:

```
ClassName.staticConstant
```

Thus, the *static* constant representing the color blue can be accessed this way:

```
Color.BLUE
```

At first, this may appear to go against our earlier discussion of encapsulation and the restrictions on clients directly accessing object data. Remember we said that the client needed to use accessor ("gets") and mutator ("sets") methods to access object data. The reasoning behind encapsulation is to protect the object data from corruption by the client. However, in this case, the *static* data is constant, so the client is unable to change it. For the client, directly accessing the class constant is easier and faster than calling a method.

3.7 Using Predefined Classes

As we mentioned earlier, Java provides a wealth of predefined classes that you can use to add functionality to your program. In this section, we'll discuss a few commonly used Java classes:

- *String,* which provides a data type for character strings, along with methods for searching and manipulating strings

- *System* and *PrintStream,* which provide data members and methods for printing data on the Java console

- *NumberFormat* and *DecimalFormat,* which allow you to format numbers for output

- *Math,* which provides methods for performing mathematical operations, including generating random numbers

- Object wrappers, which provide an object equivalent to primitive data types so they can be used in your program as if they were objects

- *JOptionPane,* which allows you to use dialog boxes to display messages to the user or to get input from the user

- *Scanner,* which provides methods for reading input from the Java console

3.7.1 Java Packages

Java provides more than 2,000 classes for use in your programs. The classes are arranged in **packages**, grouped according to functionality.

Table 3.2 describes some of the Java packages that we will cover in this book. You can find more details on these classes on Sun Microsystems' Java Web site *http://java.sun.com.*

Many of the commonly used classes, such as *String* and *Math,* reside in the *java.lang* package. Any class in the *java.lang* package is automatically available to your program.

TABLE 3.2   Commonly Used Java Packages

Package	Categories of Classes
java.lang	Basic functionality common to many programs, such as the *String* class, *Math* class, and object wrappers for the primitive data types
java.awt	Graphics classes for drawing and using colors, and old-style user interface components
javax.swing	New-style user interface components that have a consistent look and feel across platforms
java.text	Classes for formatting numeric output
java.util	Date and time functionality, the *Scanner* class, and other miscellaneous classes

To use a class that is not in the *java.lang* package, you need to tell the compiler in which package the class resides; in other words, you need to tell the compiler where to find the class definition. To do this, you include an **import** statement in your program. The *import* statement is inserted at the top of the program after your introductory comments, but before the *class* statement that begins the program. (Yes, we've defined classes already in the programs we wrote in the last two chapters. We've even written a *static* class method, *main.*)

For example, if you want to use the *DecimalFormat* class to format a floating-point number for output, you would import the *DecimalFormat* class from the *java.text* package as follows:

```
import java.text.DecimalFormat;
```

If you're using more than one class from a package, you can import the whole package by using an asterisk in place of the class name, as follows:

```
import java.text.*;
```

3.7.2   The *String* Class

As we've discussed, Java provides the *char* primitive data type, which stores one character. Almost every program, however, needs a data type that stores more than one character. Programs need to process names, addresses, or labels of many kinds. For example, many programs involve a

TABLE 3.3   *String* Class Constructors

String Class Constructor Summary
String(String str)
allocates a *String* object with the value of *str*, which can be a *String* object or a *String* literal.
String( )
allocates an empty *String* object.

login procedure where the user has to enter a user ID and a password. The program reads the user ID and password, compares them to values stored in a database, and allows the user to continue only if the user ID and password match the database values.

To handle this type of data, Java provides a *String* class. Because the *String* class is part of the *java.lang* package, it is automatically available to any Java program and you do not need to use the *import* statement. The *String* class provides several constructors, as well as a number of methods to manipulate, search, compare, and concatenate *String* objects.

Let's look at two of the *String* class constructors shown in Table 3.3. Example 3.6 shows how to use these two constructors in a program.

```
 1 /* Demonstrating the String methods
 2    Anderson. Franceschi
 3 */
 4 public class StringDemo
 5 {
 6   public static void main ( String [ ] args )
 7   {
 8     String s1 = new String( "OOP in Java " );
 9     System.out.println( "s1 is: " + s1 );
10     String s2 = "is not that difficult. ";
11     System.out.println( "s2 is: " + s2 );
12
13     String s3 = s1 + s2; // new String is s1, followed by s2
14     System.out.println( "s1 + s2 returns: " + s3 );
15
16     System.out.println( "s1 is still: " + s1 ); // s1 is unchanged
17     System.out.println( "s2 is still: " + s2 ); // s2 is unchanged
18
19     String greeting1 = "Hi"; // instantiate greeting1
20     System.out.println( "\nThe length of " + greeting1 + " is "
```

```
21                                + greeting1.length( ) );
22
23      String greeting2 = new String( "Hello" ); // instantiate greeting2
24      int len = greeting2.length( );   // len will be assigned 5
25      System.out.println( "The length of " + greeting2 + " is " + len );
26
27      String empty = new String( );
28      System.out.println( "The length of the empty String is "
29                            + empty.length( ) );
30
31      String greeting2Upper = greeting2.toUpperCase( );
32      System.out.println( );
33      System.out.println( greeting2 + " converted to upper case is "
34                            + greeting2Upper );
35
36      String invertedName = "Lincoln, Abraham";
37
38      int comma = invertedName.indexOf( ',' ); // find the comma
39      System.out.println( "\nThe index of " + ',' + " in "
40                            + invertedName + " is " + comma );
41
42      // extract all characters up to comma
43      String lastName = invertedName.substring( 0, comma );
44      System.out.println( "Dear Mr. " + lastName );
45   }
46 }
```

EXAMPLE 3.6   Demonstrating *String* Methods

When this program runs, it will produce the output shown in Figure 3.11.

The first constructor

```
String( String str )
```

allocates a *String* object and sets its value to the sequence of characters in the argument *str*, which can be a *String* object or a *String* literal. Line 8 instantiates the *String s1* and sets its value to "OOP in Java". Similarly, line 23 instantiates a *String* named *greeting2*, and assigns it the value "Hello".

The second constructor:

```
String( )
```

creates an empty *String*, in other words, a *String* containing no characters. You can add characters to the *String* later. This constructor will come in handy in programs where we build up our output, piece by piece. Line 27 uses the second constructor to instantiate an empty *String* named *empty*.

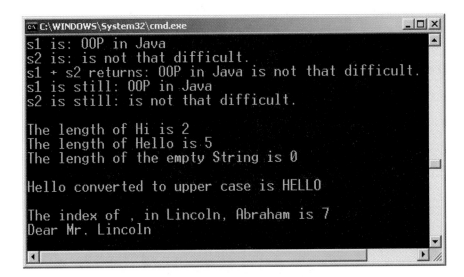

Figure 3.11

Output from Example 3.6

```
C:\WINDOWS\System32\cmd.exe                              _ □ ×
s1 is: OOP in Java
s2 is: is not that difficult.
s1 + s2 returns: OOP in Java is not that difficult.
s1 is still: OOP in Java
s2 is still: is not that difficult.

The length of Hi is 2
The length of Hello is 5
The length of the empty String is 0

Hello converted to upper case is HELLO

The index of , in Lincoln, Abraham is 7
Dear Mr. Lincoln
```

Additionally, because *Strings* are used so frequently in programs, Java provides special support for instantiating *String* objects without explicitly using the *new* operator. We can simply assign a *String* literal to a *String* object reference. Lines 10 and 19 assign *String* literals to the *s2* and *greeting1 String* references.

Java also provides special support for appending a *String* to the end of another *String* through the **concatenation operator** (+) and the **shortcut version of the concatenation operator** (+=). This concept is illustrated in Example 3.6. Lines 8–11 declare, instantiate, and print two *String* objects, *s1*, and *s2*. Line 13 concatenates *s1* and *s2* and the resulting *String* is assigned to the *s3 String* reference, which is printed at line 14. Finally, we output *s1* and *s2* again at lines 16 and 17 to illustrate that their values have not changed.

Note that the *String* concatenation operator is the same character as the arithmetic addition operator. In some cases, we need to make clear to the compiler which operator we want to use. For example, this statement uses both the *String* concatenation operator and the arithmetic addition operator:

```
System.out.println( "The sum of 1 and 2 is " + ( 1 + 2 ) );
```

Notice that we put *1 + 2* inside parentheses to let the compiler know that we want to add the two *ints* using the arithmetic addition operator (+). The addition will be performed first because of the higher operator precedence of parentheses. Then it will become clear to the compiler that the other +

TABLE 3.4   *String* Methods

String Class Method Summary	
Return value	**Method name and argument list**
int	length( )
	returns the length of the *String*
String	toUpperCase( )
	converts all letters in the *String* to upper case
String	toLowerCase( )
	converts all letters in the *String* to lower case
char	charAt(int index)
	returns the character at the position specified by *index*
int	indexOf(String searchString)
	returns the index of the beginning of the first occurrence of *searchString* or −1 if *searchString* is not found
int	indexOf(char searchChar)
	returns the index of the first occurrence of *searchChar* in the *String* or −1 if *searchChar* is not found
String	substring(int startIndex, int endIndex)
	returns a substring of the *String* object beginning at the character at index *startIndex* and ending at the character at index (*endIndex* − 1)

operator is intended to be a *String* concatenation operator because its operands are a *String* and an *int*.

Some useful methods of the *String* class are summarized in Table 3.4.

The length Method

The *length* method returns the number of characters in a *String*. Sometimes, the number of characters in a user ID is limited, for example, to eight, and this method is useful to ensure that the length of the ID does not exceed the limit.

The *length* method is not *static*, so it is called using a *String* object reference and the dot operator, as illustrated in lines 21, 24, and 29 of Example 3.6. At lines 21 and 29, the *length* method is called inside an output statement and the respective return values from the *length* method are output. At line 24, we call the *length* method for the *greeting2* object and assign the return value to the *int* variable *len*. Then at line 25, we output the value of the variable *len*. As shown in Figure 3.11, the length of "*Hi*" is 2, the length of "*Hello*" is 5, and the length of the empty *String* is 0.

The toUpperCase and toLowerCase Methods

The *toUpperCase* method converts all the letters in a *String* to upper case, while the *toLowerCase* method converts all the letters in a *String* to lower case. Digits and special characters are unchanged.

At line 31 of Example 3.6, the *toUpperCase* method is called using the object reference *greeting2*, and the return value is assigned to a *String* named *greeting2Upper*, which is then printed at lines 33 and 34.

The indexOf Methods

The *indexOf* methods are useful for searching a *String* to see if specific *Strings* or characters are in the *String*. The methods return the location of the first occurrence either of a single *char* or the first character of a *String*.

The location, or **index**, of any character in a *String* is counted from the first position in the *String*, which has the index value of 0. Thus in this *String*,

```
String greeting = "Ciao";
```

the *C* is at index 0; the *i* is at index 1; the *a* is at index 2; and the *o* is at index 3. Because indexes begin at 0, the maximum index in a *String* is 1 less than the number of characters in the *String*. So the maximum index for *greeting* is *greeting.length( ) − 1*, which is *3*.

In Example 3.6, line 38 retrieves the index of the first comma in the *String* *invertedName* and assigns it to the *int* variable *comma*; the value of *comma*, here 7, is then output at lines 39 and 40.

The charAt and substring Methods

The *charAt* and *substring* methods are useful for extracting either a single *char* or a group of characters from a *String*.

The *charAt* method returns the character at a particular index in a *String*. One of the uses of this method is for extracting just the first character of a *String*, which might be advantageous when prompting the user for an answer to a question. For example, we might ask users if they want to play again. They can answer "y," "yes," or "you bet!"

Our only concern is whether the first character is a *y*, so we could use this method to put the first character of their answer into a *char* variable. Assuming the user's answer was previously assigned to a *String* variable named *answerString*, we would use the following statement to extract the first character of *answerString*:

```
char answerChar = answerString.charAt( 0 );
```

In Chapter 5, we'll see how to test whether *answerChar* is a *y*.

The *substring* method returns a group of characters, or **substring**, from a *String*. The original *String* is unchanged. As arguments to the *substring* method, you specify the index at which to start extracting the characters and the index of the first character not to extract. Thus, the *endIndex* argument is one position past the last character to extract. We know this sounds a little awkward, but setting up the arguments this way actually makes the method easier to use, as we will demonstrate.

In Example 3.6, we want to extract the last name in the *String inverted-Name*. Line 38 finds the index of the comma and assigns it to the *int* variable *comma*, then line 43 extracts the substring from the first character (index 0) to the index of the comma (which conveniently won't extract the comma), and assigns it to the *String* variable *lastName*. When the variable *lastName* is output at line 44, its value is *Lincoln*, as shown in Figure 3.11.

When you are calculating indexes and the number of characters to extract, be careful not to specify an index that is not in the *String*, because that will generate a run-time error, *StringIndexOutOfBoundsException*.

COMMON ERROR TRAP

Specifying a negative start index or a start index past the last character of the *String* will generate a *StringIndexOutOfBoundsException*. Specifiying a negative end index or an end index greater than the length of the *String* will also generate a *StringIndexOutOfBoundsException*.

REFERENCE POINT

You can read more about the *String* class in Appendix F and on Sun Microsystems' Java Web site *http://java.sun.com*.

CODE IN ACTION

In the Chapter 3 folder on the CD-ROM included with this book, you will find a Shockwave movie showing a step-by step illustration of how to instantiate an object and call both instance and *static* methods. Double-click on *UsingAClass.html* to start the movie.

Skill Practice
with these end-of-chapter questions

3.10.1 Multiple Choice Exercises

Questions 1, 6, 7, 8, 11

3.10.2 Reading and Understanding Code

Questions 14, 15, 16

3.10.3 Fill in the Code

Questions 24, 25, 27

3.10.4 Identifying Errors in Code

Questions 37, 38, 39, 43

3.10.5 Debugging Area

Question 45

3.7.3 Using *System.out*

In order to print program output to the screen, we have been using statements like

```
System.out.println( "Hello World" );
```

and

```
System.out.println( "The value of b is " + b );
```

It is now time to look at these statements in depth and understand them completely.

System is an existing Java class in the *java.lang* package. One of its fields is a *static* constant, *out*, which is an object of the class *PrintStream*. *PrintStream* is also an existing Java class; it can be found in the *java.io* package. Because *out* is *static*, we refer to it using the class name, *System*, and the dot notation:

```
System.out
```

The *PrintStream* class methods *print* and *println* take arguments of any primitive type, a *String* object, or an object reference. The only difference between *print* and *println* is that *println* will also print a *newline* character after it writes the output. Both *print* and *println* write to the **standard output device**, which by default is the Java console. Table 3.5 shows two methods of the *PrintStream* class, which can be used with *System.out*.

Example 3.7 demonstrates various ways to use the *print* and *println* methods:

```
1 /*  Testing the print and println methods
2     Anderson, Franceschi
3 */
4
5 public class PrintDemo
6 {
7   public static void main( String [ ] args )
8   {
9     System.out.println( "Combine the arguments using concatenation" );
10    System.out.println( "A double: " + 23.7 + ", and an int: " + 78 );
11
12    System.out.print( "\nJava is case sensitive: " );
13    System.out.println( 'a' + " is different from " + 'A' );
14
15    System.out.println( "\nCreate a variable and print its value" );
16    String s = new String( "The grade is" );
17    double grade = 3.81;
18    System.out.println( s + " " + grade + "\n" );
19
20    Date d = new Date( 4, 5, 2005 );
21    System.out.println( "Explicitly calling toString, d is "
22                           + d.toString( ) );
23    System.out.println( "Implicitly calling toString, d is " + d );
24  }
25 }
```

EXAMPLE 3.7   Demonstrating the *print* and *println* Methods

Lines 10 and 13 show how *print* or *println* can be used with various data types such as *double*, *int*, and *char*. Variables and expressions can also be used instead of literals, as shown in line 18, where the *String s* and the *double* variable *grade* are output.

We can also print objects. All classes have a *toString* method, which converts the object to a *String* for printing. The *toString* method is called automatically whenever an object is used as a *String*. Notice that our *Date* class, introduced earlier in the chapter, had a *toString* method that returned the object data as a *String* in the format *mm/dd/yyyy*.

TABLE 3.5 *PrintStream* **Methods for Use with** *System.out*

Useful *PrintStream* Methods	
Return value	**Method name and argument list**
void	print(argument)
	prints *argument* to the standard output device. The *argument* can be any primitive data type or a *String* object.
void	println(argument)
	prints *argument* to the standard output device, then prints a *newline* character. The *argument* can be any primitive data type or a *String* object.

The *toString*'s method's API is

```
String toString( )
```

After the *Date* object reference *d* is instantiated at line 20, it is printed at line 21 and again at line 23. At line 21, the method *toString* is called explicitly; at line 23, it is called automatically. Therefore, the outputs of lines 21 and 23 are identical. The output of Example 3.7 is shown in Figure 3.12.

REFERENCE POINT

You can read more about the *System* and *PrintStream* classes in Appendix F and on Sun Microsystems' Java Web site *http://java.sun.com*.

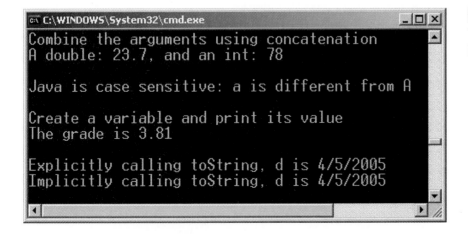

Figure 3.12

The Output from Example 3.7

3.7.4 Formatting Output

In a computer program, numbers represent a real-life entity, for instance, a price or a winning percentage. Floating-point numbers, however, are accurate to many decimal places and, as a result of some computations, can end up with more significant digits than our programs need. For example, the price of an item after a discount could look like 3.466666666666666, when all we really want to display is $3.47; that is, with a leading dollar sign and two significant digits after the decimal point.

The *NumberFormat* class and the *DecimalFormat* class allow you to specify the number of digits to display after the decimal point and to add dollar signs and percentage signs (%) to your output.

The NumberFormat Class

The *NumberFormat* class provides, among others, methods to format a number as currency or a percentage. The *NumberFormat* class is part of the *java.text* package, so you need to include the following *import* statement at the top of your program.

```
import java.text.NumberFormat;
```

The methods of the *NumberFormat* class to format currency and percentages are shown in Table 3.6.

As you can see from the first two method headers, their return type is a *NumberFormat* object. The *NumberFormat* class is an *abstract* class. We cannot instantiate an object using a constructor from an *abstract* class (more on that topic in Chapter 10). We will need to use one of two methods to create a *NumberFormat* object.

TABLE 3.6 Useful Methods of the *NumberFormat* Class

NumberFormat Method Summary	
Return value	**Method name and argument list**
NumberFormat	getCurrencyInstance( ) *static* method that creates a format object for printing money.
NumberFormat	getPercentInstance( ) *static* method that creates a format object for printing percentages.
String	format (double number) returns a *String* representation of *number* formatted according to the object used to call the method.

Once we've created a *NumberFormat* object, we can use the *format* method from the *NumberFormat* class to display a value using the *NumberFormat* object as a pattern. The *format* method takes one argument, which is the variable or value that we want to print; it returns the formatted version of the value as a *String* object, which we can then print.

Example 3.8 is a complete program illustrating how to use these three methods.

```
1  /*  Demonstration of currency and percentage formatting
2        using the NumberFormat class.
3        Anderson, Franceschi
4  */
5
6  // we need to import the NumberFormat class from java.text
7  import java.text.NumberFormat;
8
9  public class DemoNumberFormat
10 {
11   public static void main( String [ ] args )
12   {
13     double winningPercentage = .67;
14     double price = 78.99;
15
16     // get a NumberFormat object for printing a percentage
17     NumberFormat percentFormat = NumberFormat.getPercentInstance( );
18
19     // call format method using the NumberFormat object
20     System.out.print( "The winning percentage is " );
21     System.out.println( percentFormat.format( winningPercentage ) );
22
23     // get a NumberFormat object for printing currency
24     NumberFormat priceFormat = NumberFormat.getCurrencyInstance( );
25
26     // call format method using the NumberFormat object
27     System.out.println( "\nThe price is: "
28                         + priceFormat.format( price ) );
29   }
30 }
```

EXAMPLE 3.8   Demonstrating the *NumberFormat* Class

When this program is run, the output looks like the window shown in Figure 3.13.

Figure 3.13
Output from Example 3.8

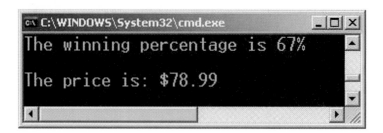

The DecimalFormat Class

The *DecimalFormat* class, also part of the *java.text* package, provides, among others, methods to format a number with a specified number of significant digits after the decimal point. To use the *DecimalFormat* class, you should include the following *import* statement in your program:

```
import java.text.DecimalFormat;
```

The *DecimalFormat* class is not an *abstract* class, and we can instantiate an object using one of its constructors. Here, we will use a simple constructor, one that takes a *String* object as an argument. This *String* object represents how we want our formatted number to look when it's printed. The header for that constructor is shown in Table 3.7.

Once we have instantiated a *DecimalFormat* object with the constructor, that object can be used to call the same *format* method as in the *Number-Format* class. (The *DecimalFormat* class is actually a **subclass** of *Number-Format*, because it inherits from *NumberFormat*. We'll discuss inheritance in Chapter 10.)

The pattern that we use to instantiate the *DecimalFormat* object consists of special characters and symbols and creates a "picture" of how we want the

TABLE 3.7   A *DecimalFormat* Constructor

DecimalFormat Class Constructor
DecimalFormat(String pattern)
instantiates a *DecimalFormat* object with the output *pattern* specified in the argument.

TABLE 3.8   Special Characters for *DecimalFormat* Patterns

Common Pattern Symbols for a *DecimalFormat* Object	
Symbol	Meaning
0	Required digit. If there is no digit in the number for this position, print a zero.
#	Digit, don't print anything if the digit is 0.
.	Decimal point.
,	Comma separator.
$	Dollar sign.
%	Multiply by 100 and display a percentage sign.

number to look when printed. Some of the more commonly used symbols and their meanings are listed in Table 3.8.

Example 3.9 demonstrates the use of these *DecimalFormat* patterns.

```
 1 /* Demonstrating the DecimalFormat class
 2      Anderson, Franceschi
 3 */
 4
 5 // import the DecimalFormat class from the java.text package;
 6 import java.text.DecimalFormat;
 7
 8 public class DemoDecimalFormat
 9 {
10   public static void main( String [ ] args )
11   {
12     // first, instantiate a DecimalFormat object specifying a
13     // pattern for currency
14     DecimalFormat pricePattern = new DecimalFormat( "$##0.00" );
15
16     double price1 = 78.66666666;
17     double price2 = 34.5;
18     double price3 = .3333333;
19     int price4 = 3;
20     double price5 = 100.23;
```

(continued)

```
21
22      // then print the values using the pattern
23      System.out.println( "The first price is: "
24              + pricePattern.format( price1 ) );
25      System.out.println( "\nThe second price is: "
26              + pricePattern.format( price2 ) );
27      System.out.println( "\nThe third price is: "
28              + pricePattern.format( price3 ) );
29      System.out.println( "\nThe fourth price is: "
30              + pricePattern.format( price4 ) );
31      System.out.println( "\nThe fifth price is: "
32              + pricePattern.format( price5 ) );
33
34      // instantiate another new DecimalFormat object
35      // for printing percentages
36      DecimalFormat percentPattern = new DecimalFormat( "#0.0%" );
37
38      double average = .980;
39      System.out.println( "\nThe average is: "
40              + percentPattern.format( average ) );
41      // notice that the average is multiplied by 100
42      // to print a percentage.
43
44
45      // now instantiate another new DecimalFormat object
46      // for printing time as two digits
47      DecimalFormat timePattern = new DecimalFormat( "00" );
48
49      int hours = 5, minutes = 12, seconds = 0;
50      System.out.println( "\nThe time is "
51              + timePattern.format( hours ) + ":"
52              + timePattern.format( minutes ) + ":"
53              + timePattern.format( seconds ) );
54
55      // now instantiate another DecimalFormat object
56      // for printing numbers in the millions.
57      DecimalFormat bigNumber = new DecimalFormat( "#,###,###" );
58
59      int millions = 1234567;
60      System.out.println( "\nmillions is "
61              + bigNumber.format( millions ) );
62   }
63 }
```

EXAMPLE 3.9   Demonstrating the *DecimalFormat* Class

Figure 3.14
Output from Example 3.9

When this program runs, the output looks like the window in Figure 3.14.

In Example 3.9, line 14 instantiates the *DecimalFormat* object, *pricePattern*, which will be used to print prices. In the pattern:

`"$##0.00"`

the first character of this pattern is the dollar sign ($), which we want to precede the price. The first two #'s specify that leading zeroes should not be printed. The 0 specifies that there should be at least one digit to the left of the decimal point. If there is no value to the left of the decimal point, then print a zero. The two 0's that follow the decimal point specify that two digits should be printed to the right of the decimal point; that is, if more than two digits are to the right of the decimal point, round to two digits; if the last digit is a 0, print the zero, and if there is no fractional part to the number, print two zeroes. Using this pattern, we see that in lines 23–24, *price1* is rounded to two decimal places. In lines 25–26, *price2* is printed with a zero in the second decimal place.

In lines 29–30, we print *price4*, which is an integer. The *format* method API calls for a *double* as the argument; however, because all numeric data types can be promoted to a *double*, any numeric data type can be sent as an argument. The result is that two zeroes are added to the right of the decimal point.

Finally, we use the *pricePattern* pattern to print *price5* in lines 31–32, which needs no rounding or padding of extra digits.

Next, line 36 instantiates a *DecimalFormat* object, *percentPattern*, for printing percentages to one decimal point (`"#0.0%"`). Lines 38–40 define the variable *average*, then print it using the *format* method. Notice that the format method automatically multiplies the value of *average* by 100.

REFERENCE POINT

You can read more about the *DecimalFormat* class and the *NumberFormat* class in Appendix F and on Sun Microsystems' Java Web site *http://java.sun.com*.

Line 47 defines another pattern, `"00"`, which is useful for printing the time with colons between the hour, minutes, and seconds. When the time is printed on lines 50–53, the hours, minutes, and seconds are padded with a leading zero, if necessary.

Line 57 defines our last pattern, `"#,###,###"`, which can be used to print integer values in the millions. Lines 60–61 print the variable *millions* with commas separating the millions and thousands digits.

3.7.5   The *Math* Class and Random Numbers

The *Math* class is also part of the *java.lang* package. As such, it is automatically available to any Java program; you do not need to use the *import* statement. The *Math* class provides two *static* constants (*E* and *PI*), as well as a number of *static* methods that save the programmer from writing some complex mathematical code.

The two constants, *E* and *PI*, are both *doubles* and represent, respectively, *e* (the base of the natural logarithm, i.e., log e = 1) and ***pi***, the ratio of the circumference of a circle to its diameter. Approximate values of *e* and *pi*, as we know them, are 2.78 and 3.14, respectively.

Because *E* and *PI* are *static* data members of the *Math* class, they are referenced using the name of the *Math* class and the dot notation as follows:

```
Math.E
Math.PI
```

Useful methods of the *Math* class are shown in Table 3.9.

All the methods of the *Math* class are also *static*; so they are called using the class name, *Math*, and the dot notation as follows:

```
Math.abs( -5 )
```

TABLE 3.9   Useful Methods of the *Math* Class

Math Class Method Summary	
Return value	**Method name and argument list**
dataTypeOfArg	abs(arg)
	returns the absolute value of the argument *arg*, which can be a *double, float, int,* or *long*.
double	log(double a)
	returns the natural logarithm (in base e) of its argument, *a*. For example, log(1) returns 0 and log(*Math.E*) returns 1.
dataTypeOfArgs	min(argA, argB)
	returns the smaller of the two arguments. The arguments can be *doubles, floats, ints,* or *longs*.
dataTypeOfArgs	max(argA, argB)
	returns the larger of the two arguments. The arguments can be *doubles, floats, ints,* or *longs*.
double	pow(double base, double exp)
	returns the value of *base* raised to the *exp* power.
double	random( )
	returns a random number greater than or equal to 0 and less than 1.
long	round(double a)
	returns the closest integer to its argument, *a*.
double	sqrt(double a)
	returns the positive square root of *a*.

Example 3.10 demonstrates how these *Math* constants and the *abs* method can be used in a Java program. In lines 9 and 10, we print the values of *e* and *pi* using the *static* constants of the *Math* class. Then in lines 12 and 15, we

Figure 3.15
Output from
Example 3.10

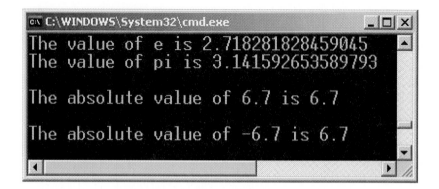

call the *abs* method, which returns the absolute value of its argument. We then print the results in lines 13 and 16. The output of Example 3.10 is shown in Figure 3.15.

```
1  /*  A demonstration of the Math class methods and constants
2      Anderson, Franceschi
3  */
4
5  public class MathConstants
6  {
7    public static void main( String [ ] args )
8    {
9      System.out.println( "The value of e is " + Math.E );
10     System.out.println( "The value of pi is " + Math.PI );
11
12     double d1 = Math.abs( 6.7 ); // d1 will be assigned 6.7
13     System.out.println( "\nThe absolute value of 6.7 is " + d1 );
14
15     double d2 = Math.abs( -6.7 ); // d2 will be assigned 6.7
16     System.out.println( "\nThe absolute value of -6.7 is " + d2 );
17   }
18 }
```

EXAMPLE 3.10   *Math* Class Constants and the *abs* Method

The operation and usefulness of most *Math* class methods are obvious. But several methods—*pow, round, min/max,* and *random*—require a little explanation.

The pow Method

Example 3.11 demonstrates how some of these *Math* methods can be used in a Java program.

```
 1 /*  A demonstration of some Math class methods
 2       Anderson, Franceschi
 3 */
 4
 5 public class MathMethods
 6 {
 7   public static void main( String [ ] args )
 8   {
 9     double d2 = Math.log( 5 );
10     System.out.println( "\nThe log of 5 is " + d2 );
11
12     double d4 = Math.sqrt( 9 );
13     System.out.println( "\nThe square root of 9 is " + d4 );
14
15     double fourCubed = Math.pow( 4, 3 );
16     System.out.println( "\n4 to the power 3 is " + fourCubed );
17
18     double bigNumber = Math.pow( 43.5, 3.4 );
19     System.out.println( "\n43.5 to the power 3.4 is " + bigNumber );
20   }
21 }
```

EXAMPLE 3.11   A Demonstration of Some *Math* Class Methods

The *Math* class provides the *pow* method for raising a number to a power. The *pow* method takes two arguments, the first is the base and the second is the exponent.

Although the argument list for the *pow* method specifies that the base and the exponent are both *doubles,* you can, in fact, send arguments of any numeric type to the *pow* method because all numeric types can be promoted to a *double*. No matter what type the arguments are, however, the return value is always a *double*. Thus, when line 15 calls the *pow* method with two integer arguments, the value of *fourCubed* will be *64.0*. If you prefer that the return value be 64, you can cast the return value to an *int*.

Figure 3.16

Output from Example 3.11

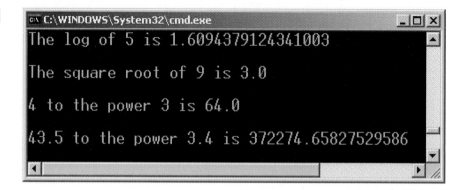

Line 18 shows how to use the *pow* method with arguments of type *double*. The output of Example 3.11 is shown in Figure 3.16.

The round Method

The *round* method converts a *double* to its nearest integer using these rules:

- any factional part .0 to .4 is rounded down

- any fractional part .5 and above is rounded up

Lines 9–13 in Example 3.12 use the *round* method with various numbers. Figure 3.17 shows the output.

```
1 /*  A demonstration of the Math round method
2     Anderson, Franceschi
3 */
4
5 public class MathRounding
6 {
7   public static void main( String [ ] args )
8   {
9     System.out.println( "23.4 rounded is " + Math.round( 23.4 ) );
10     System.out.println( "23.49 rounded is " + Math.round( 23.49 ) );
11     System.out.println( "23.5 rounded is " + Math.round( 23.5 ) );
12     System.out.println( "23.51 rounded is " + Math.round( 23.51 ) );
13     System.out.println( "23.6 rounded is " + Math.round( 23.6 ) );
14   }
15 }
```

EXAMPLE 3.12   A Demonstration of the *Math round* method

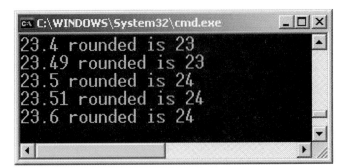

Figure 3.17
Output from
Example 3.12

The min and max Methods

The *min* and *max* methods return the smaller or larger of their two arguments, respectively. Example 3.13 demonstrates how the *min* and *max* methods can be used in a Java program. Figure 3.18 shows the output. Thus the statement on line 9 of Example 3.13

```
int smaller = Math.min( 8, 2 );
```

will assign 2 to the *int* variable *smaller*. At line 12, a similar statement using the *max* method will assign 8 to the *int* variable *larger*.

```
1  /*  A demonstration of min and max Math class methods
2       Anderson, Franceschi
3  */
4
5  public class MathMinMaxMethods
6  {
7    public static void main( String [ ] args )
8    {
9      int smaller = Math.min( 8, 2 );
10     System.out.println( "The smaller of 8 and 2 is " + smaller );
11
12     int larger = Math.max( 8, 2 );
13     System.out.println( "The larger of 8 and 2 is " + larger );
14
15     int a = 8, b = 5, c = 12;
16     int tempSmaller = Math.min( a, b );   // find smaller of a & b
17     int smallest = Math.min( tempSmaller, c ); // compare result to c
18     System.out.println( "The smallest of " + a + ", " + b + ", and "
19                          + c + " is " + smallest );
20   }
21 }
```

EXAMPLE 3.13   A Demonstration of the *min* and *max* Methods

Figure 3.18
Output from
Example 3.13

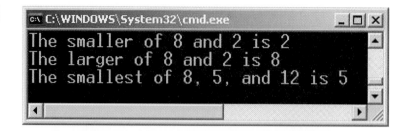

The *min* method can also be used to compute the smallest of three variables. After declaring and initializing the three variables (*a*, *b*, and *c*) at line 15, we assign to a temporary variable named *tempSmaller* the smaller of the first two variables, *a* and *b*, at line 16. Then, at line 17, we compute the smaller of *tempSmaller* and the third variable, *c*, and assign that value to the *int* variable *smallest*, which is output at lines 18 and 19.

The pattern for finding the largest of three numbers is similar, and we leave that as an exercise at the end of the chapter.

The random Method

The *random* method generates random numbers. Random numbers come in handy for many operations in a program, such as rolling dice, dealing cards, timing the appearance of a nemesis in a game, or other simulations of seemingly random events.

There's one problem in using random numbers in programs, however: Computers are **deterministic**. In essence, this means that given a specific input to a specific set of instructions, a computer will always produce the same output. The challenge, then, is how to generate random numbers while using a deterministic system. Many talented computer scientists have worked on this problem, and some innovative and complex solutions have been proposed.

The Java *Math* class's *random* method, however, takes one of the simpler approaches. It uses a mathematical formula to generate a sequence of numbers, using the current system time to *seed* the formula with an initial value. As such, the *random* method generates numbers that appear to be random, but are not actually random. These numbers are called **pseudo-random** numbers, and they work just fine for our purposes.

The *random* method returns a *double* value between 0 and up to, but not including, 1. Thus, it might return something like

0.4885534304610798

or

0.1545153340677723

Let's take rolling a die as an example. To simulate the roll of a six-sided die, we need to simulate random occurrences of the numbers 1 through 6. The return values from the *random* method described above, however, don't look anything like the roll of a die. So we need to convert the return value of the *random* method into the range of numbers we need for our program.

To accomplish this, we'll convert the return value from the *random* method into an integer value between 1 and 6. Let's start by multiplying the return value by 6, then casting the result to an integer.

```
(int) ( Math.random( ) * 6 )
```

In essence, this operation converts the fractional return value from the *random* method into one of six "equally occurring" values. Because the minimum return value of the *random* method is 0, the smallest result at this point will be 0 (which is 0.0 * 6), and because the *random* method's return value never equals 1, the highest value we can generate is 5 (which is 0.99 * 6). So now we have values ranging from 0 to 5. Those are six values, but not the right six values. We need to perform one more operation: add 1 to the result to shift the range of values to 1 through 6.

In Example 3.14, line 12 does the trick:

```
int die = 1 + (int) ( Math.random( ) * 6 );
```

Let's put the first random number we received above (0.4885534304610798) through this formula:

```
int die = 1 + (int)( Math.random( ) * 6 )
        = 1 + (int)( 0.4885534304610798 * 6 )
        = 1 + (int)( 2.931320582766479 )
        = 1 + 2
        = 3
```

Thus, we can see that if the return value from the *random* method is 0.4885534304610798, we will translate it into a 3.

In general, we will need to generate values between a given integer a and up to, but not including, another integer b. In order to use the *random* method properly, let's consider the following:

If x is a number between 0 and 1, then $x * (b - a)$ is a number between 0 and $(b - a)$. Then, $a + x * (b - a)$ is a number between a and b.

Therefore, the pattern to generate a random number between a and up to, but not including, b is

```
int randomNumber = a + (int)( Math.random( ) * ( b - a ) );
```

So for the die example, the value of a will be 1 and the value of b will be 7 (remember that we want to generate a number up to, but not including, b).

Thus, this statement generates a random number between 1 and 100 inclusive:

```
int randomNumber = 1 + (int)( Math.random( ) * ( 101 - 1 ) );
```

Line 16 of Example 3.14 will generate a random number between 20 and 200 inclusive.

```
 1 /*  A demonstration of the random method of the Math class
 2      Anderson, Franceschi
 3 */
 4
 5 public class MathRandomMethod
 6 {
 7   public static void main( String [ ] args )
 8   {
 9     double d = Math.random( );
10     System.out.println( "The random number generated is " + d );
11
12     int die = 1 + (int)( Math.random( ) * 6 );
13     System.out.println( "\nThe die roll is " + die );
14
15     int start = 20, end = 201;
16     int number = start + (int)( Math.random( ) * ( end - start ) );
17     System.out.println( "\nThe random number between " + start
18                         + " and " + ( end - 1 )  + " is " + number );
19   }
20 }
```

EXAMPLE 3.14   A Demonstration of the *random* Method

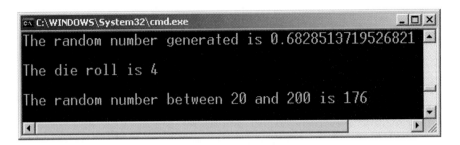

Figure 3.19
Output from
Example 3.14

When the *MathRandomMethod* program executes, it produces output similar to the window shown in Figure 3.19. The random numbers generated
may vary from one execution of the program to the next.

 REFERENCE POINT

You can read more about
the *Math* class in Appendix
F and on Sun Micro-
systems' Java Web site
http://java.sun.com.

Skill Practice
with these end-of-chapter questions

3.10.1   Multiple Choice Exercises

Question 13

3.10.2   Reading and Understanding Code

Questions 17, 18, 19, 20, 21, 22, 23

3.10.3   Fill in the Code

Questions 28, 29, 30

3.10.4   Identifying Errors in Code

Questions 35, 36, 40, 41, 42

3.10.5   Debugging Area

Questions 44, 46, 47, 48, 49

3.10.6   Write a Short Program

Question 53

3.7.6   The *Integer, Double,* and Other Wrapper Classes

In Chapter 2, we discussed primitive data types and how they can be used in a program. In this chapter, we've discussed classes and class methods and how useful and convenient classes are in representing and encapsulating data into objects.

Most programs use a combination of primitive data types and objects. Some class methods, however, will accept only objects as arguments. So we need some way to convert a primitive data type into an object. Conversely, there are times when we need to convert an object into a primitive data type. For example, let's say we have a Graphical User Interface where we ask users to type their age into a text box or a dialog box. We expect the age to be an *int* value; however, text boxes and dialog boxes return their values as *Strings*. To use an age in our program, we will need to convert the value of that *String* object into an *int*.

For these situations, Java provides **wrapper classes**. A wrapper class "wraps" the value of a primitive type, such as *double* or *int*, into an object. These wrapper classes define an instance variable of that primitive data type, and also provide useful constants and methods for converting between the objects and the primitive data types. Table 3.10 lists the wrapper classes for each primitive data type.

TABLE 3.10   Wrapper Classes for Primitive Data Types

Primitive Data Type	Wrapper Class
double	*Double*
float	*Float*
long	*Long*
int	*Integer*
short	*Short*
byte	*Byte*
char	*Character*
boolean	*Boolean*

All these classes are part of the *java.lang* package. So, the *import* statement is not needed in order to use them in a program.

To convert a primitive *int* variable to an *Integer* wrapper object, we can instantiate the *Integer* object using the *Integer* constructor.

```
int intPrimitive = 42;
Integer integerObject = new Integer( intPrimitive );
```

However, because this is a common operation, Java provides special support for converting between a primitive numeric type and its wrapper class. Instead of using the *Integer* constructor, we can simply assign the *int* variable to an *Integer* object reference. Java will automatically provide the conversion for us. This conversion is called **autoboxing**. In Example 3.15, the conversion is illustrated in lines 9 and 10. The *int* variable, *intPrimitive*, and the *Integer* object, *integerObject*, are output at lines 12 and 13 and have the same value (42). The output is shown in Figure 3.20.

Similarly, when an *Integer* object is used as an *int*, Java also provides this conversion, which is called **unboxing**. Thus, when we use an *Integer* object in an arithmetic expression, the *int* value is automatically used. Line 15 of Example 3.15 uses the *Integer* object *integerObject* in an arithmetic expression, adding the *Integer* object to the *int* variable *intPrimitive*. As shown in Figure 3.20, the result is the same as if both operands were *int* variables.

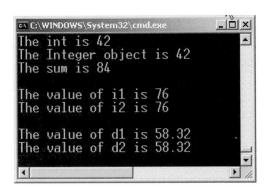

Figure 3.20

Output from Example 3.15

TABLE 3.11   Methods of the *Integer* and *Double* Wrapper Classes

Useful Methods of the *Integer* Wrapper Class	
Return value	**Method name and argument list**
int	parseInt(String s)
	converts the *String* s to an *int* and returns that value
Integer	valueOf(String s)
	converts the *String* s to an *Integer* object and returns that object
Useful Methods of the *Double* Wrapper Class	
Return value	**Method name and argument list**
double	parseDouble(String s)
	converts the *String* s to a *double* and returns that value
Double	valueOf(String s)
	converts the *String* s to a *Double* object and returns that object

Similar operations are possible using other numeric primitives and their associated wrapper classes.

In addition to automatic conversions between primitive types and wrapper objects, the *Integer* and *Double* classes provide methods, shown in Table 3.11, that allow us to convert between primitive types and objects of the *String* class.

The *parseInt*, *parseDouble*, and *valueOf* methods are *static* and are called using the *Integer* or *Double* class name and the dot notation. The *parse* methods convert a *String* to a primitive type, and the *valueOf* methods convert a *String* to a wrapper object. For example, line 18 of Example 3.15 converts the *String* "76" to the *int* value 76. Line 19 converts the *String* "76" to an *Integer* object.

Similarly, line 23 converts the *String* "58.32" to a *double*, and line 24 converts the same *String* to a *Double* object.

```
1 /* A demonstration of the Wrapper classes and methods
2    Anderson, Franceschi
3 */
4
5 public class DemoWrapper
6 {
7   public static void main( String [ ] args )
8   {
9     int intPrimitive = 42;
10    Integer integerObject = intPrimitive;
11
12    System.out.println( "The int is " + intPrimitive );
13    System.out.println( "The Integer object is " + integerObject );
14
15    int sum = intPrimitive + integerObject;
16    System.out.println( "The sum is " + sum );
17
18    int i1 = Integer.parseInt( "76" );    // convert "76" to an int
19    Integer i2 = Integer.valueOf( "76" ); // convert "76" to Integer
20    System.out.println( "\nThe value of i1 is " + i1 );
21    System.out.println( "The value of i2 is " + i2 );
22
23    double d1 = Double.parseDouble( "58.32" );
24    Double d2 = Double.valueOf( "58.32" );
25    System.out.println( "\nThe value of d1 is " + d1 );
26    System.out.println( "The value of d2 is " + d2 );
27  }
28 }
```

EXAMPLE 3.15   A Demonstration of the Wrapper Classes

The usefulness of these wrappers will become clear in the next section of this chapter, where we discuss dialog boxes.

3.7.7 Input and Output Using *JOptionPane* Dialog Boxes

As our programs become more complex, we will need to allow the users of our programs to input data. User input can be read into your program in several ways:

- from a dialog box
- from a Graphical User Interface (GUI)

 REFERENCE POINT

You can read more about the wrapper classes in Appendix F and on Sun Microsystems' Java Web site *http://java.sun.com*.

- from the Java console
- from a file

The Java programming language provides classes for all types of data input. In this chapter, we will concentrate on two ways to input data: from a dialog box and from the Java console. In Chapter 6 and Chapter 11, we explore how to input data from a file, and in Chapter 12, we learn how to input data through a GUI.

Java provides the *JOptionPane* class for creating dialog boxes—those familiar pop-up windows that prompt the user to confirm an action or notify the user of an error. The *JOptionPane* class is in the *javax.swing* package, so you will need to provide an *import* statement in any program that uses a dialog box. Most classes in the *javax.swing* package are designed for GUIs, but *JOptionPane* dialog boxes can be used in both GUI and non-GUI programs.

Table 3.12 lists some useful *JOptionPane static* methods.

The *showInputDialog* method is used for input, that is, for prompting the user for a value and inputting that value into the program. The *showMessageDialog* method is used for output, that is, for printing a message to the user. Although Java provides several constructors for dialog boxes, it is cus-

TABLE 3.12   *Input* and *Output* Methods of the *JOptionPane* Class

Useful Methods of the *JOptionPane* Class	
Return value	**Method name and argument list**
String	showInputDialog(Component parent, Object prompt)
	pops up an input dialog box, where *prompt* asks the user for input. Returns the characters typed by the user as a *String*.
void	showMessageDialog(Component parent, Object message)
	pops up an output dialog box with *message* displayed

tomary to create dialog boxes that will be used only once using the *static* methods and the *JOptionPane* class name.

Let's look first at the method *showInputDialog*, which gets input from the user. It takes two arguments: a parent component object and a prompt to display. At this point, our applications won't have a parent component object, so we'll always use *null* for that argument.

The second argument, the prompt, is usually a *String*, and lets the user know what kind of input our program needs. When writing a prompt for user input, keep several things in mind. First, be specific. If you want the user to enter his or her full name, then your prompt should say just that:

```
Please enter your first and last names.
```

If only a range of values is valid, then tell the user:

```
Please enter an integer between 0 and 10.
```

Also keep in mind that users are typically not programmers. It's important to phrase a prompt using language the user understands. Many times, programmers write a prompt from their point of view, as in this bad prompt:

```
Please enter a String:
```

Users don't know, and don't care, about *Strings* or any other data types, for that matter. Users want to know only what they need to enter to get the program to do its job.

When your prompts are clear and specific, the user makes fewer errors and therefore feels more comfortable using your program.

Next, notice that the return value of the *showInputDialog* method is a *String*.

Example 3.16 shows how the *showInputDialog* method is used to retrieve user input through a dialog box.

SOFTWARE ENGINEERING TIP

Provide the user with clear prompts for input. Prompts should be composed of words the user understands and should describe the data requested and any restrictions on valid input values.

```
1 /* Using dialog boxes for input and output of Strings
2    Anderson, Franceschi
3 */
4
5 import javax.swing.JOptionPane;
6
7 public class DialogBoxDemo1
8 {
9   public static void main( String [ ] args )
10  {
11    String name = JOptionPane.showInputDialog( null,
12                   "Please enter your first and last names" );
13    JOptionPane.showMessageDialog( null, "Hello, " + name );
14  }
15 }
```

EXAMPLE 3.16   Using Dialog Boxes with *Strings*

When lines 11 and 12 are executed, the dialog box in Figure 3.21 appears. The user types his or her name into the white box, then presses either the *En*ter key or clicks the *OK* button. At that time, the *showInputDialog* method returns a *String* representing the characters typed by the user, and that *String* is assigned to the variable *name*.

To output a message to the user, use the *showMessageDialog* method. The *showMessageDialog* method is similar to the *showInputDialog* method in that it takes a parent component object (*null* for now) and a *String* to display. Thus, in Example 3.16, line 13 uses the variable *name* to echo back to the user a greeting.

Notice that because the *showMessageDialog* is a method with a *void* return value, you call it as a standalone statement, rather than using the method call in an expression.

Figure 3.21

Dialog Box Prompting for First and Last Names

Figure 3.22
Output Dialog Box

If the user typed "Syed Ali" when prompted for his name, the output dialog box shown in Figure 3.22 would appear.

To input an integer or any data type other than a *String*, however, you need to convert the returned *String* to the desired data type. Fortunately, as we saw in the previous section, you can do this using a wrapper class and its associated *parse* method, as Example 3.17 demonstrates.

```
1 /* Demonstrating dialog boxes for input and output of numbers
2    Anderson, Franceschi
3 */
4
5 import javax.swing.JOptionPane;
6
7 public class DialogBoxDemo2
8 {
9   public static void main( String [ ] args )
10  {
11     String input = JOptionPane.showInputDialog( null,
12          "Please enter your age in years" );
13     int age = Integer.parseInt( input );
14     JOptionPane.showMessageDialog( null, "Your age is  " + age );
15
16     double average = Double.parseDouble(
17          JOptionPane.showInputDialog( null,
18          "Enter your grade point average between 0.0 and 4.0" ) );
19     JOptionPane.showMessageDialog( null, "Your average is "
20          + average );
21  }
22 }
```

EXAMPLE 3.17   Converting Input *Strings* to Numbers

Lines 11 and 12 pop up an input dialog box and assign the characters entered by the user to the *String input*. Line 13 uses the *parseInt* method of the *Integer* class to convert *input* to an integer, which is assigned to the *int* variable *age*. Line 14 then displays the value of *age* in an output dialog box.

Java programmers often combine multiple related operations into one statement in order to type less code and to avoid declaring additional variables. Lines 16, 17, and 18 illustrate this concept. At first it may look confusing, but if you look at the statement a piece at a time, it becomes clear what is happening. The *showInputDialog* method is called, returning a *String* representing whatever the user typed into the dialog box. This *String* then becomes the argument passed to *parseDouble*, which converts the *String* to a *double*. Lines 19–20 then display the value of *average* in another dialog box.

In this prompt, we included a range of valid values to help the user type valid input. However, including a range of values in your prompt does not prevent the user from entering other values. The *parseDouble* method will accept any *String* that can be converted to a numeric value. After your program receives the input, you will need to verify that the number entered is indeed within the requested range of values. In Chapter 6, we will show you techniques for verifying whether the user has entered valid values.

REFERENCE POINT

You can read more about the *JOptionPane* class in Appendix F and on Sun Microsystems' Java Web site *http://java.sun.com*.

With either *Double.parseDouble* or *Integer.parseInt*, the value the user types must be convertible to the appropriate data type. If not, an exception is generated. For example, if the user enters *A* for the grade point average, the method generates a *NumberFormatException*. We'll discuss how you can intercept and handle exceptions in Chapter 11.

The various input and output dialog boxes from a sample run of Example 3.17 are shown in Figure 3.23.

3.7.8 Input from the Console Using the *Scanner* Class

A dialog box is one way to get input from the user. But if your program needs a lot of input, using a dialog box is cumbersome and slow. For many programs, it is more convenient and efficient to prompt the user to type input into the Java console.

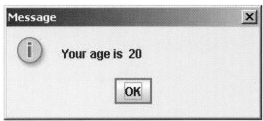

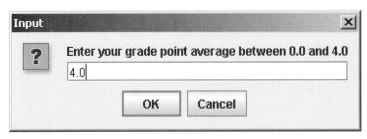

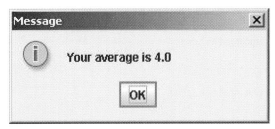

Figure 3.23
Dialog Boxes from Example 3.17

The *Scanner* class provides methods for reading *byte*, *short*, *int*, *long*, *float*, *double*, and *String* data types from the Java console. These methods are shown in Table 3.13.

The *Scanner* class is defined in the *java.util* package, so your programs will need to include the following *import* statement:

```
import java.util.Scanner;
```

In order to use the *Scanner* class, you must first instantiate a *Scanner* object and associate it with a data source. Just as we use the *System.out* output stream to print to the Java console, we will use the *System.in* input stream

TABLE 3.13   Selected Methods of the *Scanner* Class

Return value	Method name and argument list
byte	nextByte( )
	returns the next input as a *byte*
short	nextShort( )
	returns the next input as a *short*
int	nextInt( )
	returns the next input as an *int*
long	nextLong( )
	returns the next input as a *long*
float	nextFloat( )
	returns the next input as a *float*
double	nextDouble( )
	returns the next input as a *double*
boolean	nextBoolean( )
	returns the next input as a *boolean*
String	next( )
	returns the next token in the input line as a *String*
String	nextLine( )
	returns the input line as a *String*

to read from the Java console. Thus, our data source will be *System.in*. The following statement will instantiate a *Scanner* object named *scan* and associate *System.in* as the data source.

```
Scanner scan = new Scanner( System.in );
```

Once the *Scanner* object has been instantiated, you can use it to call any of the *next*. . . methods to input data from the Java console. The specific *next* . . . method you call depends on the type of input you want from the user. Each of the *next*. . . methods returns a value from the input stream. You will need to assign the return value from the *next*. . . methods to a variable to complete the data input. Obviously, the data type of the variable must match the data type of the value returned by the *next*. . . method.

The *next*. . . methods just perform input. They do not tell the user what data to enter. Before calling any of the *next* methods, therefore, you need to prompt the user for the input you want. You can print a prompt using the *System.out.print* method.

Line 13 of Example 3.18 prompts the user to enter his or her first name. Line 14 captures the user input and assigns the word entered by the user to the *String* variable *firstName*, which is printed in line 15. Similarly, line 17 prompts the user for his or her age; line 18 captures the integer entered by the user and assigns it to the *int* variable *age*, and line 19 outputs the value of *age*. Reading other primitive data types follows the same pattern. Line 21 prompts for the user's grade point average (a *float* value). Line 22 captures the number entered by the user and assigns it to the *float* variable *gpa*, and line 23 outputs the value of *gpa*.

When this program executes, the prompt is printed on the console and the cursor remains at the end of the prompt. Figure 3.24 shows the output

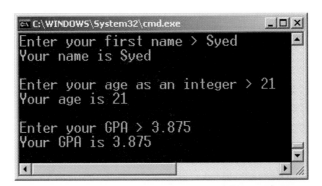

Figure 3.24

Data Input with Example 3.18

when these statements are executed and the user enters *Syed*, presses *Enter*, enters 21, presses *Enter*, and enters 3.875, and presses *Enter* again.

```
1 /*  A demonstration of reading from the console using Scanner
2       Anderson, Franceschi
3 */
4
5 import java.util.Scanner;
6
7 public class DataInput
8 {
9   public static void main( String [ ] args )
10   {
11       Scanner scan = new Scanner( System.in );
12
13       System.out.print( "Enter your first name > " );
14       String firstName = scan.next( );
15       System.out.println( "Your name is " + firstName );
16
17       System.out.print( "\nEnter your age as an integer > " );
18       int age = scan.nextInt( );
19       System.out.println( "Your age is " + age );
20
21       System.out.print( "\nEnter your GPA > " );
22       float gpa = scan.nextFloat( );
23       System.out.println( "Your GPA is " + gpa );
24   }
25 }
```

EXAMPLE 3.18   Reading from the Console using *Scanner*

SOFTWARE ENGINEERING TIP

End your prompts with some indication that input is expected, and include a trailing space for better readability.

The methods *nextByte*, *nextShort*, *nextLong*, *nextDouble*, and *nextBoolean* can be used with the same pattern as *next*, *nextInt*, and *nextFloat*.

Note that we end our prompt with a space, an angle bracket, and another space. The angle bracket indicates that we are waiting for input, and the spaces separate the prompt from the input. Without the trailing space, the user's input would immediately follow the prompt, which is more difficult to read, as you can see in Figure 3.25.

Figure 3.25

Prompt and Input Running Together

As you review Table 3.13, you may notice that the *Scanner* class does not provide a method for reading a single character. To do this, we can use the *next* method, which returns a *String*, then extract the character from the *String* using the *charAt(0)* method call, as shown in Example 3.19. Line 14 captures a *String* from the user and assigns it to the *String* variable *initialS*, then line 15 assigns the first character of *initialS* to the *char* variable *initial*; *initial* is then output at line 16 as shown in Figure 3.26.

```
 1 /*  A demonstration of how to get character input using Scanner
 2      Anderson, Franceschi
 3 */
 4
 5 import java.util.Scanner;
 6
 7 public class CharacterInput
 8 {
 9   public static void main( String [ ] args )
10   {
11       Scanner scan = new Scanner( System.in );
12
13       System.out.print( "Enter your middle initial > " );
14       String initialS = scan.next( );
15       char initial = initialS.charAt( 0 );
16       System.out.println( "Your middle initial is " + initial );
17   }
18 }
```

EXAMPLE 3.19   How to Use *Scanner* for Character Input

A *Scanner* object divides its input into sequences of characters called **tokens**, using **delimiters**. The default delimiters are the standard **whitespace** characters, which among others include the space, tab, and newline characters. The complete set of Java whitespace characters is shown in Table 3.14.

By default, when a *Scanner* object tokenizes the input, it skips leading whitespace, then builds a token composed of all subsequent characters that

Figure 3.26
Output of Example 3.19

TABLE 3.14   Java Whitespace Characters

Character	Unicode equivalents
space	\u00A0, \u2007, \u202F
tab	\u0009, \u000B
line feed	\u000A
form feed	\u000C
carriage return	\u000D
file, group, unit, and record separators	\u001C, \u001D, \u001E, \u001F

do not match its delimiters until it encounters another delimiter. Thus, if you have this code,

```
System.out.print( "Enter your age as an integer > " );
int age = scan.nextInt( );
```

and the user types, for example, three spaces and a tab, *21*, and a newline:

```
<space><space><space><tab>21<newline>
```

then the *Scanner* object skips the three spaces and the tab, starts building a token with the character *2*, then adds the character *1* to the token, and stops building the token when it encounters the *newline*. Thus, *21* is the resulting token, which the *nextInt* method returns into the *age* variable.

An input line can contain more than one token. For example, if we prompt the user for his or her name and age, and the user enters the following line, then presses *Enter:*

```
<tab>Jon<space>Olsen,<space>21<space>
```

then, the leading whitespace is skipped and the *Scanner* object creates three tokens:

- *Jon*
- *Olsen,*
- *21*

Note that commas are not whitespace, so the comma is actually part of the second token. To input these three tokens, your program would use two calls to the *next* method to retrieve the two *String* tokens and a call to *nextInt* to retrieve the age.

To capture a complete line of input from the user, we use the method *nextLine*. Example 3.20 shows how *nextLine* can be used in a program. Figure 3.27 shows a sample run of the program with the user entering data.

```
1  /*  A demonstration of using Scanner's nextLine method
2      Anderson, Franceschi
3  */
4
5  import java.util.Scanner;
6
7  public class InputALine
8  {
9    public static void main( String [ ] args )
10   {
11     Scanner scan = new Scanner( System.in );
12
13     System.out.print( "Enter a sentence > " );
14     String sentence  = scan.nextLine( );
15     System.out.println( "You said: \"" + sentence + "\"" );
16   }
17 }
```

EXAMPLE 3.20   How to Use the *nextLine* Method

If the user's input (that is, the next token) does not match the data type of the *next...* method call, then an *InputMismatchException* is generated and the program stops. Figure 3.28 demonstrates Example 3.18 when the program calls the *nextInt* method and the user enters a letter, rather than an integer. In Chapter 6, we show you how to avoid this exception, and in Chapter 11, we show you how to intercept the exception and recover from it.

REFERENCE POINT

You can read more about the Scanner class in Appendix F and on Sun Microsystems' Java Web site: *http://java.sun.com.*

Figure 3.27
Output of Example 3.20

Figure 3.28

An Exception When Input Is Not the Expected Data Type

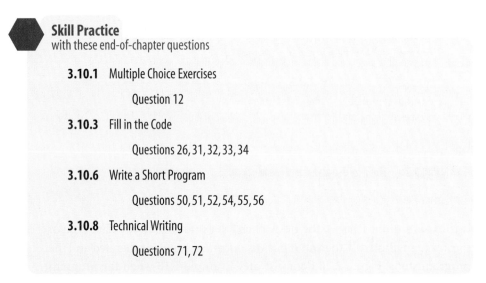

```
C:\WINDOWS\System32\cmd.exe                                _ □ ×
Enter your first name > Sarah
Your name is Sarah

Enter your age as an integer > a
Exception in thread "main" java.util.InputMismatchException
        at java.util.Scanner.throwFor(Unknown Source)
        at java.util.Scanner.next(Unknown Source)
        at java.util.Scanner.nextInt(Unknown Source)
        at java.util.Scanner.nextInt(Unknown Source)
        at DataInput.main(DataInput.java:18)
```

If the user doesn't type anything when prompted, or if the user types some characters but doesn't press *Enter*, the program will simply wait until the user does press *Enter*.

Skill Practice
with these end-of-chapter questions

3.10.1   Multiple Choice Exercises

Question 12

3.10.3   Fill in the Code

Questions 26, 31, 32, 33, 34

3.10.6   Write a Short Program

Questions 50, 51, 52, 54, 55, 56

3.10.8   Technical Writing

Questions 71, 72

3.8   Programming Activity 2: Using Predefined Classes

In this Programming Activity, you will write a short program using some of the classes and methods discussed in this chapter. Plus, given the API of a method of an additional class, you will determine how to call the method. Your program will perform the following operations:

1. a.   Prompt the user for his or her first name

    b.   Print a message saying hello to the user

    c.   Tell the user how many characters are in his or her name

2. a.   Ask the user for year of birth

   b. Calculate and print the age the user will be this year

   c. Declare a constant for average life expectancy; set its value to 76.9

   d. Print a message that tells the user the percentage of his or her expected life lived so far

3. a. Generate a random number between 1 and 20

   b. Tell the user that the program is thinking of a number between 1 and 20

   c. Wait five seconds by calling the *wait* method of the *Pause* class

To complete this Programming Activity, copy the contents of the Chapter 3 Programming Activity 2 folder on the CD-ROM accompanying this book. Open the *PracticeMethods.java* file and look for four sets of five asterisks (*****), where you will find instructions to write *import* statements and items 1, 2, and 3 for completing the Programming Activity.

In item 3, you are asked to call the *wait* method of the *Pause* class. This class is written by the authors and is included in the same folder as the *Practice-Methods.java* source file, so you can use this class without an *import* statement. The API for the *wait* method is

```
public static void wait( int numberOfSeconds )
```

Example 3.21 shows the *PracticeMethods.java* file, and Figure 3.29 shows the output from a sample run after you have completed the Programming Activity. Because item 3 generates a random number, your output may be different.

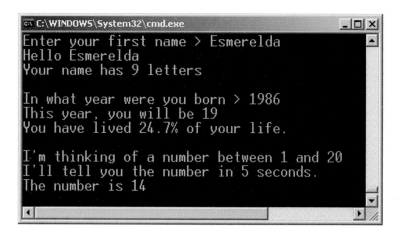

Figure 3.29

Output from a Sample Run of Programming Activity 2

```
1 /* Chapter 3 Programming Activity 2
2    Calling class methods
3    Anderson, Franceschi
4 */
5
6 // ***** add your import statements here
7
8 public class PracticeMethods
9 {
10   public static void main( String [ ] args )
11   {
12     //*****
13     // 1.  a. Create a Scanner object to read from the console
14     //      b. Prompt the user for his or her first name
15     //      c. Print a message that says hello to the user
16     //      d. Print a message that says how many letters
17     //              are in the user's name
18     // Your code goes here
19
20     //*****
21     // 2.  a. Skip a line, then prompt the user for the year
22     //          of birth.
23     //      b. Calculate and print the age the user will be this year
24     //      c. Declare a constant for average life expectancy,
25     //          set its value to 76.9
26     //      d. Print a message that tells the user the percentage
27     //          of his or her expected life lived
28     //       Use the DecimalFormat class to format the percentage
29
30     //*****
31     // 3.  a. Generate a random integer between 1 and 20
32     //      b. Skip a line, then print a message that you're
33     //          thinking of a number between 1 and 20
34     //          and that you'll tell the user the number in 5 seconds
35     //      c. Wait five seconds by calling the
36     //          wait method in the prewritten Pause class
37     //          The wait method has this API:
38     //              public static void wait( int secondsToWait )
39     //          The authors have written this class and included it in
40     //          the same directory as this file, so an import
41     //          statement is not needed
42     //      d. Print a message that tells the user the number
43
44   }
45 }
```

EXAMPLE 3.21   *PracticeMethods.java*

? DISCUSSION QUESTIONS

1. Which methods of the *Scanner* class did you choose for reading the user's name and birth year? Explain your decisions.

2. How would you change your code to generate a random number between 10 and 20?

3.9   Chapter Summary

- Object-oriented programming entails writing programs that use classes and objects. Using prewritten classes shortens development time and creates more reliable programs. Programs that use prewritten classes are called clients of the class.

- Benefits of object-oriented programming include encapsulation, reusability, and reliability.

- Classes consist of data, plus instructions that operate on that data. Objects of a class are created using the class as a template. Creating an object is called instantiating an object, and the object is an instance of the class. The *new* keyword is used to instantiate an object.

- The object reference is the variable name for an object and points to the data of the object.

- The data of a class are called instance variables or fields, and the instructions of the class are called methods. Methods of a class get or set the values of the data or provide other services of the class.

- The name of a method, along with its argument list and return value, is called the Application Programming Interface (API) of that method. Methods that are declared to be *public* can be called by any client of the class.

- By convention, class names in Java start with a capital letter. Method names, instance variables, and object names start with a lowercase letter. In all these names, embedded words begin with a capital letter.

- When your program makes a method call, control transfers to the instructions in the method until the method finishes executing. Then control is transferred back to your program.

CHAPTER SUMMARY

- Instance methods are called using the object reference and the dot notation.

- A constructor is automatically called when an object is instantiated. A constructor has the same name as the class and its job is to initialize the object's data. Classes can have multiple constructors. Constructors have no return values.

- A method's data type is called the method's return type. If the data type is anything other than the keyword *void*, the method returns a value to the program. When a value-returning method finishes executing, its return value replaces the method call in the expression.

- Accessor methods, also called *gets*, allow clients to retrieve the current value of object data. Mutator methods, also called *sets*, allow clients to change the value of object data.

- When an object reference is first declared, its value is *null*. Attempting to use a *null* object reference to call a method generates an error.

- The garbage collector runs occasionally and deletes objects that have no object reference pointing to them.

- *Static* methods, also called class methods, can be used without instantiating an object. *Static* methods can access only the *static* data of a class.

- *Static* methods are called using the class name and the dot notation.

- Java packages are groups of classes arranged according to functionality. Classes in the *java.lang* packages are automatically available to Java programs. Other classes need to be imported.

- The *String* class can be used to create objects consisting of a sequence of characters. *String* constructors accept *String* literals, *String* objects, or no argument, which creates an empty *String*. The *length* method returns the number of characters in the *String* object. The *toUpperCase* and *toLowerCase* methods return a *String* in upper or lower case. The *charAt* method extracts a character from a *String*, while the *substring* method extracts a *String* from a *String*. The *indexOf* method searches a *String* for a character or substring.

- *System.out.println* prints primitive data types or a *String* to the Java console and adds a *newline* character. *System.out.print* prints the same data types to the Java console, but does not add a *newline*. Classes provide a *toString* method to convert objects to a *String* in order to be printed.

- The *NumberFormat* and the *DecimalFormat* classes, in the *java.text* package, format numeric output. For example, you can specify the number of digits to display after the decimal point or add dollar signs and percentage signs (%).

- The *Math* class provides *static* constants *PI* and *E* and *static* methods to perform common mathematical calculations, such as generating random numbers, finding the maximum or minimum of two numbers, rounding values, and raising a number to a power.

- Wrapper classes provide an object interface for a primitive data type. The *Integer* and *Double* wrapper classes provide methods for converting between *ints* and *doubles* and *Strings*.

- The *JOptionPane* class, in the *javax.swing* package, provides the *static* methods *showMessageDialog* for popping up an output dialog box and *showInputDialog* for popping up an input dialog box.

- When prompting the user for input, phrase the prompt in language the user understands. Describe the data requested and any restrictions on valid input values.

- The *Scanner* class, in the *java.util* package, provides methods for reading input from the Java console. Methods are provided for reading primitive data types and *Strings*.

3.10   Exercises, Problems, and Projects

3.10.1   Multiple Choice Exercises

1. If you want to use an existing class from the Java class library in your program, what keyword should you use?

   ❑ *use*

   ❑ *import*

   ❑ *export*

   ❑ *include*

2. A constructor has the same name as the class name.

    ❑ true

    ❑ false

3. A given class can have more than one constructor.

    ❑ true

    ❑ false

4. What is the keyword used to instantiate an object in Java?

    ❑ make

    ❑ construct

    ❑ new

    ❑ static

5. In a given class named *Quiz*, there can be only one method with the name *Quiz*.

    ❑ true

    ❑ false

6. A *static* method is

    ❑ a class method

    ❑ an instance method

7. In the *Quiz* class, the *foo* method has the following API:

    ```
    public static double foo( float f )
    ```

    What can you say about *foo*?

    ❑ It is an instance method.

    ❑ It is a class field.

    ❑ It is a class method.

    ❑ It is an instance variable.

8. In the *Quiz* class, the *foo* method has the following API:

    ```
    public static void foo( )
    ```

How would you call that method?

- ❏ `Quiz.foo( );`
- ❏ `Quiz.foo( 8 );`
- ❏ `Quiz( foo( ) );`

9. In the *Quiz* class, the *foo* method has the following API:

   `public double foo( int i, String s, char c )`

   How many arguments does *foo* take ?

   - ❏ 0
   - ❏ 1
   - ❏ 2
   - ❏ 3

10. In the *Quiz* class, the *foo* method has the following API:

    `public double foo( int i, String s, char c )`

    What is the return type of method *foo*?

    - ❏ *double*
    - ❏ *int*
    - ❏ *char*
    - ❏ *String*

11. *String* is a primitive data type in Java.

    - ❏ true
    - ❏ false

12. Which one of the following is not an existing wrapper class?

    - ❏ *Integer*
    - ❏ *Char*
    - ❏ *Float*
    - ❏ *Double*

EXERCISES, PROBLEMS, AND PROJECTS

13. What is the proper way of accessing the constant *E* of the *Math* class?

    ❑ `Math.E( );`

    ❑ `Math.E;`

    ❑ `E;`

    ❑ `Math( E );`

3.10.2 Reading and Understanding Code

14. What is the output of this code sequence?

    ```
    String s = new String( "HI" );
    System.out.println( s );
    ```

15. What is the output of this code sequence?

    ```
    String s = "A" + "BC" + "DEF" + "GHIJ";
    System.out.println( s );
    ```

16. What is the output of this code sequence?

    ```
    String s = "Hello";
    s = s.toLowerCase( );
    System.out.println( s );
    ```

17. What is the output of this code sequence?

    ```
    int a = Math.min( 5, 8 );
    System.out.println( a );
    ```

18. What is the output of this code sequence?

    ```
    System.out.println( Math.sqrt( 4.0 ) );
    ```

19. What is the output of this code sequence? (You will need to actually compile this code and run it in order to have the correct output.)

    ```
    System.out.println( Math.PI );
    ```

20. What is the output of this code sequence?

    ```
    double f = 5.7;
    long i = Math.round( f );
    System.out.println( i );
    ```

21. What is the output of this code sequence?

    ```
    System.out.print( Math.round( 3.5 ) );
    ```

22. What is the output of this code sequence?

    ```
    int i = Math.abs( -8 );
    System.out.println( i );
    ```

23. What is the output of this code sequence?

```
double d = Math.pow( 2, 3 );
System.out.println( d );
```

3.10.3   Fill in the Code

24. This code concatenates the three *Strings* "Intro", "to", and "Programming" and outputs the resulting *String*. (Your output should be "Intro to Programming.")

```
String s1 = "Intro ";
String s2 = "to";
String s3 = " Programming";
// your code goes here
```

25. This code prints the number of characters in the *String* "Hello World."

```
String s = "Hello World";
// your code goes here
```

26. This code prompts the user for a *String*, then prints the *String* and the number of characters in it.

```
// your code goes here
```

27. This code uses only a single line *System.out.println* ... statement in order to print

"Welcome to Java Illuminated"

on one line using (and only using) the following variables:

```
String s1 = "Welcome ";
String s2 = "to ";
String s3 = "Java ";
String s4 = "Illuminated";
// your code goes here
```

28. This code uses exactly four *System.out.print* statements in order to print

"Welcome to Java Illuminated"

on the same output line.

```
// your code goes here
```

29. This code assigns the maximum of the values 3 and 5 to the *int* variable *i* and outputs the result.

```
int i;
// your code goes here
```

30. This code calculates the square root of 5 and outputs the result.

```
double d = 5.0;
// your code goes here
```

31. This code asks the user for two integer values, then calculates the minimum of the two values and prints it.

```
// your code goes here
```

32. This code asks the user for three integer values, then calculates the maximum of the three values and prints it.

```
// your code goes here
```

33. This code pops up a dialog box that prompts the user for an integer, converts the *String* to an *int*, adds 1 to the number, and pops up a dialog box that outputs the new value.

```
// your code goes here
```

34. This code asks the user for a *double*, then prints the square of this number.

```
// your code goes here
```

3.10.4   Identifying Errors in Code

35. Where is the error in this statement?

```
import text.NumberFormat;
```

36. Where is the error in this statement?

```
import java.util.DecimalFormat;
```

37. Where is the error in this code sequence?

```
String s = "Hello World";
system.out.println( s );
```

38. Where is the error in this code sequence?

```
String s = String( "Hello" );
System.out.println( s );
```

39. Where is the error in this code sequence?

```
String s1 = "Hello";
String s2 = "ello";
String s = s1 - s2;
```

40. Where is the error in this code sequence?

```
short s = Math.round( 3.2 );
System.out.println( s );
```

41. Where is the error in this code sequence?

```
int a = Math.pow( 3, 4 );
System.out.println( a );
```

42. Where is the error in this code sequence?

```
double pi = Math( PI );
System.out.println( pi );
```

43. Where is the error in this code sequence?

```
String s = 'H';
System.out.println( "s is " + s );
```

3.10.5 Debugging Area—Using Messages from the Java Compiler and *Java* JVM

44. You coded the following program in file *Test.java:*

```
public class Test
{
  public static void main( String [ ] args )
  {
    int a = 6;
    NumberFormat nf = NumberFormat.getCurrencyInstance( );
  }
}
```

When you compile, you get the following message:

```
Test.java: 6: cannot find symbol
  symbol : class NumberFormat
  location: class Test
  NumberFormat nf = NumberFormat.getCurrencyInstance( );
  ^
Test.java: 6: cannot find symbol
  symbol : variable NumberFormat
  location: class Test
  NumberFormat nf = NumberFormat.getCurrencyInstance( );
      ^
2 errors
```

Explain what the problem is and how to fix it.

45. You coded the following on lines 10–12 of class *Test.java:*

```
String s;                      // line 10
int l = s.length( );           // line 11
System.out.println( "length is " + l );      // line 12
```

When you compile, you get the following message:

```
Test.java:11: variable s might not have been initialized.
  int i = s.length( );
        ^

1 error
```

Explain what the problem is and how to fix it.

46. You coded the following on lines 10 and 11 of class *Test.java:*

```
double d = math.sqrt( 6 );         // line 10
System.out.println( "d = " + d );  // line 11
```

When you compile, you get the following message:

```
Test.java: 10: cannot find symbol
  symbol : variable math
  location: class Test
double d = math.sqrt( 6 );   // line 10
          ^

  1 error
```

Explain what the problem is and how to fix it.

47. You coded the following on lines 10 and 11 of class *Test.java:*

```
double d = Math.PI( );             // line 10
System.out.println( "d = " + d );  // line 11
```

When you compile, you get the following message:

```
Test.java:10: cannot find symbol
symbol : method PI ( )
location: class java.lang.Math
        double d = Math.PI( );   // line 10
          ^

1 error
```

Explain what the problem is and how to fix it.

48. You coded the following on lines 10 and 11 of class *Test.java:*

```
double d = Math.e;                 // line 10
System.out.println( "d = " + d );  // line 11
```

When you compile, you get the following message:

```
Test.java:10: cannot find symbol
  symbol : variable e
  location: class java.lang.Math
double d = Math.e;                    // line 10
           ^

  1 error
```

Explain what the problem is and how to fix it.

49. You imported the *DecimalFormat* class and coded the following in the class *Test.java:*

```
double grade = .895;
DecimalFormat percent =
  new DecimalFormat( "##.0%" );

System.out.println( "Your grade is "
  + grade );
```

The code compiles properly and runs, but the result is not what you expected. You expect this output:

```
Your grade is 89.5%
```

But instead, the output is

```
Your grade is 0.895
```

Explain what the problem is and how to fix it.

3.10.6 Write a Short Program

50. Write a program that reads two words representing passwords from the Java console and outputs the number of characters in the smaller of the two. For example, if the two words are *open* and *sesame*, then the output should be *4*, the length of the shorter word, *open*.

51. Write a program that reads a name that represents a domain name from the Java console. Your program should then concatenate that name with *www.* and *.com* in order to form an Internet domain name and output the result. For instance, if the name entered by the user is *yahoo*, then the output will be *www.yahoo.com*.

52. Write a program that reads a word from the Java console. Your program should then output the same word, output the word in upper-

case letters only, output that word in lowercase letters only, and then, at the end, output the original word.

53. Write a program that generates two random numbers between 0 and 100 and prints the smaller of the two numbers.

54. Write a program that takes a *double* as an input from the Java console, then computes and outputs the cube of that number.

55. Write a program that reads a filename from a dialog box. You should expect that the filename has one . (dot) character in it, separating the filename from the file extension. Retrieve the file extension and output it. For instance, if the user inputs *index.html*, you should output *html*; if the user inputs *MyClass.java*, you should output *java*.

56. Write a program that reads a full name (first name and last name) from a dialog box; you should expect the first name and the last name to be separated by a space. Retrieve the first name and output it.

3.10.7   Programming Projects

57. Write a program that reads three integer values from the Java console representing, respectively, a number of quarters, dimes, and nickels. Convert the total coin amount to dollars and output the result with a dollar notation.

58. Write a program that reads from the Java console the radius of a circle. Calculate and output the area and the perimeter of that circle. You can use the following formulas:

area $= \pi * r^2$

perimeter $= 2 * \pi * r$

59. Write a program that generates five random integers between 60 and 100 and calculates the smallest of the five numbers.

60. Write a program that generates three random integers between 0 and 50, calculates the average, and prints the result.

61. Write a program that reads two integers from the Java console: one representing the number of shots taken by a basketball player, the other representing the number of shots made by the same player. Calculate the shooting percentage and output it with the percent notation.

62. Write a program that takes three *double* numbers from the Java console representing, respectively, the three coefficients a, b, and c of a quadratic equation. Solve the equation using the following formulas:

$x1 = (-b + \text{square root } (b^2 - 4\ ac)) / (2a);$

$x2 = (-b - \text{square root } (b^2 - 4\ ac)) / (2a);$

Run your program on the following sample values:

$a = 1.0, b = 3.0, c = 2.0$

$a = 0.5, b = 0.5, c = 0.125$

$a = 1.0, b = 3.0, c = 10.0$

Discuss the results for each program run, in particular what happens in the last case.

63. Write a program that takes two numbers from the Java console representing, respectively, an investment and an interest rate (you will expect the user to enter a number such as .065 for the interest rate, representing a 6.5% interest rate). Your program should calculate and output (in $ notation) the future value of the investment in 5, 10, and 20 years using the following formula:

future value = investment * (1 + interest rate)^{year}

We will assume that the interest rate is an annual rate and is compounded annually.

64. Write a program that reads from the Java console the (x, y) coordinates for two points in the plane. You can assume that all numbers are integers. Using the *Point* class from Java (you may need to look it up on the Web), instantiate two *Point* objects with your input data, then output the data for both *Point* objects.

65. Write a program that reads a *char* from the Java console. Look up the *Character* class on the Web, in particular the method *getNumericValue*. Using the *getNumericValue* method, find the corresponding Unicode encoding number and output the character along with its corresponding Unicode value. Find all the Unicode values for characters a to z and A to Z.

66. Write a program that reads a telephone number from a dialog box; you should assume that the number is in this format: nnn-nnn-nnnn. You should output this same telephone number but with spaces instead of dashes, that is: nnn nnn nnnn.

67. Write a program that reads a sentence from a dialog box. The sentence has been encrypted as follows: only the first five even-numbered characters should be counted; all other characters should be discarded. Decrypt the sentence and output the result. For example, if the user inputs "Hiejlzl3ow", your output should be *Hello*.

68. Write a program that reads a commercial Web site URL from a dialog box; you should expect that the URL starts with *www* and ends with *.com*. Retrieve the name of the site and output it. For instance, if the user inputs *www.yahoo.com*, you should output *yahoo*.

3.10.8   Technical Writing

69. At this point, we have written and debugged many examples of code. When you compile a Java program with the Java compiler, you get a list of all the errors in your code. Do you like the Java compiler? What do you like about messages it displays when your code does not compile?

70. Computers, computer languages, and application programs existed before object-oriented programming. However, OOP has become an industry standard. Discuss the advantages of using OOP compared to using only basic data types in a program.

71. Explain and discuss a situation where you would use the method *parseInt* of the class *Integer*.

72. In addition to the basic data types (*int, float, char, boolean, . . .*), Java provides many prewritten classes, such as *Math, NumberFormat,* and *DecimalFormat.* Why is this an advantage? How does this impact the way a programmer approaches a programming problem in general?

3.10.9   Group Project (for a group of 1, 2, or 3 students)

73. Write a program that calculates a monthly mortgage payment; we will assume that the interest rate is compounded monthly.

    You will need to do the following:

    ❑ Prompt the user for a *double* representing the annual interest rate.

❑ Prompt the user for the number of years the mortgage will be held (typical input here is 10, 15, or 30).

❑ Prompt the user for a number representing the mortgage amount borrowed from the bank.

❑ Calculate the monthly payment using the following formulas:

- Monthly payment = $(mIR * M) / (1 - (1 / (1 + mIR)^{(12*nOY)}))$, where:

  - mIR = monthly interest rate = annual interest rate / 12

  - nOY = number of years

  - M = mortgage amount

❑ Output a summary of the mortgage problem, as follows:

- the annual interest rate in percent notation

- the mortgage amount in dollars

- the monthly payment in dollars, with only two significant digits after the decimal point

- the total payment over the years, with only two significant digits after the decimal point

- the overpayment, i.e., the difference between the total payment over the years and the mortgage amount, with only two significant digits after the decimal point

- the overpayment as a percentage (in percent notation) of the mortgage amount

CHAPTER 4

Introduction to Applets and Graphics

CHAPTER CONTENTS

Introduction

To this point, we've written Java applications, which run as standalone programs. Now we'll write a few Java applets, which are run by an Internet browser or an applet viewer.

As we discussed in Chapter 1, applets were originally designed to add interactivity to a Web page. For example, a computer chess game on the Web can be run as an applet.

Another advantage to applets is the ease with which you can add graphics to a program. Up to this point, the input and output of our applications have been text—words and numbers. There was one exception, however: Programming Activity 1 in Chapter 3. That application opened a window and drew figures along with the text. How did we do that? We used graphics.

Graphical output is part of many programs today. One compelling reason for using graphics in a program is the ability to present data in a format that is easy to compehend. For example, our application could output average monthly temperatures as text, like this:

```
Jan    31
Feb    24
Mar    45
Apr    56
May    69
Jun    76
Jul    88
Aug    87
Sep    75
Oct    65
Nov    43
Dec    23
```

Or we could produce the bar chart shown in Figure 4.1.

The bar chart presents the same information as the text output, but it adds a visual component that makes it easier to compare the monthly temperatures—for example, to find the highest or lowest temperature or to spot temperature trends throughout the year. The colors also add information,

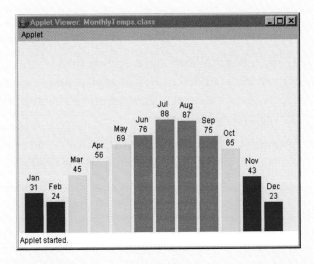

Figure 4.1
Bar Chart of Monthly Temperatures

with the low temperatures shown in blue, the moderate temperatures shown in yellow, and the high temperatures shown in red.

In this chapter, we begin by adding graphical output to applets. Later, when we cover GUIs in Chapter 12, we'll show you how to add graphical output to a Java application.

4.1   Applet Structure

The *JApplet* class, an existing Java class of the *swing* package, provides the basic functionality of an applet. An applet class that we write is an extension of the *JApplet* class. In Java, the *extends* keyword specifies that one class is an extension of another and *inherits* the properties of the other class. Inheritance is one of the ways to reuse classes. We will cover inheritance in detail in Chapter 10.

The *main* method is not used in applets. Instead, applets use two important methods: *init* and *paint*. These standard applet methods are called automatically when the browser or applet viewer launches the applet. The *init* method is called first, then the *paint* method is called. The *paint* method is also called automatically any time the applet window needs to redraw itself. Examples of automatic redrawing would be if the user resizes the applet window or after another window, which was covering part or all of the applet window, is closed or is moved away from the applet window.

There is more to learn about applets than what is covered in this chapter. We will keep our description of applets simple so that you can concentrate on the graphical aspects. In subsequent chapters, we will cover additional concepts related to applets.

Example 4.1 shows the standard pattern for an applet. This applet shell is available to you on the CD accompanying this book.

```
1 /* An applet shell
2    Anderson, Franceschi
3 */
4
5 import javax.swing.JApplet;
6 import java.awt.Graphics;
7
8 public class ShellApplet extends JApplet
9 {
10   // declare variables here
11
12   public void init( )
13   {
14     // initialize data here
15   }
16
17   public void paint( Graphics g )
18   {
19     super.paint( g );
20     // include graphics code here
21   }
22 }
```

EXAMPLE 4.1   The *ShellApplet* Class

Lines 5 and 6 import the two classes that are used in this example: *JApplet*, used at line 8, and *Graphics*, used at line 17. The *Graphics* class is part of the *awt* (Abstract Window Toolkit) package.

Line 8 looks similar to the class header in our Java applications, but it includes two additional words: *extends JApplet*. In this case, we are inheriting from the *JApplet* class. Among other things, our *ShellApplet* class inherits the methods of the *JApplet* class. This means that we don't need to start from scratch to create an applet, so we can write applets that much faster. The *JApplet* class is called the **superclass**, and the *ShellApplet* is called the **subclass**.

The *init* method, at lines 12–15, is a good place to put initialization code, such as assigning initial values to your class instance variables. In our applets, we will define instance variables of the class immediately following the class definition statement. If your applet does not have any instance variables, and so doesn't need to perform any initialization, then the *init* method is optional.

The *paint* method, at lines 17–21, is where you put code to display words and graphics that should appear in the applet window. The first statement in the *paint* method is *super.paint(g)*. This statement calls the *paint* method of our superclass, the *JApplet* class, so that it can perform its initialization of the applet window.

The *paint* method's only parameter is a *Graphics* object. This object is automatically generated by the browser or applet viewer, which sends it to the *paint* method. The *Graphics* object represents the graphics context, which, among other things, includes the applet window. The *Graphics* class contains the methods we will need to make text and shapes appear in the applet window.

Skill Practice
with these end-of-chapter questions

4.7.1   Multiple Choice Exercises

Questions 1, 2, 3, 4

4.7.4   Identifying Errors in Code

Questions 26, 27

4.7.5   Debugging Area

Question 28

4.7.8   Technical Writing

Question 38

4.2   Executing an Applet

Like applications, applets need to be compiled before they are run. Once compiled, however, applets are unlike applications in that they do not run standalone. Applets are designed to be run by an Internet browser or an applet viewer. We tell the browser to launch an applet by opening a Web page that includes an *APPLET* tag as part of the HTML code. We tell the applet viewer to run the applet by specifying a minimum Web page that contains an *APPLET* tag.

If you are not familiar with HTML coding, the language consists of pairs of **tags** that specify formatting for the Web page. The opening tag begins the specific formatting; the closing tag, which is identical to the opening tag except for a leading forward slash (/), ends that formatting. The basic HTML tags used with applets are described in Table 4.1.

TABLE 4.1   HTML Tags

HTML Tags	Meaning
<HTML></HTML>	Marks the beginning and end of the Web page.
<HEAD></HEAD>	Marks the beginning and end of the header portion of the Web page. The header contains general descriptive information about the page.
<TITLE></TITLE>	Marks the beginning and end of the text that will be displayed on the title bar of the browser or applet viewer window.
<BODY></BODY>	Marks the beginning and end of the body of the Web page. The body contains the content of the Web page.
<APPLET></APPLET>	Identifies the applet to launch in the browser or applet viewer window. The <APPLET> tag supports attributes for specifying the applet name, location of the class file, and size of the applet window. Each attribute consists of the attribute's name followed by an equals sign (=) and the value assigned to that attribute. CODE = the class name of the applet CODEBASE = the directory in which to search for the class file WIDTH = the width of the applet's window in pixels HEIGHT = the height of the applet's window in pixels

Example 4.2 shows a minimal HTML file that you can modify to launch an applet.

```
<HTML>
<HEAD>
   <TITLE>TitleName</TITLE>
</HEAD>
<BODY>
   <APPLET CODE="ClassName.class" CODEBASE="." WIDTH=w
           HEIGHT=h></APPLET>
</BODY>
</HTML>
```

EXAMPLE 4.2   Minimal HTML Page for Launching an Applet

The *CODE* attribute of the *APPLET* tag is the name of the applet class. The *CODEBASE* attribute is the directory in which the JVM should look for the class file. In Example 4.2, the dot (.) for the *CODEBASE* value means that the class file is in the same directory as the HTML page. The *WIDTH* and *HEIGHT* attributes specify in pixels (or picture elements) the width and height of the applet window.

For example, if we had a class called *FirstApplet*, we could use a simple text editor to create the HTML file shown in Example 4.3. In this case, the applet window will be 400 pixels wide and 300 pixels high.

```
<HTML>
<HEAD>
   <TITLE>My First Applet</TITLE>
</HEAD>
<BODY>
   <APPLET CODE="FirstApplet.class" CODEBASE="." WIDTH=400
           HEIGHT=300></APPLET>
</BODY>
</HTML>
```

EXAMPLE 4.3   HTML Page for Launching an Applet Named *FirstApplet*

An applet viewer is provided as part of Sun Microsystems' Java Software Development Toolkit (SDK). The applet viewer is a minimal browser that enables us to view the applet without needing to open a Web browser.

If the name of the Web page is *FirstApplet.html*, we can run the applet viewer from the command line as follows:

```
appletviewer FirstApplet.html
```

If you are using TextPad, you can call the applet viewer directly from TextPad without needing to open a command line window. TextPad automatically creates a minimum Web page that contains an *APPLET* tag. By default, TextPad applets execute in a window that is 400 pixels wide and 300 pixels high; that is, TextPad generates an *APPLET* tag with a *WIDTH* attribute of 400 and a *HEIGHT* attribute of 300.

4.3   Drawing Shapes with *Graphics* Methods

Java's *Graphics* class, in the *java.awt* package, provides methods to draw figures such as rectangles, circles, and lines; to set the colors for drawing; and to write text in a window.

Each drawing method requires you to specify the location in the window to start drawing. Locations are expressed using an (x,y) coordinate system. Each coordinate corresponds to a pixel. The x coordinate specifies the horizontal position, beginning at 0 and increasing as you move across the window to the right. The y coordinate specifies the vertical position, starting at 0 and increasing as you move down the window. Thus for a window that is 400 pixels wide and 300 pixels high, the coordinate (0, 0) corresponds to the upper-left corner; (400, 0) is the upper-right corner; (0, 300) is the lower-left corner, and (400, 300) is the lower-right corner. Figure 4.2 shows a window with a few sample pixels and their (x,y) coordinates.

Table 4.2 shows some useful methods of the *Graphics* class for drawing shapes and displaying text in a window.

Figure 4.2

The Graphics Coordinate System

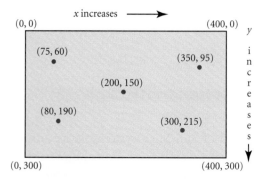

TABLE 4.2   Methods of the *Graphics* Class

	Useful Methods of the *Graphics* Class
Return value	**Method name and argument list**
void	`drawLine( int xStart, int yStart, int xEnd, int yEnd )`
	draws a line starting at (*xStart*, *yStart*) and ending at (*xEnd*, *yEnd*).
void	`drawRect( int x, int y, int width, int height )`
	draws the outline of a rectangle with its top-left corner at (*x, y*), with the specified *width* and *height* in pixels.
void	`fillRect( int x, int y, int width, int height )`
	draws a solid rectangle with its top-left corner at (*x, y*), with the specified *width* and *height* in pixels.
void	`clearRect( int x, int y, int width, int height )`
	draws a solid rectangle in the current background color with its top-left corner at (*x, y*), with the specified *width* and *height* in pixels.
void	`drawOval( int x, int y, int width, int height )`
	draws the outline of an oval inside an invisible, bounding rectangle with the specified *width* and *height* in pixels. The top-left corner of the rectangle is (*x, y*).
void	`fillOval( int x, int y, int width, int height )`
	draws a solid oval inside an invisible, bounding rectangle with the specified *width* and *height* in pixels. The top-left corner of the rectangle is (*x, y*).
void	`drawString( String s, int x, int y )`
	displays the *String s*. If you were to draw an invisible, bounding rectangle around the first letter of the *String*, (*x, y*) would be the lower-left corner of that rectangle.

As you can see, all these methods have a *void* return type, so they do not return a value. Method calls to these methods should be standalone statements; that is, the method call should be terminated by a semicolon.

The pattern for the method names is simple. The *draw* methods render the outline of the figure, while the *fill* methods render solid figures. The *clearRect* method draws a rectangle in the background color, which effectively erases anything drawn within that rectangle.

Figure 4.3 shows the relationship among the method arguments and the figures drawn.

Example 4.4 shows how to use the *drawString* method. The coordinate you specify is the lower-left corner of the first character in the *String*. If you want to display more than one line of text in the default font, add 15 to the y value for each new line. For example, the statements at lines 13 and 14 print the message "Programming is not a spectator sport!" on two lines.

There were no instance variables in this applet, so we omitted the *init* method; all the functionality of the applet is in the *paint* method.

Figure 4.4 shows the output of the applet.

```
 1 /* Drawing Text
 2    Anderson, Franceschi
 3 */
 4
 5 import javax.swing.JApplet;
 6 import java.awt.Graphics;
 7
 8 public class DrawingTextApplet extends JApplet
 9 {
10   public void paint( Graphics g )
11   {
12     super.paint( g );
13     g.drawString( "Programming is not", 140, 100 );
14     g.drawString( "a spectator sport!", 140, 115 );
15   }
16 }
```

EXAMPLE 4.4   An Applet That Displays Text

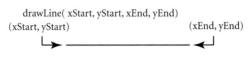

Figure 4.3

The Arguments for Drawing Lines, Rectangles, Ovals, and Text

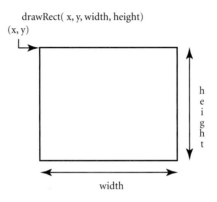

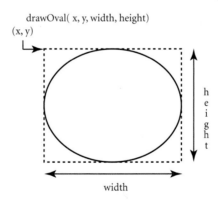

drawString(string, x, y)

To draw a line, you call the *drawLine* method with the coordinates of the beginning of the line and the end of the line. Lines can be vertical, horizontal, or at any angle. In vertical lines, the *startX* and *endX* values are the same, while in horizontal lines, the *startY* and *endY* values are the same. Statements at lines 14–16 in Example 4.5 draw a few lines.

Figure 4.4

An Applet Displaying Two Lines of Text

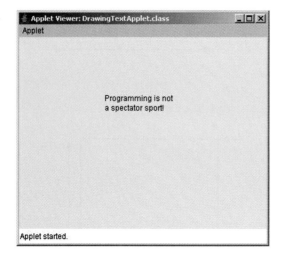

```
1 /* A Line Drawing Applet
2    Anderson, Franceschi
3 */
4
5 import javax.swing.JApplet;
6 import java.awt.Graphics;
7
8 public class LineDrawingApplet extends JApplet
9 {
10   public void paint( Graphics g )
11   {
12     super.paint( g );
13
14     g.drawLine( 100, 150, 100, 250 );  // a vertical line
15     g.drawLine( 150, 75, 275, 75 );    // a horizontal line
16     g.drawLine( 0, 0, 400, 300 );      // a diagonal line from
17                                        // the upper-left corner
18                                        // to the lower-right corner
19   }
20 }
```

EXAMPLE 4.5   An Applet That Draws Lines

Figure 4.5 shows these lines drawn in an applet window.

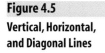

Figure 4.5

Vertical, Horizontal, and Diagonal Lines

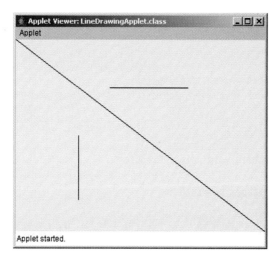

Example 4.6 shows how to use the methods for drawing shapes in an applet. To draw a rectangle, call the *drawRect* or *fillRect* methods with the (*x,y*) coordinate of the upper-left corner, as well as the width in pixels and the height in pixels. Obviously, to draw a square, you specify equal values for the width and height. Line 14 draws a rectangle 40 pixels wide and 100 pixels high; line 15 draws a solid square with sides that are 80 pixels in length.

Drawing an oval or a circle is a little more complex. As you can see in Figure 4.3, you need to imagine a rectangle bounding all sides of the oval or circle. Then the (*x,y*) coordinate you specify in the *drawOval* or *fillOval* methods is the location of the upper-left corner of the bounding rectangle. The width and height are the width and height of the bounding rectangle. Line 17 in Example 4.6 draws a filled oval whose upper-left corner is at coordinate (100, 50) and is 40 pixels wide and 100 pixels high; this filled oval is drawn exactly inside the rectangle drawn at line 14. Line 18 draws an oval 100 pixels wide and 40 pixels high, the same dimensions as the oval drawn at line 17, but rotated 90 degrees.

You draw a circle by calling the *drawOval* or *fillOval* methods, specifying equal values for the width and height. If it seems more natural to you to identify circles by giving a center point and a radius, you can convert the center point and radius into the arguments for Java's *drawOval* or *fillOval* methods as done in lines 21–24.

```
1 /* A Shape Drawing Applet
2    Anderson, Franceschi
3 */
4
5 import javax.swing.JApplet;
6 import java.awt.Graphics;
7
8 public class ShapeDrawingApplet extends JApplet
9 {
10   public void paint( Graphics g )
11   {
12     super.paint( g );
13
14     g.drawRect( 100, 50, 40, 100 );   // rectangle
15     g.fillRect( 200, 70, 80, 80 );    // solid square
16
17     g.fillOval( 100, 50, 40, 100 );   // oval inside the rectangle
18     g.drawOval( 100, 200, 100, 40 );  // same-size oval
19                                       // rotated 90 degrees
20
21     int centerX = 250, centerY = 225;
22     int radius = 25;
23     g.drawOval( centerX - radius, centerY - radius,
24                 radius * 2, radius * 2 );  // circle using radius
25                                            // and center
26   }
27 }
```

EXAMPLE 4.6   An Applet That Draws Shapes

Figure 4.6 shows the ovals and rectangles drawn in Example 4.6.

CODE IN ACTION

To see a demonstration of the *Graphics* drawing methods, look for the Shockwave movie in the Chapter 4 directory of the CD-ROM accompanying this book. Double-click on the *Graphics.html* file to start the movie.

What happens if the (*x,y*) coordinate you specify for a figure isn't inside the window? If a figure's coordinates are outside the bounds of the window, no

Figure 4.6

Geometric Shapes and Fills

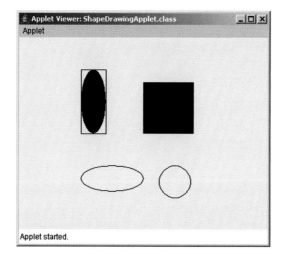

error will be generated, but the figure won't be visible. If the user resizes the window so that the coordinates are now within the newly sized window, then the figure will become visible.

Now we can write an applet that draws a picture. We've decided to draw an astronaut. Example 4.7 shows the code to do that. We started with the *AppletShell* class, changed the name of the class, and added calls to the *Graphics* methods to make our drawing. Notice that we never call the *paint* method; it is called automatically by the applet viewer or Web browser.

COMMON ERROR TRAP

Do not call the *paint* method. It is called automatically when the applet starts and every time the window contents need to be updated.

```
 1 /* An applet with graphics
 2     that draws an astronaut
 3     Anderson, Franceschi
 4 */
 5
 6 import javax.swing.JApplet;
 7 import java.awt.Graphics;
 8
 9 public class Astronaut extends JApplet
10 {
11   int sX, sY; // starting x and y coordinate
12
13   public void init( )
14   {
15     sX = 95;
16     sY = 20;
```

```
17    }
18
19    public void paint( Graphics g )
20    {
21       super.paint( g );
22
23       // helmet
24       g.drawOval( sX + 60, sY, 75, 75 );
25       g.drawOval( sX + 70, sY + 10, 55, 55 );
26
27       // face
28       g.drawOval( sX + 83,  sY + 27, 8, 8 );
29       g.drawOval( sX + 103, sY + 27, 8, 8 );
30       g.drawLine( sX + 97, sY + 35, sX + 99, sY + 43 );
31       g.drawLine( sX + 97, sY + 43, sX + 99, sY + 43 );
32       g.drawOval( sX + 90, sY + 48, 15, 6 );
33
34       // neck
35       g.drawRect( sX + 88, sY + 70, 20, 10 );
36
37       // torso
38       g.drawRect( sX + 65, sY + 80, 65, 85 );
39
40       // arms
41       g.drawRect( sX, sY + 80, 65, 20 );
42       g.drawRect( sX + 130, sY + 80, 65, 20 );
43
44       // legs
45       g.drawRect( sX + 75, sY + 165, 20, 80 );
46       g.drawRect( sX + 105, sY + 165, 20, 80 );
47
48       // flag
49       g.drawLine( sX + 195, sY + 80, sX + 195 , sY );
50       g.drawRect( sX + 195, sY, 75, 45 );
51       g.drawRect( sX + 195, sY, 30, 25 );
52
53       // caption
54       g.drawString( "One small step for man. . .",
55          sX + 25, sY + 270 );
56    }
57 }
```

EXAMPLE 4.7   An Applet that Draws an Astronaut

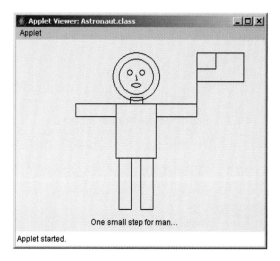

Figure 4.7

An Astronaut Made from Rectangles, Ovals, Lines, and Text

When the applet in Example 4.7 runs, our astronaut will look like the one in Figure 4.7.

To draw our astronaut, we used rectangles for the body, arms, legs, and flag; lines for the nose and the flag's stick; circles for the helmet and eyes; and an oval for the mouth. Then we used the *drawString* method to print "One small step for man…"

In line 11, we declare two instance variables of our class, *sX* and *sY*. These are the starting *x* and starting *y* values for the astronaut. In the *init* method, in lines 15 and 16, we initialize the values of *sX* and *sY*. Inside the *paint* method, the *x* and *y* arguments we send to the *fillRect*, *drawLine*, *fillOval*, and *drawString* methods are specified relative to this starting (*sX*, *sY*) coordinate. These relative values, such as *sX + 60*, are called **offsets**. By using offsets from the starting (*sX*, *sY*) coordinate, we can easily change the position of the astronaut on the screen by simply changing the values of *sX* and *sY*. We don't need to change any of the arguments sent to the *Graphics* methods.

 **SOFTWARE ENGINEERING TIP**

When drawing a figure using graphics, specify coordinates as offsets from a starting (*x, y*) coordinate.

Skill Practice
with these end-of-chapter questions

4.7.1	Multiple Choice Exercises
	Questions 6, 7, 8, 9
4.7.2	Reading and Understanding Code
	Questions 12, 13, 14, 15
4.7.3	Fill in the Code
	Questions 17, 18, 19, 20
4.7.4	Identifying Errors in Code
	Questions 21, 22
4.7.6	Write a Short Program
	Questions 31, 32, 33
4.7.8	Technical Writing
	Question 39

4.4   Using Color

All the figures we have drawn were black. That's because when our applet starts, the default drawing color is black. We can add color to the drawing by setting the **current color**, also called the **foreground color**, which is part of the graphics context represented by the *Graphics* object sent to the *paint* method. The *draw* and *fill* methods draw the figures in the current color. The current color remains in effect until it is set to another color. For example, if you set the current color to blue—then call the *drawRect*, *fillOval*, and *drawLine* methods—the rectangle, oval, and line will all be drawn in blue. Then if you set the color to yellow and call the *drawRect* method, that rectangle will be drawn in yellow.

To set the current color, use the *setColor* method of the *Graphics* class as shown in Table 4.3. This method takes a *Color* object as an argument.

TABLE 4.3   The *setColor* Method of the *Graphics* Class

Another Useful Method of the *Graphics* Class	
Return value	**Method name and argument list**
void	setColor(Color c)
	sets the current foreground color to the *Color* specified by *c*.

The *Color* class, which is in the *java.awt* package, defines colors using an RGB (Red, Green, Blue) system. Any RGB color is considered to be composed of red, green, and blue components. Each component's value can range from 0 to 255; the higher the value, the higher the concentration of that component in the color. For example, a color with red = 255, green = 0, and blue = 0 is red, and a color with red = 0, green = 0, and blue = 255 is blue.

The *Color* class provides a set of *static Color* constants representing 13 common colors. Table 4.4 lists the *Color* constants for these common colors and their corresponding red, green, and blue components. The *Color* constants that are composed of all capital letters were added when Java version 1.4.1 was released, to be consistent with the naming convention for constants; that is, the identifier consists of all capital letters and internal words are separated by underscores. The older, lowercase names for the *Color* constants are still supported, however.

Each color constant is a predefined *Color* object, so you can simply assign the constant to your *Color* object reference. You do not need to instantiate a new *Color* object. *Color* constants can be used wherever a *Color* object is expected. For example, this statement assigns the *Color* constant *Color.RED* to the object reference *red*:

```
Color red = Color.RED;
```

And this statement sets the current color to orange:

```
g.setColor( Color.ORANGE );
```

As you can see, gray consists of equal amounts of each component. The higher the value of the components, the lighter the color of gray. This makes sense because white is (255, 255, 255), so the closer a color gets to

TABLE 4.4   *Color* Constants and Their Red, Green, and Blue Components

Color Constant	Red	Green	Blue
Color.black or			
Color.BLACK	0	0	0
Color.blue or			
Color.BLUE	0	0	255
Color.cyan or			
Color.CYAN	0	255	255
Color.darkGray or			
Color.DARK_GRAY	64	64	64
Color.gray or			
Color.GRAY	128	128	128
Color.green or			
Color.GREEN	0	255	0
Color.lightGray or			
Color.LIGHT_GRAY	192	192	192
Color.magenta or			
Color.MAGENTA	255	0	255
Color.orange or			
Color.ORANGE	255	200	0
Color.pink or			
Color.PINK	255	175	175
Color.red or			
Color.RED	255	0	0
Color.white or			
Color.WHITE	255	255	255
Color.yellow or			
Color.YELLOW	255	255	0

TABLE 4.5   A *Color* Class Constructor

Color Constructor
`Color( int rr, int gg, int bb )`
Allocates a *Color* object with an *rr* red component, *gg* green component, and *bb* blue component.

white, the lighter that color will be. Similarly, the closer the gray value gets to 0, the darker the color, because (0, 0, 0) is black.

In addition to using the *Color* constants, you can instantiate your own custom colors using any of the 16 million possible combinations of the component values. The *Color* class has a number of constructors, but for our purposes, we'll need only the constructor shown in Table 4.5.

Now let's add color to our astronaut drawing. Example 4.8 shows our modified applet.

```
 1 /* An applet with graphics
 2     that draws an astronaut in color
 3     Anderson, Franceschi
 4 */
 5
 6 import javax.swing.JApplet;
 7 import javax.swing.JOptionPane;
 8 import java.awt.Graphics;
 9 import java.awt.Color;
10
11 public class AstronautWithColor extends JApplet
12 {
13
14    int sX, sY;
15    Color spacesuit;
16
17    public void init( )
18    {
19      spacesuit = new Color( 195, 175, 150 );
20
21      sX = Integer.parseInt( JOptionPane.showInputDialog
22              ( null, "Enter the starting x position") );
```

(continued)

```
23     sY = Integer.parseInt( JOptionPane.showInputDialog
24             ( null, "Enter the starting y position") );
25   }
26
27   public void paint( Graphics g )
28   {
29     super.paint( g );
30
31     // helmet
32     g.setColor( spacesuit );
33     g.fillOval( sX + 60, sY, 75, 75 );
34     g.setColor( Color.LIGHT_GRAY );
35     g.fillOval( sX + 70, sY + 10, 55, 55 );
36
37     // face
38     g.setColor( Color.DARK_GRAY );
39     g.drawOval( sX + 83,  sY + 27, 8, 8 );
40     g.drawOval( sX + 103, sY + 27, 8, 8 );
41     g.drawLine( sX + 97, sY + 35, sX + 99, sY + 43 );
42     g.drawLine( sX + 97, sY + 43, sX + 99, sY + 43 );
43     g.drawOval( sX + 90, sY + 48, 15, 6 );
44
45     // neck
46     g.setColor( spacesuit );
47     g.fillRect( sX + 88, sY + 70, 20, 10 );
48
49     // torso
50     g.fillRect( sX + 65, sY + 80, 65, 85 );
51
52     // arms
53     g.fillRect( sX, sY + 80, 65, 20 );
54     g.fillRect( sX + 130, sY + 80, 65, 20 );
55
56     // legs
57     g.fillRect( sX + 75, sY + 165, 20, 80 );
58     g.fillRect( sX + 105, sY + 165, 20, 80 );
59
60     // flag
61     g.setColor( Color.BLACK );
62     g.drawLine( sX + 195, sY + 80, sX + 195 , sY );
63     g.setColor( Color.RED );
64     g.fillRect( sX + 195, sY, 75, 45 );
65     g.setColor( Color.BLUE );
```

```
66    g.fillRect( sX + 195, sY, 30, 25 );
67
68    // caption
69    g.setColor( Color.BLACK );
70    g.drawString( "One small step for man...",
71                    sX + 25, sY + 270 );
72  }
73 }
```

EXAMPLE 4.8   An Applet That Draws an Astronaut in Color

Figure 4.8 shows our astronaut in color.

On line 9, we include an *import* statement for the *Color* class in the *java.awt* package.

For the space suit, we use a custom color named *spacesuit*, so we start by declaring the *Color* object reference on line 15, making it an instance variable. Then we instantiate the *Color* object in the *init* method on line 19 using the constructor shown in Table 4.5. To draw the astronaut in color, inside the *paint* method, we changed the *draw* methods to *fill* methods, and when we draw any figure that is part of the space suit, we make sure the current color is our custom color, *spacesuit*.

One other change we made was to prompt the user for the starting *x* and *y* values, so the user could choose where on the screen to draw the astronaut. When the applet begins running, lines 21–24 pop up dialog boxes

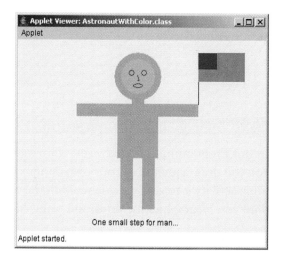

Figure 4.8

Our Astronaut in Color

that prompt the user to enter an *x* value, then a *y* value. Depending on the values the user enters, the astronaut might not fit completely in the applet window. The user can resize the window to make the whole astronaut appear.

It's important to realize that the rendering of the figures occurs in the order in which the *draw* or *fill* methods are executed. Any new figure that occupies the same space as a previously drawn figure will overwrite the previous figure. In this drawing, we intentionally draw the red rectangle of the flag before drawing the blue rectangle. If we drew the rectangles in the opposite order, the blue rectangle would not be visible because the red rectangle, drawn second, would cover the blue rectangle.

Skill Practice
with these end-of-chapter questions

4.7.1   Multiple Choice Exercises

       Questions 5, 10

4.7.2   Reading and Understanding Code

       Question 11

4.7.3   Fill in the Code

       Question 16

4.7.4   Identifying Errors in Code

       Questions 23, 24, 25

4.7.5   Debugging Area

       Questions 29, 30

4.5   Programming Activity 1: Writing an Applet with Graphics

In this Programming Activity, you will write an applet that uses graphics. You will draw a picture of your own design. The objective of this programming activity is to gain experience with the window coordinate system, the *draw* and *fill* graphics methods, and using colors.

1. Start with the *AppletShell* class, change the name of the class to represent the figure you will draw, and add an *import* statement for the *Color* class.

2. Create a drawing of your own design. It's helpful to sketch the drawing on graph paper first, then translate the drawing into the coordinates of the applet window. Your drawing should include at least two each of rectangles, ovals, circles, and lines. Your drawing should also use at least three colors, one of which is a custom color.

3. Label your drawing using the *drawString* method.

4. Prompt the user for a starting *x* value and starting *y* value for your drawing using dialog boxes.

Be creative with your drawing!

? DISCUSSION QUESTIONS

1. If the user enters 400, 400 for the starting (*x*, *y*) coordinate of the drawing, you might not be able to see the drawing. Explain why and what the user can do to make the drawing visible.

2. What is the advantage to drawing a figure using a starting (*x*, *y*) coordinate?

4.6   Chapter Summary

- Applets are Java programs that are run from an applet viewer or an Internet browser. Applets are invoked via the HTML APPLET tag.

- When an applet begins executing, its *init* method is called first. Then the *paint* method is called. The *init* method is used to initialize the applet's data. The *paint* method is used to display text and graphics on the applet window.

- The *Graphics* class in the *java.awt* package provides methods to draw figures, such as rectangles, circles, and lines; to set the colors for drawing; and to write text in a window.

- An (*x,y*) coordinate system is used to specify locations in the window. Each coordinate corresponds to a pixel (or picture element). The *x* value specifies the horizontal position, beginning at 0 and increasing as you move right across the window. The *y* value specifies the vertical position, starting at 0 and increasing as you move down the window.

- All drawing on a graphics window is done in the current color, which is changed using the *setColor* method.

CHAPTER SUMMARY

- Objects of the *Color* class, in the *java.awt* package, can be used to set the current color. The *Color* class provides *static* constants for common colors.

- Custom *Color* objects can be instantiated by using a constructor and specifying the red, green, and blue components of the color.

4.7 Exercises, Problems, and Projects

4.7.1 Multiple Choice Exercises

1. What package does the *Graphics* class belong to?

   ❑ *Graphics*

   ❑ *java.awt*

   ❑ *swing*

   ❑ *Applet*

2. How does a programmer typically get access to a *Graphics* object when coding an applet?

   ❑ One must be created with the *Graphics* constructor.

   ❑ It is an instance variable of the class *JApplet*.

   ❑ It is a parameter of the *paint* method.

3. An applet is a standalone application.

   ❑ true

   ❑ false

4. In an applet, the *paint* method is called automatically even if the programmer does not code the method call.

   ❑ true

   ❑ false

5. Look at the following code:

   ```
   Color c = Color.BLUE;
   ```

   What is *BLUE*?

   ❑ a *static* field of the class *Color*

   ❑ an instance variable of the class *Color*

❑ a *static* method of the class *Color*

❑ an instance method of the class *Color*

6. What can be stated about the line drawn by the code below?

```
g.drawLine( 100, 200, 300, 200 );
```

❑ The line is vertical.

❑ The line is horizontal.

❑ The line is a diagonal.

❑ none of the above.

7. What do the arguments 10, 20 represent in the following statement?

```
g.drawRect( 10, 20, 100, 200 );
```

❑ the (*x,y*) coordinate of the upper-left corner of the rectangle
we are drawing

❑ the width and height of the rectangle we are drawing

❑ the (*x,y*) coordinate of the center of the rectangle we are drawing

❑ the (*x,y*) coordinate of the lower-right corner of the rectangle
we are drawing

8. What do the arguments 100, 200 represent in the following statement?

```
g.drawRect( 10, 20, 100, 200 );
```

❑ the (*x,y*) coordinate of the upper-left corner of the rectangle
we are drawing

❑ the width and height of the rectangle we are drawing

❑ the height and width of the rectangle we are drawing

❑ the (*x,y*) coordinate of the lower-right corner of the rectangle
we are drawing

9. How many arguments does the *fillOval* method take?

❑ 0

❑ 2

❑ 4

❑ 5

10. In RGB format, a gray color can be coded as *A A A* where the first *A* represents the amount of red in the color, the second *A* the amount of green, and the third *A* the amount of blue. *A* can vary from 0 to 255, including both 0 and 255; how many possible gray colors can we have?

    ❏ 1

    ❏ 2

    ❏ 255

    ❏ 256

    ❏ 257

4.7.2   Reading and Understanding Code

11. In what color will the rectangle be drawn?

    ```
    g.setColor( Color.BLUE );
    g.drawRect( 10, 20, 100, 200 );
    ```

12. What is the length of the line being drawn?

    ```
    g.drawLine( 50, 20, 50, 350 );
    ```

13. What is the width of the rectangle being drawn?

    ```
    g.fillRect( 10, 20, 250, 350 );
    ```

14. What is the (x,y) coordinate of the upper-right corner of the rectangle being drawn?

    ```
    g.fillRect( 10, 20, 250, 350 );
    ```

15. What is the (x,y) coordinate of the lower-right corner of the rectangle being drawn?

    ```
    g.drawRect( 10, 20, 250, 350 );
    ```

4.7.3   Fill in the Code

16. This code sets the current color to red.

    ```
    // assume you have a Graphics object named g
    // your code goes here
    ```

17. This code draws the *String* "Fill in the Code" with the lower-left corner of the first character (the *F*) being at the coordinate (100, 250).

    ```
    // assume you have a Graphics object called g
    // your code goes here
    ```

18. This code draws a filled rectangle with a width of 100 pixels and a height of 300 pixels, starting at the coordinate (50, 30).

```
// assume you have a Graphics object called g
// your code goes here
```

19. This code draws a filled rectangle starting at (50, 30) for its upper-left corner with a lower-right corner at (100, 300).

```
// assume you have a Graphics object called g
// your code goes here
```

20. This code draws a circle of radius 100 with its center located at (200, 200).

```
// assume you have a Graphics object called g
// your code goes here
```

4.7.4   Identifying Errors in Code

21. Where is the error in this code sequence?

```
Graphics g = new Graphics( );
```

22. Where is the error in this code sequence?

```
// we are inside method paint
g.drawString( 'Find the bug', 100, 200 );
```

23. Where is the error in this code sequence?

```
// we are inside method paint
g.setColor( GREEN );
```

24. Where is the error in this code sequence?

```
// we are inside method paint
g.setColor( Color.COBALT );
```

25. Where is the error in this code sequence?

```
// we are inside method paint
g.color = Color.RED;
```

26. Where is the error in this statement?

```
import Graphics;
```

27. Where is the error in this statement?

```
import java.awt.JApplet;
```

4.7.5   Debugging Area—Using Messages from the *javac* Compiler and *java* JVM

28. You coded the following program in the file *MyApplet.java*:

```java
import javax.swing.JApplet;
import java.awt.Graphics;

public class MyApplet extends JApplet
{
    public static void paint( Graphics g )     // line 6
    {
        // some code here
    }
}
```

When you compile, you get the following message:

```
MyApplet.java:6: paint(java.awt.Graphics) in MyApplet cannot
override paint(java.awt.Graphics) in java.awt.Container;
overriding method is static
public static void paint( Graphics g )     // line 6
                    ^

1 error
```

Explain what the problem is and how to fix it.

29. You imported the *Color* class and coded the following on line 10 of the class *Test.java*:

```java
Color c = new Color( 1.4, 234, 23 );    // line 10
```

When you compile, you get the following message:

```
MyApplet.java:10: cannot find symbol
symbol  : constructor Color (double,int,int)
location : class java.awt.Color

Color c = new Color( 1.4, 234, 23 );    // line 10
              ^

1 error
```

Explain what the problem is and how to fix it.

30. You coded the following on line 10 of the class *MyApplet.java*:

```java
Color c = Color.Blue; // line 10
```

When you compile, you get the following message:

```
MyApplet.java:10: cannot find symbol
symbol  : variable Blue
location: class java.awt.Color
        Color c = Color.Blue;    // line 10
                        ^
```

```
1 error
```

Explain what the problem is and how to fix it.

4.7.6　Write a Short Program

31. Write an applet that displays the five Olympic rings.

32. Write an applet that displays a tic-tac-toe board. Include a few X's and O's.

33. Write an applet that displays a rhombus (i.e., a parallelogram with equal sides). Your rhombus should not be a square.

4.7.7　Programming Projects

34. Write an applet that displays two eyes. An eye can be drawn using an oval, a filled circle, and lines. On the applet, write a word or two about these eyes.

35. Write an applet that displays the following coins: a quarter, a dime, and a nickel. These three coins should be drawn as basic circles (of different diameters) with the currency value inside (for instance, $.25).

36. Write an applet that displays a basic house, made up of lines (and possibly rectangles). Your house should have multiple colors. On the applet, give a title to the house (for instance, "Java House").

37. Write an applet that displays a black and red bull's eye target, typically made up of several concentric circles.

4.7.8　Technical Writing

38. On the World Wide Web, an applet is a program that executes on the "client side" (a local machine such as your own PC) as opposed to the "server side" (such as a server at *www.yahoo.com*). Do you see any

potential problem executing the same program, such as an applet, on possibly millions of different computers worldwide?

39. If the *drawRect* method did not exist, but you still had the *drawLine* method available, explain how you would be able to draw a rectangle.

4.7.9 Group Project (for a group of 1, 2, or 3 students)

40. Write an applet and one HTML file calling the applet.

The applet should include the following:

❏ a drawing of a chessboard piece (it can be in a single color).

❏ a description of a particular piece of a chessboard (for instance, a rook) and its main legal moves.

In order to make the description visually appealing, you should use several colors and several fonts. You will need to look up the following on Sun's Java Web site:

❏ the *Font* class

❏ how the *Font* class constructors work

❏ the method *setFont* of the *Graphics* class

CHAPTER 5

Flow of Control, Part 1: Selection

CHAPTER CONTENTS

Introduction

In Chapter 1, we said that the order of a program's instructions is critical to producing correct results. The order in which the instructions are executed is called the **flow of control** of the program. There are essentially four types of flow of control: sequential execution, method calls, selection, and looping. Most programs use a combination of all types of flow of control.

So far, our programs have used sequential execution and method calls exclusively. In our Java applications, the JVM executed the first instruction in the *main* method, then executed the next instruction in *main*, and continued executing instructions in order until there were no more instructions to execute. Whenever one of the instructions included a method call, the instructions in the method were executed until the method returned and we resumed execution of instructions in order.

Sometimes, however, you don't want to execute every instruction. Some instructions should be executed only for certain input values, but not for others. For example, we may want to count only the odd numbers or perform only the operation that the user selects from a menu. For these applications, we need a way to determine at run time the input values we have and, therefore, which instructions we should execute.

In this chapter, we'll discuss **selection**, which gives us a way to test for certain conditions and to select the instructions to execute based on the results of the test. To perform selection, Java provides a number of alternatives: *if*, *if/else*, *if/else if*, the conditional operator (?:), and *switch*.

5.1   Forming Conditions

Often in a program, we need to compare variables or objects. For instance, we could be interested in knowing if a person's age is over 18, or if a student's average test score is above 90. If the age is over 18, that person would be allowed to shop online. If a student has an average of 90 or better, that student will be placed on the honor roll, or if a student's grade is below 60, he or she will be sent a warning.

Java provides equality, relational, and logical operators to evaluate and test whether an expression is true or false. It also provides selection statements to transfer control to a different part of the program depending on the result of that test.

5.1.1 Equality Operators

A common operation is to compare two variables or values of the same data type to determine if their values are equal. For example, we need to compare the user's input to a 'y' to determine whether he or she wants to play again. Or if we want to print a list of students who will continue next year, we need to eliminate the students who are graduating seniors.

To compare values of primitive data types, Java provides the equality operators shown in Table 5.1. Both are binary operators, meaning that they take two operands. The operands may be expressions that evaluate to a primitive numeric or *boolean* type or an object reference. The result of an expression composed of a relational operator and its two operands is a *boolean* value, that is, *true* or *false*.

For instance, if an *int* variable *age* holds the value 32, then

the expression (`age == 32`) will evaluate to *true*, and

the expression (`age != 32`) will evaluate to *false*.

The following expression can be used to eliminate seniors by testing whether the value of the *int* variable *yearInCollege* is not equal to 4:

```
yearInCollege != 4
```

The following expression can be used in a game program to determine whether the user wants to play again:

```
playAgain == 'y'
```

TABLE 5.1 Equality Operators

Equality Operator	Type	Meaning
==	binary	is equal to
!=	binary	is not equal to

Assuming the user's input is stored in the *char* variable *playAgain*, then if the user typed 'y', the expression evaluates to *true*; with any other input value, the expression evaluates to *false*.

A common error is to use the assignment operator instead of the equality operator. For example:

```
playAgain = 'y'
```

COMMON ERROR TRAP

Do not confuse the equality operator == (double equal signs) with the assignment operator = (one equal sign).

assigns the value *y* to the variable *playAgain*. Confusing the assignment and equality operators is easy to do; so easy, in fact, that we can almost guarantee that you will make this mistake at least once.

Although the equality operators can be used to compare object references, these operators cannot be used to compare objects. We discuss the comparison of objects later in the chapter.

5.1.2   Relational Operators

To compare values of primitive numeric types, Java provides the relational operators shown in Table 5.2. These operators are binary, meaning that they take two operands, each of which is an expression that evaluates to a primitive numeric type. The relational operators cannot be used with *boolean* expressions or with object references.

Again, if an *int* variable *age* holds the value 32, then

the expression (age < 32) will evaluate to *false*,

the expression (age <= 32) will evaluate to *true*,

the expression (age > 32) will evaluate to *false*, and

the expression (age >= 32) will evaluate to *true*.

TABLE 5.2   Relational Operators

Relational Operator	Type	Meaning
<	binary	is less than
<=	binary	is less than or equal to
>	binary	is greater than
>=	binary	is greater than or equal to

This expression tests whether an *int* variable *testScore* is at least 90:

```
testScore >= 90
```

This code tests whether that test score is less than 60:

```
testScore < 60
```

5.1.3   Logical Operators

A common operation in a program is to test whether a combination of conditions is true or false. For these operations, Java provides the logical operators !, &&, and ||, which correspond to the Boolean logic operators NOT, AND, and OR. These operators, which are shown in Table 5.3, take *boolean* expressions as operands. A *boolean* expression can be any legal combination of *boolean* variables; a condition using relational operators that evaluates to *true* or *false*; or a call to a method that returns a *boolean* value.

The NOT operator (!) takes one *boolean* expression as an operand and inverts the value of that operand. If the operand is *true*, the result will be *false*; and if the operand is *false*, the result will be *true*.

The AND operator (&&) takes two *boolean* expressions as operands; if both operands are *true*, then the result will be *true*; otherwise, it will be *false*.

The OR operator (||) also takes two *boolean* expressions as operands. If both operands are *false*, then the result will be *false*; otherwise, it will be *true*. The OR operator consists of two vertical bars with no intervening space. On the PC keyboard, the vertical bar is the shifted character above the *Enter* key.

The truth table for these logical operators is shown in Table 5.4.

The order of precedence of the relational and logical operators is shown in Table 5.5, along with the arithmetic operators. Note that the Unary NOT

 **REFERENCE POINT**

The complete Operator Precedence Chart is provided in Appendix B.

TABLE 5.3   Logical Operators

Logical Operator	Type	Meaning
!	unary	NOT
&&	binary	AND
||	binary	OR

TABLE 5.4   Truth Table for Logical Operators

Operands		Operations		
a	b	!a	a && b	a || b
true	true	false	true	true
true	false	false	false	true
false	true	true	false	true
false	false	true	false	false

TABLE 5.5   Operator Precedence

Operator Hierarchy	Order of Same-Statement Evaluation	Operation
( )	left to right	parentheses for explicit grouping
++, −−	right to left	shortcut postincrement
++, −−, !	**right to left**	shortcut preincrement, **logical unary NOT**
*, /, %	left to right	multiplication, division, modulus
+, −	left to right	addition or *String* concatenation, subtraction
<, <=, >, >=	**left to right**	**relational operators: less than, less than or equal to, greater than, greater than or equal to**
==, !=	**left to right**	**equality operators: equal to and not equal to**
&&	**left to right**	**logical AND**
||	**left to right**	**logical OR**
=, +=, −=, *=, /=, %=	right to left	Assignment operator and shortcut assignment operators

operator (!) has the highest precedence of the relational and logical operators, followed by the relational operators, then the equality operators, then AND (&&), then OR (||).

Example 5.1 shows these operators at work.

```
1 /* Using Logical Operators
2    Anderson, Franceschi
3 */
4
5 public class LogicalOperators
6 {
7  public static void main( String [ ] args )
8  {
9   int age = 75;
10   boolean test;
11
12   test = ( age > 18 && age < 65 );
13   System.out.println( age + " > 18 && " + age + " < 65 is " + test );
14
15   // short circuitry with AND
16   test = ( age < 65 && age > 18 );
17   System.out.println( age + " < 65 && " + age + " > 18 is " + test );
18
19   // short circuitry with OR
20   test = ( age > 65 || age < 18 );
21   System.out.println( age + " > 65 || " + age + " < 18 is " + test );
22
23   // AND has higher precedence than OR
24   test = ( age > 65 || age < 18  && false );
25   System.out.println( age + " > 65 || " + age
26                      + " < 18 && false is " + test );
27
28   // use of parentheses to force order of execution
29   test = ( ( age > 65 || age < 18 )  && false );
30   System.out.println( "( " + age + " > 65 || " + age
31                      + " < 18 ) && false is " + test );
32  }
33 }
```

EXAMPLE 5.1   How Logical Operators Work

Line 12 evaluates whether the variable *age* is greater than 18 and less than 65 and assigns the result to the *boolean* variable *test*. Since line 9 set the value of *age* to 75, the first operand (*age > 18*) evaluates to *true*. The second operand (*age < 65*) evaluates to *false*; finally,

```
true && false
```

evaluates to *false*, and *false* is assigned to *test*, which is printed at line 13. Line 16 evaluates the same expression as in line 12, but in reverse order. Now the first operand (*age < 65*) evaluates to *false*, and therefore, since the operator is the logical AND, the overall expression evaluates to *false*, independently of the value of the second operand. Because (*false && something*) always evaluates to *false*, the second operand (*age > 18*) will never be evaluated by the Java compiler. This is called **short-circuit evaluation**.

Line 20 shows an example of short-circuit evaluation for the logical OR operator. The first operand (*age > 65*) evaluates to *true*, resulting in the overall expression evaluating to *true*, independently of the value of the second operand. Because (*true || something*) always evaluates to *true*, the second operand will never be evaluated by the Java compiler.

As shown in Table 5.5, the logical AND operator has higher precedence than the logical OR operator. Thus, the expression in line 24 is not evaluated from left to right; rather, the second part of the expression (*age < 18 && false*) is evaluated first, which evaluates to *false*. Then (*age > 65 || false*) evaluates to *true*, which is assigned to *test*, and then output at lines 25–26. If we want to evaluate the expression from left to right, we have to use parentheses to force this, as in line 29. Then, (*age > 65 || age < 18*) is evaluated first and evaluates to *true*; (*true && false*) is evaluated next and evaluates to *false*.

Figure 5.1 shows the output of Example 5.1.

Figure 5.1

Output from Example 5.1

Suppose we have three *ints: x, y,* and *z,* and we want to test if *x* is less than both *y* and *z.* A common error is to express the condition this way:

```
x < y && z // incorrect comparison of x to y and z
```

Because *z* is not a *boolean* variable, this statement will generate a compiler error. Both operands of the logical AND and logical OR operators must evaluate to a *boolean* expression. The correct expression is the following:
```
x < y && x < z.
```

There are often several ways to express the same condition using the Java logical operators. For instance, suppose we have two *boolean* variables called *flag1* and *flag2* and we want to test if at least one of them is *false.*

In plain English, we would translate it as *flag1 is false OR flag2 is false*

Table 5.6 provides several equivalent expressions for the above test.

Although all the expressions in Table 5.6 are equivalent, the first expression, which is the simplest translation of the condition to test, is the easiest to understand and would be the best selection for readability.

DeMorgan's Laws

Thanks to the work of the British mathematician Augustus DeMorgan, we have a set of rules to help develop expressions that are equivalent. DeMorgan, who is known for his work in Boolean algebra and set theory, developed what are known as DeMorgan's Laws. They are the following:

```
1.  NOT( A AND B ) = ( NOT A ) OR ( NOT B )
2.  NOT( A OR B ) = ( NOT A ) AND ( NOT B )
```

COMMON ERROR TRAP

Be sure that both operands of the logical AND and logical OR operators are *boolean* expressions. Expressions such as this: x < y && z, with *x, y,* and *z* being numeric types, are illegal. Instead, use the expression:
x < y && x < z

TABLE 5.6   Examples of Equivalent Expressions

Equivalent Expressions	English Meaning
(flag1 == false) || (flag2 == false)	*flag1* is false OR *flag2* is false
!flag1 || !flag2	*!flag1* is true OR *!flag2* is true
! (flag1 && flag 2)	not both *flag1* and *flag2* are true

In Java, therefore, using the first law, we see that

> !(a && b) is equivalent to !a || !b

Using the second law, we see that

> !(a || b) is equivalent to !a && !b

These laws can be verified simply by the extended truth table shown in Table 5.7.

Thus, to use DeMorgan's Laws, you need to change the AND operator to OR and change the OR operator to AND, and apply the NOT operator (!) to each operand of a logical operator. When the operands are expressions using relational or equality operators, the negated expressions are shown in Table 5.8.

TABLE 5.7   Truth Table for DeMorgan's Laws

a	b	!a	!b	a && b	a || b	!(a && b)	!a || !b	!(a || b)	!a && !b
true	true	false	false	true	true	false	false	false	false
true	false	false	true	false	true	true	true	false	false
false	true	true	false	false	true	true	true	false	false
false	false	true	true	false	false	true	true	true	true

TABLE 5.8   The Logical NOT Operator Applied to Relational and Equality Operators

Expression	! (Expression)
a == b	a != b
a != b	a == b
a < b	a >= b
a >= b	a < b
a > b	a <= b
a <= b	a > b

TABLE 5.9   More Examples of Equivalent Expressions

Equivalent Expressions	English Meaning
(age <= 18 || age >= 65)	*age* is less than or equal to 18 or *age* is greater than or equal to 65
!(age > 18 && age < 65)	*age* is not between 18 and 65
!(age > 18) || !(age < 65)	*age* is not greater than 18 or *age* is not less than 65

For instance, suppose we have an *int* variable named *age*, representing the age of a person, and we want to assess whether *age* is less than or equal to 18 or greater than or equal to 65.

Table 5.9 provides several equivalent expressions for the above test.

Again, although all the expressions in Table 5.9 are equivalent, the first expression, which is the simplest translation of the condition to test, is the easiest to read.

SOFTWARE ENGINEERING TIP

Compose Boolean expressions so that they are easy to read and understand.

Skill Practice
with these end-of-chapter questions

5.14.1   Multiple Choice Exercises

Questions 1, 2, 3, 4, 5, 6, 7

5.14.2   Reading and Understanding Code

Questions 10, 11

5.14.4   Identifying Errors in Code

Questions 31, 32

5.2   Simple Selection with *if*

The simple selection pattern is appropriate when your program needs to perform an operation for one set of data, but not for all other data. For this situation, we use a simple *if* statement, which has this pattern:

```
if ( condition )
{
  true block
}
next statement
```

The true block can contain one or more statements and is executed only if the condition evaluates to *true*. After the true block executes, the instruction following the *if* statement is executed. If the condition is *false*, the true block is skipped and execution picks up at the next instruction after the *if* statement. If the true block contains only one statement, the curly braces are optional. Figure 5.2 illustrates the flow of control of a simple *if* statement.

In Example 5.2, we first prompt the user to enter a grade at lines 11–13. At line 15, we test whether the grade entered is greater than or equal to 60. If it is, we output "You passed" at line 16. Then, no matter what the grade was, line 18 is executed. Figures 5.3 and 5.4 show two runs of the program, one with a grade greater than or equal to 60 and one with a grade less than 60.

Figure 5.2

Flow of Control of a Simple *if* Statement

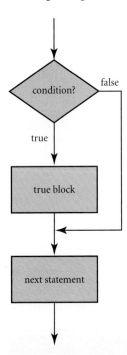

Figure 5.3

Passing Grade

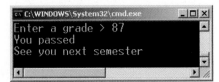

Figure 5.4
Grade Is Less Than 60

```
1 /*  Using If
2     Anderson, Franceschi
3 */
4
5 import java.util.Scanner;
6
7 public class PassingGrade
8 {
9  public static void main( String [ ] args )
10 {
11   Scanner scan = new Scanner( System.in );
12   System.out.print( "Enter a grade > " );
13   int grade = scan.nextInt( );
14
15   if ( grade >= 60 )
16      System.out.println( "You passed" );
17
18   System.out.println( "See you next semester" );
19 }
20 }
```

EXAMPLE 5.2   Working with *if* Statements

Notice the indentation of the true block (line 16). Indenting clarifies the structure of the program. It's easy to see that the message `"You passed"` is printed only if the condition is true. Notice also that we skipped a line after the end of the *if* statement; this further separates the true block from the instruction that follows the *if* statement, making it easier to see the flow of control.

Many software engineers believe it's a good practice to include the curly braces even if only one statement is included in the true block, because it increases clarity and ease of maintenance. The curly braces increase clarity

 **SOFTWARE ENGINEERING TIP**

Indent the true block in an *if* statement for clarity.

because they highlight the section of code to be executed when the condition is *true*. Program maintenance is easier because if the program requirements change and you need to add a second statement to the true block, the curly braces are already in place.

Note that there is no semicolon after the condition. If you place a semicolon after the condition, as in this **incorrect** statement,

```
if ( grade >= 60 );  // incorrect to place semicolon here
      System.out.println( "You passed" );
```

COMMON ERROR TRAP

Adding a semicolon after the condition of an *if* statement indicates that the true block is empty and can cause a logic error at run time.

the compiler will not generate an error. Instead, it will consider the semicolon to indicate that the true block is empty, because a semicolon by itself indicates a statement that does nothing. In this case, the compiler concludes that there is no instruction to execute when the condition is *true*. As a result, when the program runs, the statement

```
System.out.println( "You passed" );
```

is treated as though it follows the *if* statement, and therefore, the message `"You passed"` will be printed regardless of the value of *grade*.

5.3   Selection Using *if/else*

The second form of an *if* statement is appropriate when the data falls into two mutually exclusive categories and different instructions should be executed for each category. For these situations, we use an *if/else* statement, which has the following pattern:

```
if ( condition )
{
   true block
}
else
{
   false block
}
next statement
```

If the condition evaluates to *true*, the true block is executed and the false block is skipped. If the condition evaluates to *false*, the true block is skipped and the false block is executed. In either situation, the next statement is executed next. Figure 5.5 illustrates the flow of control of an *if/else* statement.

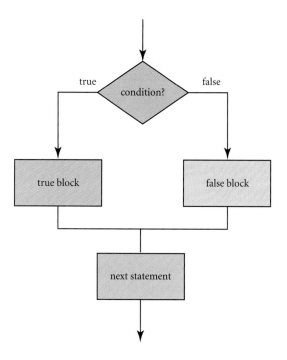

Figure 5.5
Flow of Control of an
***if/else* Statement**

If the true or false block contains only one statement, the curly braces are optional for that block.

Again, notice the indentation of the true and false blocks and that the *else* and curly braces line up under the *if*. This coding style makes it easy to see which statements belong to the true block and which belong to the false block. If the indentation is incorrect, a reader of your program may misunderstand which statements will be executed. In any event, the compiler ignores the indentation; the indentation is designed only to make it easier for humans to understand the logic of the code.

A common use of an *if/else* statement is to verify that data is valid, and to notify the user if it is not. For example, before performing an integer division, we should check that the divisor is not 0, because attempting to perform integer division with a divisor of 0 will generate a run-time exception. In Example 5.3, the *if* statement in lines 17–21 tests whether the divisor is 0. If the condition at line 17 evaluates to *true*, we notify the user that we are unable to perform the division. If the divisor is not 0, the condition evaluates to *false* and we perform the division. Note that lines 20–21 comprise

Figure 5.6

Output from Example 5.3

Figure 5.7

Output from Example 5.3

only one statement, which is the reason we do not need to include curly braces. Figures 5.6 and 5.7 show two runs of the program, first with the user entering a divisor that is not 0, then with the user entering a divisor that is 0.

```
1  /*  Using If/Else
2       Anderson, Franceschi
3  */
4
5  import java.util.Scanner;
6
7  public class Divider
8  {
9   public static void main( String [ ] args )
10  {
11     Scanner scan = new Scanner( System.in );
12     System.out.print( "Enter the dividend > " );
13     int dividend = scan.nextInt( );
14     System.out.print( "Enter the divisor > " );
15     int divisor = scan.nextInt( );
16
17     if ( divisor == 0 )
18       System.out.println( "Sorry; unable to divide by zero" );
19     else
20       System.out.println( dividend + " / " + divisor
21                            + " = " + ( dividend / divisor ) );
22  }
23 }
```

EXAMPLE 5.3   Working with *if/else* Statements

CODE IN ACTION

In the Chapter 5 folder on the CD-ROM included with this book, you will find a Shockwave movie showing a step-by-step illustration of using an *if/else* statement. Double-click on *Selection.html* to start the movie.

Skill Practice
with these end-of-chapter questions

5.14.2   Reading and Understanding Code

Questions 12, 13

5.14.3   Fill in the Code

Questions 20, 21, 22, 23, 24, 25, 26, 27, 28, 29, 30

5.14.4   Identifying Errors in Code

Questions 33, 34, 35

5.14.5   Debugging Area

Question 40

5.14.6   Write a Short Program

Questions 42, 43, 46, 48

5.14.8   Technical Writing

Question 54

5.4   Selection Using *if/else if*

The last form of an *if* statement is appropriate when the data falls into more than two mutually exclusive categories and the appropriate instructions to execute are different for each category. For this situation, Java provides the *if/else if* statement.

The *if/else if* statement follows this pattern:

```
if ( condition 1 )
{
     true block for condition 1
}
else if ( condition 2 )
{
     true block for condition 2
}
. . .
else if ( condition n )
{
     true block for condition n
}
else
{
     false block for all conditions being false
}
next statement
```

The flow of control for this form of the *if* statement is shown in Figure 5.8.

There can be any number of conditions in an *if/else if* statement. As you can see, once a condition evaluates to *true* for any value, control moves to the true block for that condition, then skips the remainder of the conditions, continuing execution at any statement that follows the *if/else if* statement. The final false block (along with the final *else*) is optional and is executed only when none of the conditions evaluates to *true*.

We can use the *if/else if* statement to determine a student's letter grade based on his or her numeric grade. Example 5.4 demonstrates a Java application that prompts a student for a test grade and translates that grade into a letter grade.

```
1 /* A program to translate a numeric grade into a letter grade
2     Anderson, Franceschi
3 */
4
5 import java.util.Scanner;
6
7 public class LetterGrade
8 {
9   public static void main( String [ ] args )
```

Figure 5.8

Flow of Control of an
***if/else if* Statement**

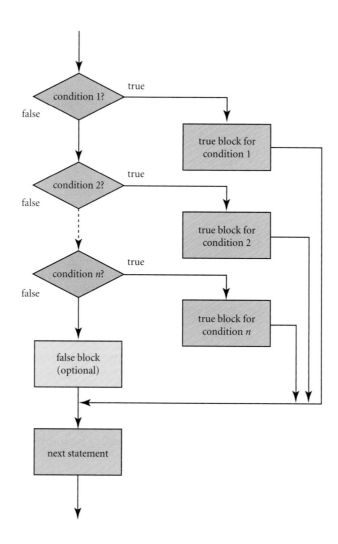

```
10   {
11      Scanner scan = new Scanner( System.in );
12
13      char letterGrade;
14
15      System.out.print( "Enter your test grade: " );
16      int grade = scan.nextInt( );
17
18      if ( grade >= 90 )
19          letterGrade = 'A';
```

```
20
21      else if ( grade >= 80 )
22           letterGrade = 'B';
23
24      else if ( grade >= 70 )
25           letterGrade = 'C';
26
27      else if ( grade >= 60 )
28           letterGrade = 'D';
29
30      else  // grade fits none of the conditions
31           letterGrade = 'F';
32
33      System.out.println( "Your test grade of " + grade
34                          + " is a letter grade of " + letterGrade );
35  }
36 }
```

EXAMPLE 5.4   A Demonstration of *if/else if*

Figure 5.9 shows the output from the program when a student enters a grade of 83.

Notice that each condition is a simple relational expression. Even though we assign a *B* letter grade when the numeric grade is between 80 and 89, the condition for a *B* letter grade (line 21) is simply:

```
if ( grade >= 80 )
```

We don't need to write the condition as

```
if ( grade >= 80 && grade < 90 )
```

because by the time the condition is tested at line 21, all numeric grades greater than or equal to 90 have been eliminated by the test condition at line 18. Any grade greater than or equal to 90 causes the condition at line

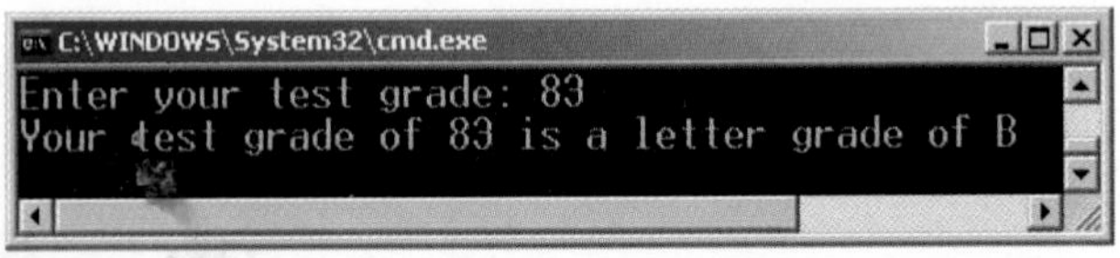

Figure 5.9

Output from Example 5.4

```
C:\WINDOWS\System32\cmd.exe
Enter your test grade: 83
Your test grade of 83 is a letter grade of B
```

18, (`grade >= 90`), to evaluate to *true*. For those grades, the flow of control is to assign an *A* to *letterGrade* at line 19, then skip the remainder of the conditions, continuing execution at the statement following the *if/else if* statement, which is line 33 in this example. Thus, if the condition at line 21 is evaluated, we know that the *grade* must be less than 90.

CODE IN ACTION

In the Chapter 5 folder on the CD-ROM included with this book, you will find a Shockwave movie showing a step-by-step illustration of using an *if/else if* statement. Double-click on *Selection.html* to start the movie.

Skill Practice
with these end-of-chapter questions

5.5 Sequential and Nested *if/else* Statements

When you need the results of one *if* statement's processing before you can evaluate the next condition, you can write multiple *if* statements either sequentially or nested within other *if* statements.

5.5.1 Sequential *if/else* Statements

Finding the Minimum or Maximum Values

To illustrate sequential *if* statements, let's look at the problem of finding the smallest of three numbers.

In Chapter 3, we found the smallest of three numbers using the *min* method of the *Math* class. We first found the smaller of two numbers, then found the smaller of that result and the third number. We can use that same logic to find the smallest of three numbers with multiple, sequential *if* statements. First we find the smaller of the first two numbers, then we find the smaller of that result and the third number. The pseudocode for this application is:

```
read number1
read number2
read number3

if number1 is less than number2
    smallest is number1
else
    smallest is number2

if number3 is less than smallest
    smallest is number3
```

Translating the pseudocode into Java, we get the application in Example 5.5, which prompts the user for three integers and outputs the smallest of the three numbers. In this application, we use two *if* statements. The first *if* statement (lines 23–26) uses an *if/else* statement to find the smaller of the first two integers and store that value into the variable *smallest*. Then, the second *if* statement (lines 28–29) compares the third integer to the value stored in *smallest*. In the second *if* statement, we don't use an *else* clause, because we need to change the value in *smallest* only if the condition is *true*, that is, if the third number is less than *smallest*. Otherwise, the smallest value is already stored in *smallest*.

```
1   /* Find the smallest of three integers
2      Anderson, Franceschi
3   */
4
5   import java.util.Scanner;
6
7   public class FindSmallest
8   {
```

```
9      public static void main( String [ ] args )
10     {
11         int smallest;
12         int num1, num2, num3;
13
14         Scanner scan = new Scanner( System.in );
15
16         System.out.print( "Enter the first integer: " );
17         num1 = scan.nextInt( );
18         System.out.print( "Enter the second integer: " );
19         num2 = scan.nextInt( );
20         System.out.print( "Enter the third integer: " );
21         num3 = scan.nextInt( );
22
23         if ( num1 < num2 )
24             smallest = num1;
25         else
26             smallest = num2;
27
28         if ( num3 < smallest )
29             smallest = num3;
30
31         System.out.println( "The smallest is " + smallest );
32     }
33 }
```

EXAMPLE 5.5   An Application with Sequential *if* Statements

When the program in Example 5.5 is run using *6, 7,* and *5* for the three integers, the output is as shown in Figure 5.10.

One more point. The code only checks that one number is less than another. What happens if two or more of the numbers are equal? The code still works! We only need to find the smallest value; we don't care which of the variables holds that smallest value.

Figure 5.10

Output from Example 5.5

5.5.2   Nested *if/else* Statements

If statements can be written as part of the true or false block of another *if* statement. These are called nested *if* statements. Typically, you nest *if* statements when more information is required beyond the results of the first *if* statement.

One difficulty that arises with nested *if* statements is specifying which *else* clause pairs with which *if* statement, especially if some *if* statements have *else* clauses and others do not. The compiler matches any *else* clause with the most previous *if* statement that doesn't already have an *else* clause. If this matching is not what you want, you can use curly braces to specify the desired *if/else* pairing.

In this code, we have one *if* statement nested within another *if* statement.

```java
if ( x == 2 )
        if ( y == x )
            System.out.println( "x and y equal 2" );
        else
            System.out.println( "x equals 2, but y does not" );
```

Without parentheses, the entire second *if* statement comprises the true block of the first condition (*x* == 2), and the *else* is paired with the second condition (*y* == *x*), because this is the most previous *if* condition that doesn't have an *else*.

However, we can force the *else* clause to be paired with the first condition by using curly braces, as follows:

```java
if ( x == 2 )
{
   if ( y == x )
       System.out.println( "x and y equal 2" );
}
else
   System.out.println( "x does not equal 2" );
```

With the curly braces added, the *if* condition (*y* == *x*), along with its true block, becomes the complete true block for the condition (*x* == 2), and the *else* clause now belongs to the first *if* condition (*x* == 2).

Why can't we just alter the indentation to indicate our meaning? Remember that indentation increases the readability of the code for humans. The compiler ignores indentation and instead follows Java's syntactic rules.

Dangling Else

A common error is writing *else* clauses that don't match any *if* conditions. This is called a **dangling else**. For example, the following code, which includes three *else* clauses and only two *if* conditions, will generate this compiler error:

```
'else' without 'if'

if ( x == 2 )

  if ( y == x )
      System.out.println( "x and y equal 2" );

  else // matches y==x
      System.out.println( "y does not equal 2" );

else // matches x==2
  System.out.println( "x does not equal 2" );


else // no matching if!
  System.out.println( "x and y are not equal" );
```

COMMON ERROR TRAP

Be sure that all *else* clauses match an *if* condition. Writing *else* clauses that don't match *if* conditions will generate an `'else'` `without 'if'` compiler error.

For a more complex and real-world example of nested *if* statements, let's generate a random number between 1 and 10. We did something similar to this in Programming Activity 2 in Chapter 2, but we just paused a few seconds, then displayed the number. Using some nested *if* statements, however, we can make this program a little more interesting. After we generate the random number, we'll prompt the user for a guess. First we'll verify that the guess is between 1 and 10. If it isn't, we'll print a message. Otherwise, we'll check whether the user has guessed the number. If so, we'll print a congratulatory message. If the user has not guessed the number, we'll display the number, then determine whether the guess was close. We'll define "close" as within three numbers. We'll print a message informing the user whether the guess was close, then we'll wish the user better luck next time. The pseudocode for this program looks like this:

```
generate a secret random number between 1 and 10
prompt the user for a guess

if guess is not between 1 and 10
    print message
else
  if guess equals the secret number
    print congratulations
```

```
else
  print the secret number
  if ( guess is not within 3 numbers )
    print "You missed it by a mile!"
  else
    print "You were close."


print "Better luck next time."
```

This pseudocode uses three nested *if* statements; the first determines if the guess is within the requested range of numbers. If it isn't, we print a message. Otherwise, the second *if* statement tests whether the user has guessed the secret number. If so, we print a congratulatory message. If not, we print the secret number, and our last nested *if* statement determines whether the guess was not within 3 numbers of the secret number. If not, we print "You missed it by a mile!"; otherwise, we print "You were close." In either case, we print "Better luck next time."

Example 5.6 is the result of translating this pseudocode into a Java application.

```
1    /* Guess a number between 1 and 10
2        Anderson, Franceschi
3    */
4
5    import java.util.Scanner;
6
7    public class GuessANumber
8    {
9      public static void main( String [ ] args )
10     {
11       int secretNumber, guess;
12
13       Scanner scan = new Scanner( System.in );
14
15       secretNumber = 1 + (int) ( Math.random( ) * 10 );
16       System.out.print( "I'm thinking of a number"
17                  + " between 1 and 10. What is your guess? " );
18       guess = scan.nextInt( );
19
```

```
20        if ( guess < 1 || guess > 10 )
21        {
22            System.out.println( "Well, if you're not going to try,"
23                                  + " I'm not playing." );
24        }
25        else
26        {
27           if ( guess == secretNumber )
28               System.out.println( "Hoorah. You win!" );
29           else
30           {
31               System.out.println( "The number was " + secretNumber );
32
33               if ( Math.abs( guess - secretNumber ) > 3 )
34                   System.out.println( "You missed it by a mile!" );
35               else
36                   System.out.println( "You were close." );
37
38               System.out.println( "Better luck next time." );
39           }
40        }
41     }
42  }
```

EXAMPLE 5.6   Nested *if* Statements

On line 33, we used the *abs* method of the *Math* class to determine whether the guess was within three integers of the secret number. By taking the absolute value of the difference between the guess and the secret number, we don't need to worry about which number is higher than the other; we will always receive a positive difference from the *abs* method.

Figure 5.11 shows the output of a sample run of this program.

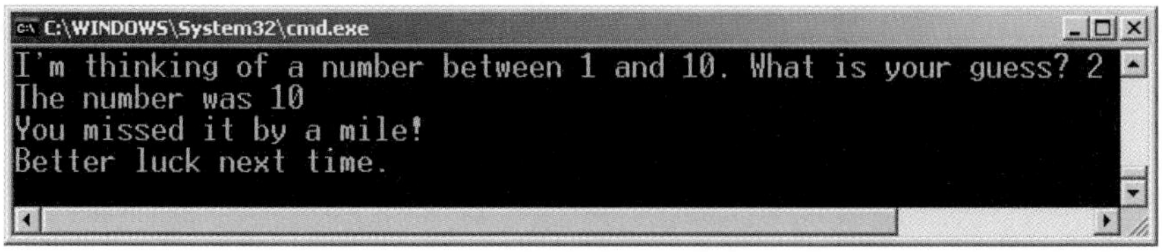

Figure 5.11

Output from the *GuessANumber* Program

```
C:\WINDOWS\System32\cmd.exe
I'm thinking of a number between 1 and 10. What is your guess? 2
The number was 10
You missed it by a mile!
Better luck next time.
```

5.6   Testing Techniques for *if/else* Statements

When an application uses *if/else* statements, the application's flow of control depends on the user's input or other data values. For one input value, the application may execute the true block, while for another input value, the application may execute the false block. Obviously, running an application only once is no guarantee that the program is correct, because if the true block was executed, then the false block was not executed, and therefore, was not tested. Similarly, if the false block was executed, then the true block was not executed, and therefore was not tested.

To test an application for correctness, we could attempt to test all execution paths. To do this, we devise a **test plan** that includes running the application with different data values designed to execute all the statements in the application.

For example, an application that determines whether an integer is positive or negative might have this code:

```
System.out.print( " Enter an integer > " );
int x = scan.nextInt( );
if  ( x > 0 )
    System.out.println( x + " is positive" );
else
    System.out.println( x + " is negative" );
```

We could test this code by running the application twice, the first time entering the value 1, and the second time entering the value -1. We see that the results for those two values are correct: 1 is positive and -1 is negative. We have executed all the statements successfully, but can we say for certain that the program is correct? What if we entered the value 0, which is considered neither a positive nor a negative integer? As written, our program determines that 0 is negative, which is incorrect.

We see, then, that testing the true and false blocks is not sufficient; we need to test the condition of the *if/else* statement as well. There are three possibilities: x is less than 0, x is equal to 0, or x is greater than 0. To test the condition, we should run the application with input values that meet these three criteria. So we should run the application one more time with the input value of 0. This will show us that the program is incorrect, because our code identifies 0 as a negative number.

To correct the program, we should add another condition $(x < 0)$ so we can separate 0 from the negative numbers. The code would then become:

```
System.out.print( " Enter an integer > " );
int x = scan.nextInt( );
if ( x > 0 )
    System.out.println( x + " is positive" );
else if ( x < 0 )
    System.out.println( x + " is negative" );
else
    System.out.println( "The integer is 0" );
```

Now if we retest the program with input values -1, 1, and 0, we get correct results for each of these values.

Another testing method is to treat the program like a black box, that is, as if the program's inner workings are unknown and unknowable to us. We devise our test plan based solely on the specifications of the program and develop input values that test the program logically. Thus, if our specifications are that we should determine whether an integer is positive or negative, we deduce that we should run the program with inputs that are a negative number, a positive number, and the special case, 0.

Both testing methods work together to ensure that a program is correct.

 **SOFTWARE ENGINEERING TIP**

When testing your program, develop input values that test all execution paths and confirm that the logic implements the program specifications.

5.7 Programming Activity 1: Working with *if/else*

In this activity, you will write an *if/else* selection statement to decide how a golfer's score compares to par.

Copy to a directory on your computer all the files in the Chapter 5 Programming Activity 1 folder on the CD-ROM accompanying this book.

Open the *PathClient.java* source file. You will add your code to the *workWithIfElse* method. Part of the method has been coded for you. Search for ***** in the source file.

You should be positioned at the code shown in Example 5.7.

```
public void workWithIfElse( int score )
{
    String result = "???";
    // ***** Student code starts here
    // If score is greater than 72, assign "over par" to result
    // If score is equal to 72, assign "par" to result
```

```
        // If score is less than 72, assign "below par" to result




        //
        // Student code ends here
        //

        firstTime = false;
        animate( score, result );
}
```

EXAMPLE 5.7   The Student Code Portion of Programming Activity 1

Where indicated in the code, you should write an *if/else* statement to perform the following function:

- In the method header of the method *workWithIfElse*, you see "(int score)". The *int* variable *score* represents a golf score. This variable will be an input from the user; the dialog box that prompts the user for the score has already been coded for you and stores the user's input in the variable *score*, which is available to your code as a parameter of the *workWithIfElse* method. Do not declare the variable *score* inside the method; just use it.

- We want to know if the golf score is "over par," "par," or "below par." Par is 72.

- Inside the *if/else* statement, you need to assign a value to the *String* variable named *result*, as follows:

   If *score* is higher than 72, then assign "over par" to *result*; if score is exactly 72, assign "par" to *result*; and if score is lower than 72, assign "below par" to *result*.

- You do not need to write the code to call the method *animate*; that part of the code has already been written for you.

Animation: The application window will display the correct path of the *if/else* statement (in green), which may or may not be the same as your path, depending on how you coded the *if/else* statement. The animation will also assess your result, that is, the value of the variable *result*, and give you feedback on the correctness of your result.

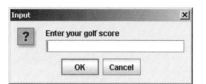

Figure 5.12
The Beginning of the Application

To test your code, compile and run the application and enter an integer in the dialog box. Try the following input values for *score*: 45, 71, 72, 73, and 89. Be sure your code produces the correct result for all input values.

When the program begins, you will see an empty graphics window and the dialog box of Figure 5.12, prompting you for an integer value.

Figure 5.13 demonstrates the correct code path when the input value is 82 and assesses that the student's code is correct.

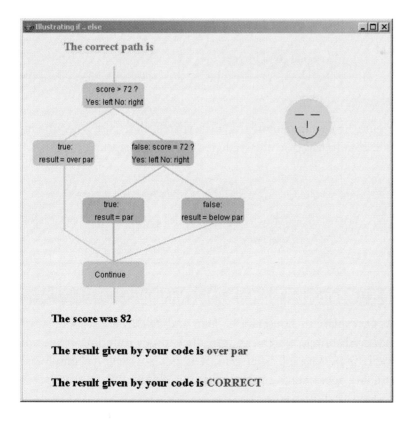

Figure 5.13
A Correct *if/else* Statement

Figure 5.14

An Incorrect *if/else* **Statement**

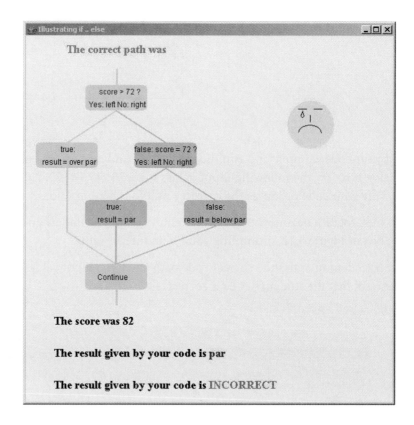

Figure 5.14 again demonstrates the correct code path when the input value is 82, but in this case, the student's code is incorrect.

DISCUSSION QUESTIONS ?

1. How many conditions did you use in the complete *if/else* statement?

2. Your code should be correct if the application gets correct results for the input values 71, 72, and 73. Explain why.

5.8   Comparing Floating-Point Numbers

As we explain in Appendix E, *floats* and *doubles* are stored using IEEE 754 standard format, which can introduce minor rounding errors when arithmetic is performed. That said, it is not advisable to simply rely on the equality operators to compare floating-point numbers.

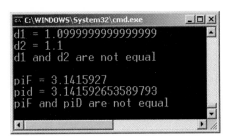

Figure 5.15
Output from Example 5.8

Let's take a look at Example 5.8, which computes 11 * .1 two ways. First, at line 11, we assign .0 to a *double* variable, *d1*, and at lines 12–22 we add .1 to *d1* eleven times. Then, at line 24, we declare a second *double* variable, *d2*, and assign it the result of multiplying .1 times 11. You would expect, then, that *d1* and *d2* would have the same value. Not so, as the output of the program shows in Figure 5.15.

You can also see the effects of rounding when comparing a *float* to a *double*. For example, at lines 35 and 36 of Example 5.8, we assign the same floating-point number (PI) to a double variable *piD* and to a float variable *piF*, then compare the two values at line 40. As you can see from the output in Figure 5.15, they do not compare as equal. The reason is that double-precision floating-point numbers are able to store a larger number of significant digits than single-precision floating-point numbers.

 **REFERENCE POINT**

Binary representation of floating-point numbers is discussed in Appendix E.

```
1 /* Using equality operators on floating-point numbers
2    Anderson, Franceschi
3 */
4
5 public class EqualityFloatingPoint
6 {
7  public static void main( String [ ] args )
8  {
9   // Part 1: Compute 11 * .1 two ways
10
11   double d1 = .0; // add .1 to 0 eleven times
12   d1 += .1;  // 1
13   d1 += .1;  // 2
14   d1 += .1;  // 3
```

```
15   d1 += .1;  // 4
16   d1 += .1;  // 5
17   d1 += .1;  // 6
18   d1 += .1;  // 7
19   d1 += .1;  // 8
20   d1 += .1;  // 9
21   d1 += .1;  // 10
22   d1 += .1;  // 11
23
24   double d2 = .1 * 11; // compute 11 * .1
25
26   System.out.println( "d1 = " + d1 );
27   System.out.println( "d2 = " + d2 );
28   if ( d1 == d2 )
29       System.out.println( "d1 and d2 are equal" );
30   else
31       System.out.println( "d1 and d2 are not equal" );
32
33   // Part 2: Compare float and double with same value
34
35   float  piF = 3.141592653589793f;
36   double piD = 3.141592653589793;
37
38   System.out.println( "\npiF = " + piF );
39   System.out.println( "pid = " + piD );
40   if ( piF == piD )
41       System.out.println( "piF and piD are equal" );
42   else
43       System.out.println( "piF and piD are not equal" );
44 }
45 }
```

EXAMPLE 5.8   Using the Equality Operator to Compare Floating-Point Numbers

Instead of using the equality operators to compare floating-point numbers, it's better to compare the absolute value of the difference to a small value, called a **threshold**. The value of the threshold should be the difference we can tolerate and still consider the numbers equal. Let's redo Example 5.8. Instead of using the equality operator, we'll use the *Math.abs* method to compute a difference between the two numbers and compare the difference to a threshold value. We'll set the threshold at .0001, meaning that if the numbers differ by less than .0001, we'll consider them equal. The results of this approach are shown in Example 5.9 and the output is given in Figure 5.16.

```
1 /* Using a threshold to compare floating-point numbers
2    Anderson, Franceschi
3 */
4
5 public class ComparingFloatingPoint
6 {
7  public static void main( String [ ] args )
8  {
9    // Part 1: Compute 11 * .1 two ways
10   double d1 = .0; // add .1 to 0 eleven times
11   d1 += .1;  // 1
12   d1 += .1;  // 2
13   d1 += .1;  // 3
14   d1 += .1;  // 4
15   d1 += .1;  // 5
16   d1 += .1;  // 6
17   d1 += .1;  // 7
18   d1 += .1;  // 8
19   d1 += .1;  // 9
20   d1 += .1;  // 10
21   d1 += .1;  // 11
22
23   double d2 = .1 * 11; // compute 11 * .1
24
25   System.out.println( "d1 = " + d1 );
26   System.out.println( "d2 = " + d2 );
27   if ( Math.abs( d1 - d2 ) < .0001 )
28      System.out.println( "d1 and d2 are considered equal" );
29   else
30      System.out.println( "d1 and d2 are not equal" );
31
32   // Part 2: Compare float and double with same value
33   float  piF = 3.141592653589793f;
34   double piD = 3.141592653589793;
35
36   System.out.println( "\npiF = " + piF );
37   System.out.println( "piD = " + piD );
38   if ( Math.abs( piF - piD ) < .0001 )
39      System.out.println( "piF and piD are considered equal" );
40   else
41      System.out.println( "piF and piD are not equal" );
42 }
43 }
```

EXAMPLE 5.9   Comparing Floating-Point Numbers Using a Threshold

Figure 5.16

Output of Example 5.9

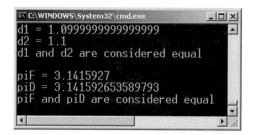

5.9   Comparing Objects

5.9.1   The *equals* Method

Often, you'll want to compare whether two objects are equal; typically, we will say that two objects are equal if they have the same data. If you use the equality operator (==) to compare object references, however, you are comparing the value of the object references. In other words, you are comparing whether the object references point to the same object, that is, the same memory location. To compare object data, you need to use the *equals* method, which all classes inherit from the *Object* class. We will cover inheritance in greater detail in Chapter 10. Many classes provide a custom version of the *equals* method. The API of the *equals* method, which is an instance method, is the following:

```
public boolean equals( Object ob )
```

Typically, the *equals* method returns *true* if the data in the parameter object matches the data in the object for which the method was called.

The program in Example 5.10 creates the *Date* object references and objects shown in Figure 5.17. The program compares the object references using the equality operator and then compares the object data using the *equals* method. The output from this program is shown in Figure 5.18.

```
1 /*  Comparing object references and data
2      Anderson, Franceschi
3 */
4
5 public class ComparingObjects
6 {
7   public static void main( String [ ] args )
8   {
9     // instantiate two Date objects with identical data
```

Figure 5.17
Date Objects and References

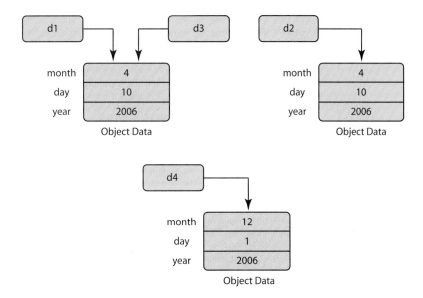

Figure 5.18
Output from Example 5.10

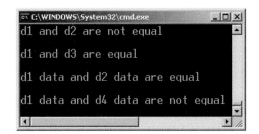

```
10    Date d1 = new Date( 4, 10, 2006 );
11    Date d2 = new Date( 4, 10, 2006 );
12
13    // assign object reference d1 to d3
14    Date d3 = d1;  // d3 now points to d1
15
16    // instantiate another object with different data
17    Date d4 = new Date( 12, 1, 2006 );
18
19    // compare references using equality operator
20    if ( d1 == d2 )
21       System.out.println( "d1 and d2 are equal\n" );
22    else
23       System.out.println( "d1 and d2 are not equal\n" );
```

```
24
25    if ( d1 == d3 )
26       System.out.println( "d1 and d3 are equal\n" );
27    else
28       System.out.println( "d1 and d3 are not equal\n" );
29
30    // compare object data using the equals method
31    if ( d1.equals( d2 ) )
32       System.out.println( "d1 data and d2 data are equal\n" );
33    else
34       System.out.println( "d1 data and d2 data are not equal\n" );
35
36    if ( d1.equals( d4 ) )
37       System.out.println( "d1 data and d4 data are equal" );
38    else
39       System.out.println( "d1 data and d4 data are not equal" );
40    }
41 }
```

EXAMPLE 5.10   Comparing Object Data

Lines 10 and 11 instantiate two *Date* objects with the same data. Line 14 sets the *d3* object reference to point to the *d1* object. Line 17 instantiates the *d4* object with different data.

COMMON ERROR TRAP

Do not use the equality operators to compare object data; instead, use the *equals* method.

In line 20, when we compare *d1* and *d2* using the equality operator, the result is *false*, because the object references *d1* and *d2* point to two different objects. However, when we compare *d1* and *d3* (line 25), the result is *true*, because *d1* and *d3* point to the same object. Thus, object references are equal only when they point to the same object.

We get different results using the *equals* method. When line 31 compares *d1* and *d2* using the *equals* method, the result is *true*, because *d1* and *d2* have identical data. As you would expect, *d1* and *d4* are not equal (line 36) because the objects have different data.

5.9.2   *String* Comparison Methods

Because *Strings* are objects, you can also compare *Strings* using the *equals* method. In addition, the *String* class provides two other methods, *equals-IgnoreCase* and *compareTo*, for comparing the values of *Strings*. These methods, along with the *equals* method are summarized in Table 5.10.

TABLE 5.10 Comparison Methods of the *String* Class

String Methods for Comparing String Values	
Return value	**Method name and argument list**
boolean	equals(String str)
	compares the value of two *Strings*. Returns *true* if the *Strings* are equal; *false* otherwise.
boolean	equalsIgnoreCase(String str)
	compares the value of two *Strings*, treating upper and lower case characters as equal. Returns *true* if the *Strings* are equal; *false* otherwise.
int	compareTo(String str)
	compares the value of the two *Strings* in lexicographic order. If the *String* object is less than the *String* argument, *str,* a negative integer is returned. If the *String* object is greater than the *String* argument, a positive number is returned; if the two *Strings* are equal, 0 is returned.

The *equalsIgnoreCase* method is similar to the *equals* method, except that it is insensitive to case. Thus, the *equalsIgnoreCase* method returns *true* if the two *String* objects have the same sequence of characters, regardless of capitalization. For example, the *equalsIgnoreCase* method considers *ABC, AbC,* and *abc* to be equal.

The *compareTo* method returns an integer value, rather than a *boolean* value. The *compareTo* method's return value represents whether the *String* object is less than, equal to, or greater than the *String* argument passed to the *compareTo* method. The *compareTo* method uses lexicographic order—the Unicode collating sequence—to compare the *Strings*. Using the Unicode collating sequence means that a character with a lower Unicode numeric value is considered less than a character with a higher Unicode numeric value. Thus, an *a* is lower than a *b;* an *A* is lower than a *B;* and *0* is lower than *1.*

 **REFERENCE POINT**

Unicode values are discussed in Appendix C.

Figure 5.19

Output from Example 5.11

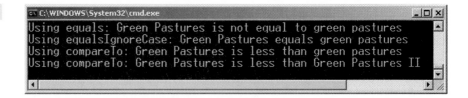

The *compareTo* method scans the two *Strings* from left to right. If it finds different characters in the same position in the two *Strings*, it immediately returns an integer value representing the difference between the Unicode values of those characters. For example, the distance between *a* and *c* is −2; the distance between *K* and *F* is 5.

If the *Strings* differ in length, but the characters they have in common are identical, then the *compareTo* method returns the difference in the length of the *Strings*.

In most cases, however, the exact return value is not important; it is sufficient to know whether the *String* object is less than, greater than, or equal to the *String* argument. In other words, all that we usually need to know is whether the return value is positive, negative, or 0.

Example 5.11 demonstrates how these methods can be used in a Java application to compare *Strings*. The output of the program is shown in Figure 5.19.

```
 1 /* Demonstration of the String comparison methods
 2    Anderson, Franceschi
 3 */
 4
 5 public class ComparingStrings
 6 {
 7   public static void main( String [ ] args )
 8   {
 9     String title1 = "Green Pastures";
10     String title2 = "Green Pastures II";
11     String title3 = "green pastures";
12
13     System.out.print( "Using equals: " );
14     if ( title1.equals( title3 ) )
15       System.out.println( title1 + " equals " + title3 );
16     else
17       System.out.println( title1 + " is not equal to " + title3 );
```

```
18
19    System.out.print( "Using equalsIgnoreCase: " );
20    if ( title1.equalsIgnoreCase( title3 ) )
21      System.out.println( title1 + " equals " + title3 );
22    else
23      System.out.println( title1 + " is not equal to " + title3 );
24
25    System.out.print( "Using compareTo: " );
26    if ( title1.compareTo( title3 ) > 0 )
27      System.out.println( title1 + " is greater than " + title3 );
28    else if ( title1.compareTo ( title3 ) < 0 )
29      System.out.println( title1 + " is less than " + title3 );
30    else
31      System.out.println( title1 + " is equal to " + title3 );
32
33    System.out.print( "Using compareTo: " );
34    if ( title1.compareTo( title2 ) > 0 )
35      System.out.println( title1 + " is greater than " + title2 );
36    else if ( title1.compareTo( title2 ) < 0 )
37      System.out.println( title1 + " is less than " + title2 );
38    else
39      System.out.println( title1 + " is equal to " + title2 );
40  }
41 }
```

EXAMPLE 5.11 Comparing *Strings*

In Example 5.11, we define three similar *Strings*: *title1 (Green Pastures)*, *title2 (Green Pastures II)*, and *title3 (green pastures)*. When we compare *title1, Green Pastures*, to *title3, green pastures*, using the *equals* method (line 14), the result is *false*, because the *Strings* do not match in case. When we perform the same comparison using the *equalsIgnoreCase* method (line 20), however, the result is *true*, because except for capitalization, these two *Strings* are identical in character sequence and length.

Using the *compareTo* method (line 34), *Green Pastures* evaluates to less than *Green Pastures II*. Although all the characters of the first *String* are found in the second *String* in the same order, the first *String* has fewer characters than the second *String*. The reason that *Green Pastures* evaluates to less than *green pastures* (line 26) is not so obvious—until you look at the Unicode character chart. The capital letters have lower numeric values than the lowercase letters, so a capital *G* is less than a lowercase *g*.

5.10   The Conditional Operator (?:)

The conditional operator (?:), while not a statement in itself, can be used in expressions. It evaluates a condition and contributes one of two values to the expression based on the value of the condition. The conditional operator is especially useful for handling invalid input and for outputting similar messages. The syntax of the conditional operator is shown below:

```
( condition ? expression1 : expression2 )
```

The value of an expression containing a conditional operator is determined by evaluating the condition, which is any expression that evaluates to *true* or *false*. If the condition evaluates to *true*, *expression1* becomes the value of the expression; if the condition evaluates to *false*, *expression2* becomes the value of the expression.

When assigning the result of that expression to a variable, the statement:

```
variable = ( condition ? expression1 : expression2 );
```

is equivalent to

```
if ( condition )
    variable = expression1;
else
    variable = expression2;
```

Some programmers like to use the conditional operator because it enables them to write compact code; other programmers feel that an *if/else* sequence is more readable.

Suppose that we want to write a simple game where we ask the user to pick between two doors. Behind one door is a prize and behind the other door is nothing. Example 5.12 shows some code to do this. We first use the conditional operator on line 17 to validate the user input. If the user enters anything other than a 2, we assign the value 1 to the variable *door*. The statement at line 17 is equivalent to this code:

```
int door;
if ( inputNum == 2 )
   door = inputNum;
else
   door = 1;
```

So, instead of using five lines to declare the variable *door* and perform the *if* statement, the conditional operator performs the same function in only one line.

We then print a message about whether the chosen door was correct. If the user has selected door number 1, we print:

```
You have chosen the wrong door
```

Otherwise, we print:

```
You have chosen the correct door
```

As you can see, depending on the value of *door*, the messages we want to print differ only in one word (*correct* or *wrong*). So on lines 19–20, we use the conditional operator in the argument of the *println* method to determine which word to insert into the message.

```
 1 /* Using the conditional operator
 2    Anderson, Franceschi
 3 */
 4
 5 import java.util.Scanner;
 6
 7 public class DoorPrize
 8 {
 9  public static void main( String [ ] args )
10  {
11   Scanner scan = new Scanner( System.in );
12
13   System.out.print( "Enter 1 or 2 to pick a door: " );
14   int inputNum = scan.nextInt( );
15   System.out.println( "You entered " + inputNum + "\n" );
16
17   int door = ( inputNum == 2 ? inputNum : 1 );
18
19   System.out.println( "You have chosen the "
20            + ( door == 1 ? "wrong" : "correct" ) + " door" );
21  }
22 }
```

EXAMPLE 5.12   Using the Conditional Operator

Figure 5.20

A Run of Example 5.12

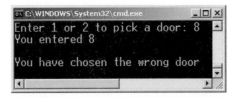

Figure 5.21

Another Run of Example 5.12

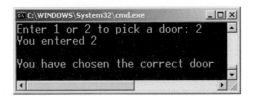

Table 5.11, Operator Precedence, shows that the conditional operator is low in precedence, being just above the assignment operators.

5.11   The *switch* Statement

The *switch* statement can be used instead of an *if/else if* statement for selection when the condition consists of comparing the value of an expression to constant integers (*byte, short,* or *int*) or characters (*char*). The syntax of the *switch* statement is the following:

```
switch ( expression )
{
    case constant1:
        statement1;

        . . .
        break; // optional
    case constant2:
        statement1;

        . . .
        break; // optional
    . . .
    default:  // optional
        statement1;

        . . .
}
```

The expression is first evaluated, then its value is compared to the *case* constants in order. When a match is found, the statements under that *case* constant are executed in sequence. The execution of statements continues until

TABLE 5.11 Operator Precedence

Operator Hierarchy	Order of Same-Statement Evaluation	Operation
( )	left to right	parentheses for explicit grouping
++, −−	right to left	shortcut postincrement
++, −−, !	right to left	shortcut preincrement, logical unary NOT
*, /, %	left to right	multiplication, division, modulus
+, −	left to right	addition or *String* concatenation, subtraction
<, <=, >, >=	left to right	relational operators: less than, less than or equal to, greater than, greater than or equal to
==, !=	left to right	equality operators: equal to and not equal to
&&	left to right	logical AND
||	left to right	logical OR
?:	**left to right**	**conditional operator**
=, +=, −=, *=, /=, %=	right to left	assignment operator and shortcut assignment operators

either a *break* statement is encountered or the end of the *switch* block is reached. If other *case* statements are encountered before a *break* statement, then their statements are also executed. This allows you to execute the same code for multiple values of the expression.

As you can see in the preceding syntax, the *break* statements are optional. Their job is to terminate execution of the *switch* statement. The *default* label and its statements, which are also optional, are executed when the value of the expression does not match any of the *case* constants. The statements under a *case* constant are also optional, so multiple *case* constants can be written in sequence if identical operations will be performed for those values. We'll use this feature in our first example of the *switch* statement.

Let's look at how a *switch* statement can be used to implement a simple calculator. We can prompt the user for two numbers on which they want to perform a calculation, and a single letter for the operation they want to perform: *a* for addition, *s* for subtraction, *m* for multiplication, or *d* for division. We can use a *switch* statement with the selected operation as the expression and *case* constants for each possible operation. For example, here's the beginning of the *switch* statement:

```
switch ( operation )
{
    case 'a':
        // perform the addition
        break;
    case 's':
        // perform the subtraction
        break;

    . . .

}
```

But what if the user enters an *A* instead of an *a*? For usability, we want to allow the user to enter the operation as either a lowercase letter or an uppercase letter. We can handle this by providing two *case* constants for each operation—the lowercase letter and the uppercase letter. Then the beginning of the *switch* statement looks like this:

```
switch ( operation )
{
    case 'a':
    case 'A':
        // perform the addition
        break;
    case 's':
    case 'S':
        // perform the subtraction
        break;

    . . .

}
```

If the user enters an uppercase *A*, we perform the addition, then the *break* ends execution of the *switch* block. If the user enters a lowercase *a*, we also perform the addition. Again, the *break* ends execution of the *switch* block.

What if the user doesn't enter any of the valid letters for the operation to perform? This is where the *default* case comes in handy. We can use the *default* case to write an error message to the user.

Example 5.13 shows the code for our simple calculator.

```
 1 /*  A simple calculator
 2      Anderson, Franceschi
 3 */
 4
 5 import java.text.DecimalFormat;
 6 import java.util.Scanner;
 7
 8 public class Calculator
 9 {
10   public static void main( String [ ] args )
11   {
12     double fp1, fp2;
13     String operationS;
14     char operation;
15
16     Scanner scan = new Scanner( System.in );
17
18     // set up the output format of the result
19     DecimalFormat twoDecimals = new DecimalFormat( "#,###,###.##" );
20
21     // print a welcome message
22     System.out.println( "Welcome to the Calculator" );
23
24     // read the two operands
25     System.out.print( "Enter the first operand: " );
26     fp1 = scan.nextDouble( );
27     System.out.print( "Enter the second operand: " );
28     fp2 = scan.nextDouble( );
29
30     // print a menu, then prompt for the operation
31     System.out.println( "\nOperations are: "
32                         + "\n\t A for addition"
33                         + "\n\t S for subtraction"
34                         + "\n\t M for multiplication"
35                         + "\n\t D for division" );
36     System.out.print( "Enter your selection: " );
37     operationS = scan.next( );
38     operation = operationS.charAt( 0 );
39
40     // perform the operation and print the result
41     switch ( operation )
42     {
```

```
43      case 'A':
44      case 'a':
45          System.out.println( "The sum is "
46                  + twoDecimals.format( fp1 + fp2 ) );
47          break;
48      case 'S':
49      case 's':
50          System.out.println( "The difference is "
51                  + twoDecimals.format( fp1 - fp2 ) );
52          break;
53      case 'M':
54      case 'm':
55          System.out.println( "The product is "
56                  + twoDecimals.format( fp1 * fp2 ) );
57          break;
58      case 'D':
59      case 'd':
60          if ( fp2 == 0 )
61            System.out.println( "Dividing by 0 is not allowed" );
62          else
63            System.out.println( "The quotient is "
64                    + twoDecimals.format( fp1 / fp2 ) );
65          break;
66      default:
67          System.out.println( operation + " is not valid." );
68      }
69   }
70 }
```

EXAMPLE 5.13   A Simple Calculator

Figure 5.22 shows the output from Example 5.13 when the user selects multiplication, and Figure 5.23 shows the output when the user enters an unsupported operation.

We declared the two numbers on which to perform the operation as *doubles* (line 12) and prompt the user using the *nextDouble* method of the *Scanner* class (lines 25–28). Because a *double* variable can hold any numeric value equal to or lower in precision than a *double*, using *doubles* for our calculator allows the user to enter two *int*s, or two *doubles*, or any combination of integers and floating-point numbers. Conversely, if we used *int* variables and the *nextInt* method of the *Scanner* class, the user would be restricted to entering integers only.

When the calculator begins, we set up a *DecimalFormat* pattern for outputting the result to a maximum of two decimal places (line 19).

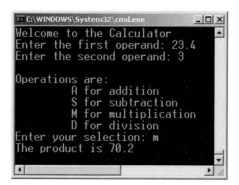

Figure 5.22

The Calculator Performing Multiplication

Figure 5.23

The Calculator with an Invalid Entry for the Operation

We also use the newline (\n) and tab (\t) escape characters to format the menu message (lines 30–35). To read the user's selection (lines 36–38), we use the *next* method of the *Scanner* class, which returns a *String*. We then extract just the first character of the *String* (via the *charAt* method of the *String* class) to produce a *char* to use as our *switch* variable.

One more note on the calculator. We need to check whether the divisor is 0 before performing division (line 60). Although we discussed earlier in the chapter that we should compare floating-point numbers by comparing the difference between the two numbers with a threshold value, in this case, we care only if the second operand is exactly 0, so we can safely compare its value to 0.0. If the second operand is 0.0, we print an error message; otherwise, we perform the division.

Let's look at another example using a simple applet that draws a balloon in the color selected by the user. The applet, shown in Example 5.14, uses a *Balloon* class written by the authors. The *Balloon* class constructor has this API:

```
public Balloon( int xStart, int yStart, int diameter, Color color )
```

Thus, a *Balloon* object is instantiated by passing the constructor the *x* and *y* start positions, the diameter, and color of the balloon. A *Balloon* object can be drawn in an applet window by calling the *draw* method of the *Balloon* class, which has this API:

```
public void draw( Graphics g )
```

In the *init* method of the applet, we prompt the user for the balloon's color using an input dialog box (lines 17–18). The user is requested to enter a single character (*r*, *b*, or *g*) to select the balloon's color. Because the *showInputDialog* method of the *JOptionPane* class returns a *String*, and we want only the first character of the *String*, we use the *charAt* method of the *String* class to extract the first character (line 19). In lines 21–40, we use a *switch* statement on that character to set the color that we will pass to the *Balloon* constructor in line 43. We include a *break* statement for each *case* constant to terminate the *switch* block after setting each color. If the user does not enter an *r*, *b*, or *g*, we use the *default* case of the *switch* statement (lines 38–39) to set the color to a default color, yellow.

In the *paint* method, we draw the balloon by calling the *draw* method of the *Balloon* class, passing it the *Graphics* object *g* associated with the applet window (line 51).

```
 1 /*  An applet that draws a balloon
 2      Anderson, Franceschi
 3 */
 4 import javax.swing.JApplet;
 5 import javax.swing.JOptionPane;
 6 import java.awt.Graphics;
 7 import java.awt.Color;
 8 public class BalloonDraw extends JApplet
 9 {
10     Balloon b1;
11     String colorSelectS;
12     char colorSelectC;
13     Color b1Color;
14
15     public void init( )
16     {
17       colorSelectS = JOptionPane.showInputDialog( "Pick a color\n"
18                         + "r for red, g for green, b for blue" );
19       colorSelectC = colorSelectS.charAt( 0 );
20
21       switch ( colorSelectC )
```

```
22         {
23                 case 'r':
24                 case 'R':
25                         b1Color = Color.RED;
26                         break;
27
28                 case 'b':
29                 case 'B':
30                         b1Color = Color.BLUE;
31                         break;
32
33                 case 'g':
34                 case 'G':
35                         b1Color = Color.GREEN;
36                         break;
37
38                 default:
39                         b1Color = Color.YELLOW;
40         }
41
42      // instantiate the balloon using the selected color
43      b1 = new Balloon( 150, 100, 50, b1Color );
44  }
45
46  public void paint( Graphics g )
47  {
48      super.paint( g );
49
50      // draw the balloon
51      b1.draw( g );
52  }
53 }
```

EXAMPLE 5.14   Drawing a Balloon in a Selected Color

Figure 5.24 shows the dialog box with the user selecting *g* for a green balloon and the applet window after the green balloon has been drawn.

CODE IN ACTION

In the Chapter 5 folder on the CD-ROM included with this book, you will find a Shockwave movie showing a step-by-step illustration of using a *switch* statement. Double-click on *Selection.html* to start the movie.

Figure 5.24

A Dialog Box Allows the User to Select the Balloon Color

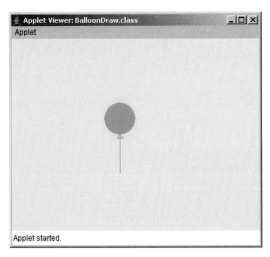

Skill Practice
with these end-of-chapter questions

5.12 Programming Activity 2: Using the *switch* Statement

In this activity, you will write a *switch* statement that selects a path depending on an input value. The framework will animate your code so that you can watch the path that the code takes in the *switch* block.

Copy to a directory on your computer all the files in the Chapter 5 Programming Activity 2 directory on the CD-ROM accompanying this book.

Search for five stars (*****) in the *MultiPathClient.java* source code to find where to add your code. The five stars are inside the method *workWithSwitch* (the method header has already been coded for you).

You should be positioned at the code shown in Example 5.15.

```java
// ***** 1 student writes this method
public void workWithSwitch( int value )
{
 //
 // Student code starts here
 //




 //
 // Student code ends here
 //

 mp.setControl( false );
 mp.resetPath( );
 mp.setCount( 0 );
 mp.setCurrent( -1 );


}
// end of workWithSwitch
```

EXAMPLE 5.15 The Student Code Portion of Programming Activity 2

Where indicated in the code, write a *switch* statement, as follows:

- In the method header of the method *workWithSwitch*, you see (int value). The *int* variable *value* represents the input from the user; the dialog box that prompts the user and reads the score has already been coded for you. This variable, *value*, is the input value for the *switch* statement; it is available to your code as a parameter of the *workWithSwitch* method. Do not declare the variable *value* inside the method; just use it.

- Write *case* statements for the following integer constants: *0, 1, 2, 3, 4*, as well as a *default* statement.

- Within each *case* statement, you should do two things:

  - Print a message to the screen indicating which value was input. The message for the *default* case should indicate that the input value is not one of the valid values.
  - Call the *animate* method. The API for the *animate* method is

    ```
    void animate( int caseConstant, int value )
    ```

    The first argument is the *case* constant, the second argument is the input variable, *value*. For instance, for the statement case 2:, your *animate* method call is

    ```
    animate( 2, value );
    ```

    For the default case, the method call should be

    ```
    animate( -1, value );
    ```

To test your code, compile and run the *MultiPathClient* application. When the program begins, you will see an empty graphics window and the dialog box of Figure 5.25, prompting you for an integer value.

To execute your *switch* statement, enter an integer in the dialog box. Depending on how you coded the *case* statements, the *break* statements, and the input value, the window will display (in green) the path of execution of your code. For example, Figure 5.26 demonstrates the code path

Figure 5.25

The Input Box of the
MultiPathClient
Application

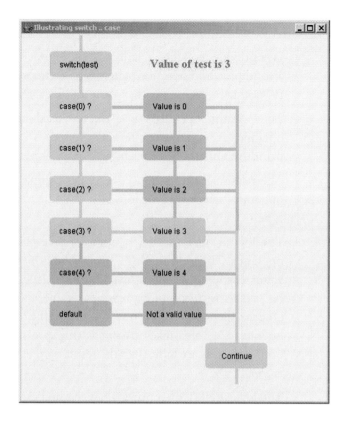

Figure 5.26

A Sample Run of the
MultiPathClient
Application

when the input value is 3. If the path is not what you expected, you will need to correct your code.

After each execution of the *switch* statement, the dialog box will reappear, prompting you for another integer. To test your code, enter each integer from 0 to 4 into the dialog box, plus some other integer value. To exit the application, click the *Cancel* button on the dialog box.

? DISCUSSION QUESTIONS

1. Explain the purpose of the *default* case in a *switch* statement.

2. Explain what happens when you omit a *break* statement in a *case* statement.

5.13   Chapter Summary

- Java provides equality, relational, and logical operators to evaluate a condition, and selection statements to choose which instructions to execute based on whether a condition evaluates to *true* or *false.*

- The equality operators (==, !=) are used to test whether two operands are equal. The operands are expressions that evaluate to a primitive numeric or *boolean* type or an object reference.

- The relational operators (<, <=, >, >=) compare the values of two operands that are expressions that evaluate to a primitive numeric type.

- The logical operators (!, &&, and ||) take *boolean* expressions as operands. The logical NOT (!) takes one operand, and inverts its value, changing *true* to *false* and *false* to *true.* The AND operator (&&) takes two *boolean* expressions as operands; if both operands are *true,* then the result is *true;* otherwise, the result is *false.* The OR operator (||) also takes two *boolean* expressions as operands. If both operands are *false,* then the result is *false;* otherwise, the result is *true.*

- The logical NOT operator (!) has the highest precedence of these operators, followed by the relational operators, then the equality operators, then the logical AND (&&), then the logical OR(||).

- DeMorgan's Laws can be used to form equivalent logical expressions to improve readability of the code.

- The *if* statement is used to perform certain operations for one set of data and do nothing for all other data.

- Curly braces are required when the true or false block of an *if* statement consists of more than one statement.

- The *if/else* statement is used to perform certain operations for one set of data and other operations for all other data.

- The *if/else if* statement is appropriate when the data falls into more than two mutually exclusive categories and the appropriate instructions to execute are different for each category.

- *if/else* statements can be coded sequentially and can be nested inside other *if/else* statements.

- When *if* statements are nested, the compiler matches any *else* clause with the most previous *if* condition that doesn't already have an *else* clause.

- Because rounding errors can be introduced in floating-point calculations, do not use the equality operators to compare two floating-point numbers. Instead, compare the absolute value of the difference between the numbers to some threshold value.

- Using the equality operator on object references compares the values of the references, not the object data. Two object references will be equal only if they point to the same object.

- Use the *equals* method to determine whether the data in two objects is equal.

- In addition to the *equals* method, two *Strings* can also be compared using the *equalsIgnoreCase* method and the *compareTo* method of the *String* class.

- The conditional operator (?:) is used in expressions where one of two values should be used depending on the evaluation of a condition. The conditional operator is useful for validating input and for outputting similar messages.

- The *switch* statement evaluates an integer or character expression, then compares the expression's value to *case* constants. When a match is found, it executes the statements until either a *break* statement or the end of the *switch* block is encountered.

5.14   Exercises, Problems, and Projects

5.14.1   Multiple Choice Exercises

1. Given the following code declaring and initializing two *int* variables *a* and *b* with respective values 3 and 5, indicate whether the value of each expression is *true* or *false*.

```
int a = 3;
int b = 5;
```

Expression	true	false
❏ `a < b`	____	____
❏ `a != b`	____	____
❏ `a == 4`	____	____
❏ `( b - a ) <= 1`	____	____
❏ `Math.abs( a - b ) >= 2`	____	____
❏ `( b % 2 == 1 )`	____	____
❏ `b <= 5`	____	____

2. Given the following code declaring and initializing three *boolean* variables *a*, *b*, and *c*, with respective values *true, true,* and *false*, indicate whether the value of each expression is *true* or *false*.

```
boolean a = true;
boolean b = true;
boolean c = false;
```

Expression	true	false
❏ `!a`	____	____
❏ `a && b`	____	____
❏ `a && c`	____	____
❏ `a || c`	____	____
❏ `!( a || b )`	____	____
❏ `!a || b`	____	____
❏ `!( !( a && c ) )`	____	____
❏ `a && !( b || c )`	____	____

3. Given two *boolean* variables *a* and *b*, are the following expressions equivalent?

    ❏ `!( !a )`

    ❏ `a`

4. Given two *boolean* variables *a* and *b*, are the following expressions equivalent?

    ❏ `!( a && b )`

    ❏ `!a || !b`

5. Given two *boolean* variables *a* and *b*, are the following expressions equivalent?

  ❑ `!( !a && !b )`

  ❑ `a && b`

6. Given two *boolean* variables *a* and *b*, are the following expressions equivalent?

  ❑ `!( !a && !b )`

  ❑ `a || b`

7. Given the following code declaring and initializing two *int* variables *a* and *b* with respective values 3 and 5, indicate whether the operand (`b < 10`) will be evaluated.

```
int a = 3;
int b = 5;
```

Expression	yes	no
❑ `a < b || b < 10`	___	___
❑ `a != b && b < 10`	___	___
❑ `a == 4 || b < 10`	___	___
❑ `a > b && b < 10`	___	___

8. Mark all the valid Java selection keywords.

  ❑ `if`

  ❑ `else if`

  ❑ `else`

  ❑ `elsif`

9. How do we compare the value of two *String* objects in Java? (Mark all that apply.)

  ❑ using the = operator

  ❑ using the == operator

  ❑ using the *equals* method

5.14.2   Reading and Understanding Code

10. What is the output of this code sequence?

```
boolean a = true;
System.out.println( a );
```

11. What is the output of this code sequence?

```
boolean a = ( true && false );
System.out.println( a );
```

12. What is the output of this code sequence?

```
if ( ( true || false ) && ( false || true ) )
    System.out.println( "Inside true block" );
System.out.println( "End of sequence" );
```

13. What is the output of this code sequence?

```
if ( 27 % 3 == 0 )
    System.out.println( "27 is divisible by 3" );
else
    System.out.println( "27 is not divisible by 3" );
System.out.println( "End of sequence" );
```

14. What is the output of this code sequence?

```
String s = "Hello";
if ( s.equals( "hello" ) )
    System.out.println( "String is hello" );
else
    System.out.println( "String is not hello" );
System.out.println( "End of sequence" );
```

15. What is the output of this code sequence?

```
int grade = 77;
if ( grade >= 90 )
    System.out.println( "A" );
else if ( grade >= 80 )
    System.out.println( "B" );
else if ( grade >= 70 )
    System.out.println( "C" );
else
    System.out.println( "D or lower" );
System.out.println( "Done" );
```

16. What is the output of this code sequence?

```
int a = 65;
boolean b = false;

if ( a >= 70 )
{
    System.out.println( "Hello 1" );
    if ( b == true )
```

```
        System.out.println( "Hello 2" );
    }
    else
    {
        System.out.println( "Hello 3" );
        if ( b == false )
            System.out.println( "Hello 4" );
    }
    System.out.println( "Done" );
```

17. What is the output of this code sequence?

```
int season = 3;
switch ( season )
{
    case  1:
            System.out.println( "Season is Winter" );
            break;
    case  2:
            System.out.println( "Season is Spring" );
            break;
    case  3:
            System.out.println( "Season is Summer" );
            break;
    case  4:
            System.out.println( "Season is Fall" );
            break;
    default:
            System.out.println( "Invalid Season" );
}
```

18. What is the output of this code sequence?

```
char c = 'e';
switch ( c )
{
    case 'H':
            System.out.println( "letter 1" );
            break;
    case 'e':
            System.out.println( "letter 2" );
            break;
    case 'l':
            System.out.println( "letters 3 and 4" );
            break;
    case 'o':
            System.out.println( "letter 5" );
            break;
```

```
        default:
            System.out.println( "letter is not in Hello" );
    }
```

19. What is the output of this code sequence?

```
int n = 3;
switch ( n )
{
    case 1:
        System.out.println( "Number 1" );
    case 2:
        System.out.println( "Number 2" );
    case 3:
        System.out.println( "Number 3" );
    case 4:
        System.out.println( "Number 4" );
    default:
        System.out.println( "Other number" );
}
```

5.14.3   Fill in the Code

For exercises 20 through 30, assume that a *boolean* variable named *a* has been declared and assigned the value *true* or *false*. You should also assume that two *int* variables named *b* and *c* have been declared and assigned some integer values.

20. If *a* is *true*, increment *b* by 1.

```
// your code goes here
```

21. If *a* is *true*, increment *b* by 2; if *a* is *false*, decrement *b* by 1.

```
// your code goes here
```

22. If *a* is *true*, change *a* to *false*; if *a* is *false*, change *a* to *true*.

```
// your code goes here
```

23. If *b* is equal to *c*, then assign *true* to *a*.

```
// your code goes here
```

24. If *b* is less than *c*, increment *b* by 1; otherwise, leave *b* unchanged.

```
// your code goes here
```

25. If *b* is a multiple of *c*, set *a* to *true*; otherwise, set *a* to *false*.

```
// your code goes here
```

26. If *c* is not equal to 0, assign to *b* the value of *b* divided by *c*.

    ```
    // your code goes here
    ```

27. If the product *b* times *c* is greater than or equal to 100, then invert *a* (if *a* is *true*, *a* becomes *false*; if *a* is *false*, *a* becomes *true*) otherwise, assign *true* to *a*.

    ```
    // your code goes here
    ```

28. If *a* is *true* and *b* is greater than 10, increment *c* by 1.

    ```
    // your code goes here
    ```

29. If both *b* and *c* are less than 10, then assign *true* to *a*; otherwise, assign *false* to *a*.

    ```
    // your code goes here
    ```

30. If *b* or *c* is greater than 5, then assign *true* to *a*; otherwise, assign *false* to *a*.

    ```
    // your code goes here
    ```

5.14.4   Identifying Errors in Code

For exercises 31 through 38, assume that two *boolean* variables named *b1* and *b2* have been declared and assigned the value *true* or *false* earlier in the program. You should also assume that two *int* variables named *a1* and *a2* have been declared and assigned some integer values earlier in the program.

31. Where is the error in this code sequence?

    ```
    b1 = a1 && a2;
    ```

32. Where is the error in this expression?

    ```
    ( b2 == b1 ) AND ( a1 <= a2 )
    ```

33. Where is the logical error in this code sequence?

    ```
    if ( a1 == 4 );
        System.out.println( "a1 equals 4" );
    ```

34. Where is the error in this code sequence?

    ```
    boolean b1 = true;
    if b1
        System.out.println( "b1 is true" );
    ```

35. Where is the error in this code sequence?

    ```
    if { b2 == true }
        System.out.println( "b2 is true" );
    ```

36. Where is the error in this code sequence?

```
if ( b1 == true )
    System.out.println( "b1 is true" );
else
    System.out.println( "b1 is false" );
else if ( a1 < 100 )
    System.out.println( "a1 is <= 100" );
```

37. Is there an error in this code sequence? Explain.

```
if ( b2 == b1 )
        System.out.println( "b2 and b1 have the same value" );
else if ( a1 == a2 )
        System.out.println( "a1 and a2 have the same value" );
else
        System.out.println( "All variables are different" );
```

38. Is there an error in this code sequence? Explain.

```
if ( b2 )
        System.out.println( "b2 is true" );
else if ( a1 <= 10 || a2 > 50 )
{
        System.out.print( "a1 <= 10 or " );
        System.out.println( "a2 > 50" );
}
else
        System.out.println( "none of the above" );
```

5.14.5   Debugging Area—Using Messages from *javac* Compiler and *java* JVM

39. You coded the following in class *Test.java:*

```
boolean b = true;
if ( b )
        System.out.println( "Inside true block" );
        System.out.println( "b was true" );
else        // line 12
        System.out.println( "Inside false block" );
```

At compile time, you get the following error:

```
Test.java:12: 'else' without 'if'

   else        // line 12
   ^

      1 error
```

Explain what the problem is and how to fix it.

40. You coded the following in the class *Test.java:*

```
int a = 32;
if ( a = 31 )      // line 9
     System.out.println( "The value of a is 31" );
else
     System.out.println( "The value of a is not 31" );
```

At compile time, you get the following error:

```
Test.java:9: incompatible types
found    : int
required: boolean
   if ( a = 31 )     // line 9
        ^

1 error
```

Explain what the problem is and how to fix it.

41. You coded the following in the class *Test.java:*

```
boolean b = true;
if ( b )
{
     System.out.println( "Inside true block" );
     System.out.println( "b was true" );
else         // line 13
     System.out.println( "Inside false block" );
}
System.out.println( "Done" );
```

At compile time, you get the following error:

```
Test.java:13: 'else' without 'if'.
else         // line 13
^

1 error
```

Explain what the problem is and how to fix it.

5.14.6   Write a Short Program

42. Write a program that takes two *ints* as input from the keyboard, representing the number of hits and the number of at-bats for a batter. Then calculate the batter's hitting percentage and check if the hitting percentage is above .300. If it is, output that the player is eligible for the All Stars Game; otherwise, output that the player is not eligible.

43. Write a program that reads a *char* as an input from the keyboard and outputs whether it comes before or after the letter *b* in Unicode order.

44. Write a program that calculates the area of the following figures:

    ❑ a square of side 0.666666667
    ❑ a rectangle of sides ⅑ and 4

    Test the two calculated areas for equality; discuss your result.

45. Write a program that reads a sentence using a dialog box. Depending on the last character of the sentence, output another dialog box identifying the sentence as declarative (ends with a period), interrogative (ends with a question mark), imperative (ends with an exclamation point), or other.

46. An email address contains the @ character. Write a program that takes a word from the keyboard and outputs whether it is an email address based on the presence of the @ character. Do not worry about what else is in the word.

47. Write a program that takes two words as input from the keyboard, representing a password and the same password again. (Often, Web sites ask users to type their password twice when they register to make sure there was no typo the first time around.) Your program should do the following:

    ❑ if both passwords match, then output "You are now registered as a new user"
    ❑ otherwise, output "Sorry, there is a typo in your password"

48. Write a program that takes a word as input from the keyboard, representing a user ID. (Often, Web sites place constraints on user IDs.) Your program should do the following:

    ❑ if the user ID contains between 6 and 10 characters inclusive, then output "Welcome barbara" (assuming barbara is the user ID entered)
    ❑ otherwise, output "Sorry, user ID invalid"

5.14.7 Programming Projects

49. Write a program that reads a Web address (for instance, *www.yahoo.com*) from the keyboard and outputs whether this Web

address is for a government, a university, a business, an organization, or another entity.

❑ If the Web address contains *gov*, it is a government Web address.

❑ If the Web address contains *edu*, it is a university Web address.

❑ If the Web address contains *com*, it is a business Web address.

❑ If the Web address contains *org*, it is an organization Web address.

❑ Otherwise, it is a Web address for another entity.

50. Write a program that reads a temperature as a whole number from the keyboard and outputs a "probable" season (winter, spring, summer, or fall) depending on the temperature.

❑ If the temperature is greater than or equal to 90, it is probably summer.

❑ If the temperature is greater than or equal to 70 and less than 90, it is probably spring.

❑ If the temperature is greater than or equal to 50 and less than 70, it is probably fall.

❑ If the temperature is less than 50, it is probably winter.

❑ If the temperature is greater than 110 or less than −5, then you should output that the temperature entered is outside the valid range.

51. Write a program that takes a *String* as input from the keyboard, representing a year. Your program should do the following:

❑ If the year entered has two characters, convert it to an *int*, add 2000 to it, and output it.

❑ If the year entered has four characters, just convert it to an *int* and output it.

❑ If the year entered has neither two nor four characters, output that the year is not valid.

52. Write a program that takes two words as input from the keyboard, representing a user ID and a password. Your program should do the following:

❑ If the user ID and the password match "admin" and "open," respectively, then output "Welcome."

❏ If the user ID matches "admin" and the password does not match "open," output "Wrong password."

❏ If the password matches "open" and the user ID does not match "admin", output "Wrong user ID."

❏ Otherwise, output "Sorry, wrong ID and password."

5.14.8   Technical Writing

53. When comparing two *doubles* or *floats* for equality, programmers calculate the difference between the two numbers and check if that difference is sufficiently small. Explain why and give a real-life example.

54. Look at the following code segment:

```
int b = 44;
if ( b = 23 )
        System.out.println( "Inside true block" );
```

In Java, this code will generate the following compiler error:

```
Test.java:9: Incompatible types
found   : int
required: boolean
if ( b = 23 )
       ^

1 error
```

In the C++ programming language, the equivalent code will compile and run and will give you the following output:

```
Inside true block
```

Discuss whether Java handles this situation better than C++ and why.

5.14.9   Group Project

55. We want to build a simple "English language" calculator that does the following:

❏ takes three inputs from the keyboard, two of them single digits (0 to 9)

❏ takes a *char* from the keyboard, representing one of five operations from the keyboard: + (addition), − (subtraction), * (multiplication), / (division), and ^ (exponentiation)

❏ outputs the description of the operation in plain English, as well as the numeric result

For instance, if the two numbers are 5 and 3, and the operation is *, then the output should be

```
five multiplied by three is 15
```

Note that the result is given as a number, not a word.

If the two numbers are 2 and 9, and the operation is −, then the output should be

```
two minus nine is -7
```

Hint: to perform the exponentiation, use the *pow* method of the *Math* class.

If the two numbers are 5 and 2, and the operation is ^, then the output should be

```
five to the power two is 25
```

Hint: to perform the exponentiation, use the *pow* method of the *Math* class.

If the two numbers are 5 and 0, and the operation is /, then the output should be

```
Division by zero is not allowed
```

Here the operation will not be performed.

If the two numbers are 25 and 3, and the operation is +, then the output should be

```
Invalid number
```

As for the operators, they should be translated into English as follows:

+   plus

−   minus

*   multiplied by

/   divided by

^   to the power

You should use the *switch ... case* selection statement to translate the input values into words.

You need to consider these special situations:

- ❏ for division, there is a special constraint: you cannot divide by 0, and you should therefore test whether the second number is

0. If it is 0, then you should output a message saying that you are not allowed to divide by 0.

❑ the "operator" is not one of the preceding five operators; in that case, output a message saying that the operator is not a valid one.

❑ one or two of the numbers is not a valid digit; again, you should output a message to that effect.

Hint: You can deal with these special situations in the *default* statement of the *switch* block and possibly use some *boolean* variables to keep track of this information, as you may need it later in your program.

CHAPTER 6

Flow of Control, Part 2: Looping

CHAPTER CONTENTS

Introduction

Have you ever watched the cashier at the grocery store? Let's call the cashier Jane. Jane's job is to determine the total cost of a grocery purchase. To begin, Jane starts with a total cost of $0.00. She then reaches for the first item and scans it to record its price, which is added to the total. Then she reaches for the second item, scans that item to record its price, which is added to the total, and so on. Jane continues scanning each item, one at a time, until there are no more items to scan. Usually, the end of an order is signaled by a divider bar laying across the conveyor belt. When Jane sees the divider bar, she knows she is finished. At that point, she tells us the total cost of the order, collects the money, and gives us a receipt.

So we see that Jane's job consists of performing some preliminary work, processing each item one at a time, and reporting the result at the end.

In computing, we often perform tasks that follow this same pattern:

1: initialize values

2: process items one at a time

3: report results

The flow of control that programmers use to complete jobs with this pattern is called **looping**, or **repetition**.

6.1   Event-Controlled Loops Using *while*

If we attempt to write pseudocode for the grocery store cashier, we may start with something like this:

```
set total to $0.00
reach for first item
if item is not the divider bar
    add price to total
reach for next item
if item is not the divider bar
    add price to total
reach for next item
if item is not the divider bar
    add price to total
... (finally)
reach for next item
```

item is the divider bar,

tell the customer the total price

We can see a pattern here. We start with an order total of $0.00. Then we repeat a set of operations for each item. We reach for the item and check whether it's the divider bar. If the item is not the divider bar, we add the item's price to the order total. We reach for the next item and check whether it's the divider bar, and so on. When we reach for the item and find that it is the divider bar, we know there are no more items to process, so the total we have at that time is the total for the whole order. In other words, we don't know the number of items that will be placed on the conveyor belt. We just process the order, item by item, until we see the divider bar, which we do not process.

In Java, the *while* loop is designed for repeating a set of instructions for each input value when we don't know at the beginning how many input values there will be. We simply process each input value, one at a time, until a signal—an event—tells us that there is no more input. This is called **event-controlled looping**. In the cashier's case, the signal for the end of input was the divider bar. In other tasks, the signal for the end of the input may be a special value that the user enters, called a **sentinel value**, or it may be that we've reached the end of an input file.

6.2   General Form for *while* Loops

The *while* loop has this syntax:

```
// initialize variables
while ( condition )
{
    // process data; loop body
}
// process the results
```

The condition is a *boolean* expression, that is, any expression that evaluates to *true* or *false*. When the *while* loop statement is encountered, the condition is evaluated; if the value is *true*, the statements in the **loop body** are executed. The condition is then reevaluated and, if *true*, the loop body is executed again. This repetition continues until the loop condition evaluates to *false*, at which time, the loop body is skipped and execution continues at the instruction following the loop body.

The curly braces are needed only if the loop body has more than one statement; that is, if more than one statement should be executed if the condition evaluates to *true*.

The flow of control of a *while* loop is shown in Figure 6.1.

Each execution of the loop body is called an **iteration** of the loop. Thus, if the loop body executes five times before the condition evaluates to *false*, we say there were five iterations of the *while* loop.

What happens if the loop condition is *false* the first time it is evaluated? Because the loop condition is evaluated before executing the *while* loop body, and the loop body is executed only if the condition is *true*, it is possible that the *while* loop body is never executed. In that case, there would be **zero iterations** of the loop.

Figure 6.1

Flow of Control of a *while* Loop

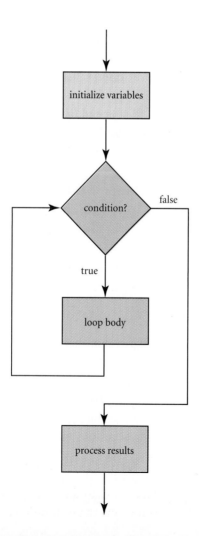

Using a *while* loop construct, the pseudocode for the cashier would look like this:

```
set total to $0.00
reach for first item
while item is not the divider bar
{
    add price to total
    reach for next item
}
// if we get here, the item is the divider bar
output the total price
```

It is also possible to construct a *while* loop whose condition *never* evaluates to *false*. That results in an **endless loop**, also known as an **infinite loop**. Because the condition always evaluates to *true*, the loop body is executed repeatedly, without end. This might happen if items other than the divider bar were placed continuously on the conveyor belt. One symptom of an endless loop is that the program doesn't terminate; it appears to "hang." However, if the program writes some output in the loop body, you will see that output spewing out on the Java console. Normally, the only recourse is for the user to abort the program.

The way to ensure that the condition will eventually evaluate to *false* is to include code, called a **loop update statement**, within the loop body that appropriately changes the variable that is being tested by the loop condition. If, for example, the loop condition tests for reading the sentinel value, the loop update statement should read the next input value.

One common logic error that causes an endless loop is putting a semicolon after the condition, as in the following:

```
while ( condition );  // semicolon causes endless loop if condition is true
```

A semicolon immediately following the condition indicates an empty loop body. Although some advanced programming techniques call for the use of an empty loop body, we will not be using those techniques in this book.

COMMON ERROR TRAP

Avoid putting a semicolon after the condition of a *while* loop. Doing so creates an empty loop body and could result in an endless loop.

6.3   Event-Controlled Looping

The *while* loop is used when we don't know how many times the loop will execute; that is, when the loop begins, we don't know how many iterations of the loop will be required. We rely on a signal, or **event**, to tell us that we have processed all the data. For example, when the cashier begins checking out an order, she doesn't (necessarily) know how many items are in the grocery cart; she only knows to stop when she sees the divider bar on the conveyor belt. We call this an event-controlled loop because we continue processing data until an event occurs, which signals the end of the data.

When we're prompting the user to enter data from the console, and we don't know at the beginning of the loop how much data the user has to be processed, we can define a special value, called the sentinel value. The sentinel value can vary from task to task and is typically a value that is outside the normal range of data for that task.

Sometimes the data our program needs is in a text file. For example, a file could store a company's monthly sales for the last five years. We may want to calculate average monthly sales or perform other statistical computations on that data. In this case, we need to read our data from the file, instead of asking the user to enter the data from the keyboard. Typically, we use a file when a large amount of data is involved because it would be impractical for a user to enter the data manually.

Reading from a file is also an event-controlled loop because we don't know at the beginning of the program how much data is in the file. Thus, we need some way to determine when we have finished processing all the data in the file. Java, and other languages, provides some indicator that we have reached the end of the file. Thus, for input from a file, sensing the end-of-file indication is the event that signals that there is no more data to read.

6.3.1   Reading Data from the User

Let's look at the general form for using a *while* loop to process data entered from the user.

```
initialize variables
read the first data item  // priming read
while  data item is not the sentinel value
{
   process the data


   read the next data item  // update read
}
report the results
```

After performing any initialization, we attempt to read the first item. We call this the **priming read** because, like priming a pump, we use that value to feed the condition of the *while* loop for the first iteration. If the first item is not the sentinel value, we process it. Processing may consist of calculating a total, counting the number of data items, comparing the data to previously read values, or any number of operations. Then we read the next data item. This is called the **update read** because we update the data item in preparation for feeding its value into the condition of the *while* loop for the next iteration. This processing, followed by an update read, continues until we do read the sentinel value, at which time, we do not execute the *while* loop body. Instead, we skip to the first instruction following the *while* loop. Note that the sentinel value is not meant to be processed. Like the divider bar for the cashier, it is simply a signal to stop processing.

We illustrate this pattern in Example 6.1, which prompts the user for integers and echoes to the console whatever the user enters. We chose the sentinel value to be −1, that is, when the user enters a −1, we stop processing.

```
 1 /*  Working with a sentinel value
 2     Anderson, Franceschi
 3 */
 4 import java.util.Scanner;
 5
 6 public class EchoUserInput
 7 {
 8    public static void main( String [ ] args )
 9    {
10       final int SENTINEL = -1;
11       int number;
12
13       Scanner scan = new Scanner( System.in );
14
15       // priming read
16       System.out.print( "Enter an integer, or -1 to stop > " );
17       number = scan.nextInt( );
18
19       while ( number != SENTINEL )
20       {
21          // processing
22          System.out.println( number );
23
24          // update read
25          System.out.print( "Enter an integer, or -1 to stop > " );
```

```
26              number = scan.nextInt( );
27         }
28
29         System.out.println( "Sentinel value detected. Goodbye" );
30    }
31 }
```

EXAMPLE 6.1   Echoing Input from the User

Figure 6.2 shows the output from this program when the user enters 23, 47, 100, and −1.

On line 10, we declare the sentinel value, −1, as a constant because the value of the sentinel will not change during the execution of the program, and it lets us clearly state via the *while* loop condition (line 19) that we want to execute the loop body only if the input is not the sentinel value.

Then on lines 16–17, we perform the priming read. The *while* loop condition on line 19 checks for the sentinel value. If the user enters the sentinel value first, we skip the *while* loop altogether and execute line 29, which prints a message that the sentinel value was entered, and we exit the program. If the user enters a number other than the sentinel value, we execute the body of the *while* loop (lines 21–26). In the *while* loop, we simply echo the user's input to the console, then perform the update read. Control then skips to the *while* loop condition, where the value the user entered in the update read is compared to the sentinel value. If this entry is the sentinel value, the loop is skipped; otherwise, the body of the loop is executed: The value is echoed, then a new value is read. This same processing continues until the user does enter the sentinel value.

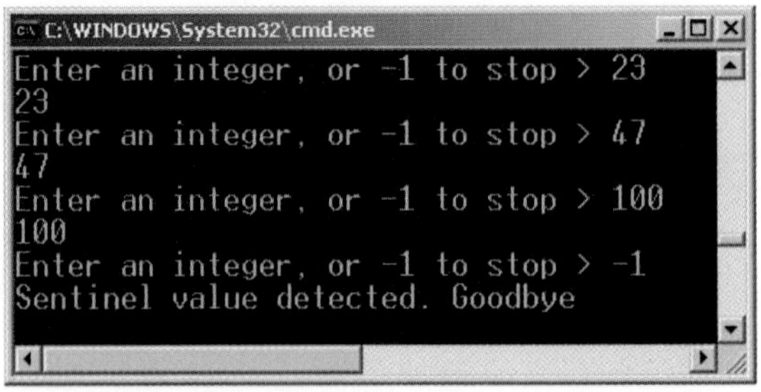

Figure 6.2

Output from Example 6.1, Using a Sentinel Value

```
C:\WINDOWS\System32\cmd.exe
Enter an integer, or -1 to stop > 23
23
Enter an integer, or -1 to stop > 47
47
Enter an integer, or -1 to stop > 100
100
Enter an integer, or -1 to stop > -1
Sentinel value detected. Goodbye
```

A common error in constructing *while* loops is forgetting the update read. Without the update read, the *while* loop continually processes the same data item, leading to an endless loop.

Another common error is omitting the priming read and, instead, reading data inside the *while* loop before the processing, as in the following pseudocode:

```
initialize variables
while  data item is not the sentinel value
{
    read the next data
    process the data
}
report the results
```

This structure has several problems. The first time we evaluate the *while* loop condition, we haven't read any data, so the result of that evaluation is unpredictable. Second, when we do read the sentinel value, we will process it, leading to incorrect results.

6.3.2 Reading Data from a Text File

The *Scanner* class enables us to read data easily from a text file. Although we will be using the *Scanner* class in this chapter, Java provides a whole set of classes in the *java.io* package to enable programmers to perform user input and output from a file. We will cover these classes in Chapter 11.

For the *Scanner* class, the general form for reading data from a text file is a little different from reading the data from the user. First, instead of reading a value and checking whether it is the sentinel value, we check whether there is more data in the file, then read a value. Second, we don't need to print a prompt because the user doesn't enter the data; we just read the next value from the file. For the *Scanner* class, the pseudocode for reading from a text file is shown below:

```
initialize variables
while we have not reached end of file
```

COMMON ERROR TRAP

Omitting the update read may result in an endless loop.

COMMON ERROR TRAP

Omitting the priming read leads to incorrect results.

REFERENCE POINT

The *java.io* package, which contains classes to perform input and output from various data streams, including files, is discussed in Chapter 11.

```
{
   read the next data item
   process the data
}
report the results
```

Scanner class methods, including a constructor for reading from a text file, are shown in Table 6.1. Another class we will use is the *File* class, which associates a file name with a file. The constructor for the *File* class is shown in Table 6.2.

The constructor shown in Table 6.1 can be used to associate a *Scanner* object with a file. The *Scanner* object will tokenize the contents of the file and return the tokens as we call the *next* methods. The *hasNext* method in the *Scanner* class returns *true* if the input has another token, and *false* otherwise. Thus, when the *hasNext* method returns *false*, we know we have reached the end of the file.

Example 6.2 reads integers from a file named *input.txt* and echoes the integers to the console. The contents of *input.txt* are shown in Figure 6.3 and the output from the program is shown in Figure 6.4.

Figure 6.3

Contents of *input.txt*

On line 14 of Example 6.2, we use the constructor of the *File* class to convert the filename, *input.txt*, to a platform-independent filename. Because we are specifying the simple filename, the JVM will look for the file in the same directory as our source file. If the file is located in another directory, we need to specify the path as well as the filename. For example, if the file were located on a disk in a Windows system, we would pass the *String* "*a:\\input.txt*" to the constructor. Notice that we need to use an escape sequence of two backslashes in order to specify the pathname, *a:\input.txt*.

The *File* class belongs to the *java.io* package, so we include an *import* statement for that class in line 5.

 REFERENCE POINT

The *String* escape sequences are discussed in Chapter 2.

In line 15, we construct a *Scanner* object associated with the *inputFile* object. If the file is not found, the constructor generates a *FileNotFoundException*. It is also possible that an *IOException* may be generated if we encounter problems reading the file. Java requires us to acknowledge that these exceptions may be generated. One way to do that is to include the phrase "throws IOException" in the header for *main* (line 10). In Chapter 11, we will discuss other ways to handle exceptions. We also import the *IOException* class on line 6.

TABLE 6.1   Selected Methods of the *Scanner* Class

Selected Methods of the *Scanner* Class	
Constructor	
`Scanner( File file )`	
creates a *Scanner* object and associates it with a file	
Return value	**Method name and argument list**
`boolean`	`hasNext( )`
	returns *true* if there is another token in the input stream; *false*, otherwise
`byte`	`nextByte( )`
	returns the next input as a *byte*
`short`	`nextShort( )`
	returns the next input as a *short*
`int`	`nextInt( )`
	returns the next input as an *int*
`long`	`nextLong( )`
	returns the next input as a *long*
`float`	`nextFloat( )`
	returns the next input as a *float*
`double`	`nextDouble( )`
	returns the next input as a *double*
`boolean`	`nextBoolean( )`
	returns the next input as a *boolean*
`String`	`next( )`
	returns the next token in the input line as a *String*

TABLE 6.2   *File* Class Constructor

A Constructor for the *File* Class
`File ( String pathname )`
constructs a *File* object with the *pathname* file name so that the file name is platform-independent

Figure 6.4

Output from Example 6.2, Reading from a File

 REFERENCE POINT

Exceptions are discussed extensively in Chapter 11. You can read more about the Scanner class in Appendix F and on Sun Microsystems' Java Web site: *http://java.sun.com.*

On line 17, the first time our *while* loop condition is evaluated, we check whether there is any data in the file. If the file is empty, the *hasNext* method will return *false*, and we will skip execution of the loop body, continuing at line 25, where we print a message and exit the program.

The body of the *while* loop (lines 19–22) calls the *nextInt* method to read the next integer in the file and echoes that integer to the console. We then reevaluate the *while* loop condition (line 17) to determine if more data is in the file. When no more integers remain to be read, the *hasNext* method returns *false*, and we skip to line 25, where we print a message and exit the program.

Notice that we do not use a priming read because the *hasNext* method essentially peeks ahead into the file to see if there is more data. If the *hasNext* method returns *true*, we know that there is another integer to read, so we perform the read in the first line of the *while* loop body (line 20).

```
 1 /* Reading a Text File
 2    Anderson, Franceschi
 3 */
 4 import java.util.Scanner;
 5 import java.io.File;
 6 import java.io.IOException;
 7
 8 public class EchoFileData
 9 {
10    public static void main( String [ ] args ) throws IOException
11    {
12       int number;
13
14       File inputFile = new File( "input.txt" );
15       Scanner scan = new Scanner( inputFile );
16
```

```
17      while ( scan.hasNext( ) )
18      {
19          // read next integer
20          number = scan.nextInt( );
21          // process the value read
22          System.out.println( number );
23      }
24
25      System.out.println( "End of file detected. Goodbye" );
26    }
27 }
```

EXAMPLE 6.2　Echoing Input from a File

6.4　Looping Techniques

You will find that the *while* loop is an important tool for performing many common programming operations on a set of input values. For example, the *while* loop can be used to calculate the sum of values, count the number of values, find the average value, find the minimum and maximum values, animate an image, and other operations.

6.4.1　Accumulation

Let's look at a common programming operation for which a *while* loop is useful: calculating the sum of a set of values. To do this, we will build a simple calculator that performs one function: addition. We will prompt the user for numbers one at a time. We'll make the sentinel value a 0; that is, when the user wants to stop, the user will enter a 0. At that point, we will print the total.

The calculator can be developed using an event-controlled *while* loop and a standard computing technique: **accumulation**. In the accumulation operation, we initialize a *total* variable to 0. Each time we input a new value, we add that value to the *total*. When we reach the end of the input, the current value of *total* is the total for all the input.

Here is the pseudocode for the addition calculator:

set total to 0

read a number　// priming read

while the number is not the sentinel value

Figure 6.5

Output from a Sample Run of the Addition Calculator

```
C:\WINDOWS\System32\cmd.exe
Welcome to the addition calculator.

Enter the first number or 0 for the total > 34
Enter the next number or 0 for the total > -10
Enter the next number or 0 for the total > 2
Enter the next number or 0 for the total > 5
Enter the next number or 0 for the total > 8
Enter the next number or 0 for the total > 0
The total is 39
```

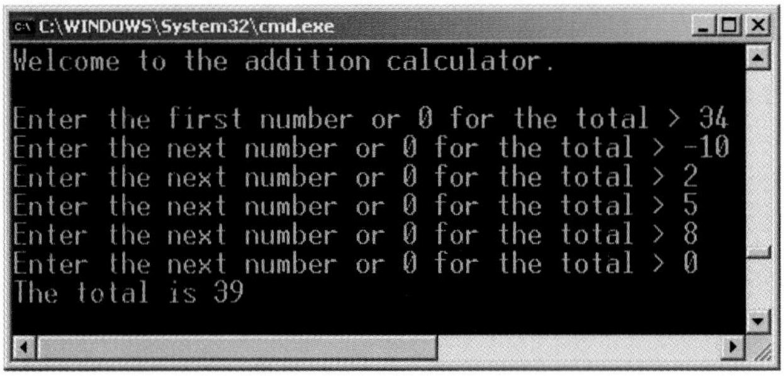

```
{
    add the number to total
    read the next number   // update read
}
output the total
```

Notice that this operation is almost identical to the grocery cashier's job in that we perform a priming read before the *while* loop. Inside the *while* loop, we process each number one at a time—adding each number to the total, then we read the next value, until we see the sentinel value, which is the signal to stop.

Example 6.3 provides the code for the addition calculator and Figure 6.5 shows the output for a sample execution of the calculator.

```
1 /*  Addition Calculator
2       Anderson, Franceschi
3 */
4
5 import java.util.Scanner;
6
7 public class Calculator
8 {
9     public static void main( String [ ] args )
10    {
11        final int SENTINEL = 0;
12        int number;
13        int total = 0;
14
15        Scanner scan = new Scanner( System.in );
16
17        System.out.println( "Welcome to the addition calculator.\n" );
18
```

```
19       System.out.print( "Enter the first number"
20                           + " or 0 for the total > " );
21       number = scan.nextInt( );
22
23       while ( number != SENTINEL )
24       {
25           total += number;
26
27           System.out.print( "Enter the next number"
28                               + " or 0 for the total > " );
29           number = scan.nextInt( );
30       }
31
32       System.out.println( "The total is " + total );
33   }
34 }
```

EXAMPLE 6.3   An Addition Calculator

Line 13 declares and initializes the *total* to *0*. This is an important step because the loop body will add each input value to the total. If the total is not set to 0 before the first input, we will get incorrect results. Furthermore, if *total* is declared but not initialized, our program will not compile.

Lines 19–21 read the first input value (the priming read). The *while* loop begins at line 23, and its condition checks for the sentinel value. The first time the *while* loop is encountered, this condition will check the value of the input from the priming read.

The loop body processes the input (line 25), which consists of adding the input value to the *total*. The final step in the loop body (lines 27–29) is to read the next input (the update read).

When the end of the loop body is reached, control is transferred back to line 23, where the loop condition is again tested with the input value read on line 29. If the condition is *true*, that is, if the input just read is not the sentinel value, then the loop body is reexecuted and the condition is retested, continuing until the input *is* the sentinel value, which causes the condition to evaluate to *false*. At that time, the loop body is skipped and line 32 is executed, which reports the results by printing the *total*.

Notice that the body of the *while* loop is indented and that the opening and closing curly braces are aligned in the same column as the *w* in the *while*. This style lets you easily see which statements belong to the *while* loop body.

COMMON ERROR TRAP

Forgetting to initialize the total to 0 will produce incorrect results.

SOFTWARE ENGINEERING TIP

Indent the body of a *while* loop to clearly illustrate the logic of the program.

COMMON ERROR TRAP

Choosing the wrong sentinel value may result in logic errors.

It is important to choose the sentinel value carefully. Obviously, the sentinel value cannot be a value that the user might want to be processed. In the addition calculator, we want to allow the user to enter positive or negative integers. We chose 0 as the sentinel value for two reasons. First, adding 0 to a total has no effect, so it is unlikely that the user will want to enter that value to be processed. Second, to the user, it is logical to enter a 0 to signal that there are no more integers to be added.

CODE IN ACTION

In the Chapter 6 folder on the CD-ROM included with this book, you will find a Shockwave movie showing a step-by-step illustration of a *while* loop with a sentinel value. Just double-click on *Loops.html* to start the movie.

6.4.2   Counting Items

Counting is used when we need to know how many items are input or how many input values fit some criterion, for example, how many items are positive numbers or how many items are odd numbers. Counting is similar to accumulation in that we start with a count of 0 and increment (add 1 to) the count every time we read a value that meets the criterion. When there are no more values to read, the count variable contains the number of items that meet our criterion.

For example, let's count the number of students who passed a test. The pseudocode for this operation is as follows:

```
set countPassed to 0
read a test score
while the test score is not the sentinel value
{
  if the test score >= 60
  {
    add 1 to countPassed
  }
  read the next test score
}
output countPassed
```

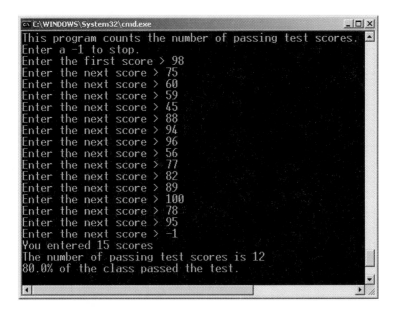

Figure 6.6

Counting Passing Test Scores

The application in Example 6.4 counts the number of students that passed a test. We also calculate the percentage of the class that passed the test. To do this, we maintain a second count: the number of scores entered. This value will be incremented each time we read a score, whereas the *countPassed* value will be incremented only if the score is greater than or equal to 60. The sentinel value is −1. A sample run of this program is shown in Figure 6.6.

```
1 /* Counting passing test scores
2    Anderson, Franceschi
3 */
4
5 import java.util.Scanner;
6 import java.text.DecimalFormat;
7
8 public class CountTestScores
9 {
10    public static void main( String [ ] args )
11    {
12      int countPassed = 0;
13      int countScores = 0;
14      int score;
15      final int SENTINEL = -1;
16
17      Scanner scan = new Scanner( System.in );
```

```
18
19      System.out.println( "This program counts "
20                  + "the number of passing test scores." );
21      System.out.println( "Enter a -1 to stop." );
22
23      System.out.print( "Enter the first score > " );
24      score = scan.nextInt( );
25
26      while ( score != SENTINEL )
27      {
28          if ( score >= 60 )
29          {
30                  countPassed++;
31          }
32
33          countScores++;
34
35          System.out.print( "Enter the next score > " );
36          score = scan.nextInt( );
37      }
38
39      System.out.println( "You entered " + countScores + " scores" );
40      System.out.println( "The number of passing test scores is "
41                      + countPassed );
42      if ( countScores != 0 )
43      {
44          DecimalFormat percent = new DecimalFormat( "#0.0%" );
45          System.out.println(
46            percent.format( (double) ( countPassed ) / countScores )
47            + " of the class passed the test." );
48      }
49   }
50 }
```

EXAMPLE 6.4   Counting Passing Test Scores

COMMON ERROR TRAP

Forgetting to initialize the count variables to 0 will produce incorrect results or a compiler error.

Lines 12 and 13 declare the variables *countPassed* and *countScores* and initialize both to 0. Initializing these values to 0 is critical; otherwise, we will get the wrong results or a compiler error.

Our *while* loop framework follows the familiar pattern. We perform the priming read for the first input (lines 23–24); our *while* loop condition checks for the sentinel value (line 26); and the last statements of the *while* loop (lines 35–36) read the next value.

In the processing portion of the *while* loop, line 28 checks if the score just read is a passing score, and if so, line 30 adds 1 to *countPassed*. For each score entered, regardless of whether the student passed, we increment *countScores* (line 33).

When the sentinel value is entered, the *while* loop condition evaluates to *false* and control skips to line 39, where we output the number of scores entered and the number of passing scores. So that we avoid dividing by 0, note that line 42 checks whether no scores were entered. Note also that in line 46 we type cast *countPassed* to a *double* to force floating-point division, rather than integer division, so that the fractional part of the quotient will be maintained.

6.4.3 Calculating an Average

Calculating an average is a combination of accumulation and counting. We use accumulation to calculate the total and we use counting to count the number of items to average.

Here's the pseudocode for calculating an average:

```
set total to 0
set count to 0
read a number
while the number is not the sentinel value
{
    add the number to total
    add 1 to the count

    read the next number
}
set the average to total / count
output the average
```

Thus, to calculate an average test score for the class, we need to calculate the total of all the test scores, then divide by the number of students who took the test.

```
average = total / count;
```

It's important to remember that if we declare *total* and *count* as integers, then the *average* will be calculated using integer division, which truncates

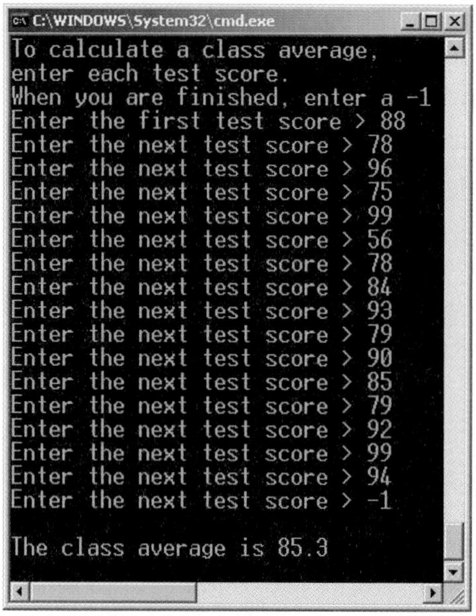

Figure 6.7

Calculating the Average Test Score

```
C:\WINDOWS\System32\cmd.exe                    _ □ ×
To calculate a class average,
enter each test score.
When you are finished, enter a -1
Enter the first test score > 88
Enter the next test score > 78
Enter the next test score > 96
Enter the next test score > 75
Enter the next test score > 99
Enter the next test score > 56
Enter the next test score > 78
Enter the next test score > 84
Enter the next test score > 93
Enter the next test score > 79
Enter the next test score > 90
Enter the next test score > 85
Enter the next test score > 79
Enter the next test score > 92
Enter the next test score > 99
Enter the next test score > 94
Enter the next test score > -1

The class average is 85.3
```

the remainder. To get a floating-point average, we need to type cast one of the variables (either *total* or *count*) to a *double* or a *float* to force the division to be performed as floating-point.

```
double average = (double) ( total ) / count;
```

The application in Example 6.5 calculates an average test score for a class of students. The output is shown in Figure 6.7.

```
 1 /* Calculate the average test score
 2    Anderson, Franceschi
 3 */
 4
 5 import java.util.Scanner;
 6 import java.text.DecimalFormat;
 7
 8 public class AverageTestScore
 9 {
10   public static void main( String [ ] args )
11   {
12     int count = 0;
13     int total = 0;
14     final int SENTINEL = -1;
15     int score;
```

```
16
17     Scanner scan = new Scanner( System.in );
18
19     System.out.println( "To calculate a class average," );
20     System.out.println( "enter each test score." );
21     System.out.println( "When you are finished, enter a -1" );
22
23     System.out.print( "Enter the first test score > " );
24     score = scan.nextInt( );
25
26     while ( score != SENTINEL )
27     {
28        total += score;    // add score to total
29        count++;           // add 1 to count of test scores
30
31        System.out.print( "Enter the next test score > " );
32        score = scan.nextInt( );
33     }
34
35     if ( count != 0 )
36     {
37         DecimalFormat oneDecimalPlace = new DecimalFormat( "##.0" );
38         System.out.println( "\nThe class average is "
39            + oneDecimalPlace.format( (double) ( total ) / count ) );
40     }
41     else
42         System.out.println( "\nNo grades were entered" );
44   }
45 }
```

EXAMPLE 6.5   Calculating an Average Test Score

In Example 6.5, lines 12 and 13 declare both *count* and *total* variables as *ints* and initialize each to 0. Again, our *while* loop structure follows the same pattern. Lines 23–24 read the first input value; the *while* loop condition (line 26) checks for the sentinel value; and the last statements in the *while* loop (lines 31–32) read the next score. For the processing portion of the *while* loop, we add the score to the total and increment the count of scores (lines 28–29). When the sentinel value is entered, we stop executing the *while* loop and skip to line 35.

In line 35, we avoid dividing by 0 by checking whether *count* is 0 (that is, if no scores were entered) before performing the division. If *count* is 0, we simply print a message saying that no grades were entered. If *count* is not 0,

COMMON ERROR TRAP

Forgetting to check whether the denominator is 0 before performing division is a logic error.

REFERENCE POINT

The difference between floating-point division and integer division is explained in Chapter 2.

we calculate and print the average. We first instantiate a *DecimalFormat* object (line 37) so that we can output the average to one decimal place. Remember that we need to type cast the *total* to a *double* (lines 38–39) to force floating-point division, rather than integer division.

6.4.4   Finding Maximum or Minimum Values

In Chapter 5, we illustrated a method for finding the maximum or minimum of three numbers. But that method won't work when we don't know how many numbers will be input. To find the maximum or minimum of an unknown number of input values, we need another approach.

In previous examples, we calculated a total for a group of numbers by keeping a running total. We started with a total of 0, then added each new input value to the running total. Similarly, we counted the number of input items by keeping a running count. We started with a count of 0 and incremented the count each time we read a new value. We can apply that same logic to calculating a maximum or minimum. For example, to find the maximum of a group of values, we can keep a "running," or current, maximum. We start by assuming that the first value we read is the maximum. In fact, it is the largest value we have seen so far. Then as we read each new value, we compare it to our current maximum. If the new value is greater, we make the new value our current maximum. When we come to the end of the input values, the current maximum is the maximum for all the input values.

Finding the minimum value, of course, uses the same approach, except that we replace the current minimum only if the new value is less than the current minimum.

Here's the pseudocode for finding a maximum value in a file:

```
read a first number and make it the maximum
while there is another number to read
{
    read the next number
    if number > maximum
```

```
    {
        set maximum to number
    }
}
output the maximum
```

Example 6.6 shows the code to find a maximum test grade in a file. As shown in Figure 6.8, the grades are stored as integers, one per line, in the file *grades.txt*. When this program runs, its output is shown in Figure 6.9.

```
 1 /* Find the maximum test grade
 2     Anderson, Franceschi
 3 */
 4
 5 import java.util.Scanner;
 6 import java.io.*;
 7
 8 public class FindMaximumGrade
 9 {
10     public static void main( String [ ] args ) throws IOException
11     {
12         int maxGrade;
13         int grade;
14
15         Scanner scan = new Scanner( new File( "grades.txt" ) );
16
17         System.out.println( "This program finds the maximum grade "
18                             + "for a class" );
19
20         if ( ! scan.hasNext( ) )
21         {
22             System.out.println( "No test grades are in the file" );
23         }
```

88
78
96
75
99
56
78
84
93
79
90
85
79
90
85
79
92
99
94

Figure 6.8
The Contents of *grades.txt*

Figure 6.9
Finding the Maximum Value

```
24       else
25       {
26          maxGrade = scan.nextInt( );   // make first grade the max
27
28          while ( scan.hasNext( ) )
29          {
30             grade = scan.nextInt( );   // read next grade
31
32             if ( grade > maxGrade )
33                maxGrade = grade;      // save as current max
34          }
35
36          System.out.println( "The maximum grade is " + maxGrade );
37       }
38    }
39 }
```

EXAMPLE 6.6   Finding the Maximum Value

In line 20, we call the *hasNext* method to test whether the file is empty. If so, we print a message (line 22) and the program ends. If, however, the file is not empty, we read the first value and automatically make it our maximum by storing the grade in *maxGrade* (line 26). In line 28, our *while* loop condition tests whether we have reached end of file. If not, we execute the body of the *while* loop (lines 30–33). We read the next grade and check whether that grade is greater than the current maximum. If so, we assign that grade to *maxGrade*; otherwise, we leave *maxGrade* unchanged. Then control is transferred to line 28 to retest the *while* loop condition.

When we do reach end of file, the *while* loop condition becomes *false*, and control is transferred to line 36, and we output *maxGrade* as the maximum value.

COMMON ERROR TRAP

Initializing a maximum or a minimum to an arbitrary value, such as 0 or 100, is a logic error and could result in incorrect results.

A common error is to initialize the maximum or minimum to an arbitrary value, such as 0 or 100. This will not work for all conditions, however. For example, let's say we are finding the maximum number and we initialize the maximum to 0. If the user enters all negative numbers, then when the end of data is encountered, the maximum will still be 0, which is clearly an error. The same principle is true when finding a minimum value. If we initialize the minimum to 0, and the user enters all positive numbers greater than 0, then at the end of our loop, our minimum value will still be 0, which is also incorrect.

Skill Practice
with these end-of-chapter questions

6.14.1   Multiple Choice Exercises

Question 1

6.14.2   Reading and Understanding Code

Questions 5, 6, 7, 8, 20

6.14.3   Fill in the Code

Questions 21, 22, 23, 24, 25, 26

6.14.4   Identifying Errors in Code

Questions 30, 31

6.14.5   Debugging Area

Question 37

6.14.6   Write a Short Program

Questions 44, 45

6.14.8   Technical Writing

Questions 70, 71

6.4.5   Animation

Animation is another operation that can be performed using *while* loops. For example, to move an object across a graphics window, we change the x or y values and draw the object in a new position in each iteration of the loop. We stop moving the object when we reach the edges of the window. Therefore, the sentinel value for the loop is that the x- or y-coordinate has reached the edge of the window.

If we want to roll a ball from left to right along an imaginary line, we can represent the ball by a filled circle. We start with an x value of 0 and some y

value; our *while* loop draws the object at the current *x*, *y* position, then increments the *x* value.

Thus, to test for the sentinel value—that is, whether the ball has reached the right edge of the window—we add the diameter of the ball to the current *x* position of the ball and compare that result to the *x*-coordinate of the right edge of the window.

For this animation, we'll use a *Circle* class written by the authors. Table 6.3 shows the constructors and methods of the *Circle* class.

Example 6.7 shows a *while* loop that simulates rolling a ball from the left edge of the window to the right edge.

```
 1 /* RollABall, Version 1
 2    Anderson, Franceschi
 3 */
 4
 5 import java.awt.Graphics;
 6 import java.awt.Color;
 7 import javax.swing.JApplet;
 8
 9 public class RollABall extends JApplet
10 {
11    private final int X = 0;             // x value of the ball
12    private final int Y = 50;            // y value of the ball
13    private final int DIAMETER = 15;    // diameter of the ball
14    private final Color COLOR = Color.BLUE; // color of the ball
15    private final int SPACER = 5;        // space between balls
16    private int sentinel;                // sentinel value for while loop
17    private Circle ball;                 // ball will be Circle object
18
19    public void init( )
20    {
21       // instantiate the ball object
22       ball = new Circle( X, Y, DIAMETER, COLOR );
23    }
24
25    public void paint( Graphics g )
26    {
27       super.paint( g );
28
29       int ballDiameter = ball.getDiameter( );
```

TABLE 6.3   The *Circle* Class API

The *Circle* Class API

Constructors

```
Circle( )
```

constructs a *Circle* object with default values; *x* and *y* are set to 0, diameter to 10, and color to black

```
Circle( int startX, int startY, int sDiameter,
          Color circleColor )
```

constructs a *Circle* object; sets *x* and *y* to *startX* and *startY*, respectively; diameter to *sDiameter*; and color to *circleColor*

Return value	Method name and argument list
`int`	`getX( )` returns the ball's current *x* value
`int`	`getY( )` returns the ball's current *y* value
`int`	`getDiameter( )` returns the current diameter of the circle
`Color`	`getColor( )` returns the current color of the circle
`void`	`setX( int newX )` sets the *x* value to *newX*
`void`	`setY( int newY )` sets the *y* value to *newY*
`void`	`setDiameter( int newDiameter )` sets the diameter to *newDiameter*
`void`	`setColor( Color newColor )` sets the circle color to *newColor*
`void`	`draw( Graphics g )` draws a filled circle with *x* and *y* being the upper-left corner of a bounding rectangle, with the diameter and color set in the object

```
30        sentinel = getWidth( ); // edge of the window is sentinel
31
32        while ( ball.getX( ) + ballDiameter < sentinel )
33        {
34            ball.draw( g );    // draw the ball
35
36            // set x to next drawing location
37            ball.setX( ball.getX( ) + ballDiameter + SPACER );
38        }
39    }
40 }
```

EXAMPLE 6.7   Roll a Ball, Version 1

In the *init* method, we instantiate the ball (line 22). It will start with an *x* value of 0 (the left edge of the screen), *y* value of 50, diameter of 15, and a blue color. In the *paint* method, we use a *while* loop (lines 32–38) to repeatedly draw a ball and increment the *x* value. The sentinel value occurs when the *x* value of the next ball (*x* + *ballDiameter* + *SPACER*) reaches the right edge of the applet window. We determine the value of the right edge of the window by calling the *getWidth* method of the *JApplet* class (line 30), which returns the width of the applet window.

We chose to increment the *x* value by the width of the ball (the diameter) plus 5 pixels so that each ball is 5 pixels apart (line 37). Let's take a closer look at that statement:

```
ball.setX( ball.getX( ) + ballDiameter + SPACER );
```

We call the *setX* method of the *Circle* class to set the *x* value of the next ball. In order to set the *x* value to a new value, we need to get the current *x* value of the *ball* object and the current diameter. We do that by calling the *getX* method and adding the *ballDiameter* value we got earlier from the *getDiameter* method (line 29). Then, by adding the diameter of the ball to the current *x* value, we calculate the *x* value of the right side of the ball. Adding the constant *SPACER* to that result puts a space of 5 pixels between the last ball drawn and the next.

Figure 6.10 shows the output when the applet is run.

This is fine for a first effort, but it isn't the effect we want. The result is just a series of balls drawn from left to right. There's another problem with

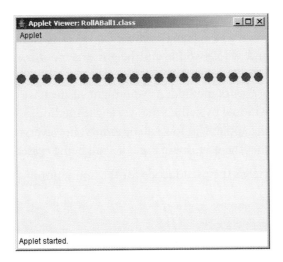

Figure 6.10

Roll a Ball, Version 1

RollABall1, which you can appreciate only if you run the applet: all the balls appear at once. There's no sense of the ball moving from left to right.

To get a rolling movement, we need to slow down the execution of the applet. To do that, we can use the *Pause* class provided by the authors and available in the directory on the CD containing this code. The *wait* method of the *Pause* class has the following API:

```
static void wait( double seconds )
```

Because the *wait* method is *static*, we invoke it using the *Pause* class name. For example, the following statement will pause the applet for approximately 3/100th of a second:

```
Pause.wait( .03 );
```

Also, we want to see only one ball at any time, and that should be the ball at the current (x, y) coordinate. To get this effect, we need to "erase" the previous ball before we draw the next ball in the new location. To erase the ball, we have two options: we can redraw the ball in the background color or we can clear the whole window by calling the *clearRect* method, which draws a rectangle in the background color. The default background color for the *JApplet* class is not one of the *Color* constants (*Color.BLUE*, etc.), so it's a difficult color to match. That being the case, we opt for the *clearRect* method, which has the following API:

```
void clearRect( int x, int y, int width, int height )
```

Using the *clearRect* method, we can erase the whole applet window by treating it as a rectangle whose (x, y) coordinate is the upper-left corner $(0, 0)$ and whose width and height are the same as the applet window. We've already seen that we can get the width of the window by calling the *getWidth* method. As you might suspect, we can get the height of the applet window by calling the *getHeight* method. Note that after we call *clearRect*, the applet window will be empty; however, we draw the next ball so quickly that the user doesn't see the ball being erased.

Here's the pseudocode for the animation:

```
set starting (x, y) coordinate
instantiate the ball object
while the x value is not the edge of the window
{
   draw the ball
   pause
   erase the ball
   set (x, y) coordinate to next drawing position
}
```

Example 6.8 shows the revised version of the rolling ball.

```
1 /* RollABall, version 2
2    Anderson, Franceschi
3 */
4
5 import java.awt.Graphics;
6 import java.awt.Color;
7 import javax.swing.JApplet;
8 import javax.swing.JOptionPane;
9
10 public class RollABall2 extends JApplet
11 {
12   private final int X = 0;            // ball starts at left of screen
13   private int y;                      // we will prompt user for y value
14   private final int DIAMETER = 15;        // diameter of ball
15   private final Color COLOR = Color.BLUE; // color of the ball
16   private final int SPACER = 2;           // space between balls
17   private Circle ball;                    // Circle object reference
```

```
18
19   public void init( )
20   {
21      y = Integer.parseInt(
22        JOptionPane.showInputDialog( "Enter the starting y value" ) );
23
24      // instantiate the ball object
25      ball = new Circle( X, y, DIAMETER, COLOR );
26   }
27
28   public void paint( Graphics g )
29   {
30      super.paint( g );
31
32      // get ball diameter and width & height of the applet window
33      int ballDiameter = ball.getDiameter( );
34      int windowWidth = getWidth( );
35      int windowHeight = getHeight( );
36
37      // rolling horizontally
38      // check whether ball is at right edge of window
39      while ( ball.getX( ) + ballDiameter < windowWidth )
40      {
41        ball.draw( g );  // draw the ball
42
43        Pause.wait( 0.03 ); // wait 3/100th of a second
44
45        // clear the window
46        g.clearRect( 0, 0, windowWidth, windowHeight );
47
48        // position to next location for drawing ball
49        ball.setX( ball.getX( ) + SPACER ); // increment x by 2
50      }
51   }
52 }
```

EXAMPLE 6.8   Roll a Ball, Version 2

In the *init* method, we prompt the user for the starting *y* value (lines 21–22) and we instantiate the ball object (line 25). Then in the *paint* method, we draw a ball (line 41), pause for approximately a 3/100ths of a second (line 43), then use the *clearRect* method to erase the window (line 46) before

Figure 6.11
Roll a Ball, Version 2

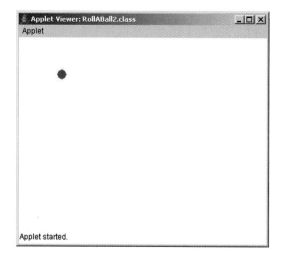

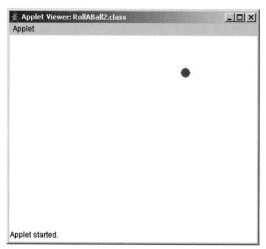

positioning to the next location for drawing a ball (lines 48–49). Now, only one ball is visible at any time, and the ball appears to roll across the screen, as shown in Figure 6.11.

6.5   Type-Safe Input Using *Scanner*

One problem with reading input using *Scanner* is that if the next token does not match the data type we expect, an *InputMismatchException* is generated, which stops execution of the program. This could be caused by a simple typo on the user's part; for example, the user may type a letter or other nonnumeric character when our program prompts for an integer. To

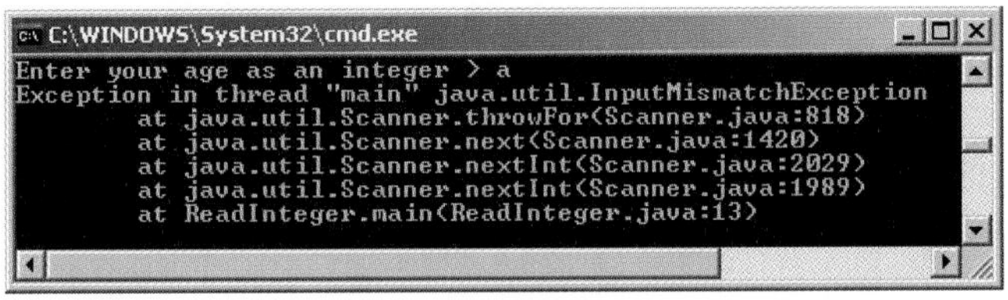

Figure 6.12

Input Failure

illustrate this problem, Example 6.9 shows a small program that prompts the user for an integer and calls the *nextInt* method of the *Scanner* class to read the integer, and Figure 6.12 shows the *InputMismatchException* generated when the user enters an *a* instead of an integer. Notice that the program ends when the exception is generated; we never execute line 15, which echoes the age to the console.

```
1 /* Reading an integer from the user
2    Anderson, Franceschi
3 */
4 import java.util.Scanner;
5
6 public class ReadInteger
7 {
8    public static void main( String [ ] args )
9    {
10         Scanner scan = new Scanner( System.in );
11
12         System.out.print( "Enter your age as an integer > " );
13         int age = scan.nextInt( );
14
15         System.out.println( "Your age is " + age );
16    }
17 }
```

EXAMPLE 6.9   Reading an Integer

We can make our program more robust by checking, before we read, that the next token matches our expected input. The *Scanner* class provides *hasNext* methods for doing this, which are shown in Table 6.4. The *hasNext* methods return *true* if the next token can be read as the data type specified. For example, if we expect an integer, we can test whether the user has typed characters that can be interpreted as an integer by calling the *hasNextInt* method. If that method returns *true*, it is safe to read the value using the *nextInt* method. If the next token is not what we need, that is, if the *has-*

TABLE 6.4   *Scanner* Methods for Testing Tokens

Selected Input Stream Testing Methods of the *Scanner* Class	
Return value	**Method name and argument list**
boolean	hasNext( ) returns *true* if there is another token in the input stream; *false*, otherwise
boolean	hasNextByte( ) returns *true* if the token in the input stream can be read as a *byte*; *false*, otherwise
boolean	hasNextShort( ) returns *true* if the token in the input stream can be read as a *short*; *false*, otherwise
boolean	hasNextInt( ) returns *true* if the token in the input stream can be read as an *int*; *false*, otherwise
boolean	hasNextLong( ) returns *true* if the token in the input stream can be read as a *long*; *false*, otherwise
boolean	hasNextFloat( ) returns *true* if the token in the input stream can be read as a *float*; *false*, otherwise
boolean	hasNextDouble( ) returns *true* if the token in the input stream can be read as a *double*; *false*, otherwise
boolean	hasNextBoolean( ) returns *true* if the token in the input stream can be read as a *boolean*; *false*, otherwise
String	nextLine( ) returns the remainder of the input line as a *String*

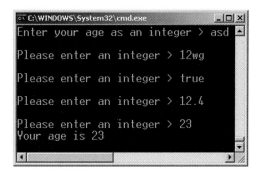

Figure 6.13

Reprompting Until the User Enters an Integer

NextInt method returns *false,* then reading that value as an *int* will generate the *InputMismatchException*. In that case, we need to notify the user that the value typed is not valid and reprompt for new input. But first we need to clear the invalid input. We can flush the invalid input by calling the *nextLine* method of the *Scanner* class, which returns any remaining tokens on the input line as a *String*. Then we just ignore that *String*. Example 6.10 shows a revised version of Example 6.9 that is type-safe, meaning we guarantee we have an integer to read before reading it.

On line 14 of Example 6.10, we prompt for the integer. Then on line 15, the *while* loop condition checks whether the user has, indeed, typed an integer value. If not, we ignore whatever the user did type by calling the *nextLine* method (line 17). On line 18, we reprompt the user. The *while* loop continues executing until the user does enter an integer and the *hasNextInt* method returns *true.* At that point, we execute line 20, which reads the integer into the *age* variable. Figure 6.13 shows the output of this program when the user enters data other than integers, then finally enters an integer.

```
1  /* Type-Safe Input Using Scanner
2     Anderson Franceschi
3  */
4
5  import java.util.Scanner;
6
7  public class TypeSafeReadInteger
8  {
9     public static void main( String [ ] args )
```

```
10    {
11        Scanner scan = new Scanner( System.in );
12        String garbage;
13
14        System.out.print( "Enter your age as an integer > " );
15        while ( ! scan.hasNextInt( ) )
16        {
17            garbage = scan.nextLine( );
18            System.out.print( "\nPlease enter an integer > " );
19        }
20        int age = scan.nextInt( );
21        System.out.println( "Your age is " + age );
22    }
23  }
```

EXAMPLE 6.10   Type-Safe Input

6.6   Constructing Loop Conditions

Constructing the correct loop condition may seem a little counterintuitive. The loop executes as long as the loop condition evaluates to *true*. Thus, if we want our loop to terminate when we read the sentinel value, then the loop condition should check that the input value is *not* the sentinel value. In other words, the loop continuation condition is the inverse of the loop termination condition. For a simple sentinel-controlled loop, the condition normally follows this pattern:

```
while ( inputValue != sentinel )
```

In fact, you can see that the loop conditions in many of the examples in this chapter use this form of *while* loop condition. Examples 6.7 and 6.8 use a similar pattern. We want to roll the ball as long as the ball is completely within the window. The loop termination condition is that the starting *x* value plus the diameter of the ball is greater than or equal to the *x* value of the right side of the window. The loop continuation condition, therefore, is that the *x* value of the ball plus the diameter is less than the *x* value of the right side of the window.

```
while ( ball.getX( ) + ballDiameter < windowWidth )
```

For some applications, there may be multiple sentinel values. For example, suppose we provide a menu for a user with each menu option being a single character. The user can repeatedly select options from the menu, with the sentinel value being *S* for stop. To allow case-insensitive input, we want to recognize the sentinel value as either *S* or *s*. To do this, we need a compound loop condition, that is, a loop condition that uses a logical AND (&&) or logical OR (||) operator.

Our first inclination might be to form the condition this way, which is **incorrect**:

```
while ( option != 'S' || option != 's' )  // INCORRECT
```

With this condition, the loop will execute forever. Regardless of what the user enters, the loop condition will be *true*. If the user types *S*, the first expression (option != 'S') is *false*, but the second expression (option != 's') is *true*. Thus, the loop condition evaluates to *true* and the *while* loop body is executed. Similarly, if the user types *s*, the first expression (option != 'S') is *true*, so the loop condition evaluates to *true* and the *while* loop body is executed.

An easy method for constructing a correct *while* loop condition consists of three steps:

1. Define the loop termination condition; that is, define the condition that will make the loop stop executing.

2. Create the loop continuation condition—the condition that will keep the loop executing—by applying the logical NOT operator (!) to the loop termination condition.

3. Simplify the loop continuation condition by applying DeMorgan's Laws, where possible.

REFERENCE POINT

DeMorgan's Laws are explained in Chapter 5.

Let's use these three steps to construct the correct loop condition for the menu program.

1. Define the loop termination condition:

   The loop will stop executing when the user enters an *S* or the user enters an *s*. Translating that into Java, we get

   ```
   ( option == 'S' || option == 's' )
   ```

2. Create the loop continuation condition by applying the ! operator:

   ```
   ! ( option == 'S' || option == 's' )
   ```

3. Simplify by applying DeMorgan's Laws:

Figure 6.14

Calculating Cell Phone Service

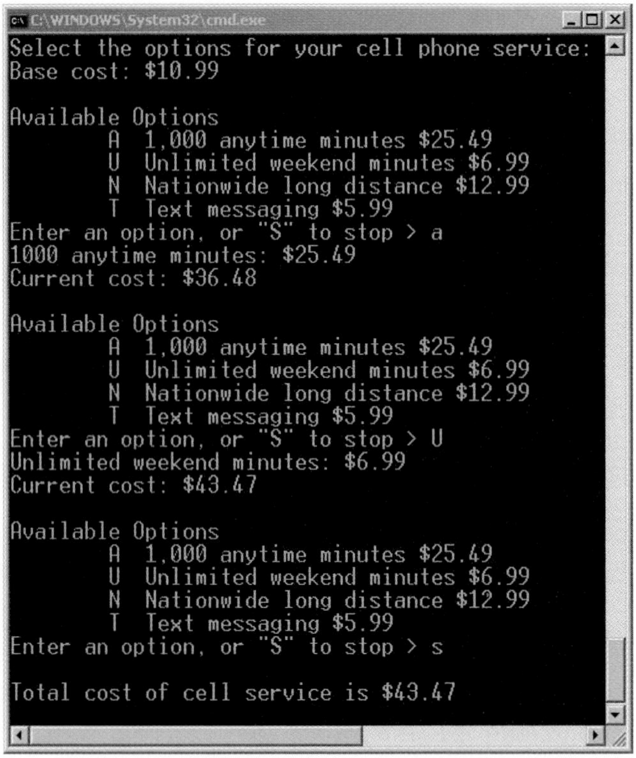

```
C:\WINDOWS\System32\cmd.exe                              _ | □ | ×
Select the options for your cell phone service:
Base cost: $10.99

Available Options
          A   1,000 anytime minutes $25.49
          U   Unlimited weekend minutes $6.99
          N   Nationwide long distance $12.99
          T   Text messaging $5.99
Enter an option, or "S" to stop > a
1000 anytime minutes: $25.49
Current cost: $36.48

Available Options
          A   1,000 anytime minutes $25.49
          U   Unlimited weekend minutes $6.99
          N   Nationwide long distance $12.99
          T   Text messaging $5.99
Enter an option, or "S" to stop > U
Unlimited weekend minutes: $6.99
Current cost: $43.47

Available Options
          A   1,000 anytime minutes $25.49
          U   Unlimited weekend minutes $6.99
          N   Nationwide long distance $12.99
          T   Text messaging $5.99
Enter an option, or "S" to stop > s

Total cost of cell service is $43.47
```

To apply DeMorgan's Laws, we change the == equality operators to !=
and change the logical OR operator (||) to the logical AND operator
(&&), producing an equivalent, but simpler expression:

```
( option != 'S' && option != 's' )
```

We now have our loop condition.

To illustrate, let's write an application that calculates the cost of cell phone
service. We'll provide a list of options, and the user will select options one
at a time until the user enters *S* or *s* to stop. This is an accumulation operation because we are accumulating the total cost of the cell phone service.
Example 6.11 shows the code for this application and Figure 6.14 shows the
output of a sample run.

```
1 /* Calculate price for cell phone service
2    Anderson, Franceschi
3 */
4
5 import java.util.Scanner;
```

```
 6 import java.text.DecimalFormat;
 7
 8 public class CellService
 9 {
10    public static void main( String [ ] args )
11    {
12       String menu = "\nAvailable Options";
13       menu += "\n\tA  1,000 anytime minutes $25.49";
14       menu += "\n\tU  Unlimited weekend minutes $6.99";
15       menu += "\n\tN  Nationwide long distance $12.99";
16       menu += "\n\tT  Text messaging $5.99";
17
18       String optionS;
19       char option;
20       double cost = 10.99; // base cost
21
22       DecimalFormat money = new DecimalFormat( "$###.00" );
23       Scanner scan = new Scanner( System.in );
24
25       System.out.println( "Select the options "
26                           + "for your cell phone service: " );
27       System.out.println( "Base cost: " + money.format( cost ) );
28
29       System.out.println( menu ); // print the menu
30       System.out.print( "Enter an option, "
31                         + "or \"S\" to stop > " );
32       option = scan.next( ).charAt( 0 );
33
34       while ( option != 'S' && option != 's' )
35       {
36          switch ( option )
37          {
38             case 'a':
39             case 'A':
40                System.out.println( "1000 anytime minutes: "
41                                    + "$25.49" );
42                cost += 25.49;
43                break;
44             case 'u':
45             case 'U':
46                System.out.println( "Unlimited weekend minutes: "
47                                    + "$6.99" );
48                cost += 6.99;
49                break;
50             case 'n':
```

```
51                  case 'N':
52                      System.out.println( "Nationwide long distance: "
53                                              + "$12.99" );
54                      cost += 12.99;
55                      break;
56                  case 't':
57                  case 'T':
58                      System.out.println( "Text messaging: "
59                                              + "$5.99" );
60                      cost += 5.99;
61                      break;
62                  default:
63                      System.out.println( "Unrecognized option" );
64              }
65
66          System.out.println( "Current cost: "
67                                  + money.format( cost ) );
68
69          System.out.println( menu ); // print the menu
70          System.out.print( "Enter an option, "
71                              + "or \"S\" to stop > " );
72          option = scan.next( ).charAt( 0 );
73          }
74
75      System.out.println( "\nTotal cost of cell service is "
76                              + money.format( cost ) );
77      }
78 }
```

EXAMPLE 6.11   A Compound Loop Condition

In Example 6.11, we use the compound condition in the *while* loop (line 34). Then within the *while* loop, we use a *switch* statement (lines 36–64) to determine which menu option the user has chosen. We handle case-insensitive input of menu options by including *case* constants for both the lowercase and uppercase versions of each letter option.

Note that we don't provide *case* statements for the sentinel values. Instead, we use the *while* loop condition to detect when the user enters the sentinel values.

Animation is another operation that may require a *while* loop with a compound condition. For example, suppose that instead of rolling our ball horizontally, we roll it diagonally down and to the right. To roll the ball diagonally down and to the right, we need to change both the *x* and the *y* values in the

COMMON ERROR TRAP

Do not check for the sentinel value inside a *while* loop. Let the *while* loop condition detect the sentinel value.

while loop body. Thus, within the while loop, we increment both *x* and *y*. We continue as long as the ball has not rolled beyond the right edge of the window and the ball has also not rolled beyond the bottom of the window.

Let's develop the condition by applying our three steps:

1. The loop termination condition is that the ball has rolled beyond either the side edge of the window or the bottom edge of the window.

```
// the ball is out of bounds
( ball.getX( ) + ballDiameter > windowWidth
      || ball.getY( ) + ballDiameter > windowHeight )
```

2. The loop continuation condition is created by applying the logical NOT operator (!) to the loop termination condition:

```
// the ball is not out of bounds
!  ( ball.getX( ) + ballDiameter > windowWidth
        || ball.getY( ) + ballDiameter > windowHeight )
```

3. Simplifying the condition by applying DeMorgan's Law, we get:

```
// the ball is in bounds
( ball.getX( ) + ballDiameter <= windowWidth
      && ball.getY( ) + ballDiameter <= windowHeight )
```

Example 6.12 shows the *RollABall3* class, which uses four *while* loops to roll the ball diagonally down to the right (*x* is incremented, *y* is incremented), then diagonally down to the left (*x* is decremented, *y* is incremented); then diagonally up to the left (*x* is decremented, *y* is decremented) and finally diagonally up to the right (*x* is incremented, *y* is decremented). We set the starting *y* value to 10 and the starting *x* value two-thirds of the way across the window. When the program runs, the ball appears to bounce off the walls of the window, as shown in Figure 6.15.

```
1  /* RollaBall, Version 3
2     Rolls the ball diagonally
3     Anderson, Franceschi
4  */
5
6  import java.awt.Graphics;
7  import java.awt.Color;
8  import javax.swing.JApplet;
9
10 public class RollABall3 extends JApplet
```

Figure 6.15

Output from *RollABall3*

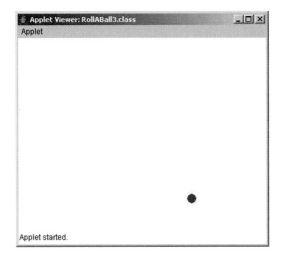

```
11   {
12       private final int X = 0;          // the x value of the ball
13       private final int Y = 10;         // the y value of the ball
14       private final int DIAMETER = 15;  // the diameter of the ball
15       private final Color COLOR = Color.BLUE; // the color of the ball
16       private final int SPACER = 2;     // space between balls
17       private Circle ball;
18
19       public void init( )
20       {
21           // instantiate the ball
22           ball = new Circle( X, Y, DIAMETER, COLOR );
23       }
24
25       public void paint( Graphics g )
26       {
27           super.paint( g );
28
29           // get ball diameter and width & height of the applet window
30           int ballDiameter = ball.getDiameter( );
31           int windowWidth = getWidth( );
32           int windowHeight = getHeight( );
33
34           // start x 2/3 across the window
35           ball.setX( windowWidth * 2 / 3 );
36
37           // rolling diagonally down to the right
38           while ( ball.getX( ) + ballDiameter <= windowWidth
```

```
39                      && ball.getY( ) + ballDiameter <= windowHeight )
40          {
41
42              ball.draw( g );  // draw the ball
43
44              Pause.wait( 0.03 ); // pause for 3/100 of a second
45              // erase the ball
46              g.clearRect( 0, 0, windowWidth, windowHeight );
47
48              ball.setX( ball.getX( ) + SPACER ); // move right
49              ball.setY( ball.getY( ) + SPACER ); // and down
50          }
51
52          // rolling diagonally down to the left
53          while ( ball.getY( )  + ballDiameter < windowHeight
54                  && ball.getX( ) > 0 )
55          {
56              ball.draw( g );  // draw the ball
57
58              Pause.wait( 0.03 ); // pause for 3/100 of a second
59              // erase the ball
60              g.clearRect( 0, 0, windowWidth, windowHeight );
61
62              ball.setX( ball.getX( ) - SPACER ); // move left
63              ball.setY( ball.getY( ) + SPACER ); // and down
64          }
65
66          // rolling diagonally up to the left
67          while ( ball.getY( ) > 0 && ball.getX( ) > 0 )
68          {
69              ball.draw( g );  // draw the ball
70
71              Pause.wait( 0.03 ); // pause for 3/100 of a second
72              // erase the ball
73              g.clearRect( 0, 0, windowWidth, windowHeight );
74
75              ball.setX( ball.getX( ) - SPACER ); // move left
76              ball.setY( ball.getY( ) - SPACER ); // and up
77          }
78
79          // rolling diagonally up to the right
80          while ( ball.getY( ) - ballDiameter > 0
81                  && ball.getX( ) + ballDiameter < windowWidth )
82          {
83              ball.draw( g );  // draw the ball
```

```
84
85              Pause.wait( 0.03 ); // pause for 3/100 of a second
86              // erase the ball
87              g.clearRect( 0, 0, windowWidth, windowHeight );
88
89              ball.setX( ball.getX( ) + SPACER ); // move right
90              ball.setY( ball.getY( ) - SPACER ); // and up
91          }
92      }
93  }
```

EXAMPLE 6.12   The *RollABall3* Class

Skill Practice
with these end-of-chapter questions

6.14.1   Multiple Choice Exercises

Questions 9, 10

6.14.3   Fill in the Code

Question 28

6.14.4   Identifying Errors in Code

Question 34

6.14.5   Debugging Area

Question 36

6.14.6   Write a Short Program

Question 53

6.7   Testing Techniques for *while* Loops

It's a good feeling when your code compiles without errors. Getting a clean compile, however, is only part of the job for the programmer. The other part of the job is verifying that the code is correct; that is, that the program produces accurate results.

It usually isn't feasible to test a program with all possible input values, but we can get a reasonable level of confidence in the accuracy of the program by concentrating our testing in three areas:

1. Does the program produce correct results with a set of known input?

2. Does the program produce correct results if the sentinel value is the first and only input?

3. Does the program deal appropriately with invalid input?

Let's take a look at these three areas in more detail:

1. Does the program produce correct results with known input?

To test the program with known input, we select valid input values and determine what the results should be by performing the program's operation either by hand or by using a calculator. For example, to test whether a total or average is computed correctly, enter some values and compare the program's output to a total or average you calculate by entering those same values into a calculator.

It's especially important to select input values that represent boundary conditions; that is, values that are the lowest or highest expected values. For example, to test a program that determines whether a person is old enough to vote in a presidential election (that is, the person is 18 or older), we should select test values of 17, 18, and 19. These values are the boundary conditions for age >= 18; the test values are one integer less, the same value, and one integer greater than the legal voting age. We then run the program with the three input values and verify that the program correctly identifies 17 as an illegal voting age and 18 and 19 as legal voting ages.

2. Does the program produce correct results if the sentinel value is the first and only input?

In our *while* loops, when we find the sentinel value, we do not execute the *while* loop. The flow of control skips the *while* loop body and picks up at the statement following the *while* loop. When the sentinel value is the first input value, our *while* loop does not execute at all. We simply skip to the statement following the *while* loop. In cases like this, the highly respected computer scientist Donald Knuth recommends that we "do exactly nothing, gracefully."

In many programs that calculate a total or an average for the input values, when no value is input, your program should either report the total or average as 0 or output a message that no values were entered. Thus, it's important to write your program so that it tolerates no input except the sentinel value and, therefore, we need to test our programs by entering the sentinel value first.

Let's revisit the earlier examples in this chapter to see how they handle the case when only the sentinel value is entered.

In the addition calculator (Example 6.3), we set the total to 0 before the *while* loop and simply report the value of total after the *while* loop. So we get the correct result (0) with only the sentinel value.

In Example 6.4 where we count the percentage of passing test scores, we handle the sole sentinel value by performing some additional checking after the *while* loop. If only the sentinel value is entered, the count will be 0. We check for this case and if we find a count of 0, we skip reporting the percentage so that we avoid dividing by 0. We use similar code in Example 6.5, where we calculate the average test score. If we detect a count of 0, we also skip the calculation of the average to avoid dividing by 0 and simply report the class average as 0.

3. Does the program deal appropriately with invalid input?

If the program expects a range of values or certain discrete values, then it should notify the user when the input doesn't fit the expected values.

In Example 6.11, we implemented a menu for calculating the cost of cell phone service. The user could enter *s*, *a*, *u*, *n*, or *t* (or the corresponding capital letters) representing their desired service options. If the user enters a letter other than those expected values, we use the *default* clause of the *switch* statement to issue an error message, "*Unrecognized option.*"

In the next section, we explain how to validate that user input is within a range of values using a *do/while* loop.

6.8 Event-Controlled Loops Using *do/while*

Another form of loop that is especially useful for validating user input is the *do/while* loop. In the *do/while* loop, the loop condition is tested at the end of the loop (instead of at the beginning, as in the *while* loop). Thus the body of the *do/while* loop is executed at least once.

The syntax of the *do/while* loop is the following:

```
// initialize variables
do
{
    // body of loop
} while ( condition );
// process the results
```

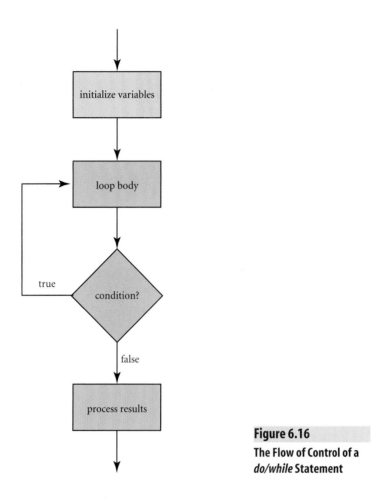

Figure 6.16

The Flow of Control of a *do/while* Statement

Figure 6.16 shows the flow of control of a *do/while* loop.

To use the *do/while* loop to validate user input, we insert the prompt for the input inside the body of the loop, then use the loop condition to test the value of the input. Like the *while* loop, the body of the loop will be reexecuted if the condition is *true*. Thus, we need to form the condition so that it's *true* when the user enters invalid values.

Example 6.13 implements a *do/while* loop (lines 14–18) that prompts the user for an integer between 1 and 10. Figure 6.17 shows the output of the program. If the user enters a number outside the valid range, we reprompt

Figure 6.17

Validating Input

the user until the input is between 1 and 10. Thus the condition for the *do/while* loop (line 18) is

```
while ( number < 1 || number > 10 )
```

```
 1 /* Validate input is between 1 and 10
 2    Anderson, Franceschi
 3 */
 4
 5 import java.util.Scanner;
 6
 7 public class ValidateInput
 8 {
 9   public static void main( String [ ] args )
10   {
11     int number;  // input value
12     Scanner scan = new Scanner( System.in );
13
14     do
15     {
16       System.out.print( "Enter a number between 1 and 10 > " );
17       number = scan.nextInt( );
18     } while ( number < 1 || number > 10 );
19
20     System.out.println( "Thank you!" );
21   }
22 }
```

EXAMPLE 6.13   Validating User Input

For validating input, you may be tempted to use an *if* statement rather than a *do/while* loop. For example, to perform the same validation as Example 6.13, you may try this **incorrect** code:

```
System.out.print( "Enter a number between 1 and 10 > " );
number = scan.nextInt( );
```

```
if ( number < 1 || number > 10 ) // INCORRECT!
{
    System.out.print( "Enter a number between 1 and 10 > " );
    number = scan.nextInt( );
}
```

COMMON ERROR TRAP

Do not use an *if* statement to validate input because it will catch invalid values entered the first time only. Use a *do/while* loop to reprompt the user until the user enters a valid value.

The problem with this approach is that the *if* statement will reprompt the user only once. If the user enters an invalid value a second time, the program will not catch it. A *do/while* loop, however, will continue to reprompt the user as many times as needed until the user enters a valid value.

CODE IN ACTION

In the Chapter 6 folder on the CD-ROM included with this book, you will find a Shockwave movie showing two step-by-step illustrations of *do/while* loops. Just double-click on *Loops.html* to start the movie.

6.9   Programming Activity 1: Using *while* Loops

In this activity, you will work with a sentinel-controlled *while* loop, performing this activity:

> Write a *while* loop to process the contents of a grocery cart and calculate the total price of the items. It is important to understand that, in this example, we do not know how many items are in the cart.

The framework will animate your code and display the current subtotal so that you can check the correctness of your code. The window will display the various *Item* objects moving down a conveyor belt toward a grocery bag. It will also display the unit price of the item and your current subtotal, as well as the correct subtotal.

For example, Figure 6.18 demonstrates the animation: We are currently scanning the first item, a milk carton, with a unit price of $2.00; thus, the correct subtotal is $2.00.

As the animation will show, *Item* objects could be milk, cereal, orange juice, or the divider bar. The number of *Item* objects in the cart is determined randomly; as you watch the animation, sometimes you will find that there are two items in the cart, sometimes six, sometimes three, and so forth. Scanning the divider bar signals the end of the items in the cart.

Figure 6.18

Animation of the *Cashier* Application

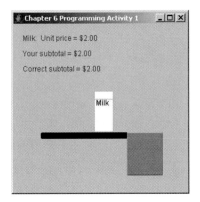

Task Instructions

Copy the files in the Chapter 6 Programming Activity 1 directory on the CD-ROM accompanying this book to a directory on your computer. Searching for five stars (*****) in the *Cashier.java* source code will show you where to add your code. You will add your code inside the *checkout* method of the *Cashier* class (the method header for the *checkout* method has already been coded for you). Example 6.14 shows a fragment of the *Cashier* class, where you will add your code:

```java
public void checkout( )
{
  /* ***** Student writes the body of this method ***** */
  //
  //  Using a while loop, calculate the total price
  //  of the groceries.
  //
  // The getNext method (in this Cashier class) returns the
  // next item on the conveyor belt, which is an Item object
  // (we do not know which item and we do not know how many items
  // are in the cart - this is randomly generated).
  // getNext does not take any arguments. Its API is:
  //       Item getNext( )
  //
  // Right after you update the current subtotal,
  // you should call the animate method.
  // The animate method takes one parameter: a double,
  // which is your current subtotal.
  // For example, if the name of your variable representing
  // the current subtotal is total, your call to the animate
  // method should be:
  //    animate( total );
```

```
//
// The instance method getPrice of the Item class
// returns the price of the Item object.
// The method getPrice does not take any arguments.
// Its API is:
//        double getPrice( )
//
// The cart is empty when the getNext method returns
// the divider Item.
// You detect the divider Item because its price
// is -0.99. So an Item with a price of -0.99
// is the sentinel value for the loop.
//
// After you scan the divider, display the total
// for the cart in a dialog box.

// End of student code
}
```

EXAMPLE 6.14   The *checkout* Method in *Cashier.java*

- You can access items in the cart by calling the *getNext* method of the *Cashier* class, which has the following API:

```
Item getNext( )
```

The *getNext* method returns an *Item* object, which represents an *Item* in the cart. As you can see, the *getNext* method does not take any arguments. Since we call the method *getNext* from inside the *Cashier* class, we call the method without an object reference. For example, a call to *getNext* could look like the following:

```
Item newItem;

newItem = getNext( );
```

The *getNext* method is already written and contains code to generate the animation; it is written in such a way that the first *Item* object on the conveyor belt may or may not be the divider. (If the first *Item* is the divider, the cart is empty.)

- After you get a new *Item*, you can "scan" the item to get its price by calling the *getPrice* method of the *Item* class. The *getPrice* method has this API:

```
double getPrice( )
```

Thus, you would get an item, then get its price using code like the following:

```
Item newItem;
double price;

newItem = getNext( );
price = newItem.getPrice( );
```

- After adding the price of an item to your subtotal, call the *animate* method of the *Cashier* class. This method will display both your subtotal and the correct subtotal so that you can verify that your code is correct.

  The animate method has the following API:

  ```
  void animate( double subtotal )
  ```

  Thus, if your variable representing the current total is *total*, you would call the animate method using the following code:

  ```
  animate( total );
  ```

- We want to exit the loop when the next *Item* is the divider. You will know that the *Item* is the divider because its price will be –0.99 (negative 0.99); thus, scanning an *Item* whose price is –0.99 should be your condition to exit the *while* loop.

- After you scan the divider, display the total for the cart in a dialog box. Verify that your total matches the correct subtotal displayed.

- To test your code, compile and run the application from the *Cashier* class.

Troubleshooting

If your method implementation does not animate or animates incorrectly, check these items:

- Verify that you have correctly coded the priming read.
- Verify that you have correctly coded the condition for exiting the loop.
- Verify that you have correctly coded the body of the loop.

DISCUSSION QUESTIONS   **?**

1.   What is the sentinel value of your *while* loop?

2.   Explain the purpose of the priming read.

6.10   Count-Controlled Loops Using *for*

Before the loop begins, if you know the number of times the loop body should execute, you can use a *count-controlled loop*. The *for* loop is designed for count-controlled loops, that is, when the number of iterations is determined before the loop begins.

6.10.1   Basic Structure of *for* Loops

The *for* loop has this syntax:

```
for ( initialization; loop condition; loop update )
{
       // loop body
}
```

Notice that the initialization, loop condition, and loop update in the *for* loop header are separated by semicolons (not commas). Notice also that there is no semicolon after the closing parenthesis in the *for* loop header. A semicolon here would indicate an empty *for* loop body. Although some advanced programs might correctly write a *for* loop with an empty loop body, the programs we write in this book will have at least one statement in the *for* loop body.

The flow of control of the *for* loop is shown in Figure 6.19. When the *for* loop is encountered, the initialization statement is executed. Then the loop condition is evaluated. If the condition is true, the loop body is executed, then the loop update statement is executed, and the loop condition is reevaluated. Again, if the condition is true, the loop body is executed, followed by the loop update, then the reevaluation of the condition, and so on, until the condition is false.

The *for* loop is equivalent to the following *while* loop:

```
// initialization
while ( loop condition )
{
   // loop body
   // loop update
}
```

As you can see, *while* loops can be used for either event-driven or count-controlled loops. A *for* loop is especially useful for count-controlled loops, however. Because all the loop control is contained in the *for* loop header,

COMMON ERROR TRAP

Use semicolons, rather than commas, to separate the statements in a *for* loop header.

COMMON ERROR TRAP

Adding a semicolon after the closing parenthesis in the *for* loop header indicates an empty loop body and will likely cause a logic error.

Figure 6.19

Flow of Control of the *for* Loop

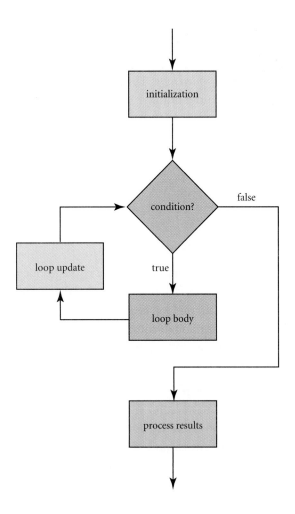

you can easily see what condition will stop the loop and how the condition will be updated after each iteration.

6.10.2 Constructing *for* Loops

Typically, we use a **loop control variable** in a *for* loop; that control variable is usually used for counting. We set its initial value in the initialization statement, increment or decrement its value in the loop update statement, and check its value in the loop condition.

For example, if we want to find the sum of five integers, we know the loop body should execute five times—once for each integer. We set our loop control variable to 1 in the initialization statement, increment the loop control variable by 1 in the loop update statement, and check if its value is less than or equal to 5 in the loop condition. When the loop update statement increments the control variable's value to 6, we will have executed the loop body five times. The pseudocode for this program is the following:

set total to 0
for i = 1 to 5 by 1
{
    read integer
    add integer to total
}
print the total

With a *for* loop, we do not need to perform a priming read because the condition for exiting the loop is controlled by a counter, not by an input value.

Example 6.15 shows the *for* loop for calculating the sum of five integers.

```
 1 /* Find the total of 5 numbers
 2    Anderson, Franceschi
 3 */
 4
 5 import java.util.Scanner;
 6
 7 public class Sum5Numbers
 8 {
 9   public static void main( String [ ] args )
10   {
11     int total = 0;  // stores the sum of the 5 numbers
12     int number;     // stores the current input
13
14     Scanner scan = new Scanner( System.in );
15
16     for ( int i = 1; i <= 5; i++ )
17     {
18       System.out.print( "Enter an integer > " );
19       number = scan.nextInt( );
20
21       total += number;  // add input to total
22     }
23
24     // process results by printing the total
```

```
25    System.out.println( "The total is " + total );
26  }
27 }
```

EXAMPLE 6.15   Finding the Sum of Five Numbers

In this example, which is a standard accumulation operation, the *for* loop initialization statement declares *i*, which will be our loop control variable. We start *i* at 1, and after each execution of the loop body, we increment *i* by 1 in the loop update statement. The loop condition checks if the value of *i* is less than or equal to 5; when *i* reaches 6, we have executed the loop body five times. Figure 6.20 shows the execution of this *for* loop.

We can also increment the loop control variable by values other than 1. Example 6.16 shows a *for* loop that increments the control variable by 2 to print the even numbers from 0 to 20.

The pseudocode for this program is the following:

set output to an empty *String*
for i = 0 to 20 by 2
{
    append i and a space to the output *String*
}
print the output *String*

We start with an empty *String* variable, *toPrint*, and with each iteration of the loop we append the next even number and a space. When the loop completes, we output *toPrint*, which prints all numbers on one line, as shown in Figure 6.21.

Figure 6.20

Finding the Sum of Five Integers

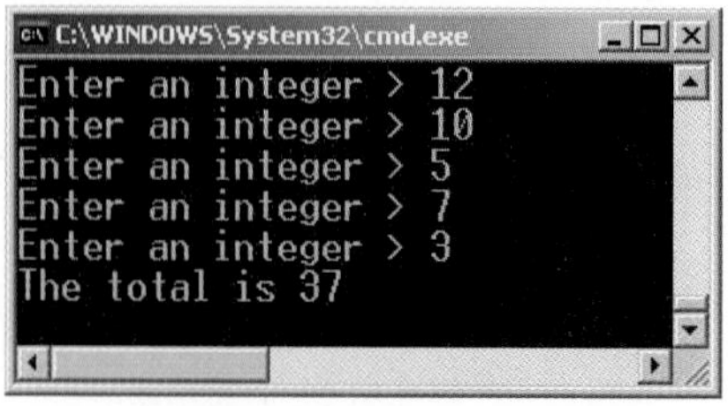

Figure 6.21
Printing Even Numbers from 0 to 20

```
1 /* Print the even numbers from zero to twenty
2    Anderson, Franceschi
3 */
4
5 public class PrintEven
6 {
7   public static void main( String [ ] args )
8   {
9     String toPrint = "";  // initialize output String
10
11    for ( int i = 0; i <= 20; i += 2 )
12    {
13        toPrint += i + " "; // append current number and a space
14    }
15
16    System.out.println( toPrint ); // print results
17  }
18 }
```

EXAMPLE 6.16   Printing Even Numbers

In this example, we initialize the loop control variable to 0, then increment *i* by 2 in the loop update statement (i += 2) to skip the odd numbers. Notice that we used the value of the loop control variable *i* inside the loop. The loop control variable can perform double duty such as this because the loop control variable is available to our code in the loop body.

The loop control variable also can be used in our prompt to the user. For example, in Example 6.15, we could have prompted the user for each integer using this statement:

```
System.out.print( "Enter integer " + i  + " > " );
```

Then the user's prompt would look like that shown in Figure 6.22.

One caution, however: If we declare the loop control variable in the *for* loop header, its value will not be available after the loop completes. It will have meaning only inside the *for* loop header and body. We'll clarify this

Figure 6.22

Adding the Loop Control Variable to the Prompt

concept in Chapter 7, when we discuss **scope**, which is the area within a program that any identifier can be used. If you want to refer to the loop control variable after the loop completes, then declare the variable before the loop begins. For example, this code could be used instead of line 11 in Example 6.16.

```
int i;
for ( i = 0; i <= 20; i += 2 )
```

Then after the loop completes, if we were to print *i*, its value would be *22*, which is the value of *i* that causes the loop condition to evaluate to *false*.

CODE IN ACTION

In the Chapter 6 folder on the CD-ROM included with this book, you will find a Shockwave movie showing a step-by-step illustration of a *for* loop. Just double-click on *Loops.html* to start the movie.

We can also decrement the loop control variable. Example 6.17 shows an application that reads a sentence entered by the user and prints the sentence backward.

The pseudocode for this program is the following:

```
set backwards to an empty String
read a sentence

for i = ( length of sentence − 1 ) to 0 by −1
{
  get character at position i in sentence
  append character to backwards
}
print backwards
```

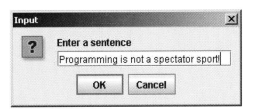

Figure 6.23
Printing a Sentence Backward

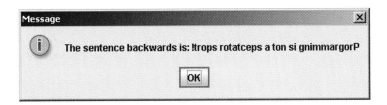

To print a sentence backward, we treat the sentence, a *String*, like a stream of characters; each iteration of the loop extracts and processes one character from the *String*, using the *charAt* method of the *String* class. Line 10 declares two *Strings*: *original*, to hold the sentence the user enters, and *backwards* (initialized as an empty *String*) to hold the reverse of the user's sentence. Lines 12–13 prompt the user for a sentence. Lines 15 through 18 make up the *for* loop, whose purpose is to copy the original sentence backward into the *String backwards*. We do this by starting the copying at the last character in the original *String* and moving backward in the *String* one character at a time until we have copied the first character in *original*. Thus, we initialize our loop variable to the position of the last character in *original* (original.length( ) - 1) and extract one character at a time, appending it to *backwards*. The loop update statement (i--) moves the loop variable backward by one position, and our loop condition (i >= 0) checks whether we have reached the beginning of the *String original*. Figure 6.23 shows the execution of the program with the user entering the sentence, "*Programming is not a spectator sport!*"

```
1 /* Print a sentence backward
2    Anderson, Franceschi
3 */
4 import javax.swing.JOptionPane;
5
6 public class Backwards
7 {
8   public static void main( String [ ] args )
9   {
10     String original, backwards = "";
```

```
11
12     original = JOptionPane.showInputDialog( null,
13                             "Enter a sentence" );
14
15     for ( int i = original.length( ) - 1; i >= 0; i-- )
16     {
17         backwards += original.charAt( i );
18     }
19
20     JOptionPane.showMessageDialog( null,
21                 "The sentence backwards is: " + backwards );
22   }
23 }
```

EXAMPLE 6.17   Printing a Sentence Backward

We can display some interesting graphics using *for* loops. The applet in Example 6.18 draws the bull's-eye target shown in Figure 6.24. To make the bull's-eye target, we draw 10 concentric circles (circles that have the same center point), beginning with the largest circle and successively drawing a smaller circle on top of the circles already drawn. Thus, the bull's-eye target circles have the same center point, but different diameters. The pseudocode for this program is

for diameter = 200 to 20 by −20
{
    instantiate a circle
    draw the circle

Figure 6.24
Drawing a Bull's-eye Target

```
   if color is black
       set color to red
   else
       set color to black
}
```

We can again use the *Circle* class introduced in Section 6.4.5, when we rolled a ball.

Translating the pseudocode into Java, we get the code shown in Example 6.18.

 **REFERENCE POINT**

The API for the *Circle* class is given in Section 6.4.5

```
 1 /* Bull's-eye target
 2    Anderson, Franceschi
 3 */
 4
 5 import javax.swing.JApplet;
 6 import java.awt.Color;
 7 import java.awt.Graphics;
 8
 9 public class Bullseye extends JApplet
10 {
11    // center of bullseye
12    private int centerX = 200, centerY = 150;
13    // color of first circle
14    private Color toggleColor = Color.BLACK;
15    // each circle will be a Circle object
16    private Circle circle;
17
18    public void paint( Graphics g )
19    {
20      super.paint( g );
21
22      for ( int diameter = 200; diameter >= 20; diameter -= 20 )
23      {
24        // instantiate circle with current diameter and color
25        circle = new Circle( centerX - diameter / 2,
26                             centerY - diameter / 2,
27                             diameter, toggleColor );
28
29        circle.draw( g ); // draw the circle
30
31        if ( toggleColor.equals( Color.BLACK ) )
32          toggleColor = Color.RED;   // if black, change to red
33        else
```

```
34              toggleColor = Color.BLACK; // if red, change to black
35      }
36    }
37 }
```

EXAMPLE 6.18   Drawing a Bull's-Eye Target

Our *for* loop initialization statement in line 22 sets up the diameter of the largest circle as 200 pixels and the loop update statement decreases the diameter of each circle by 20 pixels. The smallest circle we want to draw should have a diameter of 20 pixels, so we set the loop condition to check that the diameter is greater than or equal to 20. We need to start with the largest circle rather than the smallest circle so that new circles we draw don't hide the previously drawn circles.

Drawing the bull's-eye target circles illustrates two common programming techniques: conversion between units and a toggle variable.

We need to convert between units because the *Circle* class constructor takes as its arguments the upper-left (x, y) coordinate and the width and height of the circle's bounding rectangle (this is consistent with the *fillOval* method of the *Graphics* class). However, all our circles have the same center point, but not the same upper-left x and y coordinates. Given the diameter and the center point of the circle, however, we can calculate the (x, y) coordinate of the upper-left corner. Figure 6.25 shows how we make the conversion.

The difference between the center point and the upper-left corner of the bounding rectangle is the radius of the circle, which is half of the diameter (`diameter / 2`). So, the upper-left x value is the x value of the center point minus half the diameter (`centerX - diameter / 2`). Similarly, the upper-left y value is the y value of the center point minus half the diameter (`centerY - diameter / 2`).

Thus, we instantiate each circle using the following statement:

```
circle = new Circle( centerX - diameter / 2,
                     centerY - diameter / 2,
                     diameter, toggleColor );
```

SOFTWARE ENGINEERING TIP

Use a toggle variable when you need to alternate between two values.

To alternate between red and black circles, we use a **toggle variable**, which is a variable whose value alternates between two values. We use a *Color* object for our toggle variable, *toggleColor*, and initialize it to *Color.BLACK*. After drawing each circle, we switch the color (lines 31–34). If the current color is black, we set it to red; otherwise, the color must be red, so we set the color to black.

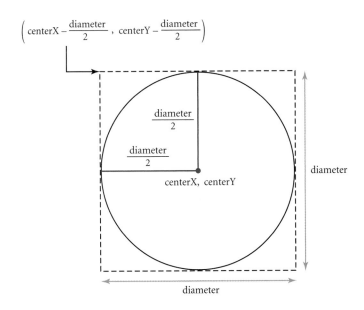

$$\left(centerX - \frac{diameter}{2} \; , \; centerY - \frac{diameter}{2} \right)$$

Figure 6.25
Converting Circle Coordinates

Skill Practice
with these end-of-chapter questions

6.10.3   Testing Techniques for *for* Loops

One of the most important tests for *for* loops is that the starting and ending values of the loop variable are set correctly. For example, to execute a *for* loop five times, we could set the initial value of the loop variable to 0 and use the condition (i < 5), or we could set the initial value of the loop variable to 1 and use the condition (i <= 5). Either of these *for* loop headers will cause the loop to execute five times.

```
for ( int i = 0; i < 5; i++ ) // executes 5 times
```

or

```
for ( int i = 1; i <= 5; i++ ) // executes 5 times
```

However, the following *for* loop header is incorrect; the loop will execute only four times.

```
for ( int i = 1; i < 5; i++ ) // INCORRECT! executes only 4 times
```

Thus to test the *for* loop in Example 6.15 that prompts for five integers, we need to verify that the program outputs exactly five prompts. To test that we are prompting the user five times, we can enter the integers 1, 2, 3, 4, and 5 at the prompts. Another option, shown in Figure 6.26, is to append a number to the prompt, which does double duty. Besides keeping the user informed of the number of integers entered so far, it also helps to verify that we have the correct number of prompts.

Like *while* loops, the body of a *for* loop may not be executed at all. If the loop condition is *false* the first time it is tested, the body of the *for* loop is skipped. Thus, when testing, we want to simulate input that would cause the loop condition to be *false* when the *for* loop statement is first encountered. For example, in the *Backwards* class in Example 6.17, we need to test the *for* loop with an empty sentence. In other words, when the prompt

Figure 6.26

Counting Five Prompts

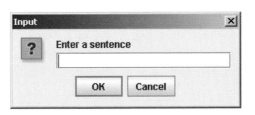

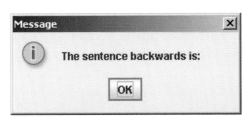

Figure 6.27
The Backwards Class with
an Empty Sentence

appears to enter a sentence, we simply press the *Enter* key. If you try this, you will find that the application still works, as Figure 6.27 shows.

The program works correctly with an empty sentence because the *for* loop initialization statement is

```
int i = original.length( ) − 1;
```

Because the length of an empty *String* is 0, this statement sets *i* to −1. The loop condition (`i >= 0`) is *false*, so the loop body is never executed. The flow of control skips to the statement following the loop,

```
JOptionPane.showMessageDialog( null,
          "The sentence backwards is: " + backwards );
```

which prints an empty *String*. Although it would be more user-friendly to check whether the sentence is empty and print a message to that effect, the program does indeed do exactly nothing, gracefully.

6.11   Nested Loops

Loops can be nested inside other loops; that is, the body of one loop can contain another loop. For example, a *while* loop can be nested inside another *while* loop or a *for* loop can be nested inside another *for* loop. In fact, the nested loops do not need to be the same loop type; that is, a *for* loop can be nested inside a *while* loop and a *while* loop can be nested inside a *for* loop.

REFERENCE POINT

Nested *for* loops are useful for processing data stored in two-dimensional arrays, which are discussed in Chapter 9. Simple *for* loops are useful to process data stored in standard arrays; standard arrays are discussed in Chapter 8.

Nested loops may be useful if you are performing multiple operations, each of which has its own count or sentinel value. For example, we may be interested in processing data in a statistics table containing rows and columns. In order to process all the data, we could loop from the first row to the last row; inside that loop, we would process each row by looping from the first column to the last column of that row. A statistics table can be stored in what is called a two-dimensional array, a subject we discuss in Chapter 9.

Going back to Jane, our grocery cashier, her workday can be modeled using nested loops. In Programming Activity 1, we wrote the code for our cashier to calculate the total cost of the contents of one customer's grocery cart. But cashiers check out multiple customers, one after another. While the line of people in front of the cashier is not empty, she will help the next customer. For each customer, she will set the total order to $0.00 and start scanning items and add the prices to the total. While the current customer still has items in the cart, Jane will scan the next item. When Jane finishes processing a customer's cart, she will check to see if there is a customer waiting in line. If there is one, she will set the total to $0.00 and start scanning the next customer's items.

Thus, the cashier's job can be described using a *while* loop nested inside another *while* loop. The pseudocode for these nested loops is shown below:

```
look for a customer
while there is a customer in line
{
  set total to $0.00
  reach for first item
  while item is not the divider bar
  {
      add price to total
      reach for next item
  }
  // if we get here, the item is the divider bar
  output the total price

  look for another customer
}
```

The important point to understand with nested loops is that the inner (or nested) loop executes completely (executes all its iterations) for each single iteration of the outer loop.

Let's look at a simple example that uses nested *for* loops. Suppose we want to print five rows of numbers as shown below:

```
1
1 2
1 2 3
1 2 3 4
1 2 3 4 5
```

We can see a pattern here. In the first line, we print one number; in the second line, we print two numbers, and so on. In other words, the quantity of numbers we print and the line number are the same. The pseudocode for this pattern is the following:

```
for line = 1 to 5 by 1
{
    for number = 1 to line by 1
    {
      print number and a space
    }
    print a new line
}
```

Translating this pseudocode into nested *for* loops, we get the code shown in Example 6.19.

```
1  /*  Printing numbers using nested for loops
2       Anderson, Franceschi
3  */
4
5  public class NestedForLoops
6  {
7    public static void main( String [ ] args )
8    {
9        // outer for loop prints 5 lines
10       for ( int line = 1; line <= 5; line++ )
11       {
```

```
12        // inner for loop prints one line
13        for ( int number = 1; number <= line; number++ )
14        {
15          // print the number and a space
16          System.out.print( number + " " );
17        }
18
19        System.out.println( );    // print a new line
20      }
21  }
22 }
```

EXAMPLE 6.19   Nested *for* Loops

Notice that the inner *for* loop (lines 12–17) uses the value of *line*, which is set by the outer *for* loop (lines 9–20). Thus, for the first iteration of the outer loop, *line* equals 1, so the inner loop executes once, printing the number 1 and a space. Then we print a new line because line 19 is part of the outer *for* loop. The outer loop then sets the value of *line* to 2, and the inner loop starts again at 1 and executes two times (until *number* equals the line number in the outer loop). Then we again print a new line. This operation continues until the *line* exceeds 5, when the outer loop terminates. The output from Example 6.19 is shown in Figure 6.28.

Let's look at another example of a nested loop. We'll let the user enter positive integers, with a 0 being the sentinel value. For each number, we'll find all its factors; that is, we will find all the integers that are evenly divisible into the number, except 1 and the number itself.

If a number is evenly divisible by another, the remainder after division will be 0. The modulus operator (%) will be useful here, because it calculates the remainder after integer division. Thus, to find all the factors of a number,

Figure 6.28

Output from Example 6.19

we can test all integers from 1 up to the number to see if the remainder after division is 0. But let's think about whether that's a good approach. The number 1 will be a factor for every number, because every number is evenly divisible by 1. So we can test integers beginning at 2. Then, because 2 is the smallest factor, there's no need to test integers higher than *number / 2*. Thus, our range of integers to test will be from 2 to *number / 2*.

For this example, we'll use a *for* loop nested inside a *while* loop. The pseudocode for this example is

```
read first number  // priming read
while number is not 0
{
    print "The factors for number are "
    for factor = 2 to ( number / 2 ) by 1
    {
        if number % factor is 0
            print factor and a space
    }
    print a new line

    read next number  // update read
}
```

But what happens if we don't find any factors for a number? In that case, the number is a prime number. We can detect this condition by using a *boolean* variable called a **flag**. We set the flag to *false* before starting the *for* loop that checks for factors. Inside the *for* loop, we set the flag to *true* when we find a factor. In other words, we signal (or flag) the fact that we found a factor. Then after the *for* loop terminates, we check the value of the flag. If it is still *false*, we did not find any factors and the number is prime. Our pseudocode for this program now becomes

```
read first number   // priming read
while number is not 0
{
    print "The factors for number are "
```

```
set flag to false
for factor = 2  to ( number / 2 ) by 1
{
   if number % factor is 0
   {
      print factor and a space
      set flag to true
   }
}

if  flag is false
   print "number is prime"

print a new line

read next number   // update read
}
```

Since we want to read positive numbers only, the lines "read first number" and "read next number" in the pseudocode above will actually be more complex than a simple statement. Indeed, we will prompt the user to enter a positive number until the user does so. In order to do that, we will use a *do/while* loop to validate the input from the user. Therefore, inside the *while* loop, we nest not only a *for* loop, but also a *do/while* loop. In the interest of keeping the pseudocode simple, we did not show that *do/while* loop. However, it is included in the code in Example 6.20 at lines 17–23 and 45–51.

Translating this pseudocode into Java, we get the code shown in Example 6.20; the output of a sample run of the program is shown in Figure 6.29.

Figure 6.29

Output of Finding Factors

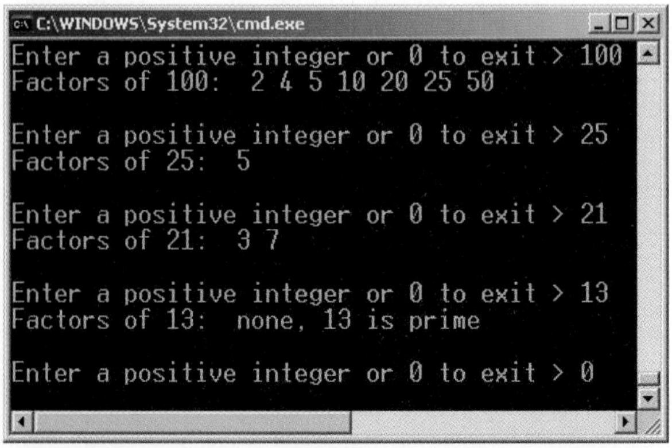

```
C:\WINDOWS\System32\cmd.exe                        _ |□| x|
Enter a positive integer or 0 to exit > 100
Factors of 100:  2 4 5 10 20 25 50

Enter a positive integer or 0 to exit > 25
Factors of 25:   5

Enter a positive integer or 0 to exit > 21
Factors of 21:   3 7

Enter a positive integer or 0 to exit > 13
Factors of 13:   none, 13 is prime

Enter a positive integer or 0 to exit > 0
```

```
1 /* Factors of integers
2    with checks for primes
3    Anderson, Franceschi
4 */
5 import java.util.Scanner;
6
7 public class Factors
8 {
9    public static void main( String [ ] args )
10   {
11     int number;              // positive integer entered by user
12     final int SENTINEL = 0;
13     boolean factorsFound; // flag signals whether factors are found
14
15     Scanner scan = new Scanner( System.in );
16
17     // priming read
18     do
19     {
20       System.out.print( "Enter a positive integer "
21                         + "or 0 to exit > " );
22       number = scan.nextInt( );
23     } while ( number < 0 );
24
25     while ( number != SENTINEL )
26     {
27       System.out.print( "Factors of " + number + ":   " );
28       factorsFound = false;  // reset flag to no factors
29
30       for ( int factor = 2; factor <= number / 2; factor++ )
31       {
32         if ( number % factor == 0 )
33         {
34           System.out.print( factor + " " );
35           factorsFound = true;
36         }
37       } // end of for loop
38
39       if ( ! factorsFound )
40           System.out.print( "none, " + number + " is prime" );
41
42       System.out.println( );  // print a new line
43       System.out.println( );  // print a second new line
44
45       // read next number
46       do
```

```
47        {
48             System.out.print( "Enter a positive integer "
49                              + "or 0 to exit > " );
50             number = scan.nextInt( );
51        } while ( number < 0 );
52    } // end of while loop
53    }
54 }
```

EXAMPLE 6.20   Finding Factors

6.12   Programming Activity 2: Using *for* Loops

In this activity, you will write a *for* loop:

> For this Programming Activity, we will again calculate the total cost of the items in a grocery cart. This time, however, we will write the program for the Express Lane. In this lane, the customer is allowed up to 10 items. The user will be asked for the number of items in the grocery cart. Your job is to write a *for* loop to calculate the total cost of the items in the cart.

Like Programming Activity 1, the framework will animate your *for* loop, displaying the items in the cart moving down a conveyor belt towards a cashier station (a grocery bag). It will also display the unit price of the item, the correct subtotal, and your current subtotal. By comparing the correct subtotal to your subtotal, you will be able to check whether your code is calculating the correct value.

Figure 6.30 demonstrates the animation. The cart contains five items. The third item, a carton of orange juice, is being scanned at a unit price of $3.00, bringing the correct subtotal for the cart to $8.50.

Instructions

Copy the files in the Chapter 6 Programming Activity 2 directory on the CD-ROM accompanying this book to a directory on your computer. Searching for five stars (*****) in the *Cashier.java* code will show you where to add your code. You will add your code inside the *checkout* method of the *Cashier* class (the method header for the *checkout* method has already been coded for you). Example 6.21 shows a fragment of the *Cashier* class, where you will add your code:

```
public void checkout( int numberOfItems )
{
    /* ***** Student writes the body of this method ***** */
```

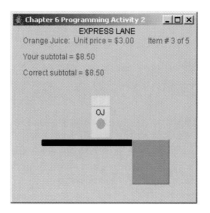

Figure 6.30
Sample Animation

```
//
// The parameter of this method, numberOfItems,
// represents the number of items in the cart. The
// user will be prompted for this number.
//
// Using a for loop, calculate the total price
// of the groceries for the cart.
//
// The getNext method (in this Cashier class) returns the next
// item in the cart, which is an Item object (we do not
// know which item will be returned; this is randomly generated).
// getNext does not take any arguments. Its API is
//     Item getNext( )
//
// As the last statement of the body of your for loop,
// you should call the animate method.
// The animate method takes one parameter:  a double,
// which is your current subtotal.
// For example, if the name of your variable representing
// the current subtotal is total, your call to the animate
// method should be:
//     animate( total );
//
// The getPrice method of the Item class
// returns the price of the Item object as a double.
// The getPrice method does not take any arguments. Its API is
//     double getPrice( )
//
// After you have processed all the items, display the total
// for the cart in a dialog box.
```

```
//
//  End of student code
//
}
```

EXAMPLE 6.21   The *checkout* Method in the *Cashier* Class

To write the body of your *for* loop, you can use the following methods:

- You can access items in the cart using the *getNext* method of the *Cashier* class, which has the following API:

```
Item getNext( )
```

The *getNext* method returns an *Item* object, which represents an *Item* in the cart. As you can see, the *getNext* method does not take any arguments. Since we call the method *getNext* from inside the *Cashier* class, we can simply call the method without an object reference. For example, a call to *getNext* could look like the following:

```
Item newItem;

newItem = getNext( );
```

- After you get a new *Item*, you can "scan" the item to get its price by calling the *getPrice* method of the *Item* class. The *getPrice* method has this API:

```
double getPrice( )
```

Thus, you would get the next item, then get its price using code like the following:

```
Item newItem;
double price;

newItem = getNext( );
price = newItem.getPrice( );
```

When you have finished writing the code for the *checkout* method, compile and run the application from the *Cashier* class. When the application finishes executing, verify that your code is correct by:

- checking that your subtotal matches the correct subtotal displayed
- checking that you have processed all the items in the cart by verifying that the current item number matches the total number of items. For example, if the cart has five items, check that the message in the upper-right corner of the screen displays: Item # 5 of 5.

Troubleshooting

If your method implementation does not animate or animates incorrectly, check these items:

- Verify that you have correctly coded the header of your *for* loop.
- Verify that you have correctly coded the body of the loop.

1. Explain why a *for* loop is appropriate for this activity.

2. Explain how you set up your *for* loop, that is, what initialization statement did you use, what was your condition, and what was the loop update statement?

6.13   Summary

- Looping repeats a set of operations for each input item while a condition is *true*.

- The *while* loop is especially useful for event-controlled looping. The *while* loop executes a set of operations in the loop body as long as the loop condition is *true*. Each execution of the loop body is an iteration of the loop.

- If the loop condition evaluates to *false* the first time it is evaluated, the body of the *while* loop is never executed.

- If the loop condition never evaluates to *false*, the result is an infinite loop.

- In event-controlled looping, processing of items continues until the end of input is signaled either by a sentinel value or by reaching the end of the file.

- A sentinel value is a special input value that signals the end of the items to be processed. With a sentinel value, we perform a priming read before the *while* loop. The body of the loop processes the input, then performs an update read of the next data item.

- When reading data from an input file, we can test whether we have reached the end of the file by calling a *hasNext* method of the *Scanner* class.

SUMMARY

- In the accumulation programming technique, we initialize a total variable to 0 before starting the loop. In the loop body, we add each input value to the total. When the loop completes, the current total is the total for all processed input values.

- In the counting programming technique, we initialize a count variable to 0 before starting the loop. In the loop body, we increment the count variable for each input value that meets our criteria. When the loop completes, the count variable contains the number of items that met our criteria.

- To find an average, we combine accumulation and counting. We add input values to the total and increment the count. When the loop completes, we calculate the average by dividing the total by the count. Before computing the average, however, we should verify that the divisor (that is, the count) is not 0.

- To find the maximum or minimum values in a set of input, we assign the first input to a running maximum or minimum. In the loop body, we compare each input value to our running maximum or minimum. If the input value is less than the running minimum, we assign the input value to the running minimum. Similarly, if the input value is greater than the running maximum, we assign the input value to the running maximum. When the loop completes, the running value is the maximum or minimum value of all the input values.

- To animate an image, the loop body draws the image, pauses for a short interval, erases the image, and changes the starting x or y values to the next location for drawing the image.

- To avoid generating exceptions when the user types characters other than the data type expected, use the *hasNext* methods of the *Scanner* class.

- To construct a loop condition, construct the inverse of the loop termination condition.

- When testing a program that contains a loop, test that the program produces correct results by inputting values and comparing the results with manual calculations. Also test that the results are correct if the *while* loop body never executes. Finally, test the results with input that is invalid.

- The *do/while* loop checks the loop condition after executing the loop body. Thus, the body of a *do/while* loop always executes at least once. This type of loop is useful for validating input.

- The *for* loop is useful for count-controlled loops, that is, loops for which the number of iterations is known when the loop begins.

- When the *for* loop is encountered, the initialization statement is executed. Then the loop condition is evaluated. If the condition is *true,* the loop body is executed. The loop update statement is then executed and the loop condition is reevaluated. Again, if the condition is *true,* the loop body is executed, followed by the loop update, then the reevaluation of the condition, and so on, until the condition evaluates to *false.*

- Typically, we use a loop counting variable in a *for* loop. We set its initial value in the initialization statement, increment or decrement its value in the loop update statement, and check its value in the loop condition.

- The loop update statement can increment or decrement the loop variable by any value.

- In a *for* loop, it is important to test that the starting and ending values of the loop variable are correct. Also test with input for which the *for* loop body does not execute at all.

6.14   Exercises, Problems, and Projects

6.14.1   Multiple Choice Exercises

1. How do you discover that you have an infinite loop in your code?
   - ❏ The code does not compile.
   - ❏ The code compiles and runs but gives the wrong result.
   - ❏ The code runs forever.
   - ❏ The code compiles, but there is a runtime error.

2. If you want to execute a loop body at least once, what type of loop would you use?
   - ❏ *for* loop
   - ❏ *while* loop

❑ *do/while* loop

❑ none of the above

3. What best describes a *for* loop?

❑ It is a count-controlled loop.

❑ It is an event-controlled loop.

❑ It is a sentinel-controlled loop.

4. You can simulate a *for* loop with a *while* loop.

❑ true

❑ false

6.14.2   Reading and Understanding Code

5. What is the output of this code sequence? (The user successively enters 3, 5, and −1)

```
System.out.print( "Enter an int > " );
int i = scan.nextInt( );
while ( i != -1 )
{
    System.out.println( "Hello" );

    System.out.print( "Enter an int > " );
    i = scan.nextInt( );
}
```

6. What is the output of this code sequence? (The user successively enters 3, 5, and −1.)

```
int i = 0;
while ( i != -1 )
{
    System.out.println( "Hello" );
    System.out.print( "Enter an int > " );
    i = scan.nextInt( );
}
```

7. What is the output of this code sequence? (The user successively enters 3, 5, and −1.)

```
System.out.print( "Enter an int > " );
int i = scan.nextInt( );
while ( i != -1 )
```

```
{
    System.out.print( "Enter an int > " );
    i = scan.nextInt( );

    System.out.println( "Hello" );
}
```

8. What are the values of *i* and *sum* after this code sequence is executed?

```
int sum = 0;
int i = 17;
while ( i % 10 != 0 )
{
    sum += i;
    i++;
}
```

9. What are the values of *i* and *product* after this code sequence is executed?

```
int i = 6;
int product = 1;
do
{
    product *= i;
    i++;
} while ( i < 9 );
```

10. What are the values of *i* and *product* after this code sequence is executed?

```
int i = 6;
int product = 1;
do
{
    product *= i;
    i++;
} while ( product < 9 );
```

11. What is the output of this code sequence?

```
for ( int i = 0; i < 3; i++ )
    System.out.println( "Hello" );
System.out.println( "Done" );
```

12. What is the output of this code sequence?

```
for ( int i = 0; i <= 2; i++ )
    System.out.println( "Hello" );
System.out.println( "Done" );
```

13. What is the value of *i* after this code sequence is executed?

```java
int i = 0;
for ( i = 0; i <= 2; i++ )
    System.out.println( "Hello" );
```

14. What is the value of *i* after this code sequence is executed?

```java
int i = 0;
for ( i = 0; i < 2034; i++ )
    System.out.println( "Hello" );
```

15. What are the values of *i* and *sum* after this code sequence is executed?

```java
int i = 0;
int sum  = 0;
for ( i = 0; i < 5; i++ )
{
    sum += i;
}
```

16. What are the values of *i* and *sum* after this code sequence is executed?

```java
int i = 0;
int sum  = 0;
for ( i = 0; i < 40; i++ )
{
    if ( i % 10 == 0 )
        sum += i;
}
```

17. What is the value of *sum* after this code sequence is executed?

```java
int sum  = 0;
for ( int i = 1; i < 10; i++ )
{
    i++;
    sum += i;
}
```

18. What is the value of *sum* after this code sequence is executed?

```java
int sum  = 0;
for ( int i = 10; i > 5; i-- )
{
    sum += i;
}
```

19. What is printed when this code sequence is executed?

```java
for ( int i = 0; i < 5; i++ )
```

```
{
    System.out.println( Math.max( i, 3 ) );
}
```

20. What are the values of *i* and *sum* after this code sequence is executed?

```
int i = 0;
int sum  = 0;
while ( i != 7 )
{
    sum += i;
    i++;
}
```

6.14.3   Fill in the Code

21. This *while* loop generates random integers between 3 and 7 until a 5 is generated and prints them all out, excluding 5.

```
int i = (int) ( 5 * Math.random( ) + 3 );
// your code goes here
```

22. This *while* loop takes an integer input from the user, then prompts for additional integers and prints all integers that are greater than or equal to the original input until the user enters 20, which is not printed.

```
System.out.print( "Enter a starting integer > " );

int start = scan.nextInt( );

// your code goes here
```

23. This *while* loop takes integer values as input from the user and finds the sum of those integers until the user types in the value −1 (which is not added).

```
System.out.print( "Enter an integer value, "
                    + "enter -1 to stop > " );
int value = scan.nextInt( );
// your code goes here
```

24. This loop calculates the sum of the first four positive multiples of 7 using a *while* loop (the sum will be equal to $7 + 14 + 21 + 28 = 70$)

```
int sum = 0;
int countMultiplesOf7 = 0;
int count = 1;
// your code goes here
```

25. This loop takes words as input from the user and concatenates them until the user types in the word "end" (which is not concatenated). The code then outputs the concatenated *String*.

```
String sentence = "";
String word;
// your code goes here

while ( ! word.equals( "end" ) )
{
    // and your code goes here

}
System.out.println( "The sentence is " + sentence );
```

26. This loop reads integers from a file (already associated with the *Scanner* object reference *scan*) and computes the sum. We don't know how many integers are in the file.

```
int sum = 0;
// your code goes here
```

27. Here is a *while* loop; write the equivalent *for* loop.

```
int i = 0;
while ( i < 5 )
{
    System.out.println( "Hi there" );
    i++;
}

// your code goes here
```

28. This loop reads integers from the user until the user enters either 0 or 100. Then it prints the sum of the numbers entered (excluding the 0 or 100).

```
// your code goes here
```

29. This loop calculates the sum of the integers from 1 to 5 using a *for* loop.

```
int sum = 0;
// your code goes here
```

6.14.4   Identifying Errors in Code

30. Where is the problem with this code sequence (although this code sequence does compile)?

```
int i = 0;
while ( i < 3 )
    System.out.println( "Hello" );
```

31. Where is the error in this code sequence that is supposed to read and echo integers until the user enters –1? (The –1 should not be echoed.)

```
int num;
while ( num != -1 )
{
    System.out.print( "Enter an integer > " );
    num = scan.nextInt( );
    System.out.println( num );
}
```

32. The following code sequence intends to print *Hello* three times; however, it does not. Where is the problem in this code sequence?

```
for ( int i = 0; i < 3; i++ );
    System.out.println( "Hello" );
```

33. Where is the error in this code sequence which is intended to print *Hello* 10 times?

```
for ( int i = 10; i > 0; i++ )
    System.out.println( "Hello" );
```

34. Where is the problem with this code sequence? The code is intended to generate random numbers between 1 and 10 until the number is either a 7 or a 5.

```
int number =  1 + (int) ( Math.random( ) * 10 );
while ( number != 5 || number != 7 )
{
    number =  1 + (int) ( Math.random( ) * 10 );
}
System.out.println( "The number is " + number );
```

35. Where is the error with this code sequence?

```
int sum = 0;
for ( int i = 1; i < 6; i++ )
    sum += i;

System.out.println( "The value of i is " + i );
```

6.14.5   Debugging Area—Using Messages from the *javac* Compiler and Java JVM

36. You coded the following in the class *Test.java*:

```
int i = 0;
int sum = 0;
do
{
    sum += i;
} while ( i < 3 )    // line 10
```

At compile time, you get the following error:

```
Test.java:10: ';' expected
while( i < 3 )   // line 10
              ^

1 error
```

Explain what the problem is and how to fix it.

37. You coded the following in the class *Test.java*:

```
int i = 0;
while ( i < 3 )
{
   System.out.println( "Hello" );
   i--;
}
```

The code compiles but never terminates.

Explain what the problem is and how to fix it.

38. You coded the following in the class *Test.java*:

```
for ( int i = 0; i++; i < 3 )     // line 5
   System.out.println( "Hello" );
```

At compile time, you get the following error:

```
Test.java:5: not a statement
for ( int i = 0; i++; i < 3 )     // line 5
                   ^

1 error
```

Explain what the problem is and how to fix it.

39. You coded the following in the class *Test.java*:

```
for ( int i = 1; i < 3; i++ )         // line 5
   System.out.println( "Hello" );
```

The code compiles and runs, but only prints *Hello* twice, whereas we expected to print *Hello* three times.

Explain what the problem is and how to fix it.

40. You coded the following in the class *Test.java*:

```
int product = 1;
for ( int i = 1, i < 5, i++ )          // line 8
    product *= i;
System.out.println( "Product is " + product ); // line 10
```

At compile time, you get the following errors:

```
Test.java:8: ';' expected
for ( int i = 1, i < 5, i++ ) // line 8
               ^
Test.java:10: ')' expected
System.out.println( "Product is " + product ); // line 10
                                           ^
2 errors
```

Explain what the problem is and how to fix it.

41. You coded the following in the class *Test.java*:

```
for ( int i = 0; i < 3; i++ )
    System.out.println( "Hello" );
System.out.println( "i = " + i );   // line 8
```

At compile time, you get the following error:

```
Test.java:8: cannot find symbol
symbol  : variable i
location: class Test
        System.out.println( "i = " + i ); // line 8
                                     ^
1 error
```

Explain what the problem is and how to fix it.

42. You coded the following in the class *Test.java*:

```
int i = 0;
for ( int i = 0; i < 3; i++ ) // line 6
    System.out.println( "Hello" );
```

At compile time, you get the following error:

```
Test.java:6: i is already defined in main( java.lang.String[] )
```

```
for( int i = 0; i < 3; i++ )       // line 6
             ^
1 error
```

Explain what the problem is and how to fix it.

6.14.6   Write a Short Program

43. Write a program that prompts the user for a value greater than 10 as an input (you should loop until the user enters a valid value) and finds the square root of that number and the square root of the result, and continues to find the square root of the result until we reach a number that is smaller than 1.01. The program should output how many times the square root operation was performed.

44. Write a program that expects a word containing the @ character as an input. If the word does not contain an @ character, then your program should keep prompting the user for a word. When the user types in a word containing an @ character, the program should simply print the word and terminate.

45. Write a program that reads *double* values from a file named *input.txt* and outputs the average.

46. Write a program that outputs the sum of all the integers between 10 and 20, inclusive, that is, 10 + 11 + 12 ... + 19 + 20.

47. Write a program that outputs the product of all the integers between 3 and 7, inclusive, that is, 3 * 4 * 5 * 6 * 7.

48. Write a program that counts how many multiples of 7 are between 33 and 97, inclusive.

49. Write a program that reads a value (say *n*) from the user and outputs *Hello World n* times. Verify that the user has entered an integer. If the input is 3, the output will be *Hello World* printed three times.

50. Write a program that takes a word as an input from the keyboard and outputs each character in the word, separated by a space.

51. Write a program that takes a value as an input from the keyboard and outputs the factorial of that number; the factorial of an integer *n* is *n* * (*n*–1) * (*n*–2) * ... * 3 * 2 * 1. For instance, the factorial of 4 is 4 * 3 * 2 * 1, or 24.

52. Using a loop, write a program that takes 10 integer values from the keyboard and outputs the minimum value of all the values entered.

53. Write an applet that displays a rectangle moving horizontally from the right side of the window to the left side of the window.

6.14.7   Programming Projects

54. Write a program that inputs a word representing a binary number (0s and 1s). First, your program should verify that it is indeed a binary number, that is, the number contains only 0s and 1s. If that is not the case, your program should print a message that the number is not a valid binary number. Then, your program should count how many 1s are in that word and output the count.

55. Perform the same operations as question 54, with the following modification: If the word does not represent a valid binary number, the program should keep prompting the user for a new word until a word representing a valid binary number is input by the user.

56. Write a program that inputs a word representing a binary number (0s and 1s). First, your program should check that it is indeed a binary number, that is, the number contains only 0s and 1s. If that is not the case, your program should output that the number is not a valid binary number. If that word contains exactly two 1s, your program should output that that word is "accepted," otherwise that it is "rejected."

57. Perform the same operations as question 56 with the following modification: If the word does not represent a valid binary number, the program should keep prompting the user for a new word until a word representing a valid binary number is input by the user.

58. Write a program that inputs a word representing a binary number (0s and 1s). First, your program should check that it is indeed a binary number, that is, that it contains only 0s and 1s. If that is not the case, your program should output that the number is not a valid binary number. If that word contains at least three consecutive 1s, your program should output that that word is "accepted," otherwise that it is "rejected."

59. Perform the same operations as question 58 with the following modification: If the word does not represent a valid binary number, the

program should keep prompting the user for a new word until a word representing a valid binary number is input by the user.

60. Write a program that takes Web site names as keyboard input until the user types the word *stop* and counts how many of the Web site names are commercial Web site names (i.e., end with *.com*), then outputs that count.

61. Using a loop, write a program that takes 10 values representing exam grades (between 0 and 100) from the keyboard and outputs the minimum value, maximum value, and average value of all the values entered. Your program should not ignore values less than 0 or greater than 100.

62. Write a program that takes an email address as an input from the keyboard and, using a loop, steps through every character looking for an @ sign. If the email address has exactly one @ character, then print a message that the email address is valid; otherwise, print a message that it is invalid.

63. Write a program that takes a user ID as an input from the keyboard and steps through every character, counting how many digits are in the user ID; if there are exactly two digits, output that the user ID is valid, otherwise that it is invalid.

64. Write a program that takes an integer value as an input and converts that value to its binary representation; for instance, if the user inputs 17, then the output will be 10001.

65. Write a program that takes a word representing a binary number (0s and 1s) as an input and converts it to its decimal representation; for instance, if the user inputs 101, then the output will be 5; you can assume that the *String* is guaranteed to contain only 0s and 1s.

66. Write a program that simulates an XOR operation. The input should be a word representing a binary number (0s and 1s). Your program should XOR all the digits from left to right and output the results as "True" or "False." In an XOR operation, *a* XOR *b* is *true* if *a* or *b* is *true* but not both; otherwise, it is *false*. In this program, we will consider the character "1" to represent true and a "0" to represent false. For instance, if the input is 1011, then the output will be 1 (1 XOR 0 is 1, then 1 XOR 1 is 0, then 0 XOR 1 is 1, which causes the output to

be "True"). You can assume that the input word is guaranteed to contain only 0s and 1s.

67. Write a program that takes a sentence as an input (using a dialog box) and checks whether that sentence is a palindrome. A palindrome is a word, phrase, or sentence that is symmetrical; that is, it is spelled the same forward and backward. Examples are "otto," "mom," and "Able was I ere I saw Elba." Your program should be case-insensitive; that is, "Otto" should also be counted as a palindrome.

68. Write a program that takes an HTML-like sequence as an input (using a dialog box) and checks whether that sequence has the same number of opening brackets (<) and closing brackets (>).

69. Write an applet that shows a small circle getting bigger and bigger. Your applet should allow the user to input the starting radius and the ending radius (and also verify that the starting radius is smaller than the ending radius).

6.14.8   Technical Writing

70. In programming, a programmer can make syntax errors that lead to a compiler error; these errors can then be corrected. Other errors can lead to a runtime error; these errors can also be corrected. Logic errors, however, can lead to an incorrect result or no result at all. Discuss examples of logic errors that can be made when coding loops and the consequences of these logic errors.

71. Discuss how you would detect whether you have an infinite loop in your code.

6.14.9   Group Project

72. Often on a Web page, the user is asked to supply personal information, such as a telephone number. Your program should take an input from the keyboard representing a telephone number. We will consider that the input is a valid telephone number if it contains exactly 10 digits and any number of dash (-) and whitespace characters. Keep prompting the user for a telephone number until the user gives you a valid one. Once you have a valid telephone number, you should assume that the digits (only the digits, not the hyphen[s] nor the whitespace) in the telephone number may have been encrypted by shifting each number by a constant value. For instance, if the shift is

2, a 0 becomes a 2, a 1 becomes a 3, a 2 becomes a 4, . . . , an 8 becomes a 0, and a 9 becomes a 1. However, we know that the user is from New York where the decrypted area code (after the shift is applied), represented by the first three digits of the input, is 212. Your program needs to decrypt the telephone number and output the decrypted telephone number with the format 212-xxx-xxxx, as well as the shift value of the encryption. If there was an error in the input and the area code cannot be decrypted to 212, you should output that information.

CHAPTER 7

Object-Oriented Programming, Part 2: User-Defined Classes

CHAPTER CONTENTS

Introduction

When you see the title of this chapter, you might say, "Finally, we get to write our own classes." Actually, we've been writing classes all along. All Java source code belongs to a class. The classes we've been writing are application and applet classes. Now it's time to write some service classes—classes that encapsulate data and methods for use by applications, applets, or even other service classes. These are called **user-defined classes** because we, rather than the Java authors, create them.

First, let's take a moment to examine why we want to create user-defined classes.

We have written a lot of programs using Java's primitive data types (*boolean, char, int, double*, etc.), but the real world requires manipulation of more complex data than just individual *booleans* or *ints*. For example, if you are the programmer for an online bookstore, you will need to manipulate data associated with books. Books typically have an ISBN, a title, an author, a price, an in-stock quantity, and perhaps other pieces of data. We can create a *Book* class so that each object will hold the data for one book. For example, the ISBN, the title, and the author can be represented by *Strings*, the price by a *double*, and the in-stock quantity by an *int*. If we create this *Book* class, our program will be able to store and manipulate all the data of a book as a whole. This is one of the concepts of object-oriented programming.

By incorporating into the class the methods that work with the book data, we also are able to hide the details involved with handling that data. An application can simply call the methods as needed. Thus, creating your own classes can simplify your program.

Finally, a well-written class can be reused in other programs. Thus, user-defined classes speed up development.

7.1   Defining a Class

Classes encapsulate the data and functionality for a person, place, or thing, or more generally, an object. For example, a class might be defined to represent a student, a college, or a course.

To define a class, we use the following syntax:

```
accessModifier class ClassName
{
    // class definition goes here
}
```

This syntax should look familiar as the first line in our applications and applets. You may also notice that our class names have been nouns and have started with a capital letter: *Astronaut, Calculator, CellService,* and so forth. These names follow the conventions encouraged by the Java developers.

SOFTWARE ENGINEERING TIP

Use a noun for the class name and start the class name with a capital letter.

Inside the curly braces we define the data of the class, called its **fields**, and the methods. An important function performed by the class methods is maintaining the values of the class data for the **client programs**, which are the users of the class, in that the clients create objects and call the methods of the class. Our applications and applets have been clients of many Java classes, such as *String, DecimalFormat,* and *Math.* The fields and methods of a class are called the **members** of the class.

For each class and for each member of a class, we need to provide an **access modifier** that specifies where the class or member can be used (see Table 7.1). The possible access modifiers are *public, private,* and *protected,* or no modifier at all, which results in package access. The *public* access modifier allows the class or member to be used, or **referenced**, by methods of the same or other classes. The *private* access modifier specifies that the class or member can be referenced only by methods of the same class. Package access specifies that the

TABLE 7.1   Access Modifiers

Access Modifier	Class or member can be referenced by . . .
public	methods of the same class, as well as methods of other classes
private	methods of the same class only
protected	methods in the same class, as well as methods of subclasses and methods in classes in the same package
no modifier (package access)	methods in the same package only

class or member can be accessed by methods in classes that are in the same package. Later in the chapter, we will learn how to create our own package. We'll defer discussing the *protected* access modifier until Chapter 10, where we cover inheritance.

Typically, the *accessModifier* for a class will be *public*, and we know that a *public* class must be stored in a file named *ClassName.java* where *ClassName* is the name of the class. Not all classes will be *public*, however; we will introduce *private* classes in Chapter 12, where we cover GUIs.

Let's start to define a class that represents an automobile, which we can use to calculate miles per gallon. We'll name the class *Auto*, and we'll use the *public* access modifier so that any application can use this class. The class header will look like the following:

```
public class Auto
{

}
```

When we write a class, we will make known the *public* method names and their APIs so that a client program will know how to instantiate objects and call the methods of the class. We will not publish the implementation (or code) of the class, however. In other words, we will publish the APIs of the methods, but not the method bodies. This is called **data hiding**. A client program can use the class without knowing how the class is implemented, and we, as class authors, can change the implementation of the methods as long as we don't change the interface, or APIs.

7.2   Defining Instance Variables

The instance variables of a class hold the data for each object of that class. Thus, we also say that the instance variables represent the properties of the object. Each object, or instance of a class, gets its own copy of the instance variables, each of which can be given a value appropriate to that object. The values of the instance variables, therefore, can represent the state of the object.

Instance variables are defined using the following syntax:

```
accessModifier dataType identifierList;
```

The *private* modifier is typically used for the nonconstant instance variables of the class. This permits only methods of the same class to set or change the values of the instance variables. In this way, we achieve encapsulation; the class provides a protective shell around the data.

SOFTWARE ENGINEERING TIP

Define instance variables of a class as *private* so that only methods of the class will be able to set or change their values.

The data type of an instance variable can be any of Java's primitive types or a class type.

The *identifierList* consists of one or more names for instance variables of the same data type and can optionally assign initial values to the instance variables. If more than one instance variable name is given, a comma is used as a separator. By convention, identifier names for instance variables are nouns and begin with a lowercase letter; internal words begin with a capital letter. Each instance variable and class variable must be given a name that is unique to the class. It is legal to use the same names for instance variables in different classes, but within a class, the same name cannot be used for more than one instance variable or class variable.

Optionally, you can declare an instance variable to be a constant (*final*).

The following statements are examples of instance variable definitions:

```
private String name = "";    // an empty String
private final int PERFECT_SCORE = 100, PASSING_SCORE = 60;
private int startX, startY, width, height;
```

SOFTWARE ENGINEERING TIP

Use nouns for identifier names for instance variables. Begin the identifier with a lowercase letter and capitalize internal words.

What criteria should you use to select the instance variables of the class? The answer is to select the data that all objects will have in common. For example, for a *Student* class, you might select the student name, grade point average, and projected graduation date. For a *Calculator* class, you might select two operands, an operator, and a result.

Thus, for our *Auto* class, we will define instance variables to hold the model of the automobile, the number of miles the auto has been driven, and the gallons of gas used. Thus, our *Auto* class definition now becomes the following:

```
public class Auto
{
    private String model;
    private int milesDriven;
    private double gallonsOfGas;
}
```

SOFTWARE ENGINEERING TIP

Define instance variables for the data that all objects will have in common.

7.3   Writing Class Methods

We declared the instance variables of the *Auto* class as *private* so that only the methods of the *Auto* class will be able to access or change the values of the instance variables directly. Clients of the *Auto* class will need to use the methods of the class to access or change any of the instance variables. So we'll need to write some methods.

Methods have this syntax:

```
accessModifier returnType methodName( parameter list ) // method header
{
     // method body
}
```

where *parameter list* is a comma-separated list of data types and variable names.

The method header syntax should be familiar because we've seen the API for many class methods. One difference is just a matter of semantics. The method caller sends **arguments**, or **actual parameters**, to the method; the method refers to these arguments as its **formal parameters**.

> **SOFTWARE ENGINEERING TIP**
>
> Use verbs for method names. Begin the method name with a lowercase letter and begin internal words with a capital letter.

Because methods provide a function for the class, typically method names are verbs. Like instance variables, the method name should begin with a lowercase letter with internal words beginning with a capital letter.

The access modifier for methods that provide services to the client will be *public*. Methods that provide services only to other methods of the class are typically declared to be *private*.

> **SOFTWARE ENGINEERING TIP**
>
> Declare methods that provide services to clients as *public*. Methods that will be called only by other methods of the class should be declared *private*.

The return type of a method is the data type of the value that the method returns to the caller. The return type can be any of Java's primitive data types, any class type, or *void*. Methods with a return type of *void* do not return a value to the caller.

The body of each method, which consists of the code that performs the method's function, is written between the beginning and ending curly braces. Unlike *if* statements and loops, however, these curly braces are not optional; the curly braces are required, regardless of the number of statements in the method body.

> **COMMON ERROR TRAP**
>
> Forgetting to enclose the body of a method in curly braces generates one or more compiler errors.

Several compiler errors can result from forgetting one or both of the curly braces. You might receive either of these messages:

```
illegal start of expression
```

or

```
';' expected
```

In the method body, a method can declare variables, call other methods, and use any of the program structures we've discussed: *if/else* statements, *while* loops, *for* loops, *switch* statements, and *do/while* loops.

All objects of a class share one copy of the class methods.

We have actually written methods already. For example, we've written the method *main*. Its definition looks like this:

```
public static void main( String [ ] args )
{
      // application code
}
```

We know that the *static* keyword means that the Java Virtual Machine can call *main* to start the application running without first instantiating an object. The return type is *void* because *main* does not return a value. The parameter list expects one argument, a *String* array. We discuss arrays in the next chapter.

We have not previously written a value-returning method. A value-returning method sends back its results to the caller using a *return* statement in the method body. The syntax for the *return* statement is

```
return expression;
```

As you would expect, the data type of the expression must match the return type of the method. Recall that a value-returning method is called from an expression, and when the method completes its operation, its return value replaces the method call in the expression.

If the data type of the method is *void*, as in *main*, we have a choice of using the *return* statement without an expression, as in this statement:

```
return;
```

or omitting the *return* statement altogether. Given that control automatically returns to the caller when the end of the method is reached, most programmers omit the *return* statement in *void* methods.

7.4 Writing Constructors

A constructor is a special method that is called when an object is instantiated using the *new* keyword. A class can have several constructors. The job of the class constructors is to initialize the fields of the new object.

The syntax for a constructor is the following:

```
accessModifier ClassName( parameter list )
{
    // constructor body
}
```

Notice that a constructor has the same name as the class and has no return type—not even *void*.

It's important to use the *public* access modifier for the constructors so that applications can instantiate objects of the class.

The constructor can either assign default values to the instance variables or the constructor can accept initial values from the client through parameters when the object is instantiated.

Providing a constructor for a class is optional. If you don't write a constructor, the compiler provides a **default constructor**, which is a constructor that takes no arguments. This default constructor assigns default initial values to all instance variables; this is called **autoinitialization**. Numeric variables are given the value of 0, characters are given the value *space*, *boolean* variables are given the value *false*, and object references are given the value *null*. Table 7.2 shows the values the default constructor assigns to instance variables.

If we do provide a constructor, any instance variables our constructor does not initialize will still be given the predefined default value.

TABLE 7.2   Default Initial Values of Instance Variables

Data Type	Initial Value
byte	0
short	0
int	0
long	0
float	0.0
double	0.0
char	space
boolean	false
object reference	null

Example 7.1 shows version 1 of our *Auto* class with two constructors.

```
1 /* Auto class, Version 1
2    Anderson, Franceschi
3 */
4
5 public class Auto
6 {
7    // instance variables
8    private String model;        //  model of auto
9    private int milesDriven;     //  number of miles driven
10   private double gallonsOfGas; //  number of gallons of gas
11
12   // Default constructor:
13   //  initializes model to "unknown";
14   //  milesDriven is autoinitialized to 0
15   //        and gallonsOfGas to 0.0
16   public Auto( )
17   {
18      model = "unknown";
19   }
20
21   // Overloaded constructor:
22   // allows client to set beginning values for
23   //   model, milesDriven, and gallonsOfGas.
24   public Auto( String startModel,
25                int startMilesDriven,
26                double startGallonsOfGas )
27   {
28      model = startModel;
29
30      // validate startMilesDriven parameter
31      if ( startMilesDriven >= 0 )
32         milesDriven = startMilesDriven;
33      else
34      {
35         System.err.println( "Miles driven is negative." );
36         System.err.println( "Value set to 0." );
37      }
38
39      // validate startGallonsOfGas parameter
40      if ( startGallonsOfGas >= 0.0 )
41         gallonsOfGas = startGallonsOfGas;
42      else
```

```
43         {
44               System.err.println( "Gallons of gas is negative" );
45               System.err.println( "Value set to 0.0." );
46         }
47     }
48 }
```

EXAMPLE 7.1   The *Auto* Class, Version 1

Our default constructor (lines 12–19) does not set values for the *miles-Driven* and *gallonsOfGas* instance variables. Because *ints* and *doubles* are autoinitialized to 0 and 0.0, respectively, we just accept those default values.

However, it is necessary for our constructor to set the *model* instance variable to a valid *String* value. Because *Strings* are object references, they are autoinitialized to *null*. Any attempt to call a method using the *model* instance variable with a *null* value would generate a *NullPointerException*.

As mentioned earlier, you can provide multiple constructors for a class. We provide a second constructor (lines 21–47) that lets the client set initial values for all the instance variables. Because the class is the caretaker of its fields, it is the class's responsibility to ensure that the data for each object is valid. Thus, when the constructor sets initial values for the instance variables, it should first check whether its parameters are, indeed, valid values. What constitutes a valid value for any instance variable depends in part on the data type of the variable and in part on the class and is a design decision. For our *Auto* class, we have decided that *milesDriven* and *gallonsOfGas* cannot be negative. If the constructor finds that the *startMilesDriven* or *startGallonsOfGas* parameters are negative, it prints an error message to *System.err*—which by default is the Java console—and sets the instance variables to default values. Some methods in the Java class library generate an exception when a parameter value is invalid; others substitute a default value for the invalid parameter. Again, how your classes handle invalid argument values is a design decision.

 REFERENCE POINT

Exceptions are covered in
Chapter 11.

When we provide multiple constructors, we are **overloading** a method. To overload a method, we provide a method with the same name but with a different number of parameters, or with the same number of parameters but with at least one parameter having a different data type. The name of the method, along with the number, data types, and order of its parameters, is called the method's **signature**. Thus, to overload a method, the new method must have a different signature. Notice that the return type is not part of the signature.

When a client calls a method that is overloaded, Java determines which version of the method to execute by looking at the number, data types, and order of the arguments in the method call. Example 7.2 shows a client program that instantiates three *Auto* objects.

```
 1 /* Auto Client, Version 1
 2    Anderson, Franceschi
 3 */
 4
 5 public class AutoClient
 6 {
 7   public static void main( String [ ] args )
 8   {
 9      System.out.println( "Instantiate sedan" );
10      Auto sedan = new Auto( );
11
12      System.out.println( "\nInstantiate suv" );
13      Auto suv = new Auto( "Trailblazer", 7000, 437.5 );
14
15      System.out.println( "\nInstantiate mini" );
16      // attempt to set invalid value for gallons of gas
17      Auto mini = new Auto( "Mini Cooper", 200, -1.0 );
18   }
19 }
```

EXAMPLE 7.2   The *Auto* Client, Version 1

Line 10 causes the default constructor to be called because no arguments are passed to the constructor. Line 13 causes the overloaded constructor to be called because it passes three arguments to the constructor. If the client attempted to instantiate a new object with a number of parameters other than 0 or 3, the compiler would generate an error because there is no constructor that matches those arguments. In general, the arguments sent to an overloaded method must match the formal parameters of some version of that method.

The number of constructors you provide is a design decision and depends on the class. Providing multiple constructors gives the client a choice of ways to create an object. It is good practice to provide, at minimum, a default constructor. The reason for this will become clear as we explore

 **SOFTWARE ENGINEERING TIP**

Provide, at the minimum, a default constructor and a constructor that accepts initial values for all instance variables.

Figure 7.1

Output from *Auto* Client, Version 1

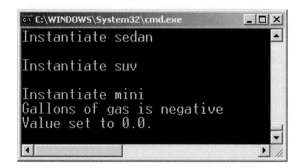

classes in more depth. It is also good practice to provide another constructor that accepts values for all the instance variables.

On line 17, we instantiate an *Auto* object with an invalid argument for gallons of gas. As Figure 7.1 shows, the constructor prints an error message. The object is still created, but the value of its *gallonsOfGas* instance variable is 0.0.

Beware of this common error: declaring a *void* return type for a constructor. Remember that constructors have no return type at all. For example, the following invalid constructor definition declares a return type of *void:*

```
// Error! void return value specified
public void Auto( String model,
                  int startMilesDriven,
                  double startGallonsOfGas )
{
    // body of constructor
}
```

This is a difficult error to find. The class file will compile without an error because the compiler doesn't recognize this method as a constructor. Instead, the client program will get a compiler error when it attempts to instantiate an *Auto* object. For example, this statement in a client program

```
Auto gm = new Auto( "Prius", 350, 15.5 );
```

would generate this compiler error:

```
C:\AutoClient.java:15: cannot find symbol
symbol  : constructor Auto (java.lang.String,int,double)
location: class Auto
        Auto gm = new Auto("Prius", 350, 15.5 );
                      ^
1 error
```

COMMON ERROR TRAP

Specifying a return value for a constructor will cause a compiler error in the client program when the client attempts to instantiate an object of that class.

Notice that both constructors access the instance variables directly. Instance variables have **class scope**, which means that they can be accessed anywhere in the class. The **scope** of an identifier is the range of code in which that identifier can be accessed. Thus, any method of the class can access any of the instance variables directly. In our *Auto* class, any method can access the instance variables *model*, *milesDriven*, and *gallonsOfGas*.

Methods have class scope as well. Any method can call any of the other methods in the class, regardless of whether the methods have been declared *private*, *public*, or *protected*.

In addition to accessing the instance variables, a method can also access its own parameters. When a method begins executing, its parameters have been declared and have been given the values of the arguments sent by the caller of the method.

The parameters have **local scope** in that a method can access its parameters directly. We call this local scope because the parameters are local to a method; that is, a method can access its own parameters, but attempting to access another method's parameters generates a compiler error.

Table 7.3 summarizes the rules of scope.

Attempting to use an identifier that is not in scope will generate the following compiler error:

```
cannot find symbol
```

TABLE 7.3   Rules of Scope

A method in a class can access
• the instance variables of its class
• any parameters sent to the method
• any variable the method declares within its body from the point of declaration until the end of the method or until the end of the block in which the variable was declared, whichever comes first
• any methods in the class

You may wonder why the compiler calls an identifier a **symbol**. The Java compiler generates a **symbol table** as it reads your code. Each identifier you declare is put into the symbol table, along with the identifier's data type and where in the program it was defined. This symbol table allows the compiler to track the identifiers that are in scope at any given time. Thus, if an identifier is not in scope, the compiler will not be able to find that symbol in its table for that section of code.

When the client in Example 7.2 runs, it instantiates three objects, but there is nothing more our application can do with them. To allow our client to manipulate the *Auto* objects further, we need to provide more methods.

Skill Practice
with these end-of-chapter questions

7.18.1 Multiple Choice Exercises

Questions 1, 2, 3, 4, 5, 6, 7

7.18.3 Fill in the Code

Questions 28, 30, 31

7.18.5 Debugging Area

Questions 47, 48, 49

7.18.8 Technical Writing

Question 73

7.5 Writing Accessor Methods

Because clients cannot directly access *private* instance variables of a class, classes usually provide *public* accessor methods for the instance variables. These methods have a simple, almost trivial, standard form:

```
public returnType getInstanceVariable( )
{
   return instanceVariable;
}
```

The standard name of the method is *get*, followed by the instance variable's name with an initial capital letter. The method takes no arguments and simply returns the current value of the instance variable. Thus, the return type is the same data type as the instance variable.

You can see this simple pattern in the accessor methods for version 2 of our *Auto* class, shown in Example 7.3 (lines 49–68).

```
1 /* Auto class, Version 2
2    Anderson, Franceschi
3 */
4
5 public class Auto
6 {
7     // instance variables
8     private String model;        //  model of auto
9     private int milesDriven;     //  number of miles driven
10    private double gallonsOfGas; //  number of gallons of gas
11
12    // Default constructor:
13    //   initializes model to "unknown";
14    //   milesDriven is autoinitialized to 0
15    //         and gallonsOfGas to 0.0
16    public Auto( )
17    {
18        model = "unknown";
19    }
20
21    // Overloaded constructor:
22    // allows client to set beginning values for
23    //    model, milesDriven, and gallonsOfGas.
24    public Auto( String startModel,
25                 int startMilesDriven,
26                 double startGallonsOfGas )
27    {
28        model = startModel;
29
30        // validate startMilesDriven parameter
31        if ( startMilesDriven >= 0 )
32           milesDriven = startMilesDriven;
33        else
34        {
35           System.err.println( "Miles driven is negative." );
36           System.err.println( "Value set to 0." );
37        }
```

```
38
39        // validate startGallonsOfGas parameter
40        if ( startGallonsOfGas >= 0.0 )
41            gallonsOfGas = startGallonsOfGas;
42        else
43        {
44            System.err.println( "Gallons of gas is negative" );
45            System.err.println( "Value set to 0.0." );
46        }
47    }
48
49    // Accessor method:
50    // returns current value of model
51    public String getModel( )
52    {
53        return model;
54    }
55
56    // Accessor method:
57    // returns current value of milesDriven
58    public int getMilesDriven( )
59    {
60        return milesDriven;
61    }
62
63    // Accessor method:
64    //  returns current value of gallonsOfGas
65    public double getGallonsOfGas( )
66    {
67        return gallonsOfGas;
68    }
69 }
```

EXAMPLE 7.3   *Auto* Class, Version 2

In the client code in Example 7.4, we've added a few statements to call the accessor methods for the two *Auto* objects we've instantiated. Then we print the values, as shown in Figure 7.2.

```
1 /* Auto Client, version 2
2    Anderson, Franceschi
3 */
4
5 public class AutoClient
```

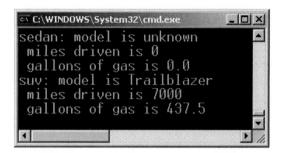

Figure 7.2
Output from *Auto* Client, Version 2

```
6  {
7      public static void main( String [ ] args )
8      {
9          Auto sedan = new Auto( );
10         String sedanModel = sedan.getModel( );
11         int sedanMiles = sedan.getMilesDriven( );
12         double sedanGallons = sedan.getGallonsOfGas( );
13         System.out.println( "sedan: model is " + sedanModel
14                     + "\n miles driven is " + sedanMiles
15                     + "\n gallons of gas is " + sedanGallons );
16
17         Auto suv = new Auto( "Trailblazer", 7000, 437.5 );
18         String suvModel = suv.getModel( );
19         int suvMiles = suv.getMilesDriven( );
20         double suvGallons = suv.getGallonsOfGas( );
21         System.out.println( "suv: model is " + suvModel
22                     + "\n miles driven is " + suvMiles
23                     + "\n gallons of gas is " + suvGallons );
24     }
25 }
```

EXAMPLE 7.4   *Auto* Client, Version 2

 **SOFTWARE ENGINEERING TIP**

Provide *public* accessor methods for any instance variable for which the client should be able to retrieve the value. Each accessor method returns the current value of the corresponding instance variable.

Because the *sedan* object was instantiated by calling the default constructor, its model is *unknown* and the miles driven and gallons of gas are set to default values. On the other hand, the *suv* object data reflects the values sent to the overloaded constructor when the *suv* object was instantiated.

Thus, version 2 of our *Auto* class lets our clients instantiate objects and get the values of the instance variables. But we still need to give the client a way to change the instance variables. In order to do this, we provide mutator methods.

7.6   Writing Mutator Methods

As we have discussed, we declare the instance variables as *private* to encapsulate the data of the class: We allow only the class methods to directly set the values of the instance variables. Thus, it is customary to provide a *public* **mutator** method for any instance variable that the client will be able to change.

The general form of a mutator method is the following:

```
public void setInstanceVariable( dataType newValue )
{
    // validate newValue, then assign to the instance variable
}
```

SOFTWARE ENGINEERING TIP

Provide a mutator method for any instance variable that you want to allow the client to change. If the argument sent to the method is not a valid value for the instance variable, one option is for the mutator method to print a message to *System.err* and leave the value of the instance variable unchanged.

We declare mutator methods as *public* so that client programs can use the methods to change the values of the instance variables. We do not return a value, so we declare the return type as *void*. By convention, the name of each mutator method starts with the lowercase word, *set*, followed by the instance variable name with an initial capital letter. For obvious reasons, the data type of the method's parameter should match the data type of the instance variable being set.

Whenever possible, the body of your mutator method should validate the parameter value passed by the client. If the parameter value is valid, the mutator assigns that value to the instance variable; otherwise, one option is for the mutator to print a message on the system error device (*System.err*), which, by default, is the Java console.

Example 7.5 shows version 3 of our *Auto* class.

```
 1 /* Auto class, Version 3
 2    Anderson, Franceschi
 3 */
 4
 5 public class Auto
 6 {
 7    // instance variables
 8    private String model;          //  model of auto
 9    private int milesDriven;       //  number of miles driven
10    private double gallonsOfGas;   //  number of gallons of gas
11
12    // Default constructor:
13    //  initializes model to "unknown";
```

```
14      //  milesDriven is autoinitialized to 0
15      //        and gallonsOfGas to 0.0
16      public Auto( )
17      {
18        model = "unknown";
19      }
20
21      // Overloaded constructor:
22      // allows client to set beginning values for
23      //   model, milesDriven, and gallonsOfGas.
24      public Auto( String startModel,
25                     int startMilesDriven,
26                     double startGallonsOfGas )
27      {
28        model = startModel;
29        setMilesDriven( startMilesDriven );
30        setGallonsOfGas( startGallonsOfGas );
31      }
32
33      // Accessor method:
34      // returns current value of model
35      public String getModel( )
36      {
37        return model;
38      }
39
40      // Accessor method:
41      // returns current value of milesDriven
42      public int getMilesDriven( )
43      {
44        return milesDriven;
45      }
46
47      // Accessor method:
48      //  returns current value of gallonsOfGas
49      public double getGallonsOfGas( )
50      {
51        return gallonsOfGas;
52      }
53
54      // Mutator method:
55      // allows client to set model
56      public void setModel( String newModel )
57      {
```

```
58        model = newModel;
59    }
60
61    // Mutator method:
62    // allows client to set value of milesDriven;
63    // prints an error message if new value is less than 0
64    public void setMilesDriven( int newMilesDriven )
65    {
66      if ( newMilesDriven >= 0 )
67        milesDriven = newMilesDriven;
68      else
69      {
70        System.err.println( "Miles driven cannot be negative." );
71        System.err.println( "Value not changed." );
72      }
73    }
74
75    // Mutator method:
76    // allows client to set value of gallonsOfGas;
77    // prints an error message if new value is less than 0.0
78    public void setGallonsOfGas( double newGallonsOfGas )
79    {
80      if ( newGallonsOfGas >= 0.0 )
81        gallonsOfGas = newGallonsOfGas;
82      else
83      {
84        System.err.println( "Gallons of gas cannot be negative." );
85        System.err.println( "Value not changed." );
86      }
87    }
88 }
```

EXAMPLE 7.5   *Auto* Class, Version 3

SOFTWARE ENGINEERING TIP

Write the validation code for instance variables in mutator methods and have the constructor call the mutator methods to set initial values.

The mutator methods for the *milesDriven* (lines 61–73) and *gallonsOfGas* (lines 75–87) instance variables validate that the parameter value is greater than 0. If not, the methods print a message to *System.err* and do not change the value of the instance variable. In previous versions of our *Auto* class, the constructor performed the same validation. Now that the mutator methods perform this validation, the constructor can call the mutator methods to set initial values. In this way, we eliminate duplicate code; the validation of each parameter's value is performed in one place. If later we decide to impose other restrictions on any instance variable's value, we will need to change the code in only one place. In this way, a client cannot set invalid values for *milesDriven* or *gallonsOfGas*, either when the object is instantiated or by calling a mutator method.

```
1  /* Auto Client, Version 3
2     Anderson, Franceschi
3  */
4
5  public class AutoClient
6  {
7    public static void main( String [ ] args )
8    {
9      Auto suv = new Auto( "Trailblazer", 7000, 437.5 );
10
11     // print initial values of instance variables
12     System.out.println( "suv: model is " + suv.getModel( )
13             + "\n miles driven is " + suv.getMilesDriven( )
14             + "\n gallons of gas is " + suv.getGallonsOfGas( ) );
15
16     // call mutator method for each instance variable
17     suv.setModel( "Sportage" );
18     suv.setMilesDriven( 200 );
19     suv.setGallonsOfGas( 10.5 );
20
21     // print new values of instance variables
22     System.out.println( "\nsuv: model is " + suv.getModel( )
23             + "\n miles driven is " + suv.getMilesDriven( )
24             + "\n gallons of gas is " + suv.getGallonsOfGas( ) );
25
26     // attempt to set invalid value for milesDriven
27     suv.setMilesDriven( -1 );
28     // print current values of instance variables
29     System.out.println( "\nsuv: Model is " + suv.getModel( )
30             + "\n miles driven is " + suv.getMilesDriven( )
31             + "\n gallons of gas is " + suv.getGallonsOfGas( ) );
32   }
33 }
```

EXAMPLE 7.6   *Auto* Client, Version 3

In Example 7.6, our client instantiates one *Auto* object, *suv* (line 9), and prints the values of its instance variables (lines 11–14). Then we call each mutator method, setting new values for each instance variable (lines 16–19). We again print the values of the instance variables (lines 21–24) to show that the values have been changed. Then, in line 27, we attempt to set an invalid value for *milesDriven*. As Figure 7.3 shows, the mutator method prints an error message and does not change the value, which we verify by again printing the values of the instance variables (lines 28–31).

When a method begins executing, the parameters have been defined and have been assigned the values sent by the client. When the client calls the *setModel* method at line 17, the *newModel* parameter has the value *Sportage* when the method starts executing.

A common error in writing mutator methods is using the instance variable name for the parameter name. When a method parameter has the same name as an instance variable, the parameter "hides" the instance variable. In other words, the parameter has **name precedence**, so any reference to that name refers to the parameter, not to the instance variable.

For example, the intention in this incorrectly coded method is to set a new value for the *model* instance variable:

```
// Incorrect!  parameter hides instance variable
public void setModel( String model )
{
    model = model;
}
```

Because the parameter, *model*, has the same identifier as the *model* instance variable, the result of this method is to assign the value of the parameter to the parameter! This is called a ***No-op***, which stands for "No operation," because the statement has no effect. To avoid this logic error, choose a different name

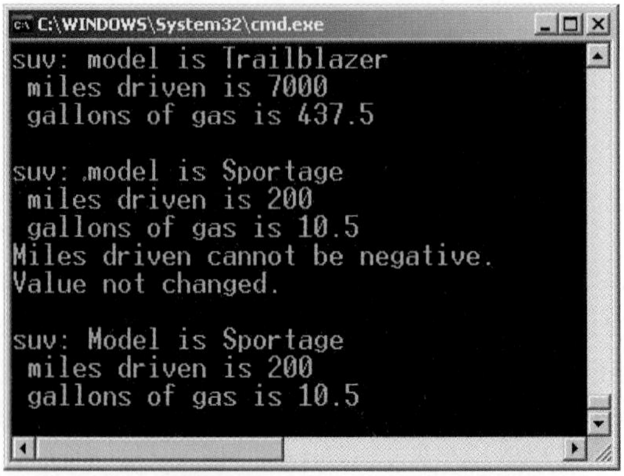

Figure 7.3

Output from *Auto* Client, Version 3

```
C:\WINDOWS\System32\cmd.exe
suv: model is Trailblazer
 miles driven is 7000
 gallons of gas is 437.5

suv: model is Sportage
 miles driven is 200
 gallons of gas is 10.5
Miles driven cannot be negative.
Value not changed.

suv: Model is Sportage
 miles driven is 200
 gallons of gas is 10.5
```

for the parameter. To avoid name conflicts, we name each parameter using the pattern *newInstanceVariable*.

A similar common error is to declare a variable with the same name as the instance variable, as shown in the following incorrectly coded method:

```
// Incorrect! declared local variable hides instance variable
public void setModel( String newModel )
{
      String model; // declared variable hides instance variable
      model = newModel;
}
```

Any variable that a method declares is a local variable because its scope is local to the method. Thus, the declared variable, *model*, is a local variable to the *setModel* method.

With the code shown above, the *model* local variable hides the instance variable with the same name, so the method assigns the parameter value to the local variable, not to the instance variable. The result is that the value of the *model* instance variable is unchanged.

The instance variable, *model*, is defined already in the class. Thus, the method should simply assign the parameter value to the instance variable without attempting to declare the instance variable (again) in the method.

Finally, another common error is declaring the parameter, as shown below:

```
// Incorrect! Declaring the parameter; parameters are declared already
public void setModel( String newModel )
{
      String newModel; // local variable has same name as parameter
      model = newModel;
}
```

This code generates this compiler error:

```
newModel is already defined in setModel(java.lang.String)
```

COMMON ERROR TRAP

Be aware that a method parameter or local variable that has the same name as an instance variable hides the instance variable.

COMMON ERROR TRAP

Do not declare the parameters of a method inside the method body. When the method begins executing, the parameters exist and have been assigned the values set by the client in the method call.

7.7   Writing Data Manipulation Methods

Now we finally get down to the business of the class. Usually you will define a class not only to encapsulate the data, but also to provide some service. Thus, you would provide one or more methods that perform the functionality of the class. These methods might calculate a value based on the instance variables or manipulate the instance variables in some way. The

API of these methods depends on the function being performed. If a method merely manipulates the instance variables, it requires no parameters because instance variables are accessible from any method and, therefore, are in scope.

For example, in our *Auto* class, part of the functionality of our class is to calculate miles per gallon, so we provide a *calculateMilesPerGallon* method in our *Auto* class, version 4, shown in Example 7.7.

```
1   /* Auto class, Version 4
2      Anderson, Franceschi
3   */
4
5   public class Auto
6   {
7       // instance variables
8       private String model;         //  model of auto
9       private int milesDriven;      //  number of miles driven
10      private double gallonsOfGas;  //  number of gallons of gas
11
12      // Default constructor:
13      //   initializes model to "unknown";
14      //   milesDriven is autoinitialized to 0
15      //        and gallonsOfGas to 0.0
16      public Auto( )
17      {
18         model = "unknown";
19      }
20
21      // Overloaded constructor:
22      // allows client to set beginning values for
23      //   model, milesDriven, and gallonsOfGas.
24      public Auto( String startModel,
25                   int startMilesDriven,
26                   double startGallonsOfGas )
27      {
28         model = startModel;
29         setMilesDriven( startMilesDriven );
30         setGallonsOfGas( startGallonsOfGas );
31      }
32
33      // Accessor method:
34      // returns current value of model
35      public String getModel( )
```

```
36        {
37           return model;
38        }
39
40        // Accessor method:
41        // returns current value of milesDriven
42        public int getMilesDriven( )
43        {
44           return milesDriven;
45        }
46
47        // Accessor method:
48        // returns current value of gallonsOfGas
49        public double getGallonsOfGas( )
50        {
51           return gallonsOfGas;
52        }
53
54         // Mutator method:
55         // allows client to set model
56         public void setModel( String newModel )
57         {
58            model = newModel;
59         }
60
61         // Mutator method:
62         // allows client to set value of milesDriven;
63         // prints an error message if new value is less than 0
64         public void setMilesDriven( int newMilesDriven )
65         {
66           if ( newMilesDriven >= 0 )
67              milesDriven = newMilesDriven;
68           else
69           {
70             System.err.println( "Miles driven cannot be negative." );
71             System.err.println( "Value not changed." );
72           }
73         }
74
75         // Mutator method:
76         // allows client to set value of gallonsOfGas;
77         // prints an error message if new value is less than 0.0
78         public void setGallonsOfGas( double newGallonsOfGas )
79         {
80           if ( newGallonsOfGas >= 0.0 )
```

```
81              gallonsOfGas = newGallonsOfGas;
82          else
83          {
84            System.err.println( "Gallons of gas cannot be negative." );
85            System.err.println( "Value not changed." );
86          }
87        }
88
89        // Calculates miles per gallon.
90        //   if no gallons of gas have been used, returns 0.0;
91        //   otherwise, returns miles per gallon
92        //        as milesDriven / gallonsOfGas
93        public double calculateMilesPerGallon( )
94        {
95          if ( gallonsOfGas != 0.0 )
96            return milesDriven / gallonsOfGas;
97          else
98            return 0.0;
99        }
100   }
```

EXAMPLE 7.7   *Auto* Class, Version 4

Our class now provides the method to calculate mileage for an *Auto* object. The *calculateMilesPerGallon* method (lines 89–99) needs no parameters since it accesses only instance variables of the class, which are in scope. As you can see from the code, we guard against dividing by 0 by checking the value of *gallonsOfGas* before using it as the divisor. If *gallonsOfGas* is not equal to zero, we divide *milesDriven* by *gallonsOfGas* and return the result as a *double*. Otherwise, we return 0.0.

Example 7.8 shows a client program that instantiates an *Auto* object, calls the *calculateMilesPerGallon* method, and prints the return value, as shown in Figure 7.4.

Figure 7.4

Output from *Auto* Client, Version 4

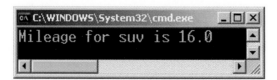

```
 1 /* Auto Client, Version 4
 2    Anderson, Franceschi
 3 */
 4
 5 public class AutoClient
 6 {
 7    public static void main( String [ ] args )
 8    {
 9      Auto suv = new Auto( "Trailblazer", 7000, 437.5 );
10
11      double mileage = suv.calculateMilesPerGallon( );
12      System.out.println( "Mileage for suv is "
13                          + mileage );
14    }
15 }
```

EXAMPLE 7.8   *Auto* Client, Version 4

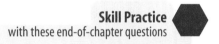

Skill Practice
with these end-of-chapter questions

7.18.1 Multiple Choice Exercises

Questions 8, 9, 10, 11, 12, 13

7.18.2 Reading and Understanding Code

Questions 17, 18, 19, 20, 24, 26

7.18.3 Fill in the Code

Questions 32, 33, 36, 37

7.18.4 Identifying Errors in Code

Questions 38, 39, 43, 45

7.18.5 Debugging Area

Question 52

7.8   Programming Activity 1: Writing a Class Definition, Part 1

In this programming activity, you will write the methods for an *Airport* class. Then you will run a prewritten client program that instantiates several *Airport* objects, calls the methods that you have written, and displays the values of the objects' data.

The *Airport* class has two instance variables: the airport code and the number of gates.

In the Chapter 7 Programming Activity 1 folder on the CD-ROM accompanying this book, you will find three source files: *Airport.java*, *AirportClient.java*, and *Pause.java*, as well as the *.class* files for *AirportClient* and *Pause*. Copy these files to a directory on your computer. Note that all files should be in the same directory.

Load the *Airport.java* source file; you'll notice that the class already contains some source code. The method names and APIs are described in comments. Your job is to define the instance variables and write the methods. It is important that you define the method headers exactly as described, including method name, return value, and parameters, because our *AirportClient* class will call each method to test it. Search for five asterisks in a row (*****). This will position you at the seven places in the class definition where you will add your code. The *Airport.java* code is shown here in Example 7.9.

```
1 /* Airport class
2    Anderson, Franceschi
3 */
4
5 public class Airport
6 {
7    // 1. ***** Define the instance variables   *****
8    //   airportCode is a String
9    //   gates is an integer
10
11
12
13    // 2. ***** Write this method *****
14    // Default constructor:
15    // method name: Airport
```

```
16    // return value:  none
17    // parameters: none
18    // function: sets the airportCode to an empty String
19
20
21
22    // 3. ***** Write this method *****
23    // Overloaded constructor:
24    // method name: Airport
25    // return value: none
26    // parameters:  a String startAirportCode and an int startGates
27    // function:
28    //       calls the setAirportCode method,
29    //       passing startAirportCode parameter;
30    //       calls the setGates method, passing startGates parameter
31
32
33
34
35    // 4. ***** Write this method *****
36    // Accessor method for the airportCode instance variable
37    // method name: getAirportCode
38    // return value: String
39    // parameters: none
40    // function: returns airportCode
41
42
43
44    // 5. ***** Write this method *****
45    // Accessor method for the gates instance variable
46    // method name: getGates
47    // return value: int
48    // parameters: none
49    // function: returns gates
50
51
52
53    // 6. ***** Write this method *****
54    // Mutator method for the airportCode instance variable
55    // method name: setAirportCode
56    // return value: void
57    // parameters: String newAirportCode
```

```
58    // function: assigns airportCode the value of the
59    //           newAirportCode parameter
60
61
62
63    // 7. ***** Write this method *****
64    // Mutator method for the gates instance variable
65    // method name: setGates
66    // return value:  void
67    // parameters: int newGates
68    // function: validates the newGates parameter.
69    //    if newGates is greater than or equal to 0,
70    //        sets gates to newGates;
71    //        otherwise, prints an error message to System.err
72    //        and does not change value of gates
73
74
75
76
77    }  // end of Airport class definition
```

EXAMPLE 7.9   *Airport.java*

When you finish writing the methods for the *Airport* class, compile the source file. When *Airport.java* compiles without errors, load the *Airport-Client.java* file. This source file contains *main*, so you will execute the application from this file. When the application begins, you should see the window shown in Figure 7.5.

Figure 7.5

**Programming Activity 1
Opening Window**

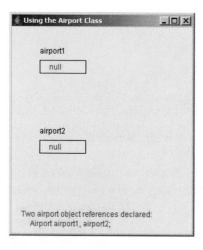

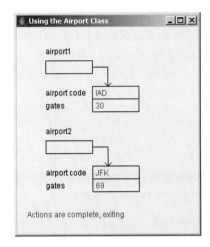

Figure 7.6
AirportClient When
Complete

As you can see, the *AirportClient* has declared two *Airport* object references, *airport1* and *airport2*. The references are *null* because no *Airport* objects have been instantiated.

The client application, *AirportClient*, will instantiate the *Airport* objects and call the methods you have written for the *Airport* class. As the application does its work, it displays a status message at the bottom of the window that indicates which method it has called. It also displays the current values of both *Airport* objects. You can check your work by comparing the values in the objects with the status message. Figure 7.6 shows the *AirportClient* application when it has finished instantiating *Airport* objects and calling *Airport* methods.

? DISCUSSION QUESTIONS

1. Why is *main* in a different source file from the *Airport* class definition?

2. Explain the importance of using standard naming conventions for accessor and mutator methods.

7.9   The Object Reference *this*

When an object is instantiated, a copy of each of the instance variables is created. However, all objects of a class share one copy of the methods. How, then, does a method know for which object the method was called? In other words, how does a method know which instance variables it should get, set, or use to calculate a value? The answer is the special object reference named *this*.

When a method begins executing, the JVM sets the object reference, *this*, to refer to the object for which the method has been called. That object is called the **implicit parameter**. When a method references an instance variable, it will access the instance variable that belongs to the object that the implicit parameter references. In other words, by default, any instance variable referred to by a method is considered to be *this.instanceVariable*.

Preceding an instance variable name with *this* is optional; when just the instance variable name is used (without any object reference), *this* is assumed. Consequently, we usually omit the *this* reference and use just the instance variable name.

However, in methods where you need to avoid ambiguity in variable names, you can precede an instance variable name with *this*. That approach comes in handy as a way to avoid one of the common errors we discussed earlier in the chapter: A parameter to a mutator method with the same name as the instance variable being changed hides the instance variable. We can eliminate this problem by using the *this* reference with the instance variable, which effectively "uncovers" the instance variable name.

For instance, some programmers would code the *setModel* mutator as follows:

```java
public void setModel( String model )
{
   this.model = model;
}
```

Above, we give the parameter, *model*, the same name as the instance variable it represents. Then in the assignment statement, we use the *this* reference to distinguish the instance variable from the parameter. Now it is clear that the parameter value, *model*, should be assigned to the instance variable, *this.model*.

7.10 The *toString* and *equals* Methods

In addition to constructors, mutator methods, and accessor methods, a well-designed class usually implements the *toString* and *equals* methods.

The *toString* method is called automatically when an object reference is used as a *String*. For example, the *toString* method for an object is called when the object reference is used with, or as, a parameter to *System.out.println*. The function of the *toString* method is to return a printable representation of the object data.

The *equals* method is designed to compare two objects for equality; that is, it typically returns *true* if the corresponding instance variables in both objects are equal in value.

All classes inherit a version of the *toString* and the *equals* methods from the *Object* class, but these versions do not provide the functionality we describe earlier. Thus, it is good practice to provide new versions of these methods. To do that, we use the same header as the methods in the *Object* class, but provide a new method body. This is called **overriding a method**. We discuss overriding methods in more detail in Chapter 10, where we cover inheritance.

The *toString* method returns a *String* representing the object's fields and takes no parameters. Its API is the following:

```
public String toString( )
```

Example 7.10 shows version 5 of the *Auto* class with implementations of the *toString* method (lines 98–106) and the *equals* method (lines 108–119).

```
 1 /* Auto class, version 5
 2    Anderson, Franceschi
 3 */
 4
 5 import java.text.DecimalFormat;
 6
 7 public class Auto
 8 {
 9     // instance variables
10     private String model;        //  model of auto
11     private int milesDriven;     //  number of miles driven
12     private double gallonsOfGas; //  number of gallons of gas
13
14     // Constructors:
15     //  initializes model to "unknown";
16     //  milesDriven is autoinitialized to 0
17     //        and gallonsOfGas to 0.0
18     public Auto( )
19     {
20        model = "unknown";
21     }
22
23     // allows client to set beginning values for
24     //   model, milesDriven, and gallonsOfGas.
25     public Auto( String startModel,
26                  int startMilesDriven,
27                  double startGallonsOfGas )
```

```
28     {
29        model = startModel;
30        setMilesDriven( startMilesDriven );
31        setGallonsOfGas( startGallonsOfGas );
32     }
33
34     // Accessor methods:
35     // returns current value of model
36     public String getModel( )
37     {
38        return model;
39     }
40
41     // returns current value of milesDriven
42     public int getMilesDriven( )
43     {
44        return milesDriven;
45     }
46
47     // returns current value of gallonsOfGas
48     public double getGallonsOfGas( )
49     {
50        return gallonsOfGas;
51     }
52
53     // Mutator methods:
54     // allows client to set model
55     public void setModel( String newModel )
56     {
57        model = newModel;
58     }
59
60     // allows client to set value of milesDriven
61     // prints an error message if new value is less than 0
62     public void setMilesDriven( int newMilesDriven )
63     {
64        if ( newMilesDriven >= 0 )
65          milesDriven = newMilesDriven;
66        else
67        {
68          System.err.println( "Miles driven cannot be negative." );
69          System.err.println( "Value not changed." );
70        }
71     }
72
```

```
73   // allows client to set value of gallonsOfGas;
74   // prints an error message if new value is less than 0.0
75   public void setGallonsOfGas( double newGallonsOfGas )
76   {
77     if ( newGallonsOfGas >= 0.0 )
78       gallonsOfGas = newGallonsOfGas;
79     else
80     {
81       System.err.println( "Gallons of gas cannot be negative." );
82       System.err.println( "Value not changed." );
83     }
84   }
85
86   // Calculates miles per gallon.
87   //   if no gallons of gas have been used, returns 0.0;
88   //   otherwise, returns miles per gallon
89   //          as milesDriven / gallonsOfGas
90   public double calculateMilesPerGallon( )
91   {
92     if ( gallonsOfGas != 0.0 )
93       return milesDriven / gallonsOfGas;
94     else
95       return 0.0;
96   }
97
98   // toString: returns a String of instance variable values
99   public String toString( )
100  {
101    DecimalFormat gallonsFormat = new DecimalFormat( "#0.0" );
102    return "Model: " + model
103            + "; miles driven: " + milesDriven
104            + "; gallons of gas: "
105            + gallonsFormat.format( gallonsOfGas );
106  }
107
108  // equals: returns true if fields of parameter object
109  //         are equal to fields in this object
110  public boolean equals( Auto autoA )
111  {
112    if ( model.equals( autoA.model )
113        && milesDriven == autoA.milesDriven
114        && Math.abs( gallonsOfGas - autoA.gallonsOfGas )
115          < 0.0001 )
116      return true;
117    else
```

```
118          return false;
119      }
120 }
```

EXAMPLE 7.10   *Auto* Class, Version 5

In the *toString* method (lines 98–106), we begin by instantiating a *Decimal-Format* object for formatting the gallons of gas as a floating-point number with one decimal place. Note that *gallonsFormat* is a local variable for the *toString* method; that is, only the *toString* method can use the *gallonsFormat* object. To use the *DecimalFormat* class, we import the class on line 5. We then build the *String* to return by concatenating labels for each instance variable with the values of the instance variables. The *toString* method can be used in a client class containing the *main* method, for instance, to print *Auto* objects using a single statement instead of calling all the class accessor methods.

The *equals* method has the following API:

```
public boolean equals( Auto autoA )
```

To implement our *equals* method (lines 108–119), we compare each instance variable in the parameter object, *autoA*, with the same instance variable in the object that was used to call the *equals* method (that is, *this*). We return *true* if the corresponding instance variables in each object have the same values; otherwise, we return *false*.

Notice that line 112 calls the *equals* method of the *String* class to compare the values of *model* in the objects because *model* is a *String* object reference. Notice also that because instance variables are in scope for methods, our *equals* method is able to directly access the instance variables of both this object and the *Auto* object, *autoA*, sent as a parameter.

Example 7.11 puts version 5 of the *Auto* class to work. We instantiate two objects that differ only in the model. On line 10, we explicitly call *toString* to print the fields of the *sporty* object. On line 14, we implicitly call the *toString* method; *toString* is called automatically because the *compact* object is the argument sent to the *println* method, which converts the object to a *String*. On lines 16–19, we compare the two objects using the *equals* method and print the results. The output is shown in Figure 7.7.

```
1  /* Auto Client, version 5
2     Anderson, Franceschi
3  */
4
```

Figure 7.7

Output from Example 7.11

```
C:\WINDOWS\System32\cmd.exe                                    _ □ X
Model: Spyder; miles driven: 0; gallons of gas: 0.0

Model: Accent; miles driven: 0; gallons of gas: 0.0

sporty and compact are not equal
```

```
5  public class AutoClient
6  {
7    public static void main( String [ ] args )
8    {
9        Auto sporty = new Auto( "Spyder", 0, 0.0 );
10       System.out.println( sporty.toString( ) );
11
12       Auto compact = new Auto( "Accent", 0, 0.0 );
13       System.out.println( );
14       System.out.println( compact );
15
16       if ( compact.equals( sporty ) )
17         System.out.println( "\nsporty and compact are equal" );
18       else
19         System.out.println( "\nsporty and compact are not equal" );
20     }
21 }
```

EXAMPLE 7.11   *Auto* Client, Version 5

CODE IN ACTION

In the Chapter 7 folder on the CD-ROM included with this book, you will find a Shockwave movie showing a step-by-step illustration of defining a class. Double-click on *Oop.html* to start the movie.

7.11 *Static* Class Members

As we have mentioned, a separate set of instance variables is created for each object that is instantiated. In addition to instance variables, classes can define **class variables**, which are created only once, when the JVM initializes the class. Thus, class variables exist before any objects are instantiated, and each class has only one copy of its class variables.

You can designate a class variable by using the keyword *static* in its definition. Also, *static* variables that are constants are usually declared to be *public* because they typically are provided to allow the client to set preferences for the operations of a class. For example, we can directly use the *INFOR-MATION_MESSAGE static* constant in the *JOptionPane* class to specify the type of icon to display in a dialog box.

Another purpose for *static* variables is to make it easier to use the class. For example, the *PI* and *E static* constants in the *Math* class are provided so that our applications do not need to define those commonly used values. Also, as we saw in the programming activity in Chapter 2, the maximum and minimum values for data types are made available as the *MAX_VALUE* and *MIN_VALUE public static* constants of the *Integer*, *Double*, and *Character* wrapper classes.

If, however, you define a *static* variable for your class that is not a constant, it is best to define it as *private* and provide accessor and mutator methods, as appropriate, for client access to the *static* variable.

We finish our *Auto* class, with version 6 shown in Example 7.12, by defining a *private static* variable to count the number of objects that have been instantiated during the application. We call this class variable *countAutos* and initialize it to 0 (line 14). Because a constructor is called whenever an object is instantiated, we can update the count by incrementing the value of *countAutos* in the class constructors (lines 24 and 37).

When you define a *static* variable for your class, its accessor and mutator methods must be defined as **static methods**, also called **class methods**. To do this, insert the keyword *static* in the method headers after the access modifier. We provide a *static* accessor method for the client to get the count of *Auto* objects (lines 59–63). We do not provide a mutator method, however, because clients of the class should not be able to update the value of *count-Autos* except via the constructors, which update the count automatically.

Methods that are defined to be *static* are subject to the following important restrictions, which are summarized in Table 7.4:

- *static* methods can reference only *static* variables.
- *static* methods can call only *static* methods.
- *static* methods cannot use the object reference *this*.

Again, it makes sense that *static* methods cannot access instance variables because *static* methods are associated with the class, not with any object. Further, a *static* method can be called before any objects are instantiated, so

TABLE 7.4	Access Restrictions for *static* and Non-*static* Methods	
	static method	Non-*static* Method
Access instance variables?	no	yes
Access *static* class variables?	yes	yes
Call *static* class methods?	yes	yes
Call non-*static* instance methods?	no	yes
Use the reference *this*?	no	yes

there will be no instance variables to access. Attempting to access an instance variable *xxx* from a *static* method will generate this compiler error:

```
non-static variable xxx cannot be referenced from a static context
```

Notice that the *getCountAutos* method (lines 59–63) is declared to be *static* and references only the *static countAutos* variable.

A non-*static*, or **instance**, method, on the other hand, can reference both class variables and instance variables, as well as class methods and instance methods.

At this point, we can explain a little more about the *main* method. Its header is:

```
public static void main( String [ ] args )
```

Because *main* is defined as *static*, the JVM can execute *main* without first creating an object.

```
1  /* Auto class, version 6
2     Anderson, Franceschi
3  */
4
5  import java.text.DecimalFormat;
6
7  public class Auto
8  {
9     // instance variables
10    private String model;         //  model of auto
11    private int milesDriven;      //  number of miles driven
12    private double gallonsOfGas;  //  number of gallons of gas
13
14    private static int countAutos = 0;  // static class variable
```

```
15
16    // Constructors:
17    //  initializes model to "unknown";
18    //  milesDriven is autoinitialized to 0
19    //        and gallonsOfGas to 0.0;
20    // increments countAutos
21    public Auto( )
22    {
23       model = "unknown";
24       countAutos++;    // increment static count of Auto objects
25    }
26
27    // allows client to set beginning values for
28    // model, milesDriven, and gallonsOfGas;
29    // increments countAutos
30    public Auto( String startModel,
31                 int startMilesDriven,
32                 double startGallonsOfGas )
33    {
34       model = startModel;
35       setMilesDriven( startMilesDriven );
36       setGallonsOfGas( startGallonsOfGas );
37       countAutos++;    // increment static count of Auto objects
38    }
39
40    // Accessor methods
41    // returns current value of model
42    public String getModel( )
43    {
44       return model;
45    }
46
47    // returns current value of milesDriven
48    public int getMilesDriven( )
49    {
50       return milesDriven;
51    }
52
53    // returns current value of gallonsOfGas
54    public double getGallonsOfGas( )
55    {
56       return gallonsOfGas;
57    }
58
```

```
59      // returns countAutos
60      public static int getCountAutos( )
61      {
62        return countAutos;
63      }
64
65      // Mutator methods:
66      // allows client to set model
67      public void setModel( String newModel )
68      {
69          model = newModel;
70      }
71
72      // allows client to set value of milesDriven;
73      // prints an error message if new value is less than 0
74      public void setMilesDriven( int newMilesDriven )
75      {
76        if ( milesDriven >= 0 )
77           milesDriven = newMilesDriven;
78        else
79        {
80           System.err.println( "Miles driven cannot be negative." );
81           System.err.println( "Value not changed." );
82        }
83      }
84
85      // allows client to set value of gallonsOfGas;
86      // prints an error message if new value is less than 0.0
87      public void setGallonsOfGas( double newGallonsOfGas )
88      {
89        if ( gallonsOfGas >= 0.0 )
90           gallonsOfGas = newGallonsOfGas;
91        else
92        {
93           System.err.println( "Gallons of gas cannot be negative." );
94           System.err.println( "Value not changed." );
95        }
96      }
97
98      // Calculates miles per gallon.
99      // if no gallons of gas have been used, returns 0.0;
100     // otherwise, returns miles per gallon
101     //    as milesDriven / gallonsOfGas
102     public double calculateMilesPerGallon( )
103     {
```

```
104      if ( gallonsOfGas != 0.0 )
105          return milesDriven / gallonsOfGas;
106      else
107          return 0.0;
108    }
109
110    // toString: returns a String with values of instance variable
111    public String toString( )
112    {
113      DecimalFormat gallonsFormat = new DecimalFormat( "#0.0" );
114      return "Model: " + model
115            + "; miles driven: " + milesDriven
116            + "; gallons of gas: "
117            + gallonsFormat.format( gallonsOfGas );
118    }
119
120    // equals: returns true if fields of parameter object
121    //         are equal to fields in this object
122    public boolean equals( Auto autoA )
123    {
124      if ( model.equals( autoA.model )
125          && milesDriven == autoA.milesDriven
126          && Math.abs( gallonsOfGas - autoA.gallonsOfGas )
127            < 0.0001 )
128          return true;
129      else
130          return false;
131    }
132 }
```

EXAMPLE 7.12   *Auto* Class, Version 6

Example 7.13 shows version 6 of our *AutoClient* class. In line 11, we call the *getCountAutos* method before instantiating any objects, then in line 17, we call the *getCountAutos* method again after instantiating one object. As Figure 7.8 shows, the *getCountAutos* method first returns 0, then 1. Notice that

Figure 7.8

Output from Example 7.13

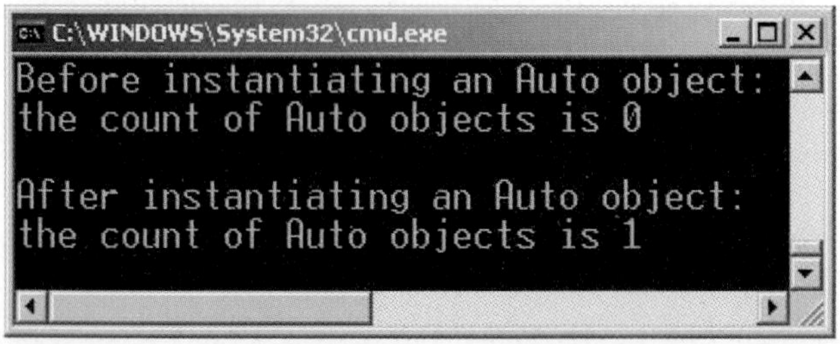

in both calls to the *static* method, we use the dot operator with the class name rather than an object reference.

```
1  /* Auto Client, version 6
2     Anderson, Franceschi
3  */
4
5  public class AutoClient
6  {
7    public static void main( String [ ] args )
8    {
9      System.out.println( "Before instantiating an Auto object:"
10                         + "\nthe count of Auto objects is "
11                         + Auto.getCountAutos( ) );
12
13     Auto sporty = new Auto( "Spyder", 0, 0.0 );
14
15     System.out.println( "\nAfter instantiating an Auto object:"
16                         + "\nthe count of Auto objects is "
17                         + Auto.getCountAutos( ) );
18   }
19 }
```

EXAMPLE 7.13 *Auto* **Client, Version 6**

Well, there it is. We've finished defining our *Auto* class. Although it's a large class, we were able to build the *Auto* class incrementally using stepwise refinement.

7.12 Graphical Objects

Let's revisit the astronaut from Chapter 4. Remember that we prompted the user for the starting (x, y) coordinate, then drew the astronaut at that location. In terms of the structure of the applet, we prompted for the starting x and y values in the *init* method and drew the astronaut in the *paint* method. The code for the astronaut and the applet was intertwined, or tightly coupled. We couldn't run the applet without drawing the astronaut, and we couldn't draw the astronaut without running the applet.

Now that we know how to design our own classes, we can separate the astronaut from the applet. We can define the astronaut as its own *Astronaut* class and make the applet the client of the *Astronaut* class. This will allow us to encapsulate the astronaut's data and the code for drawing the astronaut within the *Astronaut* class. It also promotes reuse of the *Astronaut* class by other programmers, who might want to create *Astronaut* objects for different applications.

The *Astronaut* class is shown in Example 7.14. We started by identifying the instance variables of the *Astronaut* class. Obviously, we need the starting (x, y) coordinate to draw the astronaut, so we define two *int* instance variables to hold those values (lines 11–12).

In addition, we added one more instance variable, *scale* (line 13), to allow the client to draw astronauts of different sizes. For example, a scaling factor of 1.0 will draw the astronaut at full size, 0.5 will draw the astronaut at half size, and 2.0 will draw a double-sized astronaut.

Our default constructor (lines 15–23) sets the starting x and y values to 0 and the scaling factor to 1.0 so that by default the astronaut is drawn in the upper-left corner of the window at full size. The overloaded constructor (lines 25–33) accepts values for these instance variables.

We provide one mutator method to change both x and y values (lines 36–40), as well as another mutator to change the scaling factor (lines 42–45).

We moved the code that draws the astronaut from the applet's *paint* method into its own method, which we named *draw* (lines 47–128). Because the astronaut is drawn using methods of the *Graphics* class, the applet client will need to pass its *Graphics* object as an argument to the *draw* method. Also, because the space suit color is used only in the *draw* method, we made it a local variable (line 56). If we wanted to let the client choose the space suit color, we could define another instance variable for it and add a corresponding parameter to the overloaded constructor.

Inside the *draw* method, we made a few changes to make the astronaut easier to scale. First, we converted the starting x and y coordinates to the center of the astronaut's head. In this way, the calculations for scaling the astronaut are simplified because we can capitalize on the astronaut's symmetry. Next we drew each part of the astronaut by multiplying any length measurement by the scaling factor. Finally, because the scaling factor is a *double* and the *Graphics* methods expect integer arguments, we type cast our calculated measurement to an *int* when needed.

We did not provide accessor methods or write a *toString* or an *equals* method for the *Astronaut* class. For a graphical object, these methods are less useful, given that the major purpose of graphical objects is to be drawn.

```
1   /* An Astronaut Class
2      Anderson, Franceschi
3   */
4
5   import java.awt.Graphics;
6   import java.awt.Color;
7
8   public class Astronaut
9   {
10    // the starting x and y coordinates for the astronaut
11    private int sX;
12    private int sY;
13    private double scale; // scaling factor, 1.0 is full size
14
15    // Default constructor:
16    // sets starting x and y coordinates to 0
17    // sets scaling factor to 1.0
18    public Astronaut( )
19    {
20      sX = 0;  // draw in upper-left corner
21      sY = 0;
22      scale = 1.0;  // draw full size
23    }
24
25    // Overloaded constructor:
26    // sets starting x and y coordinates
27    //  and scaling factor to values set by client
28    public Astronaut( int startX, int startY, double startScale )
29    {
30      sX = startX;
31      sY = startY;
32      scale = startScale;
33    }
34
35    // Mutator methods:
36    public void setCoordinates( int newX, int newY )
37    {
38      sX = newX;
39      sY = newY;
40    }
41
```

```
42    public void setScale( double newScale )
43    {
44      scale = newScale;
45    }
46
47    // draw method:
48    // draws astronaut using starting (x,y) coordinate
49    //  and scaling factor
50    public void draw( Graphics g )
51    {
52      // convert between start x, y coordinates and center of head
53      int oX = sX + (int) (65 * 2 * scale);
54      int oY = sY + (int) (75 * scale);
55
56      Color spacesuit = new Color( 195, 175, 150 );
57      // helmet
58      g.setColor( spacesuit );
59      g.fillOval( oX - (int) (75 * scale / 2),
60                  oY - (int) (75 * scale / 2),
61                  (int) (75 * scale), (int) (75 * scale) );
62      g.setColor( Color.LIGHT_GRAY );
63      g.fillOval( oX - (int) (55 * scale / 2),
64                  oY - (int) (55 * scale / 2),
65                  (int) (55 * scale), (int) (55 * scale) );
66
67      // face
68      g.setColor( Color.DARK_GRAY );
69      g.drawOval( oX - (int) ( (55 * scale / 4 )
70                + (8 * scale / 2) ),
71                  oY - (int) (55 * scale / 4), (int) (8 * scale),
72                  (int) (8 * scale) );
73      g.drawOval( oX + (int) ( (55 * scale / 4 )
74                - (8 * scale / 2) ),
75                  oY - (int) (55 * scale / 4), (int) (8 * scale),
76                  (int) (8 * scale) );
77      g.drawLine( oX,  oY - (int) (6 * scale),
78                  oX + (int) (2  *  scale),
79                  oY + (int) (6 * scale) );
80      g.drawLine( oX, oY + (int) (6 * scale),
81                  oX + (int) (2  *  scale),
82                  oY + (int) (6 * scale) );
83      g.drawOval( oX - (int) (15 * scale / 2),
84                  oY + (int) (55 * scale / 4),
85                  (int) (15 * scale), (int) (6 * scale) );
86
```

```
87      // neck
88      g.setColor( spacesuit );
89      g.fillRect( oX - (int) (20 * scale / 2),
90                  oY + (int) (-1 + 75 * scale / 2),
91                  (int) (20 * scale), (int) (1 + 10 * scale) );
92
93      // torso
94      g.fillRect( oX - (int) (65 * scale / 2),
95                  oY +(int) (-1 + 75 * scale / 2 + 10 * scale),
96                  (int) (65 * scale), (int) (1 + 85 * scale) );
97
98      // arms
99      g.fillRect( oX - (int) (65 * 3 * scale / 2),
100                 oY + (int) (75 * scale / 2 + 10 * scale),
101                 (int) (1 + 65 * scale), (int) (20 * scale) );
102     g.fillRect( oX + (int) (-1 + 65 * scale / 2),
103                 oY + (int) (75 * scale / 2 + 10 * scale),
104                 (int) (1 + 65 * scale), (int) (20 * scale) );
105
106     // legs
107     g.fillRect( oX - (int) (55 * scale / 2),
108                 oY + (int) (-1 + 75 * scale / 2 + 95 * scale),
109                 (int) (20 * scale), (int) (80 * scale) );
110     g.fillRect( oX + (int) (55 * scale / 2 - 20 * scale),
111                 oY + (int) (- 1 + 75 * scale / 2 + 95 * scale ),
112                 (int) (20 * scale), (int) (80 * scale) );
113
114     // flag
115     g.setColor( Color.BLACK );
116     g.drawLine( oX + (int) (65 * scale / 2 + 65 * scale),
117                 oY + (int) (75 * scale / 2 + 10 * scale),
118                 oX + (int) (65 * scale / 2 + 65 * scale),
119                 oY );
120     g.setColor( Color.RED );
121     g.fillRect( oX + (int) (65 * scale / 2 + 65 * scale),
122                 oY - (int) (75 * scale / 2),
123                 (int) (75 * scale), (int) (45 * scale) );
124     g.setColor( Color.BLUE );
125     g.fillRect( oX + (int) (65 * scale / 2 + 65 * scale ),
126                 oY - (int) (75 * scale / 2),
127                 (int) (30 * scale), (int) (25 * scale) );
128 }
129 }
```

EXAMPLE 7.14   The *Astronaut* Class

Figure 7.9

The *AstronautClient* Window

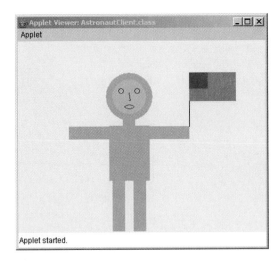

Now, we can create the applet class, which will be the client of the *Astronaut* class. Our simplified *AstronautClient* applet is shown in Example 7.15. The applet has one instance variable, which is an *Astronaut* object reference, *astro*. We instantiate the *Astronaut* object in the *init* method (lines 15–16) and call the *Astronaut*'s *draw* method in the applet's *paint* method (line 23), passing to *draw* the *Graphics* object reference *g* that was passed to *paint*. The applet window is shown in Figure 7.9.

```
1   /* Astronaut client
2      Anderson, Franceschi
3   */
4
5   import javax.swing.JApplet;
6   import java.awt.Graphics;
7
8   public class AstronautClient extends JApplet
9   {
10    // instance variable is an Astronaut
11    private Astronaut astro;
12
13    public void init( )
14    {
15      // instantiate the Astronaut object
16      astro = new Astronaut( 50, 12, 1 );
17    }
18
```

```
19    public void paint( Graphics g )
20    {
21        super.paint( g );
22
23        astro.draw( g ); // draw the astronaut
24    }
25 }
```

EXAMPLE 7.15   The *AstronautClient* Applet

An advantage to separating the *Astronaut* class from the *AppletClient* class is that it is now easy to draw two or more astronauts. Example 7.16 shows the code for the *AstronautClient2* class, which draws two astronauts, one full size and one half size. To add a second astronaut, all we needed to do was declare a second *Astronaut* object reference (line 11), instantiate it in *init* (line 17), and call the *draw* method for the second astronaut in the applet's *paint* method (line 26).

There is one other small change we needed to make. With two astronauts, we need a larger window, so we call the *setSize* method (line 18), passing it the new width and height of the applet window. The *setSize* method is inherited from the *JApplet* class. As such, it is a method of our *Astronaut-Client2* class, so we call *setSize* without an object reference. Figure 7.10 shows the output from the applet.

Figure 7.10

The *AstronautClient2* Window

```
1  /* Astronaut client with two astronauts
2     Anderson, Franceschi
3  */
4
5  import javax.swing.JApplet;
6  import java.awt.Graphics;
7
8  public class AstronautClient2 extends JApplet
9  {
10    // instance variables
11    private Astronaut astro1, astro2;
12
13    public void init( )
14    {
15      // instantiate the Astronaut objects
16      astro1 = new Astronaut( 25, 10, 1.0 );  // full size
17      astro2 = new Astronaut( 225, 155, 0.5 ); // half size
18      setSize( 500, 300 ); // set the window size
19    }
20
21    public void paint( Graphics g )
22    {
23       super.paint( g );
24
25       astro1.draw( g ); // draw first Astronaut
26       astro2.draw( g ); // draw second Astronaut
27    }
28 }
```

EXAMPLE 7.16   The *AstronautClient2* Class with Two Astronauts

7.13   Enumeration Types

Enumeration types are designed to increase the readability of programs. The enumeration type, *enum*, is a special kind of class declaration. It allows us to define a set of named constant objects that can be used instead of numbers in a program.

Enum types are useful for managing ordered sets where each member of the set has a name. Examples are the days of the week, months of the year, and playing cards. To represent these sets in a program, we often use numbers, such as 1 through 7 for the days of the week or 1 through 12 for the months of the year. The problem is that to input or output these values, we need to convert between our internal numeric representation (for example,

1–7) and the words that users recognize (Sunday, Monday, Tueday, etc.). The *enum* type allows us to instantiate a constant object for each value in a set. The set of objects will be ordered so that we can refer to the objects by name, without the need for using numbers.

The *enum* functionality is built into *java.lang*, so we can define *enum* types without using an *import* statement.

The syntax for creating a set of *enum* objects is

```
enum EnumName { obj1, obj2, . . . };
```

where obj1, obj2, etc. are names for the constant objects.

For example, the following statement defines an *enum* type to represent the days of the week:

```
enum Days { Sun, Mon, Tue, Wed, Thur, Fri, Sat };
```

When that statement is executed, an object is instantiated for each name in the list. Each name in the list, therefore, is a reference to an object of the *enum* type *Days*.

Note that the values in the initialization list are object references (*Sun*), not *String* literals ("*Sun*").

Each object has an instance variable that holds a numeric value, which is determined by its position in the list of *enum* objects. By default, the first object has the value 0, the second object has the value 1, and so on. Because the objects are an ordered set, for example, the object *Thur* is higher in value than *Wed*. We can use the *enum* objects, however, without relying on the specific value of each object.

The *enum* objects are instantiated as constant objects, meaning that their values cannot be changed.

To refer to any of the constant objects in an *enum* type, we use the following dot syntax:

```
enumType.enumObject
```

Thus, to refer to the *Wed* object in our *Days enum* type, we use this syntax:

```
Days.Wed
```

Once we have defined an *enum* type, we can declare an object reference of that type. For example, the following statement defines a *Days* object reference *d*:

```
Days d;
```

COMMON ERROR TRAP

Do not use *String* literals in the initialization list for *enum* types.

TABLE 7.5   Useful Methods for *enum* Constants

Useful Methods for *enum* Objects	
Return type	**Method name and argument list**
int	compareTo (Enum eObj)
	compares two *enum* objects and returns a negative number if *this* object is less than the argument, a positive number if *this* object is greater than the argument, and 0 if the two objects are the same
boolean	equals(Enum eObj)
	returns *true* if this object is equal to the argument *eObj*; returns *false* otherwise
int	ordinal( )
	returns the numeric value of the *enum* object. By default, the value of the first object in the list is 0, the value of the second object is 1, and so on
String	toString( )
	returns the name of the *enum* constant
enum	valueOf(String enumName)
	static method that returns the *enum* object whose name is the same as the *String* argument *enumName*

Like any other object reference, the value of *d* will be *null* initially. To assign a value to the reference *d*—for example, *Thur*—we use the following statement:

```
d = Days.Thur;
```

Table 7.5 lists some useful methods that can be called with *enum* objects, and Example 7.17 demonstrates the use of these methods.

```
1 /* Demonstration of enum
2    Anderson, Franceschi
3 */
4
5 public class EnumDemo
6 {
7   public enum Days { Sun, Mon, Tue, Wed, Thur, Fri, Sat };
```

```
 8
 9   public static void main( String [ ] args )
10   {
11     Days d1, d2;  // declare two Days object references
12
13     d1 = Days.Wed;
14     d2 = Days.Fri;
15
16     System.out.println( "Comparing objects using equals" );
17     if ( d1.equals( d2 ) )
18       System.out.println( d1 + " equals " + d2 );
19     else
20       System.out.println( d1 + " does not equal " + d2 );
21
22     System.out.println( "\nComparing objects using compareTo" );
23     if ( d1.compareTo( d2 ) > 0 )
24       System.out.println( d1 + " is greater than " + d2 );
25     else if ( d1.compareTo( d2 ) < 0 )
26       System.out.println( d1 + " is less than " + d2 );
27     else
28       System.out.println( d1 + " is equal to " + d2 );
29
30     System.out.println( "\nGetting the  ordinal value" );
31     System.out.println( "The value of " + d1 + " is "
32                         + d1.ordinal( ) );
33
34     System.out.println( "\nConverting a String to an object" );
35     Days day = Days.valueOf( "Mon" );
36     System.out.println( "The value of day is " + day );
37   }
38 }
```

EXAMPLE 7.17   A Demonstration of *enum* Methods

Line 7 defines the *enum* type *Days*; this instantiates the seven constant objects representing the days of the week. On line 11, we declare two object references of the *Days enum* type. Then on lines 13 and 14, we assign *d1* a reference to the *Wed* object, and we assign *d2* a reference to the *Fri* object.

Line 17 compares *d1* and *d2* using the *equals* method. Because *Wed* and *Fri* are different objects, the *equals* method returns *false*. Lines 18 and 20 implicitly call the *toString* method, which prints the name of the objects.

Lines 23 and 25 call the *compareTo* method, which returns a negative number, indicating that *Wed* is lower in value than *Fri*.

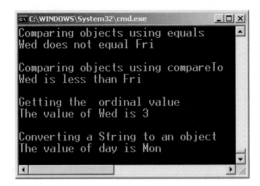

We then retrieve the value of the *d1* object by calling the *ordinal* method (lines 31–32), which returns 3 because *Wed* is the fourth object in the *enum* list.

Finally, line 35 converts from a *String* to an *enum* object using the *valueOf* method. Notice that the *valueOf* method is *static*, so we call it using our *enum* type, *Days*.

REFERENCE POINT

Exceptions are covered in Chapter 11.

If the *String* passed to the *valueOf* method is not a name in our set of defined *enum* objects, the *valueOf* method generates an *IllegalArgument-Exception*. In Chapter 11, we show you how to intercept an exception and reprompt the user for a valid name.

The output from Example 7.17 is shown in Figure 7.11.

We can use *enum* objects in *switch* statements to make the *case* constants more meaningful, which in turn makes the code more readable. Example 7.18 uses our *Days enum* class to display the daily specials offered in the cafeteria.

```
 1 /** Specials of the Day
 2     Anderson Franceschi
 3 */
 4
 5 import java.util.Scanner;
 6
 7 public class DailySpecials
 8 {
 9   public enum Days { Sun, Mon, Tue, Wed, Thur, Fri, Sat };
10
11   public static void main( String [ ] args )
```

```
12   {
13       Scanner scan = new Scanner( System.in );
14
15       System.out.print( "Enter a day\n"
16                         + "(Sun, Mon, Tue, Wed, Thur, Fri, Sat) > " );
17       String inputDay = scan.next( );
18       Days day = Days.valueOf( inputDay );
19
20       switch ( day )
21       {
22         case Mon:
23             System.out.println( "The special for "
24                                 + day + " is barbeque chicken." );
25             break;
26
27         case Tue:
28             System.out.println( "The special for "
29                                 + day + " is tacos" );
30             break;
31
32         case Wed:
33             System.out.println( "The special for "
34                                 + day + " is chef's salad" );
35             break;
36
37         case Thur:
38             System.out.println( "The special for "
39                                 + day + " is a cheeseburger" );
40             break;
41
42          case Fri:
43             System.out.println( "The special for "
44                                 + day + " is fish fillet" );
45             break;
46
47         default: // if day is Sat or Sun
48             System.out.println( "Sorry, we're closed on "
49                                 + day );
50       }
51   }
52 }
```

EXAMPLE 7.18   *DailySpecials* Class

Figure 7.12

Output from *DailySpecials*

Figure 7.12 shows the output from Example 7.18 when the user enters *Fri*.

In the *DailySpecials* program, we prompt the user for a day (lines 15–17), then read the *String* entered by the user and convert it to an *enum* object by calling the *valueOf* method at line 18.

Once we have a valid *enum* value, we can use it as a *switch* variable (line 20).

Notice that we use each *enum* object name in a *case* label without qualifying it with the *Days* type. Including the *enum* type in a *switch* statement generates the following compiler error:

```
an enum switch case label must be the unqualified name of an
enumeration constant
```

Skill Practice
with these end-of-chapter questions

7.18.1   Multiple Choice Exercises

Questions 14, 15, 16

7.18.2   Reading and Understanding Code

Questions 21, 22, 23, 25, 27

7.18.3   Fill in the Code

Questions 29, 34, 35

7.18.4   Identifying Errors in Code

Questions 40, 41, 42, 44, 46

7.18.5   Debugging Area

Questions 50, 51, 53, 54

7.18.6   Write a Short Program

Questions 55, 56, 57, 58, 59, 60, 61, 62

7.18.8   Technical Writing

Question 72

7.14 Programming Activity 2: Writing a Class Definition, Part 2

In this programming activity, you will complete the definition of the *Airport* class. Then you will run a prewritten client program that instantiates several *Airport* objects, calls the methods that you have written, and displays the values of the objects' data.

Copy into a directory on your computer all the files from the Chapter 7 Programming Activity 2 folder on the CD-ROM accompanying this book. Note that all files should be in the same directory.

Load the *Airport.java* source file; you'll notice that the class already contains the class definition from Programming Activity 1. Your job is to complete the class definition by adding a *static* class variable (and its supporting code) and writing the *toString* and *equals* methods. It is important to define the *static* class variable and the methods exactly as described in the comments because the *AirportClient* class will call each method to test its implementation. Searching for five asterisks in a row (*****) will position you at the six places in the class definition where you will add your code. The *Airport.java* code is shown here in Example 7.19:

```
1 /* Airport class
2    Anderson, Franceschi
3 */
4
5 public class Airport
6 {
7
8   // instance variables
9   private String airportCode;
10  private int gates;
11
12  // 1. ***** Add a static class variable *****
13  //   countAirports is an int
14  //   assign an initial value of 0
15
16
17  // 2. ***** Modify this method *****
18  // Default constructor:
19  // method name: Airport
20  // return value:  none
21  // parameters: none
22  // function: sets the airportCode to a blank String
```

```
23    //    ***** add 1 to countAirports class variable
24    public Airport( )
25    {
26       airportCode = "";
27
28    }
29
30    // 3. ***** Modify this method *****
31    // Overloaded constructor:
32    // method name: Airport
33    // return value: none
34    // parameters:  a String airport code and an int startGates
35    // function: assigns airportCode the value of the
36    //     startAirportCode parameter;
37    //     calls the setGates method,
38    //     passing the startGates parameter
39    //    ***** add 1 to countAirports class variable
40    public Airport( String startAirportCode, int startGates )
41    {
42       airportCode = startAirportCode;
43       setGates( startGates );
44
45    }
46
47    // Accessor method for the airportCode instance variable
48    // method name: getAirportCode
49    // return value: String
50    // parameters: none
51    // function: returns airportCode
52    public String getAirportCode( )
53    {
54       return airportCode;
55    }
56
57    // Accessor method for the gates instance variable
58    // method name: getGates
59    // return value: int
60    // parameters: none
61    // function: returns gates
62    public int getGates( )
63    {
64       return gates;
65    }
66
67    // 4. ***** Write this method *****
```

```
68   // Accessor method for the countAirports class variable
69   // method name: getCountAirports
70   // return value: int
71   // parameters: none
72   // function: returns countAirports
73
74
75
76
77   // Mutator method for the airportCode instance variable
78   // method name: setAirportCode
79   // return value: void
80   // parameters: String newAirportCode
81   // function: assigns airportCode the value of the
82   //                    newAirportCode parameter
83   public void setAirportCode( String newAirportCode )
84   {
85      airportCode = newAirportCode;
86   }
87
88   // Mutator method for the gates instance variable
89   // method name: setGates
90   // return value:  void
91   // parameters: int newGates
92   // function: validates the newGates parameter.
93   //   if newGates is greater than 0, sets gates to newGates;
94   //   otherwise, prints an error message to System.err
95   //   and does not change value of gates
96   public void setGates( int newGates )
97   {
98      if ( newGates  >=  0 )
99        gates = newGates;
100     else
101     {
102       System.err.println( "Gates must be at least 0" );
103       System.err.println( "Value of gates unchanged." );
104     }
105  }
106
107  // 5. ***** Write this method *****
108  // method name:  toString
109  // return value: String
110  // parameters: none
111  // function:  returns a String that contains the airportCode
112  //     and gates
```

```
113
114
115
116
117
118
119   // 6. ***** Write this method *****
120   // method name: equals
121   // return value: boolean
122   // parameter:  Airport object
123   // function:  returns true if airportCode
124   //    and gates in this object
125   //    are equal to those in the parameter object;
126   //    returns false otherwise
127
128
129
130
131
132
133
134   }  // end of Airport class definition
```

EXAMPLE 7.19   The *Airport.java* File

When you finish modifying the *Airport* class, compile the source file. When *Airport.java* compiles without any errors, load and compile the *AirportClient.java* file. This source file contains *main*, so you will execute the application from this file. When the application begins, you should see the window shown in Figure 7.13.

As you can see, the *AirportClient* has declared two *Airport* object references, *airport1* and *airport2*. The references are *null* because no *Airport* objects have been instantiated. Note also that the value of the *countAirports* class variable is displayed.

The *AirportClient* application will call methods of the *Airport* class to instantiate the two *Airport* objects, call the *toString* and *equals* methods, and get the value of the *static* class variable, *countAirports*. As the application does its work, it displays a status message at the bottom of the window indicating which method has been called and it also displays the current

Figure 7.13

AirportClient Opening Window

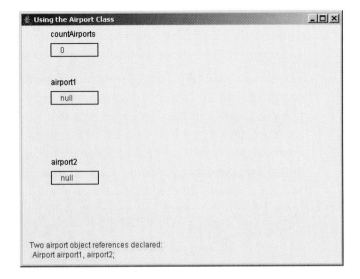

state of the *Airport* objects. You can check your work by comparing the state of the objects with the status message.

DISCUSSION QUESTIONS

1. Explain why the *countAirports* class variable has a value of 0 before any *Airport* objects have been instantiated.

2. How does a client call the *getCountAirports* method?

3. Explain why the client calls the *equals* method rather than directly comparing the object references *airport1* and *airport2* using the following *if* statement:

   ```
   if ( airport1 == airport2 )
   ```

7.15 Creating Packages

As we have mentioned, one of the advantages of a well-written class is that it can be reused. Ideally, as you write programs, you will look for functionality that is common to many programs. It is a good practice to encapsulate this functionality into a class so that you can reuse that code in future programs. Java provides the concept of a package for this purpose.

A **package** is a collection of related classes that can be imported into programs. We have imported classes from multiple Java packages: *java.awt*, *java.util*, *java.text*, and others. We can also create our own packages, which

SOFTWARE ENGINEERING TIP

Put classes that provide reusable functionality into a package.

allows us to reuse a class without needing to physically store that class in the same directory as our other source files. Instead, we create the package and *import* the class from that package into our source file.

Let's look at an example of a class that can provide reusable functionality to our programs. In Chapter 6, we demonstrated how to detect and recover from an error when the user enters data that is a different type from what we expect. For example, if we prompt the user for an integer and the user enters a letter instead, the default behavior of the *Scanner* class is to generate an *InputMismatchException*. Our solution in Chapter 6 was to check whether the user's input matched our expected data type before attempting to read the value. For example, we inserted the following code to read an *int*:

```
System.out.print( "Enter . . . as an integer > " );
while ( ! scan.hasNextInt( ) )
{
   String garbage = scan.nextLine( );
   System.out.print( "\nPlease enter an integer > " );
}
int x = scan.nextInt( );
```

Although looping until the user enters a valid value solves the input mismatch problem, that's a lot of code to include in our program every time we need to read data that is a primitive data type.

Instead, we can create a class that provides the functionality we need, but which hides the complexity of the validation code. When we need input from the user, we'll call the methods of that class instead of coding the *while* loop. Example 7.20 shows the code for a *ConsoleIn* class that provides methods for type-safe reading of primitive types. We also include a method for reading *Strings*. Although any input can be interpreted as a *String*, we include this method for completeness, so that this class can be used for all input.

```
 1 /** Type-Safe Input Using Scanner
 2 *    Anderson, Franceschi
 3 */
 4 package com.jbpub.af;
 5
 6 import java.util.Scanner;
 7
 8 public class ConsoleIn
 9 {
10     private Scanner scan;
11
12     public ConsoleIn( )
```

```
13       {
14          scan = new Scanner( System.in );
15       }
16
17       public int readInt( String prompt )
18       {
19          System.out.print( prompt + " > " );
20          while ( ! scan.hasNextInt( ) )
21          {
22             String garbage = scan.nextLine( );
23             System.out.println( "Input is not an integer" );
24             System.out.print( prompt + " > " );
25          }
26          return scan.nextInt( );
27       }
28
29       public float readFloat( String prompt )
30       {
31          System.out.print( prompt + " > " );
32          while ( ! scan.hasNextFloat( ) )
33          {
34             String garbage = scan.nextLine( );
35             System.out.println( "Input is not "
36                                 + "a floating-point number" );
37             System.out.print( prompt + " > " );
38          }
39          return scan.nextFloat( );
40       }
41
42       public double readDouble( String prompt )
43       {
44          System.out.print( prompt + " > " );
45          while ( ! scan.hasNextDouble( ) )
46          {
47             String garbage = scan.nextLine( );
48             System.out.println( "Input is not "
49                                 + "a floating-point number" );
50             System.out.print( prompt + " > " );
51          }
52          return scan.nextDouble( );
53       }
54
55       public long readLong( String prompt )
56       {
57          System.out.print( prompt + " > " );
```

```
58        while ( ! scan.hasNextLong( ) )
59        {
60          String garbage = scan.nextLine( );
61          System.out.println( "Input is not an integer" );
62          System.out.print( prompt + " > " );
63        }
64        return scan.nextLong( );
65     }
66
67     public short readShort( String prompt )
68     {
69        System.out.print( prompt + " > " );
70        while ( ! scan.hasNextShort( ) )
71        {
72          String garbage = scan.nextLine( );
73          System.out.println( "Input must be an integer "
74                              + "between  -32768 and 32767" );
75          System.out.print( prompt + " > " );
76        }
77        return scan.nextShort( );
78     }
79
80     public byte readByte( String prompt )
81     {
82        System.out.print( prompt + " > " );
83        while ( ! scan.hasNextByte( ) )
84        {
85          String garbage = scan.nextLine( );
86          System.out.println( "Input must be an integer "
87                              + "between  -128 and 127" );
88          System.out.print( prompt + " > " );
89        }
90        return scan.nextByte( );
91     }
92
93     public boolean readBoolean( String prompt )
94     {
95        System.out.print( prompt + " > " );
96        while ( ! scan.hasNextBoolean( ) )
97        {
98          String garbage = scan.nextLine( );
99          System.out.println( "Input must be "
100                             + "\"true\" or \"false\"" );
101         System.out.print( prompt + " > " );
102       }
```

```
103             return scan.nextBoolean( );
104         }
105
106     public char readChar( String prompt )
107     {
108         System.out.print( prompt + " > " );
109         String charIn = scan.next( );
110         while ( charIn.length( ) > 1 )
111         {
112             System.out.println( "Input is not "
113                                 + "a single character " );
114             System.out.print( prompt + " > " );
115             charIn = scan.next( );
116         }
117         return charIn.charAt( 0 );
118     }
119
120     public String readString( String prompt )
121     {
122         System.out.print( prompt + " > " );
123         return scan.next( );
124     }
125 }
```

EXAMPLE 7.20   *ConsoleIn* Class

We provide a constructor for the class (lines 12–15) that instantiates an object of the *Scanner* class and associates it with the console (*System.in*).

We also provide *read* methods for each primitive data type. Each method accepts one *String* argument, which the client can use as a prompt to let the user know what input to provide. The general API of each method is

```
public  dataType readDataType( String prompt )
```

Let's look at the *readInt* method (lines 17–27). Its API is

```
public int readInt( String prompt )
```

Line 19 displays the prompt and appends a space, the > character, and another space. Lines 20 through 25 consist of a *while* loop that tests whether the input the user entered is an integer. The *hasNextInt* method of the *Scanner* class returns *true* if the input is an integer. So if the *hasNextInt* method returns *false*, we flush the bad input by calling the *nextLine* method of the *Scanner* class to ignore the returned data. We then print an error message and reprompt the user. This process repeats until the user types an integer, at which time, the *hasNextInt* method returns *true*. We then skip to line 26, which reads and returns the integer the user entered. The methods for reading the other primitive data types follow the same pattern.

The only methods that operate a little differently are the *readString* and *readChar* methods. Because any data can be interpreted as a *String*, the *readString* method does not need to verify the input. Instead, the *readString* method (lines 120–124) prints the prompt and calls the *next* method of the *Scanner* class to read the input.

Similarly, the *readChar* (lines 106–118) method reads the next token, then verifies that only one character has been entered. If the length of the token is greater than 1, we reprompt the user for another input. When the user does enter one character, we convert the first character of the returned *String* to a *char*.

Now that we have the *ConsoleIn* class, we can put the class into a package to make it available for use in other programs.

To create a package, you insert a *package* statement into the source file as the first line after the header comments. The *package* statement has the following syntax:

```
package packageName;
```

In the *ConsoleIn* class, we define our package as *com.jbpub.af* (line 4). Because many programmers create packages, we need to avoid a situation, called **name collision**, where multiple programmers choose the same name for their packages. The convention, therefore, is to name your package using your domain name. Specifically, the package name should use the reverse of the domain name (without the *www*). Thus, because our domain name is *www.jbpub.com*, we begin all our package names with *com.jbpub*. For this package, we append a dot and *af*. Each part of the package name represents a directory. So our package will be stored in the directory structure *com\jbpub\af* or *com/jbpub/af*, depending on the operating system. In an *import* statement, the dots in the package name separate the directory names in a platform-independent way.

The next step in creating a package is to create the directory where you want to place the package. Later on, as you create more classes you can put these classes in that same package or create a new package in the same directory.

For our package, we created the *com* directory, then created a subdirectory, *jbpub*, and an *af* subdirectory in the *jbpub* directory.

The next step is to copy the source file into the package directory and compile it. We copied the *ConsoleIn.java* source file into the *af* directory and compiled it.

So that the compiler can find the package you just created, the final step is to modify your *CLASSPATH* environment variable, which tells the Java compiler where to look for packages. This step is system-dependent. We've included instructions for Windows 2000 and Linux systems. For other operating systems, consult your system documentation or Sun Microsystems' Java Web site.

For a Windows 2000 machine, we suggest the following steps:

Let's assume that you have decided to put the packages you create into the *My Documents* folder. For the package *com.jbpub.af*, you would create the directories in such a way that *af* will be a subdirectory of *jbpub*, itself a subdirectory of *com*, itself a subdirectory of *My Documents*.

Open the *Control Panel* and select the *System* icon. (On Windows XP, in the *Control Panel*, you will need to select the *Performance and Maintenance* icon before you can select the *System* icon.) From the *Advanced* tab, select the *Environment Variables* button. You will see two windows. In the top window, labeled *User variables*, look for *classpath* under the *variable* column.

If you see *classpath*, click the *edit* button. Append a semicolon and the pathname to the *My Documents* folder to the value that *classpath* currently has.

If *classpath* does not appear under the *variable* column, click the *new* button. Type *classpath* into the *Variable name* text box and type the pathname to the *My Documents* folder into the *Variable value* text box. You will probably need to add the current directory, designated by a dot (.), to the value.

When you finish, the *classpath* variable value might look like this:

```
.;c:\documents and settings\yourusername\my documents\
```

The initial dot (.) indicates that the compiler should look first in the current directory for classes.

On a typical Linux machine, we suggest using the following steps:

Let's assume that you have decided to put the packages that you create in the following directory, where *studentName* would be your user ID:

```
/home/studentName/myOwnClasses
```

At the Unix prompt, type the following command. (We use the # sign below to represent the Unix prompt.)

```
# export CLASSPATH=$CLASSPATH:/home/studentName/myOwnClasses
```

This statement appends */home/studentName/myOwnClasses* to the *CLASSPATH* environment variable. To check that this command was successful, at the Unix prompt type:

```
# echo $CLASSPATH
```

Your result should look something like this:

```
/usr/local/java/jre/lib:.:/home/studentName/myOwnClasses
```

You can see three directory paths separated by a colon (:):

- `/usr/local/java/jre/lib` is the directory (depending on your machine and your versions of Unix and Java, it could very well be another one) where the Java Class Library is located.
- `.` (dot) is the current directory.
- `/home/studentName/myOwnClasses` is the directory where you are planning to place the packages that you create.

Once the package is created, you can import the class to use its functionality. Example 7.21 shows client code that uses the *ConsoleIn* class to read an integer.

```
 1 /*  ConsoleIn Client
 2     Anderson, Franceschi
 3 */
 4 import com.jbpub.af.ConsoleIn; // import ConsoleIn from package
 5
 6 public class ConsoleInClient
 7 {
 8   public static void main( String [ ] args )
 9   {
10     ConsoleIn console = new ConsoleIn( );
11
12     int age = console.readInt( "Enter your age" );
13     System.out.println( "Your age is " + age );
14   }
15 }
```

EXAMPLE 7.21   *ConsoleInClient* Class

In Example 7.21, we import the *ConsoleIn* class on line 4. Line 10 instantiates a *ConsoleIn* object, then line 12 uses that object reference to call the *readInt* method. Figure 7.14 shows the output of the *ConsoleInClient* class when the user enters invalid input, then valid input.

Figure 7.14
Output from the
ConsoleInClient **Class**

In most corporations and organizations, programmers share code and frequently use classes developed by another programmer. If the class is well designed and well documented, it will be easy for others to use that class. After all, that is essentially what we have been doing by using existing Java classes. It has been easy to understand what functions these existing classes perform, what they encapsulate, how the constructors work, what the methods do, and how to use the classes. The reason that these classes are easy to understand and use is not only that they are well designed and written, but also that the available documentation, particularly on Sun Microsystems' Java Web site, is clear, easy to understand, complete, and represents these classes well.

We, too, will learn how to produce HTML-based documentation similar to the documentation available on Sun Microsystems' Java Web site.

Indeed, there is a tool, called **Javadoc**, provided in the Java Software Development Kit (SDK), to do just that. Javadoc is an executable program (actually *javadoc.exe*) located in the *bin* directory. It is invoked much the same way as the *javac* compiler, except that instead of creating *.class* files, it creates *.html* files that document the class.

For instance, to generate documentation for our *Auto* class, we would type the following at the command line:

```
javadoc Auto.java
```

If we want to generate documentation for all the source files in the directory, we would type:

```
javadoc *.java
```

Table 7.6 shows the files generated for the *Auto* class.

If you double-click on *index.html*, you will open a Web page with the same look as the ones on Sun's Java Web site.

TABLE 7.6   HTML Files Generated by Javadoc

File name	Short description
Auto.html	*Auto* class documentation (without frames)
allclasses-frame.html	List of the classes with links (with frames)
allclasses-noframe.html	List of the classes with links (without frames)
constant-values.html	Constants of the class with links
deprecated-list.html	List of deprecated methods
help-doc.html	How these files are organized
index-all.html	Links to class, constructors, methods
index.html	*Auto* class documentation (with frames)
overview-tree.html	Class hierarchy
packages.html	Links to *Auto*
resources	Directory containing one or more GIFs
stylesheet.css	Style sheet
package-list	List of packages

REFERENCE POINT

The full documentation for using Javadoc can be found at *http://java.sun.com.*

We will review a few basic Javadoc features here. Full documentation on Javadoc is available on Sun's Web site.

To write comments that will be included in the Javadoc documentation, we use a special form of block comment ahead of any class, field, constructor, or method. The syntax for including Javadoc comments is

```
/**
Javadoc comment here
*/
```

As we already know, the syntax for a Java block comment is

```
/*
Java block comment here
*/
```

So a Javadoc comment is just a special Java block comment. The *javac* compiler will simply ignore it, but the Javadoc executable will look for it and generate the appropriate documentation. Javadoc discards all whitespace characters and the * at the beginning of each line until a non–whitespace

TABLE 7.7   Selected Javadoc Tags

Tag	Most common syntax	Explanation
@param	@param variableName description	Adds a parameter to the parameter section
@return	@return text	Adds a description for the return type

character and non * character is encountered. The industry convention is to start every line of a Javadoc comment with a *. Therefore, we recommend the following syntax:

```
/**
*   A Javadoc comment here
*   A second Javadoc comment here
*  . . . .
*/
```

Class documentation comprises two parts:

- A description section

- A tag section

Javadoc recognizes two types of tags: block tags and inline tags. We will discuss block tags only.

Block tags start with the character @. Table 7.7 lists two block tags, *@param* and *@return*, along with an explanation of each.

In the description section and inside the tag section, the text should be written in HTML; therefore, HTML tags such as
 (break) or <B> (bold) can be used. The tag <BR> inserts a new line; the tag <B> will change the text style to bold until the end tag </B> is encountered.

Example 7.22 shows a simplified version of our *Auto* class incorporating some documentation comments:

```
1 /*  Simplified Auto Class with Javadoc comments
2      Anderson, Franceschi
3 */
4
5 public class SimplifiedAuto
6 {
7  private String model;
8  private int milesDriven;
9  private double gallonsOfGas;
```

SOFTWARE ENGINEERING TIP

When coding a documentation block, use an * at the beginning of each line to indicate that this is a documentation comment.

```
10
11
12
13  /**
14   * Default constructor:<BR>
15   * initializes model to "unknown"<BR>
16   * milesDriven are autoinitialized to 0, and gallonsOfGas to 0.0
17   */
18  public SimplifiedAuto( )
19  {
20     model = "unknown";
21  }
22
23  /**
24   * Overloaded constructor:<BR>
25   * Allows client to set beginning values for model,
26   *    milesDriven, and gallonsOfGas<BR>
27   * This constructor takes three parameters<BR>
28   * Calls mutator methods to validate new values
29   * @param startModel the model of the car
30   * @param startMilesDriven the number of miles driven
31   * @param startGallonsOfGas the number of gallons of gas used
32   */
33  public SimplifiedAuto( String startModel, int startMilesDriven,
34                         double startGallonsOfGas )
35  {
36     model = startModel;
37     setMilesDriven( startMilesDriven );
38     setGallonsOfGas( startGallonsOfGas );
39  }
40
41  /**
42   * Mutator method:<BR>
43   * Allows client to set value of milesDriven<BR>
44   * Prints an error message if new value is less than 0<BR>
45   * <B>setMilesDriven</B> does not change the value
46   * of <B>milesDriven</B> if newMilesDriven has negative value
47   * @param newMilesDriven the new number of miles driven
48   */
49  public void setMilesDriven( int newMilesDriven )
50  {
51     if ( newMilesDriven > 0 )
52         milesDriven = newMilesDriven;
53     else
54     {
```

```
55            System.err.println( "Miles driven cannot be negative." );
56            System.err.println( "Value not changed." );
57     }
58  }
59
60  /**
61   * Mutator method:<BR>
62   * Allows client to set value of gallonsOfGas<BR>
63   * If new value is less than 0, prints an error message<BR>
64   *     and does not change the value of <B>gallonsOfGas</B>
65   * @param newGallonsOfGas the new number of gallons of gas used
66   */
67  public void setGallonsOfGas( double newGallonsOfGas )
68  {
69     if ( newGallonsOfGas >= 0 )
70          gallonsOfGas = newGallonsOfGas;
71     else
72     {
73         System.err.println( "Gallons of gas cannot be negative." );
74         System.err.println( "Value not changed." );
75     }
76  }
77
78  /**
79   * equals method:<BR>
80   * Compares two SimplifiedAuto objects for the same field values
81   * @param a1 another SimplifiedAuto object
82   * @return a boolean, true if this object
83   * has the same field values as the parameter a1
84   */
85  public boolean equals( SimplifiedAuto a1 )
86  {
87      return ( model.equals( a1.model ) &&
88              milesDriven == a1.milesDriven &&
89              Math.abs( gallonsOfGas - a1.gallonsOfGas )
90              < 0.001 );
91  }
92  }
```

EXAMPLE 7.22   The *SimplifiedAuto* Class

SOFTWARE ENGINEERING TIP

When you write a class, add a few documentation comments, and generate the Web-style documentation. Show the Web pages to friends or colleagues and ask them if they fully understand what the class encapsulates and what it is about. Ask them a few questions about the constructor and the methods. This is a good way to check if your class is well designed and ready for reuse.

Figure 7.15 shows the generated *index.html* file, and Figure 7.16 shows the generated documentation for the *setMilesDriven* method.

Figure 7.15

SimplifiedAuto Class
Web-Style Documen-
tation

Package **Class** Tree Deprecated Index Help

PREV CLASS   NEXT CLASS   FRAMES   NO FRAMES
SUMMARY: NESTED | FIELD | CONSTR | METHOD   DETAIL: FIELD | CONSTR | METHOD

Class SimplifiedAuto

```
java.lang.Object
  └ SimplifiedAuto
```

```
public class SimplifiedAuto
extends java.lang.Object
```

Constructor Summary

SimplifiedAuto()
    Default constructor:
initializes model to "unknown"
milesDriven are autoinitialized to 0, and gallonsOfGas to 0.0

SimplifiedAuto(java.lang.String startModel, int startMilesDriven, double startGallonsOfGas)
    Overloaded constructor:
Allows client to set beginning values for model, milesDriven, and gallonsOfGas
This constructor takes three parameters
Calls mutator methods to validate new values

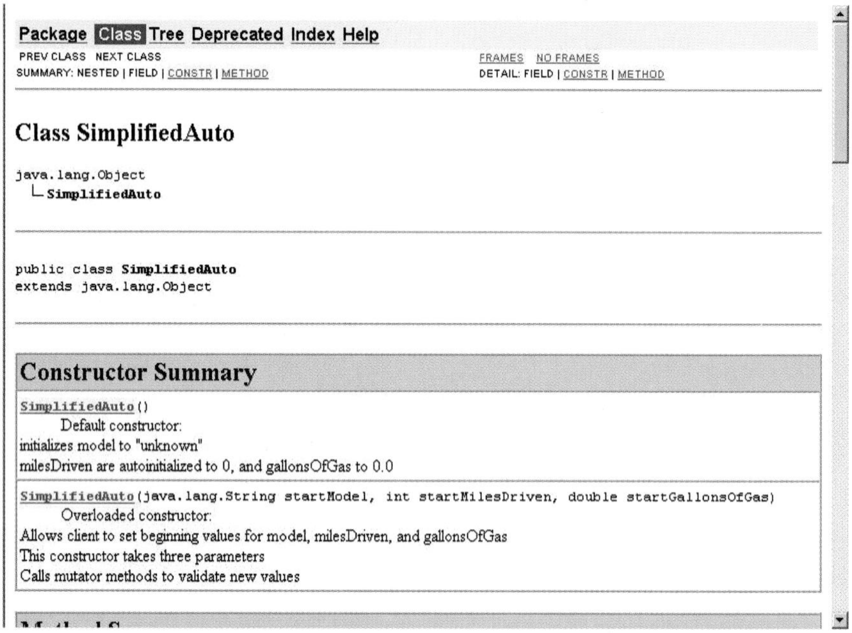

Figure 7.16

Web-Style Documenta-
tion for the *Mutator*
Methods

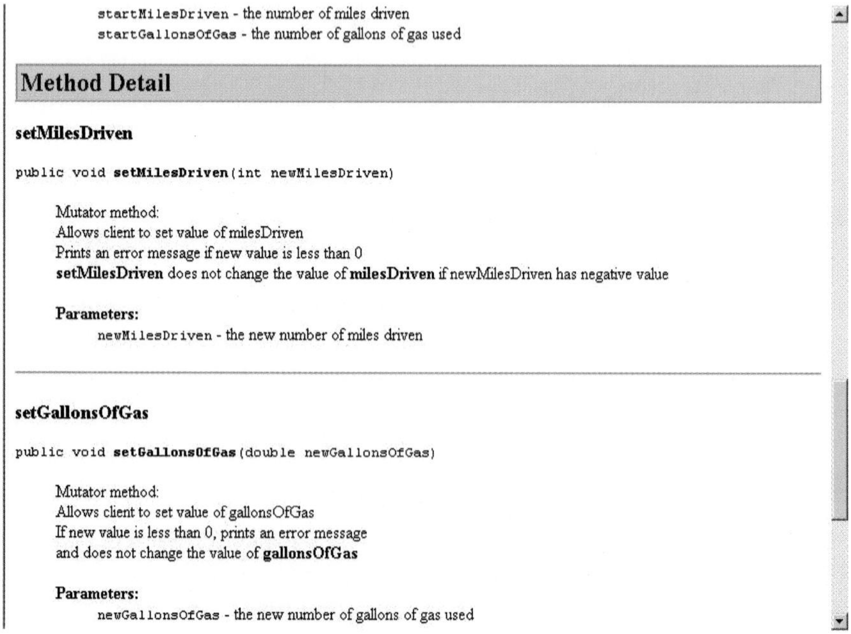

startMilesDriven - the number of miles driven
startGallonsOfGas - the number of gallons of gas used

Method Detail

setMilesDriven

```
public void setMilesDriven(int newMilesDriven)
```

    Mutator method:
    Allows client to set value of milesDriven
    Prints an error message if new value is less than 0
    setMilesDriven does not change the value of **milesDriven** if newMilesDriven has negative value

    Parameters:
        newMilesDriven - the new number of miles driven

setGallonsOfGas

```
public void setGallonsOfGas(double newGallonsOfGas)
```

    Mutator method:
    Allows client to set value of gallonsOfGas
    If new value is less than 0, prints an error message
    and does not change the value of **gallonsOfGas**

    Parameters:
        newGallonsOfGas - the new number of gallons of gas used

7.17 Chapter Summary

- The members of a Java class include its instance variables, class variables, and methods.

- One copy of each instance variable is created for every object instantiated from the class. One copy of each class variable and method is shared by all objects of the class.

- By convention, class names are nouns and begin with a capital letter; all internal words begin with a capital letter, and other letters are lowercase. Method names are verbs and begin with a lowercase letter; internal words begin with a capital letter, and all other letters are lowercase. Nonconstant instance variables are nouns and follow the same capitalization rules as methods. Constant fields have all capital letters with internal words separated by an underscore.

- The *public* access modifier allows the class or member to be accessed by other classes. The *private* access modifier specifies that the class or member can be accessed only by other members of the same class. Package access allows other classes in the same package to access the class or class members.

- Classes, constructors, *final* class variables, and class methods typically are declared as *public*, and instance variables are typically declared as *private*.

- Instance variables reflect the properties that all objects will have in common. Instance variables are defined by specifying an access modifier, data type, and identifier, and optionally, an initial value. Instance variables can be declared to be *final*.

- A method is defined by providing a method header, which specifies the access modifier, a return type, method name, and parameter list. The method body is enclosed in curly braces. Value-returning methods return the result of the method using one or more *return* statements. A method with a *void* return type does not return a value.

- The scope of an identifier is the range of code in which that identifier can be accessed. Instance variables and methods have class scope in that they can be accessed anywhere in the class.

- A method can reference the instance variables of its class, the parameters sent to the method, and local variables declared by the method and can call other methods of its class.

- A method can be overloaded by defining another method with the same name but a different signature, that is, with a different number of parameters or with parameters of different data types.

- Constructors are responsible for initializing the instance variables of the class.

- If you don't provide a constructor, the compiler provides a default constructor, which is a constructor that takes no arguments. This default constructor assigns default initial values to all the instance variables. Numeric variables are given the value of 0, characters are given the value *space*, *boolean* variables are given the value of *false*, and object references are given the value of *null*. Local variables declared in methods are not given initial values automatically.

- Accessor methods are named *getIV*, where *IV* is an instance variable name; the return data type is the same as the instance variable and the body of the method simply returns the value of the instance variable.

- Mutator methods are named *setIV*, where *IV* is an instance variable name; the return data type is *void*, and the method takes one argument, which is the same data type as the instance variable and contains the new value for the instance variable. The body of the method should validate the new value and, if the new value is valid, assign the new value to the instance variable.

- When a method begins executing, the JVM sets the object reference *this* to refer to the object for which the method has been called.

- The *toString* method is called automatically when an object reference is used as a *String* and its job is to provide a printable representation of the object data.

- The *equals* method compares two objects for equality, that is, it should return *true* only if the corresponding instance variables in both objects are equal in value, and *false* otherwise.

- *Static* class variables are created when the class is initialized. Thus, class variables exist before any objects are instantiated, and each class has only one copy of the class variables. *Static* variables that are constants are usually declared to be *public* because they typically are provided to allow the client to set preferences for the operations of a class.

- *Static* class methods can reference only *static* variables, can call only *static* methods, and cannot use the object reference *this*.

- A non-*static,* or instance, method can reference both class and instance variables, as well as class and instance methods, and the reference *this*.

- A graphical object usually has instance variables for the starting (*x*, *y*) coordinate. It also provides a *draw* method that takes a *Graphics* object as a parameter and includes the code to draw the graphical object.

- Enumeration types can be defined to give meaning to ordered sets that are represented in a program by numbers. For each name in an *enum* type initialization list, a constant object is created with an instance variable having a sequential numeric value. References can be defined of the *enum* type. Objects of the *enum* type can be compared, printed, and requested to return their numeric value.

- Javadoc, which is part of the Java SDK, generates documentation for classes. To use Javadoc, you enclose a description of each class, method, and field in a block comment beginning with /** and ending with */. In addition, you can describe each parameter using the *@param* tag and return values using the *@return* tag.

7.18   Exercises, Problems, and Projects

7.18.1   Multiple Choice Exercises

1. What can you say about the name of a class?

   ❑ It must start with an uppercase letter.

   ❑ The convention is to start with an uppercase letter.

2. What can you say about the name of constructors?

   ❑ They must be the same name as the class name.

   ❑ They can be any name, just like other methods.

3. What is a constructor's return type?

   ❑ *void.*

   ❑ *Object.*

   ❑ The class name.

   ❑ A constructor does not have a return type.

4. It is legal to have more than one constructor in a given class.

   ❑ true

   ❑ false

5. In a class, if a field is *private,*

   ❑ it can be accessed directly from any class.

   ❑ it can be accessed directly only from inside its class.

6. In a typical class, what is the general recommendation for access modifiers?

   ❑ Instance variables are *private* and methods are *private.*

   ❑ Instance variables are *private* and methods are *public.*

   ❑ Instance variables are *public* and methods are *private.*

   ❑ Instance variables are *public* and methods are *public.*

7. In a class, fields

   ❑ can only be basic data types

   ❑ can only be basic data types or existing Java types (from existing classes)

   ❑ can be basic data types, existing Java types, or user-defined types (from user-defined classes)

8. Accessors and mutators are

   ❑ instance variables of a class

   ❑ used to access and modify field variables of a class from outside the class

   ❑ constructor methods

9. Accessor methods typically take

   ❑ no parameter

   ❑ one parameter, of the same type as the corresponding field

10. Mutator methods typically take

    ❑ no parameter

    ❑ one parameter, of the same type as the corresponding field

11. Accessor methods typically

    ❑ are *void* methods

    ❑ return the same type as the corresponding field

12. Mutator methods typically

    ❑ are *void* methods

    ❑ return the same type as the corresponding field

13. When coding a method that performs calculations on fields of that class, then

    ❑ these fields must be passed as parameters to the method.

    ❑ these fields do not need to be passed as parameters to the methods because the class methods have direct access to them.

14. What is the keyword used for declaring a constant?

    ❑ *static*

    ❑ *final*

    ❑ *constant*

15. What is the keyword used for declaring a class variable or method?

    ❑ *static*

    ❑ *final*

    ❑ *class*

16. What can you say about *enum*?

    ❑ It is part of the package *java.lang*.

    ❑ It can be used for self-documentation, improving the readability of your code.

❑ An *enum* object is a constant object.

❑ All of the above.

7.18.2   Reading and Understanding Code

For questions 17 and 18, consider that inside the class *Sky*, we have already coded the following:

```
public class Sky
{
    private Color color;
    public Sky( Color c )
    {
        color = c;
    }
}
```

17. Consider the following method header:

    ```
    public Color getColor( )
    ```

    Is this method a constructor, mutator, or accessor?

18. Consider the following method header:

    ```
    public void setColor( Color c )
    ```

    Is this method a constructor, mutator, or accessor?

    For questions 19 to 24, consider that the class *Airplane* has two methods with the following method headers; we also have a default constructor already coded.

    ```
    public static double foo1( String s )
    public String foo2( char c )
    ```

19. What is the return type of method *foo1*?

20. What is the return type of method *foo2*?

21. Is method *foo1* a class or instance method? Explain.

22. Is method *foo2* a class or instance method? Explain.

23. Write a line or two of code to call method *foo1* from a client class.

24. Write a line or two of code to call method *foo2* from a client class. Assume we have instantiated an object named *a1*.

25. Inside method *main*, we see code like

    ```
    Airplane.foo3( 34.6 );
    ```

From this, reconstruct the header of method *foo3* (which belongs to the class *Airplane*); make appropriate assumptions if necessary.

26. Inside method *main*, we see code like

```
Airplane a = new Airplane( );
int n = a.foo4( "Hello" );
```

From this, reconstruct the header of method *foo4* (which belongs to class *Airplane*).

27. If you have defined the following *enum* constants:

```
enum Seasons { Winter, Spring, Summer, Fall };
```

What is the output of the following code sequence?

```
System.out.println( Seasons.Spring.ordinal( ) );
```

7.18.3   Fill in the Code

28. Declare two instance variables *grade*, which is an integer, and *letterGrade*, which is a *char*.

```
// declare grade here

// declare letterGrade here
```

29. Declare a class field for a federal tax rate, a constant, with value .07.

```
// declare federal tax rate constant; value is 0.07
```

For questions 30 to 37, we will assume that class *TelevisionChannel* has three fields: *name*, a *String*; *number*, an integer; and *cable*, a *boolean* which represents whether the channel is a cable channel.

30. Code a default constructor for that class: initialize the fields to an empty string, 0, and *false*, respectively.

```
// your default constructor code goes here
```

31. Code a constructor for that class that takes three parameters.

```
// your constructor code goes here
```

32. Code the three accessors for that class.

```
// your code goes here
```

33. Code the three mutators for that class.

```
// your code goes here
```

34. Code the *toString* method.

```
// your code goes here
```

35. Code the *equals* method.

```
// your code goes here
```

36. Code a method returning the number of digits in the channel number. For instance, if the channel number is 21, the method returns 2; if the channel number is 412, the method returns 3.

```
// your code goes here
```

37. Code a method returning the word *cable* if the current object represents a cable channel and returning the word *network* if the current object does not represent a cable channel.

```
// your code goes here
```

7.18.4   Identifying Errors in Code

For questions 38 to 45, consider that inside the class *Gift*, we have already coded the following:

```java
public class Gift
{
    private String description;
    private double price;
    private String occasion;
    private boolean taxable;

    public static final double TAX_RATE = 0.05;

    public Gift( String d, double p, String o, boolean t )
    {
        description = d;
        price = p;
        occasion = o;
        taxable = t;
    }

    public void setPrice( double p )
    {
        price = p;
    }
```

```
      public void setTaxable( boolean t )
      {
         taxable = t;
      }
   }
```

38. We are coding the following inside the class *Gift*; where is the error?

```
public void getPrice( )
{
   return price;
}
```

39. We are coding the following inside the class *Gift*; where is the error?

```
public void setOccasion( String occasion )
{
   occasion = occasion;
}
```

40. We are coding the following inside the class *Gift*; where is the error?

```
public String toString( )
{
   System.out.println( "description = " + description );
   System.out.println( "price = " + price );
   System.out.println( "occasion = " + occasion );
   System.out.println( "taxable = " + taxable );
}
```

41. We are coding the following inside the class *Gift*; where is the error?

```
public boolean equals( Gift g )
{
   return ( this = g );
}
```

42. We are coding the following inside the class *Gift*; where is the error?

```
public void setTaxRate( double newTaxRate )
{
   TAX_RATE = newTaxRate;
}
```

43. We are coding the following inside the class *Gift*; where is the error?

```
public double calcTax( TAX_RATE )
{
   return ( TAX_RATE * price );
}
```

44. We are coding the following in the *main* method inside the class *Gift-Client*; where is the error?

```
Gift g = new Gift( "radio", 59.99, "Birthday", false );
Gift.setPrice( 99.99 );
```

45. We are coding the following in the *main* method inside the class *Gift-Client*; where is the error?

```
Gift g = new Gift( "radio", 59.99, "Birthday", false );
g.setTaxable( ) = true;
```

46. Where are the errors in the following statement?

```
enum Months = { "January", "February", "March" };
```

7.18.5   Debugging Area—Using Messages from the *Java Compiler and Java* JVM

For questions 47 and 48, consider the following class *Grade*:

```java
public class Grade
{
  private char letterGrade;

  public Grade( char lg )
  {
    letterGrade = lg;
  }
  public char getLetterGrade( )
  {
    return  letterGrade;
  }
  public void setLetterGrade( char lg )
  {
    letterGrade = lg;
  }
}
```

47. In the *main* method of the class *GradeClient*, you have coded

```
Grade g = new Grade( 'B' );
g.letterGrade = 'A';          // line 10
```

When you compile, you get the following message:

```
GradeClient.java:10: letterGrade has private access in Grade
g.letterGrade = 'A';
  ^
1 error
```

Explain what the problem is and how to fix it.

48. In the *main* method of the class *GradeClient*, you have coded

```
Grade g = new Grade( "A" );  // line 10
```

When you compile, you get the following message:

```
GradeClient.java:10: cannot find symbol
symbol  : constructor Grade (java.lang.String)
location: class Grade
Grade g = new Grade( "A" );
          ^
1 error
```

Explain what the problem is and how to fix it.

49. You coded the following definition for the class *Grade*:

```
public class Grade
{
    private char letterGrade;

    public char Grade( char startLetter )
    {
       letterGrade = startLetter;
    } // line 10
}
```

When you compile, you get the following message:

```
Grade.java:10: missing return statement
 }
 ^
1 error
```

Explain what the problem is and how to fix it.

50. You coded the following definition for the class *Grade*:

```
public class Grade
{
  private char letterGrade;
  public Grade( char lg )
  {
    letterGrade = lg;
  }
  public String toString( )    // line 10
  {                            // line 11
     return letterGrade;       // line 12
  }                            // line 13
}
```

When you compile, you get the following message:

```
Grade.java:12: incompatible types
found   : char
required: java.lang.String
 return letterGrade;
        ^

1 error
```

Explain what the problem is and how to fix it.

51. You coded the following definition for the class *Grade*:

```
public class Grade
{
  private char letterGrade;
  public Grade( char lg )
  {
    letterGrade = lg;
  }
  public String toString( )   // line 10
  {                           // line 11
    return ( lg );            // line 12
  }                           // line 13
}
```

When you compile, you get the following message:

```
Grade.java:12: cannot find symbol
symbol  : variable lg
location: class Grade
 return lg;
        ^

1 error
```

Explain what the problem is and how to fix it.

52. You coded the following definition for the class *Grade*:

```
public class Grade
{
  private char letterGrade;
  public Grade( char letterGrade )
  {
    letterGrade = letterGrade;
  }
  public char getLetterGrade( )
```

```
   {
     return letterGrade;
   }
}
```

In the *main* method of the class *GradeClient*, you have coded:

```
Grade g1 = new Grade( 'A' );
System.out.println( g1.getLetterGrade( ) );
```

The code compiles properly and runs, but the result is not what you expected.

The client's output is a space, not an *A*.

Explain what the problem is and how to fix it.

53. You have defined the following *enum* constants:

```
enum Seasons { Winter, Spring, Summer, Fall };
```

In the *main* method of the class *Test*, you have coded

```
Seasons s = Seasons.Spring;
if ( s.equals( Winter ) )    // line 10
      System.out.println( "It is cold" );
else
      System.out.println( "The weather is fine" );
```

When you compile, you get the following message:

```
Test.java:10: cannot find symbol
symbol  : variable Winter
location: class Test
  if ( s.equals( Winter ) )  // line 10
                 ^
1 error
```

Explain what the problem is and how to fix it.

54. You have defined the following *enum* constants:

```
enum Seasons { Winter, Spring, Summer, Fall };
```

In the *main* method of the class *Test*, you have coded

```
Seasons.Fall = Autumn;   // line 10
```

When you compile, you get the following message:

```
Test.java:10: cannot assign a value to final variable Fall
   Seasons.Fall = Autumn;  // line 10
        ^
Test.java:10: cannot find symbol
symbol  : variable Autumn
location: class Test
   Seasons.Fall = Autumn;  // line 10
                   ^
2 errors
```

Explain what the problem is and how to fix it.

7.18.6   Write a Short Program

55. Write a class encapsulating the concept of a team (for example, "Orioles"), assuming a team has only one attribute: the team. Include a constructor, the accessor and mutator, and methods *toString* and *equals*. Write a client class to test all the methods in your class.

56. Write a class encapsulating the concept of a television set, assuming a television set has the following attributes: a brand and a price. Include a constructor, the accessors and mutators, and methods *toString* and *equals*. Write a client class to test all the methods in your class.

57. Write a class encapsulating the concept of a course grade, assuming a course grade has the following attributes: a course and a letter grade. Include a constructor, the accessors and mutators, and methods *toString* and *equals*. Write a client class to test all the methods in your class.

58. Write a class encapsulating the concept of a course, assuming a course has the following attributes: a code (for instance, CS1), a description, and a number of credits (for instance, 3). Include a constructor, the accessors and mutators, and methods *toString* and *equals*. Write a client class to test all the methods in your class.

59. Write a class encapsulating the concept of a student, assuming a student has the following attributes: a name, a social security number, and a GPA (for instance, 3.5). Include a constructor, the accessors and mutators, and methods *toString* and *equals*. Write a client class to test all the methods in your class.

60. Write a class encapsulating the concept of Web site statistics, assuming Web site statistics have the following attributes: number of visitors and type of site (commercial, government, etc.). Include a constructor, the accessors and mutators, and methods *toString* and *equals*. Write a client class to test all the methods in your class.

61. Write a class encapsulating the concept of a corporate name (for example, "IBM"), assuming a corporate name has only one attribute: the corporate name itself. Include a constructor, the accessors and mutators, and methods *toString* and *equals*. Also include a method returning a potential domain name by adding *www.* at the beginning and *.com* at the end of the corporate name (for instance, if the corporate name is IBM, that method should return *www.ibm.com*). Write a client class to test all the methods in your class.

62. Write a class encapsulating the concept of a file, assuming a file has only a single attribute: the name of the file. Include a constructor, the accessors and mutators, and methods *toString* and *equals*. Also, code a method returning the extension of the file, that is, the letters after the last dot in the file (for instance, if the filename is *Test.java*, then the method should return *java*); if there is no dot in the filename, then the method should return "*unknown extension.*" Write a client class to test all the methods in your class.

7.18.7 Programming Projects

63. Write a class encapsulating the concept of the weather forecast, assuming that it has the following attributes: the temperature and the sky conditions, which could be sunny, snowy, cloudy, or rainy. Include a constructor, the accessors and mutators, and methods *toString* and *equals*. Temperature, in Fahrenheit, should be between -50 and $+150$; the default value is 70, if needed. The default sky condition is sunny. Include a method that converts Fahrenheit to Celsius. Celsius temperature = (Fahrenheit temperature $-$ 32) * 5 / 9. Also include a method which checks whether the weather attributes are consistent (there are two cases where they are not consistent: when the temperature is below 32 and it is not snowy, and when the temperature is above 100 and it is not sunny). Write a client class to test all the methods in your class.

64. Write a class encapsulating the concept of a domain name, assuming a domain name has a single attribute: the domain name itself (for instance, *www.yahoo.com*). Include a constructor, the accessors and mutators, and methods *toString* and *equals*. Also include the following methods: one returning whether or not the domain name starts with *www*; another returning the extension of the domain name (i.e., the letters after the last dot, for instance *com*, *gov*, or *edu*; if there is no dot in the domain name, then you should return "*unknown*"); and another returning the name itself (which will be the characters between *www* and the extension; for instance, *yahoo* if the domain is *www.yahoo.com*—if there are fewer than two dots in the domain name, then your method should return "*unknown*"). Write a client class to test all the methods in your class.

65. Write a class encapsulating the concept of an HTML page, assuming an HTML statement has only a single attribute: the HTML code for the page. Include a constructor, the accessors and mutators, and methods *toString* and *equals*. Include the following methods: one checking that there is a > character following each < character, one counting how many images are on the page (i.e., the number of IMG tags), and one counting how many links are on the page (i.e., the number of times we have "A HREF"). Write a client class to test all the methods in your class.

66. Write a class encapsulating the concept of coins, assuming that coins have the following attributes: a number of quarters, a number of dimes, a number of nickels, and a number of pennies. Include a constructor, the accessors and mutators, and methods *toString* and *equals*. Also code the following methods: one printing the total amount of money in dollar notation with two significant digits after the decimal point, and others returning the money in quarters (for instance, 0.75 if there are three quarters), in dimes, in nickels, and in pennies. Write a client class to test all the methods in your class.

67. Write a class encapsulating the concept of a user-defined *double*, assuming a user-defined *double* has only a single attribute: a *double*. Include a constructor, the accessor and mutator, and methods *toString* and *equals*. Add a method, taking one parameter specifying how many significant digits we want to have, and returning a *double*

representing the original *double* truncated so that it includes the specified number of significant digits after the decimal point (for instance, if the original *double* is 6.9872 and the argument of the method is 2, this method will return 6.98). Write a client class to test all the methods in your class.

68. Write a class encapsulating the concept of a circle, assuming a circle has the following attributes: a *Point* representing the center of the circle, and the radius of the circle, an integer. Include a constructor, the accessors and mutators, and methods *toString* and *equals*. Also include methods returning the perimeter (2 * π * radius) and area (π * radius^2) of the circle. Write a client class to test all the methods in your class.

69. Write a class encapsulating the concept of a rational number, assuming a rational number has the following attributes: an integer representing the numerator of the rational number, and another integer representing the denominator of the rational number. Include a constructor, the accessors and mutators, and methods *toString* and *equals*. You should not allow the denominator to be equal to 0; you should give it the default value 1 in case the corresponding argument of the constructor or a method is 0. Also include methods performing multiplication of a rational number by another and addition of a rational number to another, returning the resulting rational number in both cases. Write a client class to test all the methods in your class.

70. Write a class encapsulating the concept of an investment, assuming the investment has the following attributes: the amount of the investment, and the interest rate at which the investment will be compounded. Include a constructor, the accessors and mutators, and methods *toString* and *equals*. Also include a method returning the future value of the investment depending on how many years we hold it before selling it, which can be calculated using the formula:

```
future value =  investment ( 1 + interest rate )numberOfYears
```

We will assume that the interest rate is compounded annually. Write a client class to test all the methods in your class.

71. Write a class encapsulating the concept of a telephone number, assuming a telephone number has only a single attribute: a *String* rep-

resenting the telephone number. Include a constructor, the accessor and mutator, and methods *toString* and *equals*. Also include methods returning the area code (the first three digits/characters of the phone number; if there are fewer than three characters in the phone number or if the first three characters are not digits, then this method should return "*unknown area code*"). Write a client class to test all the methods in your class.

7.18.8 Technical Writing

72. An advantage of object-oriented programming is code reuse, not just by the programmer who wrote the class, but by other programmers. Describe the importance of proper documentation and how you would document a class so that other programmers can use it easily.

73. Java has a number of naming conventions for classes, methods, field variables. Is this important? Why is it good to respect these conventions?

7.18.9 Group Project (for a group of 1, 2, or 3 students)

74. Write a program that solves a quadratic equation in all cases, including when both roots are complex numbers. For this, you need to set up the following classes:

Complex, which encapsulates a complex number

ComplexPair, which encapsulates a pair of complex numbers

Quadratic, which encapsulates a quadratic equation

SolveEquation, which contains the *main* method

Along with the usual constructors, accessors, and mutators, you will need to code additional methods:

In the *Complex* class, a method that determines whether a complex object is real

In the *ComplexPair* class, a method that determines whether both complex numbers are identical

In the *Quadratic* class, a method to solve the quadratic equation and return a *ComplexPair* object

Additionally, you need to include code in the *main* method to solve several examples of quadratic equations input from the keyboard.

Your output should make comments as to what type of roots we get (double real root, distinct real roots, distinct complex roots). You should check that your code works in all four basic cases:

❏ The quadratic equation is actually a linear equation.

❏ Both roots are complex.

❏ There is a double real root.

❏ There are two distinct real roots.

CHAPTER 8

Single-Dimensional Arrays

CHAPTER CONTENTS

Introduction

Up to this point, we have been working with individual, or scalar, variables; that is, each variable has held one value at a time. To process a group of variables of the same type—for example, counting the number of odd integers entered by the user—we used a *while* loop or a *for* loop.

Thus, to find the average high temperature for the last year, we would use a *for* loop:

```java
double dailyTemp;
double total = 0.0;
for ( int i = 1; i <= 365; i++ )
{
    System.out.print( "Enter a temperature" );
    dailyTemp = scan.nextDouble( );
    total += dailyTemp;
}
double average = total / 365;
```

We defined one variable, *dailyTemp*, to hold the data. We read each temperature into our *dailyTemp* variable, added the temperature to our total, then read the next value into the *dailyTemp* variable, added that temperature to the total, and so on, until we finished reading and processing all the temperatures. Each time we read a new temperature, it overwrote the previous temperature, so that at the end of the loop, we had access to the last temperature only.

But suppose we want to perform multiple operations on those temperatures. Perhaps we want to find the highest or lowest temperature or find the median. Or suppose we don't know what operations we will perform, or in what order, until the user chooses them from a menu. In those cases, one scalar variable, *dailyTemp*, won't work; we want to store all the temperatures in memory at the same time. An array allows us to do just that without declaring several variables individually.

An **array** is a sequence of variables of the same data type. The data type could be any Java primitive data type, such as *int*, *float*, *double*, *byte*, *boolean*, *char*, *short*, or *long*, or it could be a class. Each variable in the array, called an **element**, is accessed using the array name and a subscript, called an **index**, which refers to the element's position in the array.

Arrays are useful for many applications: for example, calculating statistics on a group of data values or processing data stored in tables, such as matrices or game boards.

8.1 Declaring and Instantiating Arrays

In Java, arrays are implemented as objects, so creating an array takes two steps:

1. declaring the object reference for the array

2. instantiating the array

In arrays of primitive types, each element in the array contains a value of that type. For example, in an array of *doubles*, each element contains a *double* value. In arrays of objects, each element is an object reference, which stores the location of an object.

8.1.1 Declaring Arrays

To declare an array, you specify the name of the array and the data type, as you would for any other variable. Adding an empty set of brackets ([ ]) indicates that the variable is an array.

Here is the syntax for declaring an array:

```
datatype [ ] arrayName;
```

For example, the following statement creates a reference to an array that will hold daily high temperatures:

```
double [ ] dailyTemps; // each element is a double
```

The brackets can be placed before or after the array name. So the following syntax is also valid:

```
datatype arrayName [ ];
```

Thus, we could have declared the array above using the following statement:

```
double dailyTemps [ ];
```

Although you will see Java code written using either syntax, we prefer the first format with the brackets right after the data type, because it's easier to read as "a *double* array."

To declare an array to hold the titles of all tracks on a CD, you might declare it this way:

```
String [ ] cdTracks; // each element is a String object reference
```

SOFTWARE ENGINEERING TIP

An array's data type can be any primitive type or any predefined or user-defined class. The important thing to remember is that each element of an array with a class data type is a reference to the object; it is not the object itself.

Similarly, this statement declares an array to hold the answers to a true/false test:

```
boolean [ ] answers; // each element is a boolean value
```

Using our *Auto* class from Chapter 7, this statement declares an array to hold *Auto* objects:

```
Auto [ ] cars; // each element is an Auto object reference
```

You can declare multiple arrays of the same data type in one statement by inserting a comma after each array name, using this syntax:

```
datatype [ ] arrayName1, arrayName2;
```

For example, the following statement will declare three integer arrays to hold quiz scores for current courses:

```
int [ ] cs101, bio201, hist102;  // all elements are int values
```

COMMON ERROR TRAP

Putting the size of the array inside the brackets in the array declaration will generate a compiler error.

Note that an array declaration does not specify how many elements the arrays will have. The declaration simply specifies an object reference for the array and the data type of the elements. Thus, **declaring an array does not allocate memory for the array**.

8.1.2   Instantiating Arrays

As we mentioned earlier, Java arrays are objects, so to allocate memory for an array, you need to instantiate the array using the *new* keyword. Here is the syntax for instantiating an array:

```
arrayName = new datatype [size];
```

> where size is an expression that evaluates to an integer and
> specifies the number of elements in the array.

The following statements will instantiate the arrays declared earlier:

```
dailyTemps = new double [365]; // dailyTemps has 365 elements

cdTracks = new String [15];    // cdTracks has 15 elements

int numberOfQuestions = 30;
answers = new boolean [numberOfQuestions]; // answers has 30 elements

cars = new Auto [3];           // cars has 3 elements

cs101 = new int [5];           // cs101 has 5 elements

bio201 = new int [4];          // bio201 has 4 elements

hist102 = new int [6];         // hist102 has 6 elements
```

When an array is instantiated, the elements are given initial values automatically.

Numeric elements are set to 0; *boolean* elements are set to *false*; *char* elements are set to a space; and object references are set to *null*.

Thus, all the elements in the *dailyTemps* array are given an initial value of 0.0; the elements in the *cs101*, *bio201*, and *hist102* arrays are given an initial value of 0; the elements of the *answers* array are given an initial value of *false*; and the elements of the *cdTracks* and *cars* arrays are given an initial value of *null*.

8.1.3 Combining the Declaration and Instantiation of Arrays

Arrays also can be instantiated when they are declared. To combine the declaration and instantiation of an array, use this syntax:

```
datatype [ ] arrayName = new datatype [size];
```

    where size is an expression that evaluates to an integer and
    specifies the number of elements in the array.

Thus, this statement:

```
double [ ] dailyTemps = new double [365];
```

is equivalent to:

```
double [ ] dailyTemps;
dailyTemps = new double [365];
```

TABLE 8.1 Default Initial Values of Array Elements

Element Data Type	Initial Value
double	0.0
float	0.0
int, long, short, byte	0
char	space
boolean	false
object reference	null

Similarly, this statement:

```
String [ ] cdTracks = new String [15];
```

is equivalent to:

```
String [ ] cdTracks;
cdTracks = new String [15];
```

8.1.4   Assigning Initial Values to Arrays

Java allows you to instantiate an array by assigning initial values when the array is declared. To do this, you specify the initial values using a comma-separated list within curly braces:

```
datatype [ ] arrayName = { value0, value1, value2, ... };
```

> where *valueN* is an expression that evaluates to the data type
> of the array and is the value to assign to the element at index *N*.

Note that we do not use the *new* keyword and we do not specify a size for the array. The number of elements in the array is determined by the number of values in the initialization list.

For example, this statement declares and instantiates an array of odd numbers:

```
int nine = 9;
int [ ] oddNumbers = { 1, 3, 5, 7, nine, nine + 2, 13, 15, 17, 19 };
```

Because 10 values are given in the initialization list, this array has 10 elements. Notice that the values can be an expression, for example, *nine* and *nine + 2*.

Similarly, we can declare and instantiate an array of objects by providing objects in the list, as shown below. The *cars* array of *Auto* objects has three elements.

```
Auto sportsCar = new Auto( "Ferrari", 0, 0.0 );
Auto [ ] cars = { new Auto( "BMW", 100, 15.0 ), sportsCar, new Auto( ) };
```

8.2   Accessing Array Elements

Elements of an array are accessed using this syntax:

```
arrayName[exp]
```

> where exp is an expression that evaluates to an integer.

Exp is the element's position, or **index**, within the array. The index of the first element in the array is always 0; the index of the last element is always 1 less than the number of elements.

TABLE 8.2 Accessing Array Elements	
Element	**Syntax**
Element 0	`arrayName[0]`
Element *i*	`arrayName[i]`
Last element	`arrayName[arrayName.length - 1]`

Arrays have a read-only, integer instance variable, **length**, which holds the number of elements in the array. To access the number of elements in an array named *arrayName*, use this syntax:

`arrayName.length`

Thus, to access the last element of an array, use this syntax:

`arrayName[arrayName.length - 1]`

Note that regardless of the data type of the elements in an array, the *length* of an array is always an integer, because *length* represents the number of elements in the array.

Table 8.2 summarizes the syntax for accessing elements of an array.

For example, suppose we want to analyze our monthly cell phone bills for the past six months. We want to calculate the average bill, the total payments for the six months, and the lowest and highest bills. We can use an array of *doubles* with six elements, as shown in Example 8.1.

 **COMMON ERROR TRAP**

Note that for an array, *length*—with no parentheses—is an instance variable, whereas for *Strings*, *length( )*—with parentheses—is a method. Note also that the instance variable is named *length*, rather than *size*.

```
 1  /* Array of Cell Phone Bills
 2     Anderson, Franceschi
 3  */
 4
 5  public class CellBills
 6  {
 7    public static void main( String [ ] args )
 8    {
 9      // declare and instantiate the array
10      double [ ] cellBills = new double [6];
11
12      // assign values to array elements
13      cellBills[0] = 45.24;
14      cellBills[1] = 54.67;
15      cellBills[2] = 42.55;
```

```
16      cellBills[3] = 44.61;
17      cellBills[4] = 65.29;
18      cellBills[5] = 49.75;
19
20      System.out.println( "The first monthly cell bill is "
21                            + cellBills[0] );
22      System.out.println( "The last monthly cell bill is "
23                            + cellBills[cellBills.length - 1] );
24   }
25 }
```

EXAMPLE 8.1   The *cellBills* Array

In lines 9–10, we declare and instantiate the *cellBills* array. Because the elements of *cellBills* are *doubles*, instantiating the array also initializes each element to 0.00 and sets the value of *cellBills.length* to 6. Thus, Figure 8.1 represents the *cellBills* array after line 10 is executed.

Lines 12–18 store values into each element of the array. The element at index *i* of the array is *cellBills[i]*. Remember that the first element of an array is always at index 0. Thus, the last element is *cellBills[5]*, or equivalently, *cellBills[cellBills.length – 1]*. Figure 8.2 shows how the *cellBills* array looks after lines 13–18 are executed.

Lines 20–21 print the value of the first element, and lines 22–23 print the value of the last element. The output of Example 8.1 is shown in Figure 8.3.

Array indexes *must* be between 0 and *arrayName.length – 1*. Attempting to access an element of an array using an index less than 0 or greater than *arrayName.length – 1* will compile without errors, but will generate an *ArrayIndexOutOfBoundsException* at run time. By default, this exception halts execution of the program.

Figure 8.1

The *cellBills* Array After Instantiation

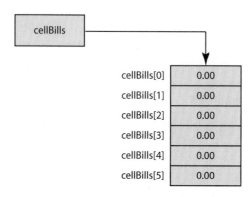

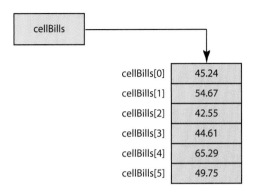

Figure 8.2
The *cellBills* Array After Assigning Values

Figure 8.3
Output of Example 8.1

For example, all the following expressions are invalid:

```
// invalid indexes for the cellBills array!!

cellBills[-1]                   // the lowest valid index is 0

cellBills[cellBills.length]     // the highest valid index is
                                // cellBills.length - 1

cellBills[150]                  // the highest valid index is 5
```

 **COMMON ERROR TRAP**

Attempting to access an element of an array using an index less than 0 or an index greater than *arrayName.length - 1* will generate an *ArrayIndexOutOfBoundsException* at run time.

Instantiating an array with a class data type involves two steps.

1. Instantiate the array.

2. Instantiate the objects.

Remember that the elements of an array with a class data type are object references. When the array is instantiated, all elements are set to *null*. Thus, the second step needs to be instantiating each object and assigning its reference to an array element.

Example 8.2 illustrates how to work with an array of objects. In this example, we reuse the *Auto* class from Chapter 7.

```
1 /* Working with an Array of Objects
2    Anderson, Franceschi
3 */
4
5 public class AutoArray
6 {
7   public static void main( String [ ] args )
8   {
9     // 1. instantiate cars array
10    Auto [ ] cars = new Auto [3];
11
12    // 2. instantiate Auto objects
13    Auto sportsCar = new Auto( "Ferrari", 100, 15.0 );
14    cars[0] = sportsCar;    // assign sportsCar to element 1
15    cars[1] = new Auto( );  // default Auto object
16    // cars[2] has not been instantiated and is null
17
18    // call Auto methods
19    System.out.println( "cars[0] is a " + cars[0].getModel( ) );
20
21    Auto myCar = cars[1];
22    System.out.println( "myCar has used " + myCar.getGallonsOfGas( )
23                        + " gallons of gas" );
24
25    // attempt to call method when Auto object is not instantiated
26    System.out.println( "cars[2] is a " + cars[2].getModel( ) );
27  }
28 }
```

EXAMPLE 8.2   Working with an Array of Objects

COMMON ERROR TRAP

With an array of objects, be sure that an array element points to an instantiated object before attempting to use that element to call a method of the class. Otherwise, a *NullPointerException* will be generated.

At lines 9–10, we declare and instantiate *cars*, an array of three *Auto* objects. At this point, each element has the value of *null*. Thus, our second step is to instantiate objects of the *Auto* class and assign their references to the array elements.

At lines 13–14, we instantiate the *Auto* object *sportsCar* and assign the *sportsCar* reference to element 0. At line 15, we instantiate a default *Auto* object and assign its reference to element 1. We do not instantiate an object for element 2, which remains *null*.

We then call methods of the *Auto* class. Because the array elements are object references, to call a method for an object in an array, we use the array name and index, along with the dot notation. This is illustrated in line 19, where we print the model of element 0 by calling the *getModel* method. In

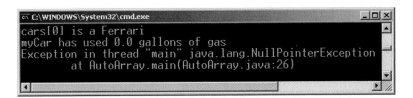

Figure 8.4
Output of Example 8.2

lines 21–23, we assign element 1 to the *Auto* reference *myCar*, then call the *getGallonsOfGas* method using the *myCar* reference.

Finally, line 26 attempts to retrieve the model of element 2; however, because *cars[2]* is *null*, a *NullPointerException* is generated. Figure 8.4 shows the output of this program.

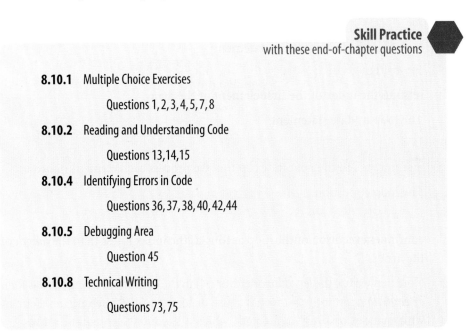

Skill Practice
with these end-of-chapter questions

8.10.1   Multiple Choice Exercises

Questions 1, 2, 3, 4, 5, 7, 8

8.10.2   Reading and Understanding Code

Questions 13, 14, 15

8.10.4   Identifying Errors in Code

Questions 36, 37, 38, 40, 42, 44

8.10.5   Debugging Area

Question 45

8.10.8   Technical Writing

Questions 73, 75

8.3   Aggregate Array Operations

Once the array is declared and instantiated, it would be convenient if we could just use the array name to perform operations on the whole array, such as printing the array, copying the array to another array, inputting values to the array, and so on. Unfortunately, Java does not support these aggregate operations on arrays.

For example, attempting to print the array using the array name will *not* print all the elements of the array. Instead, this statement:

```
System.out.println( cellBills ); // incorrect attempt to print array!
```

calls the *toString* method of the *Array* class, which simply prints the name of the object's class and the hash code of the array name, for example, [D@310d42.

8.3.1 Printing Array Elements

To print all elements of an array, we need to use a loop that prints each element individually. A *for* loop is custom-made for processing all elements of an array in order. In fact, the following *for* loop header is a standard way to process all elements in an array:

```
for ( int i = 0; i < arrayName.length; i++ )
```

Note that the initialization statement:

```
int i = 0;
```

sets *i* to the index of the first element of the array.

The loop update statement:

```
i++;
```

increments *i* to the next index so that we process each element in order.

The loop condition:

```
i < arrayName.length
```

COMMON ERROR TRAP

In a *for* loop, using the condition:

`i <= arrayName.length`

will generate an *ArrayIndexOutOfBoundsException* because the index of the last element of an array is *arrayName.length – 1*.

continues execution of the loop as long as the index is less than the *length* of the array.

Note that we use the *less than* operator (<) in the condition. Using the *less than or equal to* operator (<=) would cause us to attempt to reference an element with an index of *arrayName.length*, which is beyond the end of the array.

Inside the *for* loop, we refer to the current element being processed as

```
arrayName[i]
```

Example 8.3, whose output is shown in Figure 8.5, demonstrates how to print each element in an array.

```
1 /* Printing Array Elements
2      Anderson, Franceschi
3 */
```

```
4
5 public class PrintingArrayElements
6 {
7   public static void main( String [ ] args )
8   {
9     double [ ] cellBills = new double [6];
10    cellBills[0] = 45.24;
11    cellBills[1] = 54.67;
12    cellBills[2] = 42.55;
13    cellBills[3] = 44.61;
14    cellBills[4] = 65.29;
15    cellBills[5] = 49.75;
16
17    System.out.println( "Element\tValue" );
18    for ( int i = 0; i < cellBills.length; i++ )
19    {
20      System.out.println( i + "\t" + cellBills[i] );
21    }
22  }
23 }
```

EXAMPLE 8.3   Printing All Elements of an Array

In lines 9–15, we instantiate the *cellBills* array and assign values to its six elements. In line 18, we use the standard *for* loop header. Inside the *for* loop (line 20), we print each element's index and value.

8.3.2   Reading Data into an Array

Similarly, we can use the standard *for* loop to input data into an array. In Example 8.4, we use a *for* loop to prompt the user for each monthly cell phone bill and to assign the input value to the appropriate array elements.

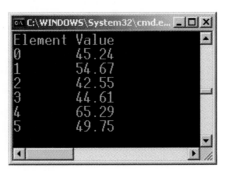

Figure 8.5
Output of Example 8.3

```
1 /* Reading data into an array
2    Anderson, Franceschi
3 */
4
5 import java.util.Scanner;
6
7 public class ReadingDataIntoAnArray
8 {
9   public static void main( String [ ] args )
10  {
11    Scanner scan = new Scanner( System.in );
12
13    double [ ] cellBills = new double[6];
14    for ( int i = 0; i < cellBills.length; i++ )
15    {
16      System.out.print( "Enter bill amount for month "
17                        + ( i + 1 ) + "\t" );
18      cellBills[i] = scan.nextDouble( ); // read current bill
19    }
20  }
21 }
```

EXAMPLE 8.4   Reading Data from the Console into an Array

At lines 14–19, our *for* loop prompts the user for a value for each element in the *cellBills* array. Note that our prompt uses the expression $(i + 1)$ for the month number. Although array indexes start at 0, people start counting at 1. If we used the array index in the prompt, we would ask the user for the bills for months 0 to 5. By adding 1 to the array index, we are able to prompt the user for months 1 through 6, which are the month numbers that the user expects.

SOFTWARE ENGINEERING TIP

Prompt for data in terms the user understands.

The output of Example 8.4 is shown in Figure 8.6.

Figure 8.6

Reading Data into an Array

```
C:\WINDOWS\System32\cmd.exe                    _ □ ×
Enter bill amount for month 1      62.33
Enter bill amount for month 2      54.27
Enter bill amount for month 3      71.19
Enter bill amount for month 4      59.03
Enter bill amount for month 5      62.65
Enter bill amount for month 6      65.08
```

8.3.3   Summing the Elements of an Array

To sum the elements of the array, we again use the standard *for* loop, as shown in Example 8.5.

```java
1 /* Summing Array Elements
2    Anderson, Franceschi
3 */
4
5 import java.text.NumberFormat;
6
7 public class SummingArrayElements
8 {
9  public static void main( String [ ] args )
10  {
11    double [ ] cellBills = new double [6];
12    cellBills[0] = 45.24;
13    cellBills[1] = 54.67;
14    cellBills[2] = 42.55;
15    cellBills[3] = 44.61;
16    cellBills[4] = 65.29;
17    cellBills[5] = 49.75;
18
19    double totalBills = 0.0;  // initialize total
20    for ( int i = 0; i < cellBills.length; i++ )
21    {
22      totalBills += cellBills[i];
23    }
24
25    NumberFormat priceFormat = NumberFormat.getCurrencyInstance( );
26    System.out.println( "Total for the bills: "
27                       + priceFormat.format( totalBills ) );
28 }
29 }
```

EXAMPLE 8.5   Summing the Elements of an Array

We fill the *cellBills* array with values at lines 12–17. We declare the *double* variable *totalBills* and initialize it to 0.0 at line 19. The *for* loop, at lines 20–23, adds each element of the array to *totalBills*. We use the *NumberFormat* class to format the value of *totalBills* as currency for output (lines 25–27). The output of Example 8.5 is shown in Figure 8.7.

Figure 8.7

**Calculating the Total of
All Elements**

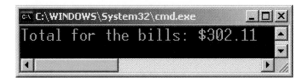

8.3.4 Finding Maximum or Minimum Values

Suppose we want to find a month that has the lowest bill. That would require finding a minimum value in the array and noting its index. Similarly, to find a month with the highest bill, we would need to find a maximum value in the array and note its index.

To find a maximum or minimum value in an array, we use a variation of the standard *for* loop. Example 8.6 finds a highest array value and its array index for our *cellBills* array of monthly cell bills.

```
1 /* Finding the maximum array value
2    Anderson, Franceschi
3 */
4
5 import java.text.NumberFormat;
6
7 public class MaxArrayValue
8 {
9  public static void main( String [ ] args )
10  {
11    double [ ] cellBills = new double [6];
12    cellBills[0] = 45.24;
13    cellBills[1] = 54.67;
14    cellBills[2] = 42.55;
15    cellBills[3] = 44.61;
16    cellBills[4] = 65.29;
17    cellBills[5] = 49.75;
18
19    int maxIndex = 0;   // initialize to index of first element
20    for ( int i = 1; i < cellBills.length; i++ )
21    {
22     if ( cellBills[i] > cellBills[maxIndex] )
23       maxIndex = i;  // save index of maximum value
24    }
25
26    NumberFormat priceFormat = NumberFormat.getCurrencyInstance( );
27    System.out.println ( "The highest bill, "
```

```
28                          + priceFormat.format( cellBills[maxIndex] )
29                          + ", was found at index " + maxIndex );
30  }
31 }
```

EXAMPLE 8.6   Finding a Maximum Value in an Array

We start by assuming that the first element is a maximum value. So we initialize an integer variable, *maxIndex*, to 0, at line 19. Then, at lines 20–24, starting at element 1, we step through the array, comparing the value of each element with the element at *maxIndex*. Whenever we find a value higher than the current maximum, we assign its index to *maxIndex* (line 23). When the *for* loop completes, *maxIndex* holds the index of the array element with a highest value. We then print both that index and the corresponding array value at lines 26–29. The output is shown in Figure 8.8.

What happens if the array has only one value? Will we still get the correct result? The answer is yes, because the single element will be at index 0. We start by assigning 0 to *maxIndex*. Then the *for* loop body will not execute because the condition will evaluate to *false*. So *maxIndex* will not be changed and remains set to 0.

What happens if more than one element holds the highest value? We find the index of the first element only, because our condition requires that the element value must be greater than the current maximum to change *maxIndex*.

8.3.5   Copying Arrays

Suppose we create a second array to hold a copy of our cell phone bills, as shown in the following statement:

```
double [ ] billsBackup = new double [6];
```

At this point, all elements of the *billsBackup* array are initialized automatically to 0.0. Figure 8.9 shows the current state of the *cellBills* and *billsBackup* arrays.

The highest bill, $65.29, was found at index 4

Figure 8.8

Output of Example 8.6

Figure 8.9

The *cellBills* and *billsBackup* Arrays

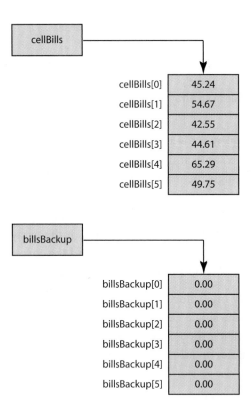

Then, if we want to copy the elements of the *cellBills* array to the corresponding elements of the *billsBackup* array, we might be tempted to use the assignment operator:

```
billsBackup = cellBills; // incorrect attempt to copy array elements!
```

This won't work. Because arrays are objects, the assignment operator copies the *cellBills* object reference to the *billsBackup* object reference. Both *cellBills* and *billsBackup* now point to the same object. The array data was not copied. In fact, we just lost the original *billsBackup* array. With no object reference pointing to it, the array is a candidate for garbage collection, as shown in Figure 8.10.

If we were to assign a new value to an element in the *billsBackup* array, we would change the element in the *cellBills* array also, because they are now the same array.

This statement:

```
billsBackup[4] = 38.00;
```

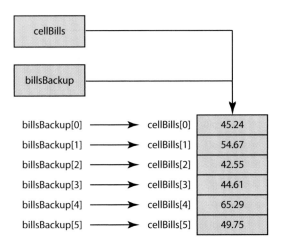

Figure 8.10
Assigning *cellBills* to
billsBackup

has the effect shown in Figure 8.11.

Example 8.7 shows how to copy the elements in one array to another array.

```
1 /* Copying Array Elements to Another Array
2    Anderson, Franceschi
3 */
4
5 public class CopyingArrayElements
6 {
7  public static void main( String [ ] args )
8  {
9    double [ ] cellBills = { 45.24, 54.67, 42.55, 44.61, 65.29, 49.75 };
10
11   double billsBackup [ ] = new double [cellBills.length];
12   for ( int i = 0; i < cellBills.length; i++ )
13   {
14     billsBackup[i] = cellBills[i]; // copy each element
15   }
16
```

Figure 8.11

Altering *billsBackup* Alters *cellBills* Array

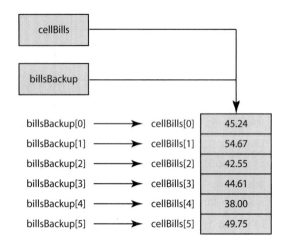

```
17    billsBackup[4] = 38.00;  // change value in billsBackup
18
19    System.out.println( "cellBills\nElement\tValue " );
20    for ( int i = 0; i < cellBills.length; i++ )
21    {
22      System.out.println ( i + "\t" + cellBills[i] );
23    }
24
25    System.out.println( "\nbillsBackup\nElement\tValue " );
26    for ( int i = 0; i < billsBackup.length; i++ )
27    {
28      System.out.println ( i + "\t" + billsBackup[i] );
29    }
30  }
31 }
```

EXAMPLE 8.7   Copying Array Elements into Another Array

At line 9, we instantiate the array *cellBills* using an initialization list. At line 11, we declare and instantiate the array *billsBackup* to have the same size as the original array *cellBills*. At lines 12–15, we use a standard *for* loop to copy one element at a time from the *cellBills* array to the *billsBackup* array.

Now the *billsBackup* array and the *cellBills* array are separate arrays with their own copies of the element values, as shown in Figure 8.12. Changing an element in one array will have no effect on the value of the corresponding element in the other array.

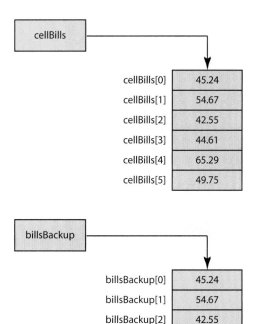

Figure 8.12
Arrays After Copying Each Element

We illustrate this by assigning a new value to an element in the array *bills-Backup* (line 17). Finally, we use two *for* loops to print the contents of both arrays. As Figure 8.13 shows, the value is changed only in the array *billsBackup*.

Be aware, however, that when you copy an array whose elements are objects, even using the *for* loop structure, you are copying object references. The result is that the corresponding elements of each array will point to the same object. If an object in one array is changed, that change will be reflected in the other array as well.

8.3.6   Changing the Size of an Array

Arrays are assigned a length when they are instantiated, and the *length* of an array becomes a constant value. But what if we want to change the number of elements in an array after it has been instantiated?

For example, our *cellBills* array contains six elements, holding six months' worth of cell phone bills. If we decide to collect a year's worth of cell phone

Figure 8.13

Output of Example 8.7

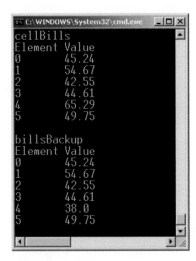

bills, we would need an array with 12 elements. We could instantiate a new version of the *cellBills* array with 12 elements, using this statement:

```
cellBills = new double [12];
```

That statement instantiates a new array of *doubles* all initialized to 0.0. But what happened to the original array of six elements? Since the *cellBills* reference now refers to the new, 12-element array, the 6-element array has no object reference pointing to it, so there is no way we can access the array's values. That is not the result we intended!

To expand the size of an array while maintaining the values of the original array, we can use the following technique:

1. Instantiate an array with the new size, giving the new array a temporary reference.

2. Copy the elements from the original array to the new array.

3. Point the original array reference to the new array.

4. Assign a *null* value to the temporary array reference.

Thus, instead of immediately pointing *cellBills* to the new array, we should instantiate a 12-element array using a temporary array name, copy the six elements from the *cellBills* array into the 12-element array, assign the *cell-Bills* reference to the new array, and assign *null* to the temporary array reference. The following code will do that:

```
double [ ] temp = new double [12];   //instantiate new array

// copy all elements from cellBills to temp
for ( int i = 0; i < cellBills.length; i++ )
{
     temp[i] = cellBills[i]; // copy each element
}

cellBills = temp; // assign temp to cellBills
temp = null;      // temp no longer points to cellBills
```

The last statement sets *temp* to *null* so that we don't have two references to the *cellBills* array. Also, by setting *temp* to *null*, we indicate to the garbage collector that the *temp* object reference is no longer needed.

This is a tedious operation. And what if after having increased the size of an array, we find later in our program that we need to increase the size again? Clearly, arrays are not meant to be expanded via this artificial process. In Chapter 9, we introduce the *ArrayList* class, which allows for automatic expansion.

 REFERENCE POINT

The *ArrayList* class is discussed in Chapter 9; it offers array functionality with automatic expansion as needed.

8.3.7   Comparing Arrays for Equality

To compare whether two arrays are equal, first determine if they are equal in length, and then use a *for* loop to compare the corresponding elements in each array, that is, compare element 0 in the first array to element 0 in the second array; compare element 1 in the first array to element 1 in the second array; and so on. If all elements in the first array are equal to the corresponding elements in the second array, then the arrays are equal. Example 8.8 compares two arrays of *doubles*, a primitive data type.

```
1 /* Comparing Arrays of basic data types
2    Anderson, Franceschi
3 */
4
5 public class ComparingArrays
6 {
```

```
 7  public static void main( String [ ] args )
 8  {
 9    double [ ] cellBills1 = { 45.24, 54.67, 42.55, 44.61, 65.29, 49.75 };
10    double [ ] cellBills2 = { 45.24, 54.67, 41.99, 44.61, 65.29, 49.75 };
11
12    boolean isEqual = true;
13    if ( cellBills1.length != cellBills2.length )
14    {
15      isEqual = false; // arrays are not the same size
16    }
17    else
18    {
19      for ( int i = 0; i < cellBills1.length && isEqual; i++ )
20      {
21        if ( Math.abs( cellBills1[i] - cellBills2[i] ) > 0.001 )
22        {
23          isEqual = false; // elements are not equal
24        }
25      }
26    }
27
28    if ( isEqual )
29      System.out.println( "cellBills1 and cellBills2 are equal" );
30    else
31      System.out.println( "cellBills1 and cellBills2 are not equal" );
32  }
33 }
```

EXAMPLE 8.8   Comparing Arrays of Primitive Data Types

Before we begin the *for* loop, we declare at line 12 a *boolean* variable, *isEqual*, and set it to *true*. In this way, we assume the arrays are equal. Then, our first step is to compare whether the two arrays have the same length (line 13). If they are not the same size, the arrays cannot be equal, so we set *isEqual* to *false* and execution skips to line 28. If the two arrays are the same size, we use a *for* loop at lines 19–25 to test whether the corresponding elements in each array are equal. Note that we have added a second test to the *for* loop condition (*isEqual*). If any corresponding elements are not equal, we set *isEqual* to *false* at line 23. This will cause the condition of the *for* loop to evaluate to *false*, and we exit the *for* loop. Thus, when the *for* loop finishes executing, if any corresponding elements did not match, *isEqual* will be

Figure 8.14
Output of Example 8.8

false. If both arrays are the same size and all corresponding elements are equal, we never change the value of *isEqual*, so it remains *true.* The output from this example is shown in Figure 8.14.

Naturally, if the elements of the arrays are *ints, booleans,* or *chars,* we would use the equality operator (!=) at line 21 as in:

```
if ( intArray1[i] != intArray2[i] )
```

assuming the two arrays we are comparing have names *intArray1* and *intArray2.*

If the elements of the arrays are objects, your *for* loop should call the *equals* method of the objects' class. Thus, to compare two arrays of *Auto* objects, named *cars1* and *cars2,* we would use the following code instead of the condition at line 21:

```
if ( ! cars1[i].equals( cars2[i] ) )
```

A pitfall to avoid is attempting to test whether two arrays are equal using the equality operator (==). This code:

```
if ( cellBills == billsBackup )
```

will not compare the data of the two arrays. It will compare whether the *cellBills* and *billsBackup* object references are equal; that is, whether they point to the same array.

Similarly, the *equals* method inherited from *Object* also returns the wrong results.

This code:

```
if ( cellBills.equals( billsBackup ) )
```

will return *true* only if both object references point to the same array.

 **COMMON ERROR TRAP**

Because arrays are objects, attempting to compare two arrays using the equality operator (==) will compare whether the two array references point to the same array in memory, not whether the data in the two arrays are equal. Calling the *equals* method inherited from the *Object* class yields similar results.

8.3.8   Displaying Array Data as a Bar Chart

One way to display array data is graphically, by drawing a bar chart. For example, the bar chart in Figure 8.15 displays the data in the *cellBills* array.

Each bar is simply a rectangle. Example 8.9 shows the code to generate Figure 8.15.

```
 1 /* BarChart Applet
 2    Anderson, Franceschi
 3 */
 4
 5 import javax.swing.JApplet;
 6 import java.awt.Graphics;
 7 import java.awt.Color;
 8
 9 public class BarChartApplet extends JApplet
10 {
11   final int LEFT_MARGIN = 20;         // starting x coordinate
12   final int BASE_Y_BAR  = 150;        // bottom of the bars
13   final int BASE_Y_VALUE = 175;       // bottom of the values
14   final int BAR_WIDTH = 30;           // width of each bar
15   final int SPACE_BETWEEN_BARS = 5;   // pixels between bars
16   double [ ] cellBills = { 45.24, 54.67, 42.55, 44.61, 65.29, 49.75 };
17
18   public void paint( Graphics g )
19   {
20     super.paint( g );
21
```

Figure 8.15

The *cellBills* Array as a Bar Chart

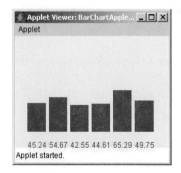

```
22   g.setColor( Color.BLUE );           // bars will be blue
23   int xStart = LEFT_MARGIN;            // x value for first bar
24
25   for ( int i = 0; i < cellBills.length; i++ )
26   {
27     g.fillRect( xStart, BASE_Y_BAR - ( int )( cellBills[i] ),
28               BAR_WIDTH, ( int )( cellBills[i] ) );
29
30     g.drawString( Double.toString( cellBills[i] ),
31                 xStart, BASE_Y_VALUE );
32
33     // move to starting x value for next bar
34     xStart += BAR_WIDTH + SPACE_BETWEEN_BARS;
35   }
36 }
37 }
```

EXAMPLE 8.9   Displaying Array Values as a Bar Chart

To create the bar chart, we use our standard *for* loop at lines 25–35 in the *paint* method and call the *fillRect* method of the *Graphics* class to draw a rectangle for each element (lines 27–28). We use the *drawString* method at lines 30–31 to print the value of each element.

As you recall, the *fillRect* method takes four arguments: the upper-left *x* value, the upper-left *y* value, the rectangle's width, and the rectangle's height.

We can determine the argument values for the *fillRect* method for each element using the following approach, as illustrated in Figure 8.16:

- width: The width of the bar is a constant value. For our bar chart, we chose a width of 30 pixels; the constant *BAR_WIDTH* stores that value (line 14).

- height: The height for each bar is the value of the array element being charted. Because the *fillRect* method expects an integer value for the height, however, we will need to type cast each *cellBills* element to an *int*. Thus, in the *fillRect* method call (lines 27–28), we represent the height of a bar as:

```
( int )( cellBills[i] )
```

REFERENCE POINT

The *fillRect* and *drawString* methods of the *Graphics* class are discussed in Chapter 4.

- Upper-left *y* value: Similarly, the upper-left *y* value will be the height of the bar subtracted from the base *y* value for all the bars; the base *y* value for all the bars is the constant *BASE_Y_BAR* defined in line 12. We subtract the value of the element from the base of the bar because *y* values increase from the top of the window to the bottom. Thus, in our *fillRect* method call, we represent the upper-left *y* value of a bar as:

```
BASE_Y_BAR - ( int )( cellBills[i] )
```

- Upper-left *x* value: We'll start the first bar at the left side of the window, plus a left margin value, represented by the constant *LEFT_MARGIN* (line 11). After we draw each bar, our *for* loop needs to move the starting *x* value to the position of the next bar. To do this, at line 34, we increment the starting *x* value by the width of the bar, *BAR_WIDTH* (defined on line 14), plus the space between bars, *SPACE_BETWEEN_BARS* (defined on line 15).

The arguments to the *drawString* method of the *Graphics* class are the *String* to display and the base *x* and *y* values. At lines 30–31, we convert the *cellBills* element to a *String* using the *toString* method of the *Double* wrapper class. The base *x* value is the same as the starting *x* value for the

Figure 8.16

Arguments for Drawing Each Bar

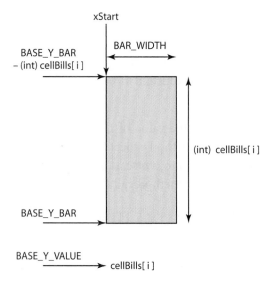

element's bar, and the base *y* coordinate, *BASE_Y_VALUE*, is the base position for printing the array values (defined on line 13).

CODE IN ACTION

In the Chapter 8 folder on the CD-ROM included with this book, you will find a Shockwave movie showing step-by-step illustrations of working with arrays. Double-click on *Arrays.html* to start the movie.

Skill Practice
with these end-of-chapter questions

8.10.1   Multiple Choice Exercises

Questions 6, 9, 10

8.10.2   Reading and Understanding Code

Questions 16, 17, 18, 19, 20, 21

8.10.3   Fill in the Code

Questions 27, 28, 29, 30, 31

8.10.4   Identifying Errors in Code

Questions 39, 41, 43

8.10.5   Debugging Area

Questions 46, 47, 48

8.10.8   Technical Writing

Question 76

8.4   Programming Activity 1: Working with Arrays

In this activity, you will work with a 15-element integer array. Specifically, you will write the code to perform the following operations:

1. fill the array with random numbers between 50 and 80

2. print the array

3. set every array element to a specified value

4. count the number of elements with a specified value

5. find the minimum value in the array

The framework for this Programming Activity will animate your algorithm so that you can check the accuracy of your code. For example, Figure 8.17 shows the application counting the elements having the value 73.

Figure 8.17

Animation of the Programming Activity

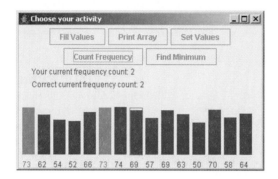

At this point, the application has found the value 73 in elements 0 and 5 and is comparing the value 73 with the value 69 in element 7.

Instructions

In the Chapter 8 Programming Activity 1 directory on the CD-ROM accompanying this book, you will find the source files needed to complete this activity. Copy all the files to a directory on your computer. Note that all files should be in the same directory.

Open the *ArrayPractice1.java* source file. Searching for five stars (*****) in the source code will position you at the sample method and the four other locations where you will add your code. We have provided the sample code for task number 1, which you can use as a model for completing the other tasks. In every task, you will fill in the code for a method that will manipulate an existing array of 15 integers. You should not instantiate the array; we have done that for you. Example 8.10 shows the section of the *ArrayPractice1* source code where you will add your code.

Note that for the *countFrequency* and *findMinimum* methods, we provide a dummy *return* statement (*return 0;*) We do this so that the source code will compile. In this way, you can write and test each method separately, using step–wise refinement. When you are ready to write the *countFrequency* and

findMinimum methods, just replace the dummy *return* statements with the
appropriate *return* statement for that method.

```
// ***** 1. The first method has been coded as an example
/** Fills the array with random numbers between 50 and 80.
*    The instance variable arr is the integer array
*    to be filled with values
*/
public void fillValues( )
{
    for ( int i = 0; i < arr.length; i++ )
    {
        arr[i] = ( int ) ( Math.random( ) * 31 ) + 50;
        animate( -1 );  // needed to create visual feedback
    }
}
// end of fillValues method


// ***** 2. student writes this method
/** Prints the array to the console with elements separated
*      by a space
*     The instance variable arr is the integer array to be printed
*/
public void printArray( )
{
 // Note:  to animate the algorithm, put this method call as the
 // last statement in your for loop:
 //                 animate( i );
 //     where i is the index of the current array element
 // Write your code here:



} // end of printArray method


// ***** 3. student writes this method
/** Sets all the elements in the array to parameter value
*    The instance variable arr is the integer array to be processed
*    @param value   the value to which to set the array elements
*/
public void setValues( int value )
{
 // Note:  to animate the algorithm, put this method call as the
 // last statement in your for loop
 //                 animate( i );
 //     where i is the index of the current array element
```

```
 // Write your code here:


} // end of setValues method

// ***** 4. student writes this method
/** Counts number of elements equal to parameter value
*     The instance variable arr is the integer array to be processed
*        @param  value    the value to count
*        @return    the number of elements equal to value
*/
public int countFrequency( int value )
{
 // Note:  to animate the algorithm, put this method call as the
 // last statement in your for loop
 //          animate( i, count );
 //          where i is the index of the current array element
 //                 count is the variable holding the frequency
 // Write your code here:


    return 0; // replace this line with your return statement

} // end of countFrequency method

// ***** 5. student writes this method
/** Finds and returns the minimum value in arr
*     The instance variable arr is the integer array to be processed
*     @return the minimum value found in arr
*/
public int findMinimum(  )
{
 // Note:  to animate the algorithm, put this method call as the
 // last statement in your for loop
 //        animate( i, minimum );
 //            where i is the index of the current array element
 //               minimum is the variable holding the minimum
 // Write your code here:


    return 0; // replace this line with your return statement

} // end of findMinimum method

// End of student code
```

EXAMPLE 8.10   Location of Student Code in *ArrayPractice1*

Our framework will animate your algorithm so that you can watch your code work. For this to happen, be sure that your *for* loop calls the *animate* method. The argument that you send to *animate* and the location of the call to *animate* will differ depending on the task you are coding. Detailed instructions for each task are included in the code.

To test your code, compile and run the *ArrayPractice1* source code. Figure 8.18 shows the graphics window when the program begins. Because the values of the array are randomly generated, the values will be different each time the program runs. To test any method, click the appropriate button.

Troubleshooting

If your method implementation does not animate, follow these tips:

- Verify that the last statement in your *for* loop is a call to the *animate* method and that you passed the appropriate arguments to the *animate* method.

- Verify that your *for* loop has curly braces. For example, the *animate* method call is outside the body of this *for* loop:

```
for ( int i = 0; i< arr.length; i++ )
    System.out.println ( arr [i] );
    animate( i );  // this statement is outside the for loop
```

Remember that without curly braces, the *for* loop body consists of only the first statement following the *for* loop header. Enclosing both statements within curly braces will make the *animate* method call part of the *for* loop body.

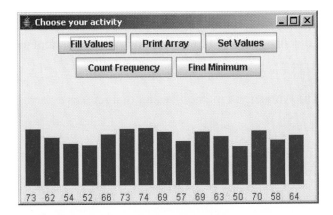

Figure 8.18
The Graphics Window When the Application Begins

```
for ( int i = 0; i< arr.length; i++ )
{
    System.out.println ( arr [i] );
    animate( i );
}
```

- Verify that you did not instantiate a new array. Perform all operations on the array passed to the method as a parameter.

DISCUSSION QUESTIONS **?**

1. Could you use the following *for* loop header in every method? Explain why or why not.

   ```
   for ( int i = 0; i < arr.length; i++ )
   ```

2. How would you modify the *findMinimum* method to return the index of the minimum value?

8.5   Using Arrays in Classes

8.5.1   Using Arrays in User-Defined Classes

An array can be used inside a user-defined class just like any other variable. In particular,

- An array can be an instance variable.

- An array can be a parameter to a method.

- A method can return an array.

- An array can be a local variable inside a method.

COMMON ERROR TRAP

If you think of the brackets as being part of the data type of the array, then it's easy to remember that the brackets are included in the method header—where the data types of parameters are given—but that brackets are not included in method calls, where the data itself is given.

To define a method that takes an array as a parameter, use this syntax:

```
accessModifier returnType methodName( dataType [ ] arrayName )
```

The syntax for a method header that returns an array is

```
accessModifier dataType [ ] methodName( parameterList )
```

To pass an array as an argument to a method, just use the array name without brackets as the argument value:

```
methodName( arrayName )
```

In Example 8.11, we define a class named *CellPhone* that illustrates the use of arrays in a class.

```
1 /** CellPhone class
2  *    Anderson, Franceschi
3  */
4
5 import java.text.DecimalFormat;
6
7 public class CellPhone
8 {
9    public final int MONTHS = 6;  // default number of months
10   private String phoneNumber;
11   private double [ ] cellBills;
12
13   /** Default constructor
14    *    creates cellBills with MONTHS elements
15    */
16   public CellPhone( )
17   {
18      phoneNumber = "";
19      cellBills = new double [MONTHS];
20   }
21
22   /** Constructor
23    * @param   number   cell phone number
24    * @param   bills    array of monthly bills
25    */
26   public CellPhone( String number, double [ ] bills )
27   {
28      phoneNumber = number;
29
30      // instantiate array with same length as parameter
31      cellBills = new double [bills.length];
32
33      // copy parameter array to cellBills array
34      for ( int i = 0; i < cellBills.length; i++ )
35      {
36         cellBills[i] = bills[i];
37      }
38   }
39
40   /** Returns the phone number
41    *    @return the phone number
42    */
```

```
43    public String getPhoneNumber( )
44    {
45      return phoneNumber;
46    }
47
48    /** Returns an array of cell phone bills
49     *   @return  copy of cellBills array
50     */
51    public double [ ] getCellBills( )
52    {
53      double [ ] temp = new double [cellBills.length];
54      for ( int i = 0; i < cellBills.length; i ++ )
55      {
56        temp[i] = cellBills[i];
57      }
58      return temp;
59    }
60
61    /**  Calculates total of all cell phone bills
62     *    @return  total of all elements in cellBills array
63     */
64    public double calcTotalBills( )
65    {
66      double total = 0.0;  // initialize total to 0.0
67
68      for ( int i = 0; i < cellBills.length; i++ )
69      {
70        total += cellBills[i];  // add current element to total
71      }
72      return total;
73    }
74
75    /** Finds a maximum bill
76     *  @return largest value in cellBills array
77     */
78    public double findMaximumBill( )
79    {
80      double max = cellBills[0]; // assume first element is max
81
82      for ( int i = 1; i < cellBills.length; i++ )
83      {
84        if ( cellBills[i] > max )
85          max = cellBills[i];  // save new maximum
86      }
87      return max;
88    }
```

```
89
90    /** Returns printable version of CellPhone object
91     *   @return phone number plus each month's bill
92     */
93    public String toString( )
94    {
95      String returnValue = phoneNumber + "\n";
96      DecimalFormat money = new DecimalFormat( "$##0.00" );
97      for ( int i = 0; i < cellBills.length; i++ )
98      {
99          returnValue += money.format( cellBills[i] ) + "\t";
100     }
101     returnValue += "\n";
102
103     return returnValue;
104   }
105
106   /**  Compares two CellPhone objects for equality
107    *   @param CellPhone object
108    *   @return  true if objects are equal; false, otherwise
109    */
110   public boolean equals( CellPhone c )
111   {
112     if ( !( phoneNumber.equals( c.phoneNumber ) ) )
113         return false;
114
115     if ( cellBills.length != c.cellBills.length )
116         return false; // arrays are not the same length
117
118     for ( int i = 0; i < cellBills.length; i++ )
119     {
120         if ( cellBills[i] != c.cellBills[i] )
121            return false;
122     }
123     return true;
124   }
125 }
```

EXAMPLE 8.11   The *CellPhone* Class

Our *CellPhone* class defines three instance variables in lines 9–11: the
phone number (a *String* named *phoneNumber*), monthly bills (an array of
doubles named *cellBills*), and a constant named *MONTHS*, whose value, 6,
represents the number of monthly cell bills, and therefore the length of the

cellBills array if a *CellPhone* object is instantiated using the default constructor. Note that since *MONTHS* is a constant, we made it *public*.

When your class has instance variables that are arrays, you will need to take a little extra care to ensure that encapsulation is not violated.

Let's start with initialization of the array. The overloaded constructor of the *CellPhone* class, whose method header is at line 26, includes an array parameter. With parameters of primitive types, the constructor can simply assign the value of the parameter to the instance variable. As we have seen, however, the name of an array is an object reference, which contains the location of the array in memory. If the constructor merely assigns the array parameter, *bills*, to our array instance variable, *cellBills*, as in the following code:

```
cellBills = bills;  // incorrect! Client still has reference!
```

then *bills* and *cellBills* would point to the same array. That means that the client still has a reference to the array, and the client can change the array values without going through the mutator methods of the class. For example, if the client executes this statement:

```
bills[2] = 75.00;
```

then *cellBills[2]* also gets the value 75.00, because they are the same array. This is clearly a violation of encapsulation, which means that a client can change the *private* fields of a class only by calling the mutator methods of the class.

To avoid this problem, our constructor instantiates a new *cellBills* array that is the same size as the array passed as a parameter, and then copies the elements of the parameter array into the new *cellBills* array (lines 30–37).

**SOFTWARE
ENGINEERING TIP**

Sharing array references with the client violates encapsulation. To return an array from a method, copy the elements of the instance variable array to a temporary array and return a reference to the temporary array. Similarly, to accept an array as a parameter to a method, instantiate a new array and copy the elements of the parameter array to the new array.

There are similar considerations in implementing the accessor method of an array instance variable. With instance variables of primitive types, the accessor methods simply return the value of the instance variable. Our accessor for *cellBills* (lines 48–59) has an array as a return value. If we return the *cellBills* reference, however, we run into the same problem with encapsulation; that is, if our accessor for the *cellBills* instance variable uses this statement:

```
return cellBills;
```

we give the client a reference to the *cellBills* array, and the client can directly change the values of the array without calling the mutator methods of the class. Just as the constructor instantiated a new array and copied the parameter array's value to the new array, the accessor method should instantiate a new array, copy the *cellBills* array to it, and return a reference to the new array. Thus, at line 53, we declare and instantiate a local array variable named *temp*. At lines 54–57, we copy the contents of *cellBills* into *temp*, and return *temp* at line 58.

We also provide a method *calcTotalBills* (lines 61–73) that calculates the total of the monthly bills using the accumulation technique discussed earlier in the chapter and a *findMaximumBill* method (lines 75–88), which finds a maximum value in the *cellBills* array, also using techniques discussed earlier in the chapter.

Our *toString* method (lines 90–104) builds up a *String* named *returnValue* by first including *phoneNumber*, then formatting each bill using a *DecimalFormat* pattern for money and concatenating that value, plus a tab, to *returnValue*.

The *equals* method (lines 106–124) compares the phone number and each element of the *cellBills* array in the object with the phone number and corresponding element in the *cellBills* array in the parameter object.

We can test our *CellPhone* class with the client class shown in Example 8.12. The output is shown in Figure 8.19.

```java
 1 /**  Client to exercise the CellPhone class
 2 *  Anderson, Franceschi
 3 */
 4
 5 import java.text.DecimalFormat;
 6
 7 public class CellPhoneClient
 8 {
 9   public static void main( String [ ] args )
10   {
11     double [ ] bills = new double[3]; // array of cell phone bills
12     bills[0] = 24.60; // assign values
13     bills[1] = 48.75;
14     bills[2] = 62.50;
15
16     // instantiate CellPhone object using default constructor
17     CellPhone c1 = new CellPhone( );
18
19     // instantiate two identical CellPhone objects
20     CellPhone c2 = new CellPhone( "555-555-5555", bills );
21     CellPhone c3 = new CellPhone( "555-555-5555", bills );
22
23     // print data from c1 and c2
24     System.out.println( "c1 = " + c1.toString( ) );
```

```
25        System.out.println( "c2 = " + c2.toString( ) );
26
27        // find and print maximum bill
28        DecimalFormat money = new DecimalFormat( "$##0.00" );
29        System.out.println( "\nThe highest bill is "
30                          + money.format( c2.findMaximumBill( ) ) );
31
32        // find and print total of all bills
33        System.out.println( "\nThe total of all bills is "
34                          + money.format( c2.calcTotalBills( ) ) );
35
36        System.out.println( ); // print blank line
37        // call equals method
38        if ( c2.equals( c3 ) )
39            System.out.println( "c2 and c3 are equal" );
40        else
41            System.out.println( "c2 and c3 are not equal" );
42
43        // test encapsulation
44        // set new value in original array
45        bills[2] = 100.00;
46        // print c2 to show value in object not changed
47        System.out.println( "\nafter client changes original array\n"
48                          + "c2 = "  + c2.toString( ) );
49
50        // test encapsulation further
51        // get array of cell bills and store in new array
52        double [ ] billsCopy = c2.getCellBills( );
53
54        billsCopy[1] = 50.00;  // change value of one element
55        // print c2 to show value in object not changed
56        System.out.println( "\nafter client changes returned array\n"
57                          + "c2 = "  + c2.toString( ) );
58    }
59 }
```

EXAMPLE 8.12   The *CellPhoneClient* Class

In the *CellPhoneClient*, we instantiate three *CellPhone* objects. We instantiate *c1* using the default constructor (line 17), giving it an empty phone number and six months of bills initialized to 0.00, as shown in line 24, when we use the *toString* method to print *c1*'s data. We set up a *bills* array with three values (lines 11–14) and pass *bills* to the overloaded constructor (lines 20–21) to instantiate *c2* and *c3* with identical data. We then use *toString* to print *c2*'s data (line 25).

Figure 8.19

Output from the
CellPhoneClient Class

We then call the *findMaximumBill* method and print its return value (lines 27–30). Next, we call the *calcTotalBills* method and print its return value (lines 32–34).

A call to the *equals* method to compare *c2* and *c3* (lines 37–41) returns a value of *true*, because the two objects have the same data.

Finally, we test encapsulation two ways. First, we change a value in the *bills* array, then print *c2* again to verify that its data has not changed (lines 43–48). Second, we call the accessor method for the *cellBills* array and change a value in the array returned from the method call. We again print *c2* to verify that its data is unchanged (lines 50–57). Testing the *CellPhone* class with such an example is helpful in checking that we have correctly implemented the class.

8.5.2   Retrieving Command Line Arguments

The syntax of an array parameter for a method might look familiar to you. We've seen it repeatedly in Java applications in the header for the *main* method:

```
public static void main( String [ ] args )
```

As you can see, *main* receives a *String* array as a parameter. That array of *Strings* holds the arguments, if any, that the user sends to the program from the command line. An argument might be the name of a file for the program to read or some configuration parameters that specify preferences in how the application should perform its function.

The sample program in Example 8.13 demonstrates how to retrieve the parameters sent to a Java application. Because *args* is a *String* array, we can use the *length* field to get the number of parameters (lines 8–9), and we use our standard *for* loop format (lines 10–13) to retrieve and print each parameter, as shown in Figure 8.20.

```
1   /** Print Command Line arguments
2    *   Anderson, Franceschi
3    */
4   public class CommandLineArguments
5   {
6     public static void main( String [ ] args )
7     {
8       System.out.println( "The number of parameters is "
9                               + args.length );
10      for ( int i = 0; i < args.length; i ++ )
11      {
12          System.out.println( "args[" + i + "]: "  + args[i] );
13      }
14    }
15  }
```

EXAMPLE 8.13   Retrieving Command Line Arguments

Figure 8.20 shows the output produced when we invoke the program as

```
java CommandLineArguments input.txt output.txt
```

Skill Practice
with these end-of-chapter questions

8.10.1   Multiple Choice Exercises

Question 11

8.10.2   Reading and Understanding Code

Questions 22, 23, 24, 25, 26

8.10.3   Fill in the Code

Questions 32, 33, 34, 35

8.10.6   Write a Short Program

Questions 49, 50, 51, 52, 53, 54, 55, 56, 58, 59, 60, 61

Figure 8.20
Output from Example
8.13

8.6 Searching and Sorting Arrays

Arrays are great instruments for storing a large number of related values. As seen earlier in this chapter, we can use arrays to store daily temperatures, CD titles, telephone bills, quiz grades, and other sets of related values. Once the data is stored in an array, we will want to manipulate that data: A very common operation is searching an array for a specific value.

8.6.1 Sequential Search of an Unsorted Array

Let's assume you are the manager of a DVD rental store. Each member customer gets a card with a unique member ID. You have decided to pick five member IDs at random and give those members a free gift the next time they visit the store. So you set up a *DVDWinners* class with an array instance variable that holds the winners' member IDs. Then you fill the array with member IDs chosen randomly from entry cards members have filled out. When a member rents a DVD, you can look through the *winners* array for the member's ID. If the member's ID is in the *winners* array, you give the member a gift. Otherwise, you know the member is not a winner.

The *DVDWinners* class is shown in Example 8.14.

```
 1 /** Winners of Free DVD Rentals
 2  *    Anderson, Franceschi
 3  */
 4
 5 public class DVDWinners
 6 {
 7   public final int DEFAULT_WINNERS = 5;
 8   private int [ ] winners;  // array to hold winning member numbers
 9
10   /** Default constructor instantiates winners array
11    *     with 5 elements and randomly generates winning member IDs
12    */
13   public DVDWinners( )
14   {
15     winners = new int [DEFAULT_WINNERS];
```

```
16   fillWinners( ); // generate winner member IDs
17   }
18
19   /** Overloaded constructor, instantiates winners array
20    *      and randomly generates winning member IDs
21    *      @param startNumberOfWinners number of winners
22    */
23   public DVDWinners( int startNumberOfWinners )
24   {
25    winners  = new int [startNumberOfWinners];
26    fillWinners( ); // generate winner member IDs
27   }
28
29   /** Utility method generates winner member IDs
30    *      and stores them in the winners array
31    */
32   private void fillWinners( )
33   {
34    for ( int i = 0; i < winners.length; i++ )
35    {
36     winners[i] = ( int )( Math.random( ) * 5000 ) + 1;
37    }
38   }
39
40   /** Performs sequential search of winners array
41    *    @param key    member ID to find in winners array
42    *    @return       index of key if found, -1 if not found
43    */
44   public int findWinners( int key )
45   {
46    for ( int i = 0; i < winners.length; i++ )
47    {
48     if ( winners[i] == key )
49        return i;
50    }
51    return -1;
52   }
53
54   /** Returns printable version of DVDWinners object
55    *    @return       winning numbers separated by a tab
56    */
57   public String toString( )
58   {
59    String returnValue = "";
60    for ( int i = 0; i < winners.length; i++ )
```

```
61    {
62       returnValue += winners[i] + "\t";
63    }
64    return returnValue;
65  }
66 }
```

EXAMPLE 8.14   The *DVDWinners* Class

Both constructors randomly generate values to fill the array by calling the utility method, *fillWinners* (lines 29–38). In the interest of keeping things simple, we have coded the *fillWinners* method in such a way that it does not necessarily generate different numbers; however, the likelihood of two winning numbers being equal is very small. We declare the *fillWinners* method as *private* because it is designed to be called only by the methods of this class.

Our *findWinners* method (lines 40–52) performs a **Sequential Search**, which compares the member ID to each element in the array one by one. The *findWinners* method accepts a parameter, *key*, which is the member ID to search for in the array. If *key* is found, *findWinners* returns the index of that array element. If *key* is not found, that is, if none of the elements in the array matches the value of *key*, *findWinners* returns −1. Since −1 is not a valid array index, it's a good value to use to indicate that the search was unsuccessful.

Notice that if the current array element matches the *key*, the *findWinners* method returns immediately to the caller (line 49); that is, the method stops executing. The return value is the index of the element that matched the *key*. If, however, the method finishes executing all iterations of the *for* loop, then the method has looked at every element in the array without finding a match. In that case, the method returns a −1 (line 51), indicating that the *key* was not found.

Example 8.15 shows a client application that uses our *DVDWinners* class.

```
 1 /** Client for the DVDWinners class
 2     Anderson, Franceschi
 3 */
 4 import java.util.Scanner;
 5
 6 public class DVDWinnersClient
 7 {
 8  public static void main( String [ ] args )
 9  {
10   // instantiate the winningIDs array
```

```
11   DVDWinners winningIDs = new DVDWinners( );
12
13   // prompt for the member ID
14   Scanner scan = new Scanner( System.in );
15   System.out.print( "Enter the member's ID > " );
16   int searchID = scan.nextInt( );
17
18   // determine whether member is a winner
19   int result = winningIDs.findWinners( searchID );
20
21   switch ( result ) // determine winner's prize
22   {
23    case -1:
24      System.out.println( "Sorry, member is not a winner." );
25      break;
26    case 0:
27      System.out.println( "You win 3 free rentals!" );
28      break;
29    case 1:
30      System.out.println( "You win 2 free rentals!" );
31      break;
32    case 2:
33      System.out.println( "You win 1 free rental!" );
34      break;
35    case 3:
36      System.out.println( "You win free popcorn!" );
37      break;
38    case 4:
39      System.out.println( "You win a free box of candy" );
40      break;
41   }
42
43   System.out.println( "\nThe winners are "
44                       + winningIDs.toString( ) );
45  }
46 }
```

EXAMPLE 8.15   Client Application for the *DVDWinners* Class

We instantiate a *DVDWinners* object reference named *winningIDs* (lines 10–11). We then prompt for a member ID (lines 15–16) and call the *findWinners* method (line 19) to perform the sequential search. Using the return value from the *findWinners* method, we use a *switch* statement (lines 21–41) to determine the prize for the winner. If *findWinners* returns –1, we

Figure 8.21

Output When Member ID Is Not Found

Figure 8.22

Output When Member ID Is Found

determine that the member is not a winner (lines 23–25). Otherwise, we determine the prize based on the index returned from the *findWinners* method. Figures 8.21 and 8.22 show two possible outputs of running the *DVDWinnersClient* application.

8.6.2   Selection Sort

The member IDs in the preceding *winners* array were in random order, so when a member was not a winner, our *findWinners* method needed to look at every element in the array before discovering that the ID we were looking for was not in the array. This is not efficient, since most members are not winners. The larger the array, the more inefficient a sequential search becomes. We could simplify the search by arranging the elements in numeric order, which is called **sorting the array**. Once the array is sorted, we can use various algorithms to speed up a search. Later in this chapter, we discuss how to search a sorted array.

In this chapter, we present two basic sorting algorithms, **Selection Sort** and **Bubble Sort**.

Selection Sort derives its name from the algorithm used to sort the array. We select a largest element in the array and place it at the end of the array. Then we select a next–largest element and put it in the next-to-last position in the array. To do this, we consider the unsorted portion of the array as a **subarray**. We repeatedly select a largest value in the current subarray and move it to the end of the subarray, then consider a new subarray by eliminating the elements that are in their sorted locations, until the subarray has only one element. At that time, the array is sorted.

In more formal terms, we can state the Selection Sort algorithm this way:

To sort an array with n elements in ascending order:

1. Consider m elements as a subarray with $m = n$ elements.
2. Find the index of a largest value in this subarray.
3. Swap the values of the element with the largest value and the element in the last position in the subarray.
4. Consider a new subarray of $m = m - 1$ elements by eliminating the last element in the previous subarray.
5. Repeat steps 2 through 4 until $m = 1$.

For example, let's walk through a Selection Sort on the following array. At the beginning, the entire array is the subarray (shown here with shading).

We begin by considering the entire array as an unsorted subarray. We find that the largest element is 26 at index 1.

Unsorted subarray

Value	17	26	5	2
Index	0	1	2	3

Next we move element 1 to the last element by swapping the values of the elements at indexes 1 and 3.

The value 26 is now in the right place, and we consider elements 0 through 2 as the unsorted subarray.

Unsorted subarray   Sorted element

Value	17	2	5	26
Index	0	1	2	3

The largest element in the new subarray is 17 at index 0. So we move element 0 to the last index of the subarray (index 2) by swapping the elements at indexes 0 and 2.

The value 17 is now in the right place, and we consider elements 0 and 1 as the new unsorted subarray.

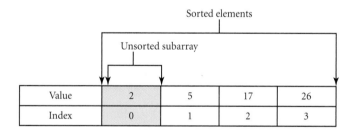

The largest element in the new subarray is 5 at index 0. We move element 0 to the last index of the subarray (index 1) by swapping the elements at indexes 0 and 1.

The value 5 is now in the right place, and we consider element 0 as the new subarray. But because there is only one element in the subarray, the subarray is sorted. Thus the whole array is sorted, and our job is done.

A critical operation in a Selection Sort is swapping two array elements. Before going further, let's examine the algorithm for swapping two array elements.

To swap two values, we need to define a temporary variable that is of the same data type as the values being swapped. This variable will temporarily hold the value of one of the elements, so that we don't lose the value during the swap.

The algorithm, presented here in pseudocode, involves three steps:

To swap elements *a* and *b*:

1. Assign the value of element *a* to the temporary variable
2. Assign the value of element *b* to element *a*
3. Assign the value in the temporary variable to element *b*

For instance, if an array named *array* has *int* elements, and we want to swap the element at index 3 with the element at index 6, we will use the following code:

```
int temp = array[3];    // line 1
array[3] = array[6];    // line 2
array[6] = temp;        // line 3
```

The order of these operations is critical; changing the order might result in loss of data and erroneous data stored in the array.

The following illustrates line by line what happens during the swap:

Before line 1 is executed, our array looks like this:

Value	23	45	7	33	78	90	82	80	90	66
Index	0	1	2	3	4	5	6	7	8	9

Line 1 assigns the value of element 3 to *temp*. After line 1 is executed, the value of *temp* is 33. The array is unchanged.

Value	23	45	7	33	78	90	82	80	90	66		33
Index	0	1	2	3	4	5	6	7	8	9		temp

Line 2 assigns the value of element 6 (82) to element 3. After line 2 is executed, both element 6 and element 3 have the same value. But that's OK, because we saved the value of element 3 in *temp*.

Value	23	45	7	82	78	90	82	80	90	66		33
Index	0	1	2	3	4	5	6	7	8	9		temp

Line 3 assigns the value we saved in *temp* to element 6. After line 3 is executed, the values of elements 3 and 6 have been successfully swapped.

COMMON ERROR TRAP

When swapping elements, be sure to save a value before replacing it with another value to avoid losing data.

Value	23	45	7	82	78	90	33	80	90	66		33
Index	0	1	2	3	4	5	6	7	8	9		temp

Example 8.16 shows the *Sorter* class, which provides a *static selectionSort* method for an integer array.

```
 1 /* Sort Utility Class
 2 * Anderson, Franceschi
 3 */
 4
 5 public class Sorter
 6 {
 7   /** Uses Selection Sort to sort
 8   *      an integer array in ascending order
 9   *    @param the array to sort
10   */
11   public static void selectionSort( int [ ] array )
12   {
13     int temp; // temporary location for swap
14     int max;  // index of maximum value in subarray
15
16     for ( int i = 0; i < array.length; i++ )
17     {
18       // find index of largest value in subarray
19       max = indexOfLargestElement( array, array.length - i );
20
21       // swap array[max] and array[array.length - i - 1]
22       temp = array[max];
23       array[max] = array[array.length - i - 1];
24       array[array.length - i - 1] = temp;
25     }
26   }
27
28   /** Finds index of largest element
29   *    @param   size  the size of the subarray
30   *    @ return  the index of the largest element in the subarray
31   */
32   private static int indexOfLargestElement( int [ ] array, int size )
33   {
34     int index = 0;
35     for( int i = 1; i < size; i++ )
36     {
37       if ( array[i] > array[index] )
38           index = i;
39     }
40     return index;
41   }
42 }
```

EXAMPLE 8.16   The *Sorter* Class

Figure 8.23

Using Selection Sort

Part of the Selection Sort algorithm is finding the index of the largest element in a subarray, so we implement the Selection Sort with two methods. At lines 7–26, is the *selectionSort* method, which implements the Selection Sort algorithm. To perform its work, the *selectionSort* method calls the utility method, *indexOfLargestElement* (lines 28–41), which returns the index of the largest element in a subarray. This method uses the algorithm discussed earlier in the chapter for finding a maximum value in an array. We declare this method *private* because its only function is to provide a service to the *selectionSort* method. The *indexOfLargestElement* method must also be declared as *static* because the *selectionSort* method is *static*, and thus can call only *static* methods.

In Example 8.17, the client code instantiates an integer array and prints the array before and after the Selection Sort is performed. Because *selectionSort* is a *static* method, we call it using the *Sorter* class name. The output of a sample run is shown in Figure 8.23.

```
 1 /** Client for Selection Sort
 2 *    Anderson, Franceschi
 3 */
 4
 5 public class SelectionSortClient
 6 {
 7   public static void main( String [ ] args )
 8   {
 9     // instantiate an array and fill with random values
10     int [ ] numbers = new int [6];
11     for ( int i = 0; i < numbers.length; i++ )
12     {
13       numbers[i] = ( int ) ( Math.random( ) * 5000 ) + 1;
14     }
15
```

```
16    System.out.println( "Before Selection Sort, the array is" );
17    for ( int i = 0; i < numbers.length; i++ )
18       System.out.print( numbers[i] + "\t" );
19    System.out.println( );
20
21    Sorter.selectionSort( numbers ); // sort the array
22
23    System.out.println( "\nAfter Selection Sort, the array is" );
24    for ( int i = 0; i < numbers.length; i++ )
25       System.out.print( numbers[i] + "\t" );
26    System.out.println( );
27  }
28 }
```

EXAMPLE 8.17   Using Selection Sort

8.6.3   Bubble Sort

The basic approach to a Bubble Sort is to make multiple passes through the array. In each pass, we compare adjacent elements. If any two adjacent elements are out of order, we put them in order by swapping their values.

To sort an array of n elements in ascending order, Bubble Sort implements a double loop:

- The outer loop executes $n - 1$ times.
- For each iteration of the outer loop, the inner loop steps through all the unsorted elements of the array and does the following:
  - Compares the current element with the next element in the array.
  - If the next element is smaller, it swaps the two elements.

Outer loop counter	Index of element(s) at the sorted position
0	n - 1
1	n - 2, n - 1
2	n - 3, n - 2, n - 1
...	...
$n - 3$	2, 3, 4, ..., n - 3, n - 2, n - 1
$n - 2$	1, 2, 3, 4, ..., n - 3, n - 2, n - 1

At this point, $n - 1$ elements have been moved to their correct positions. That leaves only the element at index 0, which is therefore automatically at the correct position within the array. The array is now sorted.

As the outer loop counter goes from 0 to $n - 2$, it iterates $n - 1$ times.

The pseudocode for the Bubble Sort is

```
for i = 0 to last array index – 1 by 1
    for j = 0 to ( last array index – i –1 ) by 1
        if (2 consecutive elements are in the wrong order)
            swap them
```

For example, let's walk through a Bubble Sort on the following array. At the beginning, the unsorted array is

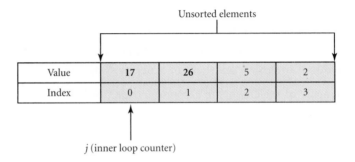

The value of the outer loop counter (i) is 0, and the value of the inner loop counter (j) is also 0. We compare elements 17 (index $j = 0$) and 26 (index $j + 1 = 1$). Since 17 is smaller than 26, we do not swap them.

The inner loop counter (j) is incremented, and its value is now 1.

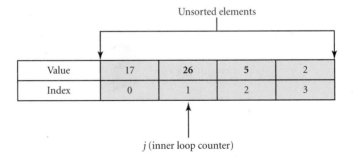

We compare elements 26 (index $j = 1$) and 5 (index $j + 1 = 2$). Since 26 is larger than 5, we swap them. The inner loop counter (j) is incremented, and its value is now 2.

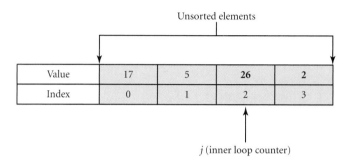

We compare elements 26 (index $j = 2$) and 2 (index $j + 1 = 3$). Since 26 is larger than 2, we swap them.

The inner loop counter (j) is incremented, and its value is now 3; therefore, we exit the inner loop. (We have reached the end of the unsorted subarray, which at this point is the whole array.) At the end of one execution of the inner loop, the value 26 has "bubbled up" to its correct position within the array.

We now go back to the outer loop, and the outer loop counter (i) is incremented; its value is now 1. We reenter the inner loop and the value of the inner loop counter (j) is reinitialized to 0.

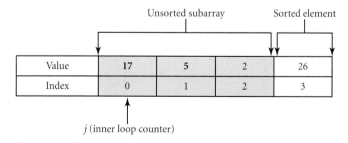

We compare elements 17 (index $j = 0$) and 5 (index $j + 1 = 1$). Since 17 is larger than 5, we swap them. The inner loop counter (j) is incremented, and its value is now 1.

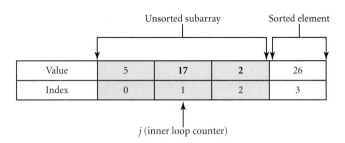

We compare elements 17 (index $j = 1$) and 2 (index $j + 1 = 2$). Since 17 is larger than 2, we swap them.

The inner loop counter (j) is incremented, and its value is now 2; therefore, we exit the inner loop. (We have reached the end of the unsorted subarray.) At this point, the element 17 has "bubbled up" to its correct position within the array.

We go back to the outer loop, and the outer loop counter (i) is incremented; its value is now 2, and this will be the last iteration of the outer loop. We reenter the inner loop and the value of the inner loop counter (j) is reinitialized to 0.

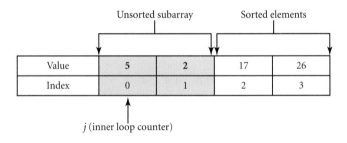

We compare elements 5 (index $j = 0$) and 2 (index $j + 1 = 1$). Since 2 is smaller than 5, we swap them.

The inner loop counter (j) is incremented, and its value is now 1; therefore, we exit the inner loop. (We have reached the end of the unsorted subarray.) At this point, the element 5 has "bubbled up" to its correct position within the array.

We go back to the outer loop, and the outer loop counter (i) is incremented; its value is now 3, and therefore, we exit the outer loop. For the four elements in the array; we executed the outer loop three times.

The array is now sorted.

 **COMMON ERROR TRAP**

When looping through an array, be careful not to access an element outside the bounds of the array. Your code will compile, but will generate an *ArrayIndexOutOfBoundsException* at run time.

	Automatically sorted	Sorted elements		
Value	2	5	17	26
Index	0	1	2	3

Here is the code for the Bubble Sort algorithm. You will be asked to implement this code in Programming Activity 2, which will animate the Bubble Sort visually so that you can see how it works.

```java
/** Performs a Bubble Sort on an integer array
*/
public void bubbleSort( )
{
   int temp;

   for ( int i = 0; i < winners.length - 1; i++ )
   {
      for ( int j = 0; j < winners.length - i - 1; j++ )
      {
         if ( winners[j] > winners[j + 1] )
         {
            // swap the 2 elements
            temp = winners[j + 1];
            winners[j + 1] = winners[j];
            winners[j] = temp;
         }
      } // end inner for loop
   } // end outer for loop
} // end bubbleSort method
```

The *bubbleSort* method makes *n – 1* passes through the array, but because each pass sorts adjacent elements, it is possible that the array might be completely sorted before all the passes have been completed. An important performance improvement in the Bubble Sort algorithm would be to stop when the array is completely sorted.

If the array is completely sorted, a pass through the inner loop will not perform any swaps. Thus, we could improve the algorithm by checking in the outer loop whether any swapping has occurred in the inner loop. If not, we can exit the method. To detect whether any swapping takes place, we use a *boolean* flag variable, *arraySorted*. We set *arraySorted* to *true* at the beginning of the outer loop (because no swapping has taken place yet) and set it to *false* in the inner loop when two elements are swapped.

Example 8.18 shows our *Sorter* class with the improved Bubble Sort algorithm implemented in lines 43–71.

```
 1 /* Sort Utility Class
 2    Anderson, Franceschi
 3 */
 4
 5 public class Sorter
 6 {
 7 /**  Performs a Selection Sort on
 8 *       an integer array
 9 *     @param the array to sort
10 */
11 public static void selectionSort( int [ ] array )
12 {
13    int temp; // temporary location for swap
14    int max;  // index of maximum value in subarray
15
16    for ( int i = 0; i < array.length; i++ )
17    {
18    // find index of largest value in subarray
19    max = indexOfLargestElement( array, array.length - i );
20
21    // swap array[max] and array[array.length - i - 1]
22    temp = array[max];
23    array[max] = array[array.length - i - 1];
24    array[array.length - i - 1] = temp;
25    }
26 }
27
28 /**  Finds index of largest element
29 *     @param    size  the size of the subarray
30 *     @ return  the index of the largest element in the subarray
31 */
32 private static int indexOfLargestElement( int [ ] array, int size )
33 {
34    int index = 0;
35    for( int i = 1; i < size; i++ )
36    {
```

```
37          if ( array[i] > array[index] )
38              index = i;
39       }
40     return index;
41   }
42
43   /**  Performs a Bubble Sort on an integer array,
44    *       stopping when array is sorted
45    *     @param array to sort
46    */
47   public static void bubbleSort( int [ ] array )
48   {
49     int temp = 0;
50     boolean arraySorted = false;
51
52     for ( int i = 0; i < array.length - 1 && !arraySorted;
53                               i++ )
54     {
55        arraySorted = true;    // start a new iteration;
56                               //  maybe the array is sorted
57
58        for ( int j = 0; j < array.length - i - 1; j++ )
59        {
60           if ( array[j] > array[j + 1] )
61           {
62              // swap the adjacent elements
63              //   and set arraySorted to false
64              temp = array[j + 1];
65              array[j + 1] = array[j];
66              array[j] = temp;
67              arraySorted = false; // note that we swapped
68           }
69        }
70     }
71   }
72 }
```

EXAMPLE 8.18   *Sorter* **Class with Bubble Sort**

Example 8.19 shows a client program that instantiates an integer array, fills it with random values, and then prints the array before and after performing the Bubble Sort. Figure 8.24 shows a sample run, using the Bubble Sort algorithm to sort an array of integers.

Figure 8.24

Using Bubble Sort

```
1 /** Client for Bubble Sort
2     Anderson, Franceschi
3 */
4
5 public class BubbleSortClient
6 {
7   public static void main( String [ ] args )
8   {
9     // instantiate an array and fill with random values
10    int [ ] numbers = new int [6];
11    for ( int i = 0; i < numbers.length; i++ )
12    {
13      numbers[i] = ( int ) ( Math.random( ) * 5000 ) + 1;
14    }
15
16    System.out.println( "Before Bubble Sort, the array is" );
17    for ( int i = 0; i < numbers.length; i++ )
18      System.out.print( numbers[i] + "\t" );
19    System.out.println( );
20
21    Sorter.bubbleSort( numbers ); // sort the array
22
23    System.out.println( "\nAfter Bubble Sort, the array is" );
24    for ( int i = 0; i < numbers.length; i++ )
25          System.out.print( numbers[i] + "\t" );
26    System.out.println( );
27  }
28 }
```

EXAMPLE 8.19   Using Bubble Sort

8.6.4   Sorting Arrays of Objects

We saw earlier in the chapter that data items to be sorted can be primitive data types, such as integers or *doubles*. But they can also be objects. With an array of objects, it is important to understand that we need to sort the object themselves, not the array elements, which are merely the object references, or memory locations of the objects.

Arrays of object references are sorted using a sort key, which is one of the instance variables of the objects. For instance, if we have email objects, they can be sorted by date received, or by author, by subject, and so on. It is important to note that when we sort objects, the integrity of the objects must be respected; for instance, when we sort a collection of email objects by sender, we sort a collection of email objects, not a collection of senders.

Thus, to perform the Bubble Sort on the *cars* array of *Auto* objects, we need to decide which field (or fields) of the *Auto* object determines the order of the objects. If we say that the *model* is the sort field, then the comparison statement would compare the models in two objects, that is, two *Strings*. As you recall from Chapter 5, the *compareTo* method of the *String* class compares the values of two *Strings*. It returns a positive number if the *String* for which the method is invoked is greater than the *String* passed as an argument.

REFERENCE POINT

The *compareTo* method of the *String* class is discussed in detail in Chapter 5.

To sort the *cars* array using a Bubble Sort, we would need to make several revisions to the *bubbleSort* method. First, the data type of the array must be declared as an *Auto* in the parameter list. Second, *temp* needs to be defined as an *Auto* reference, and finally, we need to substitute the *compareTo* method in the statement that compares adjacent array elements.

The revised bubble sort code becomes:

```java
/* * Bubble sorts an array of Autos
*       @param    arr    an array of Autos
*/
public static void bubbleSort( Auto [ ] arr )
{
  Auto temp;

  for ( int i = 0; i < arr.length - 1; i++ )
  {
    for ( int j = 0; j < arr.length - i - 1; j++ )
    {
      if ( arr[j].getModel( ).compareTo( arr[j + 1].getModel( ) ) > 0 )
      {
        // swap the 2 adjacent elements
        temp = arr[j + 1];
```

```
      arr[j + 1] = arr[j];
      arr[j] = temp;
    } // end if statement
  } // end inner for loop
 } // end outer for loop
} // end bubbleSort method
```

If instead of comparing the models, we want to compare other fields in the object, then we would need to provide a method of the *Auto* class that performs the comparison. When you write a class whose objects are likely to be sorted, you are responsible for providing a method that can be used to compare two objects of that class.

8.6.5 Sequential Search of a Sorted Array

Earlier in the chapter, the *DVDWinners* class sequentially searched an array. The algorithm assumed the elements were not in order. If we sort the array, a Sequential Search can be implemented more efficiently for the case when the search key is not present in the array. Instead of searching the entire array before discovering that the search key is not in the array, we can stop as soon as we pass the location where that element would be if it were in the array. In other words, if the array is sorted in ascending order, we can recognize an unsuccessful search when we find an element in the array that is greater than the search key. Because the array is sorted in ascending order, all the elements after that array element are larger than that element, and therefore are also larger than the search key.

To implement this algorithm, we can add another test to the *for* loop condition, so that we exit the loop as soon as we find an element that is greater than the search key. The improved algorithm shown below could be used to replace the *findWinners* method shown in Example 8.14 for Sequential Search of a sorted *winners* array:

```
public int findWinners( int key )
{
   for ( int i = 0; winners[i] <= key && i < winners.length; i++ )
   {
      if ( winners[i] == key )
         return i;
   }
```

```
return -1; // end of array reached without finding key
           // or an element larger than the key was found
}
```

In fact, if the array is sorted, it can be searched even more efficiently using an algorithm called Binary Search, which we explain in the next section.

8.6.6   Binary Search of a Sorted Array

If you've played the "Guess a Number" game, you probably have used the concept of a **Binary Search**. In this game, someone asks you to guess a secret number between 1 and 100. For each number you guess, they tell you whether the secret number is larger or smaller than your guess. A good strategy is to guess the number in the middle, which in this example is 50. Whether the secret number is larger or smaller than 50, you will have eliminated half of the possible values. If the secret number is greater than 50, then you know your next guess should be 75 (halfway between 50 and 100). If the secret number is less than 50, your next guess should be 25 (halfway between 1 and 50). If you continue eliminating half the possible numbers with each guess, you will quickly guess the secret number. This approach works because we are "searching" a sorted set of numbers (1 to 100).

Similarly, a Binary Search of a sorted array works by eliminating half the remaining elements with each comparison. First, we look at the middle element of the array. If the value of that element is the search key, we return its index. If, however, the value of the middle element is greater than the search key, then the search key cannot be found in elements with array indexes higher than that element. Therefore, we will search the left half of the array only. Similarly, if the value of the middle element is lower than the search key, then the search key cannot be found in elements with array indexes lower than the middle element. Therefore, we will search in the right half of the array only. As we keep searching, the subarray we search keeps shrinking in size. In fact, the size of the subarray we search is cut in half at every iteration.

If the search key is not in the array, the subarray we search will eventually become empty. At that point, we know that we will not find our search key, and we return −1.

Example 8.20 shows our Binary Search algorithm.

```
1  /** Binary Search
2   *   Anderson, Franceschi
3   */
4
5  import java.util.Scanner;
6
7  public class BinarySearcher
8  {
9    public static void main( String [ ] args )
10   {
11     // define an array sorted in ascending order
12     int [ ] numbers = { 3, 6, 7, 8, 12, 15, 22, 36, 45,
13                         48, 51, 53, 64, 69, 72, 89, 95 };
14
15     Scanner scan  = new Scanner( System.in );
16     System.out.print( "Enter a value to search for > " );
17     int key = scan.nextInt( );
18
19     int index = binarySearch( numbers, key );
20     if ( index != -1 )
21         System.out.println( key + " found at index " + index );
22     else
23         System.out.println( key + " not found" );
24   }
25
26   public static int binarySearch( int [ ] arr, int key )
27   {
28     int start = 0;
29     int end = arr.length - 1;
30     int middle;
31
32     while ( end >= start )
33     {
34       middle = ( start + end ) / 2; // element in middle of array
35
36       if ( arr[middle] == key )
37       {
38         return middle;       // key found at middle
39       }
40       else if ( arr[middle] > key )
41       {
42         end = middle - 1;   // search left side of array
```

```
43            }
44         else
45         {
46            start = middle + 1; // search right side of array
47         }
48      }
49      return -1;
50   }
51 }
```

EXAMPLE 8.20   Binary Search of a Sorted Array

We start by declaring and initializing an integer array with 17 sorted elements (lines 12–13). We then prompt the user for a search key and call the
binarySearch method (lines 16–19).

The *binarySearch* method is coded at lines 26–50. The local variables *start*
and *end* store the first and last index of the subarray to search. Because we
begin by searching the entire array, we initialize these to the indexes of the
first and last element of the array that was passed as a parameter. The local
variable *middle*, declared at line 30, will store the index of the middle element in the subarray to search.

The search is performed in a *while* loop (lines 32–48), whose condition
determines whether the subarray is empty. If the subarray is not empty,
we calculate the value for *middle* by adding the indexes of the first and
last elements and dividing by 2 (line 34). Next we test whether the value
at the *middle* index is equal to the key. If so, we have found the key and
we return its index, which is *middle* (lines 36–39). If not, we test
whether the value in the middle of the subarray is greater than the key.
If so, we reduce the subarray to the elements with indexes less than *middle* (lines 40–43) and greater than or equal to *start*. If the value in the
middle of the subarray is less than the key, we reduce the subarray to the
elements with indexes greater than *middle* (lines 44–47) and smaller
than or equal to *end*.

When the *while* loop continues, we reevaluate the condition to determine
whether the subarray is empty, and if not, continue making our comparisons and either returning the index of the search key or reducing the size of
the subarray. If the search key is not in the array, the subarray eventually
becomes empty, and we exit the *while* loop and return –1 (line 49). Figure
8.25 shows the output when the search key is found.

Figure 8.25

Output from Example 8.20

Let's run through the Binary Search algorithm on the key *7* to illustrate how the algorithm works when the key is found in the array. Here is the array *numbers*:

Value	3	6	7	8	12	15	22	36	45	48	51	53	64	69	72	89	95
Index	0	1	2	3	4	5	6	7	8	9	10	11	12	13	14	15	16

When the *binarySearch* method is called, it sets *start* to 0 and *end* to *arr.length – 1*, which is 16. Thus, the value of *middle* is 8.

The element at index 8 (45) is greater than 7, so we set *end* to 7 (*middle – 1*), and we will now search the left subarray, highlighted below. The value of *middle* is now 3 ((0 + 7) / 2).

Value	3	6	7	8	12	15	22	36	45	48	51	53	64	69	72	89	95
Index	0	1	2	3	4	5	6	7	8	9	10	11	12	13	14	15	16

The element at index 3 (8) is greater than 7, so we set *end* to 2 (*middle – 1*) and keep searching in the left subarray, highlighted below. The value of *middle* is now 1 ((0 + 2) / 2).

Value	3	6	7	8	12	15	22	36	45	48	51	53	64	69	72	89	95
Index	0	1	2	3	4	5	6	7	8	9	10	11	12	13	14	15	16

The element at index 1 (6) is smaller than 7, so we set *start* to 2 (*middle + 1*) and search in the right subarray, highlighted below. The value of *middle* is now 2 ((2 + 2) / 2).

Value	3	6	7	8	12	15	22	36	45	48	51	53	64	69	72	89	95
Index	0	1	2	3	4	5	6	7	8	9	10	11	12	13	14	15	16

The element at index 2 (7) is equal to 7. We have found the value and return its index, 2.

Let's now run the preceding example on the key 34 to illustrate how the algorithm works when the key is not found in the array.

Here is the array *numbers* again:

Value	3	6	7	8	12	15	22	36	45	48	51	53	64	69	72	89	95
Index	0	1	2	3	4	5	6	7	8	9	10	11	12	13	14	15	16

Again, when the *binarySearch* method is called, it sets *start* to 0 and *end* to *arr.length* − 1, which is 16. Thus, *middle* is assigned the value 8 for the first comparison.

The element at index 8 (45) is greater than 34, so we set *end* to 7 (*middle* − 1), and keep searching in the left subarray. The value of *middle* becomes 3 for the next comparison.

Value	3	6	7	8	12	15	22	36	45	48	51	53	64	69	72	89	95
Index	0	1	2	3	4	5	6	7	8	9	10	11	12	13	14	15	16

The element at index 3 (8) is smaller than 34, so we search in the right sub-array highlighted below. The value of *middle* is now 5.

Value	3	6	7	8	12	15	22	36	45	48	51	53	64	69	72	89	95
Index	0	1	2	3	4	5	6	7	8	9	10	11	12	13	14	15	16

The element at index 5 (15) is smaller than 34, so we search in the right subarray. The value of *middle* is now 6.

Value	3	6	7	8	12	15	22	36	45	48	51	53	64	69	72	89	95
Index	0	1	2	3	4	5	6	7	8	9	10	11	12	13	14	15	16

The element at index 6 (22) is smaller than 34, so we search in the right subarray. The value of *middle* is now 7.

Value	3	6	7	8	12	15	22	36	45	48	51	53	64	69	72	89	95
Index	0	1	2	3	4	5	6	7	8	9	10	11	12	13	14	15	16

At this point, *start*, *end*, and *middle* all have the value 7. The element at index 7 (36) is larger than 34, so we assign *end* the value *middle – 1*, which is 6. This makes *end* less than *start* and consequently makes the *while* loop condition evaluate to *false*. We have not found 34, so we return −1.

8.7   Programming Activity 2: Searching and Sorting Arrays

In this activity, you will work again with a 15-element integer array, performing these activities:

1. Write a method to perform a Sequential Search of an array.

2. Write a method to implement the Bubble Sort algorithm to sort an array.

The framework for this Programming Activity will animate your algorithm so that you can watch your algorithm work and check the accuracy of your code. For example, Figure 8.26 demonstrates the Bubble Sort at work. At this point, the program has completed three passes through the array and is comparing the values of elements 5 and 6.

Figure 8.26

The Bubble Sort at Work

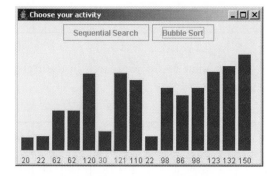

Instructions

In the Chapter 8 Programming Activity 2 directory on the CD-ROM accompanying this book, you will find the source files needed to complete this activity. Copy all the files to a directory on your computer. Note that all files should be in the same directory.

Open the *ArrayPractice2.java* source file. Searching for five stars (*****) in the source code will position you at the two locations where you will add your code. Your first task is to complete the *sequentialSearch* method, which searches the *arr* array, an instance variable of the *ArrayPractice2* class. The array *arr* has already been instantiated for you and filled with random values. The second task is to complete the *bubbleSort* method. Example 8.21 shows the section of the *ArrayPractice2* source code where you will add your code. Note that in each method, you are asked to call the *animate* method so that your method code can be animated as it works. Note also that for the *sequentialSearch* method, we provide a dummy *return* statement (*return 0;*). We do this so that the source code will compile. In this way, you can write and test each method separately, using stepwise refinement. When you are ready to write the *sequentialSearch* method, just replace the dummy *return* statement with the appropriate *return* statement for that method.

```java
//  1 ***** student writes this method
/**  Searches for key in integer array named arr
//     arr is an instance variable of the class and has been
//     instantiated and filled with random values.
//  @param key value to search for
//  @return  if key is found, the  index of the first element
//     in array whose value is key; if key is not found,
//     the method returns -1
*/
public int sequentialSearch( int key )
{
  // Note:  To animate the algorithm, put this method call as the
  // first statement in your for loop
  //  animate( i, 0 );
  //       where i is the index of the current array element


    return 0; // replace this statement with your return statement
```

```
} // end of sequentialSearch

// 2. *****  student writes this method
/** Sorts arr in ascending order using the bubble sort algorithm
*/
public void bubbleSort( )
{
// Note:  To animate the algorithm, put this method call as the
// last statement in your innermost for loop
//   animate( i, j );
//            where i is the value of the outer loop counter
//            and j is the value of the inner loop counter,
//            or the index of the current array element


} // end of bubbleSort
```

EXAMPLE 8.21   Student Section of *ArrayPractice2*

When you have finished writing your code, compile and run the application. Figure 8.27 shows the graphics window when the application begins. To test any method, click on the appropriate button.

Troubleshooting

If your method implementation does not animate, consider these tips:

- Verify that your *for* loop calls the *animate* method as instructed in the method comments.

Figure 8.27
Opening Window of
ArrayPractice2

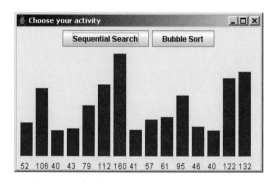

- Verify that you did not instantiate a new array. Perform all operations on the instance variable array named *arr*.

? DISCUSSION QUESTIONS

1. The *bubbleSortImproved* method always executes the outer loop one more iteration after the array is sorted. Explain why this happens.

2. The sequential search finds only the first occurrence of the parameter *key*. How would you modify the *sequentialSearch* method to count the occurrences of *key*?

8.8   Using Arrays as Counters

In some circumstances, it is useful to use an array of integers as an ordered group of accumulators, or counters. For example, suppose you are analyzing a survey that has four possible answers, 0 through 3. You want to count how many people selected each answer. You could set up four counters and use an *if/else* statement to increment the appropriate counter. The pseudocode would be:

```
read first survey
while ( not end of surveys )
{
   if answer is 0
      increment counter0
   else if answer is 1
      increment counter1
   else if answer is 2
      increment counter2
   else if answer is 3
      increment counter3

   read next survey
}
```

That would work if you have only a few possible answers, but what if you had 100 or more answers? You would end up writing a very long *if/else* statement.

Instead, you could set up an array of counters and let the counter for answer 0 be *array[0]*, the counter for answer 1 be *array[1]*, and so on. This approach—using an array of counters—is simpler to code and saves processing time.

As another example, suppose we want to throw a die 500 times and count the number of times each outcome occurs; that is, we want to count the number of ones, twos, threes, fours, fives, and sixes that are rolled. To do this, we set up a simple *Die* class shown in Example 8.22, with a method for rolling a value. Then we set up the client class, *DieCount*, shown in Example 8.23, that has an array with six integer elements, each element will hold the number of times a particular roll occurs.

```
1 /** Die class
2 *   Anderson, Franceschi
3 */
4
5 public class Die
6 {
7    private int face;
8
9    /** rolls the die
10   *  @return  the value of the roll: 1 - 6
11   */
12   public int roll( )
13   {
14       face =  1 + (int)( Math.random( ) * 6 );
15       return face;
16   }
17 }
```

EXAMPLE 8.22   The *Die* Class

```
1 /** DieCount Class
2 *   Anderson, Franceschi
3 */
4
5 public class DieCount
6 {
7   public static void main( String [ ] args )
8   {
9      final int FACES = 6, NUMBER_OF_ROLLS = 500;
10
11     // instantiate the counter array
12     // which sets initial values to 0
13     int [ ] rollCount = new int [FACES];
14
15     // instantiate the Die
16     Die d1 = new Die( );
```

```
17
18       // roll the die 500 times
19       for ( int i = 1; i <= NUMBER_OF_ROLLS; i++ )
20       {
21          int myRoll = d1.roll( );
22          rollCount[myRoll - 1]++;  // increment the counter for roll
23       }
24
25       // print count for each roll
26       System.out.println( "Roll\tCount" );
27       for ( int i = 0; i < rollCount.length; i++ )
28       {
29          System.out.println( ( i + 1 ) + "\t" + rollCount[i] );
30       }
31    }
32 }
```

EXAMPLE 8.23   The *DieCount* Class

In the *Die* class, we haven't written a constructor, because the only job for the constructor in this simple class is to set a value for the *face* instance variable. The default constructor provided by the compiler will do just that, so we'll take that default constructor. The only method, therefore, is *roll* (lines 9–16), which generates a random number between 1 and 6 to simulate the roll of a die.

In the *DieCount* class, we instantiate our array of six counters, *rollCount*, on line 13, which autoinitializes each element to 0—exactly what we want for counters.

To count the number of times each roll occurs, we use a *for* loop that iterates 500 times, with each iteration calling the *roll* method of the *Die* class. We then need to count each roll. That's where our array of counters, *rollCount*, comes in.

Since the *rollCount* array has six elements, the index of the first element is 0, and the index of the last element is 5. We will use *rollCount[0]* to hold the number of times we rolled a 1, *rollCount[1]* to hold the number of times we rolled a 2, and continue that way until we use *rollCount[5]* to hold the number of times we rolled a 6. Thus, to get the index of the appropriate counter, we need to decrement the roll by 1. So our statement to increment the count for a roll (line 22) becomes

```
rollCount[myRoll - 1]++;
```

After rolling the die 500 times and counting each roll, we print the total times each roll occurred (lines 25–30). Note that we increment the loop variable to

Figure 8.28

Output from *DieCount*

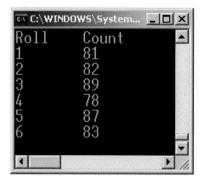

convert between our counter index and the roll number. The output from a sample run of this program is shown in Figure 8.28. Because the program generates the rolls randomly, your output may be slightly different.

Our algorithm is not ideal, however. We need to subtract 1 from the index in order to increment the counter, and we need to add 1 to the index to print the outcome.

A better approach would be to create the array with seven elements. Then we can use elements 1 through 6 as the counters for the rolls 1 through 6. The index and the roll number will be the same. What happens to element 0? Nothing. We just ignore it.

The revised *DieCount2* class is shown in Example 8.24.

```
 1 /** DieCount2 Class
 2 *    Anderson, Franceschi
 3 */
 4
 5 public class DieCount2
 6 {
 7   public static void main( String [ ] args )
 8   {
 9       final int FACES = 7, NUMBER_OF_ROLLS = 500;
10
11       // instantiate the counter array
12       // which sets initial values to 0
13       int [ ] rollCount = new int [FACES];
14
15       // instantiate the Die
16       Die d1 = new Die( );
17
18       // roll the die 500 times
```

```
19       for ( int i = 1; i <= NUMBER_OF_ROLLS; i++ )
20       {
21         int myRoll = d1.roll( );
22         rollCount[myRoll]++;  // increment the counter for roll
23       }
24
25       // print count for each roll
26       System.out.println( "Roll\tCount" );
27       for ( int i = 1; i < rollCount.length; i++ )
28       {
29         System.out.println(  i  + "\t" + rollCount[i] );
30       }
31    }
32 }
```

EXAMPLE 8.24   The *DieCount2* Class

Notice the changes to the code in this example. First, we set *FACES* to 7 (line 9), so we will instantiate an array with seven elements. Then we can use the roll of the die as the index into the counter array to increment the appropriate count (line 22). One last change is that when we loop through the *rollCount* array to print the counters, we initialize our loop counter to 1 (line 27), since we are not using element 0 as a counter and we simply use *i* as the roll number.

It's true that we're allocating an extra integer (four bytes of memory) which is never used, but we're eliminating 500 subtract operations and 500 addition operations! The program is more efficient, easier to write, and easier to read.

Skill Practice
with these end-of-chapter questions

8.10.1   Multiple Choice Exercises

Question 12

8.10.4   Identifying Errors in Code

Question 44

8.10.6   Write a Short Program

Question 57

8.10.8   Technical Writing

Question 74

8.9   Chapter Summary

- An array is a sequence of variables of the same data type. The data type can be any Java primitive data type, such as *int*, *float*, *double*, *byte*, *boolean*, or *char*, or it can be a class.

- Each element in the array is accessed using the array name and an index, which refers to the element's position in the array.

- Arrays are implemented as objects. Creating an array consists of declaring an object reference for the array and instantiating the array. The size of the array is given when the array is instantiated.

- In arrays of primitive types, each element of the array contains a value of that type. In arrays of objects, each element is an object reference.

- When an array is instantiated, the elements are given initial values automatically, depending on the data type. Numeric types are set to 0; *boolean* types are set to *false*; *char* types are set to a space, and object references are set to *null*.

- Instantiating an array of object references involves two steps, instantiating the array, and instantiating the objects.

- Arrays can be instantiated when they are declared by assigning initial values in a comma-separated list within curly braces. The number of values in the initialization list determines the number of elements in the array.

- Array elements are accessed using the array name and an index. The first element's index is 0 and the last element's index is the size of the array -1.

- Arrays have an integer instance variable, *length*, which holds the number of elements in the array.

- Attempting to access an element of an array using an index less than 0 or greater than *arrayName.length – 1* will generate an *ArrayIndexOutOfBoundsException* at run time.

- Aggregate array operations, such as printing and copying arrays, are not supported for arrays. Using a *for* loop, you can process each array element individually.

- To change the size of an array, instantiate an array of the desired size with a temporary name, copy the appropriate elements from the original array to the new array, and assign the new array reference to the original array. Assign *null* to the temporary array name.

- Arrays can be passed as arguments to methods and can also be the return type of methods.

- When an array is an instance variable of a class, the constructor should instantiate a new array and copy the elements of the parameter array into the new array.

- A Sequential Search determines whether a particular value, the search key, is in an array by comparing the search key to each element in the array.

- A Selection Sort arranges elements in the array in order by value by reducing the array into successively smaller subarrays and placing the largest element in each subarray into the last position of the subarray.

- A Bubble Sort puts elements of an array in order by making multiple passes through the array and putting adjacent elements in order.

- To sort an array of objects, you can use the class method provided to compare objects' values.

- A sorted array can be searched more efficiently using a Binary Search, which successively reduces the number of elements to search by half.

- Arrays of integers can be used as an ordered group of counters.

8.10   Exercises, Problems, and Projects

8.10.1   Multiple Choice Exercises

1. What are the valid ways to declare an integer array named *a*? (Check all that apply.)

    - ❑ `int [ ] a;`
    - ❑ `int a[ ];`
    - ❑ `array int a;`
    - ❑ `int array a;`

2. What is the index of the first element of an array?

❏ −1

❏ 0

❏ 1

3. An array *a* has 30 elements; what is the index of its last element?

❏ 29

❏ 30

❏ 31

4. What is the default value of the elements in an array of *ints* after declaration and instantiation of the array?

❏ 0

❏ *null*

❏ undefined

5. How do you access the element of array *a* located at index 6?

❏ `a{6}`

❏ `a( 6 )`

❏ `a[6]`

6. Which of the following assertions is true?

❏ An array cannot be sized dynamically.

❏ An array can be sized dynamically, but cannot be resized without instantiating it again.

❏ An array can be sized dynamically and can also be resized without instantiating it again.

7. How do you retrieve the number of elements in an array *a*?

❏ `a.length( )`

❏ `a.length`

❏ `a.size( )`

❏ `a.size`

8. All the elements of an array must be of the same type.

❏ true

❏ false

9. Array aggregate assignment is possible in Java.

   ❏ true

   ❏ false

10. Aggregate comparison of arrays is possible in Java.

   ❏ true

   ❏ false

11. An array can be returned by a method.

   ❏ true

   ❏ false

12. A Sequential Search on a sorted array is typically faster than a Sequential Search on an unsorted array.

   ❏ true

   ❏ false

8.10.2   Reading and Understanding Code

13. What is the output of this code sequence?

```
double [ ] a = { 12.5, 48.3, 65.0 };
System.out.println( a[1] );
```

14. What is the output of this code sequence?

```
int [ ] a = new int [6];
System.out.println( a[4] );
```

15. What is the output of this code sequence?

```
double [ ] a = { 12.5, 48.3, 65.0 };
System.out.println( a.length );
```

16. What is the output of this code sequence?

```
int [ ] a = { 12, 48, 65 };

for ( int i = 0; i < a.length; i++ )
   System.out.println( a[i] );
```

17. What is the output of this code sequence?

```
int [ ] a = { 12, 48, 65 };

for ( int i = 0; i < a.length; i++ )
   System.out.println( "a[" + i + "] = " + a[i] );
```

18. What is the output of this code sequence?

```
int s = 0;
int [ ] a = { 12, 48, 65 };

for ( int i = 0; i < a.length; i++ )
   s += a[i];

System.out.println( "s = " + s );
```

19. What is the output of this code sequence?

```
int [ ] a = new int[10];

for ( int i = 0; i < a.length; i++ )
   a[i] = i + 10;

System.out.println( a[4] );
```

20. What is the output of this code sequence?

```
double [ ] a = { 12.3, 99.6, 48.2, 65.8 };
double temp = a[0];

for ( int i = 0; i < a.length; i++ )
{
   if ( a[i] > temp )
      temp = a[i];
}
System.out.println( temp );
```

21. What is the output of this code sequence?

```
int [ ] a = { 12, 48, 65, 23 };
int temp = a[1];
a[1] = a[3];
a[3] = temp;

for ( int i = 0; i < a.length; i++ )
   System.out.print( a[i] + " " );
```

22. What does this method do?

```
public int foo( int [ ] a )
{
   int temp = 0;

   for ( int i = 0; i < a.length; i++ )
   {
```

```
        if ( a[i] == 5 )
                temp++;
    }
    return temp;
}
```

23. What does this method do?

```
public int foo( int [ ] a )
{
    for ( int i = 0; i < a.length; i++ )
    {
            if ( a[i] == 10 )
                return i;
    }
    return -1;
}
```

24. What does this method do?

```
public boolean foo( int [ ] a )
{
    for ( int i = 0; i < a.length; i++ )
    {
            if ( a[i] < 0 )
                return false;
    }
    return true;
}
```

25. What does this method do?

```
public String [ ] foo( String [ ] a )
{
    String [ ] temp = new String[a.length];
    for ( int i = 0; i < a.length; i++ )
    {
            temp[i] = a[i].toLowerCase( );
    }
    return temp;
}
```

26. What does this method do?

```
public boolean [ ] foo( String [ ] a )
{
    boolean [ ] temp = new boolean[a.length];

    for ( int i = 0; i < a.length; i++ )
```

```
        {
                if ( a[i].contains( "@" ) )
                        temp[i] = true;
                else
                        temp[i] = false;
        }
        return temp;
}
```

8.10.3   Fill in the Code

27. This code assigns the value 10 to all the elements of an array *a*.

```
int [ ] a = new int[25];
for ( int i = 0; i < a.length; i++ )
{
        // your code goes here


}
```

28. This code prints all the elements of array *a* that have a value greater than 20.

```
double [ ] a = { 45.2, 13.1, 12.8, 87.4, 99.0, 100.1, 43.8, 2.4 };

for ( int i = 0; i < a.length; i++ )
{
        // your code goes here


}
```

29. This code prints the average of the elements of array *a*.

```
int [ ] a = { 45, 13, 12, 87, 99, 100, 43, 2 };
double average = 0.0;

for ( int i = 0; i < a.length; i++ )
{
        // your code goes here


}

// ... and your code continues here
```

30. This code calculates and prints the dot product of two arrays (Σ a[i] * b[i]).

```
int [ ] a = { 3, 7, 9 };
int [ ] b = { 2, 9, 4 };
int dotProduct = 0;

for ( int i = 0; i < a.length; i++ )
{
      // your code goes here

}
```

31. This code prints the following three lines:

```
a[0] = 3
a[1] = 6
a[2] = 10
```

```
int [ ] a = { 3, 6, 10 };

for ( int i = 0; i < a.length; i++ )
{
      // your code goes here

}
```

32. This method returns *true* if an element in an array of *Strings* passed as a parameter contains the substring *IBM*; otherwise, it returns *false*.

```
public boolean foo( String [ ] a )
{
   // your code goes here
}
```

33. This method returns the number of elements in an array passed as a parameter that are multiples of 7.

```
public int foo( int [ ] a )
{
   // your code goes here
}
```

34. This method returns *true* if the first two elements of the array passed as a parameter have the same value; otherwise, it returns *false*.

```
public boolean foo( String [ ] a )
{
      // your code goes here
}
```

35. This method takes an array of *ints* as a parameter and returns an array of *booleans*. For each element in the parameter array whose value is 0, the corresponding element of the array returned will be assigned *false*; otherwise, the element will be assigned *true*.

```
public boolean [ ] foo( int [ ] a )
{
 // your code goes here
}
```

8.10.4 Identifying Errors in Code

36. Where is the error in this code sequence?

```
double [ ] a = { 3.3, 26.0, 48.4 };
a[4] = 2.5;
```

37. Where is the error in this code sequence?

```
double [ ] a = { 3.3, 26.0, 48.4 };
System.out.println( a[-1] );
```

38. Where is the error in this code sequence?

```
double [ ] a = { 3.3, 26.0, 48.4 };
System.out.println( a{1} );
```

39. Where is the error in this code sequence?

```
double [ ] a = { 3.3, 26.0, 48.4 };
for ( int i = 0; i <= a.length; i++ )
        System.out.println( a[i] );
```

40. Where is the error in this code sequence?

```
double a[3] = { 3.3, 26.0, 48.4 };
```

41. Where is the error (although this code will compile and run) in this code sequence?

```
int a[4] = { 3, 26, 48, 5 };
int b[4] = { 3, 26, 48, 5 };

if ( a != b )
        System.out.println( "Array elements are NOT identical" );
```

42. Where is the error in this code sequence?

```
int [ ] a = { 3, 26, 48, 5 };
a.length = 10;
```

43. Where is the logic error in this code sequence?

```
int [ ] a = { 3, 26, 48, 5 };
System.out.println( "The array elements are " + a );
```

44. Where is the error in this code sequence?

```
Integer i1 = new Integer( 10 );
Integer i2 = new Integer( 15 );
Double d1 = new Double( 3.4 );
String s = new String( "Hello" );
Integer [ ] a = { i1, i2, d1, s };
```

8.10.5 Debugging Area

45. You coded the following on line 26 of the class *Test.java:*

```
int a[6] = { 2, 7, 8, 9, 11, 16 };    // line 26
```

When you compile, you get the following message:

```
Test.java :26 : ']' expected
      int a[6] = { 2, 7, 8, 9, 11, 16 };   // line 26
           ^
      1 error
```

Explain what the problem is and how to fix it.

46. You coded the following on lines 26, 27, and 28 of the class *Test.java*:

```
int [ ] a = { 2, 7, 8, 9, 11, 16 };    // line 26 of class Test.java
for ( int i = 0; i <= a.length; i++ ) // line 27 of class Test.java
      System.out.println( a[i] );      // line 28 of class Test.java
```

The code compiles properly, but when you run, you get the following message:

```
Exception in thread "main" java.lang.ArrayIndexOutOfBoundsException
at Test.main ( Test.java : 28 )
```

Explain what the problem is and how to fix it.

47. You coded the following in the class *Test.java*:

```
int [ ] a = { 1, 2, 3 };
int [ ] b = { 1, 2, 3 };
if ( a == b )
      System.out.println( "Arrays are equal" );
else
      System.out.println( "Arrays are NOT equal" );
```

The code compiles properly and runs, but the result is not what you expected; the output is

```
Arrays are NOT equal
```

Explain what the problem is and how to fix it.

48. You coded the following in the class *Test.java*:

```
int [ ] a = { 1, 2, 3 };
System.out.println( a );
```

The code compiles properly and runs, but the result is not what you expected; the output is similar to the following:

[I@f0326267

Explain what the problem is and how to fix it.

8.10.6   Write a Short Program

49. Write a value-returning method that returns the number of elements in an integer array.

50. Write a value-returning method that returns the product of all the elements in an integer array.

51. Write a *void* method that sets to 0 all the elements of an integer array.

52. Write a *void* method that multiplies by 2 all the elements of an array of *floats*.

53. Write a method that returns the percentage of elements greater than or equal to 90 in an array of *ints*.

54. Write a method that returns the difference between the largest and smallest elements in an array of *doubles*.

55. Write a method that returns the sum of all the elements of an array of *ints* that have an odd index.

56. Write a method that returns the percentage of the number of elements that have the value *true* in an array of *booleans*.

57. Write a method that returns *true* if an array of *Strings* contains the String "Hello"; *false* otherwise.

58. Write a method that prints all the elements of an array of *chars* in reverse order.

59. Write a *void* method that returns an array composed of all the elements in an array of *chars* in reverse order.

60. Write an array-returning method that takes a *String* as a parameter and returns the corresponding array of *chars*.

61. Code an array-returning method that takes an array of *ints* as a parameter and returns an array of *booleans*, assigning *true* for any element of the parameter array greater than or equal to 100; and *false* otherwise.

8.10.7   Programming Projects

62. Write a class encapsulating the concept of statistics for a baseball team, which has the following attributes: a number of players, a list of number of hits for each player, a list of number of at-bats for each player.

    Write the following methods:

    ❏ A constuctor with two equal-length arrays as parameters, the number of hits per player, and the number of at-bats per player.

    ❏ Accessors, mutators, *toString*, and *equals* methods.

    ❏ Generate and return an array of batting averages based on the attributes above.

    ❏ Calculate and return the total number of hits for the team.

    ❏ Calculate and return the number of players with a batting average greater than .300.

    Write a client class to test all the methods in your class.

63. Write a class encapsulating the concept of student grades on a test, assuming student grades are composed of a list of integers between 0 and 100.

    Write the following methods:

    ❏ A constructor with just one parameter, the number of students; all grades can be randomly generated

    ❏ Accessor, mutator, *toString*, and *equals* methods

    ❏ A method returning an array of the grades sorted in ascending order

❏ A method returning the highest grade

❏ A method returning the average grade

❏ A method returning the median grade (*Hint:* The median grade will be located in the middle of the sorted array of grades.)

❏ A method returning the mode (the grade that occurs most often). (*Hint:* Create an array of counters; count how many times each grade occurs; then pick the maximum in the array of counters; the array index is the mode.)

Write a client class to test all the methods in your class.

64. Write a class encapsulating the concept of daily temperatures for a week.

Write the following methods:

❏ A constructor accepting an array of seven temperatures as a parameter

❏ Accessor, mutator, *toString*, and *equals* methods

❏ A method returning how many temperatures were below freezing

❏ A method returning an array of temperatures above 100 degrees

❏ A method returning the largest change in temperature between any two consecutive days

Write a client class to test all the methods in your class.

65. Write a class encapsulating the concept of a tic-tac-toe game as follows:

Two players will be playing, player 1 and player 2.

The board is represented by an array of 9 integer elements: elements at indexes 0, 1, and 2 represent the first row; elements at indexes 3, 4, and 5 represent the second row; elements at indexes 6, 7, and 8 represent the third row.

The value 0 in the array indicates that this space is available; the value 1 indicates the space is occupied by player 1; and the value 2 indicates that this space is occupied by player 2.

In the *main* method of your client class, your program will simulate a tic-tac-toe game from the command line (or a *JOptionPane* dialog box), doing the following:

❏ Create a *TicTacToe* object and instantiate it.

❏ In a loop, prompt for plays, as *ints*, from the user. At each iteration of the loop, you will need to call methods of the *TicTacToe* class to update the *TicTacToe* object. You need to keep track of who is playing (player 1 or 2), enforce the rules, check if either player has won the game. It is clear that if anyone has won the game, it is the last player who played.

❑ If a player wins, you will need to exit the loop and present the result of the game. If the game ends in a tie, you should output that result.

In your *TicTacToe* class, you will need to code the following methods:

❑ A default constructor instantiating the array representing the board.

❑ A method that allows a player to make a move; it takes two arguments: the player number and the position played on the board.

❑ A method checking if a play is legal.

❑ A method checking if a player has won the game; you can break up that method into several methods if you like (for instance, check if a player has won the game by claiming an entire horizontal row).

❑ A method that checks whether the game is a tie (if no player has won and all squares have been played, the game is tied).

❑ A method that displays the results of the game ("Player 1 won," "Player 2 won," or "Tie game").

Write a client class, where the *main* method is located, to test all the methods in your class and enable the user to play.

66. When a new user logs in for the first time on a Web site, the user has to submit personal information, such as user_id, password, name, email address, telephone number, and so forth. Typically, there are two fields for passwords, requiring the user to enter the password twice, to ensure that the user did not make a typo in the first password field.

Write a class encapsulating the concept of processing a form with the following elements:

User_id

Password

Reenter password

Email address

Name

Street address

City

State

Zip

Telephone

In your class, write the following methods:

❑ A constructor with one parameter, a sequence of 10 words in an array of *Strings*, your only instance variable.

❑ Accessor, mutator, *toString*, and *equals* methods.

❑ A method checking that no *Strings* in the array are empty. (All fields are mandatory.) If at least one is empty, it returns *false*, otherwise, it returns *true*.

❑ A method returning the number of characters in the user_id.

❑ A method checking if the two *Strings* representing the passwords (representing the password typed in twice) are identical; if they are, it returns *true*; if not, it returns *false*.

❑ A method checking if the *String* representing the email address actually "looks like" an email address; to simplify, we can assume that an email address contains one and only one @ character and contains one or more periods after the @ character. If it does "look like" an email address, then the method returns *true*; otherwise, it returns *false*.

❑ A method checking if the *String* representing the state has exactly two characters. If it does, it returns *true;* otherwise, it returns *false*.

Write a client class to test all the methods in your class.

67. We want to write a program that performs some syntax checking on HTML code; for simplicity reasons, we will assume that the HTML code is syntactically correct if the number of < characters in any word is the same as the number of > characters in that word. We will also

assume that the syntax is correct if the first word is *<HTML>* and the last word is *</HTML>*.

Write a class encapsulating that concept, including the following methods:

- ❑ A constructor with one parameter, an array of the words in the HTML sentence, your only instance variable. Your constructor should then get user input from the console for that same number of words and store them in an array of *Strings*, your only data member.

- ❑ Accessor, mutator, *toString*, and *equals* methods.

- ❑ A method returning how many words are in the array.

- ❑ A method returning *true* if the first word is *<HTML>* and the last word is *</HTML>*; *false* otherwise.

- ❑ A method checking if each array element contains the same number of < characters as > characters; if that is the case, the method returns *true*; otherwise, it returns *false*. For this, we suggest the following method to help you:

  - ▪ Write an *int*-returning method that takes a *String* and a *char* as parameters and returns how many times that *char* appears in the *String*; you can convert the *String* to an array of *chars* and loop through it, or use another strategy of your choice.

- ❑ A method counting and returning the number of IMG tags overall.

Write a client class to test all the methods in your class.

68. Write a class encapsulating the concept of converting integer grades to letter grades (A, B, C, D, or F), assuming grades are composed of a list of integers between 0 and 100.

Write the following methods:

- ❑ A constructor with just one parameter, the number of students; all grades can be randomly generated.

- ❑ Accessor, mutator, *toString*, and *equals* methods.

- ❑ A method returning an array of *chars* corresponding to the integer grades (90 or above should be converted to A, 80 or above to B, 70 or above to C, 60 or above to D, and 59 or less to F).

❑ A method returning the number of As.

❑ A method returning an array of *ints* counting how many As, Bs, Cs, Ds, and Fs were received.

Write a client class to test all the methods in your class.

69. Write a class encapsulating the concept of printing a letter as a 7 × 5 grid of either spaces or asterisks (*). That letter is made up of a list of thirty-five 1s and 0s, which will be stored in an array representing the letter, the only instance variable of the class.

For instance, below is what the input file would look like for the letter I. A 1 will print as a *, and a 0 as a space.

After every 5 elements have been printed, you will need to print a new line.

If the input is

0 1 1 1 0 0 0 1 0 0 0 0 1 0 0 0 0 1 0 0 0 0 1 0 0 0 0 1 0 0 0 1 1 1 0

When printed, that letter would look like this:

```
***
  *
  *
  *
  *
  *
***
```

Write the following methods:

❑ A constructor with 1 parameter, an array of thirty-five 0s or 1s, your only instance variable. Be sure to enforce the constraint of having only 1s and 0s.

❑ Accessor, mutator, *toString*, and *equals* methods.

❑ A method printing out the letter as in the output example above.

❑ A method returning the number of 1s.

❑ A method returning the percentage of 0s.

Write a client class to test all the methods in your class.

70. Write a class encapsulating the concept of a team of baseball players, assuming a baseball player has the following attributes: name, a position, and a batting percentage. In addition to that class, you will need

to design and code a *Player* class to encapsulate the concept of a baseball player.

In your class encapsulating the team, you should write the following methods:

❏ A constructor taking an array of *Player* objects as its only parameter and assigning that array to the array data member of the class, its only instance variable. In your client class, when you test all your methods, you can hard-code nine baseball *Player* objects.

❏ Accessor, mutator, *toString*, and *equals* methods.

❏ A method checking that all positions are different, returning *true* if they are, *false* if they are not.

❏ A method returning the batting percentage of the team.

❏ A method checking that we have a pitcher (that is, the name of the position) on the team; if we do not have any, it returns *false*; otherwise, it returns *true*.

❏ A method returning the array of *Player* objects sorted in ascending order using the batting percentage as the sorting key.

❏ A method checking if a certain person (a parameter of the method) is on the team, based on the name of that person. If the person is on the team, the method returns *true*; otherwise, it returns *false*.

Write a client class to test all the methods in your class.

71. Write a class encapsulating a similar concept to the one used in the die counting problem of section 8.8. Here, we want to roll two dice; the total of the numbers rolled will be between 2 and 12. We want to keep track of how many times each possible roll was rolled.

Write the following methods:

❏ A constructor with no parameter; it randomly generates two numbers between 1 and 6, representing the dice.

❏ Accessor, mutator, *toString*, and *equals* methods.

❏ A method returning the total of the two dice.

❏ A method checking if the two dice have identical values; if they do, it returns *true*; otherwise, it returns *false*.

The number of times we roll the dice should be an input from the user at the command line (not inside the program). Your program should output the total for each possible roll (from 2 to 12), as well as the number of times the two dice had identical values.

Write a client class to test all the methods in your class.

72. Write an applet that creates two *Die* objects and rolls the two dice 5,000 times. Display the results showing the frequency of each possible total in a bar chart. Pick a scale that is appropriate for the maximum height of your bar chart.

8.10.8   Technical Writing

73. What do you think are advantages and disadvantages of arrays?

74. Describe in pseudocode how you would implement a sorting algorithm to sort an array of *Objects*. (The *Objects* will be sorted based on the value of one of their data members.)

75. When you try to use an array index that is out of bounds, your code will compile, but you will generate a run–time exception. Discuss whether this is an advantage or a disadvantage, and why.

76. When instantiating an array, you can assign the number of elements in the array dynamically, using a variable (as opposed to using a constant). Discuss a situation where that would be useful.

8.10.9   Group Project (for a group of 1, 2, or 3 students)

77. Security is an important feature of information systems. Often, text is encrypted before being sent, and then decrypted upon receipt. We want to build a class (or several classes) encapsulating the concept of encryption. You will need to test that class with a client program where the *main* method is located.

For this project, encrypting consists of translating each character into another character. For instance, if we consider the English alphabet, including characters *a* through *z*, each character is randomly encrypted into another, which could be the same character. (If you like, you can design your program so that no character is encrypted into itself.) To represent this concept, we can have an array of characters for the original alphabet, and another array of characters for the encrypted alphabet. For example, we could have

Original alphabet	Encrypted alphabet
a	u
b	p
c	h
d	a
e	s
f	x
g	z
h	b
i	j
. . .	. . .

To encrypt a word, each letter in the word is replaced by the corresponding letter in the encryted alphabet. For example, the word *caged* would be encrypted into *huzsa*. To decrypt a word, the letters in the encrypted word are replaced by the corresponding letter in the original alphabet. For example, the encrypted word *xssa* would be decrypted as *feed*.

If we have 26 different characters in the original alphabet, then we will have 26 different characters in the encrypted alphabet. Furthermore, the encrypted alphabet should be randomly generated.

In your *main* method, you should prompt the user for a sentence. Your program should encrypt the sentence, output the encrypted sentence, then decrypt it, and output the decrypted sentence, which should be identical to the original sentence that was input by the user.

For extra credit, use an array to keep track of the number of occurrences of each character. Convert these occurrences to percentages, and then use these percentages to attempt to decrypt a large, encrypted message.

CHAPTER 9

Multidimensional Arrays and the *ArrayList* Class

CHAPTER CONTENTS

Introduction

In Chapter 8, we learned that arrays could be useful when we have a lot of data to store in memory. If we write a program to perform statistics on last year's temperatures, it is convenient to set up an array of *doubles* of size 365 to store the daily temperature data.

But what if in addition to analyzing daily temperatures, we want to analyze temperatures by the week, or by a particular day of the week? For instance, if we sail on weekends, we could want to know how many times the temperature was above 65 degrees on Saturdays and Sundays. If we are considering investing in air conditioning at home, we might be interested in knowing how many weeks had temperatures above 90 degrees. If we are avid skiers, we could be interested in the number of weeks with temperatures lower than 32 degrees.

In this situation, we would want to organize our data along two dimensions: weeks and days of the week. If we were to visualize the data as a table, we could imagine a table made up of 52 rows, each row representing a week. Each row would have seven columns, representing the days of the week. This table is shown in Figure 9.1. Or we could imagine a table of seven rows, each row representing a day of the week, and 52 columns, each column representing a week of the year. In either case, we can represent the rows and columns of our temperature table using a two-dimensional array. More generally, **multidimensional** arrays allow us to represent data organized along *n* dimensions with a single array.

Figure 9.1

Temperature Data for the Previous 52 Weeks

	Sunday	Monday	Tuesday	Wednesday	Thursday	Friday	Saturday
Week 1	35	28.6	29.3	38	43.1	45.6	49
Week 2	51.9	37.9	34.1	37.1	39	40.5	43.2
...							
...							
...							
...							
...							
Week 51	56.2	51.9	45.3	48.7	42.9	35.5	38.2
Week 52	33.2	27.1	24.9	29.8	37.7	39.9	38.8

9.1   Declaring and Instantiating Multidimensional Arrays

Just like single-dimensional arrays, multidimensional arrays are implemented as objects, so creating a multidimensional array takes the same two steps as creating a single-dimensional array:

1. declaring the object reference for the array

2. instantiating the array

In arrays with elements of primitive types, each element of the array contains a value of that type. For example, in an array of *doubles*, each element contains a *double* value. In arrays with a class data type, each element is an object reference, which points to the location of an object of that class.

9.1.1   Declaring Multidimensional Arrays

To declare a multidimensional array, we use the same syntax as for a single-dimensional array, except that we include an empty set of brackets for each dimension.

Here is the syntax for declaring a two-dimensional array:

```
datatype [ ][ ] arrayName;
```

Here is the syntax for declaring a three-dimensional array:

```
datatype [ ][ ][ ] arrayName;
```

In order to keep things simple, we will concentrate on two-dimensional arrays at this point. We will discuss three- and four-dimensional arrays later in the chapter.

The following statement declares an array to hold the daily high temperatures for the last 52 weeks:

```
double [ ][ ] dailyTemps;
```

The brackets can be placed before or after the array name. So the following syntax for declaring a two-dimensional array is also valid:

```
datatype arrayName [ ][ ];
```

We prefer to put the brackets right after the data type, because it's easier to read.

To store quiz grades for students, we could declare a two-dimensional array, where each row will store the quiz grades for a particular student and each column will store the grades for a particular quiz:

```
char [ ][ ] quizzes;    // each element is a char
```

The syntax is the same whether we declare arrays with basic data types or class types.

Imagine that we are interested in keeping track of a fleet of cars within a multinational corporation. The corporation operates in various countries, and in each of these countries, some employees have a company car. For this situation, we can declare a two-dimensional array where the first dimension will represent the country and the second dimension will represent the employee. Using our *Auto* class from Chapter 7, the following statement declares this two-dimensional array to hold *Auto* objects:

```
Auto [ ][ ] cars;
```

You can also declare multiple multidimensional arrays of the same data type in one statement by inserting a comma after each array name, using this syntax:

```
datatype [ ][ ] arrayName1, arrayName2;
```

For example, the following statement will declare two integer arrays to hold the number of stolen bases for two baseball players for each game in their career:

```
int [ ][ ] brian, jon;
```

The first dimension represents the games (per season), and the second dimension represents the season.

Notice that when we declare a multidimensional array, we do not specify how many elements the array will have. Declaring a multidimensional array does not allocate memory for the array; this is done in step 2, when we instantiate the array.

For example, this code from the file *Test.java:*

```
double [7][52] dailyTemps;
```

COMMON ERROR TRAP

Specifying the size of any of the dimensions of a multidimensional array in the declaration will generate a compiler error.

will generate the following compiler errors:

```
Test.java:5: ']' expected
  double [7][52] dailyTemps;
          ^
Test.java:5: not a statement
  double [7][52] dailyTemps;
          ^
2 errors
```

9.1.2   Instantiating Multidimensional Arrays

Just like instantiating single-dimensional arrays, you instantiate a multidimensional array using the *new* keyword. Here is the syntax for instantiating a two-dimensional array:

```
arrayName = new datatype [exp1][exp2];

   where exp1 and exp2 are expressions that evaluate to integers and
   specify, respectively, the number of rows and the number of columns in
   the array.
```

This statement allocates memory for the array. The number of elements in a two-dimensional array is equal to the number of rows multiplied by the number of columns.

For example, if we instantiate the following *dailyTemps* array with 52 rows and 7 columns, the array will have 52 * 7, or 364 elements:

```
dailyTemps = new double [52][7]; // dailyTemps has 52 rows
                                 // and 7 columns,
                                 // for a total of 364 elements
```

These statements will instantiate the other arrays declared above:

```
int numberOfStudents = 25;
int numberOfQuizzes = 10;
quizzes = new char [numberOfStudents][numberOfQuizzes];
// quizzes has 25 rows and 10 columns
// for a total of 250 elements

cars = new Auto [5][50];
// cars has 5 rows and 50 columns
// cars will store 250 Auto objects

brian = new int [80][20];
// brian has 80 rows and 20 columns
// there are 80 games per season
// brian played baseball for 20 seasons

jon = new int [80][10];
// jon has 80 rows and 10 columns
// jon played baseball for 10 seasons
```

When a multidimensional array is instantiated, the elements are given initial values automatically. Elements of arrays with numeric types are initialized to 0, elements of *char* type are initialized to a space, elements of

REFERENCE POINT

The initial values automatically given to array elements depend on the data type of the array and are discussed in Chapter 8.

boolean type are initialized to *false*, and elements of class types are initialized to *null*.

9.1.3   Combining the Declaration and Instantiation of Multidimensional Arrays

Multidimensional arrays, like single-dimensional arrays, can also be instantiated when they are declared. To combine the declaration and instantiation of a two-dimensional array, use this syntax:

```
datatype [ ][ ] arrayName = new datatype [exp1][exp2];
```

> where exp1 and exp2 are expressions that evaluate to integers and specify, respectively, the number of rows and columns in the array.

Thus, this statement:

```
double [ ][ ] dailyTemps = new double [52][7];
```

is equivalent to:

```
double [ ][ ] dailyTemps;
dailyTemps = new double [52][7];
```

Similarly, this statement:

```
char [ ][ ] quizzes = new char [25][10];
```

is equivalent to:

```
char [ ][ ] quizzes;
quizzes = new char [25][10];
```

Furthermore, this statement:

```
Auto [ ][ ] cars = new Auto [5][50];
```

is equivalent to:

```
Auto [ ][ ] cars;
cars = new Auto [5][50];
```

9.1.4   Assigning Initial Values to Multidimensional Arrays

We can instantiate a two-dimensional array by assigning initial values when the array is declared. To do this, we specify the initial values using comma-separated lists of initial values, enclosed in an outer set of curly braces:

```
datatype [ ][ ] arrayName =
    { { value00, value01, ... }, { value10, value 11, }, ... };
```

where *valueMN* is an expression that evaluates to the data type of the array and is the value to assign to the element at row M and column N.

The list contains a number of sublists, separated by commas. The number of these sublists determines the number of rows in the array. For each row, the number of values in the corresponding sublist determines the number of columns in the row. Thus, Java allows a two-dimensional array to have a different number of columns in each row. For example, in our *Auto* array, each country (row) could have a different number of employees (columns) with company cars.

Indeed, a two-dimensional array is an array of arrays. The first dimension of a two-dimensional array consists of an array of array references, with each reference pointing to a single-dimensional array. Thus, a two-dimensional array is composed of an array of rows, where each row is a single-dimensional array. Therefore, each row can have a different number of elements, or columns.

For example, this statement declares and instantiates a two-dimensional array of integers:

```
int [ ][ ] numbersList1 = { { 0, 5, 10 },
                            { 0, 3, 6, 9 } };
```

Because two sublists are given, this two-dimensional array has two rows. The first sublist specifies three values, and therefore, the first row will have three columns; the second sublist specifies four values, and therefore, the second row will have four columns.

Figure 9.2 shows the *numbersList1* array after the statement above is executed.

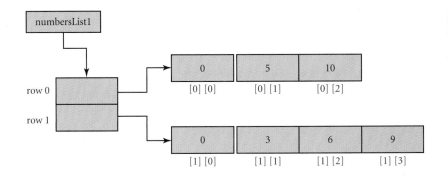

Figure 9.2
The *numbersList1* Array After Instantiation

An initialization list can be given only when the array is declared. If a two-dimensional array has already been instantiated, attempting to assign values to an array using an initialization list will generate a compiler error. For example, this code from the file *Test.java:*

```
int [ ][ ] grades = new int [2][3];
grades = { { 89, 73, 98 },
           { 88, 65, 92 } };
```

will generate the following compiler error:

```
Test.java:6: illegal start of expression
  grades = { { 89, 73, 98 },
           ^

1 error
```

We can declare and instantiate an array of objects by providing object references in the list:

```
Auto sportsCar = new Auto( "Ferrari", 0, 0.0 );
Auto sedan1 = new Auto( "BMW", 0, 0.0 );
Auto sedan2 = new Auto( "BMW", 100, 15.0 );
Auto sedan3 = new Auto( "Toyota", 0, 0.0 );
Auto rv1 = new Auto( "Jeep", 0, 0.0 );

Auto [ ][ ] cars = { { sportsCar, sedan1 },
                     { rv1, new Auto( ) },
                     { sedan2, sedan3 } };
```

This array of *Auto* objects has three rows with two columns in each row. The elements of the array *cars* are object references to *Auto* objects.

COMMON ERROR TRAP

An initialization list can be given only when the two-dimensional array is declared. Attempting to assign values to an array using an initialization list after the array is instantiated will generate a compiler error.

In most situations, the number of columns will be the same for each row. However, there are situations where it is useful to have a different number of columns for each row. For instance, Dr. Smith, a college professor, keeps track of grades using a two-dimensional array. The rows represent the courses she teaches and the columns represent the grades for the students in those sections. Grades are A, B, C, D, or F, so she declares the array with *char* elements. Dr. Smith teaches four courses: CS1, CS2, Database Management, and Operating Systems. Thus, she has four rows in the array. But in each course, Dr. Smith has a different number of students: There are 23 students in CS1, 16 in CS2, 12 in Database Management, and 28 in Operating Systems. So the first row will have 23 columns, the second row 16 columns, the third row 12 columns, and the fourth and last row will have 28 columns.

Using an initialization list, it is easy to instantiate a two-dimensional array with a different number of columns for every row. But sometimes the data is retrieved dynamically, read from a file for example, and it is not possible to use an initialization list.

To instantiate a two-dimensional array with a different number of columns for each row, you can do the following:

- first, instantiate the two-dimensional array.

- second, instantiate each row, as a single-dimensional array.

For the preceding example, we can use the following code:

```
char [ ][ ] grades;          // declare the array
grades = new char [4][ ];    // instantiate the array;
                             // grades has 4 null array elements


grades[0] = new char [23];   // instantiate row 0; 23 char elements
grades[1] = new char [16];   // instantiate row 1; 16 char elements
grades[2] = new char [12];   // instantiate row 2; 12 char elements
grades[3] = new char [28];   // instantiate row 3; 28 char elements
```

The second statement:

```
grades = new char [4][ ];
```

instantiates the two-dimensional array *grades* as an array having four rows, none of which has been instantiated yet. Because a two-dimensional array is an array of arrays, each element of the first dimension of the *grades* array is an array reference. Thus, before being instantiated, each element of the first dimension of the *grades* array has the value *null*.

As explained earlier, in a two-dimensional array, each row is a single-dimensional array. The last four statements instantiate each row, *grades[0]*, *grades[1]*, *grades[2]*, and *grades[3]*, each row having a different number of elements, or columns. The elements in these arrays are *char*s, initialized to a space.

Later in this chapter, we will define a general pattern for processing two-dimensional array elements so that it applies to all situations: an identical number of columns for each row, or a different number of columns for each row.

9.2   Accessing Multidimensional Array Elements

Elements of a two-dimensional array are accessed using this syntax:

```
arrayName[exp1][exp2]
```

> where *exp1* and *exp2* are expressions that evaluate to integers.

Exp1 is the element's row position, or **row index**, within the two-dimensional array. *Exp2* is the element's column position, or **column index**, within the two-dimensional array. The row index of the first row is always 0; the row index of the last row is always 1 less than the number of rows. The column index of the first column is always 0. The column index of the last column is always 1 less than the number of columns in that row.

Because a two-dimensional array is an array of arrays, the length of a two-dimensional array is its number of arrays, or rows. We access the number of rows in a two-dimensional array using the following syntax:

```
arrayName.length
```

Similarly, the length of each row is the number of columns (or elements) in that row's array. To access the number of columns in row *i* of a two-dimensional array named *arrayName*, use this syntax:

```
arrayName[i].length
```

Table 9.1 summarizes the syntax for accessing elements of a two-dimensional array.

TABLE 9.1   Accessing Two-Dimensional Array Elements

Array Element	Syntax
Row 0, column j	`arrayName[0][j]`
Row i, column j	`arrayName[i][j]`
Last row, column j	`arrayName[arrayName.length - 1][j]`
Last row, last column	`arrayName[arrayName.length - 1]` `        [arrayName[arrayName.length - 1].length - 1]`
Number of rows in the array	`arrayName.length`
Number of columns in row *i*	`arrayName[i].length`

Suppose we want to analyze the monthly cell phone bills for the past three months for a family of four persons. The parents, Joe and Jane, each have a cell phone, and so do the children, Mike and Sarah. We want to calculate the average monthly bill for each person, the total payments for the three months, and determine which family member had the lowest and highest bills. We could use a two-dimensional array of *doubles* with three rows and four columns. The rows will represent the months and the columns will represent the family members. For example, we could have the following mapping for the row and column indexes:

> row 0 : July
> row 1 : August
> row 2 : September
>
> column 0 : Joe
> column 1 : Jane
> column 2 : Mike
> column 3 : Sarah

We could visualize our two-dimensional array as the table shown in Table 9.2.

We'll name the array *familyCellBills*. Each element in the array will be referenced as *familyCellBills[i][j]*, where *i* is the index of the row (the month), and *j* is the index of the column (the person). Remember that the first element in a row or column is at index 0, so the first element in the first row is at index [0][0].

In lines 13–15 of Example 9.1, we declare and instantiate the *familyCellBills* array. Because the elements of *familyCellBills* are *doubles*, instantiating the array also initializes each element to 0.0. Lines 18–31 store values into each

TABLE 9.2   Visualizing a Two-Dimensional Array

	Joe	Jane	Mike	Sarah
July	45.24	54.67	32.55	25.61
August	65.29	49.75	32.08	26.11
September	75.24	54.53	34.55	28.16

Figure 9.3

The *familyCellBills* Array After Assigning Values

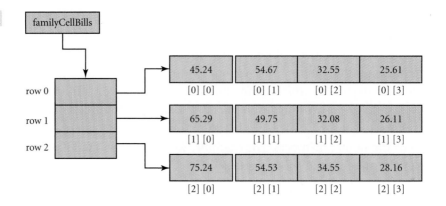

element of the array. Figure 9.3 shows how the *familyCellBills* array looks after lines 18–31 are executed.

```
1 /* Two-Dimensional Array of Cell Phone Bills
2    Anderson, Franceschi
3 */
4
5 public class FamilyCellBills
6 {
7  public static void main( String [ ] args )
8  {
9   // declare constants for the number of rows and columns
10   final int NUMBER_OF_MONTHS = 3;
11   final int NUMBER_OF_PERSONS = 4;
12
13   // declare and instantiate the array
14   double [ ][ ] familyCellBills =
15     new double [NUMBER_OF_MONTHS][NUMBER_OF_PERSONS];
16
17   // assign values to array elements
18   familyCellBills[0][0] = 45.24;  // row 0
19   familyCellBills[0][1] = 54.67;
20   familyCellBills[0][2] = 32.55;
21   familyCellBills[0][3] = 25.61;
22
23   familyCellBills[1][0] = 65.29;  // row 1
24   familyCellBills[1][1] = 49.75;
25   familyCellBills[1][2] = 32.08;
26   familyCellBills[1][3] = 26.11;
27
28   familyCellBills[2][0] = 75.24;  // row 2
```

```
29   familyCellBills[2][1] = 54.53;
30   familyCellBills[2][2] = 34.55;
31   familyCellBills[2][3] = 28.16;
32
33   System.out.println( "The first monthly cell bill for the first "
34      + "family member is\n"
35      + familyCellBills[0][0] );
36   System.out.println( "The last monthly cell bill for the last "
37      + "family member is\n"
38      + familyCellBills[NUMBER_OF_MONTHS - 1][NUMBER_OF_PERSONS - 1] );
39
40   int numRows = familyCellBills.length;
41   System.out.println( "\nThe number of rows is " + numRows );
42
43   for ( int i = 0; i < numRows; i++ )
44   {
45    System.out.print( "The number of columns in row " + i + " is " );
46    System.out.println( familyCellBills[i].length );
47   }
48  }
49 }
```

EXAMPLE 9.1   The *familyCellBills* Array

Note that the last element is *familyCellBills[2][3]*, with a row index that is 1 less than *familyCellBills.length*, and a column index that is 1 less than *familyCellBills[2].length*, which is the number of columns in the last row. More generally, for a two-dimensional array named *arr*, the last element is:

```
arr[arr.length - 1][arr[arr.length - 1].length - 1]
```

Lines 33–38 output the first and last element of the array *familyCellBills*.

Line 40 assigns the number of rows in the *familyCellBills* array to the *int* variable *numRows*. The variable *numRows* now has the value 3 and is output at line 41.

At lines 43–47, a *for* loop outputs the number of columns in each row of *familyCellBills*. Figure 9.4 shows the output of this example.

Row indexes of a two-dimensional array *must* be between 0 and *arrayName.length – 1*. Attempting to access an element of an array using a row index less than 0 or greater than *arrayName.length – 1* will compile without errors, but will generate an *ArrayIndexOutOfBoundsException* at run time. By default, this exception halts execution of the program.

Figure 9.4

Output of Example 9.1

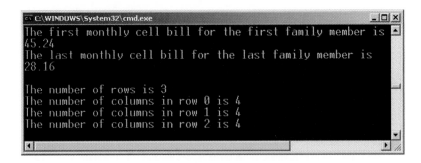

For example, all the following expressions are invalid:

```
// invalid row indexes for the familyCellBills array!!

familyCellBills[-1][2]
// the lowest valid row index is 0

familyCellBills[cellBills.length][2]
// the highest valid row index is familyCellBills.length - 1
```

Similarly, column indexes of a two-dimensional array *must* be between 0 and *arrayName[i].length – 1*, where *i* is the row index. Attempting to access an element of row *i* in a two-dimensional array using a column index less than 0 or greater than *arrayName[i].length – 1* will compile without errors, but will generate an *ArrayIndexOutOfBoundsException* at run time.

For example, all the following expressions are invalid:

```
// invalid column indexes for the familyCellBills array!!

familyCellBills[1][-1]
// the lowest valid column index is 0

familyCellBills[1][familyCellBills[1].length]
// the highest valid column index of row i is
// familyCellBills[i].length - 1
```

 **COMMON ERROR TRAP**

Attempting to access an element of a two-dimensional array using a row index less than 0 or greater than *arrayName.length – 1* will generate an *ArrayIndexOutOfBoundsException* at run time. Similarly, attempting to access an element of row *i* of a two-dimensional array using a column index less than 0 or greater than *arrayName[i].length – 1* also will generate an *ArrayIndexOutOfBounds-Exception*.

Example 9.2 illustrates how to work with an array of objects. In this example, we reuse the *Auto* class from Chapter 7. At lines 17–20, we declare and initialize *cars*, a two-dimensional array of *Auto* objects. Before using an element of *cars*, that *Auto* element has to be instantiated; failure to do so could generate a *NullPointerException* at run time.

Figure 9.5
Output of Example 9.2

There are three rows in *cars*: the first row has three columns, and the second and third rows have two columns each. Line 22 retrieves the array element at row 1 and column 0—here *sportsCar*—and assigns it to the *Auto* object reference *retrievedCar*, which is then printed at lines 25–26, where *toString* is called implicitly. Figure 9.5 shows the output of this example.

```
1 /* Working with a Two-Dimensional Array of Objects
2    Anderson, Franceschi
3 */
4
5 public class TwoDimAutoArray
6 {
7  public static void main( String [ ] args )
8  {
9    // instantiate several Auto object references
10   Auto sedan1 = new Auto( "BMW", 0, 0.0 );
11   Auto sedan2 = new Auto( "BMW", 100, 15.0 );
12   Auto sedan3 = new Auto( "Toyota", 0, 0.0 );
13   Auto sportsCar = new Auto( "Ferrari", 0, 0.0 );
14   Auto rv1 = new Auto( "Jeep", 0, 0.0 );
15   Auto rv2 = new Auto( "Ford", 200, 30.0 );
16
17   // declare and initialize two-dimensional array of Autos
18   Auto [ ][ ] cars = { { sedan1, sedan2, sedan3 },
19                        { sportsCar, new Auto( ) },
20                        { rv1, rv2 } };
21
22   Auto retrievedCar = cars[1][0];
23   // retrievedCar gets the sportsCar object reference
24
25   System.out.println( "cars[1][0]'s description is:\n"
26                       + retrievedCar );
27  }
28 }
```

EXAMPLE 9.2   Two-Dimensional Array of *Auto* Objects

Skill Practice
with these end-of-chapter questions

9.10.1   Multiple Choice Exercises

Questions 1,2,3,4,5,6,7,8

9.10.2   Reading and Understanding Code

Questions 14,15,16,17,18

9.10.3   Fill in the Code

Questions 33,34

9.10.4   Identifying Errors in Code

Questions 50,51,52,53

9.10.5   Debugging Area

Question 59

9.10.6   Write a Short Program

Question 65

9.10.8   Technical Writing

Question 94

9.3   Aggregate Two-Dimensional Array Operations

As with single-dimensional arrays, Java does not support aggregate operations on multidimensional arrays. For example, you cannot print the contents of an array using only the array name. Instead, you need to process each element individually.

9.3.1   Processing All the Elements of a Two-Dimensional Array

To process all the elements of a two-dimensional array, we use nested *for* loops that access and process each element individually. Often, the most logical way to process all elements is in row order, and within each row, in column order. We could also process elements one column at a time if that is more logical for the problem at hand.

In our nested *for* loops, the outer *for* loop will process the rows and the inner *for* loop will process the columns within each row. We will use *i* for the row index and *j* for the column index.

For the outer *for* loop, we can use the same header as we use to process single-dimensional arrays:

```
for ( int i = 0; i < arrayName.length; i++ )
```

Note that the initialization statement of the outer loop:

```
int i = 0;
```

sets *i* to the index of the first row of the two-dimensional array. Then the outer loop update statement increments *i*, so that we process each row in order.

The outer loop condition:

```
i < arrayName.length
```

continues execution of the outer loop as long as the row index is less than the *length* of the two-dimensional array, which represents the number of rows. Note that we use the *less than* operator (<), instead of the *less than or equal to* operator (<=). Using the less than or equal to operator would cause us to illegally attempt to reference an element with a row index of *arrayName.length*.

The *for* loop header for the inner loop, which processes the columns of the current row, is as follows:

```
for ( int j = 0; j < arrayName[i].length; j++ )
```

The initialization statement of the inner loop:

```
int j = 0;
```

sets *j* to the index of the first column of the current row. Then the inner loop update statement increments *j* to the next column index, so that we process each column of the current row in order.

The inner loop condition:

```
j < arrayName[i].length
```

continues execution of the inner loop as long as the column index is less than the *length* of the current row (row *i*). Given that each row can have a different number of columns, this will ensure that we do not attempt to access an element beyond the last column index of the current row.

Figure 9.6

Output of Example 9.3

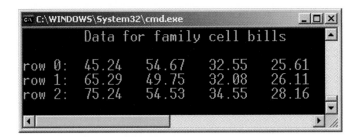

Note, again, that we use the _less than_ operator (<), not the _less than or equal to_ operator (<=), which would cause us to illegally attempt to reference an element with a column index of _arrayName[i].length_.

> **COMMON ERROR TRAP**
>
> In the outer _for_ loop, using the following condition:
>
> `i <= arrayName.length`
>
> will generate an _ArrayIndexOutOfBoundsException_ because the last row of a two-dimensional array is _arrayName.length – 1_. Similarly, in the inner _for_ loop, using the condition:
>
> `j <= arrayName[i].length`
>
> will generate an _ArrayIndexOutOfBoundsException_ because the last column of row _i_ in a two-dimensional array is `arrayName[i].length – 1.`

Inside the inner _for_ loop, we refer to the current element being processed as:

`arrayName[i][j]`

Thus, the general pattern for processing the elements of a two-dimensional array called _arrayName_ in row-first, column-second order using nested _for_ loops is:

```
for ( int i = 0; i < arrayName.length; i++ )
{
    for ( int j = 0; j < arrayName[i].length; j++ )
    {
        // process element arrayName[i][j]
    }
}
```

Example 9.3 illustrates how to print all the elements of the two-dimensional array _familyCellBills_ in row order. The array is declared and initialized at lines 10–12. At lines 16–23, the nested _for_ loops, using the standard pattern described earlier, print all the elements of the array. Figure 9.6 shows the output of the program.

```
1 /* Processing a Two-Dimensional Array of Cell Phone Bills
2    Anderson, Franceschi
3 */
4
5 public class OutputFamilyCellBills
6 {
7  public static void main( String [ ] args )
8  {
9    // declare and initialize the array
10   double [ ][ ] familyCellBills = { {45.24, 54.67, 32.55, 25.61},
```

```
11                                    {65.29, 49.75, 32.08, 26.11},
12                                    {75.24, 54.53, 34.55, 28.16} };
13
14    System.out.println( "\tData for family cell bills" );
15
16    for ( int i = 0; i < familyCellBills.length; i++ )
17    {
18      System.out.print( "\nrow " + i + ":\t" );
19      for ( int j = 0; j < familyCellBills[i].length; j++ )
20      {
21        System.out.print( familyCellBills[i][j] + "\t" );
22      }
23    }
24    System.out.println( );
25  }
26 }
```

EXAMPLE 9.3   Two-Dimensional Array Processing

9.3.2   Processing a Given Row of a Two-Dimensional Array

What if we want to process just one row of a two-dimensional array? For instance, we could be interested in calculating the sum of the cell bills for the whole family for a particular month, or identifying who had the highest cell bill in a particular month.

The general pattern for processing the elements of row i of a two-dimensional array called *arrayName* uses a single *for* loop:

```
for ( int j = 0; j < arrayName[i].length; j++ )
{
     // process element arrayName[i][j]
}
```

Example 9.4 shows how to sum all the elements of a particular row of the two-dimensional array *familyCellBills*.

```
1 /* Processing One Row of a Two-Dimensional Array
2    Anderson, Franceschi
3 */
4
5 import java.util.Scanner;
6 import java.text.NumberFormat;
7
8 public class SumARowFamilyCellBills
9 {
```

```
10  public static void main( String [ ] args )
11  {
12    // declare and initialize the array
13    double [ ][ ] familyCellBills = { {45.24, 54.67, 32.55, 25.61},
14                                      {65.29, 49.75, 32.08, 26.11},
15                                      {75.24, 54.53, 34.55, 28.16} };
16
17    String [ ] months = { "July", "August", "September" };
18    for ( int i = 0; i < months.length; i++ )
19      System.out.println( "Month " + i + " : " + months[i] );
20
21    Scanner scan = new Scanner( System.in );
22    int currentMonth;
23    do
24    {
25      System.out.print( "Enter a month number between 0 and 2 > " );
26      currentMonth = scan.nextInt( );
27    } while ( currentMonth < 0 || currentMonth > 2 );
28
29    double monthlyFamilyBills = 0.0;
30    for ( int j = 0; j < familyCellBills[currentMonth].length; j++ )
31    {
32      // add current family member bill to total
33      monthlyFamilyBills += familyCellBills[currentMonth][j];
34    }
35
36    NumberFormat priceFormat = NumberFormat.getCurrencyInstance( );
37    System.out.println( "\nThe total family cell bills during "
38                        + months[currentMonth] + " is "
39                        + priceFormat.format( monthlyFamilyBills ) );
40  }
41 }
```

EXAMPLE 9.4   Processing One Row in a Two-Dimensional Array

Since the rows correspond to the months, we declare and initialize at line 17 a single-dimensional *String* array named *months* in order to make our prompt more user-friendly. At lines 18–19, we print a menu for the user, providing month names and the corresponding indexes. At lines 23–27, we use a *do/while* loop to prompt the user for a month index until the user enters a valid value between 0 and 2.

To calculate the total of the family cell bills for the month index that the user inputs, we first initialize the variable *monthlyFamilyBills* to 0.0 at line

Figure 9.7

Output of Example 9.4

29. We then use a single *for* loop at lines 30–34, following the pattern described earlier, to sum all the family member bills for the month chosen by the user. We then format and output the total at lines 36–39. Figure 9.7 shows the output of the program when the user chooses 1 for the month.

9.3.3 Processing a Given Column of a Two-Dimensional Array

If we want to determine the highest cell bill for Mike or calculate the average cell bill for Sarah, we will need to process just one column of the two-dimensional array.

The general pattern for processing the elements of column *j* of a two-dimensional array called *arrayName* uses a single *for* loop:

```java
for ( int i = 0; i < arrayName.length; i++ )
{
   if ( j < arrayName[i].length )
      // process element arrayName[i][j]
}
```

Because rows may have a different number of columns, a given row *i* may not have a column *j*. Thus, we need to check that the current column number is less than *arrayName[i].length* before we attempt to access *arrayName[i][j]*.

Because our two-dimensional array *familyCellBills* has the same number of columns (4) in every row, no extra precaution is necessary here. It is a good software engineering practice, however, to verify that the column index is valid before attempting to process the array element.

Example 9.5 shows how to find the maximum value of all the elements of a particular column.

SOFTWARE ENGINEERING TIP

Before processing an element in a column, check whether the current row contains an element in that column. Doing so will avoid an *ArrayIndexOutOf-BoundsException*.

```java
1 /* Processing One Column of a Two-Dimensional Array
2    Anderson, Franceschi
3 */
4
5 import java.util.Scanner;
```

```java
6  import java.text.NumberFormat;
7
8  public class MaxMemberBill
9  {
10   public static void main( String [ ] args )
11   {
12    // declare and initialize the array
13    double [ ][ ] familyCellBills = { {45.24, 54.67, 32.55, 25.61},
14                                      {65.29, 49.75, 32.08, 26.11},
15                                      {75.24, 54.53, 34.55, 28.16} };
16
17    String [ ] familyMembers = { "Joe", "Jane", "Mike", "Sarah" };
18    for ( int i = 0; i < familyMembers.length; i++ )
19         System.out.println( "Family member " + i + " : "
20                              + familyMembers[i] );
21
22    Scanner scan = new Scanner( System.in );
23    int currentMember;
24    do
25    {
26     System.out.print( "Enter a family member between 0 and 3 > " );
27     currentMember = scan.nextInt( );
28    } while ( currentMember < 0 || currentMember > 3 );
29
30    double memberMaxBill = familyCellBills[0][currentMember];
31    for ( int i = 1; i < familyCellBills.length; i++ )
32    {
33     if ( currentMember < familyCellBills[i].length )
34     {
35      // update memberMaxBill if necessary
36      if ( familyCellBills[i][currentMember] > memberMaxBill )
37        memberMaxBill = familyCellBills[i][currentMember];
38     }
39    }
40
41    NumberFormat priceFormat = NumberFormat.getCurrencyInstance( );
42    System.out.println ( "\nThe max cell bill for "
43                          + familyMembers[currentMember] + " is "
44                          + priceFormat.format( memberMaxBill ) );
45   }
46  }
```

EXAMPLE 9.5   Processing a Column in a Two-Dimensional Array

At line 17, we declare and initialize a single-dimensional *String* array named *familyMembers* to make our prompt more user-friendly. At lines

24–28, we again use a *do/while* loop to prompt the user for a valid family member index.

To calculate the maximum value of the family member cell bills, we first initialize the variable *memberMaxBill* to the first element in the column (*familyCellBills[0][currentMember]*) at line 30. We then use a standard *for* loop at lines 31–39, following the pattern described earlier to update the value of *memberMaxBill* as necessary. There is one minor difference; we do not need to start the row at index 0 because we initialized *memberMaxBill* to the value of the element in row 0 of the column *currentMember*. Note that we assume that there is an element at column 0 of each row, that is, each row has been instantiated. The value of the variable *memberMaxBill* is then formatted and printed at lines 41–44. Figure 9.8 shows the output of the program.

9.3.4   Processing A Two-Dimensional Array One Row at a Time

Earlier, we calculated the sum of the elements of a given row of a two-dimensional array. But what if we are interested in calculating that sum for each row? In this case, we need to initialize our total variable before we process each row and print the results after we process each row.

The general pattern for processing each row of a two-dimensional array called *arrayName* using nested *for* loops is

```
for ( int i = 0; i < arrayName.length; i++ )
{
   // initialize processing variables for row i
   for ( int j = 0; j < arrayName[i].length; j++ )
   {
      // process element arrayName[i][j]
   }
   // finish the processing of row i
}
```

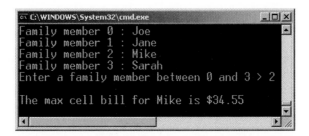

Figure 9.8

Output of Example 9.5

There are two important additions to the general pattern for processing all elements of the array:

- Before processing each row, that is, before the inner loop, we need to initialize the processing variables for the current row. If we are summing elements, we initialize the total variable to 0. If we are calculating a minimum or maximum value, we initialize the current minimum or maximum to the value of the first element of the current row.

- When we reach the end of each row, that is, after each completion of the inner loop, we finish processing the current row. For instance, we may want to print the sum or maximum value for that row.

Example 9.6 shows how to sum the elements of each row of the two-dimensional array *familyCellBills*.

```
 1 /* Processing Each Row of a Two-Dimensional Array
 2     Anderson, Franceschi
 3 */
 4
 5 import java.util.Scanner;
 6 import java.text.NumberFormat;
 7
 8 public class SumEachRowFamilyCellBills
 9 {
10  public static void main( String [ ] args )
11  {
12   // declare and initialize the array
13   double [ ][ ] familyCellBills = { {45.24, 54.67, 32.55, 25.61},
14                                     {65.29, 49.75, 32.08, 26.11},
15                                     {75.24, 54.53, 34.55, 28.16} };
16
17   String [ ] months = { "July", "August", "September" };
18
19   NumberFormat priceFormat = NumberFormat.getCurrencyInstance( );
20   double currentMonthTotal;
21   for ( int i = 0; i < familyCellBills.length; i++ )
22   {
23    currentMonthTotal = 0.0;  // initialize total for row
24    for ( int j = 0; j < familyCellBills[i].length; j++ )
25    {
26     // add current family member bill to current monthly total
27     currentMonthTotal += familyCellBills[i][j];
```

```
28    }
29    // print total for row
30    System.out.println( "The total for " + months[i] + " is "
31                        + priceFormat.format( currentMonthTotal ) );
32    }
33  }
34 }
```

EXAMPLE 9.6   Processing Each Row in a Two-Dimensional Array

Again, the rows correspond to the months, and we declare and initialize at line 17 a *String* array named *months* in order to make the output user-friendly.

To calculate the total of the family cell bills for each month, we use nested *for* loops at lines 21–32, following the pattern described earlier.

Inside the outer *for* loop, we initialize the *currentMonthTotal* at line 23 before processing each row. Without this statement, the variable *current-MonthTotal* would continue to accumulate, as if we were summing all the elements of the array instead of calculating a separate sum for each row.

After the inner loop finishes, we complete the processing of row *i* by printing the value of *currentMonthTotal* at lines 29–31. Figure 9.9 shows the output of the program.

COMMON ERROR TRAP

Failing to initialize the row processing variables before each row is a logic error and will generate incorrect results.

9.3.5   Processing a Two-Dimensional Array One Column at a Time

Processing each column of a two-dimensional array requires a little extra checking. If the number of columns in each row differs, we must be careful not to attempt to access an element with an out-of-bounds column index. Generally, we will need to determine the number of columns in the largest row in the array before coding the outer loop header.

For example, suppose you are keeping track of your test grades in three classes: Intro to Java, Database Management, and English Composition. You have two test grades in Intro to Java, four in Database Management,

Figure 9.9
Output of Example 9.6

and three in English Composition. We can use a two-dimensional array to store these test grades as follows:

```
int [ ][ ] grades = { { 89, 75 },
                      { 84, 76, 92, 96 },
                      { 80, 88, 95 } };
```

There are three rows in the array *grades*. The maximum number of columns in any row is four; therefore, in order to process all the columns, our outer loop should loop from column index 0 to column index 3. Our inner loop should check that the current column number exists in the row before attempting to process the element.

Let's assume, at this point, that we stored the maximum number of columns in an *int* variable called *maxNumberOfColumns*. The general pattern for processing elements of a two-dimensional array, *arrayName*, one column at a time is:

```
// maxNumberOfColumns holds the number of columns
// in the largest row of familyCellBills
for ( int j = 0; j < maxNumberOfColumns; j++ )
{
    for ( int i = 0; i < arrayName.length; i++ )
    {
        if ( j < arrayName[i].length )
        {
            // process element arrayName[i][j]
        }
    }
}
```

The outer loop condition:

```
j < maxNumberOfColumns
```

continues execution of the outer loop as long as the column index is less than the maximum number of columns of the two-dimensional array, which has been computed and assigned to the variable *maxNumberOfColumns*.

The inner loop condition:

```
i < arrayName.length
```

continues execution of the inner loop as long as the row index is less than the number of rows.

Again, because each row may have a different number of columns, a given row *i* may not have a column *j*. Thus, using the following *if* condition, we check that an element in column *j* exists—*j* is less than *array-Name[i].length*—before we attempt to access *arrayName[i][j]*:

```
if ( j < arrayName[i].length )
```

Example 9.7 shows how this pattern can be implemented in a program.

```
 1 /* Processing Each Column in a Two-Dimensional Array
 2    Anderson, Franceschi
 3 */
 4
 5 public class GradesProcessing
 6 {
 7  public static void main( String [ ] args )
 8  {
 9    int [ ][ ] grades = { { 89, 75 },
10                          { 84, 76, 92, 96 },
11                          { 80, 88, 95 } };
12
13    // compute the maximum number of columns
14    int maxNumberOfColumns = grades[0].length;
15    for ( int i = 1; i < grades.length; i++ )
16    {
17     if ( grades[i].length > maxNumberOfColumns )
18         maxNumberOfColumns = grades[i].length;
19    }
20    System.out.println( "The maximum number of columns in grades is "
21                        + maxNumberOfColumns );
22
23    for ( int j = 0; j < maxNumberOfColumns; j++ )
24    {
25     System.out.print( "\nColumn " + j + ": " );
26     for ( int i = 0; i < grades.length; i++ )
27     {
28      if ( j < grades[i].length )
29          System.out.print( grades[i][j] );
30      System.out.print( "\t" );
31     }
32    }
33    System.out.println( );
34  }
35 }
```

EXAMPLE 9.7   Processing a Two-Dimensional Array in Column Order

Figure 9.10

The Output of Example 9.7

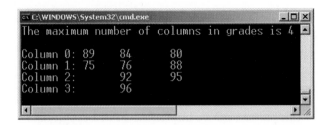

The array *grades* is declared and initialized at lines 9–11. Lines 13–19 compute the maximum number of columns in a row and store the value in the *int* variable *maxNumberOfColumns*. First, we initialize *maxNumberOfColumns* to the number of columns of row 0 at line 14. At lines 15 to 19, we loop through each remaining row in *grades* and update *maxNumberOfColumns* if we find that the current row has more columns than *maxNumberOfColumns*.

At lines 23–32, we use nested loops to print all the elements of *grades* in column order, following the general pattern described earlier. The output of the program is shown in Figure 9.10.

9.3.6 Displaying Two-Dimensional Array Data as a Bar Chart

Another way to display two-dimensional array data is graphically, by drawing a bar chart. For example, the bar chart in Figure 9.11 displays the data in the *familyCellBills* array.

 **REFERENCE POINT**

Chapter 8 provides instructions on drawing a bar chart from the data in a single-dimensional array.

Each bar is a rectangle. So to create a bar chart, we use our standard nested *for* loops, and call the *fillRect* method of the *Graphics* class to draw a rectangle for each element. We use the *drawString* method to print the value of each element. To change colors for each row, we set up an array of *Color* objects, and loop through the array to set the current color for each row iteration. Furthermore, each time we process a row, we must reset the (x, y) coordinate of the first bar of the current row.

Example 9.8 shows the applet code that displays the bar chart shown in Figure 9.11.

```
1 /* Displaying a Two-Dimensional Array as a Bar Chart
2     Anderson, Franceschi
3 */
4
```

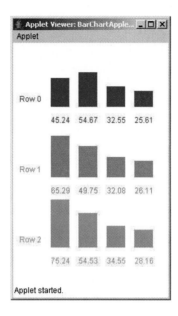

Figure 9.11
The *familyCellBills* Array
as a Bar Chart

```
 5 import javax.swing.JApplet;
 6 import java.awt.Graphics;
 7 import java.awt.Color;
 8
 9 public class BarChartApplet extends JApplet
10 {
11   final int LEFT_MARGIN = 60;          // starting x value
12   final int BASE_Y_BAR  = 100;         // bottom of the bars
13   final int BASE_Y_VALUE = 125;        // bottom of the values
14   final int BAR_WIDTH = 30;            // width of each bar
15   final int SPACE_BETWEEN_BARS = 15;   // pixels between bars
16   final int ROW_HEIGHT = 110;          // pixels between rows
17   double [ ][ ] familyCellBills = { {45.24, 54.67, 32.55, 25.61},
18                                     {65.29, 49.75, 32.08, 26.11},
19                                     {75.24, 54.53, 34.55, 28.16} };
20   Color [ ] colors = { Color.BLUE, Color.RED, Color.GREEN };
21
22   public void init( )
23   {
24     setSize( 250, 375 );
25   }
26
27   public void paint( Graphics g )
```

```
28  {
29   int xStart = LEFT_MARGIN;     // x value for 1st column (bars)
30   int yStart = BASE_Y_VALUE;    // y value for 1st row (data)
31   int yStartBar = BASE_Y_BAR;   // y value for 1st row (bars)
32
33   for ( int i = 0; i < familyCellBills.length; i++ )
34   {
35    g.setColor( colors[i] );   // set color for current row
36    g.drawString( "Row " + i, xStart - LEFT_MARGIN + 10,
37                  (int) ( yStart - .3 * ROW_HEIGHT ) );
38
39    for ( int j = 0; j < familyCellBills[i].length; j++ )
40    {
41      g.fillRect( xStart, yStartBar - (int) ( familyCellBills[i][j] ),
42                  BAR_WIDTH, (int) ( familyCellBills[i][j] ) );
43
44      g.drawString( Double.toString( familyCellBills[i][j] ),
45                    xStart, yStart );
46
47      // move to starting x value for next bar
48      xStart += BAR_WIDTH + SPACE_BETWEEN_BARS;
49    }
50
51    // new row:  increase yStart and yStartBar
52    yStart += ROW_HEIGHT;        // increment yStart for next row
53    yStartBar += ROW_HEIGHT;     // increment yStartBar for next row
54    xStart = LEFT_MARGIN;        // reset xStart for next row
55   }
56  }
57 }
```

EXAMPLE 9.8   Applet Displaying a Two-Dimensional Array as a Bar Chart

The *Color* single-dimensional array *colors* that we use to determine the color of each row of bars is declared and initialized at line 20. It has the same number of rows as *familyCellBills*. The first row of bars will be displayed in blue, the second row in red, and the third row in green.

In the *paint* method, at the beginning of the outer loop and before the inner loop, we set the color for the current row (line 35) by using the row number as an index into the *colors* array. At lines 36–37, we display the row number.

In the body of the inner loop (lines 39–49), we draw the rectangle for the element value at row *i* and column *j* of *familyCellBills*, then display a *String* representing the same value. We then increment *xStart* to the location of the next bar to draw.

After the inner loop and before restarting the outer loop, we update the values of *yStart*, *yStartBar*, and *xStart* (lines 51–54) so that they are properly set for processing the next row. Earlier, we said that initializing variable values for the next row is usually done at the beginning of the outer loop body before entering the inner loop, but it also can be done after the inner loop and before re-entering the outer loop, as shown here.

CODE IN ACTION

In the Chapter 9 folder on the CD-ROM included with this book, you will find a Shockwave movie showing step-by-step illustrations of working with two-dimensional arrays. Double-click on *MultiDimArrays.html* to start the movie.

Skill Practice
with these end-of-chapter questions

9.10.2   Reading and Understanding Code

Questions 19, 20, 21, 22, 23, 24, 25, 26, 27, 28

9.10.3   Fill in the Code

Questions 35, 36, 37, 38, 39, 40, 41, 42, 43, 44, 45

9.10.4   Identifying Errors in Code

Question 54

9.10.5   Debugging Area

Questions 60, 61, 62

9.10.6   Write a Short Program

Questions 66, 67, 68, 69, 70, 71, 72, 73, 74, 75, 76, 77, 78, 79

9.4   Two-Dimensional Arrays Passed to and Returned from Methods

Writing methods that take two-dimensional arrays as parameters and/or return two-dimensional arrays is similar to working with single-dimensional arrays.

The syntax for a method that accepts a two-dimensional array as a parameter is the following:

```
returnType methodName(  arrayType [ ][ ] arrayParameterName )
```

The caller of the method passes the name of the array without any brackets.

The syntax for a method that returns a two-dimensional array is the following:

```
returnArrayType [ ][ ]  methodName(  parameterList )
```

The caller of the method passes the argument list and assigns the return value to a reference to a two-dimensional array of the appropriate data type.

Combining both possibilities, the syntax for a method that accepts a two-dimensional array as a parameter and whose return value is a two-dimensional array is the following:

```
returnArrayType [ ][ ]  methodName(  arrayType [ ][ ] arrayParameterName )
```

The caller of the method simply passes the name of the array without any brackets and assigns the return value to a reference to a two-dimensional array of the appropriate data type.

For example, suppose we want to tally votes in an election. We have four candidates running in six districts. We want to know how many votes each candidate received and how many votes were cast in each district. Thus, we can set up a two-dimensional array with each row representing a district and each column representing a candidate, with the values in each element representing the votes a candidate received in that district. To get our tally, we need to compute the sum of each row to find the number of votes per district and the sum of each column to find the number of votes per candidate.

To do this, we create a class, _Tally,_ that has a two-dimensional array instance variable, _voteData,_ storing the votes. The _Tally_ class also has a method, _arrayTally,_ that will compute the sums for each column and row of _voteData._ The sums will be returned from the method as a two-dimensional array with two rows. The first row will hold the totals for each column of _voteData,_ and the second row will hold the totals for each row of _voteData._

Example 9.9 shows the *Tally* class.

```
 1 /** Two-Dimensional Arrays as Method Parameters
 2  *    and Return Values: the Tally class
 3  *    Anderson, Franceschi
 4  */
 5
 6 public class Tally
 7 {
 8   int [ ][ ] voteData;
 9
10   /** overloaded constructor
11    *   @param    newVoteData    an array of vote counts
12    */
13   public Tally( int [ ][ ] newVoteData )
14   {
15     voteData = new int [newVoteData.length][ ];
16     for ( int i = 0; i < newVoteData.length; i++ )
17         voteData[i] = new int [newVoteData[i].length];
18
19     for ( int i = 0; i < newVoteData.length; i++ )
20     {
21       for ( int j = 0; j < newVoteData[i].length; j++ )
22       {
23         voteData[i][j] = newVoteData[i][j];
24       }
25     }
26   }
27
28   /** arrayTally method
29    *   @return    a two-dimensional array of votes
30    */
31   public int [ ][ ] arrayTally( )
32   {
33     // create array of tallies, all elements are 0
34     int [ ][ ] returnTally = new int [2][ ];
35     returnTally[0] = new int [voteData[0].length];
36     returnTally[1] = new int [voteData.length];
37
38     for ( int i = 0; i < voteData.length; i++ )
39     {
40       for ( int j = 0; j < voteData[i].length; j++ )
41       {
```

```
42            returnTally[0][j] += voteData[i][j];  // add to column sum
43            returnTally[1][i] += voteData[i][j];  // add to row sum
44        }
45    }
46    return returnTally;
47  }
48 }
```

EXAMPLE 9.9   The *Tally* Class

The overloaded constructor, coded at lines 10–26, receives the two-dimensional array argument *newVoteData*. After instantiating *voteData* at line 15, we copy *newVoteData* into *voteData* one element at a time at lines 19–25.

We coded the *arrayTally* method at lines 28–47. Our first job is to instantiate the *returnArray*, which is the array the method will return to the caller. We know that the array will have two rows, one holding the sums of the columns and one holding the sums of the rows. Because each row in the *returnArray* will have a different number of columns, we instantiate the array with two rows, but do not give a value for the number of columns (line 34). We then instantiate each row with the appropriate number of columns (lines 35–36). Row 0, the sums of the columns, will have the same number of columns as the *voteData* array. In the interest of keeping this example simple, we have assumed that *voteData* has the same number of columns in every row, that is, each candidate was on the ballot in each district. Thus, that number is therefore equal to the number of columns in the first row, *voteData[0].length* (line 35). Row 1, the sum of the rows, will have the same number of columns as the number of rows in the *voteData* array.

In lines 38–45, we loop through the parameter array, computing the sums. We add each element's value to the sum for its column (line 42) and the sum for its row (line 43). When we finish, we return the *returnTally* array to the caller (line 46).

Example 9.10 shows a client program that instantiates a *Tally* object reference and calls the *arrayTally* method.

```
1 /** Tally votes: the VoteTally class
2 *    Anderson, Franceschi
3 */
4
5 public class VoteTally
6 {
```

```
7   public static void main( String [ ] args )
8   {
9     // votes are for 4 candidates in 6 districts.
10    int [ ][ ] votes = { { 150, 253, 125, 345 },
11                         { 250, 750, 234, 721 },
12                         { 243, 600, 212, 101 },
13                         { 234, 243, 143, 276 },
14                         { 555, 343, 297, 990 },
15                         { 111, 426, 834, 101 } };
16    // candidate names
17    String [ ] candidates = { "Smith", "Jones",
18                              "Berry", "Chase" };
19
20    // instantiate a Tally object reference
21    Tally tally = new Tally( votes );
22
23    // call arrayTally method to count the votes
24    int [ ][ ] voteCounts = tally.arrayTally( );
25
26    // print totals for candidates
27    System.out.println( "Total votes per candidate" );
28    for ( int i = 0; i < candidates.length; i++ )
29      System.out.print( candidates[i] + "\t" );
30    System.out.println( );
31    for ( int j = 0; j < voteCounts[0].length; j++ )
32      System.out.print( voteCounts[0][j] + "\t" );
33    System.out.println( );
34
35    // print totals for districts
36    System.out.println("\nTotal votes per district" );
37    for ( int i = 0; i < voteCounts[1].length; i++ )
38      System.out.print( ( i + 1 ) + "\t" );
39    System.out.println( );
40    for ( int i = 0; i < voteCounts[1].length; i++ )
41      System.out.print( voteCounts[1][i] + "\t" );
42    System.out.println( );
43  }
44 }
```

EXAMPLE 9.10   The *VoteTally* Class

We start by defining our two-dimensional array, *votes*, which holds the votes for each candidate for each district (lines 9–15). Most likely, we would read these values from a file, but for simplicity, we hard-coded the values in

Figure 9.12

Output from Example 9.10

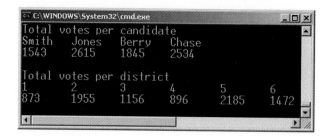

the initialization list. We also define a single-dimensional array of *Strings*, *candidates*, which holds the candidates' names (lines 16–18). Each name in the *candidates* array corresponds to the column in the *votes* array that holds that candidate's votes.

On lines 20–21, we instantiate the *Tally* object *tally*, passing the two-dimensional array *votes* to the *Tally* overloaded constructor. Notice that for the argument, we use only the array name, *votes*, without brackets.

On line 24, we call the *arrayTally* method, assigning the return value to a two-dimensional array reference named *voteCounts*.

Lines 26–33 print the totals per candidate by printing the elements in row 0 of the returned array, and lines 35–42 print the totals per district by printing the elements in row 1 of the returned array. The output is shown in Figure 9.12.

9.5   Programming Activity 1: Working with Two-Dimensional Arrays

In this activity, you will work with a 4-row, 20-column, two-dimensional array of integers. Specifically, you will write methods to perform the following operations:

1. Fill the array with random numbers between 50 and 80.

2. Print the array.

3. Set every array element of a given row to a specified value. The value is a parameter of a method.

4. Find the minimum value in a given column of the array. The column is a parameter of a method.

5. Count the number of elements of the array having a specified value. The value is a parameter of a method.

The framework for this Programming Activity will animate your algorithm so that you can check the accuracy of your code. For example, Figure 9.13 shows the application counting the elements having the value 56:

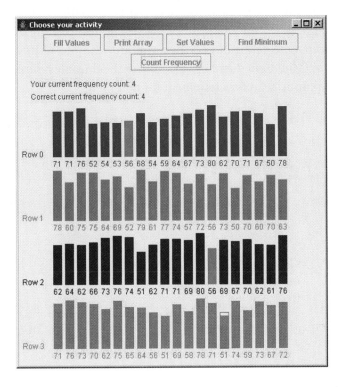

Figure 9.13

Animation of the Programming Activity

At this point, the application has found the value 56 in four array elements: one in each row.

Instructions

In the Chapter 9 Programming Activity 1 directory on the CD-ROM accompanying this book, you will find the source files needed to complete this activity. Copy all the files to a directory on your computer. Note that all files should be in the same directory.

Open the *TwoDimArrayPractice1.java* source file. Searching for five stars (*****) in the source code will position you at the sample method and the four other locations where you will add your code. We have provided the sample code for task number 1, which you can use as a model for completing the other tasks. In every task, you will fill in the code for a method that will manipulate an existing array of 4 rows and 20 columns. You should not instantiate the array; we have done that for you. Example 9.11 shows the section of the *TwoDimArrayPractice1* source code where you will add your code.

Note that for the *countFound* and *findMinimum* methods, we provide a dummy *return* statement: (*return 0;*) We do this so that the source code will compile. In this way, you can write and test each method separately, using step–wise refinement. When you are ready to write the *countFound* and *findMinimum* methods, just replace the dummy *return* statements with the appropriate *return* statement for that method.

```java
// ***** 1.  This method has been coded as an example
/** Fills the array with random numbers between 50 and 80
*   The instance variable named intArray is the integer array to be
*   filled with values
*/
public void fillValues( )
{
 for ( int row = 0; row < intArray.length; row++ )
 {
     System.out.print( row + "\t" );
     for ( int column = 0; j < intArray[row].length; column++ )
     {
      intArray[row][column] = ( int ) ( Math.random( ) * 31 ) + 50;
      animate( row, column );  // needed for visual feedback
     }
     System.out.println( );
 }
} // end of fillValues method

// ***** 2.  Student writes this method
/** Prints array to the console, elements are separated by a space
*   The instance variable named intArray is the integer array to be
*   printed
*/
public void printArray( )
{
 // Note:  To animate the algorithm, put this method call as the
 // last element in your inner for loop
 //            animate( row, column );
 //      where row is the index of the array's current row
 // and column is the index of the array's current column
 // Write your code here:

} // end of printArray method
```

```java
// ***** 3.  Student writes this method
/** Sets all the elements in the specified row to the specified value
* The instance variable named intArray is the integer array
*  @param value       the value to assign to the element of the row
*  @param row         the row in which to set the elements to value
*/
public void setValues( int value, int row )
{
 // Note:  To animate the algorithm, put this method call as the
 // last element in your for loop
 //           animate( row, column );
 //      where row is the index of the array's current row
 //      where column is the index of the array's current column
 // Write your code here:

} // end of setValues method

// ***** 4.  Student writes this method
/** Finds minimum value in the specified column
*  The instance variable named intArray is the integer array
*  @param column       the column to search
*  @return             the minimum value found in the column
*/
public int findMinimum( int column )
{
 // Note:  To animate the algorithm, put this method call as the
 // last element in your for loop
 //           animate( row, column, minimum );
 //   where row is the index of the array's current row
 //         column is the index of the array's current column
 //         minimum is the variable storing the current minimum
 // Write your code here:

  return 0; // replace this line with your return statement

} // end of findMinimumn method

// ***** 5.  Student writes this method
/** Finds the number of times value is found in the array
*  The instance variable named intArray is the integer array
*  @param value       the value to count
*  @return            the number of times value was found
*/
public int countFound( int value )
```

```
{
// Note:  To animate the algorithm, put this method call as the
// last element in your inner for loop
//              animate( row, column, num );
// where row is the index of the array's current row
//       column is the index of the array's current column
//       num is the local variable storing the current frequency
//         count
// Write your code here:


 return 0;  // replace this line with your return statement


}
// end of countFound method
```

EXAMPLE 9.11   Location of Student Code in *TwoDimArrayPractice1*

The framework will animate your algorithm so that you can watch your code work. For this to happen, be sure that your single or nested *for* loops call the method *animate*. The arguments that you send to *animate* are not always the same and the location of the call to *animate* will differ depending on the task you are coding. Detailed instructions for each task are included in the code.

To test your code, compile and run the *TwoDimArrayPractice1* source code. Figure 9.14 shows the graphics window when the program begins. Because the values of the array are randomly generated, the values will be different each time the program runs. To test any method, click on the appropriate button.

Troubleshooting

If your method implementation does not animate, check these tips:

- Verify that the last statement in your single *for* loop or inner *for* loop is a call to the *animate* method and that you passed the appropriate arguments. For example:

```
animate( row, column );
```

- Verify that your exit conditions for your *for* loops are correct. Sometimes the exit condition depends on the length of the array

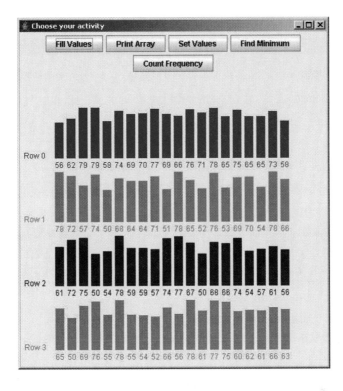

Figure 9.14
The Graphics Window When the Application Begins

(i.e., the number of rows in the array), sometimes it depends on the number of columns in the current row of the array.

? DISCUSSION QUESTIONS

1. With a two-dimensional array, for which operations would you use nested *for* loops and for which operations would you use a single *for* loop?

2. When performing an operation on a given row, which index is fixed and which index is used as the looping variable? When performing an operation on a given column, which index is fixed and which index is used as the looping variable?

9.6 Other Multidimensional Arrays

To this point, we have discussed arrays with one and two dimensions. Sometimes, however, we might need an array with more than two dimensions. For example, we might be interested in keeping track of sales on a per-year, per-week, and per-day basis. In this case, we would use a three-dimensional array as follows:

TABLE 9.3	Structure of an *n*-Dimensional Array
Dimension	**Array Element**
first	`arrayName[`i_1`]` is an (n - 1)-dimensional array
second	`arrayName[`i_1`][`i_2`]` is an (n - 2)-dimensional array
kth	`arrayName[`i_1`][`i_2`][`i_3`][..][`i_k`]` is an (n - k) multi-dimensional array
(*n* - 2)th	`arrayName[`i_1`][`i_2`][`i_3`][..][`i_{n-2}`]` is a two-dimensional array
(*n* - 1)th	`arrayName[`i_1`][`i_2`][`i_3`][..][`i_{n-1}`]` is a single-dimensional array
*n*th	`arrayName[`i_1`][`i_2`][`i_3`][..][`i_{n-1}`][`i_n`]` is an array element

1st dimension: year

2nd dimension: week

3rd dimension: day of the week

Earlier in this chapter, we explained that a two-dimensional array is an array of single-dimensional arrays. Similarly, a three-dimensional array is an array of two-dimensional arrays. And a four-dimensional array is an array of three-dimensional arrays. More generally, an *n*-dimensional array is an array of (*n* − *1*)-dimensional arrays.

Table 9.3 shows how an *n*-dimensional array is structured dimension by dimension; i_1, i_2, ..., i_n are used as generic indexes for the first dimension, second dimension, ..., n^{th} dimension.

If we keep track of sales over a period of 10 years, then we would have a 10-by-52-by-7 array. The principles discussed for a two-dimensional array still apply; we just have three dimensions instead of two. The following code sequence illustrates how to declare, instantiate, and access elements of this three-dimensional array:

```
double [ ][ ][ ] sales;              // declare a three-dimensional array

sales = new double [10][52][7];      // instantiate the array

sales[0][0][0] = 638.50;             // access the first element

sales[4][22][3] = 928.20;            // access another element

sales[9][51][6] = 1234.90;           // access the last element
```

To process elements of a single-dimensional array, we use a simple *for* loop; for a two-dimensional array, we use a double *for* loop. For a three-dimensional array, we use a triple *for* loop.

The general pattern for processing elements in a three-dimensional array is

```
for ( int i = 0; i < arrayName.length; i++ )
{
   for ( int j = 0; j < arrayName[i].length; j++ )
   {
      for ( int k = 0; k < arrayName[i][j].length; k++ )
      {
         // access and process the element arrayName[i][j][k]
      }
   }
}
```

The following code sequence will print the elements of the three-dimensional array *sales*:

```
for ( int i = 0; i < sales.length; i++ )
{
   for ( int j = 0; j < sales[i].length; j++ )
   {
      for ( int k = 0; k < sales[i][j].length; k++ )
      {
         // access the element at sales[i][j][k]
         System.out.println( sales[i][j][k] + "\t" );
      }
      // skip a line when second dimension index changes
      System.out.println( );
   }
   // skip a line when first dimension index changes
   System.out.println( );
}
```

If we are interested in keeping track of sales on a state-by-state basis, we can use a four-dimensional array as follows:

1st dimension: state

2nd dimension: year

3rd dimension: week

4th dimension: day of the week

The following code sequence illustrates how to declare, instantiate, and access the elements of such a four-dimensional array:

```
double [ ][ ][ ][ ] stateSales;              // declare a four-dimensional
                                             // array

stateSales = new double [50][10][52][7];     // instantiate the array

stateSales[0][0][0][0] = 58.50;              // access the first element

sales[34][4][22][3] = 98.30;                 // access another element

sales[49][9][51][6] = 137.70;                // access the last element
```

To process elements of a four-dimensional array, we use a quadruple *for* loop. That quadruple *for* loop pattern parallels the ones for the two-dimensional and three-dimensional arrays. For a four-dimensional array called *arrayName*, it is:

```
for ( int i = 0; i < arrayName.length; i++ )
{
    for ( int j = 0; j < arrayName[i].length; j++ )
    {
        for ( int k = 0; k < arrayName[i][j].length; k++ )
        {
            for ( int l = 0; l < arrayName[i][j][k].length; l++ )
            {
                // process element arrayName[i][j][k][l]
            }
        }
    }
}
```

9.7   The *ArrayList* Class

As we have seen, single-dimensional and multidimensional arrays are useful in many situations. However, they have limitations.

Let's say you are designing a search engine for a large Web site, for example, an online bookstore. The user will type a word in a text field box, your code will access a database, retrieve all the books with titles that contain this word, and return them to the user.

We could store the book information in an array of books. One problem, however, is that we don't know how many books we will have. There could be 3, 32, 500, or 5,000 books, or maybe even more. Without knowing the number of books, we do not know what size to make the array. The safest bet would be to create the array with the maximum possible number of elements, that is, the maximum number of books that we anticipate. If we actually have fewer books than we anticipated, however, we will waste space.

If we end up with more books than we anticipated, we would need to increase the size of an array. As we demonstrated in Chapter 8, changing the size of an array is a tedious process. We will have to instantiate a new array and copy the elements of the original array to the new array.

The *ArrayList* class, in the *java.util* package, solves these problems. An *ArrayList* object can store any number of objects and automatically expands its capacity as needed. Note that all *ArrayList* elements are objects. Thus, for example, we could have an *ArrayList* of *Book* objects, or an *ArrayList* of *Auto* objects, or an *ArrayList* of *Strings*. If we want to store primitive data types in an *ArrayList*, then we need to use one of the wrapper classes such as *Integer*, *Double*, or *Character*.

 REFERENCE POINT

Wrapper classes are explained in Chapter 3, along with the concepts of autoboxing and unboxing.

Because the *ArrayList* class is in the *java.util* package, programs using an *ArrayList* object will need to provide the following *import* statement:

```
import java.util.ArrayList;
```

9.7.1   Declaring and Instantiating *ArrayList* Objects

Here is the syntax for declaring an *ArrayList* of objects:

```
ArrayList<ClassName> arrayListName;
```

Inside the brackets, we declare the class type of the objects that will be stored in the *ArrayList*. A space is optional between the *ArrayList* class name and the opening bracket.

For example, these two statements declare an *ArrayList* of *Strings* and an *ArrayList* of *Auto* objects:

```
ArrayList<String> listOfStrings;
ArrayList<Auto> listOfCars;
```

Two constructors of the *ArrayList* class are shown in Table 9.4.

If you know how many elements you will store in the *ArrayList* object, you can use the overloaded constructor to specify the initial capacity; otherwise, simply use the default constructor. As you add elements to the *ArrayList* object, its capacity will increase automatically, as needed.

TABLE 9.4   *ArrayList* Constructors

ArrayList Constructor Summary
Constructor name and argument list
`ArrayList<ClassName>( )`
constructs an *ArrayList* object with an initial capacity of 10
`ArrayList<ClassName>( int initialCapacity )`
constructs an *ArrayList* object with the specified initial capacity

Here is the syntax for instantiating an *ArrayList* using the default constructor:

```
arrayListName = new ArrayList<ClassName>( );
```

   where `ClassName` is the class type of the objects that will be stored in the `ArrayList` and `arrayListName` has been declared previously as an `ArrayList` reference for that class.

These statements will instantiate the *ArrayList* objects declared earlier, with an initial capacity of 10:

```
listOfStrings = new ArrayList<String>( );
listOfCars = new ArrayList<Auto>( );
```

In *ArrayLists*, there is a distinction between capacity and size. The **capacity** of an *ArrayList* is the number of elements allocated to the list. The **size** is the number of those elements that are filled with objects. Thus, when you instantiate an *ArrayList* using the default constructor, its capacity is 10, but its size is 0. In other words, the *ArrayList* has room for 10 objects, but no objects are currently stored in the list.

These statements will declare, then instantiate, an *ArrayList* of *Astronaut* objects with an initial capacity of 5, using the overloaded constructor:

```
ArrayList<Astronaut> listOfAstronauts1;
listOfAstronauts1 = new ArrayList<Astronaut>( 5 );
```

In this case, the capacity of *listOfAstronauts1* is 5 and its size is 0.

We can also combine the declaration and instantiation of an *ArrayList* object into one statement. Here is the syntax using the default constructor:

```
ArrayList<ClassName> arrayListName = new ArrayList<ClassName>( );
```

These statements will declare and instantiate two *ArrayList* objects, of *Integers* and *Astronauts*, respectively:

```
ArrayList<Integer> listOfInts = new ArrayList<Integer>( );
ArrayList<Astronaut> listOfAstronauts2 = new ArrayList<Astronaut>( );
```

9.7.2   Methods of the *ArrayList* Class

Like arrays, the *ArrayList* class uses indexes to refer to elements. Among others, it provides methods that provide the following functions:

- add an item at the end of the list
- replace an item at a given index
- remove an item at a given index
- remove all the items in the list
- search the list for a specific item
- retrieve an item at a given index
- retrieve the index of a given item
- check to see if the list is empty
- return the number of items in the list, that is, its size
- optimize the capacity of the list by setting its capacity to the number of items in the list

Some of the most useful methods are shown in Table 9.5.

Note that some of the method headers include *E* as their return type or parameter data type (as opposed to a class name or simply the *Object* class). *E* represents the data type of the *ArrayList*. Thus, for an *ArrayList* of *Integer* objects, *E* is an *Integer*; and the *get* method, for example, returns an *Integer* object. Similarly, for an *ArrayList* of *Auto* objects, *E* is an *Auto* object. In this case, the *get* method returns an *Auto* object.

9.7.3   Looping Through an *ArrayList* Using an Enhanced *for* Loop

The general pattern for processing elements of an *ArrayList* of *ClassName* objects called *arrayListName* using a *for* loop is

```
ClassName currentObject;
for ( int i = 0; i < arrayListName.size( ); i++ )
{
    currentObject = arrayListName.get( i );
    // process currentObject
}
```

TABLE 9.5 *ArrayList* Methods

Useful Methods of the *ArrayList* Class	
Return value	**Method name and argument list**
boolean	add(E element) appends the specified *element* to the end of the list
void	clear( ) removes all the elements from this list
int	size( ) returns the number of elements in this list
E	remove(int index) removes and returns the element at the specified *index* position in the list
E	get(int index) returns the element at the specified *index* position in the list; the element is not removed from the list
E	set(int index, E element) replaces the element at the specified *index* position in this list with the specified *element*
void	trimToSize( ) sets the capacity to the list's current size

For instance, to process elements of an *ArrayList* of *Auto* object references called *listOfAutos* using a standard *for* loop, the general pattern is:

```
Auto currentAuto;
for ( int i = 0; i < listOfAutos.size( ); i++ )
{
    currentAuto = listOfAutos.get( i );
    // process currentAuto
}
```

Java provides a simplified way to process the elements of an *ArrayList*, called the **enhanced *for* loop**. The general pattern for processing elements of an *ArrayList* of *ClassName* objects called *arrayListName* using the enhanced *for* loop is:

```
for ( ClassName currentObject : arrayListName )
{
      // process currentObject
}
```

A variable of the class type of the objects stored in the *ArrayList* is declared in the enhanced *for* loop header, followed by a colon and name of the *ArrayList*. The enhanced *for* loop enables looping through the *ArrayList* objects automatically. Your code does not call the *get* method; inside the body of the loop, *currentObject* is directly available for processing.

For example, to process elements of an *ArrayList* of *Autos* called *cars* using the enhanced *for* loop, the general pattern is:

```
for ( Auto currentAuto : cars )
{
    // process currentAuto
}
```

Example 9.12 shows how to create and use an *ArrayList* of *Integers*. Line 11 declares and instantiates the *ArrayList* object reference *list* using the default constructor. Three elements are added to *list* using the *add* method at lines 12–14. As the argument to the *add* method, we use *Integer* object references at lines 12 and 13, and an *int* at line 14. As we explained in Chapter 3, the autoboxing feature of Java eliminates the need to convert an *int* to an *Integer* object. This is done automatically when an *int* variable is used where an *Integer* object is expected.

At lines 17–18, we print the elements of *list* using a traditional *for* loop, using the *get* method to retrieve the element at the current index. At lines 22–23, we use the enhanced *for* loop to print the elements. At lines 27–28, we also use the enhanced *for* loop to print the elements; but this time, we use an *int* as the looping variable, using the unboxing feature of Java, which converts *Integer* objects to *int* values, as needed. At line 31, we use the *set* method to change the value of the element at index 1 to 100, also using autoboxing. At line 37, we use the *remove* method to delete the element at index 0 and assign it to the variable *removed*, using unboxing again.

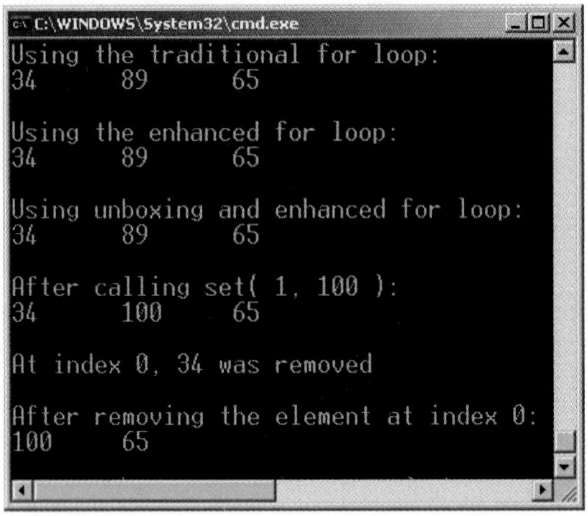

Figure 9.15
Output of Example 9.12

```
C:\WINDOWS\System32\cmd.exe                    _ □ ×
Using the traditional for loop:
34        89        65

Using the enhanced for loop:
34        89        65

Using unboxing and enhanced for loop:
34        89        65

After calling set( 1, 100 ):
34        100       65

At index 0, 34 was removed

After removing the element at index 0:
100       65
```

The output of this example is shown in Figure 9.15.

```
 1 /* A Simple ArrayList of Integers
 2    Anderson, Franceschi
 3 */
 4
 5 import java.util.ArrayList;
 6
 7 public class ArrayListOfIntegers
 8 {
 9  public static void main( String [ ] args )
10  {
11    ArrayList<Integer> list = new ArrayList<Integer>( );
12    list.add( new Integer( 34 ) );
13    list.add( new Integer( 89 ) );
14    list.add( 65 ); // autoboxing
15
16    System.out.println( "Using the traditional for loop:" );
17    for ( int i = 0; i < list.size( ); i++ )
18      System.out.print( list.get( i ) + "\t" );
19    System.out.println( );
20
21    System.out.println( "\nUsing the enhanced for loop:" );
22    for ( Integer currentInteger : list )
```

```
23      System.out.print( currentInteger + "\t" );
24   System.out.println( );
25
26   System.out.println( "\nUsing unboxing and enhanced for loop:" );
27   for ( int currentInt : list ) // unboxing
28      System.out.print( currentInt + "\t" );
29   System.out.println( );
30
31   list.set( 1, 100 );
32   System.out.println( "\nAfter calling set( 1, 100 ):" );
33   for ( int currentInt : list ) // unboxing
34      System.out.print( currentInt + "\t" );
35   System.out.println( );
36
37   int removed = list.remove( 0 );
38   System.out.println( "\nAt index 0, " + removed + " was removed" );
39   System.out.println( "\nAfter removing the element at index 0:" );
40   for ( int currentInt : list ) // unboxing
41      System.out.print( currentInt + "\t" );
42   System.out.println( );
43   }
44 }
```

EXAMPLE 9.12   Using *ArrayList* Methods

9.7.4   Using the *ArrayList* Class in a Program

Now let's see how we can use the *ArrayList* class in a Java program. Going back to our example of a bookstore and a search engine, we want to design and code a simple program that enables users to search for books.

We will have three classes in this program:

- a *Book* class, encapsulating the concept of a book

- a *BookStore* class, encapsulating the concept of a bookstore

- a *BookSearchEngine* class, including the *main* method, which provides the user interface.

In the interest of keeping things simple, our *Book* class will contain only three instance variables: the book title, which is a *String*; the book's author, which is also a *String*; and the book price, which is a *double*.

Example 9.13 shows a simplified *Book* class with constructors, accessor methods, and a *toString* method.

```
1 /* Book class
2    Anderson, Franceschi
3 */
4
5 public class Book
6 {
7  private String title;
8  private String author;
9  private double price;
10
11  /** default constructor
12  */
13  public Book( )
14  {
15    title = "";
16    author = "";
17    price  = 0.0;
18  }
19
20  /** overloaded constructor
21  *   @param newTitle   the value to assign to title
22  *   @param newAuthor  the value to assign to author
23  *   @param newPrice   the value to assign to price
24  */
25  public Book( String newTitle, String newAuthor, double newPrice )
26  {
27    title = newTitle;
28    author = newAuthor;
29    price  = newPrice;
30  }
31
32  /** getTitle method
33  *    @return the title
34  */
35  public String getTitle( )
36  {
37    return title;
38  }
39
40  /** getAuthor method
```

```
41  *    @return the author
42  */
43  public String getAuthor( )
44  {
45    return author;
46  }
47
48  /** getPrice method
49  *    @return the price
50  */
51  public double getPrice( )
52  {
53    return price;
54  }
55
56  /** toString
57  * @return title, author, and price
58  */
59  public String toString( )
60  {
61    return ( "title: " + title + "\t"
62            + "author: " + author + "\t"
63            + "price: " + price );
64  }
65 }
```

EXAMPLE 9.13   The *Book* Class

Our *BookStore* class, shown in Example 9.14, will simply have one instance variable: an *ArrayList* of *Book* objects, representing the collection of books in the bookstore, which we name *library*.

In most cases, when an *ArrayList* is filled with data, that data will come from a database or a file. In the interest of focusing on the *ArrayList* class and its methods, we have hard-coded the objects for the *ArrayList library* in the *BookStore* class, rather than reading them from a database or a file.

In the default constructor (lines 11 to 24), we instantiate the *library* instance variable, then add six *Book* objects to *library* using the *add* method from the *ArrayList* class. At line 23, we call the *trimToSize* method to set the capacity of *library* to its current size, which is 6, in order to minimize the memory resources used.

The *toString* method is coded from lines 26 to 37. It generates and returns a *String* representing all the books in *library*, one book per line. In order to do that, we use an enhanced *for* loop from lines 32 to 35. The header of that loop, at line 32, follows the general pattern of the enhanced *for* loop header by declaring a *Book* variable named *tempBook*, followed by a colon, followed by *library*, the *ArrayList* object to loop through.

The *searchForTitle* method, coded from lines 39 to 53, performs the task of searching for a keyword within the title of each *Book* object stored in *library*. The keyword, a *String*, is the parameter of the method and is named *searchString*. This method returns an *ArrayList* of *Book* objects. We create another *ArrayList* of *Books*, which we name *searchResult* at line 45 and loop through *library* using an enhanced *for* loop from lines 46 to 50. Inside the body of the loop, we use the *indexOf* method of the *String* class to test if the current *Book* object contains the keyword *searchString* in its *title* instance variable. If it does, we add that *Book* object to *searchResult*. Finally, we call the method *trimToSize* to set the capacity of *searchResult* to the current number of elements, then return the *ArrayList* to the caller.

```
 1 /*  BookStore class
 2     Anderson, Franceschi
 3 */
 4
 5 import java.util.ArrayList;
 6
 7 public class BookStore
 8 {
 9   private ArrayList<Book> library;
10
11   /** default constructor
12   *   instantiates ArrayList of Books
13   */
14   public BookStore( )
15   {
16     library = new ArrayList<Book>( );
17     library.add( new Book( "Intro to Java", "James", 56.99 ) );
18     library.add( new Book( "Advanced Java", "Green", 65.99 ) );
19     library.add( new Book( "Java Servlets", "Brown", 75.99 ) );
20     library.add( new Book( "Intro to HTML", "James", 29.49 ) );
21     library.add( new Book( "Intro to Flash", "James", 34.99 ) );
22     library.add( new Book( "Advanced HTML", "Green", 56.99 ) );
```

```
23   library.trimToSize( );
24   }
25
26   /** toString
27    *  @return  each book in library, one per line
28    */
29   public String toString( )
30   {
31     String result = "";
32     for( Book tempBook : library )
33     {
34       result += tempBook.toString( ) + "\n";
35     }
36     return result;
37   }
38
39   /** Generates list of books containing searchString
40    *  @param searchString    the keyword to search for
41    *  @return          the ArrayList of books containing the keyword
42    */
43   public ArrayList<Book> searchForTitle( String searchString )
44   {
45     ArrayList<Book> searchResult = new ArrayList<Book>( );
46     for ( Book currentBook : library )
47     {
48       if ( ( currentBook.getTitle( ) ).indexOf( searchString ) != -1 )
49           searchResult.add( currentBook );
50     }
51     searchResult.trimToSize( );
52     return searchResult;
53   }
54 }
```

EXAMPLE 9.14   The *BookStore* Class

Our *BookSearchEngine* class, shown in Example 9.15, contains the *main* method: it creates a *BookStore* object, asks the user for a keyword, and searches for partial matches in our *BookStore* object.

A *BookStore* object, *bs*, is declared and instantiated at line 12. At lines 14–15, the user is then prompted for a keyword that will be used to search for books whose title contains that keyword. Lines 16 and 17 simply output the collection of *Books* in the *BookStore* object *bs*; later, when the search results are output, we can compare that output to the original list of *Books*

Figure 9.16

Results of a Search for the Keyword "Java"

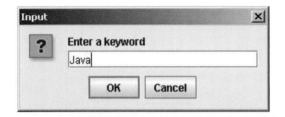

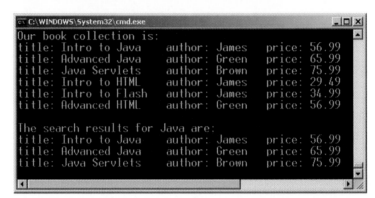

to check our results. At line 19, we call the *searchForTitle* method with *keyword* as its argument; the *ArrayList* of *Book* objects returned is assigned to the variable *results*. At lines 23–24, we loop through *results* and output its contents, again using the enhanced *for* loop. Figure 9.16 shows a run of the program with the user searching for books containing the word "Java."

```
1 /* BookSearchEngine class
2    Anderson, Franceschi
3 */
4
5 import java.util.ArrayList;
6 import javax.swing.JOptionPane;
7
8 public class BookSearchEngine
9 {
10  public static void main( String [ ] args )
11  {
12   BookStore bs = new BookStore( );
13
14   String keyword = JOptionPane.showInputDialog( null,
15                     "Enter a keyword" );
16   System.out.println( "Our book collection is:" );
17   System.out.println( bs.toString( ) );
```

```
18
19   ArrayList<Book> results = bs.searchForTitle( keyword );
20
21   System.out.println( "The search results for " + keyword
22                       + " are:" );
23   for( Book tempBook : results )
24        System.out.println( tempBook.toString( ) );
25  }
26 }
```

EXAMPLE 9.15   A Search Engine for Books

9.8   Programming Activity 2: Working with the *ArrayList* Class

In this activity, you will work with an *ArrayList* object. Specifically, you will write the code to perform the following operations:

1. Fill the *ArrayList* object with *Auto* elements.

2. Print the *Auto* elements contained in the *ArrayList* object.

3. Set the *model* instance variable of every *Auto* element in the *ArrayList* object to a specified model.

4. Find the maximum number of miles of all *Auto* elements contained in the *ArrayList* object.

5. Count the number of *Auto* elements in the *ArrayList* objects with a specified model.

The framework for this Programming Activity will animate your algorithm so that you can check the accuracy of your code. For example, Figure 9.17 shows the application counting the number of *Auto* elements in the *ArrayList* object having a model value equal to "Ferrari." The application accesses each element in the *ArrayList* in order, checking the *model* for the desired value, "Ferrari." At this point, the current element being accessed is a *BMW* and the application has found two *Auto* elements with the *model* value, "Ferrari."

Instructions

In the Chapter 9 Programming Activity 2 directory on the CD-ROM accompanying this book, you will find the source files needed to complete this activity. Copy all the files to a directory on your computer. Note that all files should be in the same directory.

Figure 9.17

Animation of the Programming Activity

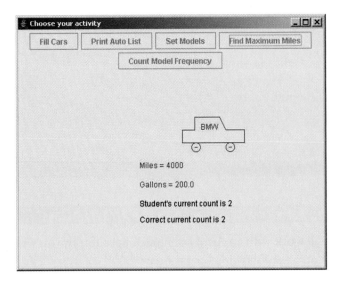

Open the *ArrayListPractice.java* source file. Searching for five stars (*****) in the source code will position you to the sample method and the four other locations where you will add your code. We have provided the sample code for task number 1. In every task, you will fill in the code for a method that will manipulate an existing *ArrayList* of *Auto* elements. You should not instantiate the *ArrayList* object; we have done that for you. Example 9.16 shows the section of the *ArrayListPractice* source code where you will add your code.

Note that for the *countFound* and *findMaximumMilesDriven* methods, we provide a dummy *return* statement (*return 0;*). We do this so that the source code will compile. In this way, you can write and test each method separately, using step-wise refinement. When you are ready to write the *countFound* and *findMaximumMilesDriven* methods, just replace the dummy *return* statements with the appropriate *return* statement for that method.

```
// ***** 1.  This method has been coded as an example
/** Fills the carList with hard-coded Auto objects
*     The instance variable carList is the ArrayList
*          to be filled with Auto objects
*/
public void fillWithCars( )
{
  // clear carList before adding cars
  carList.clear( );
  // Reset the number of Autos to 0
```

```java
   // This is needed so that the animation feedback works correctly
   Auto.clearNumberAutos( );

   Auto car1 = new Auto( "BMW", 0, 0.0 );
   Auto car2 = new Auto( "Ferrari", 100, 500.0 );
   Auto car3 = new Auto( "Jeep", 1000, 90.0 );
   Auto car4 = new Auto( "Ferrari", 10, 3.0 );
   Auto car5 = new Auto( "BMW", 4000, 200.0 );
   Auto car6 = new Auto( "Ferrari", 1000, 50.0 );

   carList.add( car1 );
   carList.add( car2 );
   carList.add( car3 );
   carList.add( car4 );
   carList.add( car5 );
   carList.add( car6 );
   animate( );
}
// end of fillWithCars method

// ***** 2.  Student writes this method
/** Prints carList to console, elements are separated by a space
*      The instance variable carList is the ArrayList to be printed
*/
public void printAutoList( )
{
  // Note:  To animate the algorithm, put this method call as the
  // last statement in your for loop
  //              animate( car );
  // where car is the variable name for the current Auto object
  // as you loop through the ArrayList object
  // Write your code here:

}
// end of printAutoList method

// ***** 3.  Student writes this method
/** Sets the model of all the elements in carList to parameter value
* The instance variable carList is the ArrayList to be modified
* @param model the model to assign to all Auto objects in carList
*/
public void setModelValues( String model )
{
  // Note:  To animate the algorithm, put this method call as the
  // last statement in your for loop
  //              animate( car );
  // where car is the variable name for the current Auto object
  // as you loop through the ArrayList object
```

```
// Write your code here:


}
// end of setModelValues method

// ***** 4.  Student writes this method
/** Finds maximum number of miles driven
*    Instance variable carList is the ArrayList to search
*  @return     the maximum miles driven by all the Auto objects
*/
public int findMaximumMilesDriven( )
{
 // Note:  To animate the algorithm, put this method call as the
 // last statement in your for loop
 //           animate( car, maximum );
 //  where car is the variable name for the current Auto object
 //  and maximum is the int variable storing the current maximum
 //  number of miles for all Auto elements you have already tested
 //  as you loop through the ArrayList object
 // Write your code here:

  return 0; // replace this statement with your return statement


}
// end of findMaximumMilesDriven method

// ***** 5.  Student writes this method
/** Finds number of times parameter model is found in the carList
*    Instance variable carList is the ArrayList in which we search
*  @param model      the model to count
*  @return           the number of times model was found
*/
public int countFound( String model )
{
 // Note:  To animate the algorithm, put this method call as the
 // last statement in your for loop
 //           animate( car, num );
 //  where car is the variable name for the current Auto object
 //  and num is the int variable storing the current number of
 //  Auto elements whose model is equal to the method's parameter
 //  as you loop through the ArrayList object
 // Write your code here:

  return 0; // replace this statement with your return statement


}
// end of countFound method
```

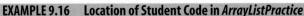

EXAMPLE 9.16   Location of Student Code in *ArrayListPractice*

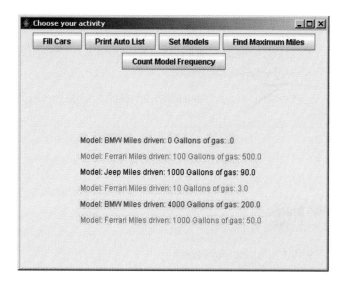

Figure 9.18

The Graphics Window When the Application Begins

The framework will animate your code so that you can watch it work. For this to happen, be sure that your *for* loops call the *animate* method. The arguments that you send to *animate* are not always the same, but the location of the call to *animate* is always the same, that is, the last statement of your *for* loop. Detailed instructions for each task are included in the code.

To test your code, compile and run the *ArrayPractice* source code. Figure 9.18 shows the graphics window when the program begins. Because the *Auto* elements of the *ArrayList* object are hard coded, the values will be the same each time the program runs. To test any method, click on the appropriate button.

Troubleshooting

If your method implementation does not animate, check these tips:

- Verify that the last statement in your single *for* loop or inner *for* loop is a call to the *animate* method and that you passed the loop variable(s) as the argument(s), as in the following:

```
animate( car );              // or
animate( car, maximum );     // or
animate( car, num );
```

- Verify that the headers of your *for* loops are correct. It should always be the same.

- Verify that you update the variables *maximum* and *num* correctly.

DISCUSSION QUESTIONS   **?**

1. Change the code in the *fillWithCars* method so that there are more or fewer *Auto* objects in the *ArrayList*. How does the number of *Auto* objects impact how the other methods are coded? Explain.

2. Explain how looping through an *ArrayList* is different from looping through an array.

Skill Practice
with these end-of-chapter questions

9.9 Chapter Summary

- Arrays can be single-dimensional, two-dimensional, three-dimensional, or more generally *n*-dimensional.

- In a two-dimensional array, each row is an array.

- Each element in a two-dimensional array is accessed using the array name, a row index, and a column index that refer to the element's position in the array.

- Concepts such as declaration, instantiation, initial values, indexing, and aggregate operations from single-dimensional arrays also apply to two-dimensional arrays.

- Two-dimensional arrays can be instantiated by assigning initial values in a comma-separated list of comma-separated lists at the declaration.

- Each row in a two-dimensional array can have a different number of columns.

- A two-dimensional array has an instance variable, *length*, which holds the number of rows in the array.

- Each row of a two-dimensional array has an instance variable, *length*, which holds the number of elements in that row.

- The *ArrayList* class is part of the *java.util* package.

- An *ArrayList* can be thought of as an expandable single-dimensional array of objects.

- To define an *ArrayList* to hold elements of primitive data types, use the wrapper classes.

- An *ArrayList* object expands automatically as needed as objects are added.

- We access an element of an *ArrayList* via its index.

- We can process each element in an *ArrayList* using the enhanced *for* loop.

CHAPTER SUMMARY

9.10 Exercises, Problems, and Projects

9.10.1 Multiple Choice Exercises

1. What is/are the valid way(s) to declare a two-dimensional integer array named *a*? (Check all that apply.)

   ❏ `int [ ][ ] a;`

   ❏ `int a [ ][ ];`

   ❏ `array [ ] int a;`

   ❏ `int array [ ] a;`

2. A two-dimensional array is an array of arrays.

   ❏ true

   ❏ false

3. In a two-dimensional array, every row must have the same number of columns.

   ❏ true

   ❏ false

4. What is the default value of the elements of a two-dimensional array of *booleans* after declaration and instantiation of the array?

   ❏ *true*

   ❏ *false*

   ❏ undefined

5. How do you access the element of array *a* located at row 2 and column 4?

   ❏ `a{2}{4}`

   ❏ `a( 2,4 )`

   ❏ `a[2][4]`

   ❏ `a[4][2]`

6. How do you retrieve the number of rows in a two-dimensional array *a*?

   ❏ `a.rows`

   ❏ `a.length`

   ❏ `a.rows( )`

   ❏ `a.size`

7. How do you retrieve the number of columns in row 2 in a two-dimensional array *a*?

   ❑ `a.length`

   ❑ `a[2].length`

   ❑ `a.size`

   ❑ `a[2].size`

8. All the elements of a two-dimensional array must be of the same type.

   ❑ true

   ❑ false

9. An *ArrayList* can be returned by a method.

   ❑ true

   ❑ false

10. It is possible to declare and instantiate an *ArrayList* of a user-defined class type.

    ❑ true

    ❑ false

11. As we add objects to an *ArrayList*, how can we be sure it has enough capacity?

    ❑ Use the *setCapacity* method.

    ❑ Use the *trimToSize* method.

    ❑ We don't need to do anything; capacity expands automatically as needed.

12. Where does the *add* method of the *ArrayList* class add an object?

    ❑ at the beginning of the list.

    ❑ at the end of the list.

13. To what package does the class *ArrayList* belong?

    ❑ *java.io*

    ❑ *java.util*

❑ *java.array*

❑ *java.list*

9.10.2   Reading and Understanding Code

For questions 14 to 24, consider the following two-dimensional array declaration and initialization:

```
String [ ][ ] cities = { {"New York", "LA", "San Francisco", "Chicago" },
                         { "Munich", "Stuttgart", "Berlin", "Bonn" },
                         { "Paris", "Ajaccio", "Lyon" },
                         { "Montreal", "Ottawa", "Vancouver" } };
```

14. How many rows are in the array *cities*?

15. What is the value of the expression *cities[2][1]*?

16. What is the index of the last row in the array *cities*?

17. What are the row and column indexes of *Chicago* in the array *cities*?

18. What is the output of this code sequence?

```
System.out.println( cities[3][2] );
```

19. What is the output of this code sequence?

```
for ( int j = 0; j < cities[1].length; j++ )
    System.out.println( cities[1][j] );
```

20. What is the output of this code sequence?

```
for ( int i = 0; i < cities.length; i++ )
    System.out.println( cities[i][1] );
```

21. What is the output of this code sequence?

```
for ( int i = 0; i < cities.length; i++ )
{
    for ( int j = 0; j < cities[i].length; j++ )
        System.out.print( cities[i][j] + "\t" );
    System.out.println( );
}
```

22. What is the output of this code sequence?

```
for ( int i = 0; i < cities.length; i++ )
{
    for ( int j = 0; j < cities[i].length; j++ )
    {
        if ( cities[i][j].length( ) == 6 )
```

```
            System.out.println( cities[i][j] );
    }
}
```

23. What is the output of this code sequence?

```
int count  = 0;
for ( int i = 0; i < cities.length; i++ )
{
    for ( int j = 0; j < cities[i].length; j++ )
    {
        if ( cities[i][j].length( ) == 7 )
            count++;
    }
}
System.out.println( "count is " + count );
```

24. What is the output of this code sequence?

```
for ( int i = 0; i < cities.length; i++ )
{
    for ( int j = 0; j < cities[i].length; j++ )
    {
        if ( cities[i][j].charAt( 0 ) == 'S' )
            System.out.println( cities[i][j] );
    }
}
```

25. What does this method do?

```
public static int foo( double [ ][ ] a )
{
    int b = 0;
    for ( int i = 0; i < a.length; i++ )
    {
        for ( int j = 0; j < a[i].length; j++ )
            b++;
    }
    return b;
}
```

26. What does this method do?

```
public static boolean foo( char [ ][ ] a )
{
    int b = a[0].length;
    for ( int i = 1; i < a.length; i++ )
    {
        if ( a[i].length != b )
```

```
            return false;
    }
    return true;
}
```

27. What does this method do?

```
public static int foo( String [ ][ ] a )
{
    int b = 0;
    for ( int i = 0; i < a.length; i++ )
    {
        b++;
    }
    return b;
}
```

28. What does this method do?

```
public static int [ ] foo( float [ ][ ] a )
{
    int [ ] temp = new int [a.length];
    for ( int i = 0; i < a.length; i++ )
        temp[i] = a[i].length;
    return temp;
}
```

29. What does this method do?

```
public static int foo( ArrayList<Integer> a )
{
    int b = 0;
    for ( Integer i : a )
    {
        b++;
    }
    return b;
}
```

30. After the following code sequence is executed, what are the contents and index of each element of *a*?

```
ArrayList<Integer> a = new ArrayList<Integer>( );
a.add( 7 );
a.add( 4 );
a.add( 21 );
```

31. After the following code sequence is executed, what are the contents and index of each element of *a*?

```
ArrayList<Integer> a = new ArrayList<Integer>( );
a.add( 7 );
a.add( 4 );
a.add( 21 );
a.set( 1, 45 );
```

32. After the following code sequence is executed, what are the contents and index of each element of *a?*

```
ArrayList<Integer> a = new ArrayList<Integer>( );
a.add( 7 );
a.add( 4 );
a.add( 21 );
a.add( 1, 45 );
```

9.10.3   Fill in the Code

For questions 33 to 37, consider the following statement:

```
String [ ][ ] geo = { { "MD", "NY", "NJ", "MA", "ME", "CA", "MI", "OR" },
                      { "Detroit", "Newark", "Boston", "Seattle" } };
```

33. This code prints the element at row index 1 and column index 2 of the two-dimensional array *geo.*

```
// your code goes here
```

34. This code prints the element of the array *geo* whose value is "CA."

```
// your code goes here
```

35. This code prints all the states (i.e., the first row) that start with an *M* in the array *geo.*

```
for ( int j = 0; j < geo[0].length; j++ )
{

    // your code goes here


}
```

36. This code prints all the cities (i.e., the second row) in the array *geo.*

```
for ( int j = 0; j < geo[1].length; j++ )
{

    // your code goes here


}
```

37. This code prints all the elements of the array *geo*.

```
for ( int i = 0; i < geo.length; i++ )
{
      // your code goes here


}
```

For questions 38 to 41, consider the following statement:

```
int [ ][ ] a = { { 9, 6, 8, 10, 5},
                 { 7, 6, 8, 9, 6 },
                 { 4, 8, 10, 6, 6 } };
```

38. This code calculates and prints the sum of all the elements in the array *a*.

```
int sum = 0;
for ( int i = 0; i < a.length; i++ )
{
      // your code goes here


}
System.out.println( "sum is " + sum );
```

39. This code counts and prints the number of times the value 8 appears in the array *a*.

```
int count = 0;
for ( int i = 0; i < a.length; i++ )
{
      // your code goes here


}
System.out.println( "# of 8s in a: " + count );
```

40. This code counts and prints the number of times the value 6 appears in the second row (i.e., the row whose index is 1) of array *a*.

```
int count = 0;

// your code for the for loop header goes here
{
      if ( a[1][j] == 6 )
            count++;
}
System.out.println( "# of 6s in the 2nd row: " + count );
```

41. This code calculates the sum of the elements in the second column (i.e, the column with index 1) of array *a*.

```
int sum  = 0;
for ( int i = 0; i < a.length; i++ )
{

     // your code goes here

}
System.out.println( "sum is " + sum );
```

42. This method returns *true* if an element in an array of *Strings* is equal to "Java"; otherwise, it returns *false*.

```
public static boolean foo( String [ ][ ] a )
{
     // your code goes here
}
```

43. This method returns the product of all the elements in an array.

```
public static int foo( int [ ][ ] a )
{
   // your code goes here
}
```

44. This method returns *true* if there is at least one row in the array that has exactly five columns; otherwise, it returns *false*.

```
public static boolean foo( char [ ][ ] a )
{
   // your code goes here
}
```

45. This method takes an array of *ints* as a parameter and returns a single-dimensional array of *booleans*. The length of the array returned should be equal to the number of rows in the two-dimensional array parameter. The element at index *i* of the returned array will be *true* if there is a 0 in the corresponding row of the parameter array; otherwise, it will be *false*. Assume that every row in *a* has the same number of columns.

```
public static boolean [ ] foo( int [ ][ ] a )
{
   // your code goes here
   // every row has the same number of columns

}
```

For questions 46 to 49, consider the following statements:

```
ArrayList<String> languages = new ArrayList<String>( );
languages.add( "SQL" );
languages.add( "Java" );
languages.add( "HTML" );
languages.add( "PHP" );
languages.add( "Perl" );
```

46. This code prints the number of elements in *languages.*

    ```
    // your code goes here
    ```

47. This code retrieves the *String* "HTML" from *languages* (without deleting it) and assigns it to the *String* variable *webLanguage.*

    ```
    // your code goes here
    ```

48. This code replaces "HTML" *with* "C++" in *languages.*

    ```
    // your code goes here
    ```

49. This code prints all the elements of *languages* that start with the letter *P.*

    ```
    for ( String s : languages )
    {
      // your code goes here

    }
    ```

9.10.4   Identifying Errors in Code

50. Where is the error in this code sequence?

    ```
    double [ ][ ] a = { 3.3, 26.0, 48.4 };
    ```

51. Where is the error in this code sequence?

    ```
    int [ ][ ] a = { { 3, 26, 4 }, { 14, 87 } };
    System.out.println( a[1][2] );
    ```

52. Where is the error in this code sequence?

    ```
    double [ ][ ] a = new double [ ][10];
    ```

53. Where is the error in this code sequence?

    ```
    int [ ][ ] a = { { 1, 2 },
                     { 10.1, 10.2 } };
    ```

54. Where is the error in this code sequence? (This code compiles and runs, but outputs garbage.)

    ```
    int [ ][ ] a = { { 3, 26, 48 }, { 5, 2, 9 } };
    System.out.println( "The array elements are " + a );
    ```

55. Where is the error in this code sequence?

```java
ArrayList<double> al;
```

56. Where is the error in this code sequence?

```java
ArrayList<Float> al = new ArrayList( )<Float>;
```

57. Where is the error in this code sequence? (The compiler may ask you to recompile.)

```java
ArrayList<Double> a;
a = new ArrayList<Float>( );
```

58. Where is the error in this code sequence?

```java
// a is an ArrayList of Strings
// a has already been declared and instantiated
a.size( ) = 10;
```

9.10.5   Debugging Area

59. You coded the following on line 14 of the *Test.java* class:

```java
int a[2][ ] = { { 2, 7 }, { 9, 2 } };       // line 14
```

When you compile, you get the following message:

```
Test.java:14: ']' expected
  int a[2][ ] = { { 2, 7 }, { 9, 2 } };
        ^

1 error
```

Explain what the problem is and how to fix it.

60. You coded the following in the *Test.java* class:

```java
int [ ][ ] a = { { 1, 2, 3, 4 },
                 { 10, 20, 30 } };

for ( int i = 0; i < a.length; i++ )
{
    for ( int j = 0; j < a[0].length; j++ )
    {
        System.out.println( a[i][j] );    // line 14
    }
}
```

The code compiles properly but when you run, you get the following output:

```
1
2
3
4
10
20
30
Exception in thread "main" java.lang.ArrayIndexOutOfBoundsException: 3
        at Test.main(Test.java: 14)
```

Explain what the problem is and how to fix it.

61. You coded the following in the *Test.java* class in order to output the smallest element in the array *a*.

```
int [ ][ ] a = { { 9, 8, 7, 6 },
                 { 10, 20, 30, 40 } };

int min = a[0][0];
for ( int i = 1; i < a.length; i++ )
{
        for ( int j = 0; j < a[i].length; j++ )
        {
                if ( a[i][j] < min )
                        min = a[i][j];
        }
}
System.out.println( "The minimum is " + min );
```

The code compiles properly, but when you run, you get the following output:

```
The minimum is 9
```

You expected the value of *min* to be 6. Explain what the problem is and how to fix it.

62. You coded the following in file *Test.java*:

```
int [ ][ ] a = { { 9, 8, 7, 6 },
                 { 10, 20, 30, 40 } };

for ( int j = 0; j <= a[1].length; j++ )
{
  if ( a[1][j] == 20 )       // line 14
```

```
    {
        System.out.println( "Found 20 at column index " + j
                                + " of second row" );
    }
}
```

The code compiles properly, but when you run, you get the following output:

```
Found 20 at column index 1 of second row
Exception in thread "main" java.lang.ArrayIndexOutOfBoundsException: 4
        at Test.main(Test.java:14)
```

Explain what the problem is and how to fix it.

63. You coded the following in the *Test.java* class:

```
public static void main( String [ ] args )
{
  // cars is an ArrayList of Auto objects
  // cars has already been declared and instantiated
  for ( Auto a ; cars )      // line 12
  {
      System.out.println( a.toString( ) );
  }   // line 15
}   // line 16
```

When you compile, you get the following message :

```
Test.java:12: ';' expected
  for ( Auto a ; cars ) // line 12
                    ^
Test.java:16: illegal start of expression
  }     // line 16
  ^
Test.java:15: ')' expected
  }       // line 15
    ^
3 errors
```

Explain what the problems are and how to fix them.

64. You coded the following in the *Test.java* class:

```
ArrayList<String> a = new ArrayList<String>( );
a.add( "Cloudy" );
a.add( "Snowy" );
a.add( "Cloudy" );
System.out.println( "Weather is " + a.get( 3 ) ); // line 14
```

The code compiles properly, but when you run, you get the following output:

```
Exception in thread "main" java.lang.IndexOutOfBoundsException:
Index: 3, Size: 3
          at java.util.ArrayList.RangeCheck(ArrayList.java:547)
          at java.util.ArrayList.get(ArrayList.java:322)
          at Test.main(Test.java:14)
```

Explain what the problem is and how to fix it.

9.10.6   Write a Short Program

65. Write a value-returning method that returns the number of rows in a two-dimensional array of *doubles*. Include code to test your method.

66. Write a value-returning method that returns the number of elements in a two-dimensional array of *floats*. Include code to test your method.

67. Write a value-returning method that returns the number of columns that have two elements in a two-dimensional array of *booleans*. Include code to test your method.

68. Write a value-returning method that returns the number of columns with *n* elements in a two-dimensional array of *chars*, where *n* is a parameter of the method. Include code to test your method.

69. Write a value-returning method that returns the sum of all the elements in a two-dimensional array of *floats*. Include code to test your method.

70. Write a method with a *void* return value that sets to 0 all the elements of the even numbered rows and sets to 1 all the elements of odd numbered rows of a two-dimensional array of *ints*. Include code to test your method.

71. Write a value-returning method that returns the sum of the elements in the last column of each row in a two-dimensional array of *ints*. Include code to test your method.

72. Write a method with a *void* return value that inverts all the elements of a two-dimensional array of *booleans* (*true* becomes *false* and *false* becomes *true*). Include code to test your method.

73. Write a method that returns the number of elements having the value *true* in a two-dimensional array of *booleans*. Include code to test your method.

74. Write a method that returns the percentage of elements having the value *false* in a two-dimensional array of *booleans*. Include code to test your method.

75. Write a method that returns the average of all elements in a two-dimensional array of *ints*. Include code to test your method.

76. Write a method that returns the *String* "regular" if all the rows of a two-dimensional array of *floats* have the same number of columns; otherwise, it returns "irregular." Include code to test your method.

77. Write a method that returns the concatenation of all elements in a two-dimensional array of *Strings*. Include code to test your method.

78. Write an array-returning method that takes a two-dimensional array of *chars* as a parameter and returns a single-dimensional array of *Strings* as follows: The array returned should have a number of elements equal to the number of rows in the parameter array; every element of the array returned should be the concatenation of all the column elements of the corresponding row in the parameter array. Include code to test your method.

79. Write an array-returning method that takes a two-dimensional array of *ints* as a parameter and returns a two-dimensional array of *chars*, assigning a letter grade corresponding to the integer grade (A if 90 or above, ..., F if less than 60). Include code to test your method.

80. Write a method that returns the sum of all the elements of an *ArrayList* of *Integer* objects. Include code to test your method.

81. Write a method that returns the *String* "odd" or "even" if the number of elements of an *ArrayList* of *Strings* is odd or even. Include code to test your method.

82. Write a method that takes an *ArrayList* of *Integer* objects and returns an *ArrayList* of *Character* objects of the same size. The returned elements of the *ArrayList* are assigned a letter grade corresponding to the integer grade of the same index element of the *ArrayList* parameter (A if 90 or above, ..., F if less than 60). Include code to test your method.

9.10.7   Programming Projects

√83. Write a class (and a client class to test it) that encapsulates statistics for summer job salaries for a group of people over several years. Your only instance variable should be a two-dimensional array of values representing salaries. Dimension 1 represents the people and dimension 2 represents the year of the summer job. Your constructor can simply take two integers representing the number of people and the number of years, then randomly generate the salaries and fill the array. You should include the following methods:

- ❑ a method returning the index of the person having made the most money over the years

- ❑ a method returning the year when the highest salary was earned

- ❑ a method returning the total amount of money made by all the people over the years.

84. Write a class (and a client class to test it) that encapsulates the evolution of the passwords of three students over four months. Your only instance variable should be a two-dimensional array of values representing the passwords. Dimension 1 represents the student and dimension 2 represents the month. (Since we are concerned about security, we are assuming that people change their password once a month; we only care about the value of the password at the end of a given month.) Your constructor can simply take a single-dimensional array of words representing the 12 passwords; they can be assigned to the two-dimensional array elements one at a time, starting with the first row. You should include the following methods:

- ❑ a method returning the index of the person who changed his or her password the most times

- ❑ a method returning the longest password

- ❑ a method changing all the passwords to "unlock"

- ❑ a method returning *true* if at least one person had a given word—the method's parameter—as his/her password in at least one month; *false* otherwise

85. Write a class (and a client class to test it) that encapsulates the evolution of the sales tax rates in the 50 U.S. states over the last 10 years. Your only

instance variable should be a two-dimensional array of values representing the sales tax rates. Dimension 1 represents the state and dimension 2 represents the year. Your constructor can simply be a default constructor, randomly generating the sales tax rates, which should be between 0 and 0.06. You should include the following methods:

- ❑ a method returning the index of the state that has the biggest average tax rate over the years

- ❑ a method returning an array of indexes of the states that have had at least one year with a tax rate less than 0.001

- ❑ a method returning the highest sales tax rate over the years for a given state (which will be a parameter).

86. Write a class (and a client class to test it) that encapsulates the evolution of the quality ratings of various hotels over the years. Hotel ratings are represented by a number of stars, which can vary from one star (lowest quality) to five stars (highest quality). Your only instance variable should be a two-dimensional array of values representing the quality ratings. Dimension 1 represents the hotel and dimension 2 represents the year. Your constructor can take two parameters representing the number of hotels and the number of years. The ratings can simply be generated randomly. You should include the following methods:

- ❑ a method returning an array of indexes of the hotels that have earned five stars at least once over the years

- ❑ a method returning the average rating of all the hotels over the years

- ❑ a method printing the indexes of the hotels that have earned five stars every year

- ❑ a method returning *true* if at least one hotel earned five stars for at least one year; *false* otherwise

87. Write a class (and a client class to test it) that encapsulates the value of the 26 letters of the English alphabet in the game of Scrabble in 10 countries. You should have three instance variables:

- ❑ a two-dimensional array of integers representing the point values of the letters in the various countries

- ❑ a single-dimensional array representing the alphabet from a to z

❏ another single-dimensional array representing 10 countries.

For the two-dimensional array, dimension 1 represents the letter and dimension 2 represents the country. Your constructor can simply be a default constructor, randomly generating the values between 1 and 10. You should include the following methods:

❏ a method returning an array of letters with their highest point value in any country

❏ a method printing the names of the countries that have at least one letter with a point value of 10

❏ a method taking a *String* as a parameter and printing the score of the word represented by that *String* in every country.

88. Write a class (and a client class to test it) that encapsulates the numbers of the various chessboard pieces in a chess game. You should have two instance variables:

❏ a two-dimensional array of integers; each array element represents how many of a particular chess piece of a particular color are on the board. In order to set it up, consider the following:

▪ The first dimension represents the color of the pieces. On a chessboard, there are white and black pieces.

▪ The second dimension represents the pieces themselves. On a chessboard, we have on each side: one king, one queen, two bishops, two knights, two rooks, and eight pawns.

❏ a single-dimensional array describing the pieces (king, queen, etc.).

Your constructor can simply be a default constructor, declaring and instantiating the two arrays to match the preceding information. You should include the following methods:

❏ a method with a *void* return value, called *playerATakesPlayerB*, updating the array based on a piece being taken by the opponent. It takes two parameters:

▪ a *boolean* parameter representing whether "white takes black" or "black takes white"

▪ an *int* parameter representing which piece gets taken

❏ a method returning how many of a particular piece are on the board (this method takes a parameter representing the piece).

❏ a method taking a *boolean* as a parameter, representing a color and returning the value of the board for that particular color. You can consider that a king is worth 0 points, a queen is worth 6 points, a rook is worth 4 points, a knight and a bishop are each worth 3 points, and a pawn is worth 1 point.

89. Write a class (and a client class to test it) that encapsulates a deck of cards. A deck of cards is made up of 52 cards. You should have three instance variables:

❏ a two-dimensional array of values representing the cards

❏ a single-dimensional array describing the suit: spades, hearts, diamonds, and clubs

❏ an instance variable representing the trump suit

For the two-dimensional array, dimension 1 represents the suit and dimension 2 represents the type of card (ace, two, three, . . ., jack, queen, king). Your constructor should take one parameter, which will represent the suit of the trump. Based on that, the cards should be given the following values:

❏ Non–trump from 2 to 10: 1 point

❏ Non–trump jack = 2

❏ Non–trump queen = 3

❏ Non–trump king = 4

❏ Non–trump ace = 5

❏ Any trump card = Non–trump value + 1

You should include the following methods:

❏ a method returning the trump suit, by name

❏ a method printing the whole deck of cards, suit by suit, with the value for each card

❏ a method taking a *String* as a parameter representing a suit, and returning the total value of the cards of that suit

90. Write a class (and a client class to test it) that encapsulates a tic-tac-toe board. A tic-tac-toe board looks like a table of three rows and three columns partially or completely filled with the characters X and O. At any point, a cell of that table could be empty or could contain an X or an O. You should have one instance variable, a two-dimensional array of values representing the tic-tac-toe board.

    Your default constructor should instantiate the array so that it represents an empty board.

    You should include the following methods:

    ❏ a method, returning a *boolean*, simulating a play with three parameters as follows: If the first parameter is *true*, then X is playing; otherwise, O is playing. The other two parameters represent what cell on the board is being played. If the play is legal, that is, the cell is a legal cell on the board and is empty, then the method should update the array and return *true*; otherwise, the array should not be updated and the method should return *false*.

    ❏ a method returning how many valid plays have been made so far.

    ❏ a method checking if a player has won based on the contents of the board; this method takes no parameter. It returns X if the "X player" has won, O if the "O player" has won, T if the game was a tie. A player wins if he or she has placed an X (or an O) in all cells in a row, all cells in a column, or all cells in one of the two diagonals.

91. Modify the *BookStore* and *BookSearchEngine* classes from the chapter.

    You should include the following additional methods and test them:

    ❏ a method returning the book with the lowest price in the library

    ❏ a method searching the library for *Books* of a given author and returning an *ArrayList* of such *Books*

    ❏ a method returning an *ArrayList* of *Books* whose price is less than a given number

92. Write a *Garage* class (and a client class to test it) with one instance variable: an *ArrayList* of *Autos* (you can use the *Auto* class from Chapter 7).

    You should include the following methods:

    ❑ a method returning the average number of miles of all cars in the garage

    ❑ a method returning "full" if the garage has 100 cars or more, "below minimum" if the garage has fewer than 25 cars, and "normal load" if the garage has between 25 and 100 cars in it

    ❑ a method returning the total number of gallons of gas used by all cars in the garage.

93. Write a *ComputerPart* class and a *ComputerKit* class (and a client class to test them).

    The *ComputerPart* class has two instance variables: a *String* representing an item (for instance, "cpu" or "disk drive"), and a *double* representing the price of that item. The *ComputerKit* class has just one instance variable: an *ArrayList* of *ComputerPart* objects (they make up a computer) representing the list of parts for the computer kit.

    You should include the following methods:

    ❑ a method returning "expensive" if the total of the prices of the *ComputerPart* objects is greater than 1,000, "cheap" if it is less than 250, "normal" if it is between 250 and 1,000

    ❑ a method returning *true* if a certain item is included in the list of parts; *false* otherwise

    ❑ a method returning how many times a particular item (for instance, "cpu," or "memory") is found in the list of parts.

9.10.8 Technical Writing

94. A two-dimensional array can have a different number of columns in every row. Do you see that as an advantage or a disadvantage? Discuss.

95. Discuss the pros and cons of using an array vs. using an *ArrayList*.

9.10.9   Group Project (for a group of 1, 2, or 3 students)

96. Design and code a program including the following classes, as well as a client class to test all the methods coded:

    A *Passenger* class, encapsulating a passenger. A passenger has two attributes: a name, and a class of service, which will be 1 or 2.

    A *Train* class, encapsulating a train of passengers: a train of passengers has one attribute, a list of passengers, which must be represented with an *ArrayList*. Your constructor will build the list of passengers by reading data from a file called *passengers.txt*. You can assume that *passengers.txt* has the following format:

    ```
    <name1>   <class1>
    <name2>   <class2>
    ...
    ```

    For instance, the file could contain:

James	1
Ben	2
Suri	1
Sarah	1
Jane	2

    ...

    You should include the following methods in your *Train* class:

    ❑ a method returning the percentage of passengers traveling in first class

    ❑ a method taking two parameters representing the price of traveling in first and second class and returning the total revenue for the train

    ❑ a method checking if a certain person is on the train; if he/she is, the method returns *true*; otherwise, it returns *false*.

CHAPTER 10

Object-Oriented Programming, Part 3: Inheritance, Polymorphism, and Interfaces

CHAPTER CONTENTS

Introduction

One of the most common ways to reuse a class is through inheritance. Inheritance helps us to organize related classes into **hierarchies**, or ordered levels of functionality. To set up a hierarchy, we begin by defining a class that contains methods and fields (instance variables and class variables) that are common to all classes in the hierarchy. Then we define new classes at the next lower level of the hierarchy, which inherit the behavior and fields of the original class. In the new classes, we define additional fields and more specific methods. The original class is called the **superclass**, and the new classes that inherit from the superclass are called **subclasses**. Some OOP developers call a superclass the **base class** and call a subclass the **derived class**.

As in life, a superclass (parent) can have multiple subclasses (children), and each subclass can be a superclass (parent) of other subclasses (children) and so on. Thus, a class can be both a subclass (child) and a superclass (parent). In contrast to life, however, Java subclasses inherit directly from only one superclass.

A subclass can add fields and methods, some of which may **override**, or hide, a field or method inherited from a superclass.

Let's look at an example. To represent a hierarchy of vehicle types, we define a *Vehicle* class as a superclass. We then define an *Automobile* class that inherits from *Vehicle*. We also define a *Truck* class, which also inherits from *Vehicle*. We further refine our classes by defining a *Pickup* class and a *TractorTrailer* class, both of which inherit from the *Truck* class. Figure 10.1 depicts our hierarchy using a UML (Unified Modeling Language) diagram. Arrows pointing from a subclass to a superclass indicate that the subclass refers to the superclass for some of its methods and fields. The boxes below the class name are available for specifying instance variables and methods for each class. For simplicity, we will leave those boxes blank.

The Java class library contains many class hierarchies. At the root of all Java class hierarchies is the *Object* class, the superclass for all classes. Thus, all classes inherit from the *Object* class.

The most important advantage to inheritance is that in a hierarchy of classes, we write the common code only once. After the common code has been tested, we can reuse it with confidence by inheriting it into the subclasses. And when that common code needs revision, we need to revise the code in only one place.

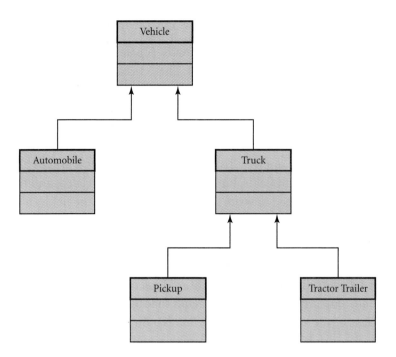

Figure 10.1
Vehicle **Class Hierarchy**

10.1   Inheritance

The syntax for defining a subclass class that inherits from another class is to add an *extends* clause in the class header:

```
accessModifier class SubclassName extends SuperclassName
{
    // class definition
}
```

The *extends* keyword specifies that the subclass inherits members of the superclass. That means that the subclass begins with a set of predefined methods and fields inherited from its hierarchy of superclasses.

Let's look at an example of inheritance that we've already used. We've used the *extends* keyword whenever we wrote an applet. For example, we defined our rolling ball applet in Chapter 6 as:

```
public class RollABall extends JApplet
```

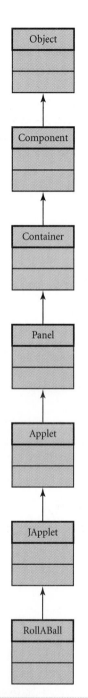

Figure 10.2

The *RollABall* Class Hierarchy

This means that the *RollABall* class inherits from the *JApplet* class.

Because our *RollABall* class extends *JApplet*, it inherits more than 275 methods and more than 15 fields. That's because the *JApplet* class is a subclass of *Applet,* which is a subclass of *Panel*, which is a subclass of *Container*, which is a subclass of *Component*, which is a subclass of *Object*. The *RollABall* class hierarchy is shown in Figure 10.2. All along the hierarchy, the subclasses inherit methods and fields, all of which become available to our applets. True, not every applet has a use for all the inherited methods and fields, but they are available if needed, and the benefit is that we don't need to write the methods or define the fields in our applets. Thus, we can build applets with a minimum of effort.

As you can see from Figure 10.2, our *RollABall* class has six superclasses. The class that a subclass refers to in the *extends* clause of the class definition is called its **direct superclass**. Thus, *JApplet* is the direct superclass of *RollABall*. Similarly, the class that *extends* the superclass is called the **direct subclass** of the superclass, so *RollABall* is a direct subclass of the *JApplet* class. A class can have multiple direct subclasses, but only one direct superclass.

10.2   Inheritance Design

We say that an "is a" relationship exists between a subclass and a superclass; that is, a subclass object "is a" superclass object. For example, we could define a student class hierarchy with a *Student* superclass and derive a *GraduateStudent* subclass. A graduate student "is a" student, but actually a special type of student. We could also define an employee class hierarchy with an *Employee* superclass and derive *Faculty* and *Staff* subclasses, because faculty and staff are both special types of employees.

To design classes for inheritance, our superclass should define fields and methods that will be common to all classes in the hierarchy. Each subclass will provide specialization by adding methods and fields. Where appropriate, subclasses can also provide new versions of inherited methods, which is called **overriding methods**.

Let's build a bank account class hierarchy. We start by defining a generic *BankAccount* superclass. The *BankAccount* class will contain the fields and methods that are common to all bank accounts. Then we will define a *CheckingAccount* class that inherits from the *BankAccount* class. The

CheckingAccount class will add instance variables and methods that specifically support checking accounts. Our class hierarchy is shown in Figure 10.3.

10.2.1   Inherited Members of a Class

As shown in Example 10.1, our *BankAccount* class has two instance variables, the *balance*, which is a *double* (line 11), and a constant *DecimalFormat* object that we will use for formatting the *balance* as money (lines 9–10). We provide two constructors. The default constructor (lines 13–19) sets the *balance* instance variable to 0.0. The overloaded constructor (lines 21–27) takes a starting balance and passes that parameter to the *deposit* method (lines 37–47), which adds any non-negative starting balance to the *balance*. If the starting balance is less than 0.0, the *deposit* method prints an error message and leaves *balance* unchanged.

The *withdraw* method (lines 49–61) validates that the *amount* parameter is not less than 0.0 and is not greater than the *balance*. If *amount* is valid, the *withdraw* method subtracts *amount* from *balance*; otherwise, it prints an error message.

Other methods of the *BankAccount* class include the *balance* accessor (lines 29–35) and the *toString* method (lines 63–69), which uses the *DecimalFormat* object, *MONEY*, to return the balance formatted as money.

SOFTWARE ENGINEERING TIP

The superclasses in a class hierarchy should contain fields and methods common to all subclasses. The subclasses should add specialized fields and methods.

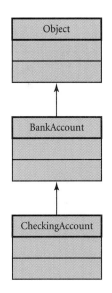

Figure 10.3

The *BankAccount* Class Hierarchy

```
 1 /**    BankAccount class, version 1
 2 *      Anderson, Franceschi
 3 *      Represents a generic bank account
 4 */
 5 import java.text.DecimalFormat;
 6
 7 public class BankAccount
 8 {
 9    public final DecimalFormat MONEY
10                   = new DecimalFormat( "$#,##0.00" );
11    private double balance;
12
13    /** Default constructor
14     *    sets balance to 0.0
15     */
16    public BankAccount( )
17    {
18      balance = 0.0;
19    }
20
```

```
21    /** Overloaded constructor
22    *    @param startBalance  beginning balance
23    */
24    public BankAccount( double startBalance )
25    {
26      deposit( startBalance );
27    }
28
29    /** Accessor for balance
30    *    @return  current account balance
31    */
32    public double getBalance( )
33    {
34      return balance;
35    }
36
37    /** Deposit amount to account
38    *    @param amount  amount to deposit;
39    *                   amount must be >= 0.0
40    */
41    public void deposit( double amount )
42    {
43      if ( amount >= 0.0 )
44        balance += amount;
45      else
46        System.err.println( "Deposit amount must be positive." );
47    }
48
49    /** withdraw amount from account
50    *    @param amount   amount to withdraw;
51    *                    amount must be >= 0.0
52    *                    amount must be <= balance
53    */
54    public void withdraw( double amount )
55    {
56      if (  amount >= 0.0 && amount <= balance )
57        balance -= amount;
58      else
59        System.err.println( "Withdrawal amount must be positive "
60                            + "and cannot be greater than balance" );
61    }
62
63    /** toString
64    *    @return  the balance formatted as money
65    */
```

```
66   public String toString( )
67   {
68      return ( "balance is " + MONEY.format( balance ) );
69   }
70 }
```

EXAMPLE 10.1   *BankAccount* class, Version 1

Now we can derive our *CheckingAccount* subclass. Example 10.2 shows version 1 of our *CheckingAccount* class. For this initial version, we simply define the *CheckingAccount* class as extending *BankAccount* (line 5). The body of our class is empty for now, so we can demonstrate the fields and methods that a subclass inherits from its superclass.

```
1 /* CheckingAccount class, version 1
2    Anderson, Franceschi
3 */
4
5 public class CheckingAccount extends BankAccount
6 { }
```

EXAMPLE 10.2   The *CheckingAccount* Class, Version 1

When a class *extends* a superclass, all the *public* fields and methods of the superclass (excluding constructors) are inherited. That means that the *CheckingAccount* class inherits the *MONEY* instance variable and the *getBalance, deposit, withdraw,* and *toString* methods from the *BankAccount* class. An inherited field is directly accessible from the subclass, and an inherited method can be called by the other methods of the subclass. In addition, *public* inherited methods can be called by a client application using a subclass object reference.

Any fields and methods that are declared *private* are not inherited, and therefore are not directly accessible by the subclass. Nevertheless, the *private* fields and methods are still part of the subclass object. Remember that a *CheckingAccount* object "is a" *BankAccount* object, so a *CheckingAccount* object has a *balance* instance variable. However, the *balance* is declared to be *private* in the *BankAccount* class, so the *CheckingAccount* methods cannot directly access the *balance*. The *CheckingAccount* methods must call the accessor and mutator methods of the *BankAccount* class to access or change the value of *balance*.

Calling methods to retrieve and change values of an instance variable may seem a little tedious, but it enforces encapsulation. Allowing the *Checking-*

Account class to set the value of *balance* directly would complicate maintenance of the program. The *CheckingAccount* class would need to be responsible for maintaining a valid value for *balance*, which means that the *CheckingAccount* class would need to know all the validation rules for *balance* that the *BankAccount* class enforces. If these rules change, then the *CheckingAccount* class would also need to change. As long as the *BankAccount* class ensures the validity of *balance*, there is no reason for the *CheckingAccount* class to duplicate that code.

Java provides the **protected** access modifier so that fields and methods can be inherited by subclasses (like *public* fields and methods), while still being hidden from client classes (like *private* fields and methods). In addition, any class in the same package as the superclass can directly access a *protected* field, even if that class is not a subclass. Because more than one class can directly access a *protected* field, *protected* access compromises encapsulation and complicates maintenance of a program. For that reason, we prefer to use *private*, rather than *protected*, for our instance variables. We will discuss the difference between *private* and *protected* in greater detail later in the chapter.

Table 10.1 summarizes the fields and methods that are inherited by a subclass. We will add to this table as we explain more about inheritance.

Example 10.3 shows a client for the *CheckingAccount* class. In line 9, we instantiate an object of the *CheckingAccount* class. After instantiation, the *c1* object has two fields: *balance* and *MONEY*, and it has four methods: *getBalance*, *deposit*, *withdraw*, and *toString*.

TABLE 10.1   Inheritance Rules

Superclass Members	Inherited by Subclass?	Directly Accessible by Subclass?	Directly Accessible by Client of Subclass?
public fields	yes	yes, by using field name	yes
public methods	yes	yes, by calling method from other subclass methods	yes
protected fields	yes	yes, by using field name	no, must use accessors and mutators
protected methods	yes	yes, by calling method from subclass methods	no
private fields	no	no, must use accessors and mutators	no, must use accessors and mutators
private methods	no	no	no

Figure 10.4
Output from *Checking-AccountClient*, **Version 1**

We illustrate this by using the *c1* object reference to call the *deposit* method in line 12 and the *withdraw* method in line 15, and to call the *toString* method implicitly in lines 13 and 16. Figure 10.4 shows the output from this program.

```
 1 /* CheckingAccount Client, version 1
 2    Anderson, Franceschi
 3 */
 4
 5 public class CheckingAccountClient
 6 {
 7   public static void main( String [ ] args )
 8   {
 9     CheckingAccount c1 = new CheckingAccount( );
10     System.out.println( "New checking account: " + c1 );
11
12     c1.deposit( 350.75 );
13     System.out.println( "\nAfter depositing $350.75: " + c1 );
14
15     c1.withdraw( 200.25 );
16     System.out.println( "\nAfter withdrawing $200.25: " + c1 );
17   }
18 }
```

EXAMPLE 10.3   *CheckingAccount* Client, Version 1

10.2.2   Subclass Constructors

Although constructors are *public*, they are not inherited by subclasses. However, to initialize the *private* instance variables of the superclass, a subclass constructor can call a superclass constructor either implicitly or explicitly.

When a class extends another class, the default constructor of the subclass automatically calls the default constructor of the superclass. This is called **implicit** invocation. Athough we did not code any constructors in our

CheckingAccount class in Example 10.2, we were able to instantiate a *CheckingAccount* object (with a 0.0 *balance*) because the Java compiler provided a default constructor for the *CheckingAccount* class, which implicitly called the default constructor of the *BankAccount* class.

To **explicitly** call the constructor of the direct superclass, the subclass constructor uses the following syntax:

```
super( argument list );
```

Thus, if we want to instantiate a *CheckingAccount* object with a starting balance other than 0.0, we need to provide an overloaded constructor for the *CheckingAccount* class. That constructor will take the starting balance as a parameter and pass that starting balance to the overloaded constructor in the *BankAccount* class.

This call to the direct superclass constructor, if used, must be the first statement in the subclass constructor. Otherwise, the following compiler error is generated:

```
call to super must be first statement in constructor
```

Example 10.4 shows version 2 of the *BankAccount* class, which for simplicity, and to help us focus on constructors, has only a default and overloaded constructor and the *toString* method. To illustrate the order in which the constructors execute, we print a message in each constructor (lines 21 and 33), indicating that it has been called.

```
 1 /**    BankAccount class, version 2
 2 *      Constructors and toString method only
 3 *      Anderson, Franceschi
 4 *      Represents a generic bank account
 5 */
 6
 7 import java.text.DecimalFormat;
 8
 9 public class BankAccount
10 {
11     public final DecimalFormat MONEY
12                 = new DecimalFormat( "$#,##0.00" );
13     private double balance;
14
15     /** Default constructor
16     *    sets balance to 0.0
17     */
18     public BankAccount( )
```

```
19    {
20       balance = 0.0;
21       System.out.println( "In BankAccount default constructor" );
22    }
23
24    /** Overloaded constructor
25     *    @param startBalance   beginning balance
26     */
27    public BankAccount( double startBalance )
28    {
29       if ( balance >= 0.0 )
30          balance = startBalance;
31       else
32          balance = 0.0;
33       System.out.println( "In BankAccount overloaded constructor" );
34    }
35
36    /** toString
37     *    @return   the balance formatted as money
38     */
39    public String toString( )
40    {
41       return ( "balance is " + MONEY.format( balance ) );
42    }
43 }
```

EXAMPLE 10.4   *BankAccount*, Version 2

Example 10.5 shows version 2 of the *CheckingAccount* class, which has both a default constructor and an overloaded constructor. Again, we have inserted messages (lines 13–14 and 24–25) to indicate when a constructor is called.

```
 1 /* CheckingAccount class, version 2
 2    Anderson, Franceschi
 3 */
 4
 5 public class CheckingAccount extends BankAccount
 6 {
 7    /** default constructor
 8     *    explicitly calls the BankAccount default constructor
 9     */
10    public CheckingAccount( )
11    {
```

```
12          super( ); // optional, call BankAccount constructor
13          System.out.println( "In CheckingAccount "
14                                  + "default constructor" );
15      }
16
17      /** overloaded constructor
18       *    calls BankAccount overloaded constructor
19       *    @param  startBalance  starting balance
20       */
21      public CheckingAccount( double startBalance )
22      {
23          super( startBalance ); // call BankAccount constructor
24          System.out.println( "In CheckingAccount "
25                                  + "overloaded constructor" );
26      }
27 }
```

EXAMPLE 10.5   *CheckingAccount* Class, Version 2

In the *SavingsAccount* default constructor, we explicitly call the default constructor of the *BankAccount* class (line 12). This statement is optional; without it, the *BankAccount* default constructor is still called implicitly.

In the *SavingsAccount* overloaded constructor, we pass the *startBalance* parameter to the *BankAccount* constructor (line 23) to initialize the *balance* instance variable. Because *balance* has *private* access in the *BankAccount* class, our *SavingsAccount* class cannot access *balance* directly. If we attempted to initialize the *balance* directly using the following statement:

```
balance = startBalance;
```

the compiler would generate the following error:

```
balance has private access in BankAccount
```

Example 10.6 shows version 2 of our *CheckingAccount* client. On line 10, we instantiate a *CheckingAccount* object using the default constructor and print the balance by implicitly calling the *toString* method on line 11. Then on line 14, we instantiate a second *CheckingAccount* object with a starting balance of $100.00. Again we verify the result by printing the balance (line 15).

```
1 /* CheckingAccount Client, version 2
2     Anderson, Franceschi
3 */
4
```

```
 5 public class CheckingAccountClient
 6 {
 7   public static void main( String [ ] args )
 8   {
 9     // use default constructor
10     CheckingAccount c1 = new CheckingAccount( );
11     System.out.println( "New checking account: " + c1 + "\n" );
12
13     // use overloaded constructor
14     CheckingAccount c2 = new CheckingAccount( 100.00 );
15     System.out.println( "New checking account: " + c2 );
16   }
17 }
```

EXAMPLE 10.6   *CheckingAccountClient*, Version 2

Figure 10.5 shows the output from this program. As you can see, when we construct the *c1* object, the *BankAccount* default constructor runs. When it finishes, we print a message indicating that the *CheckingAccount* default constructor is running. Similarly, when we construct the *c2* object, the *BankAccount* overloaded constructor runs, then we print a message from the *CheckingAccount* overloaded constructor.

Table 10.2 summarizes the inheritance rules for constructors.

Figure 10.5
Output from Example 10.6

TABLE 10.2   Inheritance Rules for Constructors

Superclass Members	Inherited by Subclass?	Directly Accessible by Subclass?	Directly Accessible by Client of Subclass Using a Subclass Reference?
constructors	no	yes, using super(arg list) in a subclass constructor	no

10.2.3   Adding Specialization to the Subclass

At this point, our *CheckingAccount* class provides no more functionality than the *BankAccount* class. But our purpose for defining a *CheckingAccount* class was to provide support for a specialized type of bank account. To add specialization to our *CheckingAccount* subclass, we define new fields and methods. For example, we can define a *monthlyFee* instance variable, as well as an accessor and mutator method for the monthly fee and a method to charge the monthly fee to the account.

Example 10.7 shows version 3 of the *CheckingAccount* class with the specialization added. This version *extends* the complete *BankAccount* class shown in Example 10.1. We added the *monthlyFee* instance variable on line 8, as well as a constant default value for the monthly fee (line 7). Our default constructor (lines 10–18) still calls the default constructor of the *BankAccount* class to initialize the *balance*, but it also initializes the *monthlyFee* to the default value.

Similarly, the overloaded constructor (lines 20–30) passes the *startBalance* parameter to the overloaded constructor of the *BankAccount* class and adds a *startMonthlyFee* parameter to accept an initial value for the *monthlyFee*, which it passes to the *setMonthlyFee* mutator method (lines 48–57).

The *applyMonthlyFee* method (lines 32–38), which charges the monthly fee to the checking account, calls the *withdraw* method inherited from the *BankAccount* class to access the *balance* instance variable, which is declared *private* in the *BankAccount* class.

```
 1  /* CheckingAccount class, version 3
 2     Anderson, Franceschi
 3  */
 4
 5  public class CheckingAccount extends BankAccount
 6  {
 7    public final double DEFAULT_FEE = 5.00;
 8    private double monthlyFee;
 9
10    /** default constructor
11     *    explicitly calls the BankAccount default constructor
12     *    set monthlyFee to default value
13     */
14    public CheckingAccount( )
15    {
```

```
16        super( ); // optional
17        monthlyFee = DEFAULT_FEE;
18     }
19
20     /** overloaded constructor
21      *  calls BankAccount overloaded constructor
22      *  @param  startBalance   starting balance
23      *  @param  startMonthlyFee starting monthly fee
24      */
25     public CheckingAccount( double startBalance,
26                             double startMonthlyFee )
27     {
28        super( startBalance ); // call BankAccount constructor
29        setMonthlyFee( startMonthlyFee );
30     }
31
32     /** applyMonthlyFee method
33      * charges the monthly fee to the account
34      */
35     public void applyMonthlyFee( )
36     {
37        withdraw( monthlyFee );
38     }
39
40     /** accessor method for monthlyFee
41      *  @return   monthlyFee
42      */
43     public double getMonthlyFee( )
44     {
45        return monthlyFee;
46     }
47
48     /** mutator method for monthlyFee
49      *  @param newMonthlyFee new value for monthlyFee
50      */
51     public void setMonthlyFee( double newMonthlyFee )
52     {
53        if ( monthlyFee >= 0.0 )
54           monthlyFee = newMonthlyFee;
55        else
56           System.err.println( "Monthly fee cannot be negative" );
57     }
58 }
```

EXAMPLE 10.7   *CheckingAccount*, Version 3

Figure 10.6

Output from *Checking-AccountClient,* **Version 3**

Example 10.8 shows version 4 of our client program, which instantiates a *CheckingAccount* object and charges the monthly fee. The output is shown in Figure 10.6.

```
1  /* CheckingAccount Client, version 3
2     Anderson, Franceschi
3  */
4
5  public class CheckingAccountClient
6  {
7    public static void main( String [ ] args )
8    {
9      CheckingAccount c3 = new CheckingAccount( 100.00, 7.50 );
10     System.out.println( "New checking account:\n"
11                          + c3.toString( )
12                          + "; monthly fee is "
13                          + c3.getMonthlyFee( ) );
14
15     c3.applyMonthlyFee( );  // charge the fee to the account
16     System.out.println( "\nAfter charging monthly fee:\n"
17                          + c3.toString( )
18                          + "; monthly fee is "
19                          + c3.getMonthlyFee( ) );
20   }
21 }
```

EXAMPLE 10.8   *CheckingAccountClient,* Version 3

10.2.4   Overriding Inherited Methods

When the methods our subclass inherits do not fulfill the functions we need, we can **override** the inherited methods by providing new versions of those methods. We have seen this feature in our applets. Whenever we wrote an *init* or *paint* method, we were overriding the corresponding method inherited from the *JApplet* class.

To override an inherited method, we provide a new method with the same header as the inherited method; that is, the new method must have the same name, the same number and type of parameters, and the same return type. Overriding a method makes the inherited version of the method invisible to the client of the subclass. We say that the overridden method is hidden from the client. When the client calls the method using a subclass object reference, the subclass version of the method is invoked.

Methods in a subclass can still access the inherited version of the method by preceding the method call with the *super* keyword, as in the following syntax:

```
super.methodName( argument list )
```

In our *CheckingAccount* class, we inherited the *toString* method from the *BankAccount* class. But this method returns only the *balance*. In Example 10.8, we needed to call the *CheckingAccount* method *getMonthlyFee* to print the value of *monthlyFee*. Furthermore, as Figure 10.6 shows, the *balance* value is formatted and the *monthlyFee* value is not. Instead, the *toString* method in the *CheckingAccount* class should return formatted versions of both the *balance* and the *monthlyFee*. We can accomplish this by overriding the inherited *toString* method.

Example 10.9 shows version 4 of the *CheckingAccount* class with the new *toString* method (lines 59–67). To format the *balance*, we call the *toString* method of the *BankAccount* class (line 65), then add the formatted value of *monthlyFee* to the *String* being returned. Notice that we didn't need to instantiate a new *DecimalFormat* object in order to format the *monthlyFee* instance variable. Because the *MONEY* object is declared to be *public* in the *BankAccount* class, we inherited the *MONEY* object, so we can simply call the *format* method using the *MONEY* object reference. An advantage to making the *MONEY* object *public* is that both the balance and the monthly fee will be printed using the same formatting rules. Another advantage is that if we want to change the formatting for printing the data, we need to make only one change: We redefine the value of the *MONEY* constant in the *BankAccount* class.

```
1  /* CheckingAccount class, version 4
2     Anderson, Franceschi
3  */
4
5  public class CheckingAccount extends BankAccount
6  {
```

```
 7     public final double DEFAULT_FEE = 5.00;
 8     private double monthlyFee;
 9
10     /** default constructor
11      *   explicitly calls the BankAccount default constructor
12      *   set monthlyFee to default value
13      */
14     public CheckingAccount( )
15     {
16        super( ); // call BankAccount constructor
17        monthlyFee = DEFAULT_FEE;
18     }
19
20     /** overloaded constructor
21      *   calls BankAccount overloaded constructor
22      *   @param  startBalance   starting balance
23      *   @param  startMonthlyFee starting monthly fee
24      */
25     public CheckingAccount( double startBalance,
26                             double startMonthlyFee )
27     {
28        super( startBalance ); // call BankAccount constructor
29        setMonthlyFee( startMonthlyFee );
30     }
31
32     /** applyMonthlyFee method
33      * charges the monthly fee to the account
34      */
35     public void applyMonthlyFee( )
36     {
37        withdraw( monthlyFee );
38     }
39
40      /** accessor method for monthlyFee
41       *  @return  monthlyFee
42       */
43      public double getMonthlyFee( )
44      {
45         return monthlyFee;
46      }
47
48     /** mutator method for monthlyFee
49      *  @param newMonthlyFee new value for monthlyFee
50      */
51     public void setMonthlyFee( double newMonthlyFee )
```

```
52      {
53        if ( monthlyFee >= 0.0 )
54           monthlyFee = newMonthlyFee;
55        else
56           System.err.println( "Monthly fee cannot be negative" );
57      }
58
59      /* toString method
60       *  @return String containing formatted balance and monthlyFee
61       *     invokes superclass toString to format balance
62       */
63      public String toString( )
64      {
65        return super.toString( )
66               + "; monthly fee is " + MONEY.format( monthlyFee );
67      }
68  }
```

EXAMPLE 10.9   *CheckingAccount* Class, Version 4

Example 10.10 shows version 4 of the *CheckingAccountClient* class. In this class, we again instantiate a *CheckingAccount* object with an initial balance of $100.00 and a monthly fee of $7.50 (line 9), then implicitly invoke the *toString* method to print the data of the object (line 10). This time, we invoke the *toString* method of the *CheckingAccount* class, which returns both the *balance* and *monthlyFee* values, formatted as money, as shown in Figure 10.7.

```
1 /* CheckingAccount Client, version 4
2     Anderson, Franceschi
3 */
4
5 public class CheckingAccountClient
6 {
7    public static void main( String [ ] args )
8    {
9      CheckingAccount c4 = new CheckingAccount( 100.00, 7.50 );
```

Figure 10.7

Output from *Checking-AccountClient*, Version 4

COMMON ERROR TRAP

Do not confuse overriding a method with overloading a method. A subclass overriding a method provides a new version of that method, which hides the superclass version. A client calling the method using a subclass object reference will invoke the subclass version. A class overloading a method provides a new version of that method, which varies in the number, and/or type of parameters. All *public* versions of overloaded methods are available to be called by the client of the class.

SOFTWARE ENGINEERING TIP

Methods that override inherited methods should explicitly call the direct superclass method whenever appropriate, in order to process inherited fields.

```
10        System.out.println( "New checking account:\n" + c4 );
11    }
12 }
```

EXAMPLE 10.10   *CheckingAccountClient*, Version 4

Table 10.3 summarizes the inheritance rules for inherited methods that have been overridden.

When you override a method, be sure that the method signature is identical to the inherited method. However, you can override an inherited method with a method that specifies a subclass object reference where the original method used a superclass reference. This is possible because a subclass object is a superclass object, so a subclass object reference can be substituted for any superclass object reference. If two methods of a class have the same name but different signatures (that is, if the number, order, or type of parameters is different), then the method is *overloaded*, not *overridden*.

For example, if in an applet, we were to write the *init* method with the following header:

```
public void init( int a )
```

then our *init* method has a different signature from the *init* method we inherited from the *JApplet* class, which does not take any parameters. In this case, we are overloading the *init* method, not overriding it. In other words, we are providing an additional version of the *init* method. The inherited version is still visible and available to be called. When the applet starts executing, the browser or applet viewer would call the *init* method of the *JApplet* class, not our *init* method.

Table 10.4 illustrates the differences between overriding *public* methods and overloading *public* methods.

TABLE 10.3   Inheritance Rules for Overridden Methods

Superclass Members	Inherited by Subclass?	Directly Accessible by Subclass?	Directly Accessible by Client of Subclass Using a Subclass Reference?
public or *protected* inherited methods that have been overridden in the subclass	no	yes, using `super.methodName( arg list )`	no

TABLE 10.4 Overriding vs. Overloading Methods

	Method Names	Argument Lists	Return Types	Directly Accessible by Subclass Client Using a Subclass Object Reference?
Overriding a *public* Method	identical	identical	identical	only the subclass version can be called
Overloading a *public* Method	identical	different in number or type of parameters	identical	all versions of the overloaded method can be called

Skill Practice
with these end-of-chapter questions

10.3   The *protected* Access Modifier

We have seen that the subclass does not inherit constructors or *private* members of the superclass. However, the superclass constructors are still available to be called from the subclass and the *private* fields of the super-class are implemented as fields of the subclass.

Although *private* fields preserve encapsulation, there is additional processing overhead involved with calling methods. Whenever a method is called, the JVM saves the return address and makes copies of the arguments. Then when a value-returning method completes, the JVM makes a copy of the return value available to the caller. The *protected* access modifier was designed to avoid this processing overhead and to facilitate coding by allowing the subclass to access any *protected* field without calling its accessor or mutator method.

Protected fields and methods also can be accessed directly by other classes in the same package, even if the classes are not within the same inheritance hierarchy.

To classes outside the package, a *protected* member of a class has the same restrictions as a *private* member. In other words, a class outside the package in which the *protected* member is declared may not call any *protected* methods and must access any *protected* fields through *public* accessor or mutator methods.

The *protected* access modifier has tradeoffs. As we mentioned, any fields declared as *protected* can be accessed directly by subclasses. Doing so, however, compromises encapsulation because multiple classes can set the value of an instance variable defined in another class.

Thus, maintaining classes that define or use *protected* members becomes more difficult. For example, we need to verify that any class that has access to the *protected* instance variable either does not set the variable's value, or if the class does change the value, that the new value is valid. Because of this added maintenance complexity, we recommend that *protected* access be used only when high performance is essential.

SOFTWARE ENGINEERING TIP

Unless high performance is a critical requirement, avoid using the *protected* access modifier because doing so compromises encapsulation and complicates the maintenance of a program. Where possible, call superclass methods to change the values of *protected* instance variables.

We also recommend that subclass methods avoid directly setting the value of a *protected* instance variable. Instead, wherever possible, call superclass methods when values of *protected* variables need to be changed.

To illustrate how *protected* access can be used in class hierarchies, let's look closely at our *CheckingAccount* class. We have been calling the *withdraw* method inherited from the *BankAccount* class to apply the monthly fee. However, the *withdraw* method leaves the *balance* unchanged if the withdrawal amount is greater than the balance. Thus, if the account does not have sufficient funds to charge the monthly fee, the bank does not get its money. We would like the *CheckingAccount* class to be able to charge the monthly fee to the account and let the balance become negative. When this happens, we will print a warning message that the account is overdrawn.

To accomplish this, we declare the *balance* instance variable to be *protected* instead of *private*. This allows us to directly access *balance* inside the *apply-*

MonthlyFee method of the *CheckingAccount* class, because *balance* is now inherited by *CheckingAccount*.

Example 10.11 shows the *BankAccount* class, version 3. The only change, compared to version 1 (Example 10.1), is that the *balance* instance variable is declared as *protected*, rather than *private* (line 11).

```java
 1 /**    BankAccount class, version 3
 2  *      Anderson, Franceschi
 3  *      Represents a generic bank account
 4  */
 5 import java.text.DecimalFormat;
 6
 7 public class BankAccount
 8 {
 9   public final DecimalFormat MONEY
10                    = new DecimalFormat( "$#,##0.00" );
11   protected double balance;
12
13   /** Default constructor
14    *   sets balance to 0.0
15    */
16   public BankAccount( )
17   {
18     balance = 0.0;
19   }
20
21   /** Overloaded constructor
22    *   @param startBalance  beginning balance
23    */
24   public BankAccount( double startBalance )
25   {
26     deposit( startBalance );
27   }
28
29   /** Accessor for balance
30    *   @return  current account balance
31    */
32   public double getBalance( )
33   {
34     return balance;
35   }
36
37   /** Deposit amount to account
```

```
38    *   @param amount   amount to deposit;
39    *                   amount must be >= 0.0
40    */
41   public void deposit( double amount )
42   {
43     if ( amount >= 0.0 )
44       balance += amount;
45     else
46       System.err.println( "Deposit amount must be positive." );
47   }
48
49   /** withdraw amount from account
50    *   @param amount   amount to withdraw;
51    *                   amount must be >= 0.0
52    *                   amount must be <= balance
53    */
54   public void withdraw( double amount )
55   {
56     if (   amount >= 0.0 && amount <= balance )
57       balance -= amount;
58     else
59       System.err.println( "Withdrawal amount must be positive "
60                           + "and cannot be greater than balance" );
61   }
62
63   /** toString
64    * @return  the balance formatted as money
65    */
66   public String toString( )
67   {
68     return ( "balance is " + MONEY.format( balance ) );
69   }
70 }
```

EXAMPLE 10.11   *BankAccount* Class, Version 3

Example 10.12 shows version 5 of the *CheckingAccount* class, which inherits from the *BankAccount* class in Example 10.11 that declares the *balance* as *protected*. The *CheckingAccount* class now inherits *balance*, and our *CheckingAccount* methods can access the *balance* variable directly. Nevertheless, in the default and overloaded constructors, we still call the superclass constructor to set the value of *balance* (lines 16 and 28). Otherwise, to avoid setting *balance* to an invalid initial value, we would need to know the validation rules for *balance* in *BankAccount* and unnecessarily duplicate that code.

Also, in the *toString* method (lines 61–69), we call the *toString* method of the *BankAccount* class. Again, we do this to be consistent with the superclass functionality and to avoid duplicating code in the *BankAccount* class.

In the *applyMonthlyFee* method (lines 32–40), however, we access *balance* directly. For this checking account, our bank will charge the monthly fee even if it results in a negative balance for the account, so we subtract *monthlyFee* from *balance*, which allows the balance to be negative, and if so, we print a warning. Notice that we change the value of *balance* directly instead of calling the *getBalance* and *withdraw* methods.

```
 1 /* CheckingAccount class, version 5
 2    Anderson, Franceschi
 3 */
 4
 5 public class CheckingAccount extends BankAccount
 6 {
 7    public final double DEFAULT_FEE = 5.00;
 8    private double monthlyFee;
 9
10    /** default constructor
11     *   explicitly calls the BankAccount default constructor
12     *   set monthlyFee to default value
13     */
14    public CheckingAccount( )
15    {
16      super( );      // call BankAccount constructor
17      monthlyFee = DEFAULT_FEE;
18    }
19
20    /** overloaded constructor
21     *  calls BankAccount overloaded constructor
22     *  @param  startBalance     starting balance
23     *  @param  startMonthlyFee starting monthly fee
24     */
25    public CheckingAccount( double startBalance,
26                            double startMonthlyFee )
27    {
28      super( startBalance );   // call BankAccount constructor
29      setMonthlyFee( startMonthlyFee );
30    }
```

```
31
32    /** applyMonthlyFee method
33     * charges the monthly fee to the account
34     */
35    public void applyMonthlyFee( )
36    {
37      balance -= monthlyFee;
38      if ( balance < 0.0 )
39        System.err.println( "Warning: account is overdrawn" );
40    }
41
42    /** accessor method for monthlyFee
43     *  @return   monthlyFee
44     */
45    public double getMonthlyFee( )
46    {
47      return monthlyFee;
48    }
49
50    /** mutator method for monthlyFee
51     *  @param newMonthlyFee new value for monthlyFee
52     */
53    public void setMonthlyFee( double newMonthlyFee )
54    {
55      if ( monthlyFee >= 0.0 )
56        monthlyFee = newMonthlyFee;
57      else
58        System.err.println( "Monthly fee cannot be negative" );
59    }
60
61    /* toString method
62     *  @return String containing formatted balance and monthlyFee
63     *     invokes superclass toString to format balance
64     */
65    public String toString( )
66    {
67      return super.toString( )
68            + "; monthly fee is " + MONEY.format( monthlyFee );
69    }
70 }
```

EXAMPLE 10.12   *CheckingAccount* Class, Version 5

Example 10.13 shows version 5 of the *CheckingAccountClient* class. In this class, we again instantiate a *CheckingAccount* object with an initial balance of $100.00 and a monthly fee of $7.50 (line 9). We then call *withdraw* (line 12), so that the resulting balance is less than the monthly fee. Next we call the *applyMonthlyFee* method (line 16). When we print the state of the object in line 17, the *balance* is negative. The output of Example 10.13 is shown in Figure 10.8.

```
1 /* CheckingAccount Client, version 5
2     Anderson, Franceschi
3 */
4
5 public class CheckingAccountClient
6 {
7    public static void main( String [ ] args )
8    {
9      CheckingAccount c5 = new CheckingAccount( 100.00, 7.50 );
10     System.out.println( "New checking account:\n" + c5 );
11
12     c5.withdraw( 95 );
13     System.out.println( "\nAfter withdrawing $95:\n" + c5 );
14
15     System.out.println( "\nApplying the monthly fee:" );
16     c5.applyMonthlyFee( );
17     System.out.println( "\nAfter charging monthly fee:\n" + c5 );
18    }
19 }
```

EXAMPLE 10.13　*CheckingAccountClient* **Class, Version 5**

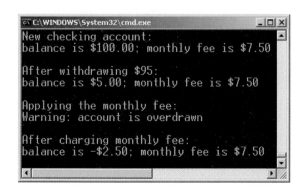

Figure 10.8
Output from *Checking-AccountClient*, Version 5

TABLE 10.5   Inheritance Rules

Superclass Members	Inherited by Subclass?	Directly Accessible by Subclass?	Directly Accessible by Client of Subclass?
public fields	yes	yes, by using field name	yes
public methods	yes	yes, by calling method from other subclass methods	yes, by calling method using a subclass object reference
protected fields	yes	yes, by using field name	no, must use accessors and mutators
protected methods	yes	yes, by calling method from subclass methods	no
private fields	no	no, must use accessors and mutators	no, must use accessors and mutators
private methods	no	no	no
constructors	no	yes, using `super( arg list )` in a subclass constructor	no
public or *protected* inherited methods that have been overridden in the subclass	no	yes, using `super.methodName( arg list )`	no

Table 10.5 compiles all the inheritance rules we have discussed.

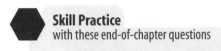

Skill Practice
with these end-of-chapter questions

10.10.2   Reading and Understanding Code

Questions 12,13,14,15,16,17,18,19,20

CODE IN ACTION

In the Chapter 10 folder on the CD-ROM included with this book, you will find a Shockwave movie showing a step-by-step illustration of how inheritance can be used in a program. Just double-click on *Inheritance.html* to start the movie.

10.4 Programming Activity 1: Using Inheritance

For this Programming Activity, you will create the *SavingsAccount* class, which inherits directly from the *BankAccount* class. The *SavingsAccount* class is similar to the *CheckingAccount* class in that both classes inherit from *BankAccount*. Figure 10.9 shows the resulting hierarchy.

The *SavingsAccount* class inherits from the version of the *BankAccount* class in which the *balance* is declared to be *private*. The *SavingsAccount* subclass adds an annual *interestRate* instance variable, as well as supporting methods to access, change, and apply the interest rate to the account balance.

Instructions

Copy the source files in the Programming Activity 1 directory for this chapter to a directory on your computer. Load the *SavingsAccount.java* source

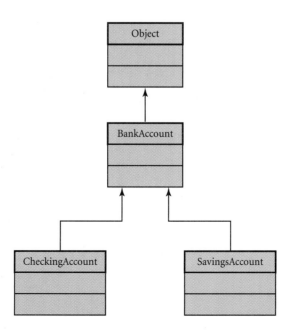

Figure 10.9
Bank Account Hierarchy

file and search for five asterisks in a row (*****). This will position you to the six locations in the file where you will add code to complete the *SavingsAccount* class. The *SavingsAccount.java* file is shown in Example 10.14.

```
1 /* SavingsAccount class
2    Anderson, Franceschi
3 */
4
5 import java.text.NumberFormat;
6
7 // 1. ***** indicate that SavingsAccount inherits
8 //          from BankAccount
9 public class SavingsAccount
10 {
11    public final double DEFAULT_RATE = .03;
12    // 2. ****** define the private interestRate instance variable
13    // interestRate, a double, represents an annual rate
14
15    // 3. ***** write the default constructor
16    /** default constructor
17     *    explicitly call the BankAccount default constructor
18     *    set interestRate to default value DEFAULT_RATE
19     *    print a message to System.out indicating that
20     *     constructor is called
21     */
22
23    // 4. ***** write the overloaded constructor
24    /** overloaded constructor
25     *    explicitly call BankAccount overloaded constructor
26     *    call setInterestRate method, passing startInterestRate
27     *    print a message to System.out indicating that
28     *     constructor is called
29     *  @param  startBalance      starting balance
30     *  @param  startInterestRate starting interest rate
31     */
32
33
34    // 5. ****** write this method:
35    /** applyInterest method, no parameters, void return value
36     *  call the deposit method, passing a month's worth of interest
36     *  remember that interestRate instance variable is annual rate
37     */
38
39
```

```
40    /** accessor method for interestRate
41     *  @return  interestRate
42     */
43    public double getInterestRate( )
44    {
45      return interestRate;
46    }
47
48    /** mutator method for interestRate
49     *  @param  newInterestRate new value for interestRate
50     *            newInterestRate must be >= 0.0
51     *              if not, print an error message
52     */
53    public void setInterestRate( double newInterestRate )
54    {
55      if ( interestRate >= 0.0 )
56        interestRate = newInterestRate;
57      else
58        System.err.println( "Interest rate cannot be negative" );
59    }
60
61    // 6. *****  write this method
62    /* toString method
63     *  @return String containing formatted balance and interestRate
64     *      invokes superclass toString to format balance
65     *      formats interestRate as percent using a NumberFormat object
66     *      To create a NumberFormat object for formatting percentages
67     *      use the getPercentInstance method in the NumberFormat class,
68     *      which has this API:
69     *          static NumberFormat getPercentInstance( )
70     */
71
72 }
```

EXAMPLE 10.14   *SavingsAccount.java*

When you have completed the six tasks, load, compile, and run the Teller application (*Teller.java*), which you will use to test your *SavingsAccount* class. When the Teller application begins, you will be prompted with a dialog box for a starting balance. If you press "Enter" or the "OK" button without entering a balance, the Teller application will use the default constructor to instantiate a *SavingsAccount* object. If you enter a starting balance, the Teller application will prompt you for an interest rate and will

Figure 10.10

The Teller Window

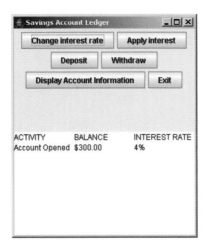

instantiate a *SavingsAccount* object using the overloaded constructor. Once the *SavingsAccount* object has been instantiated, the Teller application will open the window shown in Figure 10.10, which provides buttons you can use to call the *SavingsAccount* methods to test your code.

Below the buttons is a ledger that displays the current state of the savings account. As you click on the various buttons, the ledger will display the operation performed and the values of the balance and the interest rate when that operation is complete.

The operations performed by each button are already coded for you and are the following:

- *Change Interest Rate*—prompts for a new interest rate and calls your *setInterestRate* method

- *Apply Interest*—calls your *applyInterest* method

- *Deposit*—prompts for the deposit amount and calls the *deposit* method inherited from *BankAccount*

- *Withdraw*—prompts for the withdrawal amount and calls the *withdraw* method inherited from *BankAccount*

- *Display Account Information*—calls your *toString* method and displays the result in a dialog box

- *Exit*—exits the program.

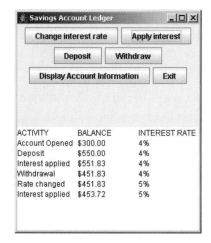

Figure 10.11
Sample Teller Window After Performing Several Operations

Figure 10.11 shows the Teller window after several operations have been performed.

1. Explain why the Teller application can call the *withdraw* and *deposit* methods using a *SavingsAccount* object reference, even though we did not define these methods.

2. Explain why your *applyInterest* method in the *SavingsAccount* class needs to call the *deposit* method of the *BankAccount* class.

10.5   *Abstract* Classes and Methods

In our Bank Account hierarchy, we could instantiate *BankAccount* objects, *CheckingAccount* objects, and *SavingsAccount* objects. In some situations, however, we will design a class hierarchy where one or more classes at the top of the hierarchy specify patterns for methods that subclasses in the hierarchy must implement. The superclasses do not implement these methods, however. In these situations, we do not intend that these superclasses will be used to instantiate objects, and we define the superclasses as *abstract*.

An *abstract* **class** is a class that is not completely implemented. Usually, an *abstract* class contains at least one *abstract* **method**, that is, a method that specifies an API that subclasses should implement, but does not provide an implementation for the method.

Because an *abstract* class is not complete, it cannot be used to instantiate objects. An *abstract* class can be extended, however, so that its subclasses can complete the implementation of the *abstract* methods and can be instantiated.

A class is declared to be *abstract* by including the *abstract* keyword in the class header, as shown in the following syntax:

`accessModifier` `abstract` `class` `ClassName`

An *abstract* method is defined by including the *abstract* keyword in the method header and by using a semicolon to indicate that there is no code for the method, as shown in the following syntax:

`accessModifier` `abstract` `returnType methodName( argument list );`

Note that we do not include opening and closing curly braces for the method body—just a semicolon to indicate that the *abstract* method does not have a body.

For example, to draw figures, we can set up the hierarchy shown in Figure 10.12. The root superclass is an abstract *Figure* class, and we derive two subclasses: *Circle* and *Square*. In the UML diagram, the name of the *Figure* class is set in italics to indicate that it is an *abstract* class.

Figure 10.12
The *Figure* Hierarchy

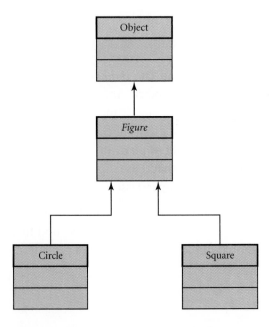

All figures will have an (*x, y*) coordinate and a color, so the *Figure* class defines three fields: two *ints, x* and *y*, and a *Color* object named *color*.

We want all classes in the hierarchy to provide a *draw* method to render the figure; however, the *Figure* class has nothing but a point to draw, so its *draw* method has nothing to do. Thus, we will not provide an implementation of the *draw* method in the *Figure* class; instead, we will define the *draw* method as an *abstract* method.

Let's look at the code for the *Figure* hierarchy in detail. Example 10.15 shows the *abstract Figure* class. We define the class as *abstract* in the class header (line 7). The constructors (lines 13–22 and lines 24–37) instantiate the *x* and *y* values and the *Color* object that all figures will have in common. The *Figure* class also provides accessor and mutator methods for its instance variables. The *abstract draw* method (lines 88–91) provides the API for the *draw* method, but no implementation—just a semicolon. The *Circle* and *Square* subclasses of the *Figure* class will provide appropriate implementations of the *draw* method.

```
 1 /** abstract Figure superclass for drawing shapes
 2 *    Anderson, Franceschi
 3 */
 4 import java.awt.Graphics;
 5 import java.awt.Color;
 6
 7 public abstract class Figure
 8 {
 9   private int x;
10   private int y;
11   private Color color;
12
13   /** default constructor
14    *    sets x and y to 0
15    *    sets color to black
16    */
17   public Figure( )
18   {
19     x = 0;
20     y = 0;
21     color = Color.BLACK;
22   }
23
24   /** overloaded constructor
25    *    sets x to startX
```

```
26   *    sets y to startY
27   *    sets the color to startColor
28   *    @param  startX       starting x pixel for figure
29   *    @param  startY       starting y pixel for figure
30   *    @param  startColor   figure color
31   */
32   public Figure( int startX, int startY, Color startColor )
33   {
34     x = startX;
35     y = startY;
36     color = startColor;
37   }
38
39   /** accessor method for color
40    *   @return current figure color
41    */
42   public Color getColor( )
43   {
44     Color tempColor = color;
45     return tempColor;
46   }
47
48   /** mutator method for color
49    *   @param newColor  new color for figure
50    */
51   public void setColor( Color newColor )
52   {
53     color = newColor;
54   }
55
56   /** accessor method for x
57    *   @return current x value
58    */
59   public int getX( )
60   {
61     return x;
62   }
63
64   /** mutator method for x
65    *   @param newX  new value for x
66    */
67   public void setX( int newX )
68   {
69     x = newX;
70   }
```

```
71
72   /** accessor method for y
73    *    @return current y value
74    */
75   public int getY( )
76   {
77      return y;
78   }
79
80   /** mutator method for y
81    *    @param newY new y value
82    */
83   public void setY( int newY )
84   {
85      y = newY;
86   }
87
88   /** abstract draw method
89    *    @param Graphics context for drawing figure
90    */
91   public abstract void draw( Graphics g );
92 }
```

EXAMPLE 10.15   The *abstract Figure* Class

When a subclass inherits from an *abstract* class, it can provide implementations for any, all, or none of the *abstract* methods. If the subclass does not completely implement all the *abstract* methods of the superclass, then the subclass must also be declared *abstract*. If, however, the subclass implements all the *abstract* methods in the superclass, and the subclass is not declared *abstract*, then the class is not *abstract* and we can instantiate objects of that subclass.

Example 10.16 shows the *Circle* class, which inherits from the *Figure* class and adds a *radius* instance variable. In the overloaded constructor, we pass the *startX*, *startY*, and *startColor* parameters to the constructor of the *Figure* class (line 34). On lines 54–63, the *Circle* class implements the *draw* method. We get the (x, y) coordinate and the color for the circle by calling the accessor methods of the *Figure* class because the *x*, *y*, and *color* instance variables are declared *private*.

```
1 /* Circle class
2 *   inherits from abstract Figure class
3 *   Anderson, Franceschi
```

COMMON ERROR TRAP

Do not include opening and closing curly braces in the definition of an *abstract* method. Including them would mean that the method is implemented, but does nothing. Instead, indicate an unimplemented method by using a semicolon.

COMMON ERROR TRAP

Attempting to instantiate an object of an *abstract* class will generate the following compiler error:

```
className is
abstract; cannot
be instantiated
```

where *className* is the name of the *abstract* class.

```java
 4 */
 5
 6 import java.awt.Graphics;
 7 import java.awt.Color;
 8
 9 public class Circle extends Figure
10 {
11    private int radius;
12
13    /** default constructor
14    *    calls default constructor of Figure class
15    *    sets radius to 0
16    */
17    public Circle( )
18    {
19       super( );
20       radius = 0;
21    }
22
23    /** overloaded constructor
24    *    sends startX, startY, startColor to Figure constructor
25    *    sends startRadius to setRadius method
26    *    @param startX       starting x pixel
27    *    @param startY       starting y pixel
28    *    @param startColor   color for circle
29    *    @param startRadius  radius of circle
30    */
31    public Circle( int startX, int startY, Color startColor,
32                   int startRadius )
33    {
34       super( startX, startY, startColor );
35       setRadius( startRadius );
36    }
37
38    /** mutator method for radius
39    *    @param newRadius   new value for radius
40    */
41    public void setRadius( int newRadius )
42    {
43       radius = newRadius;
44    }
45
46    /** accessor method for radius
47    *    @return radius
48    */
```

```
49    public int getRadius( )
50    {
51       return radius;
52    }
53
54    /** draw method
55     *  sets color and draws a circle
56     *  @param g  Graphics context for drawing the circle
57     */
58    public void draw( Graphics g )
59    {
60       g.setColor( getColor( ) );
61       g.fillOval ( getX( ), getY( ),
62                    radius * 2, radius * 2 );
63    }
64 }
```

EXAMPLE 10.16   The *Circle* Class

Similarly, Example 10.17 shows the *Square* class, which also inherits from the *Figure* class. The *Square* class adds a *length* instance variable and uses code similar to the *Circle* class to call the constructors of the *Figure* class (lines 19 and 34) and to implement its own version of the *draw* method (lines 54–63).

```
1 /* Square class
2 *   inherits from abstract Figure class
3 *   Anderson, Franceschi
4 */
5
6 import java.awt.Graphics;
7 import java.awt.Color;
8
9 public class Square extends Figure
10 {
11    private int length;
12
13    /** default constructor
14     *   calls default constructor of Figure class
15     *   sets length to 0
16     */
17    public Square( )
18    {
19      super( );
20      length = 0;
```

```
21    }
22
23    /** overloaded constructor
24    *    sends startX, startY, startColor to Figure constructor
25    *    sets startLength to setLength method
26    *    @param startX       starting x pixel
27    *    @param startY       starting y pixel
28    *    @param startColor   color for square
29    *    @param startLength length of square
30    */
31    public Square( int startX, int startY, Color startColor,
32                      int startLength )
33    {
34       super( startX, startY, startColor );
35       setLength( startLength );
36    }
37
38    /** mutator method for length
39    *    @param newLength   new value for length
40    */
41    public void setLength( int newLength )
42    {
43       length = newLength;
44    }
45
46    /** accessor method for length
47    *    @return length
48    */
49    public int getLength( )
50    {
51       return length;
52    }
53
54    /** draw method
55    *   sets color and draws a square
56    *   @param g  Graphics context for drawing square
57    */
58    public void draw( Graphics g )
59    {
60       g.setColor( getColor( ) );
61       g.fillRect( getX( ), getY( ),
62                   length, length );
63    }
64 }
```

EXAMPLE 10.17   The *Square* Class

Because we want to instantiate *Circle* and *Square* objects, we do not declare these classes *abstract* and they are forced to implement the *draw* method. Example 10.18 shows a client applet, *TrafficLight*, which paints a traffic light, shown in Figure 10.13. On lines 10 and 11, we declare two *ArrayLists*, one to hold *Circle* objects and one to hold *Square* objects. In the *init* method (lines 13–24), we instantiate both *ArrayLists* and add three *Square* objects to *squaresList* and three *Circle* objects to *circlesList*. Then in the *paint* method, we create the traffic light by calling the *draw* methods for all the *Squares* in the *squaresList* (lines 28–29), then calling the *draw* method for all the *Circles* in the *circlesList* (lines 31–32).

REFERENCE POINT

For more information on *ArrayLists*, see Chapter 9.

```
 1 /* Figure Hierarchy Client
 2    Anderson, Franceschi
 3 */
 4 import javax.swing.JApplet;
 5 import java.awt.*;
 6 import java.util.ArrayList;
 7
 8 public class TrafficLight extends JApplet
 9 {
10    private ArrayList<Circle> circlesList;
11    private ArrayList<Square> squaresList;
12
13    public void init( )
14    {
15      squaresList = new ArrayList<Square>( );
16      squaresList.add( new Square( 150, 100, Color.BLACK, 40 ) );
```

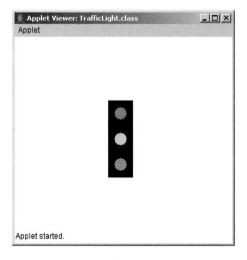

Figure 10.13
The *TrafficLight* Applet

```
17    squaresList.add( new Square( 150, 140, Color.BLACK, 40 ) );
18    squaresList.add( new Square( 150, 180, Color.BLACK, 40 ) );
19
20    circlesList = new ArrayList<Circle>( );
21    circlesList.add( new Circle( 160, 110, Color.RED, 10 ) );
22    circlesList.add( new Circle( 160, 150, Color.YELLOW, 10 ) );
23    circlesList.add( new Circle( 160, 190, Color.GREEN, 10 ) );
24    }
25
26  public void paint( Graphics g )
27  {
28    for ( Square s : squaresList )
29      s.draw( g );
30
31    for ( Circle c : circlesList )
32      c.draw( g );
33  }
34 }
```

EXAMPLE 10.18   The *TrafficLight* Applet

Java imposes a few restrictions on declaring and using *abstract* classes and methods. These rules are summarized in Table 10.6.

TABLE 10.6   Restrictions for Defining *abstract* Classes and Methods

abstract classes	• Classes must be declared *abstract* if the class contains any *abstract* methods.
	• *abstract* classes can be extended.
	• *abstract* classes cannot be used to instantiate objects.
abstract methods	• *abstract* methods can be declared only within an *abstract* class.
	• An *abstract* method must consist of a method header followed by a semicolon.
	• *abstract* methods cannot be called.
	• *abstract* methods cannot be declared as *private* or *static*.
	• A constructor cannot be declared *abstract*.

10.6   Polymorphism

An important concept in inheritance is that an object of a class is also an object of any of its superclasses. That concept is the basis for an important OOP feature, called **polymorphism**, which simplifies the processing of various objects in the same class hierarchy. The word *polymorphism*, which is derived from the word fragment *poly* and the word *morpho* in the Greek language, literally means "multiple forms."

Polymorphism allows us to use the same method call for any object in the hierarchy. We make the method call using an object reference of the superclass. At run time, the JVM determines to which class in the hierarchy the object actually belongs and calls the version of the method implemented for that class.

To use polymorphism in your application, the following conditions must be true:

- the classes are in the same hierarchy
- the subclasses override the same method
- a subclass object reference is assigned to a superclass object reference (that is, a subclass object is referenced by a superclass reference)
- the superclass object reference is used to call the method

For example, we can take advantage of polymorphism in our traffic light applet by calling the *draw* method for either a *Circle* or *Square* object using a *Figure* object reference. Although we cannot instantiate an object from an *abstract* class, Java allows us to define object references of an *abstract* class.

Example 10.19 shows the rewritten traffic light applet. Instead of using separate *ArrayLists* for *Circle* and *Square* objects, we can declare and instantiate only one *ArrayList* of *Figure* references (lines 10 and 14). As each *Circle* and *Square* object is instantiated, we add its object reference to the *ArrayList* of *Figure* references (lines 15–22).

This greatly simplifies the *paint* method (lines 25–29), which steps through *figuresList*, calling the *draw* method for each element. For the method call, it doesn't matter whether the object reference in *figuresList* is a *Circle* or *Square* reference. We just call the *draw* method using that reference. At run time, the JVM determines whether the object is a *Circle* or a *Square* and calls the appropriate *draw* method for the object type. Notice that we have interwoven the adding of *Circles* and *Squares* to *figuresList*, rather than adding all *Squares*, then adding all *Circles*. Because the *ArrayList* is composed of *Figure* references, any element can be either a *Circle* or a *Square*—because a *Circle* and a *Square* are both *Figures*. The output of this applet is identical to that of Example 10.18, as shown in Figure 10.13.

```
1 /* Figure hierarchy Client
2    Anderson, Franceschi
3 */
4 import javax.swing.JApplet;
5 import java.awt.*;
6 import java.util.ArrayList;
7
8 public class TrafficLightPolymorphism extends JApplet
9 {
10   private ArrayList<Figure> figuresList;
11
12   public void init( )
13   {
14     figuresList = new ArrayList<Figure>( );
15     figuresList.add( new Square( 150, 100, Color.BLACK, 40 ) );
16     figuresList.add( new Circle( 160, 110, Color.RED, 10 ) );
17
18     figuresList.add( new Square( 150, 140, Color.BLACK, 40 ) );
19     figuresList.add( new Circle( 160, 150, Color.YELLOW, 10 ) );
20
21     figuresList.add( new Square( 150, 180, Color.BLACK, 40 ) );
22     figuresList.add( new Circle( 160, 190, Color.GREEN, 10 ) );
23   }
24
25   public void paint( Graphics g )
26   {
27     for ( Figure f : figuresList )
28         f.draw( g );
29   }
30 }
```

EXAMPLE 10.19   Traffic Light Using Polymorphism

Thus, the four conditions for polymorphism listed earlier are true for this applet:

- The *Figure*, *Circle*, and *Square* classes are in the same hierarchy.
- The non-*abstract* classes implement the *draw* method.

- We assigned the *Circle* and *Square* objects to *Figure* references.

- We called the *draw* method using *Figure* references.

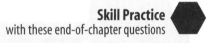

Skill Practice
with these end-of-chapter questions

10.10.1 Multiple Choice Exercises

Questions 7,10,11

10.10.4 Identifying Errors in Code

Question 31

10.10.5 Debugging Area

Questions 33,34,35

10.7 Programming Activity 2: Using Polymorphism

In this Programming Activity, you will complete the implementation of the Tortoise and the Hare race. The Tortoise runs a slow and steady race, while the Hare runs in spurts with rests in between. Figure 10.14 shows a sample run of the race. In this figure, we show only one tortoise and one

Figure 10.14
A Sample Run of the Tortoise and Hare Race

Figure 10.15

Racer **Hierarchy**

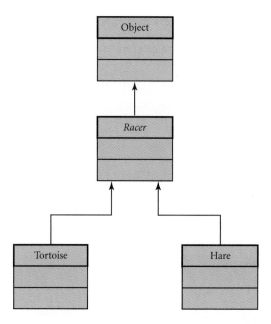

hare; however, using polymorphism we can easily run the race with any number and combination of tortoises and hares.

The class hierarchy for this Programming Activity is shown in Figure 10.15.

The code for the *Racer* class, which is the superclass of the *Tortoise* and *Hare* classes, is shown in Example 10.20. The *Racer* class has three instance variables (lines 10–12): a *String ID*, which identifies the type of racer; and *x* and *y* positions, both of which are *ints*. The class has the usual constructors, as well as accessor and mutator methods for the *x* and *y* positions and ID. These instance variables and methods are common to all racers, so we put them in the *Racer* class. Individual racers, however, will differ in the way they move and in the way they are drawn. Thus, in line 8, we declare the *Racer* class to be *abstract*, and in lines 74–81, we define two *abstract* methods, *move* and *draw*. Classes that inherit from the *Racer* class will need to provide implementations of these two methods (or be declared *abstract* as well).

```
 1 /**   Racer class
 2 *     Abstract class intended for racer hierarchy
 3 *     Anderson, Franceschi
 4 */
 5
 6 import java.awt.Graphics;
 7
```

```
 8 public abstract class Racer
 9 {
10   private String ID;   // racer ID
11   private int x;        // x position
12   private int y;        // y position
13
14   /** default constructor
15    *    Sets ID to blank
16    */
17   public Racer( )
18   {
19     ID = "";
20   }
21
22   /** Constructor
23    *    @param rID   racer ID
24    *    @param rX    x position
25    *    @param rY    y position
26    */
27   public Racer( String rID, int rX, int rY )
28   {
29     ID = rID;
30     x = rX;
31     y = rY;
32   }
33
34   /** accessor for ID
35    *    @return   ID
36    */
37   public String getID( )
38   {
39     return ID;
40   }
41
42   /** accessor for x
43    *    @return   current x value
44    */
45   public int getX( )
46   {
47     return x;
48   }
49
50   /** accessor for y
51    *    @return   current y value
52    */
```

```
53   public int getY( )
54   {
55     return y;
56   }
57
58   /** mutator for x
59    *   @param  newX   new value for x
60    */
61   public void setX( int newX )
62   {
63     x = newX;
64   }
65
66   /** mutator for y
67    *   @param  newY   new value for y
68    */
69   public void setY( int newY )
70   {
71     y = newY;
72   }
73
74   /** abstract method for Racer's move
75    */
76   public abstract void move( );
77
78   /** abstract method for drawing Racer
79    *   @param   g    Graphics context
80    */
81   public abstract void draw( Graphics g );
82 }
```

EXAMPLE 10.20   The *abstract Racer* Class

The *Tortoise* and the *Hare* classes inherit from the *Racer* class. Thus, their only job is to pass constructor arguments to the *Racer* class and implement the *draw* and *move* methods. For this Programming Activity, we have provided the *Tortoise* and *Hare* classes with the *draw* and *move* methods already written.

Your job is to add *Tortoise* and *Hare* objects to an *ArrayList* of *Racer* objects, as specified by the user. Then you will add code to run the race by stepping through the *ArrayList*, calling *move* and *draw* for each *Racer* object.

Instructions

Copy the source files in the Programming Activity 2 directory for this chapter to a directory on your computer.

1. Write the code to determine which racers will run the race. Load the *RacePoly.java* source file and search for five asterisks in a row (*****). This will position you inside the *prepareToRace* method.

   The dialog box to prompt the user for the racer type is already coded for you in the *getRacer* method. When your *switch* statement executes, the *getRacer* method has already been called and the *char* variable *input* contains the user's input. You do not need to call the *getRacer* method.

```
/** prepareToRace method
*    uses a dialog box to prompt user for racer types
*       and to start the race
*    racer types are 't' or 'T' for Tortoise,
*                     'h' or 'H' for Hare
*    's' or 'S' will start the race
*/
private void prepareToRace( )
{
    int yPos = FIRST_RACER;          // y position of first racer
    final int START_LINE = 40;       // x position of start of race
    final int RACER_SPACE = 50;      // spacing between racers
    char input;

    input = getRacer( ); // get input from user

    while ( input != 's' && input != 'S' )
    {
        /** 1. ***** Student writes this switch statement
        *    input local char variable contains the racer type
        *       entered by the user
        *    If input is 'T' or 't',
        *       add a Tortoise object to the ArrayList named racerList
        *              which is an instance variable of this class
        *    The API of the Tortoise constructor is:
        *            Tortoise( String ID, int startX, int startY )
        *    a sample call to the constructor is
        *            new Tortoise( "Tortoise", START_LINE, yPos )
        *            where START_LINE is a constant local variable
        *               representing the starting x position for the race
```

```
*          and yPos is a local variable representing
*             the next racer's y position
*
*  If input is 'H' or 'h',
*      add a Hare object to the ArrayList named racerList
*  The API of the Hare constructor is:
*          Hare( String ID, int startX, int startY )
*      a sample call to the constructor is
*          new Hare( "Hare", START_LINE, yPos )
*          where START_LINE is a constant local variable
*             representing the starting x position for the race
*          and yPos is a local variable representing
*             the next racer's y position
*
*  After adding a racer to the ArrayList racerList,
*          increment yPos by the value of
*          the constant local variable RACER_SPACE
*
*  if input is anything other than 'T', 't',
*          'H' or 'h', pop up an error dialog box
*          a sample method call for the output dialog box is:
*             JOptionPane.showMessageDialog( this, "Message" );
*/
// write your switch statement here

  /** end of student code, part 1 */

  repaint( );
  input = getRacer( );  // get input from user

} // end while

} // end prepareToRace
```

2. Next, write the code to run the race. In the *RacePoly.java* source file, search again for five asterisks in a row (*****). This will position you inside the *paint* method, where you will perform tasks 2 and 3. For task 2, you will write code to loop through the *ArrayList* of *Racers* and call the *move* and *draw* methods for each racer as they run the race. When you finish that task, search again for five asterisks in a row (*****), which will position you at the location of task 3. This task is similar to task 2, in that you need to loop through the *ArrayList* of *Racers*. However, in this task you will only call the *draw* method for

each *Racer*. This code will be executed before the race begins as racers are added to the start line.

The portion of the *paint* method where you will add your code is shown below.

```java
/** paint method
 *     @param g   Graphics context
 *     draws the finish line;
 *     moves and draws racers
 */
public void paint( Graphics g )
{
  super.paint( g );

  // draw the finish line
  finishX = getWidth( ) - 20;
  g.setColor( Color.blue );
  g.drawLine( finishX, 0, finishX, getHeight( ) );

  if ( raceIsOn )
  {
     /* 2. ***** student writes this code
      * loop through instance variable ArrayList racerList,
      *    which contains Racer object references,
      *    calling move, then draw for each racer
      * The API for move is:
      *     void move( )
      * The API for draw is:
      *     void draw( Graphics g )
      *        where g is the Graphics context
      *        passed to the paint method
      */

       /** end of student code, part 2 */
  }
  else  // display racers before race begins
  {
     /* 3. ***** student writes this code
      * loop through instance variable ArrayList racerList,
      *    which contains Racer object references,
      *    calling draw for each element. (Do not call move!)
      * The API for draw is:
      *     void draw( Graphics g )
      *        where g is the Graphics context
```

```
 *          passed to this paint method
 */
// student code goes here

/** end of student code, part 3 */
   }
 }
```

When you have finished writing the code, compile the source code and run the *RacePoly* application. Try several runs of the race with a different number of racers and with a different combination of *Tortoises* and *Hares*. Figure 10.16 shows the race with four *Tortoises* and three *Hares*.

DISCUSSION QUESTIONS ❓

1. Explain how polymorphism simplifies this application.

2. If you wanted to add another racer, for example, an aardvark, explain what code you would need to write and what existing code, if any, you would need to change.

10.8   Interfaces

In Java, a class can inherit directly from only one class, that is, a class can *extend* only one class. To allow a class to inherit behavior from multiple sources, Java provides the **interface**.

Figure 10.16
Another Run of the Race

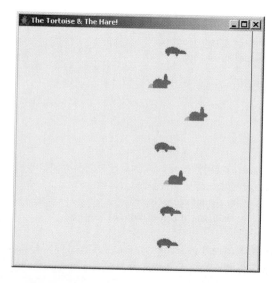

An interface typically specifies behavior that a class will *implement*. Interface members can be any of the following:

- classes

- constants

- *abstract* methods

- other interfaces

Typically, interfaces define only constants and *abstract* methods. Notice that an interface cannot have instance variables and that all methods in an interface are *abstract*.

To define an interface, use the following syntax:

```
accessModifier interface InterfaceName
{
    // body of interface
}
```

All interfaces are *abstract*; thus, they cannot be instantiated. The *abstract* keyword, however, can be omitted in the interface definition. If the interface's access modifier is *public*, its members are implicitly *public* as well.

Any field defined in an interface is *public*, *static*, and *final*. These keywords can be specified or omitted. When you define a field in the interface, you must also assign a value to the field at that time.

All methods within an interface must be *abstract*, so the method definition must consist of only a method header and a semicolon. Like the interface header, the *abstract* keyword can be omitted from the method definition.

To inherit from an interface, a class declares that it *implements* the interface in the class definition, using the following syntax:

```
accessModifier class ClassName extends SuperclassName
                        implements Interface1, Interface2, ...
```

The *extends* clause is optional if the class inherits only from the *Object* class. A class can *implement* 0, 1, or more interfaces. If a class *implements* more than one interface, the interfaces are specified in a comma-separated list of interface names. When a class *implements* an interface, the class must provide an implementation for each method contained in the interface.

In the Programming Activity of the last section, we ran the Tortoise and Hare Race. Each racer inherited from the *abstract Racer* class, which specified two *abstract* methods: *draw* and *move*. Thus, both the *Tortoise* and the *Hare* classes implemented those two methods.

Below are brief, summarized versions of the *Racer* and *Tortoise* classes from Programming Activity 2:

```
// Racer defines move and draw as abstract methods
public abstract class Racer
{
  public abstract void move( );
  public abstract void draw( Graphics g );

  // other fields and methods
}

// Tortoise inherits from Racer and implements move and draw
public class Tortoise extends Racer
{
  public void move( )
  {
    // implementation here
  }

  public void draw( Graphics g )
  {
    // implementation here
  }

  // other fields and methods
}
```

That class hierarchy worked well for running the race, but suppose we just wanted to draw a tortoise or a hare, or another animal, without racing them. In other words, we don't want to implement the *move* method, just the *draw* method.

In this case, we can define an *abstract* class, *Animal*, which contains only one *abstract* method: *draw*. To provide the optional capability of running a race, we define an interface, named *Moveable*, which includes the *abstract* method *move*. Then, if we just want to draw an animal, we define a class that *extends* the *Animal* class. If we want to make our animal a racer, we implement the *Moveable* interface.

Following are brief, summarized versions of the *Animal* class; the *Moveable* interface; a racing animal class, which we call *TortoiseRacer*; and a *Tor-*

toiseNonRacer class that can be used in another application where animal objects are drawn, but do not race.

```java
// Animal defines only one abstract method: draw
public abstract class Animal
{
  public abstract void draw( Graphics g );

  // other fields and methods
}

// Moveable defines move as an abstract method
public interface Moveable
{
  // some constants defined here
  public void move( );

}

// TortoiseRacer inherits from Animal and Moveable
//  and implements both move and draw
public class TortoiseRacer extends Animal implements Moveable
{
  public void draw( Graphics g )
  {
    // implementation here
  }

  public void move( )
  {
    // implementation here
  }

  // other fields and methods here
}

// non-racing Tortoise inherits only from Animal
//  and implements draw method only
public class TortoiseNonRacer extends Animal
{
  public void draw( Graphics g )
  {
    // implementation here
  }
```

```
  // other fields and methods here
}
```

Example 10.21 shows the actual *Animal* class, which is similar to the *Racer* class shown in Example 10.20, except that its only *abstract* method is *draw* (lines 73–76).

```
 1 /**  Animal class
 2 *     Anderson. Franceschi
 3 */
 4
 5 import java.awt.Graphics;
 6
 7 public abstract class Animal
 8 {
 9   private int x;      // x position
10   private int y;      // y position
11   private String ID;  // animal ID
12
13   /** default constructor
14   *    Sets ID to blank
15   */
16   public Animal( )
17   {
18     ID = "";
19   }
20
21   /** Constructor
22   *    @param rID    Animal ID
23   *    @param rX     x position
24   *    @param rY     y position
25   */
26   public Animal( String rID, int rX, int rY )
27   {
28     ID = rID;
29     x = rX;
30     y = rY;
31   }
32
33   /** accessor for ID
34   *    @return   ID
35   */
36   public String getID( )
37   {
```

```
38     return ID;
39   }
40
41   /** accessor for x
42    *  @return  x coordinate
43    */
44   public int getX( )
45   {
46     return x;
47   }
48
49   /** accessor for y
50    *  @return  y coordinate
51    */
52   public int getY( )
53   {
54     return y;
55   }
56
57   /** mutator for x
58    *  @param  newX  new value for x position
59    */
60   public void setX( int newX )
61   {
62     x = newX;
63   }
64
65   /** mutator for y
66    *  @param  newY  new value for y position
67    */
68   public void setY( int newY )
69   {
70     y = newY;
71   }
72
73   /** abstract method for drawing Animal
74    *  @param   g    Graphics context
75    */
76   public abstract void draw( Graphics g );
77 }
```

EXAMPLE 10.21   The *Animal* Class

Example 10.22 shows the actual *Moveable* interface, which specifies the API for the *move* method (line 10). Although all methods in an interface are *abstract*, we do not need to specify the *abstract* keyword. Also, all members of a *public* interface are *public*, so we do not need to specify an access modifier either.

In lines 7–8, we define two constants, which will be used by the racer in the *move* method to determine how fast the racer will move. A hare would increment its *x* value by the *FAST* value (5), and the tortoise would increment its *x* value by the *SLOW* value (1).

```
 1 /** Moveable interface
 2 *    Anderson, Franceschi
 3 */
 4
 5 public interface Moveable
 6 {
 7   int FAST = 5; // static constant
 8   int SLOW = 1; // static constant
 9
10   void move( ); // abstract method
11 }
```

EXAMPLE 10.22   The *Moveable* Interface

Example 10.23 shows the actual *TortoiseRacer* class, which is functionally equivalent to the *Tortoise* class in the Programming Activity. It inherits from the *Animal* class and *implements* the *Moveable* interface (line 10). It provides bodies for both the *draw* method (lines 29–53), inherited from *Animal*, and the *move* method (lines 55–63), inherited through the *Moveable* interface. Because implementing the *Moveable* interface is optional, we can also define classes that inherit from *Animal*, but do not need to provide a *move* method. In this way, we have designed for more optimal reuse of our classes.

```
 1 /**   TortoiseRacer class
 2 *     inherits from abstract Animal class
 3 *     implements Moveable interface
 4 *     Anderson, Franceschi
 5 */
 6
 7 import java.awt.Graphics;
 8 import java.awt.Color;
 9
```

```
10  public class TortoiseRacer extends Animal implements Moveable
11  {
12    /** Default Constructor: calls Animal default constructor
13    */
14    public TortoiseRacer( )
15    {
16      super( );
17    }
18
19    /** Constructor
20    *    @param rID  racer Id, passed to Animal constructor
21    *    @param rX   x position, passed to Animal constructor
22    *    @param rY   y position, passed to Animal constructor
23    */
24    public TortoiseRacer( String rID, int rX, int rY )
25    {
26      super( rID, rX, rY );
27    }
28
29    /** draw: draws the Tortoise at current (x, y) coordinate
30    *         implements abstract method in Animal class
31    *         @param g   Graphics context
32    */
33    public void draw( Graphics g )
34    {
35      int startX = getX( );
36      int startY = getY( );
37
38      g.setColor( new Color( 34, 139, 34 ) ); // dark green
39
40      //body
41      g.fillOval( startX, startY, 25, 15 );
42
43      //head
44      g.fillOval( startX + 20, startY + 5,  15, 10 );
45
46      //flatten bottom
47      g.clearRect( startX, startY + 11, 35, 4 );
48
49      //feet
50      g.setColor( new Color( 34, 139, 34 ) );  // brown
51      g.fillOval( startX + 3, startY + 10,  5, 5 );
52      g.fillOval( startX + 17, startY + 10, 5, 5 );
53    }
54
```

```
55    /** implements move method in Moveable interface
56    *    move:  calculates the new x value for the racer
57    *    Tortoise move characteristics: "slow & steady wins the race"
58    *        increment x by SLOW (inherited from Moveable interface)
59    */
60    public void move( )
61    {
62        setX( getX( ) + SLOW );
63    }
64 }
```

EXAMPLE 10.23   The *TortoiseRacer* Class

REFERENCE POINT

Interfaces are used extensively in GUI applications, as you will see in Chapter 12.

Example 10.24 shows a client applet that exercises the *TortoiseRacer* class. In this race, the tortoise, the only racer, always wins, as shown in Figure 10.17.

```
1 /** TortoiseRacer Client
2 *    Anderson, Franceschi
3 */
4
5 import javax.swing.*;
6 import java.awt.*;
7
8 public class TortoiseRacerClient extends JApplet
9 {
10    private TortoiseRacer t;
11
```

Figure 10.17

Output from Example 10.24

```
12    public void init( )
13    {
14      t = new TortoiseRacer( "Tortoise", 50, 50 );
15    }
16
17    public void paint( Graphics g )
18    {
19      for ( int i = 0; i < getWidth( ); i++ )
20      {
21        t.move( );
22        t.draw( g );
23
24        Pause.wait( .03 );
25        g.clearRect( 0, 0, getWidth( ), getHeight( ) );
26      }
27    }
28 }
```

EXAMPLE 10.24   A Client Applet for the *TortoiseRacer* Class

Skill Practice
with these end-of-chapter questions

10.10.1   Multiple Choice Exercises

Questions 3,5,6

10.10.3   Fill in the Code

Question 25

10.10.4   Identifying Errors in Code

Questions 26,27,28,29,30

10.10.8   Technical Writing

Question 57

CODE IN ACTION

In the Chapter 10 folder on the CD-ROM included with this book, you will find a Shockwave movie showing a step-by-step illustration of how *abstract* classes, polymorphism, and interfaces can be used in a program. Just double-click on *Inheritance.html* to start the movie.

10.9   Chapter Summary

- Inheritance lets us organize related classes into ordered levels of functionality, called hierarchies. The advantage is that we write the common code only once and reuse it in multiple classes.

- A subclass inherits methods and fields of its superclass. A subclass can have only one direct superclass, but many subclasses can inherit from a common superclass.

- Inheritance implements the "is a" relationship between classes. Any object of a subclass is also an object of the superclass.

- All classes inherit from the *Object* class.

- To specify that a subclass inherits from a superclass, the subclass uses the *extends* keyword in the class definition, as in the following syntax:

```
accessModifier class ClassName extends SuperclassName
```

- A subclass does not inherit constructors or *private* members of the superclass. However, the superclass constructors are still available to be called from the subclass, and the *private* fields of the superclass are implemented as fields of the subclass.

- To access private fields of the superclass, the subclass needs to use the accessor and mutator methods provided by the superclass.

- To call the constructor of the superclass, the subclass constructor uses the following syntax:

```
super( argument list );
```

If used, this statement must be the first statement in the subclass constructor.

- A subclass can override an inherited method by providing a new version of the method. The new method's API must be identical to the inherited method. To call the inherited version of the method, the subclass uses the *super* object reference using the following syntax:

```
super.methodName( argument list )
```

- Any field declared using the *protected* access modifier is inherited by the subclass. As such, the subclass can directly access the field without calling its accessor or mutator method.

- An *abstract* class can be used to specify APIs for methods that sub-classes should implement. An *abstract* class cannot be used to instantiate objects. A class is declared to be *abstract* by including the *abstract* keyword in the class header.

- An *abstract* class typically has one or more *abstract* methods. An *abstract* method specifies the API of the method, but does not provide an implementation. The API of an *abstract* method is followed by a semicolon.

- When a subclass inherits from an *abstract* class, it can provide implementations for any, all, or none of the *abstract* methods. If the subclass does not implement all the *abstract* methods of the superclass, then the subclass must also be declared as *abstract*. If, however, the subclass implements all the *abstract* methods in the superclass and is not declared *abstract*, then the class is not *abstract* and we can instantiate objects of that subclass.

- Polymorphism simplifies the processing of various objects in a hierarchy by allowing us to use the same method call for any object in the hierarchy. We assign an object reference of a subclass to a superclass reference, then make the method call using the super-class object reference. At run time, the JVM determines to which class in the hierarchy the object actually belongs and calls the appropriate form of the method for that class.

- Interfaces allow a class to inherit behavior from multiple sources. Interface members can be classes, constants, *abstract* methods, or other interfaces.

- To define an interface, use the following syntax:

```
accessModifier interface InterfaceName
{
  // body of interface
}
```

- To use an interface, a class header should include the *implements* keyword and the name of the interface, as in the following syntax:

```
accessModifier class ClassName implements InterfaceName
```

- To specify that a subclass inherits from a superclass and uses an interface, a class header should include the *implements* keyword and the name of the interface, as in the following syntax:

```
accessModifier class ClassName extends SuperclassName
                               implements InterfaceName
```

10.10   Exercises, Problems, and Projects

10.10.1   Multiple Choice Exercises:

1. The *extends* keyword applies to
   - ❏ a class inheriting from another class
   - ❏ a variable
   - ❏ a method
   - ❏ an expression

2. A Java class can inherit from two or more classes.
   - ❏ true
   - ❏ false

3. In Java, multiple inheritance is implemented using the concept of
   - ❏ an interface
   - ❏ an *abstract* class
   - ❏ a *private* class

4. Which of the following is inherited by a subclass?
   - ❏ all instance variables and methods
   - ❏ *public* instance variables and methods only
   - ❏ *protected* instance variables and methods only
   - ❏ *protected* and *public* instance variables and methods

5. What Java keyword is used in a class header when a class is defined as inheriting from an interface?
   - ❏ *inherits*
   - ❏ *includes*
   - ❏ *extends*
   - ❏ *implements*

6. A Java class can inherit from two or more interfaces.
   - ❏ true
   - ❏ false

7. How do you instantiate an object from an *abstract* class?

   ❑ With any constructor.

   ❑ With the default constructor only.

   ❑ You cannot instantiate an object from an *abstract* class.

8. When a class overrides a method, what Java keyword is used to call the method inherited from the superclass?

   ❑ *inherited*

   ❑ *super*

   ❑ *class*

   ❑ *methodName*

9. Where should the following statement be located in the body of a subclass constructor?

   ```
   super( );
   ```

   ❑ It should be the last statement.

   ❑ It should be the first statement.

   ❑ It can be anywhere.

10. If a class contains an *abstract* method, then

    ❑ The class must be declared *abstract*.

    ❑ The class is not *abstract*.

    ❑ The class may or may not be *abstract*.

    ❑ All of the above.

11. What can you tell about the following method?

    ```
    public void myMethod( )
    {
    }
    ```

    ❑ This method is *abstract*.

    ❑ This method is not *abstract*.

10.10.2   Reading and Understanding Code

For questions 12 to 20, consider the following three classes:

```java
public class A
{
 private int number;
 protected String name;
 public double price;

 public A( )
 {
   System.out.println( "A( ) called" );
 }

 private void foo1( )
 {
  System.out.println( "A version of foo1( ) called" );
 }

 protected int foo2( )
 {
  System.out.println( "A version of foo2( ) called" );
  return number;
 }

 public String foo3( )
 {
  System.out.println( "A version of foo3( ) called" );
  return "Hi";
 }
}

public class B extends A
{
  private char service;

  public B( )
  {
   super( );
   System.out.println( "B( ) called" );
  }

  public void foo1( )
```

```
    {
      System.out.println( "B version of foo1( ) called" );
    }

    protected int foo2( )
    {
      int n = super.foo2( );
      System.out.println( "B version of foo2( ) called" );
      return ( n + 5 );
    }

    public String foo3( )
    {
      String temp = super.foo3( );
      System.out.println( "B version of foo3( )" );
      return ( temp + " foo3" );
    }
}

public class C extends B
{
    public C( )
    {
      super( );
      System.out.println( "C( ) called" );
    }

    public void foo1( )
    {
      System.out.println( "C version of foo1( ) called" );
    }
}
```

12. Draw the class hierarchy.

13. What fields and methods are inherited by which class?

14. What fields and methods are not inherited?

15. What is the output of the following code sequence?

    ```
    B b1 = new B( );
    ```

16. What is the output of the following code sequence?

    ```
    B b2 = new B( );
    b2.foo1( );
    ```

17. What is the output of this code sequence?

```
B b3 = new B( );
int n = b3.foo2( );
```

18. What is the output of this code sequence?

```
// b4 is a B object reference
System.out.println( b4.foo3( ) );
```

19. What is the output of the following code sequence?

```
C c1 = new C( );
```

20. What is the output of the following code sequence?

```
// c2 is a C object reference
c2.foo1( );
```

10.10.3   Fill in the Code

For questions 21 to 25, consider the following class *F* and the interface *I:*

```
public class F
{
 private String first;
 protected String name;

 public F( )
 { }

 public F( String f, String n )
 {
  first = f;
  name = n;
 }
 public String getFirst( )
 {
  return first;
 }
 public String getName( )
 {
  return name;
 }
 public String toString( )
 {
   return ("first: " + first + "\tname: " + name);
 }
```

```
    public boolean equals( F f )
    {
      return( first.equals( f.first ) && name.equals( f.name ) );
    }
  }

  public interface I
  {
    public static final String TYPE = "human";
    public abstract int age( );
  }
```

21. The *G* class inherits from the *F* class. Code the class header of the *G* class.

    ```
    // your code goes here
    ```

22. Inside the *G* class, which inherits from the *F* class, declare a *private* instance variable for the middle initial and code a constructor with three parameters, calling the constructor of the *F* class and assigning the third parameter, a *char*, to the new instance variable.

    ```
    // your code goes here
    ```

23. Inside the *G* class, which inherits from the *F* class, code the *toString* method, which returns a printable representation of a *G* object reference.

    ```
    // your code goes here
    ```

24. Inside the *G* class, which inherits from the *F* class, code the *equals* method, which compares two *G* objects and returns *true* if they have identical instance variables; *false* otherwise.

    ```
    // your code goes here
    ```

25. The *K* class inherits from the *F* class and the *I* interface; code the class header of the *K* class.

    ```
    // your code goes here
    ```

10.10.4 Identifying Errors in Code

For questions 26 to 31, consider the following two classes, *C* and *D*, and interface *I:*

```
public abstract class C
{
  private void foo1( )
  {
    System.out.println( "Hello foo1" );
  }
```

```
 public abstract void foo2( );
 public abstract int foo3( );
}

public class D extends C
{
 public void foo2( )
 {
  System.out.println( "Hello foo2( )" );
 }
 public int foo3( )
 {
  return 10;
 }
 private void foo4( )
 {
  System.out.println( "Hello D foo4( )" );
 }
}

public interface I
{
 public static final double PI = 3.14;
}
```

26. Where is the error in this code sequence?

```
C c1 = new C( );
```

27. Where is the error in this code sequence?

```
D d1 = new D( );
d1.foo1( );
```

28. Is there an error in this code sequence? Why or why not?

```
C c2;
c2 = new D( );
```

29. Where is the error in this new class?

```
public class E extends D
{
 public void foo4( )
 {
  super.foo4( );
  System.out.println( "Hello E foo4()" );
 }
}
```

30. Where is the error in this class?

```
public class J extends I
{
}
```

31. Where is the error in this class?

```
public class K
{
 public void foo( );
}
```

10.10.5   Debugging Area

32. You coded the following class

```
public class N extends String, Integer
{
}
```

When you compile, you get the following message:

```
N.java:1: '{' expected
public class N extends String, Integer
                             ^
N.java:4: '}' expected
^
2 errors
```

Explain what the problem is and how to fix it.

For exercises 33 to 35, consider the following class:

```
public abstract class M
{
 private int n;
 protected double p;
 public abstract void foo1( );
}
```

33. You coded the following class:

```
public class P extends M
{
}
```

When you compile, you get the following message:

```
P.java:1: P is not abstract and does not override abstract method
foo1() in M
public class P extends M
       ^
1 error
```

34. You coded the following class:

```
public class P extends M
{
 public void foo1( )
 {
  System.out.println( "n is: " + n );
 }
}
```

When you compile, you get the following message:

```
P.java:5: n has private access in M
   System.out.println( "n is: " + n );
                                   ^
1 error
```

35. You coded the following classes:

```
public class P extends M
{
 public P( double newP )
 {
  p = newP;
 }
 public void foo1( )
 {
 }
}

public class Q extends P
{
 private int z;
 public Q( double newP, int newZ )
 {
  z = newZ;
  super( newP );  // line 7
 }
}
```

When you compile, you get the following message:

```
Q.java:5: cannot find symbol
symbol  : constructor P()
location: class P
 {
 ^
Q.java:7: call to super must be first statement in constructor
  super( newP );
       ^
2 errors
```

10.10.6   Write a Short Program

36. Write an applet overriding the *init* and *paint* methods of the *JApplet* class with a simple output line to the screen, which will show in what order each method is called.

For exercises 37 to 41, consider the following class:

```
public class Game
{
 private String description;

 public Game( String newDescription )
 {
  setDescription( newDescription );
 }

 public String getDescription( )
 {
  return description;
 }

 public void setDescription( String newDescription )
 {
  description = newDescription;
 }

 public String toString( )
 {
  return ( "description: " + description );
 }
}
```

37. Write a class encapsulating a PC-based game, which inherits from *Game*. A PC-based game has the following additional attributes: the minimum megabytes of RAM needed to play the game, the number of megabytes needed on the hard drive to install the game, and the minimum GHz performance of the CPU. Code the constructor and the *toString* method of the new class. You also need to include a client class to test your code.

38. Write a class encapsulating a board game, which inherits from *Game*. A board game has the following additional attributes: the number of players and whether the game can end in a tie. Code the constructor and the *toString* method of the new class. You also need to include a client class to test your code.

39. Write a class encapsulating a sports game, which inherits from *Game*. A sports game has the following additional attributes: whether the game is a team or individual game, and whether the game can end in a tie. Code the constructor and the *toString* method of the new class. You also need to include a client class to test your code.

40. Write a class encapsulating a trivia game, which inherits from *Game*. A trivia game has the following additional attributes: the ultimate money prize, and the number of questions that must be answered to win the ultimate money. Code the constructor and the *toString* method of the new class. You also need to include a client class to test your code.

41. Write a class encapsulating a board game, which inherits from *Game*. A board game has the following additional attributes: the minimum number of players, the maximum number of players, and whether there is a time limit to finish the game. Code the constructor and the *toString* method of the new class. You also need to include a client class to test your code.

For exercises 42 to 46, consider the following class:

```java
public class Store
{
  public final double SALES_TAX_RATE = 0.06;
  private String name;

  public Store( String newName )
  {
```

```
  setName( newName );
  }

  public String getName( )
  {
   return name;
  }

  public void setName( String newName )
  {
   name = newName;
  }

  public String toString( )
  {
   return ( "name: " + name );
  }
 }
```

42. Write a class encapsulating a Web store, which inherits from *Store*. A Web store has the following additional attributes: an Internet address and the programming language in which the Web site was written. Code the constructor and the *toString* method of the new class. You also need to include a client class to test your code.

43. Write a class encapsulating a music store, which inherits from *Store*. A music store has the following additional attributes: the number of titles it offers and its address. Code the constructor and the *toString* method of the new class. You also need to include a client class to test your code.

44. Write a class encapsulating a bike store, which inherits from *Store*. A bike store has the following additional attributes: the number of bicycle brands that it carries and whether it sponsors a bike club. Code the constructor and the *toString* method of the new class. You also need to include a client class to test your code.

45. Write a class encapsulating a grocery store, which inherits from *Store*. A grocery store has the following additional attributes: annual revenues and whether it is an independent store or part of a chain. Code the constructor and the *toString* method of the new class; also code a method returning the annual taxes paid by the store. You also need to include a client class to test your code.

46. Write a class encapsulating a restaurant, which inherits from *Store*. A restaurant has the following additional attributes: how many people are served every year and the average price per person. Code the constructor and the *toString* method of the new class; also code a method returning the average taxes per year. You also need to include a client class to test your code.

10.10.7   Programming Projects

47. Write a superclass encapsulating a rectangle. A rectangle has two attributes representing the width and the height of the rectangle. It has methods returning the perimeter and the area of the rectangle. This class has a subclass, encapsulating a parallelepiped, or box. A parallelepiped has a rectangle as its base, and another attribute, its length; it has two methods that calculate and return its area and volume. You also need to include a client class to test these two classes.

48. Write a superclass encapsulating a circle; this class has one attribute representing the radius of the circle. It has methods returning the perimeter and the area of the circle. This class has a subclass, encapsulating a cylinder. A cylinder has a circle as its base, and another attribute, its length; it has two methods, calculating and returning its area and volume. You also need to include a client class to test these two classes.

49. Write an *abstract* superclass encapsulating a shape: A shape has two *abstract* methods: one returning the perimeter of the shape, another returning the area of the shape. It also has a constant field named PI. This class has two non-*abstract* subclasses: one encapsulating a circle, and the other encapsulating a rectangle. A circle has one additional attribute, its radius. A rectangle has two additional attributes, its width and height. You also need to include a client class to test these two classes.

50. Write an *abstract* superclass encapsulating a vehicle: A vehicle has two attributes: its owner's name and its number of wheels. This class has two non-*abstract* subclasses: one encapsulating a bicycle, and the other encapsulating a motorized vehicle. A motorized vehicle has the following additional attributes: its engine volume displacement, in liters; and a method computing and returning a measure of horsepower—the number of liters times the number of wheels. You also need to include a client class to test these two classes.

51. Write an *abstract* superclass encapsulating some food; it has two attributes: its description and the number of calories per serving. It also has an *abstract* method taking a number of servings as a parameter and returning the number of calories. This class has two non-*abstract* subclasses: one encapsulating a liquid food (such as a drink, for instance), and the other encapsulating a fruit. A liquid food has an additional attribute: its viscosity. A fruit has an additional attribute: its season. You also need to include a client class to test these two classes.

52. Write an *abstract* superclass encapsulating a college applicant: A college applicant has two attributes: the applicant's name and the college the applicant is applying to. This class has two non-*abstract* subclasses: one encapsulating an applicant for undergraduate school, and the other encapsulating an applicant for graduate school. An applicant for undergraduate school has two additional attributes: an SAT score, and a GPA. An applicant for graduate school has one additional attribute: the college of origin. It also has a method which returns "from inside" if the college of origin is the same as the college applied to; otherwise, it returns "from outside." You also need to include a class to test these two classes.

53. Write an *abstract* superclass encapsulating a vacation: A vacation has two attributes: a budget and a destination. It has an *abstract* method returning by how much the vacation is over or under budget. This class has two non-*abstract* subclasses: one encapsulating an all-inclusive vacation, and the other encapsulating a vacation bought piece-meal. An all-inclusive vacation has three additional attributes: a brand (for instance ClubMed®); a rating, expressed as a number of stars; and a price. A piecemeal vacation has two additional attributes: a set of items (hotel, meal, airfare, . . .), and a set of corresponding costs. You also need to include a class to test these two classes.

54. Write an *abstract* superclass encapsulating a part, with two attributes: the part number, and a budget cost for it. This class has two non-*abstract* subclasses: one encapsulating a self-manufactured part, and the other encapsulating an outsourced part. A self-manufactured part has a cost and a drawing number; it has also a method returning whether it is over budget or under budget. An outsourced part has a set of suppliers, each with a price for the part. It also has a method to

retrieve the lowest-cost supplier for a part and the corresponding cost. You also need to include a class to test these two classes.

55. Write an *abstract* superclass encapsulating a number; this class has one *abstract void* method: *square.* This class has two non-*abstract* subclasses: one encapsulating a rational number, and the other encapsulating a complex number. A rational number is represented by two integers, the numerator and the denominator of the rational number. A complex number is represented by two real numbers, the real part and the complex part of the complex number. You also need to include a class to test these two classes.

10.10.8   Technical Writing

56. In a large organization, programmers develop a library of classes as they work on various projects. Discuss, in such an environment, how inheritance can be helpful in reusing code and therefore saving time.

57. Other programming languages allow multiple inheritance, that is, a class can inherit from several classes. In Java, a class can extend only one class, but can implement several interfaces. Discuss potential problems that can arise in other programming languages that allow inheritance from multiple classes.

10.10.9   Group Project (for a group of 1, 2, or 3 students)

58. Design and code a program, including the following classes, as well as a client applet class to test all the methods coded:

An *abstract Shape* class, encapsulating a shape: a shape has one *abstract* method, *draw*, which takes one parameter, a *Graphics* object. *Shape* has three subclasses:

❏ The *Line* class, encapsulating a line: A line can be represented by a starting (x, y) coordinate and an ending (x, y) coordinate. The *draw* method will draw a line between them.

❏ The *Rectangle* class, encapsulating a rectangle: A rectangle can be represented by its (x, y) top-left corner of the rectangle, its width, and its height. The *draw* method will draw the corresponding rectangle.

❑ The *Oval* class, encapsulating an oval: An oval can be represented by the (x, y) top-left corner coordinate of its bounding rectangle, its width, and its height. The *draw* method will draw the corresponding oval.

Your applet class should prompt the user for the type of shape that the user wants to draw, prompt the user for the appropriate data, and then draw the figure in the applet window.

CHAPTER 11

Exceptions and Input/Output Operations

CHAPTER CONTENTS

Introduction

Up to now, whenever our programs needed data, we have supplied that data using one of several different methods:

- Assigning values to variables in our program. This is known as **hard coding** the values of variables.
- Prompting the user for values using the *Scanner* class.
- Reading data from a text file using the *Scanner* class.
- Prompting the user for values using a *JOptionPane* dialog box.
- Generating random numbers using the *random* method of the *Math* class.

Typically, whenever we prompted the user to supply values, we asked for one value at a time. If a program needs a large number of values, however, prompting the user for each value will take a long time and will be impractical. Furthermore, as the number of values increases, the potential for input errors increases as well.

Programs often use existing data accumulated by an organization, such as a university, a government, or a corporation. Typically, the volume of data is significant, and again, data entry through the keyboard is impractical.

Furthermore, these large amounts of data typically reside in two types of storage:

- disk files
- databases

Working with databases is beyond the scope of this book. In most of this chapter, we concentrate on reading from and writing to files. We also revisit the concept of reading data from the console and examine the Java classes supporting this action.

But there is a prerequisite to all this: understanding the concept of exceptions, their associated classes, and exception handling.

11.1   Simple Exception Handling

By now you should have discovered that sometimes your program doesn't work, even though you didn't get any compiler errors. At run time, logic errors can surface. For example, we might attempt to divide an integer by 0 or try to access the 11th element in a 10-element array. Java is a robust language and does not allow these "illegal" operations to occur unnoticed.

These illegal operations generate **exceptions**. Some exceptions are generated by the Java Virtual Machine, while others are generated by constructors or other methods. For example, a method might generate an exception when it detects an attempted illegal operation or an illegal parameter.

By default, when an exception is generated in an application that does not have a graphical user interface, the program will terminate. In many cases, however, we can attempt to recover from the exception and continue running the program. This is called **handling the exception**. For the programmer to handle an exception, Java provides two tools:

- exception classes
- the *try*, *catch*, and *finally* blocks

The *Exception* class is the superclass of all exception classes, which encapsulate specific exceptions, such as integer division by 0, attempting to access an out-of-bounds array index, an illegal number format, using a *null* object reference to call a method, trying to open a file that does not exist, and others.

Figure 11.1 is an inheritance hierarchy showing only a few of the Java exception classes. The *Exception* class and *RuntimeException* and its subclasses are in the *java.lang* package. The *IOException* class and its subclass, *FileNotFoundException*, are in the *java.io* package.

11.1.1 Using *try* and *catch* Blocks

Throughout this book, we have used dialog boxes to prompt the user for input values. Example 11.1 shows a program that prompts the user for an integer. The *showInputDialog* method of the *JOptionPane* class returns the user's input as a *String* (lines 12–13), which we then convert to an *int* using the *parseInt* method of the *Integer* wrapper class (line 17).

```
1 /*  An exception generated by the parseInt method
2 *   Anderson, Franceschi
3 */
4
5 import javax.swing.JOptionPane;
6
7 public class DialogBoxInput
8 {
```

Figure 11.1

Inheritance Hierarchy for Various Exception Classes

```
 9   public static void main( String [ ] args )
10   {
11      // prompt for input; return value is a String
12      String s = JOptionPane.showInputDialog( null,
13                              "Enter an integer" );
14      System.out.println( "You entered " + s );
15
16      // attempt to convert the String to an int
17      int n = Integer.parseInt( s );
18      System.out.println( "Conversion was successful. "
19                          + "The integer is " + n );
20   }
21 }
```

EXAMPLE 11.1   Generating an Exception

Figure 11.2 shows a successful run of the program with the user input being 45.

Everything goes well as long as the user's input can be converted to an *int*. But what happens when the user types characters other than digits? Figure 11.3 shows the output from the same program when the user enters "a."

At run time, the call to the *parseInt* method (line 17) generates a *NumberFormatException*, which terminates the program. Lines 18–19 of the program are never executed. We can determine the line that generated the exception by reading the last line of the console output, which identifies the

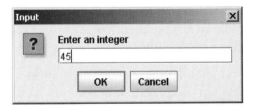

Figure 11.2

Successful Conversion of a *String* to an *int*

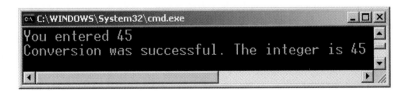

Figure 11.3

Output Showing *a*
NumberFormatException
at Run Time

```
You entered a
Exception in thread "main" java.lang.NumberFormatException: For input string: "a
"
        at java.lang.NumberFormatException.forInputString(NumberFormatException
.java:48)
        java.lang.Integer.parseInt(Integer.java:447)
        java.lang.Integer.parseInt(Integer.java:497)
        at DialogBoxInput.main(DialogBoxInput.java:17)
```

source of the exception: line 17 in the *main* method of the *DialogBoxInput* class.

Let's take a look at what happened here. The *parseInt* method has the following header:

```
public static int parseInt( String str ) throws NumberFormatException
```

The *throws NumberFormatException* clause indicates that the *parseInt* method may detect a situation for which it will generate a *NumberFormat- Exception*. In fact, if the *String* argument cannot be converted to an *int*, the *parseInt* method will generate, or **throw**, a *NumberFormatException*.

Naturally, we would like to avoid the situation when invalid user input terminates execution of our program. Typos and invalid input values can occur in any program. We need to be able to recover from these errors and continue executing.

Java provides the *try* and *catch* blocks to allow us to handle exceptions so that our code can continue to run. We put the code that might generate an exception inside the *try* block, and we put the code to recover from the exception inside a *catch* block. If an exception is thrown by the code inside the *try* block, then execution will jump to the *catch* block, where we write code to handle that exception. If nothing illegal happens in the *try* block, the code in the *catch* block will be skipped.

The minimum syntax for a *try* and *catch* block is as follows:

```
try
{
  // code that might generate an exception
}
catch ( ExceptionClass exceptionObjRef )
{
  // code to recover from the exception
}
```

The curly braces are required for both the *try* body and the *catch* body even if the bodies have only one statement, or even no statements.

Note that the *ExceptionClass* parameter of the *catch* clause specifies one and only one *ExceptionClass*. Listing zero or two or more *ExceptionClasses* in the *catch* clause will generate a compiler error.

Java distinguishes between two types of exceptions:

- unchecked, those that are subclasses of *Error* or *RuntimeException*

- checked, any other exception class

An **unchecked exception**, such as an *ArithmeticException* caused by attempting integer division by 0, a *NumberFormatException*, or a *Null-PointerException*, does not have to be handled with a *try* and *catch* block. In other words, if you omit the *try* and *catch* blocks, your code will compile without an error. If one of these unchecked exceptions is generated at run time, however, the JVM will catch it and print output similar to that shown in Figure 11.3.

Code that could generate a **checked exception**, such as an *IOException*, must be coded within a *try* block. This is required; otherwise, the program will not compile. Thus, when we perform I/O on a file, our code must deal with a potential *IOException* by using *try* and *catch* blocks. We illustrate this later in the chapter.

In the *catch* block, we can use the *Exception* parameter as an object reference to get more information about what caused the exception. Table 11.1 shows three methods inherited by the *Exception* classes.

Example 11.2 shows version 2 of the *DialogBoxInput* application, using a *try* and *catch* block to detect the exception if it occurs.

COMMON ERROR TRAP

Omitting curly braces around the *try* and *catch* blocks will generate a compiler error. A *catch* clause listing several *Exception* classes as parameters will also generate a compiler error.

TABLE 11.1   Useful Methods of Exception Classes

Useful Methods of Exception Classes	
Return value	**Method name and argument list**
String	getMessage( )
	returns a message indicating the cause of the exception
String	toString( )
	returns a *String* containing the exception class name and a message indicating the cause of the exception
void	printStackTrace( )
	prints the line number of the code that caused the exception, along with the sequence of method calls leading up to the exception

We prompt the user and echo the input on lines 14–17. Then we define a *try* block (lines 19–24) and insert the *parseInt* method call that performs the conversion. The *catch* block (lines 25–35) contains the code we want to execute if the *parseInt* method *throws* an exception.

```
 1 /*  DialogBoxInput, version 2
 2 *   Catching the exception generated by the parseInt method
 3 *   Anderson, Franceschi
 4 */
 5
 6 import javax.swing.JOptionPane;
 7
 8 public class DialogBoxInput
 9 {
10   public static void main( String [ ] args )
11   {
12     int n = 0;  // declare and initialize variable
13
14     // prompt for input
15     String s = JOptionPane.showInputDialog( null,
16                            "Enter an integer" );
17     System.out.println( "You entered " + s );
18
19     try
```

```
20      {
21        // attempt to convert the String to an int
22        n = Integer.parseInt( s );
23        System.out.println( "Conversion was successful." );
24      }
25      catch ( NumberFormatException nfe )
26      {
27        System.out.println( "Sorry. incompatible data." );
28        System.out.println( "\nOutput from getMessage: \n"
29                              + nfe.getMessage( ) );
30
31        System.out.println( "\nOutput from toString: \n"
32                              + nfe.toString( ) );
33        System.out.println( "\nOutput from printStackTrace: " );
34        nfe.printStackTrace( );
35      }
36
37      System.out.println( "\nn is " + n );
38    }
39 }
```

EXAMPLE 11.2   *DialogBoxInput* with *try* and *catch* Blocks

Figure 11.4 shows the output when the user inputs a valid value. In this case, the *try* block completes without an exception being generated, and the *catch* block is not executed. Execution of the program skips to line 37, where we print the value of the converted integer.

Figure 11.4
Output with No Exception Generated

Figure 11.5

**Output When an
Exception Is Generated**

Input
? Enter an integer
a

OK   Cancel

```
C:\WINDOWS\System32\cmd.exe
You entered a
Sorry, incompatible data.

Output from getMessage:
For input string: "a"

Output from toString:
java.lang.NumberFormatException: For input string: "a"

Output from printStackTrace:
java.lang.NumberFormatException: For input string: "a"
        at java.lang.NumberFormatException.forInputString(NumberFormatException
.java:48)
        java.lang.Integer.parseInt(Integer.java:447)
        java.lang.Integer.parseInt(Integer.java:497)
        at DialogBoxInput.main(DialogBoxInput.java:22)

n is 0
```

In contrast, Figure 11.5 shows the output when the user inputs an invalid value. In this case, the *parseInt* method throws a *NumberFormatException*. As you can see, the *try* block stops executing at line 22, and we do not print the "Conversion was successful" message. Instead, the *catch* block is executed, and we print the values from the *getMessage*, *toString*, and *printStackTrace* methods of the *NumberFormatException* class. As you can see, the only difference between the return values from the *getMessage* and *toString* methods is that the *toString* method returns the exception class name, as well as the message. You may recognize the output of the *printStackTrace* method. It is almost identical to the message that the JVM printed to the console in Example 11.1, when we didn't have a *try/catch* block.

**COMMON ERROR
TRAP**

Failing to initialize a variable that is assigned a value in a *try* block, then accessed after the *try* block, will generate a compiler error.

When the *catch* block finishes executing, we execute line 37, which prints the value of *n*, which is still 0.

Notice that we declare and initialize the variable *n* in line 12 before we enter the *try* block. If we do not initialize *n* and then try to access *n* after the *try/catch* blocks, we will receive the following compiler error:

```
variable n might not have been initialized
```

The error indicates that the only place where *n* is assigned a value is in the *try* block. If an exception occurs, the *try* block will be interrupted and we might not ever assign a value to *n*. Initializing *n*'s value before entering the *try* block solves this problem.

Although Example 11.2 detects the exception, it merely prints a message that the exception occurred; it does nothing to recover from—or handle— the exception. Example 11.3 shows version 3 of the *DialogBoxInput* class, which handles the exception by putting the *try* and *catch* blocks inside a *do/while* loop so that we continue to prompt the user for a value until the input is valid.

```
 1 /*  DialogBoxInput, version 3
 2 *   Handling an exception
 3 *   Anderson, Franceschi
 4 */
 5
 6 import javax.swing.JOptionPane;
 7
 8 public class DialogBoxInput
 9 {
10   public static void main( String [ ] args )
11   {
12     // declare and initialize variables that will be
13     // assigned values in the try block
14     int n = 0;
15     boolean goodInput = false; // flag variable
16
17     // priming read
18     String s = JOptionPane.showInputDialog( null,
19                         "Enter an integer" );
20     do
21     {
22       try
23       {
24         // attempt to convert the String to an int
25         n = Integer.parseInt( s );
26         goodInput = true;
27       }
28       catch ( NumberFormatException nfe )
29       {
30         s = JOptionPane.showInputDialog( null,
31                         s + " is not an integer. "
32                         + "Enter an integer" );
33       }
34     } while ( !goodInput );
```

```
35
36      JOptionPane.showMessageDialog( null, "The integer is " + n );
37    }
38 }
```

EXAMPLE 11.3   Recovering from the Exception

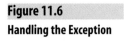

On line 15, we declare a *boolean* variable, *goodInput*, which we will use as a flag variable to indicate whether the value entered by the user could be converted to an *int*. We initialize *goodInput* to *false*; its value will remain *false* until the *parseInt* method completes without an exception, at which time we will assign the value *true* (line 26). We use the value of *goodInput* in the *while* condition of the *do/while* loop (line 34) so that we continue to reprompt the user as long as the input is invalid. Remember that if an exception occurs in the *parseInt* method, line 26 will not be executed, so *goodInput* will be set to *true* only if no exception occurs. Now our application correctly detects and recovers from invalid user input and continues processing.

In Figure 11.6, the user first enters an invalid value. We reprompt the user, and the user enters a valid value. Notice that the user doesn't see that the

Figure 11.6

Handling the Exception

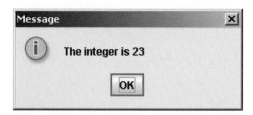

exception occurred, and also notice that our prompt clearly explains the problem to the user.

11.1.2   Catching Multiple Exceptions

If the code in the *try* block might generate multiple types of exceptions, we can provide multiple *catch* blocks, one for each possible exception. When an exception is generated, the JVM searches the *catch* blocks in order. The first *catch* block with a parameter that matches the exception thrown will execute; any remaining *catch* blocks will be skipped.

Remember that subclass objects are also objects of their superclasses, so an exception will match any *catch* block with a parameter that names any of its superclasses. For example, a *NumberFormatException* will match a *catch* block with a *RuntimeException* parameter, and all exceptions will match a *catch* block with an *Exception* parameter. Therefore, when coding several *catch* blocks, put the *catch* blocks for the specialized exceptions first, followed by more general exceptions.

SOFTWARE ENGINEERING TIP

Arrange *catch* blocks to handle the more specialized exceptions first, followed by more general exceptions.

Furthermore, after a *try* block and its associated *catch* blocks, you may optionally add a *finally* block, which will always be executed, whether an exception occurred or not. In the *finally* block, you can include some clean-up code. We will demonstrate a *finally* block when we read from a file later in this chapter.

Here is the syntax for using a *try* block, several *catch* blocks, and a *finally* block:

```
try
{
   // code that might generate an exception
}

catch ( Exception1Class e1 )
{

   // code to handle an Exception1Class exception
}
...

catch ( ExceptionNClass eN )
{
   // code to handle an ExceptionNClass exception
}

finally
```

```
{
   // code to execute regardless of whether an exception occurs
}
```

Again, the curly braces around the various blocks are required, whether these blocks contain zero, one, or more statements.

Example 11.4 shows a *Divider* class that catches two possible exceptions. First, we prompt the user for an integer (lines 20–22), then attempt to convert the input *String* to an *int* (lines 27–28). As we have seen, an invalid input value will generate a *NumberFormatException*. If we are successful in converting the input to an *int*, we use the *int* as the divisor in a division operation (lines 30–31). For simplicity, we use a predefined value (100) as the dividend. If the divisor is 0, line 31 will generate an *ArithmeticException*.

Thus, we put all this code into our *try* block (lines 25–34) and provide two *catch* blocks, one to handle the *NumberFormatException* (lines 35–40) and one to handle the *ArithmeticException* (lines 41–46).

```
 1 /* Divider
 2 *  Handling multiple exceptions
 3 *  Anderson, Franceschi
 4 */
 5
 6 import javax.swing.JOptionPane;
 7
 8 public class Divider
 9 {
10   public static void main( String [ ] args )
11   {
12     // declare and initialize variables
13     int divisor = 0;
14     int quotient = 0;
15     int dividend = 100;
16
17     // initialize flag variable
18     boolean goodInput = false;
19
20     // prompt for input
21     String s = JOptionPane.showInputDialog( null,
22                            "Enter an integer divisor" );
23     do
24     {
```

```
25      try
26      {
27        // attempt to convert the String to an int
28        divisor = Integer.parseInt( s );
29
30        // attempt the division
31        quotient = dividend / divisor;
32
33        goodInput = true;
34      }
35      catch ( NumberFormatException nfe )
36      {
37        s = JOptionPane.showInputDialog( null,
38                           s + " is not an integer. "
39                           + "Enter an integer divisor" );
40      }
41      catch ( ArithmeticException ae )
42      {
43        s = JOptionPane.showInputDialog( null,
44                         "Divisor cannot be 0. "
45                         + "Enter an integer divisor" );
46      }
47    } while ( !goodInput );
48
49    JOptionPane.showMessageDialog( null,
50                         "The result is " + quotient );
51  }
52 }
```

EXAMPLE 11.4   The *Divider* Class

Figure 11.7 shows an execution of the program. At the first prompt, the user enters 45h, which causes the *parseInt* method to throw a *NumberFormatException*. The JVM starts scanning the *catch* blocks for a matching *Exception* parameter. The first *catch* block (lines 35–40) matches the exception thrown, so the code in that *catch* block is executed and we reprompt the user for a valid integer. We then skip the *catch* block for the *ArithmeticException* and line 47 is executed, which tests the value of *goodInput*. This will still be *false* at this point, so we repeat the *do/while* loop.

This time, the user enters 0, so the *parseInt* method successfully converts 0 to an *int*. Then line 31 is executed, where we attempt to divide by 0. This

Figure 11.7

Output from Example 11.4

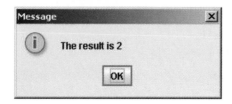

causes an *ArithmeticException*. Again, the JVM starts scanning *catch* blocks for a matching exception parameter. The JVM skips the first *catch* block, but finds a match in the second block (lines 41–46), so we execute that *catch* block. This time we inform the user that the divisor cannot be 0 and reprompt for a new value. Finally, the user enters a valid, nonzero value; we are now able to both convert the input to an *int* and perform the division without generating any exceptions. In this case, both *catch* blocks are skipped, and we display the result in a dialog box (lines 49–50).

Having provided several examples of exceptions, we must also consider this: Not every problem needs to be addressed by generating an exception. As a matter of fact, generating and handling exceptions considerably slows down execution of your code due to the processing overhead. Often, for

SOFTWARE ENGINEERING TIP

Whenever possible, use a simple *if/else* statement to detect an unchecked exception, rather than *try* and *catch* blocks. This will improve the performance of your code.

example when using Java's I/O classes, we will have no choice but to use *try* and *catch* blocks. In Example 11.4, however, we could have used a simple *if/else* statement to test the value of the divisor before attempting the division. This would solve the problem simply and efficiently without generating an exception.

How do we know if a constructor or a method *throws* an exception and what type of exception it *throws*? As always, our best source of information is the Sun Microsystems Web site. After you have identified a constructor or a method that you would like to use, simply view its API in order to determine whether it *throws* any exceptions, and if so, which ones.

REFERENCE POINT

Consult the Sun Microsystems' Java Web site *www.java.sun.com* to see if a constructor or a method *throws* an exception and, if so, what type of exception.

11.1.3   User-Defined Exceptions

There will be times when we want to design our own exception class because the predefined Java exception classes do not fit our needs.

Suppose we are interested in designing a class encapsulating email addresses. We will call that class *EmailAddress*. To keep things simple, we will say that a legal email address is a *String* containing the @ character. In order to prevent instantiation of objects with illegal email addresses, we will design our *EmailAddress* constructor so that it throws an exception if its argument, a *String*, does not contain the @ character.

In order to do that, we first design an exception class that encapsulates an illegal email exception. We call our class *IllegalEmailException* and we will *throw* the exception when the argument to the *EmailAddress* constructor does not contain the @ character. Since Java already has an *IllegalArgumentException* class, we will define our *IllegalEmailException* class as a subclass of the *IllegalArgumentException* class.

More generally, when a user-defined exception class is defined as a subclass of an existing Java exception class, such as *Exception*, *NumberFormatException*, or *IllegalArgumentException*, our class inherits the functionality of the existing exception class, which simplifies coding the new class. We *extend* the *IllegalArgumentException* class so that we can associate a specific error message with the exception. We need to code only the constructor, and the constructor's job is to pass our message to the constructor of the superclass.

Thus, the general pattern of a user-defined exception class is:

```
public class ExceptionName extends ExistingExceptionClassName
{
  public ExceptionName( String message )
```

```
   {
     super( message );
   }
 }
```

Example 11.5 shows our *IllegalEmailException* class.

```
 1 /* The IllegalEmailException class
 2    Anderson, Franceschi
 3 */
 4
 5 public class IllegalEmailException extends IllegalArgumentException
 6 {
 7   public IllegalEmailException( String message )
 8   {
 9     super( message );
10   }
11 }
```

The constructor for the class is coded at lines 7 to 10; it takes a *String* parameter and simply passes it to the superclass constructor.

The pattern for a method that throws a user-defined exception is:

```
accessModifier dataType methodName( parameter list )
                    throws ExceptionName
{
  if ( parameter list is legal )
      // process the parameter list
  else
      throw new ExceptionName( "Some message here" );
}
```

The message we pass to the *ExceptionName* constructor will identify the type of error we detected. When a client program catches the exception, the client can call the *getMessage* method of the exception class in order to retrieve that message.

Example 11.6 shows our *EmailAddress* class.

```
 1 /* The EmailAddress class
 2    Anderson, Franceschi
 3 */
 4
```

```
 5 public class EmailAddress
 6 {
 7   public static final char AT_SIGN = '@';
 8   private String email;
 9
10   public EmailAddress( String newEmail )
11                     throws IllegalEmailException
12   {
13     if ( newEmail.indexOf( AT_SIGN ) != - 1 )
14         email = newEmail;
15     else
16         throw new IllegalEmailException
17             ( "Email address does not contain " + AT_SIGN );
18   }
19
20   public String getHost( )
21   {
22     int index = email.indexOf( AT_SIGN );
23     return email.substring( index + 1, email.length( ) );
24   }
25 }
```

EXAMPLE 11.6   The *EmailAddress* Class

We coded the constructor at lines 10–18. We test if the constructor's argument, *newEmail*, contains the character *AT_SIGN* (a constant equal to @) at line 13. If it does, we proceed normally and initialize the instance variable *email* at line 14. If it does not, we throw an *IllegalEmailException* with the appropriate message at lines 16–17. In addition to the constructor, we coded the *getHost* method at lines 20–24. The *getHost* method returns the substring comprising the characters of *email* after *AT_SIGN*. Thus, for an email address of *myEmailAddress@yahoo.com*, the *getHost* method will return *yahoo.com*.

Now that we have built our own exception class and a class including a method that *throws* that exception, we are ready to use them in a client program. This is identical to using a predefined Java exception. Example 11.7 shows our *EmailChecker* class.

```
1 /* The EmailChecker class
2    Anderson, Franceschi
3 */
4
5 import java.util.Scanner;
```

```
 6
 7 public class EmailChecker
 8 {
 9   public static void main( String [ ] args )
10   {
11     Scanner scan = new Scanner( System.in );
12     System.out.print( "Enter your email address > " );
13     String myEmail = scan.next( );
14     try
15     {
16       EmailAddress address = new EmailAddress( myEmail );
17       System.out.println( "Your host is " + address.getHost( ) );
18     }
19     catch ( IllegalEmailException iee )
20     {
21       System.out.println( iee.getMessage( ) );
22     }
23   }
24 }
```

EXAMPLE 11.7   The *EmailChecker* Class

We ask the user to input an email address, *myEmail*, at lines 12–13. We then try to instantiate the *EmailAddress* object *address* at line 16, passing *myEmail* to the constructor. If *myEmail* does not contain the @ character, our *EmailAddress* constructor *throws* an *IllegalEmailException*, which this program *catches* at line 19. In this *catch* block, we print the message the *EmailAddress* constructor sent to the *IllegalEmailException* constructor. If *myEmail* contains the @ character, we continue executing inside the *try* block. Figure 11.8 shows two runs of this example,

Figure 11.8

Two Sample Runs of Example 11.7

the first generates the exception, the second completes without generating an exception.

CODE IN ACTION

In the Chapter 11 directory of the CD-ROM accompanying this book you will find a Shockwave movie showing a step-by-step illustration of *try* and *catch* blocks. Double-click on the *IO.html* file to start the movie.

Skill Practice
with these end-of-chapter questions

11.11.1   Multiple Choice Exercises

Questions 1, 2, 3, 4

11.11.8   Technical Writing

Question 65

11.2   The *java.io* Package

Java provides a number of classes in the *java.io* package for reading from files, writing to files, and for reading from the console. We will use only a few of those classes here. Table 11.2 describes a group of classes designed for data input.

TABLE 11.2   Selected Classes for Input

Input Classes	
Class	**Description**
Reader	*Abstract* superclass for input classes
InputStream	*Abstract* superclass representing an input stream of raw bytes
InputStreamReader	Class to read input data streams
FileReader	Class to read character files
BufferedReader	Class providing more efficient reading of character files
FileInputStream	Input stream to read raw bytes of data from files
ObjectInputStream	Class to read/recover objects from a file written using *ObjectOutputStream*

Figure 11.9 shows an inheritance hierarchy for the Java classes described in Table 11.2:

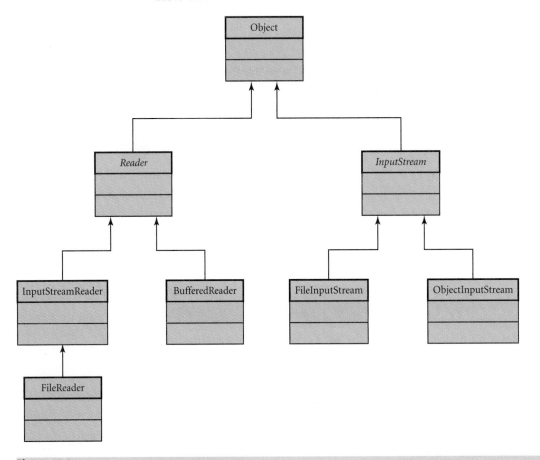

Figure 11.9
The Inheritance Hierarchy for Input Classes

Table 11.3 describes a group of classes designed for data output, and Figure 11.10 shows an inheritance hierarchy for output Java classes in Table 11.3.

11.3   Reading from the Java Console

Since the beginning, we have used the *System* class to read from and write to the Java console. We wrote to the console using the *out* object, which is a *static* field of the *System* class. *System.out* represents the standard output

TABLE 11.3   Selected Output Classes

Output Classes	
Class	**Description**
Writer	*Abstract* superclass for output classes
OutputStreamWriter	Class to write output data streams
OutputStream	*Abstract* superclass representing an output stream of raw bytes
FileWriter	Class for writing to character files
BufferedWriter	Class providing more efficient writing to character files
PrintWriter	Convenient class to print basic data types, *Strings*, and objects
PrintStream	Class providing ability to print various data types conveniently
FileOutputStream	Output stream to write raw bytes of data to files
ObjectOutputStream	Class to write objects to a file

stream, which by default is the Java console. We also used the *in* object, which is another *static* field of the *System* class, to read from the console using the *Scanner* class. We used *System.in* as an argument to the *Scanner* constructor to associate our *Scanner* object with the Java console, as in the following statement:

```
Scanner scan = new Scanner( System.in );
```

System.in represents the standard input stream, which by default is also the Java console. While *Scanner* is a convenient class for reading from the console, the Java I/O classes provide more flexibility. Using the Java I/O classes, we can treat the console input as a stream of bytes.

To do this, we use *InputStreamReader*, a subclass of the *abstract* class *Reader*, which is designed to read input data streams. *InputStreamReader* has several constructors, all of which take at least an *InputStream* argument, representing the input stream we are reading from. When we read from the console, the *InputStream* argument is *System.in*.

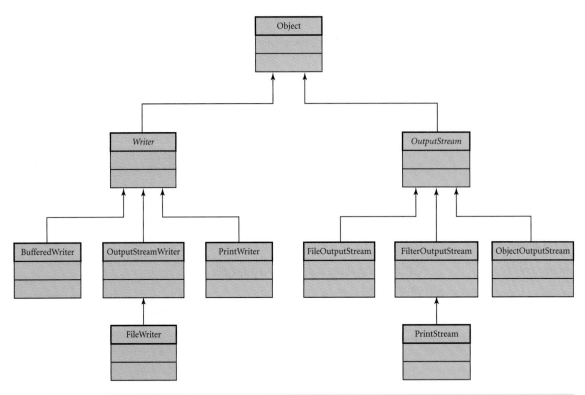

Figure 11.10
The Inheritance Hierarchy for Output Classes

InputStream has several *read* methods, inherited from the class *Reader*, which read bytes and convert them into characters.

However, an *InputStreamReader* reads just one byte at a time, and therefore is inefficient for reading entire lines of text. The class *BufferedReader*, also a subclass of the class *Reader*, uses **buffering** for efficient reading, in particular with its method *readLine*. Both constructors of the *BufferedReader* class take a *Reader* object as an argument. Because *InputStreamReader* is a subclass of *Reader*, any *InputStreamReader* object is a *Reader* object.

You may wonder what the word "buffering" means and how buffering applies to reading data. Reading data from the disk or the console is much slower than accessing data in main memory. When a class uses buffering, it reads data bytes ahead (that is, before our program asks for them) and stores the data in a temporary location in memory, called a **buffer**. Then, when our program asks for data, the input class quickly transfers the data from its buffer in memory to our input variable.

When we construct an input stream or output stream object, the JVM associates the filename, standard input stream, or standard output stream with our object. When we associate a file with an input stream or output stream, we are **opening the file**. When we are finished with a file, we call the *close* method to release the resources associated with the file. Calling the *close* method is optional. When the program finishes executing, all of its resources are released, including the resources of any unclosed files. It is good practice, in general, to call the *close* method, especially if you will be opening a number of files (or opening the same file multiple times). In contrast, the standard input stream (*System.in*), the standard output stream (*System.out*), and the standard error stream (*System.err*) are open when the program begins. They are intended to stay open and should not be closed.

SOFTWARE ENGINEERING TIP

Close files when you have finished processing their data. Do not close the standard input, output, or error devices.

The classes, constructors, and methods discussed above are shown in Table 11.4.

Example 11.8 shows how these *InputStreamReader* and *BufferedReader* classes can be used in a Java program to read a *String* from the console.

```
 1 /* Demonstrating Reading a String from the Console
 2  *  Anderson, Franceschi
 3  */
 4
 5 import java.io.InputStreamReader;
 6 import java.io.BufferedReader;
 7 import java.io.IOException;
 8
 9 public class ConsoleInput
10 {
11   public static void main( String [ ] args )
12   {
13     String stringRead = "";
14
```

TABLE 11.4   Useful Classes, Constructors, and Methods for Console Input

Classes, Constructors, and Methods for Console Input		
Class	Constructor	Exceptions Thrown
InputStreamReader	InputStreamReader(InputStream is) constructs an *InputStreamReader* object from an *InputStream* object. For console input, the *InputStream* object is *System.in*	None
BufferedReader	BufferedReader(Reader r) constructs a *BufferedReader* object from a *Reader* object—here the *Reader* object will be an *InputStreamReader* object	None
Method API		
BufferedReader	String readLine( ) reads a line of text from the current *InputStream* object, and returns the text as a *String*	IOException
BufferedReader	void close( ) releases resources associated with an open input stream	IOException

```
15      try
16      {
17        // set up for input
18        InputStreamReader isr = new InputStreamReader( System.in );
19        BufferedReader br = new BufferedReader( isr );
20
21        // prompt and read input
22        System.out.println( "Please enter a phrase or sentence > " );
23        stringRead = br.readLine( );
24      }
25      catch ( IOException ioe )
26      {
27        System.out.println( ioe.getMessage( ) );
28      }
29
30      // echo data read
31      System.out.println( "The string read was " + stringRead );
32    }
33 }
```

EXAMPLE 11.8   Reading a *String* from the Console

Lines 5, 6, and 7 import the three classes that are used in this program: *InputStreamReader*, *BufferedReader*, and *IOException*. The *String stringRead* variable is initialized at line 13, since we will be accessing that variable after the *try* block (at line 31).

As you can see from Table 11.4, the *readLine* and *close* methods of the *BufferedReader* class throw an *IOException*. This is a checked exception, so we need to put those method calls into a *try* block (lines 15–24) and provide a *catch* block (lines 25–28) to handle the *IOException*, if it occurs.

Line 18 instantiates an *InputStreamReader* object using *System.in* as the argument for the constructor. This associates our *InputStreamReader* object with the console. Line 19 instantiates a *BufferedReader* object from the *InputStreamReader* object we just instantiated. At line 23, we call the *readLine* method for the *BufferedReader* object *br*, which waits for user input. The user is expected to enter a line of input and press the *Enter* key. The text typed by the user is then returned by the *readLine* method as a *String*.

Figure 11.11 shows the output when this program runs and the user enters "Java Illuminated" at the prompt.

In the preceding program, the *InputStreamReader* object *isr* is used only as the argument of the *BufferedReader* constructor; it is not used anywhere else in the program. In this case, instead of creating an *InputStreamReader* object reference, many programmers prefer to use an anonymous *InputStreamReader* object as the argument of the *BufferedReader* constructor. In other words, instead of writing the following two statements:

```
InputStreamReader isr = new InputStreamReader( System.in );
BufferedReader br = new BufferedReader( isr );
```

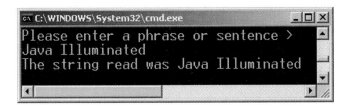

Figure 11.11
Output from Example 11.8

we could use the following single statement:

```
BufferedReader br = new BufferedReader(
                        new InputStreamReader ( System.in ) );
```

It is a matter of preference as to which code you use.

At this point, you may be thinking that performing user input from the console is not very convenient because it involves a lot of code. We can hide that complexity, however, by encapsulating all this processing into a *User-Input* class, which is similar in concept to the *Scanner* class. We can write our class so that with just one line of code, the client program can retrieve user input. Our class will provide the *try* and *catch* blocks and handle the exceptions. Also, if the client program wants to validate that the user enters only an integer value, the *UserInput* class can solve that problem too; we will keep reprompting the user to enter an integer value until the user does. Example 11.9 shows how we can build the *readInteger* method of our *UserInput* class. Other methods of the class would follow the same logic and design.

The *readInteger* method will have this API:

```
public static int readInteger( String prompt )
```

We declare the *readInteger* method to be *static* so that the user does not need to instantiate an object before reading from the console. Thus, the *readInteger* method will be invoked using the *UserInput* class name, rather than an object reference. Also notice that the user supplies the prompt as an argument to the *readInteger* method. This lets us combine the prompting and the reading into one statement.

Let's consider what we need to do with the *readInteger* method. In addition to prompting the user and reading the input, we have to do the following:

- Convert the user input into an integer value
- Reprompt the user and read new input if the conversion fails.

These steps are similar to what we did earlier in Example 11.3. Thus, the code of the *readInteger* method of class *UserInput* follows the same logic as the code in Example 11.3.

```
1 /** UserInput class
2 *    Anderson, Franceschi
3 */
```

```
 4
 5 import java.io.IOException;
 6 import java.io.InputStreamReader;
 7 import java.io.BufferedReader;
 8
 9 public class UserInput
10 {
11    /** readInteger method
12     *   @param    prompt  message for user
13     *   @return   the value read
14     */
15    public static int readInteger( String prompt )
16    {
17      int result = 0;
18      String message = "";
19
20      try
21      {
22        InputStreamReader isr = new InputStreamReader( System.in );
23        BufferedReader in = new BufferedReader( isr );
24        String str = "";
25        boolean validInt = false;
26
27        do
28        {
29          // prompt user and read value
30          System.out.print( message + prompt + " > " );
31          str = in.readLine( );
32
33          try
34          {
35            // attempt to convert to an integer
36            result = Integer.parseInt( str );
37            validInt = true;
38          }
39
40          catch ( NumberFormatException nfe )
41          {
42            message = "Invalid integer:   ";
43          }
44        } while ( !validInt );
45      }
46
47      catch ( IOException ioe )
```

```
48   {
49      System.out.println( ioe.getMessage( ) );
50   }
51
52   return result;
53 }
54
55 // other methods of the UserInput class
56 // ....
57 }
```

EXAMPLE 11.9   The *UserInput* Class

In the *readInteger* method, we use nested *try* and *catch* blocks. We open the *BufferedReader* object and call the *readLine* method in a *try* block (lines 20–45) with a corresponding *catch* block (lines 47–50) that handles an *IOException*, if it occurs. Within this *try* block is nested another *try* block (lines 33–38), into which we put the call to *parseInt* to convert the input *String* to an integer. The *NumberFormatException*, if it occurs, will be handled by the corresponding nested *catch* block (lines 40–43), which sets the value of the *String message* to indicate that the input is invalid.

As we mentioned, the *readInteger* method is *static*, so we do not require the user to instantiate an object that represents the console. Thus, we must instantiate an object of the *BufferedReader* class each time the *readInteger* method is called (lines 22–23).

Example 11.10 shows a client program that uses the *UserInput* class for console input. You can see that only one statement (line 9) is needed to prompt the user and read an integer.

```
 1 /** UserInputClient
 2 *    Anderson, Franceschi
 3 */
 4
 5 public class UserInputClient
 6 {
 7    public static void main( String [ ] args )
 8    {
 9      int age = UserInput.readInteger( "Enter your age" );
10      System.out.println( "You entered " + age );
11    }
12 }
```

EXAMPLE 11.10   A *UserInput* Client

Figure 11.12

Output from
UserInputClient

**SOFTWARE
ENGINEERING TIP**

Encapsulate complex code
into a reusable class. This
will simplify your applications and make the logic
clearer.

Figure 11.12 shows the output from the *UserInputClient* application when
the user enters an invalid integer, then a valid integer.

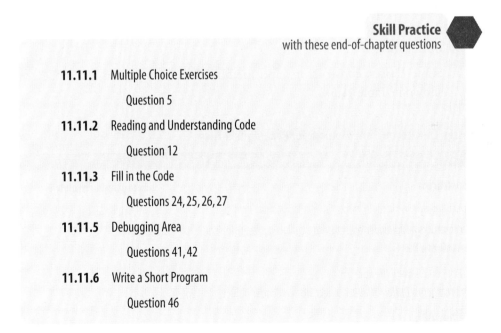

Skill Practice
with these end-of-chapter questions

11.11.1 Multiple Choice Exercises

Question 5

11.11.2 Reading and Understanding Code

Question 12

11.11.3 Fill in the Code

Questions 24, 25, 26, 27

11.11.5 Debugging Area

Questions 41, 42

11.11.6 Write a Short Program

Question 46

11.4 Reading and Writing Text Files

Java supports two file types, text and binary. In text files, data is stored as
characters; in binary files, data is stored as raw bytes. Different classes are
used for writing and reading each file type. The type of a file is determined
when the file is written to and depends on which classes were used to write

to the file. Thus, to read from an existing file, you must know the file's type in order to select the appropriate classes.

In this section, we concentrate on text files.

11.4.1   Reading Text Files

Reading from a text file one line at a time is similar to reading input from the console.

FileReader, a subclass of class *InputStreamReader*, itself a subclass of the class *Reader*, is designed to read character files. *FileReader* has several constructors; one of them takes a *String* as its only argument, representing the name of the file to be read.

However, a *FileReader* object does not use buffering to read ahead, and therefore is inefficient when reading entire lines of text. Just as we used the *BufferedReader* class to read more efficiently from the console, we will use the *BufferedReader* class and the *readLine* method to read more efficiently from a file.

Some classes, constructors, and methods for reading from a text file are shown in Table 11.5.

TABLE 11.5   Useful Classes, Constructors, and Methods for Reading Text Files

Classes, Constructors, and Methods for Reading Text Files		
Class	**Constructor**	**Exceptions Thrown**
FileReader	FileReader(String filename) constructs a *FileReader* object from a *String* representing the name of a file	FileNotFoundException
BufferedReader	BufferedReader(Reader r) constructs a *BufferedReader* object from a *Reader* object	None
	Method APIs	
BufferedReader	String readLine( ) reads a line of text from the current *InputStream* object and returns a *String*. Returns a *null String* when the end of the file is reached	IOException
BufferedReader	void close( ) releases resources allocated to the *BufferedReader* object	IOException

Usually, we do not know how much data a file contains; there could be a small amount of data, say two lines of text, or a large amount of data, say 3,000 lines. And usually, we need to process all the data in the file. For instance, a log file could store the email addresses of all the visitors (one email address per line, for instance) on our Web site for the last two years. There is no way to predict the number of lines of text in the log file.

Because we don't know how many lines are in a file, we need a signal to tell us when we have read all the data. In other words, we need a signal when we reach the end of the file. This condition will be easy to test. The *readLine* method returns a *null String* when the end of the file is detected.

Example 11.11 shows how these *FileReader* and *BufferedReader* classes can be used in a Java program to read from an existing file named *dataFile.txt*, one line at a time.

COMMON ERROR TRAP

To determine if we have reached the end of the file, be sure to test whether the return value from the *read-Line* method is a *null String*. Do not test whether the return value is the empty *String*, because the file could contain empty lines.

```
 1 /* Demonstrating how to read from a text file
 2    Anderson, Franceschi
 3 */
 4
 5 import java.io.FileReader;
 6 import java.io.BufferedReader;
 7 import java.io.IOException;
 8 import java.io.FileNotFoundException;
 9
10 public class ReadTextFile
11 {
12   public static void main( String [ ] args )
13   {
14     try
15     {
16         FileReader fr = new FileReader( "dataFile.txt" );
17         BufferedReader br = new BufferedReader( fr );
18
19         // declare String variable and prime the read
20         String stringRead = br.readLine( );
21
22         while ( stringRead != null ) // test for the end of the file
23         {
24            // print the line read
25            System.out.println( stringRead );
26            stringRead = br.readLine( );  // read next line
27         }
```

```
28
29          // release resources associated with dataFile.txt
30          br.close( );
31      }
32
33      catch ( FileNotFoundException fnfe )
34      {
35        System.out.println( "Unable to find dataFile.txt, exiting" );
36      }
37
38      catch ( IOException ioe )
39      {
40        ioe.printStackTrace( );
41      }
42    }
43 }
```

EXAMPLE 11.11   Demonstrating How to Read a Text File

Lines 5–8 import the four classes used by this program: *FileReader, Buffered-Reader, IOException,* and *FileNotFoundException.*

Line 16 instantiates a *FileReader* object using the name of the file to be read, *dataFile.txt,* as the argument of the constructor. The *FileReader* constructor throws a *FileNotFoundException* if the file does not exist. We catch this exception at line 33. Since the program cannot continue without the file, we print a message to the user that we were not able to find the file and that the program is exiting (line 35). If no exception is thrown, line 17 instantiates a *BufferedReader* object, which we use to read complete lines from the file.

On line 20, we perform our priming read for the *while* loop by reading the first line of text in the file. Because it is possible that the file is empty, we need to prime the read before entering the loop body. The *while* loop condition, at line 22, tests whether the line we just read is *null.* If so, there is nothing to read in the file and we skip the *while* loop. If *stringRead* is not *null,* we were able to read a line of text and we enter the loop body to process it.

The *stringRead String* variable is declared and initialized at line 20, because we will be accessing that variable only inside the *try* block. In this example, there is no need to declare and initialize the variable before the *try* block.

In the body of the loop, at line 25, we process the line of text read from the file. In this example, we just echo what we read to the console. At line 26, we read the next line of text, which is then tested by the *while* loop condition at line 22. If the *String* returned from the *readLine* method is not *null*, we re-enter the body of the loop to process that line of text and to read the next line. We continue looping through the file until we receive a *null String* from the *readLine* method. When the *String* is *null*, we exit the loop and resume execution at lines 29–30.

At line 30, we use the *BufferedReader* object *br* to call the *close* method, thus releasing its resources. After line 30, any attempt to read using the *br* object reference will throw an *IOException*, which we will catch at line 38. The *catch* block at lines 38–41 uses an *IOException* as its parameter, which also matches the type of exception thrown by the *readLine* method. Because we don't know whether the *close* or the *readLine* method triggered the exception, we call the *printStackTrace* method, which outputs useful debugging information.

Note how we have ordered the two *catch* blocks. If a problem is detected with the *readLine* method, it throws an *IOException*, while the *FileReader* constructor could throw a *FileNotFoundException*. Remember that when an exception occurs, the *catch* blocks are scanned, in order, for a match between the *catch* block parameter and the type of exception that occurred. Because the *FileNotFoundException* is a subclass of *IOException*, a *FileNotFoundException* will match a *catch* block for an *IOException*. Therefore, we need to put the *catch* block for the *FileNotFoundException* before the *catch* block for the *IOException*. This way, if the file *dataFile.txt* does not exist, the exception matches the *FileNotFoundException* block, and we are able to print a meaningful message for the user.

Let's assume the file *dataFile.txt* contains the Gelett Burgess poem shown in Figure 11.13.

```
I never saw a purple cow,
I never hope to see one;
But I can tell you, anyhow,
I'd rather see than be one!
```

Figure 11.13
Contents of *dataFile.txt*

Figure 11.14
Output of Example 11.11

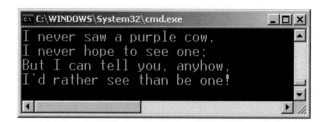

Figure 11.14
Output of Example 11.11

When the program in Example 11.8 runs, it will produce the output shown in Figure 11.14.

11.4.2   Writing to Text Files

In the previous section, we learned how to read data from a text file. But how did the data get into the file in the first place? It could be that someone put the data into the file using an editor, such as Notepad in Windows, or vi, pico, or emacs in Unix. Typing data into a file is convenient when the amount of data is small. But very often files contain a significant amount of data, typically written to the file by a computer program. For instance, a Web server writes to log files to keep track of the visitors accessing the Web site, how they got to the Web site, the time they arrived, etc. If the Web server comes under attack from a hacker, these log files can be consulted to determine where the hacker came from, who the hacker was, and other information.

In this section, we will learn how to write to a text file. But before going into the details, we must distinguish among several situations:

- Creating/writing to a new file, that is, the file does not exist.

- Writing to an existing file and replacing the contents of the file with new data.

- Writing to an existing file, but keeping the contents of the file and adding data at the end of the file. This is called **appending** to the file.

Java provides us with the necessary tools to perform all the above actions. Table 11.6 summarizes what will happen, depending on the action we perform.

In many ways, writing to a file parallels reading from a file. We instantiate a *FileWriter* object, add buffering with a *BufferedWriter* object, write to the file, and *close* the *BufferedWriter* object to release the resources associated with it.

TABLE 11.6 Writing or Appending to an Existing or New File

Operation	If the file exists ...	If the file does not exist ...
write	the current contents of the file are deleted, and writing starts at the beginning of the file	the file is created and writing starts at the beginning of the file
append	data is added to the end of the file, keeping the existing contents	the file is created and writing starts at the beginning of the file

FileWriter, a subclass of the class *OutputStreamWriter*, itself a subclass of the class *Writer*, is designed to write characters to text files. *FileWriter* has several constructors, one of which takes as its two arguments a *String* file name and a *boolean* mode, representing whether we are writing (*false*) or appending (*true*) to the file.

However, a *FileWriter* object, which is also a *Writer* object, does not use buffering to write ahead. As we used the *BufferedReader* class to read more efficiently from a file, we will use the *BufferedWriter* class to write more efficiently to a file. We use the method *write*, which takes one argument, a *String*. (There are other *write* methods, taking other arguments, but we will concentrate on just this one.) The classes, constructors, and methods discussed above are shown in Table 11.7.

Example 11.12 shows how these *FileWriter* and *BufferedWriter* classes can be used to write to a text file named *output.txt*.

```
 1 /* Demonstrating how to write to a text file
 2    Anderson, Franceschi
 3 */
 4
 5 import java.io.FileWriter;
 6 import java.io.BufferedWriter;
 7 import java.io.IOException;
 8
 9 public class WriteTextFile
10 {
11   public static void main( String [ ] args )
12   {
```

TABLE 11.7　**Useful Classes, Constructors, and Methods for Writing to a Text File**

	Classes, Constructors, and Methods for Writing to Text Files	
Class	**Constructor**	**Exceptions Thrown**
FileWriter	FileWriter(String fileName, 　　　boolean mode)	IOException
	constructs a *FileWriter* object from a *String* representing the name of a file; if *mode* is *false*, we will write to the file; if *mode* is *true*, we will append to the file	
BufferedWriter	BufferedWriter(Writer w)	None
	constructs a *BufferedWriter* object from a *Writer* object	
Method APIs		
BufferedWriter	void write(String s)	IOException
	writes a *String* to the current *OutputStream* object. This method is inherited from the *Writer class*	
BufferedWriter	void newLine( )	IOException
	writes a line separator	
BufferedWriter	void close( )	IOException
	releases the resources associated with the *BufferedWriter* object	

```
13      try
14      {
15          FileWriter fw = new FileWriter( "output.txt", false );
16          // false means we will be writing to output.txt,
17          // rather than appending to it
18
19          BufferedWriter bw = new BufferedWriter( fw );
20
21          // write four lines
22          bw.write( "I never saw a purple cow," );
23          bw.newLine( );
24          bw.write( "I never hope to see one;" );
25          bw.newLine( );
26          bw.write( "But I can tell you, anyhow," );
27          bw.newLine( );
28          bw.write( "I'd rather see than be one!" );
```

```
29          bw.newLine( );
30
31          // release resources associated with output.txt
32          bw.close( );
33          System.out.println( "File written successfully" );
34      }
35
36      catch ( IOException ioe )
37      {
38         ioe.printStackTrace( );
39      }
40   }
41 }
```

EXAMPLE 11.12   Demonstrating How to Write to a Text File

Lines 5, 6, and 7 import the *FileWriter*, *BufferedWriter*, and *IOException* classes.

Line 15 instantiates a *FileWriter* object using two arguments: *output.txt*, the name of the file we will write to, and *false*, which means that we will be writing to the file, not appending to it. If the file *output.txt* exists, its contents will be deleted and overwritten, whereas if the file does not exist, it will be created. The *FileWriter* constructor throws an *IOException*; such an exception will be thrown, for instance, if we specify a filename that is a directory.

Line 19 instantiates a *BufferedWriter* object, which we will use to write text to the file. At line 22, using the *BufferedWriter* object *bw*, we call the *write* method, passing the *String* to be written to the file. Note that we call the *newLine* method after writing the *String* to the file. We do this because the *write* method does not insert a line separator into the file. Also, we call the *newLine* method, rather than appending a "\n" to our *String*, because the line separator can be different on different platforms. This makes our code more portable. At lines 24–29, we write three more lines of text and three more line separators.

At line 32, we call the *close* method to release the *BufferedWriter* resources. Any further attempt to write to the file using the *bw* object reference will result in an *IOException* being thrown (and caught at line 36). The *catch* block at lines 36–39 uses an *IOException* as its parameter, which also matches the type of exception thrown by the *FileWriter* constructor and the *write* method. Again, because we don't know where the *IOException* may have occurred, we include code to print a stack trace in the *catch* block to help diagnose the problem.

Figure 11.15

Contents of *output.txt*

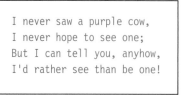

```
I never saw a purple cow,
I never hope to see one;
But I can tell you, anyhow,
I'd rather see than be one!
```

Figure 11.16

Console Output from Example 11.12

After this program is executed, the file *output.txt* will contain the text shown in Figure 11.15.

Because we wrote the text to the *output.txt* file, the only output to the console is generated by line 33, as shown in Figure 11.16.

11.4.3   Appending to Text Files

Appending text to a file is similar to writing text; the only difference is that the second argument of the *FileWriter* constructor is *true*, instead of *false*.

Example 11.13 shows how these *FileWriter* and *BufferedWriter* classes can be used in a Java program to append text to our file named *output.txt*.

```
 1 /* Demonstrating how to append to a text file
 2    Anderson, Franceschi
 3 */
 4
 5 import java.io.FileWriter;
 6 import java.io.BufferedWriter;
 7 import java.io.IOException;
 8
 9 public class AppendTextFile
10 {
11   public static void main( String [ ] args )
12   {
```

```
13      try
14      {
15          FileWriter fw = new FileWriter( "output.txt", true );
16          // true means we will be appending to output.txt,
17          // rather than writing to it
18
19          BufferedWriter bw = new BufferedWriter( fw );
20
21          // write four more lines
22          bw.write( "Ah, yes! I wrote the \"Purple Cow\" --" );
23          bw.newLine( );
24          bw.write( "I'm sorry, now, I wrote it!" );
25          bw.newLine( );
26          bw.write( "But I can tell you anyhow," );
27          bw.newLine( );
28          bw.write( "I'll kill you if you quote it!" );
29          bw.newLine( );
30
31          // release resources associated with output.txt
32          bw.close( );
33          System.out.println( "File appended successfully" );
34      }
35
36      catch ( IOException ioe )
37      {
38          ioe.printStackTrace( );
39      }
40   }
41 }
```

EXAMPLE 11.13   Demonstrating How to Append to a Text File

Example 11.13 is similar to Example 11.12. The major difference is that when we instantiate the *FileWriter* object (line 15), the second argument is *true*, which means that we will append to the file *output.txt*, instead of writing to it. If the file *output.txt* exists, we will start writing at the end of its current contents, whereas if the file does not exist, it will be created.

In this program, we append four additional lines to the file (lines 21–29).

Assuming that before this program is executed, the file *output.txt* contains the poem shown in Figure 11.15, then after this program is executed, the file *output.txt* will contain the text shown in Figure 11.17, and the output to the console is that shown in Figure 11.18.

COMMON ERROR TRAP

Opening a file for writing will cause the existing file data to be deleted. If you intend to add new data to a file while maintaining the original contents, open the file for appending.

Figure 11.17

Contents of *output.txt*

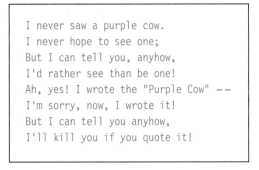

```
I never saw a purple cow.
I never hope to see one;
But I can tell you, anyhow,
I'd rather see than be one!
Ah, yes! I wrote the "Purple Cow" --
I'm sorry, now, I wrote it!
But I can tell you anyhow,
I'll kill you if you quote it!
```

Figure 11.18

Console Output from Example 11.13

11.5   Reading Structured Text Files

Sometimes a text file is organized so that each line represents data related to a particular record or object. For instance, an airline company could have data stored in a file where each line represents a flight segment, with the following comma-separated data:

- flight number
- origin airport
- destination airport
- number of passengers
- average ticket price

Such a file could contain the following data:

```
AA123,BWI,SFO,235,239.5
AA200,BOS,JFK,150,89.3
AA900,LAX,CHI,201,201.8
. . .
```

As we read the file, we should **parse** each line, that is, separate the line into the individual pieces of data (flight number, origin airport, etc.) called **tokens**. In this case, the comma is the **delimiter**, that is, a comma separates one token from the next. We will store the tokens from each line into a corresponding *FlightRecord* object.

TABLE 11.8   *StringTokenizer* Constructors

StringTokenizer Constructor Summary
Constructor name and argument list
StringTokenizer(String str)
constructs a *StringTokenizer* object for the specified *String* using space, tab, carriage return, newline, and form feed as the default delimiters
StringTokenizer(String str, String delim)
constructs a *StringTokenizer* object for the specified *String* using *delim* as the delimiters

The *StringTokenizer* class, in the *java.util* package, is designed to parse *Strings*, that is, to separate *Strings* into tokens.

11.5.1   Parsing a *String* Using *StringTokenizer*

Two constructors of the class *StringTokenizer* are shown in Table 11.8.

As you can see, the default delimiters are the whitespace characters. To parse a *String* like *AA123,BWI,SFO,235,239.5*, we instantiate our *StringTokenizer* object with two arguments; the second argument indicates that the delimiter is a comma.

Some useful methods of the *StringTokenizer* class are shown in Table 11.9.

TABLE 11.9   *StringTokenizer* Methods

Useful *StringTokenizer* Methods	
Return value	**Method name and argument List**
int	countTokens( )
	returns the number of unretrieved tokens in this object; the count is decremented as tokens are retrieved
String	nextToken( )
	returns the next token
boolean	hasMoreTokens( )
	returns *true* if more tokens are available to be retrieved; returns *false*, otherwise

Example 11.14 shows how the *StringTokenizer* class can be used in a Java program:

```
1  /* Demonstrating the StringTokenizer class
2     Anderson, Franceschi
3  */
4
5  import java.util.StringTokenizer;
6
7  public class UsingStringTokenizer
8  {
9    public static void main( String [ ] args )
10   {
11     String flightRecord1 = "AA123,BWI,SFO,235,239.5";
12     StringTokenizer stfr1 = new StringTokenizer( flightRecord1, "," );
13                                     // the delimiter is a comma
14
15     while ( stfr1.hasMoreTokens( ) )
16       System.out.println( stfr1.nextToken( ) );
17   }
18 }
```

EXAMPLE 11.14   Demonstrating the *StringTokenizer* Class

Line 5 imports the *StringTokenizer* class.

The *flightRecord1 String* variable is declared and initialized at line 11. At line 12, the *StringTokenizer* object *stfr1* is instantiated using the constructor with two arguments: the first argument, *flightRecord1*, is the *String* that we want to tokenize, and the second argument, a *String* containing just a comma, is the delimiter.

Lines 15 and 16 loop through all the tokens of *stfr1* and process them; here, we simply echo them to the console.

The *hasMoreTokens* method, called at line 15, returns *true* if the object *stfr1* has more tokens to be retrieved. If so, we execute the body of the *while* loop. The *nextToken* method, called at line 16, does several things. First, it returns the next token as a *String*. Second, it decrements the number of tokens left to be retrieved. Eventually, when all tokens have been retrieved, the *hasMoreTokens* method returns *false*, which causes us to exit the *while* loop.

When the program in Example 11.14 runs, it will produce the output shown in Figure 11.19.

Figure 11.19
Output from Example 11.14

You may wonder why we didn't use a *for* loop and the *countTokens* method, as in the following:

```
for ( int i = 0; i < stfr1.countTokens( ); i++ ) // incorrect!
    System.out.println( stfr1.nextToken( ) );
```

COMMON ERROR TRAP

This code won't work because the return value of *countTokens* is the number of tokens **remaining to be retrieved**. The body of the loop retrieves one token, so each time we evaluate the loop condition by calling *countTokens*, the count of tokens is 1 fewer. The result is that we retrieve only half of the tokens.

Using a *for* loop and the *countTokens* method in the loop condition will process only half of the tokens because *countTokens* returns a smaller number at each iteration.

We could use a *for* loop, however, if we capture the token count before the loop begins and use that value in our loop condition. Thus, the code below could be used instead of the *while* loop in Example 11.14.

```
int numberOfTokens = stfr1.countTokens( );

for ( int i = 0; i < numberOfTokens; i++ )
    System.out.println( stfr1.nextToken( ) );
```

REFERENCE POINT

You can read more about the *StringTokenizer* class on Sun Microsystems' Java Web site: *www.java.sun.com*.

11.5.2   Reading Structured Data Using *StringTokenizer*

Now we are ready to put the previous two ideas together: Let's say that we have a file named *flights.txt* containing many flight records, and we want to read the data into variables. Again, suppose that the file is the same as the file in section 11.5; that is, it looks like the following:

```
AA123,BWI,SFO,235,239.5
AA200,BOS,JFK,150,89.3
AA900,LAX,CHI,201,201.8
. . .
```

where each line represents a flight segment with the following comma-separated data: flight number, origin airport, destination airport, number of passengers, and average ticket price.

First, we will build a class called *FlightRecord*, encapsulating a flight record as reflected by the data in the file. Each line read from the file will be parsed and used to instantiate a *FlightRecord* object. Since we do not know how many lines (i.e., how many flight records) are in the file, we will place all the flight records into an *ArrayList* object as opposed to a fixed-length array.

Our simplified *FlightRecord* class is shown in Example 11.15. It has only a constructor (lines 17–35) and the *toString* method (lines 37–49).

```
 1 /* The FlightRecord class
 2    Anderson, Franceschi
 3 */
 4
 5 import java.text.DecimalFormat;
 6
 7 public class FlightRecord
 8 {
 9    public static final DecimalFormat MONEY
10                        = new DecimalFormat( "$###.00" );
11    private String flightNumber;    // ex. = AA123
12    private String origin;          // origin airport; ex. = BWI
13    private String destination;     // destination airport; ex. = SFO
14    private int numPassengers;      // number of passengers
15    private double avgTicketPrice;  // average ticket price
16
17    /** Constructor
18     *  @param   startFlightNumber    flight number
19     *  @param   startOrigin          origin airport
20     *  @param   startDestination     destination airport
21     *  @param   startNumPassengers   number of passengers
22     *  @param   startAvgTicketPrice  average ticket price
23     */
24    public FlightRecord( String startFlightNumber,
25                         String startOrigin,
26                         String startDestination,
27                         int startNumPassengers,
28                         double startAvgTicketPrice )
29    {
30      flightNumber = startFlightNumber;
31      origin = startOrigin;
32      destination = startDestination;
```

```
33     numPassengers = startNumPassengers;
34     avgTicketPrice = startAvgTicketPrice;
35   }
36
37   /** toString
38    * @return flight number, origin, destination,
39    *          number of passengers, and average ticket price
40    */
41   public String toString( )
42   {
43     return "Flight " + flightNumber
44            + ": from " + origin
45            + " to " + destination
46            + "\n\t" + numPassengers + " passengers"
47            + "; average ticket price: "
48            + MONEY.format( avgTicketPrice );
49   }
50   // accessors, mutators, and other methods ...
51 }
```

EXAMPLE 11.15   The *FlightRecord* Class

Example 11.16 shows our client class, which will read the file, *flights.txt*, parse each line using *StringTokenizer*, then instantiate a *FlightRecord* object and add it to the *ArrayList* named *listFlightRecords*.

```
 1 /* Reading structured data from a text file
 2    Anderson, Franceschi
 3 */
 4
 5 import java.io.FileReader;
 6 import java.io.BufferedReader;
 7 import java.io.FileNotFoundException;
 8 import java.io.IOException;
 9 import java.util.StringTokenizer;
10 import java.util.ArrayList;
11
12 public class ReadFlights
13 {
14   public static void main( String [ ] args )
15   {
16   // declare ArrayList to hold FlightRecord objects
17   ArrayList<FlightRecord> listFlightRecords =
18                   new ArrayList<FlightRecord>( );
19
```

```
20    try
21    {
22      FileReader fr = new FileReader( "flights.txt" );
23      BufferedReader br = new BufferedReader( fr );
24
25      // declare String variable and prime the read
26      String stringRead = br.readLine( );
27
28      while ( stringRead != null ) // end of the file?
29      {
30        // process the line read
31        StringTokenizer st = new
32              StringTokenizer( stringRead, "," );
33        String flightNumber = st.nextToken( );
34        String origin = st.nextToken( );
35        String destination = st.nextToken( );
36
37        try
38        {
39          int numPassengers =
40                Integer.parseInt( st.nextToken( ) );
41          double avgTicketPrice =
42                Double.parseDouble( st.nextToken( ) );
43
44          FlightRecord frTemp = new FlightRecord(
45                                    flightNumber,
46                                    origin,
47                                    destination,
48                                    numPassengers,
49                                    avgTicketPrice );
50
51          // add FlightRecord obj to listFlightRecords
52          listFlightRecords.add( frTemp );
53        }
54
55        catch ( NumberFormatException nfe )
56        {
57          System.out.println( "Error in flight record: "
58                            + stringRead
59                            + "; record ignored" );
60        }
61
62        // read the next line
63        stringRead = br.readLine( );
64      }
65
```

```
66      // release resources associated with flights.txt
67      br.close( );
68    }
69
70    catch ( FileNotFoundException fnfe )
71    {
72      System.out.println( "Unable to find flights.txt" );
73    }
74
75    catch ( IOException ioe )
76    {
77      ioe.printStackTrace( );
78    }
79
80    // print the FlightRecords read
81    for ( FlightRecord flight : listFlightRecords )
82        System.out.println( flight );
83  }
84 }
```

EXAMPLE 11.16   Demonstrating How to Read Structured Data from a File

Lines 5–10 import the classes needed for input and exception handling, as well as *StringTokenizer* and *ArrayList*. The *FlightRecord* class is also used in this program, but is assumed to be in the same directory as the *ReadFlights* class.

This example is similar to Example 11.11 in that we instantiate *FileReader* and *BufferedReader* objects (lines 22–23), use the *readLine* method to read a line at a time (lines 26 and 63), and handle the *FileNotFoundException* (lines 70–73) and *IOException* (lines 75–78). The difference is that instead of just printing each line of text that we read from the file, we parse that line using *StringTokenizer* and pass the data we extracted as our arguments to the *FlightRecord* constructor to instantiate a *FlightRecord* object (lines 44–49). One intermediate step is to convert the *String* tokens representing the number of passengers and average ticket price to an *int* and *double*, respectively. We catch any exceptions that occur during the conversion (lines 55–60), and we print an error message and skip any records with invalid data.

The *FlightRecord* object is then added to the *ArrayList listFlightRecords* at lines 51–52. The *ArrayList listFlightRecords* is declared and instantiated at lines 17–18, before the *try* block so that *listFlightRecords* is available for printing the *FlightRecord* objects at lines 80–82, after we finish reading the file. If the *flights.txt* file contains the data shown in Figure 11.20, the program will produce the output shown in Figure 11.21.

Figure 11.20
Contents of *flights.txt*

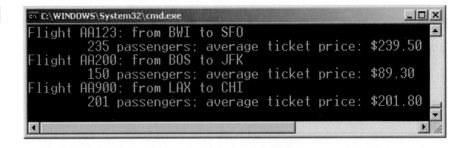

```
AA123,BWI,SFO,235,239.5

AA200,BOS,JFK,150,89.3

AA900,LAX,CHI,201,201.8
```

Figure 11.21
Output from
ReadFlights.java

```
C:\WINDOWS\System32\cmd.exe                                    _ □ ×
Flight AA123: from BWI to SFO
         235 passengers; average ticket price: $239.50
Flight AA200: from BOS to JFK
         150 passengers; average ticket price: $89.30
Flight AA900: from LAX to CHI
         201 passengers; average ticket price: $201.80
```

CODE IN ACTION

In the Chapter 11 directory of the CD-ROM accompanying this book, you will find a Shockwave movie showing a step-by-step illustration of reading from a text file. Double-click on the *IO.html* file to start the movie.

Skill Practice
with these end-of-chapter questions

11.11.1   Multiple Choice Exercises

Questions 6,7,8,9,10

11.11.2   Reading and Understanding Code

Questions 13,14,15,16,17,18,19,20,21

11.11.3   Fill in the Code

Questions 28,29,30,31,32

11.11.4   Identifying Errors in Code

Questions 37,38,39

11.11.5   Debugging Area

Questions 40,43,44,45

11.11.6   Write a Short Program

Questions 47,48,49,50,51,52,54

11.6   Programming Activity 1: Reading from a Structured Text File

In this activity, you will read from a text file using an end-of-file controlled *while* loop performing this activity:

> Read a text file containing transaction items for a bank account. Loop through all the transaction items and calculate the new balance of the bank account. Assume that we do not know the number of transaction items, i.e., lines, in the file.

The framework will display the current transaction and current balance so that you can check the correctness of your code as the program executes.

For example, Figure 11.22 demonstrates the animation: We are currently scanning a check for the amount of $200.00. The original balance was $0.00 and the new balance is –$200.00. Ideally, this is not your bank account.

Instructions

In the Chapter 11 directory on the CD-ROM accompanying this book, you will find the Programming Activity 1 directory. Copy the contents of the directory onto a directory on your disk.

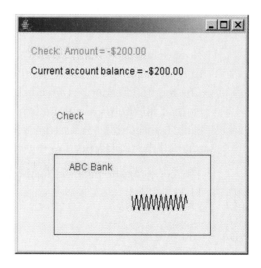

Figure 11.22
Animation Showing a $200 Check and the New Balance

Figure 11.23

Contents of the
***transactions.txt* File**

```
Check # 13 : -200.00

Check # 14 : -100.00

Withdrawal June 12 : -200.00

Withdrawal June 17 : -400.00

Withdrawal June 23 : -100.00

Deposit : 4000.00

Deposit : 100.00

Something else : -1000.00

Check # 16 : -500.00

Check # 15 : -100.00
```

- Open the file "*transactions.txt*" with a text editor. You will see that each line contains a transaction name and transaction amount separated by a colon, as shown in Figure 11.23.

- Note that the transaction amounts are positive or negative. For instance,

  - A check or a withdrawal has a negative amount.

  - A deposit has a positive amount.

  - An unknown transaction has either a positive or negative amount.

- Now open the *Accounting.java* file. Search for five stars (*****) to find the *balanceCheckBook* method where you will add your code. The method header has already been coded for you. Write the code to read all the transactions from the file *transactions.txt*, process each transaction against the account, and calculate the balance after all the transactions in that file have been processed.

The code for the *balanceCheckBook* method is shown in Example 11.17:

```
public void balanceCheckBook( )
{
  // ***** Write the body of this method *****
  //
  //  Using a while loop, read the file transactions.txt
```

```
// The file transactions.txt contains money
// transactions between you and your bank
//
//  You will need to call the method animate inside
//   the body of the loop reading the file contents
//
// The animate method takes 3 arguments:
//    a String, representing the type of transaction
//    a double, representing the transaction money amount
//    a double, representing the new checkbook balance
// So if these 3 variables are:
//     transactionName, currentAmount, and balance,
//   then the call to animate will be:
//
//   animate( transactionName, currentAmount, balance );
//
// You should make that call in the body of your while
// loop, after you have updated the checkbook balance
//


//
// end of student code
//
}
```

EXAMPLE 11.17   *balanceCheckBook* Method in *Accounting.java*

- Begin with a checkbook balance of 0.00.

- To process the transactions, you will need to read one line at a time from the *transactions.txt* file and parse the *String* that you retrieve. You can use the *StringTokenizer* class for this. The delimiter will be a colon. Then process the transaction; you do not need to check the type of transaction. Just add the amount of the transaction to the checkbook balance. Adding a negative transaction amount will decrease the balance, as expected. Be sure to use *try/catch* blocks where appropriate.

- After you have processed each transaction, call the *animate* method. This method belongs to the *Accounting* class, so you will call *animate* without using an object reference. The API of the *animate* method is the following:

```
public void animate( String currentTransaction,
                     double currentAmount,
                     double currentBalance )
```

As you can see, the *animate* method takes three arguments: *currentTransaction* is the transaction name (*"Deposit"* for example), *currentAmount* is the amount of the transaction (*-45.00*, for example), and *currentBalance* is the current balance of the checkbook. Assuming that you have a *String* variable called *transactionName*, a *double* variable called *amount*, and another *double* called *balance*, a call to *animate* will look like the following:

```
animate( transactionName, amount, balance );
```

- When you call *animate*, the window will display the current transaction graphically. It will also display the transaction amount (red if negative, blue if positive), and the current checkbook balance (in black). By adding the previous checkbook balance to the current transaction amount, you will be able to compute in your head what the current checkbook balance should be and determine if your program is working correctly.

- When you reach the end of the file, print the final balance.

To test your code, compile and run the *Accounting* application.

If you have time...

- Modify the file *transactions.txt* by deleting or adding transactions manually with a text editor. Run the program again and check that your code still gives the correct result.

- Using a text editor, modify the file *transactions.txt* by entering a positive amount to all transactions. Change the *balanceCheckBook* method so that it determines which transactions are positive and which are negative. Run the program again and check that your code still gives the correct result.

Troubleshooting

If your method implementation does not animate or animates incorrectly, check these items:

- Verify that you coded the priming read correctly.

- Verify that you coded the call to *animate* at the proper time.

- Verify that you coded the condition for exiting the loop correctly.

- Verify that you coded the body of the loop correctly.

1. How do you know when you have reached the end of the file?

2. Explain why we use the *BufferedReader* class.

3. Explain why we use the *StringTokenizer* class.

11.7 Writing and Appending to Structured Text Files

Earlier in this chapter, we learned how to write character data or *Strings* to text files. But very often, our data will be other data types, such as integers, *doubles*, *booleans*, or even objects. In this section, we will demonstrate writing primitive data types to a structured text file.

FileOutputStream, a subclass of the *OutputStream* class, is designed to write a stream of bytes to a file. It has several constructors, one of which takes a filename and a mode as its two arguments. The *boolean mode* variable specifies whether we are writing (*false*) or appending (*true*) to the file.

The *PrintWriter* class is designed for converting basic data types to characters and writing them to a text file. The *PrintWriter* class provides *print* and *println* methods for all primitive data types, as well as for *Strings* and objects. The *print* method writes the argument value to the file, whereas the *println* method writes the argument value to the file followed by a *newline* character. The constructors and method APIs are shown in Table 11.10.

Example 11.18 shows how the *PrintWriter* class can be used to write *Strings* and primitive data types to a text file named *grade.txt*.

```
 1 /* Demonstrating how to write basic data types to a text file
 2    Anderson, Franceschi
 3 */
 4
 5 import java.io.FileOutputStream;
 6 import java.io.PrintWriter;
 7 import java.io.FileNotFoundException;
 8
 9 public class WriteGradeFile
10 {
11   public static void main( String [ ] args )
12   {
13     try
```

TABLE 11.10   Useful Classes, Constructors, and Methods for Writing to a Structured Text File

Classes, Constructors, and Methods for Writing to a Structured Text File		
Class	**Constructors**	**Exceptions Thrown**
FileOutputStream	FileOutputStream(String filename, boolean mode)	FileNotFoundException
	constructs a *FileOutputStream* object from a *String* representing the name of a file; if *mode* is *false*, we will write to the file; if *mode* is *true*, we will append to the file	
PrintWriter	PrintWriter(OutputStream os)	None
	constructs a *PrintWriter* object from the *OutputStream* object	
	Method APIs	
PrintWriter	void print(int i) void print(double d) void print(char c) void print(boolean b) . . . void println (int i) void println (double d) . . .	None
	writes the argument to a text file	
PrintWriter	void close( )	None
	releases the resources associated with the *PrintWriter* object	

```
14     {
15        FileOutputStream fos = new FileOutputStream
16                          ( "grade.txt", false );
17        // false means we will be writing to grade.txt,
18        // rather than appending to it
19
20        PrintWriter pw = new PrintWriter( fos );
21
22        // write data to the file
23        pw.print( "Grade: " );
24        pw.println( 95 );
```

```
25        pw.print( "Letter grade: " );
26        pw.println( 'A');
27        pw.print( "Current GPA: " );
28        pw.println( 3.68 );
29        pw.print( "Successful student: " );
30        pw.println( true );
31
32        // release the resources associated with grade.txt
33        pw.close( );
34      }
35
36    catch ( FileNotFoundException fnfe )
37      {
38        System.out.println( "Unable to find grade.txt" );
39      }
40    }
41  }
```

EXAMPLE 11.18   Writing Primitive Data Types to a Text File

Lines 15–16 instantiate a *FileOutputStream* object to write to the file "grade.txt." The *FileOutputStream* constructor throws a *FileNotFoundException*. Our code catches that exception at lines 36–39. This is the only *catch* block because the methods of the *PrintWriter* class do not throw exceptions.

Line 20 instantiates a *PrintWriter* object, which we will use to write to the file. At lines 22 to 30, using the *PrintWriter* object *pw*, we call the methods *print* and *println*, passing various *String* and primitive data types arguments (*int, char, double,* and *boolean*) to be written to the file. When we want a *newline* character appended to the output, we call *println*, rather than *print*.

After this program is executed, the file *grade.txt* will contain the data shown in Figure 11.24.

```
Grade: 95
Letter grade: A
Current GPA: 3.68
Successful student: true
```

Figure 11.24
Contents of the *grade.txt* File

CODE IN ACTION

To see a demonstration of writing and appending to a text file, watch the Shockwave movie in the Chapter 11 directory of the CD-ROM accompanying this book. Double-click on the *IO.html* file to start the movie.

11.8   Reading and Writing Objects to a File

Throughout this book, we have emphasized the benefits of object-oriented programming. Just as we can write text and primitive data types to a file and subsequently read them from the file, we can also write objects to a file and subsequently read them as objects. This is convenient for two reasons:

- We can write these objects directly to a file without having to convert the objects to primitive data types or *Strings*.

- We can read the objects directly from a file, without having to read *Strings* and convert these *Strings* to primitive data types in order to instantiate objects.

To read objects from a file, the contents of the file must have been written as objects. So our first order of business should be to learn how to write objects to a file.

11.8.1   Writing Objects to Files

The *ObjectOutputStream* class, coupled with the *FileOutputStream* class, provides the functionality to write objects to a file. We are familiar with the *FileOutputStream* class, which we used in the last section to write structured data to a text file.

The *ObjectOutputStream* class, which is a subclass of *OutputStream*, provides a convenient way to write objects to a file. Its *writeObject* method takes one argument—the object to be written.

The classes, constructors, and methods we will use are shown in Table 11.11.

TABLE 11.11   Useful Classes, Constructors, and Methods for Writing Objects to a File

Classes, Constructors, and Methods for Writing Objects to a File		
Class	**Constructor**	**Exceptions Thrown**
`FileOutputStream`	`FileOutputStream( String filename, boolean mode )`	`FileNotFoundException`
	constructs a *FileOutputStream* object from a *String* representing the name of a file; if *mode* is *false*, we will write to the file; if *mode* is *true*, we will append to the file	
`ObjectOutputStream`	`ObjectOutputStream( ObjectStream out )`	`IOException`
	creates an *ObjectOutputStream* that writes to the *ObjectStream out*	
	Method API	
`ObjectOutputStream`	`void writeObject( Object o )`	`IOException`
	writes the object argument to a file. That object must be an instance of a class that implements the *Serializable* interface. Otherwise, a run-time exception will be generated	

We will use the *FlightRecord* class developed earlier in the chapter. However, in order for an object to be written to a file (and later to be read using the *ObjectInputStream* class), that object must implement the *Serializable* interface. When an object implements the *Serializable* interface, its state can be converted to a byte stream to be written to a file, such that this byte stream can be converted back into a copy of the object when read from the file. Therefore, our modified *FlightRecord2* class will implement *Serializable*, which is in the *java.io* package.

The *Serializable* interface has no methods to implement. As a result, the only things we have to worry about when writing a class implementing *Serializable* are the following:

- the *import* statement
- the class header showing the class *implements Serializable*

Example 11.19 shows the *FlightRecord2* class. This class is identical to the *FlightRecord* class except that it *imports Serializable* (line 5) and *implements* the *Serializable* interface (line 8).

```java
1 /* The FlightRecord2 class
2    Anderson, Franceschi
3 */
4
5 import java.io.Serializable;
6 import java.text.DecimalFormat;
7
8 public class FlightRecord2 implements Serializable
9 {
10   public static final DecimalFormat MONEY
11                          = new DecimalFormat( "$###.00" );
12   private String flightNumber;    // ex. = AA123
13   private String origin;          // origin airport; ex. = BWI
14   private String destination;     // destination airport; ex. = SFO
15   private int numPassengers;      // number of passengers
16   private double avgTicketPrice;  // average ticket price
17
18   /** Constructor
19    *  @param  startFlightNumber    flight number
20    *  @param  startOrigin          origin airport
21    *  @param  startDestination     destination airport
22    *  @param  startNumPassengers   number of passengers
23    *  @param  startAvgTicketPrice  average ticket price
24    */
25   public FlightRecord2( String startFlightNumber,
26                         String startOrigin,
27                         String startDestination,
28                         int startNumPassengers,
29                         double startAvgTicketPrice )
30   {
31     flightNumber = startFlightNumber;
32     origin = startOrigin;
33     destination = startDestination;
34     numPassengers = startNumPassengers;
35     avgTicketPrice = startAvgTicketPrice;
36   }
37
38   /** toString
```

```
39    * @return flight number, origin, destination,
40    *            number of passengers, and average ticket price
41    */
42   public String toString( )
43   {
44     return "Flight " + flightNumber
45            + ": from " + origin
46            + " to " + destination
47            + "\n\t" + numPassengers + " passengers"
48            + "; average ticket price: "
49            + MONEY.format( avgTicketPrice );
50   }
51   // accessors, mutators, and other methods ...
52 }
```

EXAMPLE 11.19   The *FlightRecord2* Class

Example 11.20 shows how the *FileOutputStream* and *ObjectOutputStream* classes can be used in a Java program to write *FlightRecord2* objects to a file named *objects*.

```
 1 /* Demonstrating how to write objects to a file
 2    Anderson, Franceschi
 3 */
 4
 5 import java.io.FileOutputStream;
 6 import java.io.ObjectOutputStream;
 7 import java.io.FileNotFoundException;
 8 import java.io.IOException;
 9
10 public class WritingObjects
11 {
12   public static void main( String [ ] args )
13   {
14   // instantiate the objects
15   FlightRecord2 fr1 = new FlightRecord2( "AA31", "BWI", "SFO",
16                                     200, 235.9 );
17   FlightRecord2 fr2 = new FlightRecord2( "CO25", "LAX", "JFK",
18                                     225, 419.9 );
19   FlightRecord2 fr3 = new FlightRecord2( "US57", "IAD", "DEN",
20                                     175, 179.5 );
21
```

```
22    try
23    {
24      FileOutputStream fos = new FileOutputStream
25                                      ( "objects", false );
26                  // false means we will write to objects
27
28      ObjectOutputStream oos = new ObjectOutputStream( fos );
29
30      // write the objects to the file
31      oos.writeObject( fr1 );
32      oos.writeObject( fr2 );
33      oos.writeObject( fr3 );
34
35      // release resources associated with the objects file
36      oos.close( );
37    }
38
39    catch ( FileNotFoundException fnfe )
40    {
41      System.out.println( "Unable to write to objects" );
42    }
43
44    catch ( IOException ioe )
45    {
46      ioe.printStackTrace( );
47    }
48  }
49 }
```

EXAMPLE 11.20   Writing Objects to a File

Lines 14–20 declare and instantiate three *FlightRecord2* objects that we will write to the *objects* file.

Lines 24–25 instantiate a *FileOutputStream* object for writing to the *objects* file, then line 28 instantiates an *ObjectOutputStream* object, which we will use to write the *FlightRecord2* objects to the file.

At lines 30–33, using the *ObjectOutputStream* object *oos*, we call the *writeObject* method, passing the three *FlightRecord2* objects we instantiated. The *writeObject* method takes a *Serializable* object as its parameter, here a *FlightRecord2* object, and writes it to the file in such a way that the stream of bytes can be read using the *readObject* method from the *Object-InputStream* class. Both the *ObjectOutputStream* constructor and the *writeObject* method can throw an *IOException*, which will be caught at line 44.

After this program is executed, the *objects* file will contain a representation of the three *FlightRecord2* objects.

One more note about writing objects to files: A file containing objects can be quite large. Not only does the object data get written to the file, but also the name of the class, a description of each data field, and other information needed to reconstruct the objects when the file is subsequently read.

The *writeObject* method, however, does not write any *static* class variables to the file. Thus, you may consider declaring any constants as *static*, if appropriate. For example, the object file we create in Example 11.20 by writing three *FlightRecord* objects is 241 bytes long. If we had not declared the constant *DecimalFormat* object *MONEY* as *static*, the size of the object file would be 1,945 bytes!

Similarly, the *writeObject* method does not write to the file any instance variable that is declared to be *transient*. Thus, you can also save space in the file by declaring an instance variable as *transient*. An instance variable is a good candidate to be declared *transient* if you can easily reproduce its value, or if the variable has a value of 0 at the time the file is created. For example, suppose our *FlightRecord* had an additional instance variable named *totalRevenue*, which stored a value we calculated by multiplying *avgTicketPrice* by *numPassengers*. Because we can easily recalculate the value for *totalRevenue*, we can declare it as *transient*; then, that instance variable will not be written to the object file.

You declare an instance variable as *transient* by inserting the keyword *transient* between the access modifier and the data type of the instance variable, as in the following syntax:

```
accessModifier transient dataType instanceVariableName
```

Thus, the following declaration would declare the *totalRevenue* instance variable as *transient*:

```
private transient double totalRevenue;
```

SOFTWARE ENGINEERING TIP

To save disk space when writing to an object file, declare the class data as *static* or *transient* where appropriate.

11.8.2 Reading Objects from Files

Reading objects from a file somewhat parallels writing objects to a file.

The class *ObjectInputStream*, a subclass of *InputStream*, coupled with *FileInputStream*, provides the functionality we need. We are already familiar with the *FileInputStream* class.

ObjectInputStream is designed to read objects from a file. The *readObject* method, which does not take any arguments, reads the next object from the file and returns it. Because the *readObject* method returns a generic *Object*, we must type cast the returned object to the appropriate class. When the end of the file is reached, the *readObject* method throws an *EOFException*. This is in contrast to reading a text file, where the *readLine* method indicates the end of the file by returning a *null String*.

The classes, constructors, and methods discussed above are shown in Table 11.12.

Example 11.21 shows how these *FileInputStream* and *ObjectInputStream* classes can be used in a Java program to read objects from a file. We assume

TABLE 11.12   Useful Classes, Constructors, and Methods for Reading Objects from a File

Classes, Constructors, and Methods for Reading Objects from a File		
Class	**Constructors**	**Exceptions Thrown**
FileInputStream	FileInputStream(String filename)	FileNotFoundException
	constructs a *FileInputStream* object from a *String* representing the name of a file	
ObjectInputStream	ObjectInputStream(InputStream in)	IOException
	constructs an *ObjectInputStream* from the *InputStream in*	
	Method API	
ObjectInputStream	Object readObject( )	IOException, ClassNotFoundException, EOFException
	reads the next object and returns it. The object must be an instance of a class that implements the *Serializable* interface. When the end of the file is reached, an *EOFException* is thrown	

that the file *objects* contains *FlightRecord2* objects, as written in the previous section.

```java
1 /* Demonstrating how to read objects from a file
2    Anderson, Franceschi
3 */
4
5 import java.io.FileInputStream;
6 import java.io.ObjectInputStream;
7 import java.io.FileNotFoundException;
8 import java.io.EOFException;
9 import java.io.IOException;
10
11 public class ReadingObjects
12 {
13   public static void main( String [ ] args )
14   {
15    try
16    {
17      FileInputStream fis = new FileInputStream( "objects " );
18      ObjectInputStream ois = new ObjectInputStream( fis );
19
20      try
21      {
22        while ( true )
23        {
24          // read object, type cast returned object to FlightRecord
25          FlightRecord2 temp = ( FlightRecord2 ) ois.readObject( );
26
27          // print the FlightRecord2 object read
28          System.out.println( temp );
29        }
30      } // end inner try block
31
32      catch ( EOFException eofe )
33      {
34       System.out.println( "End of the file reached" );
35      }
36
37      catch ( ClassNotFoundException cnfe )
38      {
39       System.out.println( cnfe.getMessage( ) );
40      }
41
```

```
42      finally
43      {
44       System.out.println( "Closing file" );
45       ois.close( );
46      }
47   } // end outer try block
48
49   catch ( FileNotFoundException fnfe )
50   {
51       System.out.println( "Unable to find objects" );
52   }
53
54   catch ( IOException ioe )
55   {
56        ioe.printStackTrace( );
57   }
58  }
59 }
```

EXAMPLE 11.21   Reading Objects from a File

Lines 5 through 9 import the needed classes from the *java.io* package. The *ClassNotFoundException* class is part of the *java.lang* package and does not need to be imported.

Line 17 associates a *FileInputStream* object with the *objects* file, and line 18 instantiates an *ObjectInputStream* object for reading the objects from the file.

The *while* loop, from line 22 to 29, reads and prints each object in the file. We will continue reading until the *readObject* method throws an *EOFException*, which will transfer control to the *catch* block (lines 32–35). Thus, our condition for the *while* loop is

```
while ( true )
```

In that *catch* block, we print a message that the end of the file was detected. Given this *while* loop construction, we do not need a priming read. Inside the *while* loop, we read an object, then print it. When the end of the file is detected, the output statement (line 28) will not be executed.

On line 25, we read an object from the file and assign it to the *FlightRecord2* object reference *temp*. Because the *readObject* method returns an *Object*, we need to type cast the return value to a *FlightRecord2* object. The *readObject* method can also throw a *ClassNotFoundException* or an *IOException*, which will be caught at lines 37 or 54, respectively.

Because an *EOFException* will occur when the end of the file is reached, the *EOFException catch* block will always execute in a normal program run. Thus, any code following the *while* loop in the *try* block will not execute. In order to be able to close the *objects* file, we need to use nested *try/catch* blocks. The inner *try* block (lines 20–30) encloses the *while* loop; its associated *catch* blocks handle the *EOFException* and *ClassNotFoundException*. The outer *try* block (lines 15–47) encloses the instantiations of the *File-InputStream* and *ObjectInputStream* objects, the inner *try* block, and the *finally* block where we close the file (line 45). We can close the file in the *finally* block because the *ois* object reference, declared in the outer *try* block, is visible (that is, in scope) inside the *finally* block.

The *catch* blocks following the outer *try* block handle any *FileNot-FoundException* and any other *IOExceptions* that occur in the inner or outer *try* blocks.

It is important to place the *catch* clause with the *EOFException* ahead of the *catch* clause with the *IOException*; otherwise, the *EOFException catch* block will never be reached because *EOFException* is a subclass of *IOException*, and therefore will match an *IOException catch* block.

Figure 11.25 shows the console output when this program is executed. Note that after we read the last object in the file and we try to read another

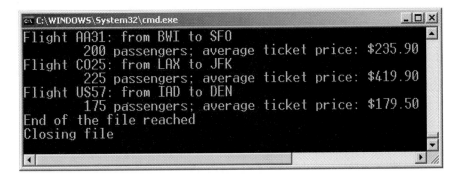

Figure 11.25

Output from Example 11.21

object, the code executes the *catch* block for the *EOFException*, then the *finally* block.

Skill Practice
with these end-of-chapter questions

11.11.1   Multiple Choice Exercises

Question 11

11.11.2   Reading and Understanding Code

Questions 22, 23

11.11.3   Fill in the Code

Questions 33, 34, 35, 36

11.11.6   Write a Short Program

Question 53

11.11.8   Technical Writing

Question 66

11.9   Programming Activity 2: Reading Objects from a File

In this activity, you will read objects from a file and perform this activity:

Read an object file containing bank account transaction objects. Loop through all the objects and calculate the new balance of the bank account. Assume that we do not know the number of transaction items, that is, objects, in the file.

Notice that this activity is identical to Programming Activity 1, except that the transactions you will read are stored in the file as objects.

The framework will display the current transaction and current balance so that you can check the correctness of your code as the program executes.

For example, Figure 11.26 demonstrates the animation: We are currently scanning a check transaction for the amount of $500.00. The original balance was $0.00 and the new balance now is –$500.00.

Task Instructions: Reading from the transactions.obj File

In the Chapter 11 directory on the CD-ROM accompanying this book, you will find a Programming Activity 2 directory. Copy the contents of the directory onto a directory on your disk.

Figure 11.26

Animation of a $500 Check and the New Balance

- Open the *Accounting.java* file. Search for five stars (*****) to find the *balanceCheckBook* method where you will add your code. The method header has been coded for you. Write the code to read the transactions from the *transactions.obj* file, and calculate the balance after all the transactions in that file have been executed. This program first writes *Transaction* objects to the file *transactions.obj*; that code is provided. You need to code the body of the *balanceCheckBook* method in order to read that file. Example 11.22 shows the student code section of the *Accounting.java* file.

```
public void balanceCheckBook( )
{
//
// ***** Student writes the body of this method *****
//
// Using a while loop, read the file transactions.obj
// The file transactions.obj contains transaction objects
//
//   You will need to call the animate method inside
//   the body of the loop that reads the objects
//
// The animate method takes 2 arguments:
//    a Transaction object, representing the transaction
//    a double, representing the new checkbook balance
//   So if these two variables are transaction and balance,
//    then the call to animate will be:
```

```
//
//   animate( transaction, balance );
//
//   You should make that call in the body of your while
//   loop, after you have updated the checkbook balance
//



//
//   end of student code
//
}
```

EXAMPLE 11.22   The *balanceCheckBook* Method

- Begin with a checkbook balance of 0.00.

- To process the transactions, you will need to read one *Transaction* object at a time from the *transactions.obj* file; you will retrieve the transaction amount using the *getAmount* method of the *Transaction* class. The API for that method is:

  ```
  public double getAmount( )
  ```

- Then process the transaction; you do not need to check the type of transaction. Just add the amount to the checkbook balance.

- After you have processed each transaction, call the *animate* method. This method belongs to the *Accounting* class, so you will call *animate* without using an object reference. The API of the *animate* method is the following:

  ```
  public void animate( Transaction currentTransaction,
                       double currentBalance )
  ```

  As you can see, the *animate* method takes two arguments:

    - *currentTransaction* is the current *Transaction* object
    - *currentBalance* is the current balance of the checkbook

  Assuming that you have a *Transaction* object reference called *transactionObject* and a *double* called *balance*, a call to *animate* will look like the following:

  ```
  animate( transactionObject, balance );
  ```

  When you call *animate*, the window will display the current transaction graphically. It will also display the transaction amount (red if negative, blue if positive) and the current check-book balance (in black). By adding the previous checkbook balance to the current transaction amount, you will be able to compute the current checkbook balance and check that your program is correct.

- Stop reading from the file when you reach the end of the file. You will need to set up a *catch* block to handle the *EOFException* that occurs when the end of the file is reached.

- Display the ending balance in a dialog box.

To test your code, compile and run the *Accounting.java* application.

If you have time . . .

- Modify the *main* method of the *Accounting* class, adding another transaction. Run the program again and verify that your code still yields the correct result. To add another transaction, you could, for instance, write this code:

```
Withdrawal w2 = new Withdrawal( -200.00 );
transactionList.add( w2 );
```

You can add a transaction of type *Check, Withdrawal, Deposit,* or *UnknownTransaction* (all of which are subclasses of the *abstract* class *Transaction*).

Troubleshooting

If your method implementation does not animate or animates incorrectly, check these items:

- Verify that you have coded the call to *animate* at the proper time.

- Verify that you have coded the condition for exiting the loop correctly.

- Verify that you have coded the body of the loop correctly.

? DISCUSSION QUESTIONS

1. Explain why we cannot simply read the *transactions.obj* file as a text file.

2. Explain why we need to type cast each object that we read from the file.

11.10   Chapter Summary

- Java provides exception classes so that unexpected, illegal operations at run time can be trapped and handled. This provides the programmer with a tool to keep the program running instead of terminating.

- When calling a constructor or method that *throws* a checked exception, you must use *try* and *catch* blocks; otherwise, the code will not compile.

- For calls to a constructor or method that *throws* an unchecked exception, *try* and *catch* blocks are optional. If *try* and *catch* blocks are not used, the exception will be caught at run time by the Java Virtual Machine.

- When a *try* block assigns a value to a variable and that variable is used after the *try/catch* block, the variable must be initialized before the *try* block is entered.

- A variable defined inside a *try* block is local to that block.

- To define your own exception, create a class that extends an existing exception class. This class will consist of a constructor that accepts a message and passes the message to the superclass constructor.

- The method that will generate the exception includes the *throws* clause in the method header. If the invalid condition is detected, the method *throws* a new object of the user-defined exception type, passing the appropriate message to the constructor.

- The *java.io* package contains classes for input and output operations.

- The *InputStreamReader* and *BufferedReader* classes provide functionality to read from the console. *System.in* represents the console.

- In order to read from a file, that file must exist; otherwise, a *FileNotFoundException* will be thrown.

- When we open a file for writing, the file is created if it does not exist. If the file already exists, the contents of the file are deleted.

- When we open a file for appending, the file is created if it does not exist. If the file already exists, we start writing at the end of the file.

- The *FileReader* and *BufferedReader* classes provide functionality to read from a text file.

- The *FileWriter* and *BufferedWriter* classes provide functionality to write to a text file.

- The *StringTokenizer* class in the *java.util* package is helpful in parsing a *String* consisting of fields separated by one or more delimiters.

- The *FileOutputStream* and *PrintWriter* classes provide functionality to write primitive data types to a text file.

- Objects can be written to a file; they must be instantiated from a class that *implements* the *Serializable* interface.

- The *Serializable* interface has no methods; therefore, no additional methods need to be implemented in a class that *implements* the *Serializable* interface.

- The *FileOutputStream* and *ObjectOutputStream* classes provide functionality to write objects to a file.

- To avoid writing class data to a file of objects, declare the data as *static* or *transient*, where appropriate.

- The *FileInputStream* and *ObjectInputStream* classes provide the functionality to read objects from a file.

- The *readObject* method returns the object read as an *Object* class reference. That object reference must be type cast to the appropriate class.

11.11 Exercises, Problems, and Projects

11.11.1 Multiple Choice Exercises

1. Why are exceptions useful?

   ❑ They can replace selection statements, thus saving CPU time.

   ❑ Exceptions enable programmers to attempt to recover from illegal situations and continue running the program.

2. Some methods that *throw* an exception require *try* and *catch* blocks, while some do not.

   ❏ True

   ❏ False

3. What keyword is found in the header of a method that could detect an error and generate an appropriate exception?

   ❏ *throw*

   ❏ *throws*

   ❏ *exception*

   ❏ *exceptions*

4. When coding a *try* and *catch* block, it is mandatory to code a *finally* block.

   ❏ True

   ❏ False

5. Most input and output related classes can be found in the package

   ❏ *java.file*

   ❏ *java.inputoutput*

   ❏ *java.io*

   ❏ *java.readwrite*

6. If we open a file for reading and the file does not exist,

   ❏ there is a compiler error.

   ❏ an exception is thrown.

   ❏ the file will be created automatically.

7. When we open a file for writing, then

   ❏ we will be adding data at the end of the file.

   ❏ the contents of the file, if any, will be deleted.

   ❏ there is a run-time error if the file does not exist.

8. When we open a file for appending, then

   ❏ we will be adding data at the end of the file.

❏ the contents of the file, if any, will be deleted.

❏ there is a run-time error if the file does not exist.

9. In the following code located inside a *try* block:

```
BufferedReader br = new BufferedReader(
                    new FileReader( "data.txt" ) );
```

❏ the code will not compile.

❏ the argument to the *BufferedReader* constructor is an anonymous object.

❏ there will be a run-time error, even if the file *data.txt* exists.

10. The *StringTokenizer* class is useful to parse strings. In what package is the *StringTokenizer* class?

❏ *java.io*

❏ *java.util*

❏ *java.string*

11. Which interface must be implemented by a class whose objects will be written to a file directly?

❏ none

❏ *Serializable*

❏ *IO*

❏ *Object*

11.11.2   Reading and Understanding Code

12. Assuming the user inputs successively "*CS1*", "*Java*", "*Illuminated*", and "*STOP*", what is the output of this code sequence?

```
try
{
  InputStreamReader isr = new InputStreamReader( System.in );
  BufferedReader br = new BufferedReader( isr );
  String result = "";

  System.out.print( "Enter a word > " );
  String s = br.readLine( );

  while ( ! s.equals( "STOP" ) )
```

```
   {
     result += s;
     result += " AND ";
     System.out.print( "Enter a word > " );
     s = br.readLine( );
   }

   System.out.println( "result is " + result );
   }
catch ( IOException ioe )
   {
    ioe.printStackTrace( );
   }
```

13. What is the output of this code sequence?

```
StringTokenizer st = new StringTokenizer( "A B C D" );

while ( st.hasMoreTokens( ) )
    System.out.print( st.nextToken( ) );
```

14. What is the output of this code sequence?

```
StringTokenizer st = new StringTokenizer( "AA:B:CC", ":" );

while ( st.hasMoreTokens( ) )
    System.out.println( st.nextToken( ) );
```

15. What is the output of this code sequence?

```
StringTokenizer st = new StringTokenizer( "A B C D" );
String result = "";

while ( st.hasMoreTokens( ) )
   {
     result += st.nextToken( );
   }
System.out.println( result );
```

For questions 16, 17, 18, and 19, you should assume that the file *data.txt* contains the following text:

```
A
B
C
A
B
A
```

16. What is the output of this code sequence?

```
try
{
  FileReader fr = new FileReader( "data.txt" );
  BufferedReader br = new BufferedReader( fr );
  String result = "";

  String s = br.readLine( );
  while ( s != null )
  {
    result += s;
    s = br.readLine( );
  }

  System.out.println( "result is " + result );
  br.close( );
}

catch ( IOException ioe )
{
  ioe.printStackTrace( );
}
```

17. What is the output of this code sequence?

```
try
{
  FileReader fr = new FileReader( "data.txt" );
  BufferedReader br = new BufferedReader( fr );
  int n = 0;

  String s = br.readLine( );
  while ( s != null )
  {
    if ( s.equals( "A" ) )
        n++;
    s = br.readLine( );
  }

  System.out.println( "The value of n is " + n );
  br.close( );
}
catch ( IOException ioe )
{
  ioe.printStackTrace( );
}
```

18. What is the output of this code sequence?

```
try
{
  FileReader fr = new FileReader( "data.txt" );
  BufferedReader br = new BufferedReader( fr );

  String s = br.readLine( );
  while ( s != null )
  {
    if ( s.equals( "A" ) )
        System.out.println( "Excellent" );
    else if ( s.equals( "B" ) )
        System.out.println( "Good" );
    else
        System.out.println( "Try to do better" );
    s = br.readLine( );
  }
  br.close( );
}
catch ( IOException ioe )
{
  ioe.printStackTrace( );
}
```

19. What is the output of this code sequence?

```
try
{
  FileReader fr = new FileReader( "data.txt" );
  BufferedReader br = new BufferedReader( fr );

  String s = br.readLine( );
  String previous = s;

  while ( s != null )
  {
    previous = s;
    s = br.readLine( );
  }

  if ( previous.equals( "A" ) )
    System.out.println( "Nice finish" );

  br.close( );
}
```

```
catch ( IOException ioe )
{
    ioe.printStackTrace( );
}
```

20. The file *data.txt* contains the following text:

    CS1

    What does the file *data.txt* contain after this code sequence is executed?

    ```
    try
    {
      FileWriter fw = new FileWriter( "data.txt", true );
      BufferedWriter bw = new BufferedWriter( fw );

      bw.write( "Java Illuminated" );
      bw.newLine( );

      bw.close( );
    }
    catch ( IOException ioe )
    {
        ioe.printStackTrace( );
    }
    ```

21. What does the file *data.txt* contain after this code sequence is executed?

    ```
    try
    {
      FileWriter fw = new FileWriter( "data.txt", false );
      BufferedWriter bw = new BufferedWriter( fw );

      String s = "ABCDEFGH";
      String temp = "";

      for ( int i = 0; i < s.length( ); i++ )
      {
        if ( i % 2 == 0 )
          bw.write( s.charAt(i) );
      }
      bw.newLine( );
      bw.close( );
    }

    catch ( IOException ioe )
    {
      ioe.printStackTrace( );
    }
    ```

22. The file *data.txt* contains the following text:

```
CS1
```

What does the file contain after the following code sequence is executed?

```
try
{
  FileOutputStream fos = new FileOutputStream( "data.txt", true );
  PrintWriter pw = new PrintWriter( fos );

  for ( int i = 0; i < 5; i++ )
     pw.println( i );

  pw.close( );
}
catch ( IOException ioe )
{
   ioe.printStackTrace( );
}
```

23. What does the file *data.txt* contain after the following code sequence is executed?

```
try
{
  FileOutputStream fos = new FileOutputStream( "data.txt", false );
  PrintWriter pw = new PrintWriter( fos );

  int s = 0;
  for ( int i = 0; i < 5; i++ )
  {
    s += i;
  }
  pw.print( "The result is " );
  pw.print( s );
  pw.close( );
}
catch ( IOException ioe )
{
   ioe.printStackTrace( );
}
```

11.11.3 Fill in the Code

24. This code segment asks the user to enter a line of text from the console and outputs it.

```
try
{
 // your code goes here

 String s = br.readLine( );
 System.out.println( s );
}
catch ( IOException ioe )
{
   ioe.printStackTrace( );
}
```

25. This code segment asks the user to enter two lines of text, concatenates them, and outputs the result.

```
try
{
 InputStreamReader isr = new InputStreamReader( System.in );
 // your code goes here
```

26. This code segment keeps asking the user to type "*Java*" at the console until the user does.

```
try
{
 InputStreamReader isr = new InputStreamReader( System.in );
 BufferedReader br = new BufferedReader( isr );
 String s = "";
 do
 {
  // your code goes here

 } while ( ! s.equals( "Java" ) );
}
catch ( IOException ioe )
{
   ioe.printStackTrace( );
}
```

27. This code segment keeps asking the user to input an integer until the user does. Hint: You may need to use nested *try* and *catch* blocks.

```java
boolean flag = true;
String s = "";
int n = 0;
try
{
 InputStreamReader isr = new InputStreamReader( System.in );
 BufferedReader br = new BufferedReader( isr );
 do
 {
   s = br.readLine( );
   // your code goes here

 } while ( flag );
}
catch ( IOException ioe )
{
   ioe.printStackTrace( );
}
```

28. This code retrieves the "*C*" in the string "*ABC$D*" using *StringTokenizer* and outputs it:

```java
StringTokenizer st = new StringTokenizer( "A$B$C$D", "$" );
String s = "";
// your code goes here

System.out.println( s );
```

For questions 29, 30, 31, and 32, you should assume that the file *data.txt* contains the following:

```
Java
Illuminated:
Programming
Is Not A
Spectator
Sport
```

29. This code sequence reads the first two lines of the file *data.txt* and outputs them to the console.

```java
try
{
 FileReader fr = new FileReader( "data.txt" );
 // your code goes here
```

30. This code sequence reads the file *data.txt* and outputs its contents to the console.

```
try
{
    FileReader fr = new FileReader( "data.txt" );
    BufferedReader br = new BufferedReader( fr );
    String result = "";
    // your code goes here


}
catch (  IOException ioe )
{
    ioe.printStackTrace( );
}
```

31. This code sequence reads the file *data.txt*, concatenates all the lines with a space between them, and outputs them as:

```
Java Illuminated: Programming Is Not A Spectator Sport
```

```
try
{
    FileReader fr = new FileReader( "data.txt" );
    BufferedReader br = new BufferedReader( fr );
    String result = "";
    // your code goes here


}
catch ( IOException ioe )
{
    ioe.printStackTrace( );
}
```

32. This code sequence reads the file *data.txt* and outputs only the lines that contain the *String* "*Sp*". Assume that we do not know the contents of the file before reading it. Here, the output will be:

```
Spectator
Sport
```

```
try
{
    FileReader fr = new FileReader( "data.txt" );
    BufferedReader br = new BufferedReader( fr );
    String result = "";
    // your code goes here
```

```
    }
    catch ( IOException ioe )
    {
      ioe.printStackTrace( );
    }
```

33. This code sequence loops through the array *grades* and writes all its elements into the file *data.txt*, one per line:

```
int [ ] grades = { 98, 76, 82, 90, 100, 75 };
try
{
   FileOutputStream fos = new FileOutputStream( "data.txt", false );
   // your code goes here


}
// and your code continues here
```

34. This code sequence loops through the array *grades,* calculates the average, and writes the average into the file *data.txt*:

```
int [ ] grades = { 98, 76, 82, 90, 100, 75 };
double average = 0.0;
for ( int i = 0; i < grades.length; i++ )
{
   // some of your code goes here


}
// and more code goes here

try
{
   FileOutputStream fos = new FileOutputStream( "data.txt", false );
   PrintWriter pw = new PrintWriter( fos );
   // and more code goes here


}
catch ( IOException ioe )
{
   ioe.printStackTrace( );
}
```

35. This code sequence writes the values of the variables *i* and *d* to the file *data.txt*, one line at a time.

```
int i = 45;
double d = 6.7;
```

```
try
{
  FileOutputStream fos = new FileOutputStream( "data.txt", false );
  PrintWriter pw = new PrintWriter( fos );
  // your code goes here

}
catch ( IOException ioe )
{
  ioe.printStackTrace( );
}
```

36. This code sequence appends the value of the variable *f* to the file *data.txt*:

```
float f = 13.5f;
try
{
  // your code goes here
```

11.11.4 Identifying Errors in Code

37. Where is the error in this code sequence?

```
StringTokenizer st = new StringTokenizer( "1 2 3" );
int i = st.nextToken( );
```

38. Where is the error in this code sequence?

```
try
{
  FileReader fr = new FileReader( "data.txt" );
  BufferedReader br = new BufferedReader( fr );
  String s = br.readLine( );
}
catch ( ArithmeticException ae )
{
  System.out.println( ae.getMessage( ) );
}
```

39. Where is the error in this code sequence?

```
try
{
  FileReader fr = new FileReader( "data.txt" );
  BufferedReader br = new BufferedReader( fr );
  br.write( "Hello" );
}
```

```
catch ( IOException ioe )
{
  ioe.printStackTrace( );
}
```

11.11.5   Debugging Area

40. You coded the following in the class *Test.java*:

```java
import java.io.InputStreamReader;
import java.io.BufferedReader;
import java.io.IOException;

public class Test
{
  public static void main( String [ ] args )
  {
      try    // line 9
      {
              InputStreamReader isr = new InputStreamReader
                                        ( System.in );
              BufferedReader br = new BufferedReader( isr );
              System.out.println( "Enter a line > " );
              String stringRead = br.readLine( );
              System.out.println( stringRead );
      }
  }
}
```

At compile time, you get the following error:

```
Test.java:9: 'try' without 'catch' or 'finally'
   try
   ^
1 error
```

Explain what the problem is and how to fix it.

41. You coded the following in the class *Test.java*:

```java
import java.io.InputStreamReader;
import java.io.BufferedReader;
import java.io.IOException;

public class Test
{
  public static void main( String [ ] args )
  {
      try
```

```
        {
                InputStreamReader isr = new InputStreamReader
                                            ( System.in );
                BufferedReader br = new BufferedReader( isr );
                System.out.println( "Enter a line > " );
                String stringRead = br.readLine( );
        }
        catch ( IOException ioe )
        {
            ioe.printStackTrace( );
        }
        System.out.println( "string read: " + stringRead );
        // line above is 22
    }
}
```

At compile time, you get the following error:

```
Test.java:22: cannot find symbol
symbol   : variable stringRead
location: class Test
    System.out.println( "string read: " + stringRead );
                                          ^
1 error
```

Explain what the problem is and how to fix it.

42. You coded the following in the class *Test.java*:

```
import java.io.InputStreamReader;
import java.io.BufferedReader;
import java.io.IOException;

public class Test
{
  public static void main( String [ ] args )
  {
        String stringRead;
        try
        {
                InputStreamReader isr = new InputStreamReader
                                            ( System.in );
                BufferedReader br = new BufferedReader( isr );
                System.out.println( "Enter a line > " );
                stringRead = br.readLine( );
        }
        catch ( IOException ioe )
```

```
        {
              ioe.printStackTrace( );
        }
        System.out.println( "string read: " + stringRead );
        // line above is line 23
    }
}
```

At compile time, you get the following error:

```
Test.java:23: variable stringRead might not have been initialized
System.out.println( "string read: " + stringRead );
                                       ^

1 error
```

Explain what the problem is and how to fix it.

43. You coded the following in the class *Test.java*:

```
String s = "A,B,C,D,E,F";
StringTokenizer st = new StringTokenizer( s, "," );

for ( int i = 0; i < st.countTokens( ); i++ )
        System.out.print( st.nextToken( ) + ":" );
```

The code compiles and runs, but the result is

```
A:B:C:
```

You expected

```
A:B:C:D:E:F:
```

Explain what the problem is and how to fix it.

44. In order to read from the file *data.txt*, you coded the following in the *Test.java* class:

```
try
{
   FileReader fr = new FileReader( "datatxt" );
   BufferedReader br = new BufferedReader( fr );
   String s = br.readLine( );
   System.out.println( "Line read is " + s );
}
catch ( IOException ioe )
{
   System.out.println( ioe.getMessage( ) );
}
```

The code compiles and runs, but here is the output:

```
datatxt (The system cannot find the file specified)
```

Explain what the problem is and how to fix it.

45. You coded the following in the class *Test.java*:

```
BufferedReader br = new BufferedReader( "data.txt" );
...
```

At compile time, you get the following error:

```
Test.java:12: cannot find symbol
symbol  : constructor BufferedReader(java.lang.String)
location: class java.io.BufferedReader
        BufferedReader br = new BufferedReader( "data.txt" );
                            ^

1 error
```

Explain what the problem is and how to fix it.

11.11.6   Write a Short Program

46. Without using the *UserInput* class from the chapter, write a program that prompts the user for input until the user inputs an integer whose value is between 0 and 100, inclusive.

47. In Internet programming, programmers receive parameters via a query string, which looks like a *String* with fields separated by the & character. Each field typically has a metadata part and a data part separated by the equal sign. An example of a query string is:

```
first=Mike&last=Jones&id=mike1&password=hello
```

Using *StringTokenizer* at least once, parse a query string and output each field on a different line after replacing the equal sign with a colon followed by a space. For example, for the sample query string above, the output should be:

```
first: Mike
last: Jones
id: mike1
password: hello
```

48. Write a program that reads a file that contains only one line; output all the characters, one character per line.

49. Write a program that reads a file and counts how many lines it contains.

50. Write a program that reads a text file that contains a grade (for instance, 87) on each line. Calculate and print the average of the grades.

51. Write a program that reads a text file and outputs every line of the file separated by a blank line.

52. An HTML file starts with <HTML> and ends with </HTML>. Write a program that reads a file and checks whether that is true.

53. Often Web sites display the visitor count ("You are visitor number 5246"). Write a program that reads a file that holds the visitor count, outputs it, and updates the file, incrementing the visitor count by 1.

54. Often on Web sites, the beginning of an article is displayed followed by the word *more* and several dots (as in *more...*). Write a program that reads the first two lines of a file, and displays them inside an applet, adding the word *more* in blue followed by three dots.

11.11.7   Programming Projects

55. Design your own *MyStringTokenizer* class that implements a method *myNextToken* as follows: When two delimiters are next to each other in the *String*, there is a token between them (this is different from the *StringTokenizer* class). For instance, if the *String* is "A,B,C,,,D" and the delimiter is a comma, you should consider that there are six tokens, with the fourth and fifth tokens being empty *Strings*. Test your class with a client program.

56. We are interested in checking the number of times a given word (for example, the word *secret*) appears in a file. You should assume that lines do not wrap, that is, a line does not continue on the next line. Warning: You could have letters arranged like *secsecret*. Design a class that encapsulates that idea. Test it with a client program.

57. Design a class that checks if the contents of two text files are identical and, if not, determines how many lines are different. Lines are different if they differ in one or more characters. Test your class with a client program.

58. Design a class that encapsulates the contents of a text file. Include the following methods in your class: *numberOfLinesInFile*, *longestLineInFile* (the line number of the line containing the maximum number of characters), *shortestLineInFile*, and *averageNumberOfCharactersPerLine*. Test your class with a client program.

59. The most common characters in an HTML file are < and >. Every < must be followed eventually by a > character before the next < character is found. There should be an equal number of both in the file. Design a class that encapsulates that idea. Test your class with a client program.

60. A file contains Web addresses, one on each line. Design a class that encapsulates the concept of counting the number of college addresses (contains .*edu*), government addresses (contains .*gov*), business addresses (contains .*com*), organization addresses (contains .*org*), or other addresses. Test your class with a client program.

61. In cryptograms, each character is encoded into another. If the text is long enough, one can, as a strategy, use the frequency of occurrence of each character. The most frequently occurring character will likely be the code for an *e*, because *e* is the most frequently used letter of the English alphabet. Design a class that attempts to determine the relative frequency of each letter by reading a file and keeping track of the number of times each of the 26 English alphabet characters appears. Also provide methods, such as *highestFrequencyCharacter* and *lowestFrequencyCharacter*. Test your class with a client program.

62. Design a class that calculates statistics on data in a file. We expect the file to contain grades represented by integer values, one per line. If you encounter a value that is not an integer, you should throw an exception, print a message to the console, skip that value, and continue processing. Store the grades that you read in an *ArrayList* so that all the grades are available for retrieval. You should also have, as a minimum, methods that return the grade average, the highest grade, the lowest grade, and ones that return all the grades as an array of letter grades. Test your class with a client class.

63. Write a class encapsulating the concept of a home, assuming that it has the following attributes: the number of rooms, the square footage, and whether it has a basement. Write a client program that creates five *Home* objects, writes them to a file as objects, then reads them from the file as objects, outputs a description of each object using the *toString* method (which the *Home* class should override), and outputs the number of *Home* objects. When reading the objects, you should assume that you do not know the number of objects in the file.

64. Write a class named *CarPlate* encapsulating the concept of a car license plate, assuming that it has the following attributes: the plate

number, the state, and its color. Write a client program that creates three *CarPlate* objects, writes them to a file as objects, then reads them from the file as objects, outputs a description of each of the objects using the *toString* method (which the *CarPlate* class should override), and outputs the number of objects. When reading the objects, you should assume that you do not know the number of objects in the file.

11.11.8   Technical Writing

65. Are exceptions a good thing or a bad thing? Argue both sides.

66. With respect to writing objects to and reading objects from a file, discuss the importance of documenting your code well.

11.11.9   Group Project for Groups of 2, 3, or More Students

67. A friend of yours owns two houses at Football City, the site of the next Super Bowl. Your friend wants to rent those two houses for the Friday, Saturday, and Sunday of the Super Bowl weekend. House #1 has 3BR (3 bedrooms), 3BA (3 baths), and house #2 has 1BR, 1BA.

    For this project, concurrency is not an issue; you should assume that two customers will never access your system at exactly the same time. You should also assume that the management-side software and the customer-side software will never run at the same time. We can assume that we run the management-side software first, then the customer-side software.

    This friend has asked you to build a file-based reservation system enabling the following:

    A. Management-side software:

       Your friend controls the rental price and may change it every day. He/she sends you a change file every day; this file may be empty, in which case there are no pricing changes. If the file is not empty, pricing has changed (for one or more houses, or for one or more days). You are in charge of this project, and therefore, you are in charge of specifying the file format; however, this must be a simple text file because your friend is not a computer person.

       You do not have to simulate the act of sending the file by your friend; you should assume that the file is a text file in your directory and that you only need to read the data.

Your management-side software needs to read this file and update a different file, with which you control the reservation system. You can create your own design for the structure of that file. Of course, prices for existing reservations cannot be changed.

Finally, your management-side software should write to a file the status of the reservations; that is, which house is rented to whom, when, and for what price.

B. Customer-side software:

The customer-side software allows a customer to make a reservation. You should prompt the customer for a possible reservation, offering whatever house is available, when, and at what price. Do not offer a customer a house that is already rented.

In this simple version, a customer makes and pays for the reservation at the same time. Also, a reservation cannot be cancelled. When a reservation is made, the customer-side software automatically updates the file controlling the reservations.

CHAPTER 12

Graphical User Interfaces

CHAPTER CONTENTS

Introduction

Many applications we use every day have a graphical user interface, or GUI (pronounced goo-ey), which allows us to control the operation of the program visually. For example, Web browsers, such as Microsoft Internet Explorer, provide menus, buttons, drop-down lists, and other visual input and output devices to allow the user to communicate with the program through mouse clicks, mouse movements, and by typing text into boxes.

GUIs enable the user to select the next function to be performed, to enter data, and to set program preferences, such as colors or fonts. GUIs also make a program easier to use because a GUI is a familiar interface to users. If you design your program's GUI well, users can quickly learn to operate your program, in many cases, without consulting documentation or requiring extensive training.

Java is very rich in GUI classes. In this chapter, we will present some of those classes, along with the main concepts associated with developing a GUI application.

12.1   GUI Applications Using *JFrame*

The first step in developing a GUI application is to create a window. We've opened graphical windows in our applets, but so far, we have not displayed a window in our applications. Instead, we've communicated with users through the Java console and dialog boxes. We will use the *JFrame* class in the *javax.swing* package to create a window for our GUI applications. The inheritance hierarchy for the *JFrame* class is shown in Figure 12.1.

REFERENCE POINT

Inheritance, including which class members are inherited, is discussed in Chapter 10.

Inheriting directly from *Object* is the *Component* class, which represents a graphical object that can be displayed. Inheriting from the *Component* class is the *Container* class, which, as its name indicates, can hold other objects. This is good because we will want to add GUI components to our window. The *Window* class, which inherits from the *Container* class, can be used to create a basic window. The *Frame* class, which inherits from the *Window* class, adds a title bar and a border to the window. The title bar contains icons that allow the user to minimize, maximize, resize, and close the window. This is the type of window we are accustomed to seeing.

We need to step down one more level of inheritance, however, to the *JFrame* class before we are ready to create our GUI application. A *JFrame* object is a *swing* component. Thus, the *JFrame* class provides the functionality of *Frame*, as well as support for the *swing* architecture. We'll explain more about the *swing* components later in this chapter. For now, Figure 12.1 shows us that a *JFrame* object is a *Component*, a *Container*, a *Window*, and a *Frame* by inheritance, so we can use a *JFrame* object to display a window that will hold our GUI components, and thus present our GUI to the user. Our typical GUI application class will be a subclass of *JFrame*, inheriting its functionality as a window and a container. Thus, the class header for our GUI applications will follow this pattern:

```
public class ClassName extends JFrame
```

Table 12.1 shows two constructors and some important methods of the *JFrame* class, some of which are inherited from its superclasses. Because our GUI applications extend the *JFrame* class, our applications inherit these methods also.

Example 12.1 shows a shell GUI application class. This class demonstrates the general format for building GUI applications, but has no components.

```
1  /*  A Shell GUI Application
2       Anderson, Franceschi
3  */
4
5  import javax.swing.JFrame;
6  import java.awt.Container;
7  // other import statements here as needed
8
9  public class ShellGUIApplication extends JFrame
10 {
11    private Container contents;
12    // declare other instance variables
13
14    // constructor
15    public ShellGUIApplication( )
16    {
17      // call JFrame constructor with title bar text
18      super( "A Shell GUI Application" );
19
```

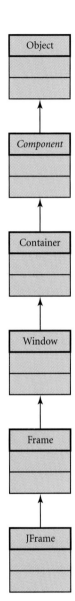

Figure 12.1
Inheritance Hierarchy for *JFrame*

TABLE 12.1   *JFrame* Constructors and Methods

Useful Constructors and Methods of the *JFrame* Class	
Class	**Constructor**
JFrame	JFrame( )
	constructs a *JFrame* object, initially invisible, with no text in the title bar
JFrame	JFrame(String titleBarText)
	constructs a *JFrame* object, initially invisible, with *titleBarText* displayed in the window's title bar
Methods	
Return value	**Method name and argument list**
Container	getContentPane( )
	returns the content pane object for this window
void	setDefaultCloseOperation(int operation)
	sets the default operation when the user closes this window, that is, when the user clicks on the X icon in the top-right corner of the window
void	setSize(int width, int height)
	sizes the window to the specified *width* and *height* in pixels
void	setVisible(boolean mode)
	displays this window if *mode* is *true*; hides the window if *mode* is *false*

```
20      // get container for components
21      contents = getContentPane( );
22
23      // set the layout manager
24
25      // instantiate GUI components and other instance variables
26
27      // add GUI components to the content pane
28
```

```
29      // set original size of window
30      setSize( 300, 200 );
31
32      // make window visible
33      setVisible( true );
34   }
35
36   public static void main( String [ ] args )
37   {
38     ShellGUIApplication basicGui = new ShellGUIApplication( );
39     basicGui.setDefaultCloseOperation( JFrame.EXIT_ON_CLOSE );
40   }
41 }
```

EXAMPLE 12.1   A Shell GUI Application Using *JFrame*

We have defined one instance variable, *contents*, which is a *Container* object reference (line 11). Our subsequent GUI applications will define instance variables for the components to be placed in the window, as well as instance variables to hold the data of the application as primitive data types or objects.

The *main* method is coded at lines 36–40. We start by instantiating an object of this application class (line 38), which invokes the constructor (lines 14–34).

At line 39, we call the *setDefaultCloseOperation* method. The *EXIT_ON_CLOSE* argument is a useful *static* constant of the *JFrame* class, which specifies that the GUI application should terminate when the user closes the window.

A constructor in a GUI application has several tasks to perform:

- Call the constructor of the *JFrame* superclass.
- Get an object reference to the content pane container. We will add our GUI components to the content pane.
- Set the layout manager. Layout managers arrange the GUI components in the window.
- Instantiate each component.
- Add each component to the content pane.
- Set the size of the window.
- Display the window.

In our constructor, at line 18, we call the *JFrame* constructor, passing as an argument, a *String* representing the text that we want to be displayed in the title bar of the window. As in any subclass, this must be the first statement in the constructor.

At line 21, we call the *getContentPane* method, inherited from the *JFrame* class, and assign its return value to *contents*. The *getContentPane* method returns a *Container* object reference; subsequent applications will add our GUI components to this container.

Although this shell application does not have any GUI components, we have inserted comments to indicate where the component-related operations should be performed. Later in this chapter, we show you how to perform these actions.

 COMMON ERROR TRAP

Be sure to call the *setSize* method to set the initial dimensions of the window and call the *setVisible* method to display the window and its contents. Omitting the call to the *setSize* method will create a default *JFrame* consisting of a title bar only. If you omit the call to the *setVisible* method, the window will not open when the application begins.

We then set the initial size of the window to a width of 300 pixels and a height of 200 pixels by calling the *setSize* method (line 30). Finally, we call the *setVisible* method (line 33) so that the window will be displayed when the constructor finishes executing. Calling the *setSize* and *setVisible* methods is not required, but if you omit either method call, you will get unfavorable results. If you omit the call to *setSize*, the window will consist of just the title bar. If you omit the call to *setVisible*, the window will not be displayed when the application begins.

The window generated by running Example 12.1 is shown in Figure 12.2. Note the text in the title bar, which was set by calling the *JFrame* constructor. When you run the program, try minimizing, maximizing, moving, resizing, and closing the window.

We have opened a window successfully, but an empty window is not very impressive. In the next section, we will show you how to start adding GUI components to the window.

Figure 12.2

The Window Generated by Example 12.1

12.2   GUI Components

We have already said that a **component** is an object having a graphical representation. Labels, text fields, buttons, radio buttons, checkboxes, and drop-down lists are examples of components. A component performs at least one of these functions:

- displays information
- collects data from the user
- allows the user to initiate program functions

Java provides an extensive set of classes that can be used to add a GUI to your applications. Table 12.2 lists some GUI components and the Java classes that encapsulate them. All classes listed in Table 12.2 belong to the *javax.swing* package.

Java supports two implementations of GUI components: AWT (Abstract Window Toolkit) and *swing*.

The AWT components are the original implementation of Java components and hand off some of the display and behavior of the component to the native windowing system. In other words, on a PC, AWT components,

TABLE 12.2   Selected GUI Components and Java Classes

Component	Purpose	Java Class
Label	Displays an image or read-only text. Labels are often paired with text fields and are used to identify the contents of the text field.	JLabel
Text field	A single-line text box for displaying information and accepting user input.	JTextField
Text area	Multiple-line text field for data entry or display.	JTextArea
Password field	Single-line text field for accepting passwords without displaying the characters typed.	JPasswordField
Button	Command button that the user clicks to signal that an operation should be performed.	JButton
Radio button	Toggle button that the user clicks to select one option in the group. Clicking on a radio button deselects any previously selected option.	JRadioButton
Checkbox	Toggle button that the user clicks to select 0, 1, or more options in a group.	JCheckBox
List	List of items that the user clicks to select one or more items.	JList
Drop-down list	Drop-down list of items that the user clicks to select one item.	JComboBox

such as buttons and frames, are rendered by the Windows windowing system; on a Macintosh computer, AWT components are rendered by the MacOS windowing system; on a Unix computer, AWT components are rendered by the X-Window system. As a result, the AWT GUI components automatically take on the appearance and behavior (commonly called the **look and feel**) of the windowing system on which the application is running. One disadvantage of AWT components, however, is that because of the inconsistencies in the look and feel among the various windowing systems, an application may behave slightly differently from one platform to another. Because AWT components rely on the native windowing system, they are often called **heavyweight** components.

The *swing* components are the second generation of GUI components, developed entirely in Java to provide a consistent look and feel from platform to platform. As such, they are often referred to as **lightweight** components. Some of the benefits of *swing* components are:

- Applications run consistently across platforms, which makes maintenance easier.

- The *swing* architecture has its roots in the model-view-controller paradigm, which facilitates programming:
    - the model represents the data for the application
    - the view is the visual representation of that data
    - the controller takes user input on the view and updates the model accordingly
- The *swing* components can be rendered in multiple windowing system styles, so your application can take on the look and feel of the platform on which it is running, if desired.

Given the advantages of *swing* over AWT, we will build our GUI applications using *swing* components exclusively. You can recognize a *swing* component because its class name begins with J. Thus, *JFrame* is a *swing* component. *Swing* components are found in the *javax.swing* package.

A summary of the inheritance hierarchy for selected *swing* components is shown in Figure 12.3. *JComponent* is the base class for all swing components, except for top-level containers such as *JFrame*. Notice that the *JFrame* class does not inherit from the *JComponent* class. However, the *JFrame* class and the *JComponents* shown in Table 12.2 do share some common superclasses: *Component* and *Container*. Thus, the *JComponents* are

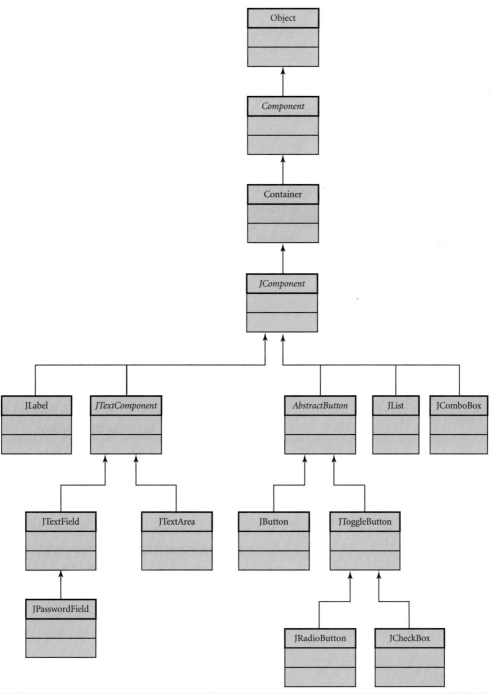

Figure 12.3
The Inheritance Hierarchy for Some GUI Classes

Containers, and as such, can contain other *JComponents* or other *Container* objects. This means that we can nest GUI components, which will help us organize the layout of our windows. We will show you how to do that later in the chapter.

Table 12.3 lists some important methods of *JComponent.* Because these methods are *public,* the GUI components shown in Figure 2.3 inherit these methods.

TABLE 12.3   *JComponent* Methods

Some Useful Methods of the *JComponent* Class	
Return value	**Method name and argument list**
void	setVisible(boolean mode)
	makes the component visible if *mode* is *true*; hides the component if *mode* is *false*. The default is visible.
void	setToolTipText(String toolTip)
	sets the tool tip text to *toolTip*. When the mouse lingers over the component, the tool tip text will be displayed.
void	setForeground(Color foreColor)
	sets the foreground color of the component to *foreColor*.
void	setBackground(Color backColor)
	sets the background color of the component to *backColor*.
void	setOpaque(boolean mode)
	sets the component's background to opaque if *mode* is *true*; sets the component's background to transparent if *mode* is *false*. If opaque, the component's background is filled with the component's background color; if transparent, the component's background is filled with the background color of the container on which it is placed. The default is transparent.
void	setEnabled(boolean mode)
	enables the component if *mode* is *true*; disables the component if *mode* is *false*. An enabled component can respond to user input.

12.3   A Simple Component: *JLabel*

Now it's time to place a component into the window. We will start with a simple component, a label, encapsulated by the *JLabel* class. A user does not interact with a label; the label just displays some information, such as a title, an identifier for another component, or an image.

Example 12.2 creates a window containing two labels, one that displays text and one that displays an image. Figure 12.4 shows the window when the application is run.

```
 1 /*  Using JLabels to display text and images
 2      Anderson, Franceschi
 3 */
 4
 5 import java.awt.Container;
 6 import javax.swing.JFrame;
 7 import javax.swing.ImageIcon;
 8 import javax.swing.JLabel;
 9 import java.awt.FlowLayout;
10 import java.awt.Color;
11
12 public class Dinner extends JFrame
13 {
14   private Container contents;
15   private JLabel labelText;
16   private JLabel labelImage;
17
18   // Constructor
19   public Dinner( )
20   {
21     super( "What's for dinner?" );      // call JFrame constructor
```

Figure 12.4
Running Example 12.2

```
22
23     contents = getContentPane( );          // get content pane
24
25     contents.setLayout( new FlowLayout( ) ); // set layout manager
26
27     // use the JLabel constructor with a String argument
28     labelText = new JLabel( "Sushi tonight?" );
29
30     // set label properties
31     labelText.setForeground( Color.WHITE );
32     labelText.setBackground( Color.BLUE );
33     labelText.setOpaque( true );
34
35     // use the JLabel constructor with an ImageIcon argument
36     labelImage = new JLabel( new ImageIcon( "sushi.jpg" ) );
37
38     // set tool tip text
39     labelImage.setToolTipText( "photo of sushi" );
40
41     // add the two labels to the content pane
42     contents.add( labelText );
43     contents.add( labelImage );
44
45     setSize( 300, 200 );
46     setVisible( true );
47   }
48
49   public static void main( String [ ] args )
50   {
51     Dinner dinner = new Dinner( );
52     dinner.setDefaultCloseOperation( JFrame.EXIT_ON_CLOSE );
53   }
54 }
```

EXAMPLE 12.2   A Simple GUI Component: *JLabel*

Java provides classes to help us organize window contents. These classes are called layout managers. They implement the *LayoutManager* interface and determine the size and position of the components within a container. We will use the simple *FlowLayout* layout manager for the next few examples; later in the chapter, we will look into two other, more–sophisticated layout managers: *BorderLayout* and *GridLayout*.

The *FlowLayout* layout manager arranges components in rows from left to right in the order in which the components are added to the container.

Whenever a newly added component does not fit into the current row, the *FlowLayout* layout manager starts a new row. With *FlowLayout*, if the user resizes the window, the components may be rearranged into fewer or more rows. We will use the default constructor of the *FlowLayout* class, which centers the components within each row.

To add components to a window, we use two methods of the *Container* class, shown in Table 12.4, to set the layout manager and add components to the window. Remember that we obtain the content pane of the *JFrame* window as a *Container* object. We call these methods using the content pane object reference.

In Example 12.2, we declare two *JLabel* instance variables at lines 15–16. At line 25, we set *FlowLayout* as the layout manager.

Next, we instantiate our *JLabel* objects. Table 12.5 shows several constructors of the *JLabel* class.

The *SwingConstants* interface, which is implemented by many *JComponents* that display text, such as labels, text fields, and buttons, provides a collection of *static int* constants that can be used for positioning and orientation of the text within a component.

 **REFERENCE POINT**

More information about the *SwingConstants* interface can be found on the Sun Microsystems Web site: www.java.sun.com.

The first *JLabel* object reference, *labelText*, is instantiated at line 28, using the constructor with a *String* argument.

The second *JLabel* object reference, *labelImage*, is instantiated at line 36, using the constructor that takes an *Icon* argument. The *ImageIcon* class

TABLE 12.4   Useful Methods of the *Container* Class

Useful Methods of the *Container* Class	
Return value	**Method name and argument list**
void	`setLayout( LayoutManager mgr )`
	sets the layout manager of the window to *mgr*
Component	`add( Component component )`
	adds the *component* to the container, using the rules of the layout manager. Returns the argument.
void	`removeAll( )`
	removes all components from the window

TABLE 12.5   Constructors of the *JLabel* Class

Useful Constructors of the *JLabel* Class	
Class	**Constructor**
JLabel	JLabel(String text) creates a *JLabel* object that displays the specified *text*
JLabel	JLabel(String text, int alignment) creates a *JLabel* object that displays the specified *text*. The *alignment* argument specifies the alignment of the text within the label component. The *alignment* value can be any of the following *static int* constants from the *SwingConstants* interface: LEFT, CENTER, RIGHT, LEADING, or TRAILING. By default, the label text is left-adjusted.
JLabel	JLabel(Icon image) creates a *JLabel* object that displays the *image*.

COMMON ERROR TRAP

As for any object reference, it is mandatory to instantiate a component before using it. Forgetting to instantiate a component before adding it to the content pane will result in a *NullPointerException* at run time.

COMMON ERROR TRAP

Be sure to place the call to the *setVisible* method as the last statement in the constructor. If you add components to the window after calling *setVisible*, those components will not be visible until the window is repainted.

encapsulates an image and implements the *Icon* interface, so an *IconImage* object can be used wherever an *Icon* argument is required. One of the *ImageIcon* constructors takes as a *String* argument the filename where the image is stored. Its API is:

```
public ImageIcon( String filename )
```

Lines 31–33 calls the *setForeground*, *setBackground*, and *setOpaque* methods inherited from the *JComponent* class to set some properties of *labelText*. On line 39, we set up a tool tip that will pop up the message "photo of sushi" when the user pauses the mouse pointer over the image. You can see this tool tip displayed in Figure 12.4.

In lines 42–43, we add the two labels to the window. Because we are using the *FlowLayout* layout manager, the labels appear in the order we added them to the component, first *labelText*, then *labelImage*, centered left to right in the window. If the user resizes the window to be about the same width as the *JLabel labelText*, the layout manager will arrange the display so that the image appears under the text (as a second row).

Note that the last statement of the constructor (line 46) is a call to the *setVisible* method to make the window visible. A common error is to call the *setVisible* method earlier in the constructor, then add more components to the window. If you do this, however, the components added after the call to the *setVisible* method will not display until the window is repainted, for example, as a result of the user resizing the window.

Skill Practice
with these end-of-chapter questions

12.18.1   Multiple Choice Exercises

Questions 1, 2, 3, 4

12.18.2   Reading and Understanding Code

Question 18

12.18.3   Fill in the Code

Question 27

12.18.4   Identifying Errors in Code

Question 42

12.18.5   Debugging Area

Questions 46, 47

12.4   Event Handling

Now we know how to open a window in an application, and we know how to display labels and images. But the user can't interact with our application yet, except to display a tool tip. We need to add some interactive GUI components, like buttons or text fields or lists. The user will then control which operations of the program will take place, and in what order, by interacting with these components.

GUI programming uses an **event-driven model** of programming, as opposed to the procedural model of programming we have been using thus far. By that, we mean that by using a GUI, we put the user in interactive control. For example, we might display some text fields, a few buttons, and a selectable list of items. Then our program will "sit back" and wait for the user to do something. When the user enters data into a text field, presses a button, or selects an item from the list, our program will respond, perform the function that the user has requested, then sit back again and wait for the user to do something else. These user actions generate **events**. Thus, the processing of our program will consist of responding to events caused by the user interacting with GUI components.

When the user interacts with a GUI component, the component **fires an event**. Java provides interfaces, classes, and methods to handle these events. Using these Java tools, we can register our application's interest in being notified when an event occurs for a particular component, and we can specify the code we want to be executed when that event occurs.

To allow a user to interact with our application through a GUI component, we need to perform the following functions:

1. write an event handler class (called a **listener**)

2. instantiate an object of that class

3. register that listener on one or more components

A typical event handler class *implements* a listener interface. The listener interfaces, which inherit from the *EventListener* interface, are supplied in the *java.awt.event* and *javax.swing.event* packages. A listener interface specifies one or more *abstract* methods that an event handler class needs to implement. The listener methods receive as a parameter an event object, which represents the event that was fired.

An application can instantiate multiple event handlers, and a single event handler can be the listener for multiple components.

Event classes are subclasses of the *EventObject* class, as shown in Figure 12.5, and are in the *java.awt.event* and *javax.swing.event* packages. From the *EventObject* class, the event classes inherit the *getSource* method, which returns the object reference of the component that fired the event. Its API is shown in Table 12.6.

Thus, with some simple *if/else* statements, an event handler that is registered as the listener for more than one component can identify which of the components fired the event and decide on the appropriate action.

The types of listeners that we can register on a component depend on the types of events that the component fires. Table 12.7 shows some user activities that generate events, the type of event object created, and the appropriate listener interface for the event handler to implement. Some of these components can fire other events, as well.

To add event handling to our *ShellGUIApplication* class, we will follow the following pattern. The code we need to add is shown in bold.

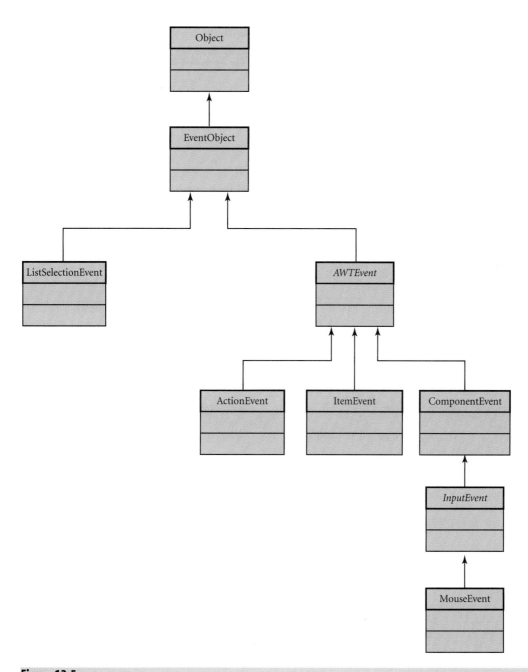

Figure 12.5
Event Class Hierarchy

TABLE 12.6   The *getSource* Method Inherited by Event Classes

Return value	Method name and argument list
Object	getSource( )
	returns the object reference of the component that fired the event

TABLE 12.7   Component Events and Listeners

JComponent	User Interaction That Generates an Event	The Event Object Created	Listener Interface the Event Handler Should Implement
JTextField	Pressing Enter	ActionEvent	ActionListener
JTextArea	Pressing Enter	ActionEvent	ActionListener
JButton	Pressing the button	ActionEvent	ActionListener
JRadioButton	Selecting a radio button	ItemEvent	ItemListener
JCheckBox	Selecting or deselecting a checkbox	ItemEvent	ItemListener
JList	Selecting an item	ListSelectionEvent	ListSelectionListener
JComboBox	Selecting an item	ItemEvent	ItemListener
Any component	Pressing or releasing mouse buttons	MouseEvent	MouseListener
Any component	Moving or dragging the mouse	MouseEvent	MouseMotionListener

```
// import statements as needed

public class ClassName1 extends JFrame
{
  // declare components and other instance variables

  // constructor
  public ClassName1( )
  {
    // call JFrame constructor
    // get content pane
    // set the layout manager
    // instantiate components and other instance variables
    // add components to the content pane
    // declare and instantiate event handler objects
```

```
      // register event handlers on components

      // set window size
      // make window visible
   }

   // private event handler class
   private class EventHandlerName implements ListenerName
   {
      // implement the methods of the listener interface
      // to process the events
   }

   public static void main( String [ ] args )
   {
      // instantiate application object
   }
}
```

Although we can define an event handler class as *public* in its own source file, we usually declare an event handler as a ***private* inner class** within the GUI application class. A *private* inner class is defined within the *public* class and has access to all the members of the *public* class. Thus, declaring our event handler as a *private* inner class simplifies our code by giving the event handler direct access to our application's GUI components.

In the constructor, we instantiate an object of our event handler class. Then we register that event handler on a component by calling an *add...Listener* method. Table 12.8 shows a few of these methods. We call the *add...Listener* method using the object reference of the component on which we want to register the listener and passing as an argument the event handler object we instantiated.

TABLE 12.8   Some Add...Listener Methods

Add...Listener Method APIs
void addActionListener(ActionListener handler)
void addItemListener(ItemListener handler)
void addListSelectionListener(ListSelectionListener handler)
void addMouseListener(MouseListener handler)
void addMouseMotionListener(MouseMotionListener handler)

12.5   Text Fields

Now we are ready for our first GUI program with user interaction. For this first example, we will build a GUI that takes an ID and a password from a user. If the ID is "open" and the password is "sesame", we display "Welcome!" Otherwise, we display "Sorry: wrong login".

We will use a *JTextField* for the ID and a *JPasswordField* for the password. For confidentiality of passwords, the *JPasswordField* does not display the characters typed by the user. Instead, as each character is typed, the *JPasswordField* displays an echo character. The default echo character is *, but we can specify a different character, if desired. We will also use a *JTextArea* to display a legal warning to potential hackers. Both *JTextField* and *JTextArea* are direct subclasses of *JTextComponent*, which encapsulates text entry from the user. *JTextField* displays a single-line field and *JTextArea* displays a multiline field.

Table 12.9 lists some useful constructors and methods of these text classes.

TABLE 12.9   Constructors and Methods of *JTextField, JTextArea,* and *JPasswordField*

Useful Constructors and Methods of the *JTextField, JTextArea,* and *JPasswordField* Classes	
Constructors	
Class	**Constructor**
JTextField	JTextField(String text, int numColumns) constructs a text field initially filled with *text,* with the specified number of columns
JTextField	JTextField(int numberColumns) constructs an empty text field with the specified number of columns
JTextArea	JTextArea(String text) constructs a text area initially filled with *text*
JTextArea	JTextArea(int numRows, int numColumns) constructs an empty text area with the number of rows and columns specified by *numRows* and *numColumns*
JTextArea	JTextArea(String text, int numRows, int numColumns) constructs a text area initially filled with *text,* and with the number of rows and columns specified by *numRows* and *numColumns*
JPasswordField	JPasswordField(int numberColumns) constructs an empty password field with the specified number of columns

TABLE 12.9   (continued)

Methods Common to *JTextField*, *JTextArea*, and *JPasswordField* Classes	
Return value	**Method name and argument list**
void	setEditable(boolean mode) sets the properties of the text component as editable or noneditable, depending on whether *mode* is *true* or *false*. The default is editable.
void	setText(String newText) sets the text of the text component to *newText*.
String	getText( ) returns the text contained in the text component.
Additional Methods of the *JPasswordField* Class	
Return value	**Method name and argument list**
void	setEchoChar(char c) sets the echo character of the password field to *c*.
char [ ]	getPassword( ) returns the text entered in this password field as an array of *char*s. Note: This method is preferred over the *getText* method for getting the password typed by the user.

Example 12.3 implements our login application, and Figure 12.6 shows the application in action.

```
1 /* Using JTextFields, JTextArea, and JPasswordField
2    Anderson, Franceschi
3 */
4
5 import javax.swing.JFrame;
6 import javax.swing.JLabel;
7 import javax.swing.JTextField;
8 import javax.swing.JPasswordField;
9 import javax.swing.JTextArea;
10 import java.awt.Container;
11 import java.awt.FlowLayout;
12 import java.awt.Color;
13 import java.awt.event.ActionListener;
14 import java.awt.event.ActionEvent;
15
```

Figure 12.6

Running Example 12.3

```
16 public class Login extends JFrame
17 {
18   private Container contents;
19   private JLabel idLabel, passwordLabel, message;
20   private JTextField id;
21   private JPasswordField password;
22   private JTextArea legal;
23
24   // Constructor
25   public Login( )
```

```
26  {
27    super( "Login Screen" );
28    contents = getContentPane( );
29    contents.setLayout( new FlowLayout( ) );
30
31    idLabel = new JLabel( "Enter id" ); // label for ID
32    id = new JTextField( "", 12 );        // instantiate ID text field
33
34    passwordLabel = new JLabel( "Enter password" ); // password label
35    password = new JPasswordField( 8 ); // instantiate password field
36    password.setEchoChar( '?' );          // set echo character to '?'
37
38    message = new JLabel( "Log in above" );  // label to hold messages
39
40    // instantiate JTextArea with legal warning
41    legal = new JTextArea( "Warning: Any attempt to illegally\n"
42              + "log in to this server is punishable by law.\n"
43              + "This corporation will not tolerate hacking,\n"
44              + "virus attacks, or other malicious acts." );
45    legal.setEditable( false );           // disable typing in this field
46
47    // add all components to the window
48    contents.add( idLabel );
49    contents.add( id );
50    contents.add( passwordLabel );
51    contents.add( password );
52    contents.add( message );
53    contents.add( legal );
54
55    // instantiate event handler for the text fields
56    TextFieldHandler tfh = new TextFieldHandler( );
57
58    // add event handler as listener for ID and password fields
59    id.addActionListener( tfh );
60    password.addActionListener( tfh );
61
62    setSize( 250, 200 );
63    setVisible( true );
64  }
65
66  // private inner class event handler
67  private class TextFieldHandler implements ActionListener
68  {
69    public void actionPerformed( ActionEvent e )
```

```
70    {
71      if ( id.getText( ).equals( "open" )
72         && ( new String( password.getPassword( ) ) ).equals( "sesame" ) )
73      {
74        message.setForeground( Color.BLACK );
75        message.setText( "Welcome!" );
76      }
77      else
78      {
79        message.setForeground( Color.RED );
80        message.setText( "Sorry: wrong login" );
81      }
82    }
83  }
84
85    public static void main( String [ ] args )
86    {
87      Login login = new Login( );
88      login.setDefaultCloseOperation( JFrame.EXIT_ON_CLOSE );
89    }
90  }
```

EXAMPLE 12.3   The *Login* Class

Lines 5–14 import the various classes that we use in this program. Line 16 declares the class, which we name *Login*, as a subclass of *JFrame*.

We declare our instance variables at lines 18–22. In addition to our three components: the *JTextField id*, the *JPasswordField password*, and the *JTextArea legal*, we also have three *JLabel* components: *idLabel*, *passwordLabel*, and *message*. The *idLabel* and *passwordLabel* components provide descriptions for the corresponding text fields. We will use the *message* label to display feedback to the user on whether the login was successful.

At line 32, we instantiate the *JTextField id* using the constructor that takes an initial value and the size of the text field. The initial value is blank, and we want the text field to accommodate 12 characters. At line 35, we instantiate the *JPasswordField password* and set its length to 8 characters. At line 36, we call the *setEchoChar* method to reset the echo character from its default of * to ?. Thus, when the user types characters into the password field, a ? will be displayed for each character typed.

At lines 40–44, we instantiate the *JTextArea legal*. By default, a user can enter data into a text area. However, since we are using this text area only to display a legal warning, we turn off the ability of the user to type into the text area by calling the *setEditable* method with the argument *false* (line 45).

At lines 47–53, we add all the components to the content pane. As Figure 12.6 shows, the components will be displayed in the window in the order we added them to the container.

After the window is displayed, our application will wait for the user to interact with the components. When the user enters a value into either the *id* or the *password* field, we want to check whether the values the user entered are correct. This will be the job of the event handler for those fields.

Pressing the *Enter* key in a text field generates an *ActionEvent*; therefore, at lines 66–83, we coded our event handler as the *private* inner class, *TextFieldHandler*, which *implements* the *ActionListener* interface. As shown in Table 12.10, the *ActionListener* interface has only one *abstract* method, *actionPerformed*, which receives an *ActionEvent* parameter.

Be sure that you code the *actionPerformed* method correctly, as shown in Table 12.10. Failure to code the header properly causes a compiler error. For example, misspelling the method name generates the following compiler error:

```
Login.TextFieldHandler is not abstract and does not override abstract
method actionPerformed(java.awt.event.ActionEvent) in
java.awt.event.ActionListener
```

In the constructor, we declare and instantiate a *TextFieldHandler* object reference, *tfh* (line 55–56). Then at lines 58–60, we register *tfh* as the listener on the *id* and *password* components. When either *id* or *password* is in focus (that is, if the mouse was last clicked on the component) and the user

COMMON ERROR TRAP

Be sure that the header of the *actionPerformed* method is coded correctly. Otherwise, your method will not override the abstract *actionPerformed* method, as required by the *ActionListener* interface.

TABLE 12.10   *ActionListener* Method API

```
public void actionPerformed( ActionEvent event )
```
An event handler that implements the *ActionListener* interface writes code in this method to respond to the *ActionEvent* fired by any registered components.

presses the *Enter* key, the component that is in focus will fire an action event and our *actionPerformed* method will be executed.

We implement the *actionPerformed* method at lines 69–82. Because we defined this event handler as a *private* inner class, the *actionPerformed* method can directly access the *id* and *password* fields. At lines 71–72, we test if the ID and password entered by the user are correct.

As shown in Table 12.9, the *getPassword* method of the *JPasswordField* class returns an array of *chars*. At line 72, to convert that array of *chars* to a *String*, we use a constructor of the *String* class with the following API, which takes an array of *chars* as an argument:

```
public String( char [ ] charArray )
```

If the user has typed correct values into both the *id* and *password* fields, our event handler sets the foreground color to black and sets the text of *message* to "Welcome!" (lines 74–75). If either the id or the password is incorrect, we set the foreground color to red and set the text of *message* to "Sorry: wrong login" (lines 79–80).

Note that we did not register our event handler for the *JTextArea*. We have disabled typing into that field, so the user cannot enter new text into that field. Also, if we did not register a listener on the *id* and *password* components, the user could still type characters into these two fields and press the *Enter* key, but no events would fire, and therefore, our application would not respond to the user's actions.

COMMON ERROR TRAP

If you do not register a listener on a component, the component will not fire an event. Thus, the event handler will not execute when the user interacts with the component.

Figure 12.6 shows the application when the window first opens, after the user enters incorrect login values, and after the user enters correct login values. We suggest you become familiar with this application. First run the application as it is written. Then, delete either line 59 or 60, which registers the listeners on the components, and test the application again. Finally, change the echo character and test the application again.

12.6   Command Buttons

Handling an event associated with a button follows the same pattern as Example 12.3. We instantiate an event handler and add that event handler as a listener for the button. Clicking on a button generates an *ActionEvent*, so our listener needs to implement the *ActionListener* interface.

In Example 12.4, we present the user with a text field and two command buttons. The user enters a number into the text field, then presses one of the two buttons. When the user clicks on the first button, we square the number; when the user clicks on the second button, we cube the number. We then display the result using a label component. To determine whether to square or cube the number, our event handler will need to identify which button was clicked by calling the *getSource* method of the *ActionEvent* class, as described in Table 12.6.

This example will demonstrate the following:

- how to handle an event originating from a button
- how to determine which component fired the event

```java
1  /* Simple Math Operations Using JButtons
2     Anderson, Franceschi
3  */
4
5  import javax.swing.*;
6  import java.awt.*;
7  import java.awt.event.*;
8
9  public class SimpleMath extends JFrame
10 {
11   private Container contents;
12   private JLabel operandLabel, resultLabel, result;
13   private JTextField operand;
14   private JButton square, cube;
15
16   public SimpleMath( )
17   {
18     super( "Simple Math" );
19     contents = getContentPane( );
20     contents.setLayout( new FlowLayout( ) );
21
22     operandLabel = new JLabel( "Enter a number" ); // text field label
23     operand = new JTextField( 5 ); // text field is 5 characters wide
24
25     // instantiate buttons
26     square = new JButton( "Square" );
27     cube = new JButton( "Cube" );
28
29     resultLabel = new JLabel( "Result:" ); // label for result
30     result = new JLabel( "???" );          // label to hold result
31
32     // add components to the window
```

```
33    contents.add( operandLabel );
34    contents.add( operand );
35    contents.add( square );
36    contents.add( cube );
37    contents.add( resultLabel );
38    contents.add( result );
39
40    // instantiate our event handler
41    ButtonHandler bh = new ButtonHandler( );
42
43    // add event handler as listener for both buttons
44    square.addActionListener( bh );
45    cube.addActionListener( bh );
46
47    setSize( 175, 150 );
48    setVisible( true );
49    }
50
51    // private inner class event handler
52    private class ButtonHandler implements ActionListener
53    {
54     // implement actionPerformed method
55     public void actionPerformed( ActionEvent ae )
56     {
57      try
58      {
59       double op = Double.parseDouble( operand.getText( ) );
60
61       // identify which button was pressed
62       if ( ae.getSource( ) == square )
63         result.setText( ( new Double( op * op ) ).toString( ) );
64       else if ( ae.getSource( ) == cube )
65          result.setText( ( new Double( op * op * op ) ).toString( ) );
66      }
67      catch ( NumberFormatException e )
68      {
69       operandLabel.setText( "Enter a number" );
70       operand.setText( "" );
71       result.setText( "???" );
72      }
73     }
74    }
75
76    public static void main( String [ ] args )
77    {
```

```
78    SimpleMath sm = new SimpleMath( );
79    sm.setDefaultCloseOperation( JFrame.EXIT_ON_CLOSE );
80  }
81 }
```

EXAMPLE 12.4   Simple Math using *JButton*

As you have seen in the previous examples, GUI applications use a number of Java classes. For Example 12.4, as well as the remaining examples in this chapter, we will use the bulk *import* statement, which replaces the individual class names with the wildcard character (*). Its syntax is:

```
import packageName.*;
```

In this way, we write only one *import* statement per package (lines 5–7).

Notice that the *java.awt.event* package is different from the *java.awt* package. You might assume that importing *java.awt.** also imports the classes in the *java.awt.event* package. That is not the case, however; we need to import both packages.

COMMON ERROR TRAP

The *java.awt.event* package is not imported with the *java.awt* package. Include *import* statements for both the *java.awt* and the *java.awt.event* packages.

At lines 51–74, we define our event handler, *ButtonHandler*, as a *private* inner class. Because clicking a button fires an *ActionEvent*, our event handler implements the *ActionListener* interface. Thus, we provide our code to handle the event in the *actionPerformed* method. Line 59 retrieves the data the user typed into the text field and attempts to convert the text to a *double*. Because the *parseDouble* method will *throw* a *NumberFormatException* if the user enters a value that cannot be converted to a *double*, we perform the conversion inside a *try* block.

The *if* statement at line 62 calls the *getSource* method using the *ActionEvent* object reference to test if the component that fired the event is the *square* button. If so, we set the text of the *result* label to the square of the number entered.

If the *square* button did not fire the event, we test if the source of the event was the *cube* button (line 64). If so, we set the text of the *result* label to the cube of the number entered. Actually, the test in line 64 is not necessary, because we registered our event handler as the listener for only two buttons. So if the source isn't the *square* button, then the *cube* button must have fired the event. However, in order to improve readability and maintenance, it is good practice to check the source of the event specifically, in particular if additional buttons or components will be added to the application later.

SOFTWARE ENGINEERING TIP

Verify the source component before processing the event.

In the constructor, at lines 40–41, we declare and instantiate the *Button-Handler* event handler, *bh*. At lines 43–45, we call the *addActionListener* method to register the handler on our two buttons.

The output of this example is shown in Figure 12.7. When you run this example, try entering a valid number into the text field, and press each button. Then try to enter text that cannot be converted to a number. Also, try deleting either statement that registers the event listener on the buttons (line 44 or 45), and run the application again.

12.7   Radio Buttons and Checkboxes

If you have ever completed a survey on the Web, you are probably acquainted with radio buttons and checkboxes.

Radio buttons prompt the user to select one of several mutually exclusive options. Clicking on any radio button deselects any previously selected option. Thus, in a group of radio buttons, a user can select only one option at a time.

Checkboxes often are associated with the instruction "check all that apply"; that is, the user is asked to select 0, 1, or more options. A checkbox is a toggle button in that if the option is not currently selected, clicking on a checkbox selects the option, and if the option is currently selected, clicking on the checkbox deselects the option.

The *JRadioButton* and *JCheckBox* classes, which belong to the *javax.swing* package, encapsulate the concepts of radio buttons and checkboxes, respectively. We will present two similar examples in order to illustrate how to use these classes and how they differ. Both examples allow the user to select the background color for a label component. We display three color options: red, green, and blue. Using radio buttons, only one option can be selected at a time. Thus, by clicking on a radio button, the user will cause the background of the label to be displayed in one of three colors. Using check-

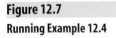

Figure 12.7

Running Example 12.4

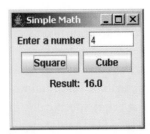

boxes, the user can select any combination of the three color options, so the label color can be set to any of eight possible combinations. Table 12.11 lists all these combinations.

Table 12.12 shows several constructors of the *JRadioButton*, *ButtonGroup*, and *JCheckBox* classes.

TABLE 12.11   Selecting Colors Using Radio Buttons vs. Checkboxes

Using Radio Buttons
(1 selection possible at a time)

Color Selection			Resulting Color
red	**green**	**blue**	
●	○	○	red
○	●	○	green
○	○	●	blue

Using Checkboxes
(0 to 3 selections possible at a time)

Color Selections			Resulting Color
red	**green**	**blue**	
☐	☐	☐	black
☑	☐	☐	red
☐	☑	☐	green
☐	☐	☑	blue
☑	☑	☐	yellow
☑	☐	☑	purple
☐	☑	☑	blue-green
☑	☑	☑	white

TABLE 12.12   Useful Constructors of the *JRadioButton*, *ButtonGroup*, and *JCheckBox* Classes

Useful Constructors of the *JRadioButton*, *ButtonGroup*, and *JCheckBox* Classes	
Constructors	
Class	**Constructor**
JRadioButton	JRadioButton(String buttonLabel)
	constructs a radio button labeled *buttonLabel*. By default, the radio button is initially deselected.
JRadioButton	JRadioButton(String buttonLabel, boolean selected)
	constructs a radio button labeled *buttonLabel*. If *selected* is *true*, the button is initially selected; if *selected* is *false*, the button is deselected.
ButtonGroup	ButtonGroup( )
	constructs a button group. Adding buttons to this group makes the buttons mutually exclusive.
JCheckBox	JCheckBox(String checkBoxLabel)
	constructs a checkbox labeled *checkBoxLabel*. By default, the checkbox is initially deselected.
JCheckBox	JCheckBox(String checkBoxLabel, boolean selected)
	constructs a checkbox labeled *checkBoxLabel*. If *selected* is *true*, the checkbox is initially selected; if *selected* is *false*, the checkbox is initially deselected.

Selecting or deselecting radio buttons and checkboxes fires an *ItemEvent*. To receive this event, our event handler needs to implement the *ItemListener* interface, which has only one method, shown in Table 12.13.

Note that selecting a radio button fires both an *ItemEvent* and an *ActionEvent*, so an alternative for radio buttons is to register a handler that implements the *ActionListener* interface. We have chosen to use an *ItemListener* for both radio buttons and checkboxes to demonstrate the similarities and differences between the two components.

TABLE 12.13   *ItemListener* Method API

```
public void itemStateChanged( ItemEvent event )
```
An event handler that implements the *ItemListener* interface writes code in this method to respond to the *ItemEvent* fired by any registered components.

Example 12.5 shows the color selection application using radio buttons.

```
1  /* Select a Color using JRadioButtons
2     Anderson, Franceschi
3  */
4
5  import javax.swing.*;
6  import java.awt.*;
7  import java.awt.event.*;
8
9  public class ChangingColors extends JFrame
10 {
11   private Container contents;
12   private JRadioButton red, green, blue;
13   private ButtonGroup colorGroup;
14   private JLabel label;
15   private Color selectedColor = Color.RED;
16
17   public ChangingColors( )
18   {
19     super( "Selecting a color" );
20     contents = getContentPane( );
21     contents.setLayout( new FlowLayout( ) );
22
23     red = new JRadioButton( "red", true );
24     green = new JRadioButton( "green" );
25     blue = new JRadioButton( "blue" );
26
27     label = new JLabel( "Watch my background" );
28     label.setForeground( Color.GRAY );
29     label.setOpaque( true );
30     label.setBackground( selectedColor );
31
32     contents.add( red );
33     contents.add( green );
34     contents.add( blue );
35     contents.add( label );
36
37     // create button group
38     colorGroup = new ButtonGroup( );
39     colorGroup.add( red );
40     colorGroup.add( green );
```

```
41   colorGroup.add( blue );
42
43   // create RadioButtonHandler event handler
44   // and register it on the radio buttons
45   RadioButtonHandler rbh = new RadioButtonHandler( );
46   red.addItemListener( rbh );
47   green.addItemListener( rbh );
48   blue.addItemListener( rbh );
49
50   setSize( 225, 200 );
51   setVisible( true );
52   }
53
54   private class RadioButtonHandler implements ItemListener
55   {
56    public void itemStateChanged( ItemEvent ie )
57    {
58     if ( ie.getSource( ) == red )
59        selectedColor = Color.RED;
60     else if ( ie.getSource( ) == green )
61        selectedColor = Color.GREEN;
62     else if ( ie.getSource( ) == blue )
63        selectedColor = Color.BLUE;
64
65     label.setBackground( selectedColor );
66    }
67   }
68
69    public static void main( String [ ] args )
70    {
71     ChangingColors cc = new ChangingColors( );
72     cc.setDefaultCloseOperation( JFrame.EXIT_ON_CLOSE );
73    }
74  }
```

EXAMPLE 12.5   Selecting Colors Using *JRadioButtons*

The various instance variables are declared at lines 11–15. The instance variable *selectedColor*, which is initialized to red, will store the choice of the user and will be used to set the background of the *JLabel* component *label*. The three radio buttons and *label* are instantiated at lines 23–27. At line 23, we use a *JRadioButton* constructor with two arguments to instantiate the radio button *red*. The first argument is the title of the radio button; the second argument, *true*, specifies that *red* is selected. Thus, when the window appears, the

Figure 12.8
Running Example 12.5

red radio button will be selected. In order to reflect the effect of the selected radio button, we set the background color of the label to red at line 30.

At lines 24 and 25, *green* and *blue* are instantiated using the *JRadioButton* constructor with only a *String* argument, specifying the radio button titles. The four components are added to the content pane at lines 32–35.

At lines 37–41, we instantiate a *ButtonGroup* object, then add the *red*, *green*, and *blue* radio buttons to *colorGroup* so that they will be mutually exclusive selections.

At lines 43–48, we instantiate our event handler, *RadioButtonHandler rbh*, and call the *addItemListener* method to register the listener *rbh* on the three radio buttons.

At lines 54–67, the *private* class *RadioButtonHandler implements* the *Item-Listener* interface. The only method of *ItemListener, itemStateChanged*, is overriden at lines 56–66. Inside *itemStateChanged*, we use an *if/else* statement to determine which radio button was selected in order to set *selected-Color* to the appropriate color.

Figure 12.8 shows a run of the example after the user has clicked on the *green* radio button. Try running the example and clicking on each radio button. Try modifying the code: for example, delete the lines adding the radio buttons to the button group, then compile and run the program again.

Example 12.6 shows the color selection application using checkboxes.

 **COMMON ERROR TRAP**

Forgetting to make *JRadioButtons* part of the same *ButtonGroup* makes them independent and not mutually exclusive.

```
1 /*  Using JCheckBoxes
2     Anderson, Franceschi
3 */
4
5 import javax.swing.*;
6 import java.awt.*;
```

```
 7 import java.awt.event.*;
 8
 9 public class MixingColors extends JFrame
10 {
11  private Container contents;
12  private JCheckBox red, green, blue;
13  private int redValue, greenValue, blueValue;
14  private JLabel label;
15
16  public MixingColors( )
17  {
18   super( "Selecting a color" );
19   contents = getContentPane( );
20   contents.setLayout( new FlowLayout( ) );
21
22   red = new JCheckBox( "red" );
23   green = new JCheckBox( "green" );
24   blue = new JCheckBox( "blue" );
25
26   label = new JLabel( "Watch my background" );
27   label.setOpaque( true );
28   label.setForeground( Color.GRAY );
29   label.setBackground( new Color ( 0, 0, 0 ) );
30
31   contents.add( red );
32   contents.add( green );
33   contents.add( blue );
34   contents.add( label );
35
36   // create CheckBoxHandler event handler
37   // and register it on the checkboxes
38   CheckBoxHandler cbh = new CheckBoxHandler( );
39   red.addItemListener( cbh );
40   green.addItemListener( cbh );
41   blue.addItemListener( cbh );
42
43   setSize( 225, 200 );
44   setVisible( true );
45  }
46
47  private class CheckBoxHandler implements ItemListener
48  {
49   public void itemStateChanged( ItemEvent ie )
50   {
51    if ( ie.getSource( ) == red )
```

```
52     {
53       if ( ie.getStateChange( ) == ItemEvent.SELECTED )
54         redValue = 255;
55       else
56         redValue = 0;
57     }
58     else if ( ie.getSource( ) == green )
59     {
60       if ( ie.getStateChange( ) == ItemEvent.SELECTED )
61         greenValue = 255;
62       else
63         greenValue = 0;
64     }
65     else if ( ie.getSource( ) == blue )
66     {
67       if ( ie.getStateChange( ) == ItemEvent.SELECTED )
68         blueValue = 255;
69       else
70         blueValue = 0;
71     }
72
73     label.setBackground(
74           new Color( redValue, greenValue, blueValue ) );
75   }
76 }
77
78 public static void main( String [ ] args )
79 {
80   MixingColors mc = new MixingColors( );
81   mc.setDefaultCloseOperation( JFrame.EXIT_ON_CLOSE );
82 }
83 }
```

EXAMPLE 12.6   Using JCheckBoxes

The various instance variables are declared at lines 11–14. The instance variables *redValue*, *greenValue*, and *blueValue* will store the red, green, and blue intensity values, depending on which checkboxes the user selects. These values will be used to set the background color of the *JLabel* component *label*.

The three checkboxes and *label* are instantiated at lines 22–26. We use a *JCheckBox* constructor with a *String* argument that specifies the checkbox titles. The four components are added to the content pane at lines 31–34.

TABLE 12.14   A Useful Method of the *ItemEvent* Class

Return value	Method name and argument list
int	getStateChange( )
	returns the state of the checkbox. If the checkbox is selected, the value *SELECTED* is returned; if the checkbox is deselected, the value *DESELECTED* is returned, where *SELECTED* and *DESELECTED* are *static int* constants of the *ItemEvent* class.

At lines 36–41, we instantiate the *CheckBoxHandler* event handler and register the *cbh* listener on the three checkboxes by calling the *addItemListener* method for each checkbox.

At lines 47–76, we define the *private* inner class, *CheckBoxHandler*, which *implements* the ItemListener interface. The only method of *ItemListener*, *itemStateChanged*, is overriden at lines 49–75. Inside *itemStateChanged*, we first use an *if/else* statement to determine which checkbox fired the event. We then use a nested *if/else* statement to determine if that checkbox has just been selected. The *getStateChange* method in the *ItemEvent* class returns this information. Its API is shown in Table 12.14. The *ItemEvent* class provides the *static int* constants SELECTED and DESELECTED for convenience in coding this method call. Every click on our checkboxes will fire an event, so calling the *getStateChange* method helps us to distinguish between the event fired when the user selects a checkbox from the event fired when the user deselects a checkbox.

If the source checkbox was selected, we set the corresponding color value to 255 (lines 54, 61, and 68). If the source checkbox was deselected, we set the corresponding color value to 0 (lines 56, 63, and 70). For example, if the *red* checkbox is the source of the event, then we check whether the *red* checkbox was selected. If so, we set *redValue* to 255. Otherwise, the *red* checkbox must have been deselected, so we set *redValue* to 0.

At lines 73–74, we set the background color of *label* to a color we instantiate using the values of *redValue*, *greenValue*, and *blueValue* for the color's respective intensities of red, green, and blue.

Figure 12.9 shows a run of the example after the user has selected the red and green checkboxes.

Figure 12.9
Running Example 12.6

12.8 Programming Activity 1: Working with Buttons

In this activity, you will work with two *JButtons* that control one electrical switch. Specifically, you will write the code to perform the following operations:

1. If the user clicks on the "OPEN" button, open the switch.

2. If the user clicks on the "CLOSE" button, close the switch.

The framework for this Programming Activity will animate your code so that you can check its accuracy. Figures 12.10 and 12.11 show the application after the user has clicked on the button labeled "OPEN" and the button labeled "CLOSE", respectively.

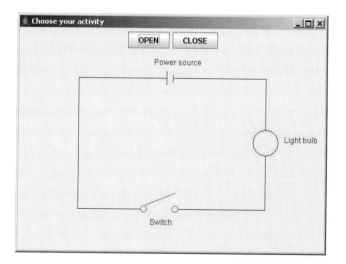

Figure 12.10
User Clicked on "OPEN"

Figure 12.11

User Clicked on "CLOSE"

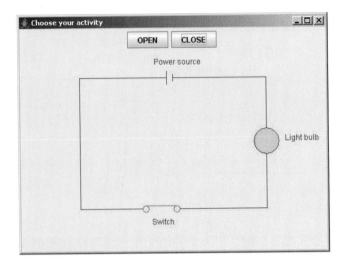

Instructions

In the Chapter 12 Programming Activity 1 directory on the CD-ROM accompanying this book, you will find the source files needed to complete this activity. Copy all the files to a directory on your computer. Note that all files should be in the same directory.

Open the *JButtonPractice.java* source file. Searching for five stars (*****) in the source code will position you to the first code section and then to the second location where you will add your code. In task 1, you will fill in the code to instantiate a button handler and register the handler on the appropriate components. In task 2, you will code the *private* class implementing the listener interface that handles the event generated when the user clicks on either button. Be careful: The class name you use for the handler in the first task needs to be the same as the name you use in the second task. Example 12.7 shows the section of the *JButtonPractice* source code where you will add your code.

```
. . .
open = new JButton( "OPEN" );
contents.add( open );
close = new JButton( "CLOSE" );
contents.add( close );

// ***** 1. Student code starts here
// declare and instantiate the button handler
// and register it on the buttons
```

```
  // end of task 1

  setSize( 500, 375 );
  setVisible( true );
}

// ***** 2. Student code restarts here
// Code a private class to implement the correct Listener
// and its required method
// To open the switch, call the open method with the statement
//   open( );
// To close the switch, call the close method with the statement
//   close( );
// The last statement of the method should be
//   animate( );


// end of task 2
```

EXAMPLE 12.7   Location of Student Code in *JButtonPractice.java*

The framework will animate your code so that you can watch your code work. For this to happen, be sure that you call the *animate* method.

To test your code, compile and run the *JButtonPractice.java* file, then click on each button.

Troubleshooting

If your method implementation does not animate, check these tips:

- Verify that the last statement in your method inside the *private* class is:

  ```
  animate( );
  ```

- Verify that your listener is registered on the components.

- Verify that you have identified the origin of the event correctly.

? DISCUSSION QUESTIONS

1. Explain why the *getSource* method is useful here.

2. Could you implement the above with *JRadioButtons* instead of *JButtons*? What interface would you implement? What would be the method of the interface that you would need to override? What type of event would you handle?

12.9   Lists

In GUIs, often users are asked to select one or more items in a list. Sometimes all items in the list are displayed by default, and sometimes clicking a button displays the items in a scrollable window. Java provides the *JList* class for the former and the *JComboBox* class for the latter.

The *JList* class encapsulates a list in which the user can select one or more items. An item is selected by clicking on it. A range of items can be selected by clicking on the first item in the range, then holding down the *Shift* key while selecting the last item in the range. You can add an item to a selected group of items by holding down the control (*CTRL*) key while clicking on that item.

When the user clicks on one or more items in a list, the *JList* component fires a *ListSelectionEvent*. Our event handler for a *JList* will implement the *ListSelectionListener* interface, which has only one method, *valueChanged*, with the API shown in Table 12.15.

Table 12.16 shows some useful constructors and methods of the *JList* class.

Example 12.8 shows how to use the *JList* class. In this application, we allow the user to choose from a list of countries. We then display a typical food from the country selected.

We construct our *JList* (line 31) by providing an array of *Strings*, *countryList*, which holds the names of the countries to be displayed in the list. When the user selects a country from the list, we display the food image in a *JLabel* component, named *foodImage*, which we instantiate at line 32.

Notice that our list of countries is arranged alphabetically to simplify finding a desired country. In this case, we have only five countries; however, with a longer list, the alphabetical ordering would make it easy for the user to find a particular item in the list. Another option is to display the most likely choice first, then display the remaining items in alphabetical order.

SOFTWARE ENGINEERING TIP

Arrange items in lists in a logical order so that the user can find the desired item quickly.

TABLE 12.15   *ListSelectionListener* Method API

```
public void valueChanged( ListSelectionEvent e )
```

An event handler that implements the *ListSelectionListener* interface writes code in this method to respond to the *ListSelectionEvent* fired by any registered components.

TABLE 12.16 Useful Methods of the *JList* Class

Useful Constructors and Methods of the *JList* Class	
Constructor	
Class	**Constructor**
JList	JList(Object [ ] arrayName)
	constructs a new *JList* component initially filled with the objects in *arrayName*. Often, the objects are *Strings*.
Methods	
Return value	**Method name and argument list**
void	setSelectionMode(int selectionMode)
	sets the number of selections that can be made at one time. The following *static int* constants of the *ListSelectionModel* interface can be used to set the selection mode:
	SINGLE_SELECTION—one selection allowed
	SINGLE_INTERVAL_SELECTION—multiple contiguous items can be selected
	MULTIPLE_INTERVAL_SELECTION—multiple contiguous intervals can be selected (This is the default.)
int	getSelectedIndex( )
	returns the index of the selected item. The index of the first item in the list is 0.
void	setSelectedIndex(int index)
	selects the item at *index*. The index of the first item in the list is 0.

For example, if most users reside in the United States, you could list "USA" first in the list, with the remaining countries alphabetized starting in the second position of the list.

We declare and instantiate the instance variable, *foods*, as an array of *Image-Icons* (lines 17–22). The *foods* array stores images of the food samplings in the same order as the countries in our list. We initialize the *foodImage* label to the first element of *foods* array (line 32). Thus, when we first display the window, the label will show the food sampling from France, which is the first country in the list. In order to match the displayed food sampling with

Figure 12.12
Running Example 12.8

the list selection, we programmatically select the first item of the *countries* list (line 36), using the method *setSelectedIndex* of the *JList* class.

For this application, we will allow the user to select only one country at a time, so we set the selection mode of the list to single selection at line 35 using the *setSelectionMode* method of the *JList* class. The argument passed to the method, *SINGLE_SELECTION*, is a *static int* constant of the *ListSelectionModel* interface.

At lines 50–56, we define our event handler as the *private* inner class, *ListHandler*, which implements the *ListSelectionListener* interface. The only method of *ListSelectionListener*, *valueChanged*, is overriden at lines 52–55. We set up the appropriate food icon to display by calling the *getSelectedIndex* method of the *JList* class. This method returns the index of the item selected by the user. Because we have set up the *foods* array in the same order as the *countries* array, we can use the return value from the *getSelectedIndex* method as the index into the *foods* array to retrieve the corresponding food image for the country selected. In this way, we pass the corresponding array element of *foods* to the *setIcon* method of *JLabel* so that the *foodImage* label will display the appropriate food sampling. Figure 12.12 shows this example running after the user has clicked on "Greece".

```
1 /* Using JList to show a sampling of international foods
2      Anderson, Franceschi
3 */
4
5 import javax.swing.*;
6 import java.awt.*;
7 import javax.swing.event.*;
8
9 public class FoodSamplings extends JFrame
10 {
11   private Container contents;
12   private JList countries;
```

```java
13   private JLabel foodImage;
14
15   private String [ ] countryList =
16              { "France", "Greece", "Italy", "Japan", "USA" };
17   private ImageIcon [ ] foods =
18              {  new ImageIcon( "cheese.jpg" ),
19                 new ImageIcon( "fetaSalad.jpg" ),
20                 new ImageIcon( "pizza.jpg" ),
21                 new ImageIcon( "sushi.jpg" ),
22                 new ImageIcon( "hamburger.jpg" ) };
23
24   public FoodSamplings( )
25   {
26    super( "Food samplings of various countries" );
27    contents = getContentPane( );
28    contents.setLayout( new FlowLayout( ) );
29
30    // instantiate the components
31    countries = new JList( countryList );
32    foodImage = new JLabel( foods[0] );
33
34    // allow single selections only
35    countries.setSelectionMode( ListSelectionModel.SINGLE_SELECTION );
36    countries.setSelectedIndex( 0 );
37
38    // add components to the content pane
39    contents.add( countries );
40    contents.add( foodImage );
41
42    // set up event handler
43    ListHandler lslh = new ListHandler( );
44    countries.addListSelectionListener( lslh );
45
46    setSize( 350, 150 );
47    setVisible( true );
48   }
49
50   private class ListHandler implements ListSelectionListener
51   {
52    public void valueChanged( ListSelectionEvent lse )
53    {
54     foodImage.setIcon( foods[countries.getSelectedIndex( )] );
55    }
56   }
57
```

```
58   public static void main( String args[ ] )
59   {
60     FoodSamplings fs = new FoodSamplings( );
61     fs.setDefaultCloseOperation( JFrame.EXIT_ON_CLOSE );
62   }
63 }
```

EXAMPLE 12.8   Using *JList* to Display Food Samplings

12.10   Combo Boxes

A *JComboBox* implements a drop-down list. When the combo box appears, one item is displayed, along with a button showing a down arrow. When the user presses on the button, the combo box "drops" open and displays a list of items, with a scroll bar for viewing more items. The user can select only one item from the list.

When the user selects an item, the list closes and the selected item is the one item displayed. A *JComboBox* fires an *ItemEvent*, so the event handler must implement the *ItemListener* interface, and thus, provide the *itemState-Changed* method.

Table 12.17 shows the APIs for a constructor and some useful methods of the *JComboBox* class. The constructor is similar to the *JList* constructor in that it takes an array of objects. The *JComboBox* class also provides the *getSelectedIndex* method, so that the event handler can determine which item the user has selected, and the *setSelectedIndex* method, which typically is used to initialize the default item displayed when the list appears. The *setMaximumRowCount* method allows us to specify how many items to display when the combo box opens. The user can use the scroll bar to move through all the items in the list.

To illustrate a combo box, we will display five possible destinations for a spring break vacation: Cancun, Colorado, Jamaica, Orlando, and Pinehurst. When the user selects a destination, information about that destination will be displayed in a text area.

The information about our vacation specials is stored in the file *specials.txt*. Each line in the file represents a vacation destination, the sponsoring organization, a brief description, and a price.

The contents of the *specials.txt* file is shown in Figure 12.13.

TABLE 12.17   Useful Constructors and Methods of the *JComboBox* Class

Useful Constructors and Methods of the *JComboBox* Class	
Constructor	
Class	**Constructor**
JComboBox	JComboBox(Object [ ] arrayName)
	constructs a new *JComboBox* component initially filled with the objects in *arrayName*. Often, the objects are *Strings*.
Methods	
Return value	**Method name and argument list**
void	setSelectedIndex(int index)
	sets the item at *index* as selected. The index of the first item in the list is 0.
int	getSelectedIndex( )
	returns the index of the selected item. The index of the first item in the list is 0.
void	setMaximumRowCount(int size)
	sets the number of rows that will be visible at one time to *size*.

```
Cancun,Club Med,all inclusive,1230

Colorado,Club Med,all inclusive,780

Jamaica,Extreme Vacations,all inclusive,1150

Orlando,Disney Vacations,unlimited pass to DisneyWorld,800

Pinehurst,Golf Concepts,unlimited golf,900
```

Figure 12.13

Contents of the *specials.txt* File

We will first create a *Vacation* class to encapsulate the information about each vacation destination. Then we will create a *VacationList* class that reads vacation information from a text file and creates an *ArrayList* of *Vacation* objects. Finally, our application will retrieve data from a *VacationList* object to create the items for our *JComboBox* dynamically.

For simplicity, in our *Vacation* class (Example 12.9), we have coded only an overloaded constructor (lines 17–32), the accessor method for the *location* instance variable (lines 34–40), and the *toString* method (lines 42–51).

```
1 /* Vacation class
2    Anderson, Franceschi
3 */
4
5 import java.text.DecimalFormat;
6
7 public class Vacation
8 {
9   public final DecimalFormat MONEY
10                     = new DecimalFormat( "$#,##0.00" );
11
12  private String location;
13  private String organization;
14  private String description;
15  private double price;
16
17  /** Constructor
18   *  @param  startLocation       location
19   *  @param  startOrganization   organization
20   *  @param  startDescription    description
21   *  @param  startPrice          price
22   */
23  public Vacation( String startLocation,
24                   String startOrganization,
25                   String startDescription,
26                   double startPrice )
27  {
28   location = startLocation;
29   organization = startOrganization;
30   description = startDescription;
31   price = startPrice;
32  }
33
34  /** getLocation
35   *  @return location
36   */
37  public String getLocation( )
38  {
```

```
39   return location;
40 }
41
42 /** toString
43  *  @return location, organization, description, and price
44  */
45 public String toString( )
46 {
47   return "Location: " + location + "\n"
48          + "Organization: " + organization + "\n"
49          + "Description: " + description + "\n"
50          + "Price: " + MONEY.format( price );
51 }
52 }
```

EXAMPLE 12.9   The *Vacation* Class

Our next step is to create the *VacationList* class, shown in Example 12.10, which we will use to read vacation information from a file and build a list of *Vacation* objects. We assume that we do not know how many records are in the file; thus, we will choose an *ArrayList* rather than an array to store the *Vacation* objects.

Again, for simplicity, we have coded just an overloaded constructor (lines 12–58), the *getLocationList* method (lines 60–69), and the *getDescription* method (lines 71–78). The only instance variable, *vacationList*, is an *ArrayList* of *Vacation* objects. The overloaded constructor takes one argument, the name of the file that contains the data.

At lines 24–47, the *while* loop reads each line of the file, creates a *Vacation* object, and adds the object to the *ArrayList*. The *getLocationList* method returns a *String* array of the *location* for each *Vacation* object. We will call this method in our GUI application to create the items for our *JComboBox*. The *getDescription* method returns the *String* representation of the *Vacation* object stored at a given index of *vacationList*. Our GUI application will call this method to display information about the vacation destination that the user has selected from the *JComboBox*.

REFERENCE POINT

The *ArrayList* class is explained in Chapter 9. *I/O* classes and the *StringTokenizer* class are discussed in Chapter 11.

```
1 /* VacationList class
2    Anderson, Franceschi
3 */
4
```

```
 5 import java.util.*;
 6 import java.io.*;
 7
 8 public class VacationList
 9 {
10   private ArrayList<Vacation> vacationList;
11
12   /** Constructor
13    *  @param  fileName  the name of the file containing the data
14    */
15   public VacationList( String fileName )
16   {
17     vacationList = new ArrayList<Vacation>( );
18     try
19     {
20       FileReader isr = new FileReader( fileName );
21       BufferedReader br = new BufferedReader( isr );
22
23       String record = br.readLine( );
24       while ( record != null )
25       {
26         // extract the fields from the records
27         StringTokenizer st = new StringTokenizer( record, "," );
28         String loc = st.nextToken( );
29         String org = st.nextToken( );
30         String desc = st.nextToken( );
31
32         try
33         {
34           double pr = Double.parseDouble( st.nextToken( ) );
35
36           Vacation vacationTemp = new Vacation( loc, org, desc, pr );
37           vacationList.add( vacationTemp );
38         }
39         catch ( NumberFormatException nfe )
40         {
41           System.out.println( "Error in vacation record: "
42                               + record + "; record ignored" );
43         }
44
45         // read the next line
46         record = br.readLine( );
47       }
48       br.close( );
```

```
49    }
50    catch ( FileNotFoundException fnfe )
51    {
52      System.out.println( "Unable to find " + fileName );
53    }
54    catch ( IOException ioe )
55    {
56      ioe.printStackTrace( );
57    }
58  }
59
60  /** getLocationList
61   *  @return array of locations
62   */
63  public String [ ] getLocationList( )
64  {
65    String [ ] temp = new String[vacationList.size( )];
66    for ( int i = 0; i < vacationList.size( ); i++ )
67         temp[i] = ( vacationList.get( i ) ).getLocation( );
68    return temp;
69  }
70
71  /** getDescription
72   *  @param  index      index of vacation in vacationList
73   *  @return description of vacation at index
74   */
75  public String getDescription( int index )
76  {
77    return ( ( vacationList.get( index ) ).toString( ) );
78  }
79 }
```

EXAMPLE 12.10   The *VacationList* Class

We are now ready to code a GUI application, shown in Example 12.11.

The instance variable, *vacations*, a *VacationList* object reference, will store
an *ArrayList* of vacation information. We instantiate *vacations* (line 20) by
passing the filename that the *main* method passed to the constructor (line
53). For simplicity in execution of the application, we have hard-coded the
filename. However, we could have accepted the filename as a command-
line argument to the application or we could have prompted the user for
the filename.

 REFERENCE POINT

Retrieving command-line
arguments is discussed in
Chapter 8.

Figure 12.14

Running Example 12.11

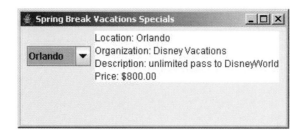

We then instantiate our *JComboBox* (line 26) by passing to the constructor the array of locations returned by the *getLocationList* method of the *VacationList* class.

At line 27, we call the *setMaximumRowCount* method of the *JComboBox* class with an argument of *4* to set the maximum number of items that the user will see when the combo box opens.

We use a *JTextArea* component, named *summary*, to display the vacation descriptions, because the descriptions are of variable length. At line 28, we instantiate the *JTextArea*, with the initial value being the description of the first *Vacation* object in *vacations*. We retrieve the first description by calling the *getDescription* method of the *VacationList* class with an index of 0. By default, a *JComboBox* displays the first item in the list, so in this way, we will match the description with the first item displayed.

At lines 42–49, we define the *ItemListenerHandler* event handler. At line 46, we call the *getSelectedIndex* method of the *JComboBox* class to determine which item the user has selected. Using that returned index, we call the *getDescription* method of the *VacationList* class to set the text of the *JTextArea* to the description matching the selected item.

Figure 12.14 shows a run of the application, after the user has clicked on "*Orlando*" inside the combo box. Try running the example, then modify the number of visible rows by changing the argument of the *setMaximumRowCount* method, and run the example again.

```
1 /* Using a JComboBox to display dynamic data
2    Anderson, Franceschi
3 */
4
5 import javax.swing.*;
6 import java.awt.*;
7 import java.awt.event.*;
```

```
 8
 9 public class VacationSpecials extends JFrame
10 {
11   private VacationList vacations;
12
13   private Container contents;
14   private JComboBox places;
15   private JTextArea summary;
16
17   public VacationSpecials( String fileName )
18   {
19     super( "Spring Break Vacations Specials" );
20     vacations = new VacationList( fileName );
21
22     contents = getContentPane( );
23     contents.setLayout( new FlowLayout( ) );
24
25     // instantiate components
26     places = new JComboBox( vacations.getLocationList( ) );
27     places.setMaximumRowCount( 4 );
28     summary = new JTextArea( vacations.getDescription( 0 ) );
29
30     // add components to content pane
31     contents.add( places );
32     contents.add( summary );
33
34     // set up event handler
35     ItemListenerHandler ilh = new ItemListenerHandler( );
36     places.addItemListener( ilh );
37
38     setSize( 350, 150 );
39     setVisible( true );
40   }
41
42   private class ItemListenerHandler implements ItemListener
43   {
44     public void itemStateChanged( ItemEvent ie )
45     {
46       int index = places.getSelectedIndex( );
47       summary.setText( vacations.getDescription( index ) );
48     }
49   }
50
51   public static void main( String [ ] args )
52   {
```

```
53   VacationSpecials vs = new VacationSpecials( "specials.txt" );
54   vs.setDefaultCloseOperation( JFrame.EXIT_ON_CLOSE );
55 }
56 }
```

EXAMPLE 12.11   The *VacationSpecials* class

Skill Practice
with these end-of-chapter questions

12.18.1	Multiple Choice Exercises
	Questions 5, 6, 7, 8
12.18.2	Reading and Understanding Code
	Questions 16, 19, 20, 21, 22, 23, 24, 25, 26
12.18.3	Fill in the Code
	Questions 28, 29, 31, 32
12.18.4	Identifying Errors in Code
	Questions 43, 44, 45
12.18.5	Debugging Area
	Questions 49, 50
12.18.6	Write a Short Program
	Questions 51, 52, 53, 54, 55, 56, 57

CODE IN ACTION

In the Chapter 12 folder on the CD-ROM included with this book, you will find a Shockwave movie showing step-by-step illustrations of working with GUI components. Double-click on *GUI.html* to start the movie.

12.11   Adapter Classes

We have learned that events are associated with event listener interfaces, and that we implement at least one interface in order to process an event. So far, we have used the *ActionListener*, *ItemListener*, and *ListSelectionLis-*

tener interfaces, each of which has only one method. For mouse events, there are two listeners: the *MouseListener* and the *MouseMotionListener*. The *MouseListener* interface specifies five methods to implement and the *MouseMotionListener* interface specifies two methods to implement. If we want to use *MouseListener* but need only one of its five methods to process a *MouseEvent*, we still have to implement the other four methods as "do-nothing" methods with empty method bodies. For convenience, Java provides **adapter classes**, each of which *implements* an interface and provides an empty body for each of the interface's methods. For mouse events, the adapter classes are *MouseAdapter* and the *MouseMotionAdapter*. Thus, instead of implementing an interface, we can extend the appropriate adapter class and override only the method or methods we need. For example, if we want to process a *MouseEvent* using only one method of the five in the *MouseListener* interface, we can simply extend the *MouseAdapter* class and override that one method. We will do that in our next example.

SOFTWARE ENGINEERING TIP

When you need to implement only a few methods of a listener interface having more than one method, consider extending the corresponding adapter class instead.

12.12 Mouse Movements

A truly interactive application allows the user to point and click using the mouse. Any mouse activity (clicking, moving, or dragging) by the user generates a *MouseEvent*. When any mouse activity occurs, we will be interested in determining where on the window the user clicked, moved, or dragged the mouse. To determine the (*x, y*) coordinate of the mouse event, we can call two methods of the *MouseEvent* class, *getX* and *getY*, which are described in Table 12.18.

Depending on the type of mouse activity, our application will implement either a *MouseListener* interface or a *MouseMotionListener* interface. As

TABLE 12.18   Useful Methods of the *MouseEvent* Class

Return value	Method name and argument list
int	getX( )
	returns the *x* value of the (*x, y*) coordinate of the mouse activity
int	getY( )
	returns the *y* value of the (*x, y*) coordinate of the mouse activity

TABLE 12.19   Methods of the *MouseListener* Interface

MouseListener Interface Method APIs
`public void mousePressed( MouseEvent e )`
called when the mouse button is pressed
`public void mouseReleased( MouseEvent e )`
called when the mouse button is released after being pressed
`public void mouseClicked( MouseEvent e )`
called when the mouse button is pressed and released
`public void mouseEntered( MouseEvent e )`
called when the mouse enters the registered component
`public void mouseExited( MouseEvent e )`
called when the mouse exits the registered component

mentioned, both of the listener interfaces have been implemented as adapter classes that we can extend. The *MouseListener* interface includes the five *abstract* methods described in Table 12.19.

To illustrate how to use the *MouseAdapter* class, we will build a simple submarine hunt game. A submarine is hidden somewhere in the window, and the user will try to sink the submarine by clicking the mouse at various locations in the window, simulating the dropping of a depth charge. Each time the user clicks the mouse, we will indicate how close that click is to the submarine. If the user clicks too far from the submarine, we will display "In the water" in the title bar and draw a blue circle where the mouse was clicked. If the user clicks close to the submarine, we will display "Close ..." in the title bar. Finally, if the submarine is hit, we will change the title bar to "Sunk!", display the submarine, and remove the listener so that the game ends.

In this game, the only mouse action we care about is a click; therefore, we are interested in only one method of the *MouseListener* interface:

mouseClicked. To simplify our code, we can extend the *MouseAdapter* class, which provides implementations for the five *MouseListener* methods, so our event handler needs to override only the *mouseClicked* method.

Example 12.12 implements the submarine hunt game. In the constructor, we randomly generate the (*x, y*) coordinate for the center of the submarine and store the generated values in the *xC* and *yC* instance variables (lines 22–24).

We also define a *boolean* flag variable, *hit*, which is initially *false* (line 14). In the event handler, we will change *hit* to *true* when the user clicks the mouse on the submarine. Then in the *paint* method, we will check the value of *hit* to determine whether to draw the sunken submarine.

In this example, we have set up the listener reference, *mh*, as an instance variable (line 16) rather than defining the reference as a local variable to the constructor, as we have done in previous examples. We define *mh* as an instance variable because when the submarine is hit, the event handler needs to access that listener to turn it off. The event handler is instantiated at line 27. In this application, we want the listener to handle mouse clicks anywhere in the window, so we register the *mouseListener* on our window (*JFrame*) component, which is the *SubHunt* object. Thus, we do not use an object reference to call the *addMouseListener* method, and line 28 is equivalent to:

```
this.addMouseListener( mh );
```

At lines 34–63, we define our mouse event handler, *MouseHandler*, as extending *MouseAdapter*. Inside the method *mouseClicked*, overriden at lines 36–62, we call the *MouseEvent* methods *getX* and *getY* to get the (*x, y*) coordinate where the mouse was clicked.

The *if/else* structure inside the *mouseClicked* method tests how far the mouse was clicked from the submarine location. It updates the title of the window accordingly at lines 45, 54, and 59.

When the submarine has been hit, we set the value of the *hit* flag variable to *true* (line 46) and we also remove *mh* as a listener to this object (line 47) by calling the *removeMouseListener* method, inherited from the *Component* class.

When the submarine has been hit, we also want to reveal the location of the submarine by drawing it. Similarly, if the mouse click is more than two lengths from the center of the submarine, we want to draw a blue circle. Both of these actions require an update to the drawing in the window, so we need the *paint* method to be called. However, our application cannot call the *paint* method explicitly. Instead, we call the *repaint* method, which forces a call to the *paint* method. The *repaint* method is inherited from the *Component* class and has the API shown in Table 12.20.

In the *paint* method (lines 65–87), we test the value of our flag variable. If *hit* is *true*, the user has clicked the mouse on the submarine, so we draw the sunken submarine and a red depth charge (lines 69–80). If *hit* is *false*, the user has not yet sunk the submarine, so we draw a filled blue circle (lines 84–85) at the location of the mouse click. Note that we do not call *super.paint(g)*, because that method erases the contents of the window, and we would lose all the previously drawn blue circles. Also note that if the submarine is not hit and the user clicked the mouse close to the submarine, we do not call *repaint*.

Figure 12.15 shows a run of this game. At this point, the user has found the submarine.

```
 1 import javax.swing.*;
 2 import java.awt.*;
 3 import java.awt.event.*;
 4
 5 public class SubHunt extends JFrame
 6 {
 7   public static int GAME_SIZE = 300;
 8   public static int SIDE = 28; // size of submarine
 9
10   private int xC;    // x coordinate of center of submarine
11   private int yC;    // y coordinate of center of submarine
12   private int x;     // current x mouse position
```

TABLE 12.20   The *repaint* Method API in the *Component* Class

Return value	Method name and argument list
void	repaint( )
	automatically forces a call to the *paint* method

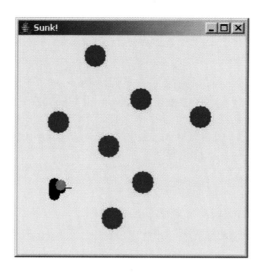

Figure 12.15
A Run of Example 12.12

```
13  private int y;      // current y mouse position
14  private boolean hit = false;    // if false, submarine not sunk
15
16  private MouseHandler mh; // mouse event handler
17
18  public SubHunt( )
19  {
20   super( "Click in the window to sink the sub" );
21
22   // generate submarine center
23   xC = SIDE / 2 + ( int ) ( Math.random( ) * ( GAME_SIZE - SIDE ) );
24   yC = SIDE / 2 + ( int ) ( Math.random( ) * ( GAME_SIZE - SIDE ) );
25
26   // instantiate event handler and register listener on window
27   mh = new MouseHandler( );
28   addMouseListener( mh );
29
30   setSize( GAME_SIZE, GAME_SIZE );
31   setVisible( true );
32  }
33
34  private class MouseHandler extends MouseAdapter
35  {
36   public void mouseClicked( MouseEvent me )
37   {
```

```
38   x = me.getX( );
39   y = me.getY( );
40
41   // is click within the submarine?
42   if ( Math.abs( x - xC ) < SIDE / 2
43        && Math.abs( y - yC ) < SIDE / 2 )
44   {
45    setTitle( "Sunk!" );
46    hit = true;
47    removeMouseListener( mh ); // remove listener
48    repaint( );
49   }
50   // is click close?
51   else if ( Math.abs( x - xC ) < 2 * SIDE
52            && Math.abs( y - yC ) < 2 * SIDE )
53   {
54    setTitle( "Close ..." );
55   }
56   else
57   // click is too far from submarine
58   {
59    setTitle( "In the water" );
60    repaint( );
61   }
62   }
63  }
64
65  public void paint( Graphics g )
66  {
67   if ( hit )
68   {
69   // draw sunken submarine
70   g.setColor( Color.BLACK );
71   g.fillRoundRect( xC - SIDE/2, yC - SIDE/2, SIDE/2, SIDE,
72                    15, 15 );
73   g.fillRoundRect( xC - SIDE/4, yC - SIDE/3, SIDE/2, SIDE/2,
74                    7 , 7 );
75   g.drawLine( xC + SIDE/4, yC - SIDE/12,
76               xC + SIDE/2, yC - SIDE/12 );
77
78   // draw red depth charge
79   g.setColor( Color.RED );
80   g.fillOval( x - SIDE/4, y - SIDE/4, SIDE/2, SIDE/2 );
81   }
```

```
82   else // draw blue circle
83   {
84     g.setColor( Color.BLUE );
85     g.fillOval( x - SIDE/2, y - SIDE/2, SIDE, SIDE );
86   }
87  }
88
89  public static void main( String [ ] args )
90  {
91    SubHunt subH = new SubHunt( );
92    subH.setDefaultCloseOperation( JFrame.EXIT_ON_CLOSE );
93  }
94 }
```

EXAMPLE 12.12   A Simple Game Using a *MouseListener*

The second interface related to mouse events is *MouseMotionListener*, which has two methods, *mouseMoved* and *mouseDragged*, shown in Table 12.21. Dragging the mouse is defined as the user moving the mouse with the mouse button pressed, but not released.

In order to illustrate how to use the *MouseMotionListener* interface with a *MouseEvent* class, we will build a simple treasure hunt game that is similar to the submarine hunt game. A treasure is hidden somewhere in the window, and the user will try to find it, not by clicking the mouse button, but by moving the mouse inside the window. Depending on how close the mouse is to the treasure, we will display a message at the mouse location so that the user can find the treasure and win the game.

If the user moves the mouse far from the treasure, we display the message "Cold". As the user moves the mouse closer and closer to the treasure, the message becomes "Lukewarm", then "Warm", and then "Hot", before we

TABLE 12.21   *MouseMotionListener* Interface Method APIs

MouseMotionListener Interface Method APIs
public void mouseMoved(MouseEvent e)
called when the mouse is moved onto a component
public void mouseDragged(MouseEvent e)
called when the mouse button is pressed on a component and the mouse is dragged

finally reveal the treasure. We then remove the specified mouse motion listener so that the game stops.

In this application, we will not code the event handler as a *private* inner class, because we will define our application class as implementing the *MouseMotionListener* interface. As a result, our application is a listener, and we register the listener on itself.

Example 12.13 implements that game and in our class definition, we include the clause *implements MouseMotionListener* (lines 9–10).

Again, we randomly generate a location for the treasure and store the generated center *x* and *y* values in the instance variables, *xCtr* and *yCtr* (lines 24–25).

The instance variables *x* and *y* (lines 17–18) will store the current location of the mouse. The *String status*, declared at line 19, will hold the message to display as the user moves the mouse closer to the treasure.

At line 29, we register this *TreasureHunt* object on itself as a *MouseMotionListener*. In this game, the only event we want to handle is that the user has moved the mouse. Because *TreasureHunt* implements the *MouseMotionListener* interface, however, we must implement both the *mouseMoved* and the *mouseDragged* methods. We are interested in the *mouseMoved* method only; thus, we implement *mouseDragged* with an empty body (lines 35–36). Note that we could not use the *MouseMotionAdapter* class because our application (which is the listener) already extends the *JFrame* class. Remember that a class can extend only one class, but can implement multiple interfaces.

The *mouseMoved* method is implemented at lines 38–66. At lines 41–42, we assign the (*x, y*) coordinate of the mouse position to the instance variables *x* and *y*, using the *getX* and *getY* methods of the *MouseEvent* class. The *if/else* structure inside the method tests how far from the treasure the mouse was moved and updates *status* accordingly. If the user has found the treasure, we remove the listener (line 48). At line 65, we call the *repaint* method to force a call to the *paint* method.

We begin the *paint* method (lines 68–83) with a call to the *paint* method of the *JFrame* superclass to clear the contents of the window. We then test if the value of *status* is "Found" (line 74). If it is, the treasure has been found and we reveal its location by drawing it. If the treasure has not been found, we display the *String status* at the current mouse location (line 82).

Figure 12.16
The User Is Getting Close to the Treasure

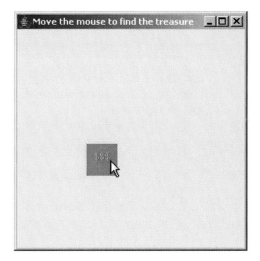

Figure 12.17
The User Has Found the Treasure

Figures 12.16 and 12.17 show the program running. In Figure 12.16, the user is getting close to the treasure, and in Figure 12.17, the user has found the treasure.

```
1 /* A Treasure Hunt using MouseMotionListener
2    Anderson, Franceschi
3 */
4
5 import javax.swing.*;
```

```
 6 import java.awt.*;
 7 import java.awt.event.*;
 8
 9 public class TreasureHunt extends JFrame
10                               implements MouseMotionListener
11 {
12  public static int GAME_SIZE = 300; // side of window
13  public static int SIDE = 40; // side of treasure
14
15  private int xCtr;  // x coordinate of center of square
16  private int yCtr;  // y coordinate of center of square
17  private int x;     // current x mouse position
18  private int y;     // current y mouse position
19  private String status = ""; // message
20
21  public TreasureHunt( )
22  {
23   super( "Move the mouse to find the treasure" );
24   xCtr = SIDE / 2 + (int) ( ( GAME_SIZE - SIDE ) * Math.random( ) );
25   yCtr = SIDE / 2 + (int) ( ( GAME_SIZE - SIDE ) * Math.random( ) );
26
27   // application registers on itself
28   // since it is a MouseMotionListener itself
29   addMouseMotionListener( this );
30
31   setSize( GAME_SIZE, GAME_SIZE );
32   setVisible( true );
33  }
34
35  public void mouseDragged( MouseEvent me )
36  { } // we do not want to process mouse drag events
37
38  public void mouseMoved( MouseEvent me )
39  {
40   // get location of mouse
41   x = me.getX( );
42   y = me.getY( );
43   // is mouse within treasure?
44   if ( Math.abs( x - xCtr ) < SIDE / 2
45         && Math.abs( y - yCtr ) < SIDE / 2 )
46   {
47       status = "Found";
48       removeMouseMotionListener( this ); // remove listener
49   }
```

```
50   // is mouse  within half-length of the treasure?
51   else if ( Math.abs( x - xCtr ) < ( 1.5 * SIDE )
52              && Math.abs( y - yCtr ) < ( 1.5 * SIDE ) )
53        status = "Hot";
54   // is mouse within 1 length of the treasure?
55   else if ( Math.abs( x - xCtr ) < ( 2 * SIDE )
56              && Math.abs( y - yCtr ) < ( 2 * SIDE ) )
57        status = "Warm";
58   // is mouse within 2 lengths of the treasure?
59   else if ( Math.abs( x - xCtr ) < ( 3 * SIDE )
60              && Math.abs( y - yCtr ) < ( 3 * SIDE ) )
61        status = "Lukewarm";
62   else // mouse is not near treasure
63        status = "Cold";
64
65   repaint( );
66   }
67
68   public void paint( Graphics g )
69   {
70    super.paint( g );
71
72    g.setColor( Color.BLUE );
73
74    if ( status.equals( "Found" ) ) // if found, draw treasure
75    {
76     g.setColor( Color.RED );
77     g.fillRect( xCtr - SIDE / 2, yCtr - SIDE / 2, SIDE, SIDE );
78     g.setColor( Color.GREEN );
79     g.drawString( "$$$", xCtr - SIDE / 4, yCtr );
80    }
81    else
82     g.drawString( status, x, y );   // display current status
83   }
84
85   public static void main( String [ ] args )
86   {
87    TreasureHunt th = new TreasureHunt( );
88    th.setDefaultCloseOperation( JFrame.EXIT_ON_CLOSE );
89   }
90   }
```

EXAMPLE 12.13   A Simple Game Using *MouseMotionListener*

12.13   Layout Managers: *GridLayout*

We have been using the *FlowLayout* layout manager because it is the easiest to use. The *FlowLayout* layout manager adds new components from left to right, creating as many rows as needed. A problem, however, is that if the user resizes the window, the components are rearranged to fit the new window size. Typically, GUIs can be quite complex and use many components, all of which need to be organized so that the user interface is effective and easy to use even if the user resizes the window. Two useful layout managers that give us more control over the organization of components within a window are the *GridLayout* and the *BorderLayout*.

Regardless of the layout manager used, the constructor of our application will still perform the following setup operations:

- declare and instantiate the layout manager
- use the *setLayout* method of the *Container* class to set the layout manager of the content pane of the *JFrame*
- instantiate components
- add components to the content pane using one of the *add* methods of the *Container* class

The *GridLayout* organizes the container as a grid. We can visualize the layout as a table made up of equally sized cells in rows and columns. Each cell can contain one component. The first component added to the container is placed in the first column of the first row; the second component is placed in the second column of the first row, and so on. When all the cells in a row are filled, the next component added is placed in the first cell of the next row.

Table 12.22 shows two constructors of the *GridLayout* class.

Example 12.14 shows how to use a *GridLayout* to display a chessboard. A two-dimensional array of *JButtons*, named *squares* (line 13), will make up the chessboard. A two-dimensional array of *Strings*, named *names*, will hold the position of each square (lines 14–22). The position of a square is composed of a letter representing the row (a–h) and a number representing the column (1–8). When the user clicks on a button of the chessboard, we will set the text of that button to display its position on the board, retrieving the name from the array *names*.

At line 30, we instantiate a *GridLayout* anonymous object using the constructor with two arguments representing the number of rows and

TABLE 12.22   *GridLayout* Constructors

	Constructors
Class	**Constructor**
GridLayout	GridLayout(int numberOfRows, int numberOfColumns)
	creates a grid layout with the number of rows and columns specified by the arguments.
GridLayout	GridLayout(int numberOfRows, int numberOfColumns, int hGap, int vGap)
	creates a grid layout with the specified number of rows and columns and with a horizontal gap of *hGap* pixels between columns and a vertical gap of *vGap* pixels between rows. Horizontal gaps are also placed at the left and right edges, and vertical gaps are placed at the top and bottom edges.

columns in the grid, here *SIDE* and *SIDE*. The constant *SIDE* is declared at line 11 and has the value 8. Still at line 30, we pass the *GridLayout* anonymous object as the argument of the *setLayout* method. Thus, components will be added cell by cell to an 8-by-8 grid, with each row being filled before starting the next row.

At line 34, we declare and instantiate the listener *bh*, a *ButtonHandler* object reference. Since we are interested in events related to buttons, our *Button-Handler private* inner class *implements* the *ActionListener* interface and overrides the *actionPerformed* method.

At line 32, we instantiate the two-dimensional array *squares*. Because we have a two-dimensional array of *JButtons*, we use nested *for* loops at lines 36–53 to instantiate the *JButtons*, add them to the content pane, and register the listener on all of the buttons. Inside the inner loop, the value of the expression $(i + j)$ will alternate between an even and odd number. Accordingly, at lines 43–45, we set the background of every other button to red.

In the *actionPerformed* method, we use nested *for* loops at lines 63–73 to identify the source of the event; that is, which button the user clicked. When a button is clicked, the condition of the *if* statement at line 67 will evaluate to *true* when the *i* and *j* indices are such that *squares[i][j]* is the button that was clicked. We then set the text of that button to its board position (line 69), using the corresponding element in the two-dimensional array *names*. Having found the source of the event, we then exit the event handler via the *return* statement (line 70) to interrupt the *for* loops, and thus to avoid unnecessary processing.

Figure 12.18

Running Example 12.14

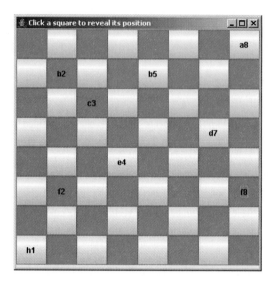

Figure 12.18 shows the example running. When you run this program, click on various squares; resize the window, and check that the layout manager maintains an 8-by-8 grid.

```
1 /* Using GridLayout to organize our window
2    Anderson, Franceschi
3 */
4
5 import javax.swing.*;
6 import java.awt.*;
7 import java.awt.event.*;
8
9 public class ChessBoard extends JFrame
10 {
11   public static final int SIDE = 8;
12   private Container contents;
13   private JButton [ ][ ] squares;
14   private String [ ][ ] names =
15   { { "a1","a2","a3","a4","a5","a6", "a7", "a8" },
16     { "b1","b2","b3","b4","b5","b6", "b7", "b8" },
17     { "c1","c2","c3","c4","c5","c6", "c7", "c8" },
18     { "d1","d2","d3","d4","d5","d6", "d7", "d8" },
19     { "e1","e2","e3","e4","e5","e6", "e7", "e8" },
20     { "f1","f2","f3","f4","f5","f6", "f7", "f8" },
21     { "g1","g2","g3","g4","g5","g6", "g7", "g8" },
22     { "h1","h2","h3","h4","h5","h6", "h7", "h8" } };
```

```
23
24  public ChessBoard( )
25  {
26   super( "Click a square to reveal its position" );
27   contents = getContentPane( );
28
29   // set layout to an 8-by-8 Grid
30   contents.setLayout( new GridLayout( SIDE, SIDE ) );
31
32   squares = new JButton[SIDE][SIDE];
33
34   ButtonHandler bh = new ButtonHandler( );
35
36   for ( int i = 0; i < names.length; i++ )
37   {
38    for ( int j = 0; j < SIDE; j++ )
39    {
40     // instantiate JButton array
41     squares[i][j] = new JButton( );
42
43     // make every other square red
44     if ( ( i + j ) % 2 == 0 )
45       squares[i][j].setBackground( Color.RED );
46
47     // add the JButton
48     contents.add( squares[i][j] );
49
50     // register listener on button
51     squares[i][j].addActionListener( bh );
52    }
53   }
54
55   setSize( 400, 400 );
56   setVisible( true );
57  }
58
59  private class ButtonHandler implements ActionListener
60  {
61   public void actionPerformed( ActionEvent ae )
62   {
63     for ( int i = 0; i < SIDE; i++ )
64     {
65       for ( int j = 0; j < SIDE; j++ )
66       {
67         if ( ae.getSource( ) == squares[i][j] )
```

```
68          {
69             squares[i][j].setText( names[i][j] );
70             return;
71          }
72       }
73     }
74   }
75 }
76
77 public static void main( String [ ] args )
78 {
79   ChessBoard myGame = new ChessBoard( );
80   myGame.setDefaultCloseOperation( JFrame.EXIT_ON_CLOSE );
81 }
82 }
```

EXAMPLE 12.14   Using *GridLayout* to Display a Chessboard

Layout managers can be set dynamically, based on user input. For example, the user could enter the size of the grid. Or based on user input, we can rearrange the components using another layout manager, such as *FlowLayout*. The user could also instruct us to remove components and add others. Our next example, the Tile Puzzle game, will illustrate some of these capabilities.

In the Tile Puzzle game, eight tiles displaying the digits 1 through 8 are scrambled on a 3-by-3 grid, leaving one cell empty. Any tile adjacent to the empty cell can be moved to the empty cell by clicking on the numbered tile. The goal is to rearrange the tiles so that the numbers are in the correct order as shown in Figure 12.19.

The Tile Puzzle game can also be played in a 4-by-4, a 5-by-5, and more generally, an *n*-by-*n* grid. Example 12.15 will set up a 3-by-3 grid for the first game, then will randomly select a 3-by-3, a 4-by-4, a 5-by-5, or a 6-by-6 grid for subsequent games. Once you understand this example, you can modify it to allow the user to specify the size of the grid.

Each cell of the grid is a button. At line 13, we declare a two-dimensional array of *JButtons* named *squares*. Each element of *squares* will be a cell in the game grid. The instance variable *side*, declared at line 14, represents the size of the grid. We initialize its value to 3 for the first game, then we will randomly generate the value for each new game. The instance variables *emptyRow* and *emptyCol*, declared at lines 16–17, identify the empty cell in the game grid.

Figure 12.19

The Winning Position of a 3-by-3 Tile Puzzle Game

The constructor (lines 19–25) calls the *setUpGame* method, passing the size of the grid (*side*) as an argument. We also call the *setUpGame* method (lines 27–60) before starting each new game.

Inside the *setUpGame* method, we assign *newSide* to *side*, and set the empty cell to the last cell in the grid at lines 29–31. We then remove all the components from the content pane by calling the *removeAll* method of the *Container* class (line 33) and set the layout manager (line 34) as a *GridLayout* with the new grid size. We instantiate the *squares* array and our event handler at lines 36 and 38. After that, we use nested *for* loops (lines 40–54) to generate each button label, instantiate the button, add it to the container, and register the event handler. Rather than randomly generating each button label, which would complicate this example, we assign the labels to the buttons in descending order.

Inside the *private* class *ButtonHandler* (lines 108–124), the *actionPerformed* method identifies the button that was clicked and calls the *tryToPlay* method at line 118 with the row and column arguments corresponding to the button that originated the event.

The *tryToPlay* method (lines 62–82) first checks if the play is legal by calling the *possibleToPlay* method (lines 84–91). If the *possibleToPlay* method returns *true*, we swap the label of the button that was clicked with the label of the button in the empty cell (lines 66–69). We also update the empty cell position (lines 71–72). We then call the *won* method (line 74) to check if this move wins the game. The *won* method (lines 93–106) checks if the tiles

Figure 12.20

Running Example 12.15

are in order. If the user has won the game, the *won* method returns *true*; otherwise, the method returns *false*. If the *won* method returns *true*, we congratulate the user by popping up a dialog box at lines 76–77.

We then randomly generate a grid size between 3 and 6 (line 78) for the next game and call the *setUpGame* method to begin the game with the new grid size at line 79.

The *possibleToPlay* method is coded at lines 84–91. If the play is legal, that is, if the button clicked is within one cell of the empty cell, the method returns *true*; otherwise, the method returns *false*.

Figure 12.20 shows the game in progress.

```
1  /* Using GridLayout dynamically
2      Anderson, Franceschi
3  */
4
5  import javax.swing.*;
6  import java.awt.*;
7  import java.awt.event.*;
8
9  public class TilePuzzle extends JFrame
10 {
11   private Container contents;
12
13   private JButton [ ][ ] squares;
14   private int side = 3; // grid size for game 1
```

```
15
16   private int emptyRow;
17   private int emptyCol;
18
19   public TilePuzzle( )
20   {
21     super( "The Tile Puzzle Game" );
22     contents = getContentPane( );
23
24     setUpGame( side );
25   }
26
27   private void setUpGame( int newSide )
28   {
29     side = newSide;
30     emptyRow = side - 1;
31     emptyCol = side - 1;
32
33     contents.removeAll( ); // remove all components
34     contents.setLayout( new GridLayout( side, side ) );
35
36     squares = new JButton [side][side];
37
38     ButtonHandler bh = new ButtonHandler( );
39
40     // for each button: generate button label,
41     // instantiate button, add to container,
42     // and register listener
43     for ( int i = 0; i < side; i++ )
44     {
45       for ( int j = 0; j < side; j++ )
46       {
47         String label = String.valueOf( ( side * side )
48                             - ( side * i + j + 1 ) );
49         squares[i][j] = new JButton( label );
50
51         contents.add( squares[i][j] );
52         squares[i][j].addActionListener( bh );
53       }
54     }
55     // set empty cell label to blank
56     squares[side - 1][side - 1].setText( "" );
57
58     setSize( 300, 300 );
59     setVisible( true );
```

```
60  }
61
62  private void tryToPlay( int row, int col )
63  {
64   if ( possibleToPlay( row, col ) )
65   {
66    // play: switch empty String and button label at row, col
67    squares[emptyRow][emptyCol].setText(
68                              squares[row][col].getText( ) );
69    squares[row][col].setText( "" );
70
71    emptyRow = row;
72    emptyCol = col;
73
74    if ( won( ) )
75    {
76     JOptionPane.showMessageDialog( TilePuzzle.this,
77            "Congratulations! You won!\nSetting up new game" );
78     int sideOfPuzzle = 3 + (int) ( 4 * Math.random( ) );
79     setUpGame( sideOfPuzzle );
80    }
81   }
82  }
83
84  private boolean possibleToPlay( int row, int col )
85  {
86   if ( ( col == emptyCol && Math.abs( row - emptyRow ) == 1 )
87         || ( row == emptyRow && Math.abs( col - emptyCol ) == 1 ) )
88    return true;
89   else
90    return false;
91  }
92
93  private boolean won( )
94  {
95   for ( int i = 0; i < side ; i++ )
96   {
97    for ( int j = 0; j < side; j++ )
98    {
99     if ( !( squares[i][j].getText( ).equals(
100                     String.valueOf( i * side + j + 1 ) ) )
101                  && ( i != side - 1 || j != side - 1 ) )
102       return false;
103    }
104   }
```

```
105   return true;
106  }
107
108  private class ButtonHandler implements ActionListener
109  {
110   public void actionPerformed( ActionEvent ae )
111   {
112    for ( int i = 0; i < side; i++ )
113    {
114     for ( int j = 0; j < side; j++ )
115     {
116      if ( ae.getSource( ) == squares[i][j] )
117      {
118       tryToPlay( i, j );
119       return;
120      }
121     }
122    }
123   }
124  }
125
126  public static void main( String [ ] args )
127  {
128   TilePuzzle myGame = new TilePuzzle( );
129   myGame.setDefaultCloseOperation( JFrame.EXIT_ON_CLOSE );
130  }
131 }
```

EXAMPLE 12.15   Setting *GridLayout* Dynamically in the Tile Puzzle Game

12.14   Layout Managers: *BorderLayout*

A *BorderLayout* organizes a container into five areas: north, south, west, east, and center, with each area holding at most one component. Thus, for each area, you can add one component or no component. The size of each area expands or contracts depending on the size of the component in that area, the sizes of the components in the other areas, and whether the other areas contain a component. Figure 12.21 shows the areas in a sample border layout.

In contrast to the *FlowLayout* and *GridLayout* layout managers, the order in which we add components to a *BorderLayout* is not important. We use a second argument in the *add* method to specify the area in which to place the component. This *add* method of the *Container* class has the API shown in Table 12.23.

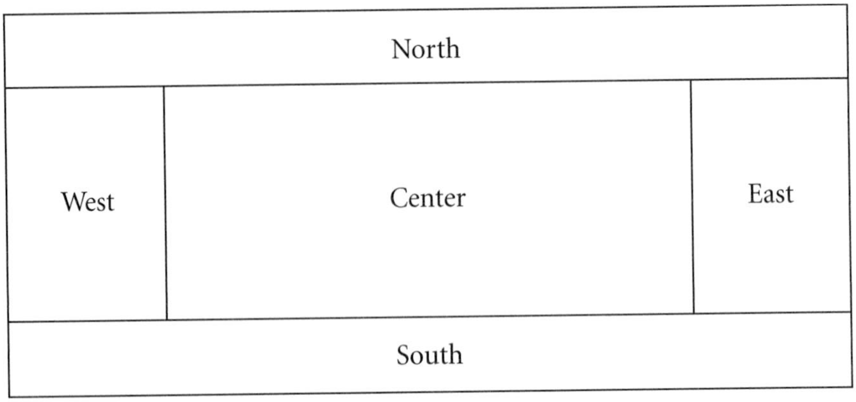

Figure 12.21

BorderLayout **Areas**

TABLE 12.23   The *Container add* Method for Using a *BorderLayout*

Return value	Method name and argument list
void	add(Component c, Object borderlayoutArea)
	adds the component *c* to the container. The area defined by *border-layoutArea* can be specified using any of the following *static String* constants in the *BorderLayout* class: NORTH, SOUTH, EAST, WEST, CENTER.

Two *BorderLayout* constructors are shown in Table 12.24. The *BorderLayout* is the default layout for a *JFrame* class, so if we want to use a border layout for our GUI application, we do not need to instantiate a new layout manager.

Example 12.16 uses a *BorderLayout* to illustrate bidding order in the card game of Bridge. There are four players: North, East, South, and West. Players take turns bidding in clockwise order, starting with the dealer. In this example, we assume the player sitting in the North position is the dealer, so North will bid first. A bid consists of a level and a suit, with the lowest bid being 1 Club and the highest bid being 7 No trump. Each new bid must be higher than the previous bid, that is, a new bid must name a higher-ranked suit at the same level, or any suit at a higher level. Suits are ranked in the following ascending order: Clubs, Diamonds, Hearts, Spades, and No trump. Thus, if the current bid is 3 Hearts, the next possible bids are, in order, 3 Spades, 3 No trump, 4 Clubs, 4 Diamonds, 4 Hearts, and so on. We will use a window managed by a *BorderLayout* manager to simulate

TABLE 12.24   *BorderLayout* Constructors

	Constructors
Class	**Constructor**
BorderLayout	BorderLayout( )
	creates a new border layout with no gaps between components.
BorderLayout	BorderLayout(int hGap, int vGap)
	creates a border layout with a horizontal gap of *hGap* pixels between components and a vertical gap of *vGap* pixels between components. Unlike *GridLayout*, horizontal gaps are not placed at the left and right edges, and vertical gaps are not placed at the top and bottom edges.

sequential bids by our four Bridge players. At any point, a player can "pass" or "double" the previous bid, but for simplicity and to illustrate bidding order only, we do not take these bids into account.

In Example 12.16, we declare four buttons representing the players (line 12); we will place one button each in the north, east, south, and west areas of the border layout. We will use the label *bid*, declared at line 13, to display the current bid in the center area.

The *String* array *suitNames*, the *int* instance variables *bidder*, *level*, and *suit*, declared and initialized at lines 15–23, will help us keep track of the bidding and enforce the bidding order. The *bidder* instance variable represents the next bidder: Its possible values of 0, 1, 2, and 3 represent North, East, South, and West, respectively. The *level* instance variable will store a value between 1 and 7, and *suit* will store a valid index for the array *suitNames*. The first legal bid in Bridge is 1 Club so we have initialized *level* to 1 and *suit* to 0.

At line 29, we set the layout of the content pane to be a *BorderLayout*. Note that this statement is optional, because *BorderLayout* is the default layout manager for a subclass of the *JFrame* class.

When instantiating *bid* at line 38, we use an overloaded *JLabel* constructor. We use the *static int* constant *CENTER* of the *SwingConstants* interface to center the text of the label within the component. By default, the text for a *JLabel* is left-aligned. Because the text on a *JButton* is centered by default, we can simply use the constructor with one argument when we instantiate the *JButtons* for the players.

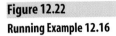

Figure 12.22

Running Example 12.16

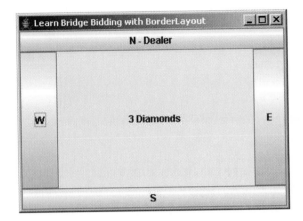

We add the four buttons and the label to the content pane in the appropriate areas at lines 40–45. The order in which we add the components is not important because we specify a border layout area as the second argument of the *add* method.

In our *ButtonHandler* event handler (lines 57–88), the *actionPerformed* method first determines the button that fired the event, translating the source button to an integer value between 0 and 3. That value is assigned to the local variable *source*. We want to allow bids only from the player whose turn it is. If *source* is not equal to *bidder*, we do not display a new bid. Also, after we have reached the highest possible bid of 7 No trump, no action will take place.

After displaying the current bid at line 79, we set up the values for the next bid (lines 81–85). We increment *bidder*, using the modulus operator to cycle through the values 0–3. We also increment *suit*, cycling through the possible indexes for the *suitNames* array. Whenever the next suit index is 0, we increment *level*.

Figure 12.22 shows the Bridge bidding example running.

```
1 /* Using BorderLayout to display Bridge bidding
2    Anderson, Franceschi
3 */
4
5 import javax.swing.*;
6 import java.awt.*;
7 import java.awt.event.*;
8
```

```
 9 public class BridgeBidding extends JFrame
10 {
11   private Container contents;
12   private JButton north, east, south, west;
13   private JLabel bid;
14
15   private String [ ] suitNames =
16   { "Club", "Diamond", "Heart", "Spade", "No trump" };
17
18   // next bidder
19   private int bidder = 0;              // north is 1st bidder
20
21   // bidding will open at 1 Club
22   private int level = 1;               // current level
23   private int suit = 0;                // index of current suit
24
25   public BridgeBidding( )
26   {
27    super( "Learn Bridge Bidding with BorderLayout" );
28    contents = getContentPane( );
29    contents.setLayout( new BorderLayout( ) );  // optional
30
31    // instantiate button objects
32    north = new JButton( "N - Dealer" );
33    east = new JButton( "E" );
34    south = new JButton( "S" );
35    west = new JButton( "W" );
36
37    // instantiate JLabel
38    bid = new JLabel( "No bid", SwingConstants.CENTER );
39
40    // order of adding components not important
41    contents.add( north, BorderLayout.NORTH );
42    contents.add( east, BorderLayout.EAST );
43    contents.add( south, BorderLayout.SOUTH );
44    contents.add( west, BorderLayout.WEST );
45    contents.add( bid, BorderLayout.CENTER );
46
47    ButtonHandler bh = new ButtonHandler( );
48    north.addActionListener( bh );
49    east.addActionListener( bh );
50    south.addActionListener( bh );
51    west.addActionListener( bh );
52
53    setSize( 350, 250 );
```

```
54   setVisible( true );
55  }
56
57  private class ButtonHandler implements ActionListener
58  {
59   public void actionPerformed( ActionEvent ae )
60   {
61    int source = 0;
62    if ( ae.getSource( ) == north )
63      source = 0;
64    else if ( ae.getSource( ) == east )
65      source = 1;
66    else if ( ae.getSource( ) == south )
67      source = 2;
68    else if ( ae.getSource( ) == west )
69      source = 3;
70
71    if ( source == bidder && level < 8 )
72    {
73      String currentBid = level + " " + suitNames[suit];
74
75      // add an "s" if level > 1 and suit is not No trump
76      if ( level > 1 && suit != suitNames.length - 1 )
77        currentBid += "s";
78
79      bid.setText( currentBid ); // set label to bid
80
81      // set up next bid
82      bidder = ( bidder + 1 ) % 4;
83      suit = ( suit + 1 ) % ( suitNames.length );
84      if ( suit == 0 )
85        level++;
86    }
87   }
88  }
89
90   public static void main( String [ ] args )
91   {
92    BridgeBidding blGui = new BridgeBidding( );
93    blGui.setDefaultCloseOperation( JFrame.EXIT_ON_CLOSE );
94   }
95 }
```

EXAMPLE 12.16   Using *BorderLayout* to Illustrate Bridge Bidding Order

12.15 Using Panels to Nest Components

Components can be nested. Indeed, since the *JComponent* class is a subclass of the *Container* class, a *JComponent* object is a *Container* object as well. As such, it can contain other components. We can use this feature to achieve more precise layouts.

The *JPanel* class is a general-purpose container, or a **panel**, and is typically used to hold other components. When nesting components, we usually place several components into a panel, and place the panel into the content pane of the current *JFrame*. Each panel has its own layout manager, which can vary from panel to panel, and the content pane for the *JFrame* application has its own layout manager, which can be different from any of the panels. We can even have multiple levels of nesting, as needed.

Figure 12.23 shows a window that uses multiple panels, along with the underlying layout of the window.

The content pane of the window is using a *GridLayout* with one row and two columns. In the first column, we have defined a panel managed by a

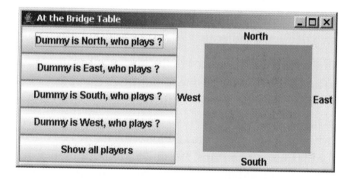

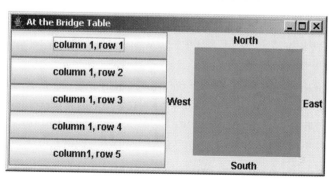

Figure 12.23

Sample Window and Underlying Layout

GridLayout having five rows and one column. We placed five buttons into the panel, then placed the panel into the first column of the content pane grid. In the second column, we have defined a panel managed by a *Border-Layout*. We put five components into the panel and added the panel as the second column of the content pane grid. Thus, we have two panels, each of which has a different layout manager, and these two panels are added to the content pane, which is itself managed by a *GridLayout*.

In a Bridge game, depending on the bidding, one of the four players will be the "dummy" and will not participate in the play for the current hand. We illustrate this concept in Example 12.17. The panel in column two of the content pane grid uses a *BorderLayout* layout manager to show four players around the Bridge table. The panel in column one of the content pane grid uses a *GridLayout* to provide five buttons.

If the user clicks on one of the first four buttons, we make the corresponding player disappear from the Bridge table (in column 2). If the user clicks the fifth button, we make all players visible. Thus, the actions we want to perform are different depending on whether the user clicks on one of the first four buttons or the "Show all players" button. So it makes sense to write two event handlers: one that listens to the first four buttons, and a second event handler that listens to the fifth button only.

In Example 12.17, we first define the layout manager for our content pane to be a *GridLayout* with one row and two columns (line 34). Then we set up the panel for the first column at lines 37–38, by instantiating the *JPanel* named *questionPanel* and setting the layout manager as a *GridLayout* with five rows and one column. At lines 40–48, we instantiate the event handler for the question buttons, instantiate the buttons, register the listener on the buttons, and add the buttons to the *questionPanel* in rows 1–4.

In lines 50–54, we set up the fifth row in this grid by instantiating the *reset* button, instantiating our separate listener for this button, and adding the button in the fifth row.

In lines 56–73, we set up column two, by instantiating the *JPanel gamePanel* and setting its layout to a *BorderLayout* with horizontal and vertical gaps of 3 pixels between elements. At lines 69–73, we add one component to each area of the *BorderLayout*, representing the four players and the Bridge table.

Finally, we add the two panels to the content pane of the application window at lines 75–77.

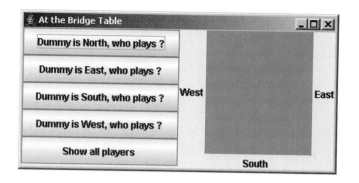

Figure 12.24
User Clicked Top Button

The *QuestionButtonHandler* event handler (lines 83–96) checks which question button was clicked and sets the visibility of the appropriate label in the *gamePanel* to *false*. The other three labels are made visible, in case they were hidden as a result of a previous button click.

The second event handler, *ResetButtonHandler* (lines 98–106), does not need to check the source of the event because the listener is registered only on the *reset* button component. Its job is to make every player's button visible.

When the application begins, we display the window shown in Figure 12.23. Figure 12.24 shows the window after the user has clicked on the top button ("Dummy is North, who plays?"). As you run the application, click on the various buttons.

```
1   /* Nesting components using layout managers
2        Anderson, Franceschi
3   */
4
5   import javax.swing.*;
6   import java.awt.*;
7   import java.awt.event.*;
8
9   public class BridgeRules extends JFrame
10  {
11    private Container contents;
12
13    // 1st row, column 1
14    private JPanel questionPanel;
15    private JButton [ ] questionButtons;
16    private String [ ] questionNames = {
17              "Dummy is North, who plays ?",
18              "Dummy is East, who plays ?",
```

```
19                    "Dummy is South, who plays ?",
20                    "Dummy is West, who plays ?" };
21
22    private JButton reset;
23
24    // 1st row, column 2
25    private JPanel gamePanel;
26    private JLabel gameTable;
27    private JLabel [ ] gameLabels;
28
29    public BridgeRules( )
30    {
31     super( "At the Bridge Table" );
32
33     contents = getContentPane( );
34     contents.setLayout( new GridLayout( 1, 2 ) );
35
36     // 1st row, col 1: question buttons and reset button
37     questionPanel = new JPanel( );
38     questionPanel.setLayout( new GridLayout( 5, 1 ) );
39
40     QuestionButtonHandler qbh = new QuestionButtonHandler( );
41     questionButtons = new JButton[questionNames.length];
42
43     for ( int i = 0; i < questionNames.length; i ++ )
44     {
45        questionButtons[i] = new JButton( questionNames[i] );
46        questionButtons[i].addActionListener( qbh );
47        questionPanel.add( questionButtons[i] );
48     }
49
50     reset = new JButton( "Show all players" );
51     ResetButtonHandler rbh = new ResetButtonHandler( );
52     reset.addActionListener( rbh );
53
54     questionPanel.add( reset );
55
56     // 1st row, column 2: gamePanel contains the players and table
57     gamePanel = new JPanel( );
58     gamePanel.setLayout( new BorderLayout( 3, 3 ) );
59     gameLabels = new JLabel[4];
60     gameLabels[0] = new JLabel( "North", SwingConstants.CENTER );
61     gameLabels[1] = new JLabel( "East", SwingConstants.CENTER );
62     gameLabels[2] = new JLabel( "South", SwingConstants.CENTER );
63     gameLabels[3] = new JLabel( "West", SwingConstants.CENTER );
```

```
64
65    gameTable = new JLabel( );
66    gameTable.setBackground( Color.GREEN );
67    gameTable.setOpaque( true );
68
69    gamePanel.add( gameLabels[0], BorderLayout.NORTH );
70    gamePanel.add( gameLabels[1], BorderLayout.EAST );
71    gamePanel.add( gameLabels[2], BorderLayout.SOUTH );
72    gamePanel.add( gameLabels[3], BorderLayout.WEST );
73    gamePanel.add( gameTable, BorderLayout.CENTER );
74
75    // add panels to content pane
76    contents.add( questionPanel );
77    contents.add( gamePanel );
78
79    setSize( 410, 200 );
80    setVisible( true );
81   }
82
83   private class QuestionButtonHandler
84                        implements ActionListener
85   {
86    public void actionPerformed( ActionEvent ae )
87    {
88     for ( int i = 0; i < questionButtons.length; i++ )
89     {
90       if ( ae.getSource( ) == questionButtons[i] )
91        gameLabels[i].setVisible( false );
92       else
93        gameLabels[i].setVisible( true );
94     }
95    }
96   }
97
98   private class ResetButtonHandler
99                        implements ActionListener
100  {
101    public void actionPerformed( ActionEvent ae )
102    {
103       for ( int i = 0; i < gameLabels.length; i++ )
104        gameLabels[i].setVisible( true );
105    }
106 }
107
108 public static void main( String [ ] args )
```

```
109   {
110     BridgeRules myNestedLayout = new BridgeRules( );
111     myNestedLayout.setDefaultCloseOperation( JFrame.EXIT_ON_CLOSE );
112   }
113 }
```

EXAMPLE 12.17   More Bridge Rules with Nested Components

Skill Practice
with these end-of-chapter questions

12.18.1	Multiple Choice Exercises
	Questions 9,10,11,12,13,14,15
12.18.2	Reading and Understanding Code
	Question 17
12.18.3	Fill in the Code
	Questions 30,33,34,35,36,37,38,39,40,41
12.18.5	Debugging Area
	Question 48
12.18.6	Write a Short Program
	Questions 58,59,60,61,62
12.18.8	Technical Writing
	Question 73

CODE IN ACTION

In the Chapter 12 folder on the CD-ROM included with this book, you will find a Shockwave movie showing step-by-step illustrations of working with GUI components. Double-click on *GUI.html* to start the movie.

12.16   Programming Activity 2: Working with Layout Managers

In this Programming Activity, you will complete the implementation of a version of the Tile Puzzle game (Example 12.15) using a more complex GUI. As it stands, the application compiles and runs, but is missing a lot of

Figure 12.25

The Starting Window When Running the Prewritten Code

code. Figure 12.25 shows the window that will open when you run the application without adding your code.

Once you have completed the five tasks of this Programming Activity, you should see the window in Figure 12.26 when you run your program and click on the "3-by-3" button.

When you click on one of the buttons labeled "3-by-3", "4-by-4", or "5-by-5", the tile puzzle will reset to a grid of that size.

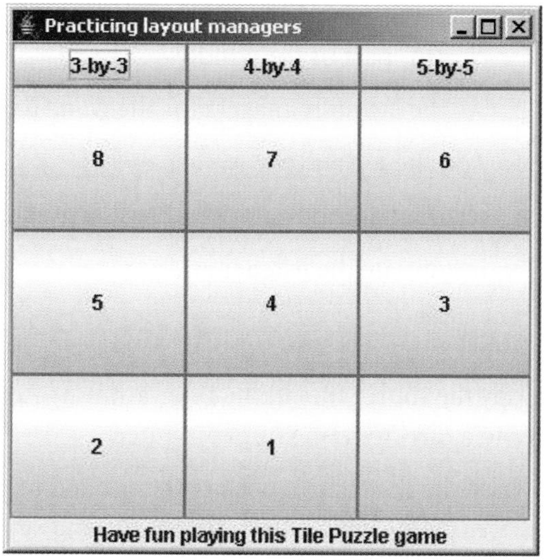

Figure 12.26

The Starting Window When the Activity Is Completed

TABLE 12.25   The *Game* Class API

Game Class API		
Constructor		
Class	**Constructor**	
Game	Game(int nSides)	
	instantiates a tile puzzle as an *nSides*-by-*nSides* grid	
Method		
Return value	**Method name and argument list**	
void	setUpGame(int nSides)	
	resets the grid as an *nSides*-by-*nSides* grid	

We provide you a prewritten *Game* class, which encapsulates a Tile Puzzle game. We have implemented the *Game* class as a *JPanel* component, so you can add it to your window as you would any other panel. It has two important methods, shown in Table 12.25. Thus, your job in this Programming Activity is not to write the game code, but to organize components in a window.

Your job is to:

1. Declare a *JPanel top* and three *JButtons* that will be added to the "north" part of the window.

2. Set the layout managers for the *game* panel and the *top* panel.

3. Add the *top* and the *game* panels.

4. Code an appropriate *private* listener class.

5. Instantiate the listener and register it on the appropriate components.

Instructions

Copy the source files in the Programming Activity 2 directory for this chapter to a directory on your computer.

1. Write the code to declare the needed instance variables. Load the *NestedLayoutPractice.java* source file and search for five asterisks in a row (*****). This will position you to the instance variables declaration.

```
// ***** Task 1: declare a JPanel named top
// also declare three JButton instance variables
// that will be added to the JPanel top
// these buttons will determine the grid size of the game:
//   3-by-3, 4-by-4, or 5-by-5


// task 1 ends here
```

2. Next, write the code to set the layout manager of the window and add
    the component *game* in the center of the window. In the *NestedLay-outPractice.java* source file, search again for five asterisks in a row
    (*****). This will position you inside the constructor.

```
// ***** Task 2: student code starts here
// instantiate the BorderLayout manager bl


// set the layout manager of the content pane contents to bl


   game = new Game( 3 );  // instantiating the Game object
// add game to the center of the content pane


// task 2 ends here
```

3. Next, write the code to instantiate the *JPanel top* component, set its
    layout, instantiate the buttons from task 1, add them to *top*, and
    finally add *top* as the north component for our overall window. In the
    NestedLayoutPractice.java source file, search again for five asterisks in
    a row (*****). This will position you inside the constructor.

```
// ***** Task 3: Student code restarts here

// instantiate the JPanel component named top

// set the layout of top to a 1-by-3 grid

// instantiate the JButtons that determine the grid size

// add the buttons to JPanel top

// add JPanel top to the content pane as its north component

// task 3 ends here
```

4. Next, write the code for the *private* inner class that implements the appropriate listener. In the *NestedLayoutPractice.java* source file, search again for five asterisks in a row (*****). This will position you between the constructor and the *main* method.

```
// ***** Task 4: Student code restarts here
// create a private inner class that implements ActionListener
// your method should identify which of the 3 buttons was the
//   source of the event.
// depending on which button was pressed,
//   call the setUpGame method of the Game class
//   with arguments 3, 4, or 5
// the API of that method is:
//   public void setUpGame( int nSides )

// task 4 ends here
```

5. Next, write the code to declare and instantiate a listener, and register it on the appropriate components. In the *NestedLayoutPractice.java* source file, search again for five asterisks in a row (*****). This will position you inside the constructor.

```
// ***** Task 5: Student code restarts here
// Note: search for and complete Task 4 before performing this task
// declare and instantiate an ActionListener

// register the listener on the 3 buttons
//   that you declared in Task 1

// task 5 ends here
```

After completing each task, compile your code.

When you have finished writing all the code, compile the source code and run the *NestedLayoutPractice* application. Try clicking on the three buttons that you added.

DISCUSSION QUESTIONS ?

1. Identify the various layout managers you used and the panels they manage.

2. Explain why the East and West areas do not show up on the window.

12.17 Chapter Summary

- A graphical user interface allows the user to interact with an application through mouse clicks, mouse movements, the keyboard, and visual input components.

- The *JFrame* class provides the capabilities for creating a window that will hold GUI components.

- A constructor in a GUI application should call the constructor of the *JFrame* superclass, get an object reference to the content pane, set the layout manager, instantiate each component and add it to the window, set the size of the window, and make the window visible.

- A component is an object having a graphical representation and that displays information, collects data from the user, or allows the user to initiate program functions.

- Java provides a set of GUI components in the *javax.swing* package.

- A *JLabel* component can display text or an image.

- The *FlowLayout* layout manager arranges components in rows from left to right, starting a new row whenever a newly added component does not fit into the current row. If the window is resized, the components are rearranged.

- Event-driven programming consists of setting up interactive components and event handlers and responding to events generated by user interaction with the components.

- To allow a user to interact with a component, we need to instantiate an object of that class, write an event handler class (called a listener), instantiate an object of the event handler class, and register that listener on the component.

- Event handlers implement a listener interface in the *java.awt.event* or the *javax.swing.event* package. The listener methods receive as a parameter an event object, which encapsulates information about the user interaction. The *getSource* method can be called to determine which component fired the event.

- Event handlers usually are instantiated as *private* inner classes so the handler will have access to the components of the application.

- A *JTextField* component displays a text field for user input. A *JPasswordField* component accepts user input without echoing the characters typed. A *JTextArea* component displays a multiple-line text input area. Events fired by these three components generate an *ActionEvent* object and require an *ActionListener* to handle the event.

- A *JButton* component implements a command button used for initiating operations. Clicking on a *JButton* component generates an *ActionEvent* object and requires an *ActionListener* to handle the event.

- *JRadioButton* components allow the user to select one of several mutually exclusive options. Clicking on any radio button deselects any previously selected option. *JRadioButton* components need to be added to a *ButtonGroup*, which manages the mutual exclusivity of the buttons. *JCheckBox* components are toggle buttons; successive clicks on a *JCheckBox* component alternately select and deselect that option. Events fired by these components generate an *ItemEvent* object and use an *ItemListener* to handle the event.

- The *JList* class encapsulates a list from which the user can select one or multiple items. Selecting an item from a *JList* component generates a *ListSelectionEvent* object and requires a *ListSelectionListener* to handle the event.

- A *JComboBox* implements a drop-down list. The user can select only one item from the list. A *JComboBox* fires an *ItemEvent*, so the event handler must implement the *ItemListener* interface.

- Adapter classes, which *implement* an interface and provide empty bodies for each method, are useful when only one of multiple component actions is processed.

- *MouseAdapter* and *MouseMotionAdapter* are adapter classes for the *MouseListener* and *MouseMotionListener* interfaces, respectively.

- The *GridLayout* layout manager arranges components into equally sized cells in rows and columns.

- A *BorderLayout* layout manager, which is the default layout manager for the *JFrame* class, organizes a container into five areas: north, south, west, east, and center, with each area holding at most one component. The size of each area expands or contracts depending on the size of the component in that area, the sizes of the components in the other areas, and whether the other areas contain a component.

- A *JPanel* component can be used as a general-purpose container. To create a complex arrangement of GUI components, we place several components into a panel and place the panel into the content pane of the current *JFrame*. Each panel and the content pane has its own layout manager.

12.18   Exercises, Problems, and Projects

12.18.1   Multiple Choice Exercises

1. An example of a GUI component class is

   ❏ *ActionEvent*

   ❏ *actionPerformed*

   ❏ *JTextField*

   ❏ *ActionListener*

2. What are the primary uses of GUI components? (Check all that apply.)

   ❏ to display information

   ❏ to facilitate the coding of methods

   ❏ to let the user control the program

   ❏ to collect information from the user

3. In what package do you find the *JButton*, *JTextField*, and *JComboBox* classes?

   ❏ *javax.swing*

   ❏ *java.swing*

   ❏ *javax.awt*

   ❏ *java.awt*

   ❏ *java.io*

4. Components can be hidden.

   ❏ true

   ❏ false

5. In order to process an event when the user clicks on a button, what should the programmer do? (Check all that apply.)

   ❑ Code a class that implements the *ActionListener* interface.

   ❑ Declare and instantiate an object reference (a listener) of the class above.

   ❑ Call the *actionPerformed* method.

   ❑ Register the listener on the button.

6. Assuming everything has been coded correctly, what happens when the user clicks a button?

   ❑ The *actionPerformed* method executes.

   ❑ The *JButton* constructor executes.

   ❑ The *main* method executes.

7. If you visit Sun Microsystems' Java Web site (*www.java.sun.com*) and look at the *KeyListener* interface, you will find that it has three methods: *keyPressed*, *keyTyped*, and *keyReleased*. We want to build a class that implements *KeyListener*. Which one of the three methods should we implement?

   ❑ *keyPressed* only

   ❑ *keyReleased* only

   ❑ *keyTyped* only

   ❑ All three methods

8. You are designing a GUI with three buttons; a different action will be taken depending on which button the user clicks. You want to code only one *private* class implementing the *ActionListener* interface. Inside the *actionPerformed* method, which method do you call to determine which button was clicked?

   ❑ *getButton*

   ❑ *getSource*

   ❑ *getOrigin*

9. A class extending the *JFrame* class can also implement a listener interface.

   ❑ true

   ❑ false

10. *NewLayout* is a layout manager.

    ❏ true

    ❏ false

11. In the following code:

    ```
    GridLayout gl = new GridLayout( 6, 4 );
    ```

    what do the arguments 6 and 4 specify?

    ❏ 6 refers to the number of columns and 4 to the number of rows.

    ❏ 4 refers to the number of columns and 6 to the number of rows.

    ❏ There will be 6 components organized in 4 different areas.

    ❏ There will be 4 components organized in 6 different areas.

12. What is the maximum number of components that a *BorderLayout* can manage?

    ❏ 2

    ❏ 3

    ❏ 4

    ❏ 5

    ❏ 6

13. In the following code:

    ```
    BorderLayout bl = new BorderLayout( 7, 3 );
    ```

    what do the arguments 7 and 3 represent?

    ❏ the horizontal and vertical gaps between the five areas of the component

    ❏ the vertical and horizontal gaps between the five areas of the component

    ❏ the number of rows and columns in the component

    ❏ the number of columns and rows in the component

14. In the following code:

    ```
    contents.add( button, BorderLayout.NORTH );
    ```

    what is the data type of the second argument?

    ❏ *int*

    ❏ *String*

❏ *BorderLayout*

❏ *NORTH*

15. Components can be nested.

❏ true

❏ false

12.18.2   Reading and Understanding Code

For questions 16 to 21, consider the following code:

```java
import javax.swing.*;
import java.awt.*;
import java.awt.event.*;

public class Game extends JFrame
{
 private JButton b1, b2, b3, b4;
 private Container contents;
 public Game( )
 {
  super( "Play this game" );
  contents = getContentPane( );
  contents.setLayout( new GridLayout( 2, 2 ) );
  b1 = new JButton( "Button 1" );
  b2 = new JButton( "Button 2" );
  b3 = new JButton( "Button 3" );
  b4 = new JButton( "Button 4" );
  contents.add( b1 );
  contents.add( b2 );
  contents.add( b3 );

  MyHandler mh = new MyHandler( );
  b1.addActionListener( mh );
  b2.addActionListener( mh );

  setSize( 400, 400 );
  setVisible( true );
 }

 private class MyHandler implements ActionListener
 {
  public void actionPerformed( ActionEvent ae )
  {
   System.out.println( "Hello" );
```

```
   if ( ae.getSource( ) == b2 )
      System.out.println( "Hello again" );
   }
  }
  public static void main( String [ ] args )
  {
   Game g = new Game( );
   g.setDefaultCloseOperation( JFrame.EXIT_ON_CLOSE );
  }
 }
```

16. How many buttons will be displayed in the window?

17. How are the buttons organized in the window?

18. What is the text in the title bar of the window?

19. What happens when the user clicks on the button that says "Button 1"?

20. What happens when the user clicks on the button that says "Button 2"?

21. What happens when the user clicks on the button that says "Button 3"?

For questions 22 to 26, consider the following code:

```
import javax.swing.*;
import java.awt.*;
import java.awt.event.*;

public class Game extends JFrame
{
  private JCheckBox c1, c2, c3;
  private int value1, value2, value3;
  private Container contents;
  public Game( )
  {
   super( "Play this game" );
   contents = getContentPane( );
   contents.setLayout( new FlowLayout( ) );
   c1 = new JCheckBox( "Choice 1" );
   c2 = new JCheckBox( "Choice 2" );
   c3 = new JCheckBox( "Choice 3" );
   contents.add( c1 );
   contents.add( c2 );
   contents.add( c3 );
   MyHandler mh = new MyHandler( );
   c1.addItemListener( mh );
   c2.addItemListener( mh );
   c3.addItemListener( mh );
```

```
      setSize( 400, 400 );
      setVisible( true );
    }

    private class MyHandler implements ItemListener
    {
      public void itemStateChanged( ItemEvent ie )
      {
        if ( ie.getSource( ) == c1 )
        {
          if ( ie.getStateChange( ) == ItemEvent.SELECTED )
            value1 = 1;
          else
            value1 = 0;
        }
        else if ( ie.getSource( ) == c2 )
        {
          if ( ie.getStateChange( ) == ItemEvent.SELECTED )
            value2 = 2;
          else
            value2 = 0;
        }
        else if ( ie.getSource( ) == c3 )
        {
          if ( ie.getStateChange( ) == ItemEvent.SELECTED )
            value3 = 4;
          else
            value3 = 0;
        }
        System.out.println( ( value1 + value2 + value3 ) );
      }
    }
    public static void main( String [ ] args )
    {
      Game g = new Game( );
      g.setDefaultCloseOperation( JFrame.EXIT_ON_CLOSE );
    }
  }
```

22. How many checkboxes will be displayed in the window?

23. How are the checkboxes organized in the window?

24. What happens when the user checks "Choice 3" only?

25. What happens when the user checks "Choice 1" and "Choice 3"?

26. What happens when the user checks all the checkboxes?

12.18.3   Fill in the Code

For questions 27 to 31, consider the following class:

```java
import javax.swing.*;
import java.awt.*;
import java.awt.event.*;

public class A extends JFrame
{
  private Container c;
  private JButton b;
  private JTextField tf;

}
```

27. Inside the constructor, this code assigns the content pane of the frame to the *Container c*:

```java
// your code goes here
```

28. Inside the constructor, this code instantiates the button *b* with the text "Button":

```java
// your code goes here
```

29. Inside the constructor, this code instantiates the text field *tf*; after instantiation, the text field should be emtpy, but have space for 10 characters:

```java
// your code goes here
```

30. Inside the constructor, and assuming that *c* has been assigned the content pane, this code sets the layout manager of the content pane to a 2-by-1 grid layout manager:

```java
// your code goes here
```

31. Inside the *actionPerformed* method of a *private* inner class implementing the *ActionListener* interface, this code changes the text of *tf* to "Button clicked" if the button *b* was clicked; otherwise, nothing happens:

```java
public void actionPerformed( ActionEvent ae )
{
  // your code goes here

}
```

32. Inside the constructor, this code registers the listener *mh* on the button *b*:

```
// the MyHandler class is a private class implementing
// ActionListener
MyHandler mh = new MyHandler( );
// your code goes here
```

For questions 33 to 41, consider the following class:

```
import javax.swing.*;
import java.awt.*;

public class B extends JFrame
{
  private Container c;
  private JPanel p1;
  private JPanel p2;
  private JButton [ ] buttons;        // length 12
  private JTextField [ ] textfields;  // length 10
  private JLabel label1;
  private JLabel label2;

}
```

Also, assume that all the instance variables have been instantiated and you are coding inside the constructor.

33. This code sets the layout manager of the content pane to be a border layout manager.

```
// your code goes here
```

34. This code adds *label1* to the north area of the window.

```
// your code goes here
```

35. This code adds *label2* to the east area of the window.

```
// your code goes here
```

36. This code sets the layout manager of the panel *p1* to be a 3-by-4 grid layout manager.

```
// your code goes here
```

37. This code places all the buttons of the array buttons inside the panel *p1*.

```
// your code goes here
```

38. This code adds the panel *p1* in the center area of the window.

```
// your code goes here
```

39. This code sets the layout manager of the panel *p2* to a 5-by-2 grid with four pixels between cells, both horizontally and vertically.

```
// your code goes here
```

40. This code places all the text fields of the array *textfields* inside the panel *p2*.

```
// your code goes here
```

41. This code adds the panel *p2* in the west area of the window.

```
// your code goes here
```

12.18.4   Identifying Errors in Code

42. Where is the error in this code sequence?

```
import java.swing.*;

public class MyGame extends JFrame
{
  // some code here
}
```

43. Where is the error in this code sequence?

```
import javax.swing.*;
import java.awt.event.*;

public class MyGame extends JFrame
{
  // some code here
 private class MyHandler extends ActionListener
 {
  public void actionPerformed( ActionEvent ae )
  { }
 }
}
```

44. Where is the error in this code sequence?

```
import javax.swing.*;
import java.awt.event.*;

public class MyGame extends JFrame
{
  // some code here
 private class MyHandler implements ItemListener
```

```
  {
   public void actionPerformed( ActionEvent ae )
   { }
  }
}
```

45. Where is the error in this code sequence?

```
import javax.swing.*;
import java.awt.event.*;

public class MyGame extends JFrame
{
 // some code here
 private class MyHandler implements ItemListener
 {
  public void itemStateChanged( ActionEvent e )
  { }
 }
}
```

12.18.5   Debugging Area

46. You coded the following in the file *MyGame.java*:

```
import javax.swing.*;
import java.awt.*;
import java.awt.event.*;

public class MyGame extends JFrame
{
 private Container c;
 private JLabel l;

 public MyGame( )
 {
  super( "My Game" );
  c = getContentPane( );
  c.setLayout( new FlowLayout( ) );
  c.add( l );   // Line 15
 }

 public static void main( String [ ] args )
 {
  MyGame mg = new MyGame( ); // Line 20
 }
}
```

The code compiles, but at run time, you get the following output:

```
Exception in thread "main" java.lang.NullPointerException
        at java.awt.Container.addImpl(Container.java:1013)
        at java.awt.Container.add(Container.java:349)
        at MyGame.<init>(MyGame.java:15)
        at MyGame.main(MyGame.java:20)
```

Explain what the problem is and how to fix it.

47. You coded the following in the file *MyGame.java*

```java
import javax.swing.*;

public class MyGame extends JFrame
{
    public MyGame( )
    {
     super( "My Game" );
     setSize( 400, 400 );
    }

    public static void main( String [ ] args )
    {
     MyGame mg = new MyGame( );
    }
}
```

The code compiles, but at run time, you cannot see the window and the code terminates.

Explain what the problem is and how to fix it.

48. You coded the following in the file *MyGame.java*

```java
import javax.swing.*;
import java.awt.*;

public class MyGame extends JFrame
{
 private Container c;
 private JTextField tf;

 public MyGame( )
 {
  super( "My Game" );
  c = getContentPane( );
  tf = new JTextField( "Hello" );
```

```
    c.add( tf, NORTH );
    setSize( 400, 400 );
    setVisible( true );
    }

    public static void main( String [ ] args )
    {
     MyGame mg = new MyGame( );
    }
}
```

When you compile your code, you get the following error:

```
MyGame.java:14: cannot find symbol
symbol   : variable NORTH
location: class MyGame
    c.add( tf, NORTH );
             ^
MyGame.java:14: internal error; cannot instantiate
add(java.awt.Component,int) a
t java.awt.Container to (javax.swing.JTextField,NORTH)
    c.add( tf, NORTH );
     ^
2 errors
```

Explain what the problem is and how to fix it.

49. You coded the following in the file *MyGame.java:*

```
import javax.swing.*;
import java.awt.*;

public class MyGame extends JFrame
{
    // Some code here
    private class MyHandler implements ActionListener
    {
     public void actionPerformed( ActionEvent ae )
     { }
    }
}
```

When you compile your code, you get the following error:

```
MyGame.java:7: cannot find symbol
symbol   : class ActionListener
```

```
location: class MyGame
      private class MyHandler implements ActionListener
                                         ^

1 error
```

Explain what the problem is and how to fix it.

50. You coded the following in the *MyGame.java* file:

```java
import javax.swing.*;
import java.awt.*;
import java.awt.event.*;

public class MyGame extends JFrame
{
  private JButton b;
  private JTextField tf;
  private Container contents;
  public MyGame( )
  {
    super( "Play this game" );
    contents = getContentPane( );
    contents.setLayout( new GridLayout( 1, 2 ) );
    b = new JButton( "Click here" );
    tf = new JTextField( "Hello" );
    contents.add( b );
    contents.add( tf );
    setSize( 400, 400 );
    setVisible( true );
  }

  private class MyHandler implements ActionListener
  {
    public void actionPerformed( ActionEvent ae )
    {
      tf.setText( "Hi" );
    }
  }
  public static void main( String [ ] args )
  {
    MyGame g = new MyGame( );
    g.setDefaultCloseOperation( JFrame.EXIT_ON_CLOSE );
  }
}
```

The code compiles and runs. However, when you click the button, the text in the text field does not change.

Explain what the problem is and how to fix it.

12.18.6   Write a Short Program

51. Write a program that displays a text field and two buttons labeled "upper case" and "lower case". When the user clicks on the upper case button, the text changes to upper case; when the user clicks on the lower case button, the text changes to lower case.

52. Write a program with two radio buttons and a text field. When the user clicks on one radio button, the text changes to lower case; when the user clicks on the other radio button, the text changes to upper case.

53. Write a program with two checkboxes and a text field. When no checkbox is selected, no text shows in the text field. When only the first checkbox is selected, the word "hello" shows in lower case. When only the second checkbox is selected, the word "HELLO" shows in upper case. When both checkboxes are selected, the word "HeLlO" shows (lower and upper case letters alternate).

54. Write a program with three radio buttons and a circle. (You can choose whether you draw the circle or if the circle is a label image.) When the user clicks on the first radio button, the circle becomes red. When the user clicks on the second radio button, the circle turns orange. When the user clicks on the third radio button, the circle becomes blue.

55. Write a program with three checkboxes and a circle drawn in black. Like the checkbox example in the chapter, each checkbox represents a color (red, blue, or green). Depending on the checkboxes selected, compute the resulting color as follows. If a checkbox is selected, assign the value 255 to the amount of the corresponding color. If a checkbox is not selected, assign 0 to the amount of the corresponding color. For example, if the checkboxes representing the colors red and blue are selected, the resulting color should be *Color(255, 0, 255)*. Color the circle appropriately.

56. Write a program that simulates a guessing game in a GUI program. Ask the user for a number between 1 and 6 in a text field, then roll a die randomly and tell the user if he or she won. Write the program in such a way that any invalid user input (i.e., not an integer between 1 and 6) is rejected and the user is asked again for input.

57. Write a program that simulates a guessing game in a GUI program. Generate a random number between 1 and 100; that number is hidden from the user. Ask the user for a number between 1 and 100 in a text field, then tell the user whether the number is too high, too low, or the correct number. Let the user continue guessing until he or she guesses the correct number.

58. Write a program that displays a 5-by-5 grid of buttons, each with a different button label. When the user clicks on a button, its text is changed to "Visible".

59. Write a program that displays a 4-by-6 grid of buttons, each with some unique text. One button is the "winning" button, which your program determines randomly, inside the constructor. When the user clicks on a button, its text is changed to "No" if the button clicked is not the winning button, or to "Won" if the button clicked is the winning button.

60. Same as exercise 59 with the following additions: Keep track of how many times the user clicks on buttons. If the user has not won after five clicks, the text on the last button clicked should be changed to "Lost". Once the user has lost or won, you should disable the game, that is, the buttons no longer respond to clicks from the user.

61. Write a program that displays in the title of the window the position of the mouse as the user moves the mouse around the window.

62. Write a program that draws a small circle that follows the mouse as the user moves the mouse around the window.

12.18.7   Programming Projects

63. Write a GUI-based tic-tac-toe game for two players.

64. Write a GUI-based program that analyzes a word. The user will type the word in a text field. Provide buttons for the following:

   ❏ One button, when clicked, displays the length of the word.

   ❏ Another button, when clicked, displays the number of vowels in the word.

   ❏ Another button, when clicked, displays the number of upper case letters in the word.

For this, you should design and code a separate (non-GUI) class encapsulating a word and its analysis, then instantiate an object of that class inside your GUI class and call the various methods as needed.

65. Write a GUI-based program that analyzes a soccer game. The user will type the names of two teams and the score of the game in four text fields. You should add appropriate labels and create buttons for the following:

    ❏ One button, when clicked, displays which team won the game.

    ❏ Another button, when clicked, displays the game score.

    ❏ Another button, when clicked, displays by how many goals the winning team won.

For this, you should design and code a separate (non-GUI) class encapsulating a soccer game, then instantiate an object of that class inside your GUI class and call the various methods as needed.

66. Write a GUI-based program that analyzes a round of golf. You will retrieve the data for 18 holes from a text file. On each line in the file will be the par for that hole (3, 4, or 5) and your score for that hole. Your program should read the file and display a combo box listing the 18 holes. When the user selects a hole, the score for that hole should be displayed in a label. Provide buttons for the following:

    ❏ One button, when clicked, displays whether your overall score was over par, under par, or par.

    ❏ Another button, when clicked, displays the number of holes for which you made par.

    ❏ Another button, when clicked, displays how many birdies you scored (a birdie on a hole is 1 under par).

For this, you should design and code a separate (non-GUI) class encapsulating the analysis, then instantiate an object of that class inside your GUI class and call the various methods as needed.

67. Write a GUI-based program that analyzes statistics for tennis players. You will retrieve the data from a text file. On each line in the file will be the name of a player, the player's number of wins for the year, and

the player's number of losses for the year. Your program should read the file and display the list of players. When the user selects a player, the winning percentage of the player should be displayed in a label. Provide buttons for the following:

- ❑ One button, when clicked, displays which player had the most wins for the year.

- ❑ Another button, when clicked, displays which player had the highest winning percentage for the year.

- ❑ Another button, when clicked, displays how many players had a winning record for the year.

For this, you should design and code a separate (non-GUI) class encapsulating the tennis statistics analysis, then instantiate an object of that class inside your GUI class and call the various methods as needed.

68. Write a GUI-based program that simulates the selection of a basketball team. You will retrieve the data from a text file containing 10 lines. On each line will be the name of a player. Your program needs to read the file and display 10 checkboxes representing the 10 players. A text area will display the team, made up of the players being selected. A basketball team has five players. Your program should not allow the user to change his or her selection after the team has five players. Every time the user checks or unchecks a checkbox, the team in the text area should be updated accordingly. Provide buttons for the following:

- ❑ One button, when clicked, displays how many players are currently on the team.

- ❑ Another button, when clicked, displays how many players remain unselected.

For this, you should design and code a separate (non-GUI) class encapsulating the player selection process, then instantiate an object of that class inside your GUI class and call the various methods as needed.

69. Write a GUI-based program that analyzes a simplified pick of the NBA (National Basketball Association) draft. You will retrieve the

data from a text file containing 10 lines. On each line will be the name of a player, the player's height, and the player's position on the court, each field separated by a space. Your program should read the file and display 10 radio buttons representing the 10 players. A text area will display the information on the player corresponding to the radio button just selected. Every time the user clicks on a radio button, the information in the text area should be updated accordingly. Provide buttons for the following:

❑ One button, when clicked, displays how many centers are available in the draft.

❑ Another button, when clicked, displays the name of the tallest player in the draft.

For this, you should design and code a separate (non-GUI) class encapsulating the set of players available for the draft, then instantiate an object of that class inside your GUI class and call the various methods as needed.

70. Write a GUI-based program that displays a team on a soccer field. You will retrieve the data from a text file containing 11 lines. Each line will contain the name of a player. Your program should read the file and display the window as shown below when it starts (you can assume that the players in the file are not in any particular order). Each cell is a button; when the user clicks on a button, the button replaces its text with the name of the player.

Left wing (11)		Striker (9)		Right wing (7)
Left midfielder (6)		Midfielder (10)		Right midfielder (8)
Left defender (3)	Stopper (4)		Sweeper (5)	Right defender (2)
		Goalie (1)		

71. Write a GUI-based program that displays a Monopoly® game. Add labels for the four train stations. Add buttons for all the Chance cells and set the text of these to a question mark. When the user clicks on one of the buttons, set its text to a message of your choice, chosen randomly from four messages.

MONOPOLY

72. Write a GUI-based, simple drawing program. This program should have two buttons: one allowing the user to draw a rectangle, the other allowing the user to draw an oval. The user draws either a rectangle or an oval by pressing the mouse, dragging it, and releasing it. The top-left (x, y) coordinate of the rectangle (or enclosing rectangle for the oval) is where the user pressed the mouse button; the bottom-right point of the rectangle (or enclosing rectangle for the oval) drawn is where the user released the mouse button. You will need to organize the window in two areas: two for the buttons, one for drawing.

12.18.8 Technical Writing

73. You are writing a program that you expect to be used by many users, all with a different computer system. Would you use layout managers or would you hard code the position of components inside your GUI? Discuss.

12.18.9   Group Project (for a group of 1, 2, or 3 students)

74. Design and code a program that simulates an auction. You should consider the following:

    A file contains a list of items to be auctioned. You can decide on the format of this file and its contents. For example, the file could look like:

    Oldsmobile, oldsmobile.gif, 100
    World Cup soccer ticket, soccerTickets.gif, 50
    Trip for 2 to Rome, trip.gif, 100

    In the file sample above, each line represents an item as follows: the first field is the item's description, the second field is the name of a file containing an image of the item, and the third field is the minimum bid. You can assume that each item's description is unique.

    Items are offered via an online-like auction. (You do not need to include any network programming; your program is a single-computer program.) Users of the program can choose which item to bid on from a list or a combo box. Along with displaying the description of the item, your program should show a picture of the item and the current highest bid (at the beginning, the current highest bid is the minimum bid). Users bid on an item by selecting the item, typing their name (you can assume that all users have a different name), and entering a price for the item. Your program should remember the highest bidder and the highest bid for each item by writing the information to a file. Furthermore, each time a bid is made, the item's highest bid, displayed on the screen, should be updated if necessary.

CHAPTER 13

Recursion

CHAPTER CONTENTS

Introduction

Small problems are easier to solve than big ones, with or without the help of a computer. For example, it is easy to see that 14 is a multiple of 7, but determining if 12,348 is a multiple of 7 requires some thinking ... or a well-programmed computer.

If we knew that 12,341 is a multiple of 7, then it would be easy to determine that 12,348 is also a multiple of 7, because 12,348 is simply 12,341 + 7. But then, it is not that easy to determine that 12,341 is a multiple of 7. But again, if we knew that 12,334 is a multiple of 7, then it would be easy to determine that 12,341 is also a multiple of 7, because 12,341 is simply 12,334 + 7. Well, if we keep subtracting 7 from the current number, eventually, either we will arrive at 0, which means that 12,348 is a multiple of 7, or we will arrive at a number less than 7 but not 0, which means that 12,348 is not a multiple of 7. Thus, we have reduced a large problem to a small problem that is easy to solve.

The idea of **recursion** is to reduce the size of a problem at each step so that we eventually arrive at a very small, easy-to-solve problem. That easy-to-solve problem is called the **base case**. The formula that reduces the size of the problem is called the **general case**. The general case takes us from solving a bigger problem to solving a smaller problem.

A method that uses recursion calls itself. In other words, in the body of a **recursive method**, there is a call to the method itself. The arguments passed are smaller in value (that is, they get us closer to the base case) than the original arguments. The recursive method will keep calling itself with arguments that are smaller and smaller in value, until eventually we reach the base case.

Any problem that can be solved recursively can also be solved using a loop, or iteration. Often, however, a recursive solution to a problem provides simpler, more elegant, and more compact code than its iterative counterpart.

13.1   Simple Recursion: Identifying the General and Base Cases

When designing a recursive solution for a problem, we need to do two things:

- define the base case
- define the rule for the general case

For example, if we want to print "Hello World" 100 times, we can do the following:

- print "Hello World" once
- print "Hello World" 99 times

Note that we do two things above: first, we print "Hello World" once, which is easy to do. Then we reduce the size of the remaining problem to printing "Hello World" 99 times. In order to print "Hello World" 99 times, we print "Hello World" once, then we print "Hello World" 98 times. Continuing the same approach, to print "Hello World" 98 times, we print "Hello World" once, then we print "Hello World" 97 times, and so on. Eventually, we will reach a point where we print "Hello World" once, then print "Hello World" 0 times. Printing "Hello World" 0 times is an easy-to-solve problem; we simply do nothing. That is our base case for this problem.

Thus, our general approach to printing "Hello World" n times (where n is greater than 0) is to print "Hello World" once, and then print "Hello World" $n - 1$ times. As we reduce the number of times we print "Hello World," we will eventually reach 0, the base case. This condition is easy to detect. Thus, we can solve the large problem by reducing the problem to smaller and smaller problems until we find a problem that we know how to solve.

The following pseudocode illustrates the approach for our recursive method.

```
void printHelloWorldNTimes ( int n )
{
  if ( n is greater than 0 )
  {
    print "Hello World"
    printHelloWorldNTimes( n − 1 )
  }
  // else do nothing
}
```

When n is greater than 0, we will execute the body of the *if* statement, printing "Hello World" once, then printing it $n - 1$ times. This is the general case for this problem. We can see that we are going from a problem of size n (print "Hello World" n times) to a problem of size $(n - 1)$ (print "Hello World" $n - 1$ times).

When n is 0 (or less), we do nothing, that is, the call to *printHelloWorldNTimes* with an argument of 0 does not generate any action. This is the base case, and this is when the recursive calls will end.

Example 13.1 shows this method.

```
1    /* Printing Hello World n times using recursion
2        Anderson, Franceschi
3    */
4
5    public class RecursiveHelloWorld
6    {
7      public static void main( String [ ] args )
8      {
9        // print "Hello World" 5 times using our recursive method
10       printHelloWorldNTimes( 5 );
11     }
12
13     // the recursive method
14     public static void printHelloWorldNTimes( int n )
15     {
16      if ( n > 0 )
17      {
18      // print "Hello World" once
19      System.out.println( "Hello World" );
20
21      // now print "Hello World" ( n - 1 ) times
22      printHelloWorldNTimes( n - 1 );
23      }
24      // if n is 0 or less, do nothing
25     }
26   }
```

EXAMPLE 13.1   Recursively Printing "Hello World" *n* Times

We coded the *printHelloWorldNTimes* method from line 13 to line 25. That method prints "Hello World" n times, where n is an *int*, the only parameter of the method. We test at line 16 for the general case: n is greater than 0. There is no *else* clause: if n is 0 or less, we have reached the base case and the method does nothing.

The code for the general case is executed at lines 18–22. At line 19, we print "Hello World" once. At line 22, we make a recursive call to the *printHelloWorldNTimes* method in order to print "Hello World" $(n - 1)$ times. The method calls itself, but with an argument that is 1 less than the original argument n.

SOFTWARE ENGINEERING TIP

If the method does nothing in the base case, it is important to document that fact to show when the recursive calls will end.

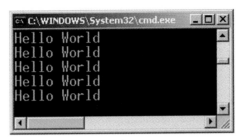

Figure 13.1
Output of Example 13.1

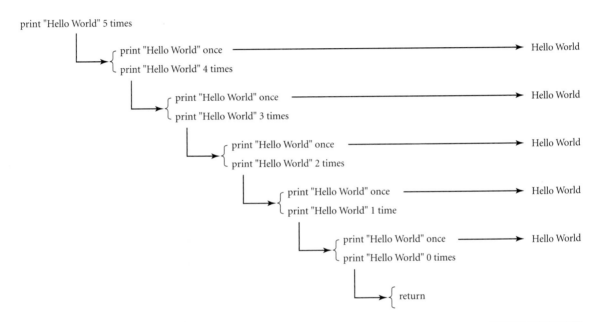

Figure 13.2
Recursive Method Calls

On line 10, we call the *printHelloWorldNTimes* method, passing the argument 5. Because *main* is *static*, it can call only *static* methods; therefore, we need to define our *printHelloWorldNTimes* method as *static*. In general, recursive methods can be defined as *static* or non-*static*.

Figure 13.1 shows the output of Example 13.1. As you can see, "Hello World" is indeed printed five times. Figure 13.2 illustrates how the recursive calls are executed and the output resulting from the calls.

Skill Practice
with these end-of-chapter questions

13.2 Recursion with a Return Value

In the example above, we coded a very simple method. Now let's look at some examples that are a little more complex, with recursive methods that return a value.

In a value-returning method the *return* statement can include a call to another value-returning method, as in:

```
public static int multiplyAbsoluteValueBy3( int n )
{
    return ( 3 * Math.abs( n ) );
}
```

In this case, the *multiplyAbsoluteValueBy3* method cannot return its value until the *abs* method returns a value, allowing the expression in the *return* statement to be fully evaluated.

The same principle applies to a value-returning method that is recursive. The return value of the recursive method often consists of an expression that includes a call to the method itself.

Thus, in the general case of the method, we could see code like:

```
return ( expression including a recursive call to the method );
```

Each execution of the recursive method must wait to return its value until its recursive call to the method returns a value. When the base case is reached, the method simply returns a value without making another recursive call. At that point, the method that invoked the method with the base case argument receives its return value, which allows that method to return a value to its caller, and so on, until the method is able to return a value to the initial caller. In this way, the return values unravel up to the initial caller.

To see how this works, let's look at an example of a recursive method that returns a value.

13.2.1   Computing the Factorial of a Number

We will define a recursive method to compute and return the factorial of a positive integer.

The factorial of a positive number is defined as follows:

$$\text{factorial}(\,n\,) = n! = n * (\,n - 1\,) * (\,n - 2\,) * (\,n - 3\,) * \ldots * 4 * 3 * 2 * 1$$

The factorial of a negative number is not defined. The factorial of 0, by convention is 1.

$$\text{factorial}(\,0\,) = 0! = 1$$

Let's define the base case and the general case for computing the factorial of a number.

In order to define the rule for the general case, we need to find a relationship between the problem at hand (computing the factorial of a number n), and a smaller, similar problem, involving, for example $(\,n - 1\,)$, $(\,n - 2\,)$, or other smaller values of n. So, here we will try to establish a relationship between factorial($\,n\,$) and factorial($\,n - 1\,$), factorial $(\,n - 2\,)$, and so on.

Let's first examine what the value of factorial($\,n - 1\,$) is. Applying the formula above, we get:

$$\text{factorial}(\,n - 1\,) = (\,n - 1\,)! = (\,n - 1\,) * (\,n - 2\,) * (\,n - 3\,) * \ldots$$
$$* 4 * 3 * 2 * 1$$

As we can see from the formulas above, there is a very simple relationship between factorial($\,n\,$) and factorial($\,n - 1$):

$$\text{factorial}(\,n\,) = n * \text{factorial}(\,n - 1\,)$$

This is the relationship we will use for the formulation of the general case.

Using this formula, at each step we reduce the size of the problem (measured by the value of the input n) from n to $(\,n - 1\,)$. In order to compute factorial($\,n\,$), we will call the factorial method with the argument $(\,n - 1\,)$ and multiply the returned value by n. The call to the factorial method with the argument ($n - 1$) will generate a recursive call to the factorial method with argument ($n - 2$), until eventually we generate a recursive call to the factorial method with the argument 0. We know how to compute factorial (0): by convention, it is 1. That is our base case and we have reached it. We will return 1, which will allow the unraveling of the recursive method calls until we solve the original problem, factorial (n).

Example 13.2 shows the code for calculating a factorial recursively. In order to keep things simple, we will also return 1 if the argument sent to the method is negative. However, we are careful in documenting our method to emphasize that the argument should be greater than or equal to 0. If we do not want to return anything when a negative argument is passed to the method, we would need to throw an exception, because the method is a value-returning method.

Here is how our *factorial (int n)* method will work;

- Base case: if *n* is negative or 0, the method returns 1

- General case: if *n* is greater than 0, the method returns *n * factorial (n –1)*

```
1 /* Computing the factorial of a number using recursion
2    Anderson, Franceschi
3 */
4
5 public class RecursiveFactorial
6 {
7   public static void main( String [ ] args )
8   {
9     // compute factorial of 5 and output it
10    System.out.println( "Factorial ( 5 ) is "
11                        + factorial( 5 ) );
12  }
13
14  /** recursive factorial method
15   *   @param    n  a positive integer
16   *   @return      the factorial of n
17   */
18  public static int factorial( int n )
19  {
20    if ( n <= 0 )    // base case
```

```
21        return 1;
22      else                 // general case
23        return ( n * factorial ( n - 1 ) );
24    }
25 }
```

EXAMPLE 13.2   Computing a Factorial Using Recursion

At lines 10–11, we make the initial call to the *factorial* method and print the result. We simply compute the factorial of 5. You can modify the example to prompt the user for another value.

We coded the *factorial* method at lines 14–24. The *factorial* method takes an *int* parameter named *n*, and returns the factorial of *n* as an *int*. At line 20, we test if *n* is less than or equal to 0. If that is true, we have reached the base case, and the *factorial* method returns 1. If *n* is greater than 0, the code skips to line 23, where we have coded the general case. We make a recursive call to the *factorial* method with an argument of ($n - 1$). The value returned by that recursive call is then multiplied by *n* and the result is returned.

Figure 13.3 shows the output of Example 13.2.

We can verify that factorial(5) is 120. Indeed,

$$5! = 5 * 4 * 3 * 2 * 1 = 120$$

To illustrate how the recursive method calls return their values, let's modify Example 3.2 to include some output statements inside the *factorial* method. In this way, we can trace the recursive calls.

We want to trace the following:

- each call to the *factorial* method and its argument
- the detection of the base case and the value returned at that point
- the expression that evaluates to the return value

Figure 13.3

Output of Example 13.2

Figure 13.4
Output of Example 13.3

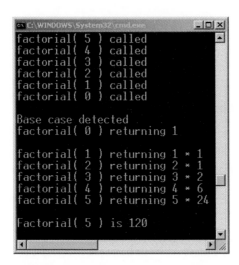

```
C:\WINDOWS\System32\cmd.exe                    _ | □ | x |
factorial( 5 ) called
factorial( 4 ) called
factorial( 3 ) called
factorial( 2 ) called
factorial( 1 ) called
factorial( 0 ) called

Base case detected
factorial( 0 ) returning 1

factorial( 1 ) returning 1 * 1
factorial( 2 ) returning 2 * 1
factorial( 3 ) returning 3 * 2
factorial( 4 ) returning 4 * 6
factorial( 5 ) returning 5 * 24

Factorial( 5 ) is 120
```

Example 13.3 is similar to Example 13.2, except that its *factorial* method includes the trace features described previously.

The *factorial* method is coded at lines 14–34. At line 20, we output a message indicating that the method has been called, along with the parameter value. When the base case is detected, we output a message indicating that the method has reached the base case and report its return value (lines 23–24). For the general case, we output the expression that will be returned by the method (lines 30–31). Figure 13.4 shows the output of Example 13.3. We can see the recursive calls to the *factorial* method with the value of the argument being reduced by 1 until the base case, 0, is reached. At that point, each recursively called method, in turn, returns a value to its caller, until the initial invocation of the method returns the value 120.

```
1 /* Computing the factorial of a number using recursion
2    Anderson, Franceschi
3 */
4
5 public class RecursiveFactorialWithTrace
6 {
7   public static void main( String [ ] args )
8   {
9     // compute factorial of 5 and output it
10    System.out.println( "\nFactorial( 5 ) is "
11                       + factorial( 5 ) );
12  }
```

```
13
14   /** recursive factorial method
15    *    @param    n  a positive integer
16    *    @return   the factorial of n
17    */
18   public static int factorial( int n )
19   {
20     System.out.println( "factorial( " + n + " ) called" );
21     if ( n == 0 )      // base case
22     {
23       System.out.println( "\nBase case detected" );
24       System.out.println( "factorial( " + n + " ) returning 1\n" );
25       return 1;
26     }
27     else               // general case
28     {
29       int factorialNMinus1 = factorial( n - 1 );
30       System.out.println( "factorial( " + n + " ) returning "
31                            + n + " * " + factorialNMinus1 );
32       return ( n * factorialNMinus1 );
33     }
34   }
35 }
```

EXAMPLE 13.3   Tracing the Recursive Calls of the *Factorial* Method

Identifying the base case is critical. When a method is called, the JVM stores the method's arguments and the caller's return address on a **stack**. When the method returns to the caller, the JVM removes the data for that method call from the stack. If a recursive method never reaches a base case, the method continues calling itself indefinitely, causing the JVM to continue placing values on the stack until memory for the stack is full. At this time, the JVM generates a *StackOverflowError*, which terminates the program.

REFERENCE POINT

We discuss stacks in Chapter 14.

For example, if we did not code the base case in our *factorial* method, the method would look like the following:

```
public static int factorial( int n )
{
   // n must be a positive integer
   return ( n * factorial ( n - 1 ) );
}
```

COMMON ERROR TRAP

Failure to code the base case will result in a run-time error.

When the method is called, the recursive calls keep being made because the base case is never reached. This eventually generates a *StackOverflowError*.

Figure 13.5

A Run of Example 13.2 If the Base Case is Not Coded

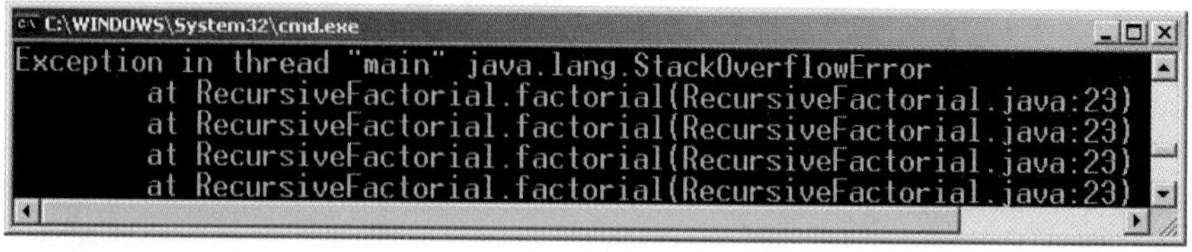

```
C:\WINDOWS\System32\cmd.exe                                    _ |□| x|
Exception in thread "main" java.lang.StackOverflowError
        at RecursiveFactorial.factorial(RecursiveFactorial.java:23)
        at RecursiveFactorial.factorial(RecursiveFactorial.java:23)
        at RecursiveFactorial.factorial(RecursiveFactorial.java:23)
        at RecursiveFactorial.factorial(RecursiveFactorial.java:23)
```

Figure 13.5 shows a run of Example 13.2 (the *RecursiveFactorial* class) with lines 20 to 22 commented out.

CODE IN ACTION

In the Chapter 13 directory of the CD-ROM accompanying this book you will find a Shockwave movie showing a step-by-step illustration of recursion. Double-click on the *Recursion.html* file to start the movie.

13.2.2   Computing the Greatest Common Divisor

A common algebra problem is to calculate the greatest common divisor, or **gcd**, of two positive integers. The gcd is the greatest positive integer that divides evenly into both numbers.

For example, consider 50 and 20. We can figure in our head that 5 divides evenly into both numbers, but so does 10. Since we can't find a number greater than 10 that divides evenly into both numbers, 10 is the gcd of 50 and 20.

It is easy to guess the gcd of two small numbers, but it is more difficult to guess the gcd of two large numbers, such as 123,450 and 60,378. The following Euclidian algorithm finds the gcd of two positive integers a and b. This algorithm derives from the fact that the gcd of two integers a and b (with $a > b$) is the same as the gcd of b and the remainder of a / b.

```
Step 1:
  r0 = a % b
  if ( r0 is equal to 0 )
      gcd ( a, b ) = b
      stop
  else
      go to step 2

Step 2:
  repeat step 1 with b and r0, instead of a and b.
```

Let's run the algorithm on our first example, 50 and 20. We substitute 50 for *a* and 20 for *b*.

```
Step 1:
   r0 = 50 % 20 = 10
   is 10 equal to 0 ?  no, go to Step 2.

Step 2:
   r0 = 20 / 10  = 0
   is 0 equal to 0 ?
      yes. gcd( 50, 20 ) = 10
      stop
```

Therefore, the gcd of 50 and 20 is 10.

Let's now run the algorithm on our second example, 123,450 and 60,378.

The remainder of 123,450 divided by 60,378 is 2,694.

2694 is not equal to 0

so we take the remainder of 60,378 divided by 2,694, which is 1,110

1,110 is not equal to 0

so we take the remainder of 2,694 divided by 1,110, which is 474

474 is not equal to 0

so we take the remainder of 1,110 divided by 474, which is 162

162 is not equal to 0

so we take the remainder of 474 divided by 162, which is 150

150 is not equal to 0

so we take the remainder of 162 divided by 150, which is 12

12 is not equal to 0

so we take the remainder of 150 divided by 12, which is 6

6 is not equal to 0

so we take the remainder of 12 divided by 6, which is 0

0 is equal to 0

so the gcd of 123, 450 and 60,378 is 6

Let's go back to our algorithm and look at Step 1 as a method taking two parameters, *a* and *b*. Step 2 is a method call to Step 1 with two different parameters, *b* and *r0*. It is very simple to calculate *r0*, since *r0* is the remainder of the division of *a* by *b*. Using the modulus operator, *r0* is *a* % *b*. Therefore, this algorithm can easily be coded as a recursive method.

Let's call the two parameters of the method, *dividend* and *divisor*, in that order.

When the remainder of the division of *dividend* by *divisor* is 0, we have reached the base case and the method returns *divisor*. The general case is when the remainder of the division of *dividend* by *divisor* is not 0. The method then calls itself with *divisor* and the remainder of the division of *dividend* by *divisor*.

Example 13.4 shows the code for the recursive implementation of the greatest common divisor solution.

```
1  /* Computing the greatest common divisor using recursion
2     Anderson, Franceschi
3  */
4
5  public class RecursiveGCD
6  {
7    public static void main( String [ ] args )
8    {
9      // compute and output gcd of 123450 and 60378
10     System.out.println( "The GCD of " + 123450 + " and "
11                         + 60378 + " is " + gcd( 123450, 60378 ) );
12   }
13
14   /** recursive gcd method
15    *    @param    dividend  the first strictly positive integer
16    *    @param    divisor   the second strictly positive integer
17    *    @return             the gcd of dividend and divisor
18    */
19   public static int gcd( int dividend, int divisor )
20   {
21     if ( dividend % divisor == 0 )        // base case
22       return divisor;
23     else                                  // general case
24       return ( gcd ( divisor, dividend % divisor ) );
25   }
26 }
```

EXAMPLE 13.4   Computing the GCD of Two Integers Using Recursion

Figure 13.6
Output of Example 13.4

We make the call to the *gcd* method at lines 10–11 with arguments 123450 and 60378 and output the result.

The *gcd* method is coded from lines 14–25. The method header shows that the *gcd* method takes two *int* parameters named *dividend* and *divisor*, and returns an *int*, the greatest common divisor of *dividend* and *divisor*. At line 21, we check for the base case by testing if the remainder of the integer division of *dividend* by *divisor* is 0. If so, the *gcd* method returns *divisor* without making another recursive call.

If the remainder is not 0, we are in the general case, so we make a recursive call at line 24 with the arguments *divisor* and the remainder of the division (*dividend % divisor*). We return the value returned by that call.

Figure 13.6 shows the output of Example 13.4.

As we did with the recursive *factorial* method, let's modify Example 13.4 to include some output statements inside the *gcd* method in order to trace the recursive calls.

The *gcd* method in Example 13.5, (lines 14–39), is the same as the *gcd* method in Example 13.4, except that each time the method is called, we print the parameter values and result of the modulus operation (lines 21–23) to verify that the method is correctly detecting the general and base cases. We also print a message when the base case is reached (lines 27–28). At lines 34–36, we output the value returned by the method in the general case.

Figure 13.7 shows the output of Example 13.5. We can see the recursive calls all the way to the base case, and the return value from each recursive call. As we can see, the return value stays the same throughout the process. Such a recursive method is called **tail recursive**.

```
1 /* Computing the greatest common divisor using recursion
2    Anderson, Franceschi
3 */
4
```

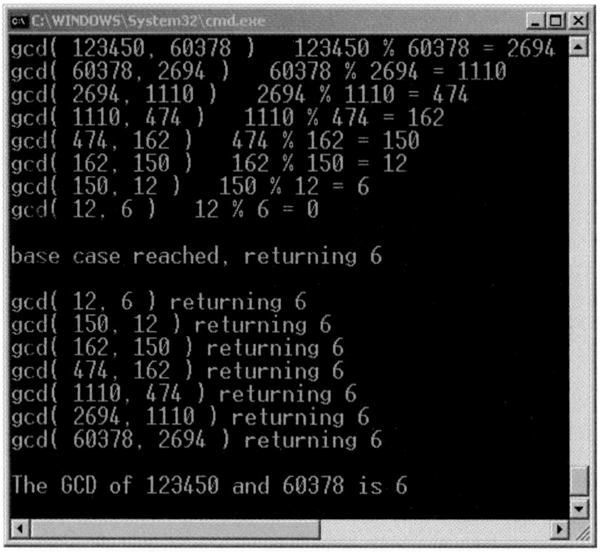

Figure 13.7

Output of Example 13.5

```
 5 public class RecursiveGCDWithTrace
 6 {
 7   public static void main( String [ ] args )
 8   {
 9     // compute gcd of 123450 and 60378 and output it
10     System.out.println( "\nThe GCD of " + 123450 + " and "
11                         + 60378 + " is " + gcd( 123450, 60378 ) );
12   }
13
14   /** recursive gcd method with trace
15   *   @param    dividend   the first strictly positive integer
16   *   @param    divisor    the second strictly positive integer
17   *   @return              the gcd of dividend and divisor
18   */
19   public static int gcd( int dividend, int divisor )
20   {
21     System.out.print( "gcd( " + dividend + ", " + divisor + " )" );
22     System.out.println( "    " + dividend + " % " + divisor + " = "
23                         + ( dividend % divisor ) );
24
25     if ( dividend % divisor == 0 )  // base case
26     {
27       System.out.println( "\nbase case reached, returning "
28                           + divisor + "\n" );
29       return divisor;
30     }
```

```
31     else                      // general case
32     {
33       int temp = gcd( divisor, dividend % divisor );
34       System.out.println( "gcd( " + divisor + ", "
35                                 + ( dividend % divisor )
36                                 + " ) returning " + temp );
37       return ( temp );
38     }
39   }
40 }
```

EXAMPLE 13.5   Tracing the Recursive Calls of the *gcd* Method

CODE IN ACTION

In the Chapter 13 folder on the CD-ROM included with this book, you will find a Shockwave movie showing step-by-step illustrations of various recursive methods. Double-click on *Recursion.html* to start the movie.

13.3   Recursion with Two Base Cases

Recursive formulations can be more complex than the examples we have discussed. The general case can involve more than one recursive call, with different arguments. This, in turn, means that we can have more than one base case.

Suppose we are playing a networked video game online. There are *n* players who would like to play. Unfortunately, that game can be played with only *p* players. We will make the assumption that *p* is an integer between 0 and *n* (for instance, *n* could be 100 and *p* could be 8). Otherwise, we simply cannot play the game.

Our problem is to determine how many different ways we can choose *p* players from among *n* players. We will call that number *Combinations(n, p)*.

The math formula for *Combinations(n, p)* is:

Combinations(n, p) = n! / ((n − p)! * p!)

Our goal here is to come up with a recursive solution to the problem and thus to code *Combinations(n, p)* recursively.

There are some obvious cases to consider. If we have the same number of players as the number who can play the game, then *p* equals *n*, and we pick all the players. There is only one way to do that, so *Combinations(n, n) = 1*.

If the game requires no players, then p equals 0, and we do not pick any players. Again, there is only one way to do that so $Combinations(n, 0) = 1$.

But what is the answer in the general case where the value of $Combinations$ (n, p) may not be so obvious?

One way to look at that problem is as follows:

Among these n potential players, let's focus on one player in particular. We will call that player Louis. We can either pick Louis or not pick Louis. Therefore, the total number of possibilities of picking p players among n potential players is equal to the sum of the following two numbers:

- the number of possibilites of picking p players, including picking Louis, among n

- the number of possibilities of picking p players, without picking Louis, among n

If we pick Louis, then we will have to choose $(p - 1)$ more players. But we cannot pick Louis again, so there are only $(n - 1)$ potential players left. The number of such possibilities is $Combinations(n - 1, p - 1)$.

If we do not pick Louis, then we still have to choose p players. But since we are not picking Louis, there are only $(n - 1)$ potential players left. The number of such possibilities is $Combinations(n - 1, p)$.

Therefore, we can write the following recursive formula:

```
Combinations( n, p ) = Combinations( n - 1, p - 1 )
                     + Combinations( n - 1, p )
```

If we look at the two terms on the right side of the above formula, we can see that:

- In the first term, both parameters, n and p, have been decreased by 1.

- In the second term, one parameter, n, has been decreased by 1, while p is unchanged.

Therefore, solving the problem of computing $Combinations(n, p)$ using this formula translates into solving two similar, but smaller, problems. That is our general case.

Our next concern is to decide what the base case or cases are. In other words, as we apply the above formula repeatedly, when will we reach an easy-to-solve problem? Since we have two recursive terms on the right side of the formula, we will have two base cases.

Let's look at the first term, *Combinations(n − 1, p − 1)*. We can see that both *n* and *p* decrease by 1 at the same time. When we start, *p* is greater than or equal to 0 and less than or equal to *n*. Therefore, as we keep applying the formula and concentrate on the first term, we can see that *p* will eventually reach 0, and that *p* will reach 0 before *n* does. As discussed earlier, *Combinations(n, 0) = 1*, because there is only one way to pick 0 players from a set of *n* players—do not pick any. This is one base case.

Let's now look at the second term, *Combinations(n − 1, p)*. We can see that *n* decreases by 1 while *p* is unchanged. We know that *p* must be less than or equal to *n* (we cannot pick more than *n* players among *n* players). As *n* decreases and *p* does not, *n* will eventually reach *p*. As discussed earlier, *Combinations(n, n) = 1*, because there is only one way to pick *n* players among *n* players—pick them all. This is our other base case.

Example 13.6 shows the code for this example.

```
 1 /* Computing the number of combinations
 2     of picking p objects among n, using recursion
 3     Anderson, Franceschi
 4 */
 5
 6 public class RecursiveCombinations
 7 {
 8   public static void main( String [ ] args )
 9   {
10     // compute and output number of combinations
11     System.out.println( "C( 5, 2 ) = "
12                         + combinations( 5, 2 ) );
13   }
14
15   /** recursive combinations method
16    *    @param   n a positive number
17    *    @param   p a positive number, less than or equal to n
18    *    @return  the number of combinations of choosing p among n
19    */
20   public static int combinations( int n, int p )
21   {
22     if ( p == 0 )             // base case # 1
23       return 1;
24     else if ( n == p )        // base case # 2
25       return 1;
26     else                      // general case
```

```
27      return ( combinations( n - 1, p - 1 )
28                 + combinations( n - 1, p ) );
29    }
30 }
```

EXAMPLE 13.6   Computing Combinations Recursively

In this example, we use the *combinations* method to compute the number of ways of picking 2 players among 5.

We call the *combinations* method with arguments, 5 and 2, and output the returned value at lines 11–12.

The *combinations* method is coded at lines 15–29. The method header, at line 20, shows that the *combinations* method takes two *int* parameters, the number of players (n) and the number of players to select (p). The return value, an *int*, is the number of combinations of picking p players among n.

At line 22, we test for the first base case ($p == 0$). If *true*, we return 1. If p is not equal to 0, we test for the second base case (n is equal to p). If that is *true*, we return 1. If p is not equal to 0 and n is not equal to p, then we are in the general case and the code skips to lines 27–28. We make two recursive calls to the *combinations* method. The first recursive call is with arguments $n - 1$ and $p - 1$. The second recursive call is with arguments $n - 1$ and p. We add the values returned by these two recursive calls and return the result.

The output of Example 13.6 is shown in Figure 13.8.

We can verify that our algorithm is correct. As discussed earlier,

Combinations(n, p) = n! / ((n − p)! * p!)

Thus,

Combinations(5, 2) = 5! / (3! * 2!) = 10

Those of us with a mathematics background can verify that

```
Combinations( n, p ) = Combinations( n − 1, p − 1 ) +
                       Combinations( n − 1, p )
```

Figure 13.8

Output of Example 13.6

```
C( 5, 2 ) = 10
```

that is,

```
n! / ( ( n – p )! * p! ) = ( n – 1 )! / ( ( n – p )! * ( p – 1 )! )
                         + ( n – 1 )! / ( ( n – 1 – p )! * p! )
```

What happens if we code for only one base case when there are two or more base cases?

When the method is called, the recursive calls will continue to be made, because the missing base cases will never be detected. This will eventually generate a *StackOverflowError*.

COMMON ERROR TRAP

There can be more than one base case. Failing to take into account all base cases can result in a *StackOverflowError* at run time.

13.4   Programming Activity 1: Checking for a Palindrome

In this activity, you will work with recursion to perform this function:

Code a recursive method to determine if a *String* is a palindrome.

A palindrome is a word, phrase, or sentence that is symmetrical, that is, it is spelled the same forward and backwards. Examples are "otto," "mom," "madam," and "able was I ere I saw elba."

How can we determine, using recursion, whether a *String* is a palindrome?

If the *String* has two or more characters, we can check if the first and last characters are identical. If they are not identical, then the *String* is not a palindrome. That is a base case.

If the first and last characters are identical, then we need to check if the substring comprised of all the characters between the first and last characters is a palindrome. That is the general case.

If the *String* is a palindrome, each recursive call will reduce the size of the argument, that is, the number of characters in the argument *String*, by 2. Eventually, the recursive calls will result in a *String* argument consisting of 0 or 1 character. Both are trivial palindromes. That is our second base case. Note that we will reach this base case only if the *String* is a palindrome. Indeed, if the *String* is not a palindrome, the recursive calls will detect the first base case as soon as the first and last characters of the *String* argument are different, and the recursive method will return *false*.

For example, to check if "madam" is a palindrome, we take the following steps:

Here is the original *String*:

We compare the first and last characters.

They are equal, so we now check the substring comprised of the characters between the first and last characters. Again, we compare the first and last characters of this substring.

They are equal, so we now check the substring comprised of the characters between the first and last characters.

There is only one character in this substring, so we have reached our second base case. The *String* "madam" is a palindrome.

Let's now check if "modem" is a palindrome.

Here is the original *String*:

We compare the first and last characters.

They are equal, so we now check the substring comprised of the characters between the first and last characters. Again, we check the first and last characters.

REFERENCE POINT

Useful methods for manipulating and comparing *Strings* are listed in Appendix F.

They are not equal, so we have reached the first base case. The *String* "modem" is not a palindrome.

Instructions

In the Chapter 13 Programming Activity 1 directory on the CD-ROM accompanying this book, you will find the source files needed to complete this activity. Copy all of the files to a directory on your computer. Note that all files should be in the same directory.

Open the *PalindromeClient.java* source file. Searching for five stars (*****) in the source code will position you to the location where you will add your code. In this task, you will fill in the code inside the *recursivePalindrome* method to determine if a *String* representing a word or a sentence is a palindrome. The method returns *true* if the *String* is a palindrome, *false* if the *String* is not a palindrome. Example 13.7 shows the section of the *PalindromeClient* source code where you will add your code.

```java
public boolean recursivePalindrome( String pal )
{
  // ***** Student writes the body of this method *****

  // Using recursion, determine if a String representing
  // a word or a sentence is a palindrome
  // If it is, return true, otherwise return false

  // We call the animate method inside the body of this method
  // The call to animate is already coded below

  animate( pal );

  //
  // Student code starts here
  //

  return true; // replace this dummy return statement

  //
  // End of student code - PA 1
  //
}
```

EXAMPLE 13.7   Location of Student Code in *PalindromeClient*

The framework will animate your code so that you get some feedback on the correctness of your code. It will display the argument *String* passed to the recursive method at each recursive call of that method. Your result will be displayed in red and the correct result will be displayed in green.

To test your code, compile and run the application; when the program begins, a dialog box will prompt you for a word or a sentence, as shown in Figure 13.9.

Click "Cancel" to exit the program; click "OK" to continue and animate your code.

If you enter an empty *String* or a *String* with more than 26 characters, the program will prompt you for another *String*. This part is already coded for you.

Figure 13.10 shows the output if you enter "able was I ere I saw elba". We can see the argument *String* of our recursive method shrinking by two characters at each recursive call until we reach a base case.

If you insert an extra "h" into the phrase above, and enter "able was I here I saw elba", which is not a palindrome, the final result of your animation is

Figure 13.9

Opening Dialog Box

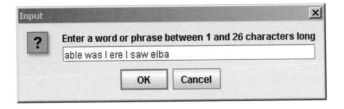

Figure 13.10

Sample Final Screen for Programming Activity 1

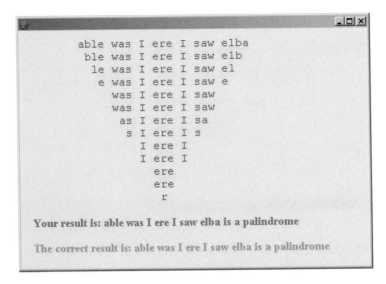

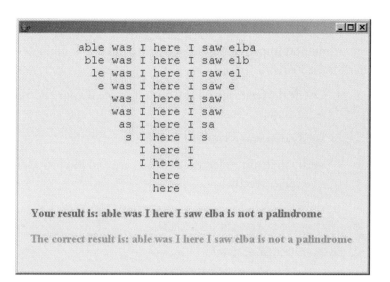

```
able was I here I saw elba
 ble was I here I saw elb
  le was I here I saw el
   e was I here I saw e
     was I here I saw
     was I here I saw
      as I here I sa
       s I here I s
         I here I
         I here I
           here
           here
```

Your result is: able was I here I saw elba is not a palindrome

The correct result is: able was I here I saw elba is not a palindrome

Figure 13.11
Sample Final Screen for Programming Activity 1

shown in Figure 13.11. When the argument *String* of our recursive method become "here", the recursive calls stop and the method returns *false*.

Task Instructions

Inside the method *recursivePalindrome* of class *PalindromeClient*, write the code to solve the palindrome problem:

- The *recursivePalindrome* method header has already been coded for you. Write the code to check if the parameter of the method, *pal*, is a palindrome. Return *true* if it is, *false* if it is not. Your method should be recursive, that is, it should call itself. We have provided a dummy *return* statement so that the code will compile. You should replace the dummy statement with your appropriate *return* statement.

- Be sure your code ignores case differences; that is, Otto and Racecar are indeed palindromes.

- The call to the *animate* method has already been written for you. It should be the first statement in the body of the method and is simply:

```
animate( pal );
```

Troubleshooting

If your method implementation does not animate or animates incorrectly, check these items:

- Check the feedback on the output to see if your code gives the correct result.
- Verify that you coded the base cases correctly.
- Verify that you coded the general case and its corresponding recursive call correctly.

1. What are the base cases for this method?
2. Is this method tail recursive?
3. What happens if you do not code one of the base cases?

13.5   Binary Search Revisited: A Recursive Solution

In Chapter 8, we presented a binary search algorithm to search a sorted array for a given value. That algorithm was iterative, using a *while* loop.

Let's look at how we can define a recursive solution to this problem. We will assume that the array is sorted in ascending order.

Again, we need to define the base cases and the general case, and the general case must reduce the size of the problem.

When searching for a value in an array, we have two possible outcomes:

- We find the value and return its array index.
- We do not find the value and return −1.

Overall, our strategy is similar to the iterative solution. First, we will look at the middle element of the array. If the value of the middle element is the value we are looking for, we will return its index. That is our first base case.

If the value of the middle element is greater than the value we are looking for, then the value we are looking for cannot be found in elements with array indexes higher than the index of the middle element. Therefore, we will continue our search in the lower half of the array only. We will do that by making a recursive call to our search method, specifying the lower half of the original array as the subarray to search.

Similarly, if the value of the middle element is lower than the value we are looking for, then the value we are looking for cannot be found in elements with array indexes lower than the index of the middle element. Therefore, we will continue our search in the upper half of the array only. We will do that by making a recursive call to our search method, specifying the upper half of the original array as the subarray to search. That is our formulation for the general case.

As we continue searching, the size of the subarray that we search will shrink with every recursive call. Indeed, every recursive call cuts the size of the subarray we search in half. In this recursive algorithm, not only does the size of the problem decrease with each recursive call, but it also decreases by a large amount.

If the value we are looking for is not in the array, the part of the array that we are searching will continue shrinking until it is empty. At that point, we know that we will not find our value in the array. We have reached our other base case, and we return –1.

Example 13.8 shows the code for a recursive binary search.

```
 1 /* Searching a sorted array using recursion
 2     Anderson, Franceschi
 3 */
 4
 5 import java.util.Scanner;
 6
 7 public class RecursiveBinarySearch
 8 {
 9   public static void main( String [ ] args )
10   {
11     // define an array sorted in ascending order
12     int [ ] numbers = { 3, 6, 7, 8, 12, 15, 22, 36, 45,
13                         48, 51, 53, 64, 69, 72, 89, 95 };
14
15     Scanner scan = new Scanner( System.in );
16     System.out.print( "Enter a value to search for > " );
17     int value = scan.nextInt( );
18
19     int index = recursiveBinarySearch
20                 ( numbers, value, 0, numbers.length - 1 );
21     if ( index != -1 )
22       System.out.println( value + " found at index " + index );
```

```
23    else
24      System.out.println( value + " not found" );
25   }
26
27   /** recursiveBinarySearch method
28    *   @param    arr   the array sorted in ascending order
29    *   @param    key   the value to search for in the subarray
30    *   @param    start the subarray's first index
31    *   @param    end   the subarray's last index
32    *   @return   the array index at which key was found,
33    *             or -1 if key was not found
34    */
35   public static int recursiveBinarySearch
36                ( int [ ] arr, int key, int start, int end )
37   {
38     if ( start <= end )
39     {
40       // look at the middle element of the subarray
41       int middle = ( start + end ) / 2;
42
43       if ( arr[middle] == key )      // found key, base case
44         return middle;
45       else if ( arr[middle] > key ) // look lower
46         return recursiveBinarySearch( arr, key, start, middle - 1 );
47       else                          // look higher
48         return recursiveBinarySearch( arr, key, middle + 1, end );
49     }
50     else                            // key not found, base case
51       return -1;
52   }
53 }
```

EXAMPLE 13.8   Searching an Array Sorted in Ascending Order

We coded the *recursiveBinarySearch* method at lines 27–52. That method takes four parameters: *arr*, the array we are searching, *key*, the value we are searching for; and *start* and *end*, which represent, respectively, the first and last index of the subarray of *arr* that we should search.

At line 38, we test if the subarray we are searching contains at least one element. If it does not, we have reached a base case and we know that we will not find *key*. Thus, we return −1 in the *else* clause at line 51. If the subarray has at least one element, we assign the index of the middle element of the subarray to *middle* at line 41. We then compare the array element at index *middle* to *key* at line 43. If they are equal, we have reached the other base case (we have found *key*) so we return *middle* at line 44.

REFERENCE POINT

Various algorithms for sorting an array are discussed in detail in Chapter 8, as is searching a sorted array using an iterative binary search algorithm.

If the array element at index *middle* is greater than *key*, we call the *recursiveBinarySearch* method with the subarray consisting of all elements with values lower than *middle* (from *start* to *middle* − *1*) at line 46. If the array element at index *middle* is smaller than *key*, then we call the *recursiveBinarySearch* method with the subarray consisting of all elements with values higher than *middle* (from *middle* + *1* to *end*) at line 48. In both cases, whatever is returned by the recursive call is returned by the method.

In *main*, we begin by instantiating our array to search. Note that the values are in ascending order (lines 12–13). We then prompt the user for the search key and make the call to the recursive binary search method, passing the entire array as the subarray to search (lines 19–20). We output the result of our search at lines 21–24.

Figure 13.12 shows the output from Example 13.8 when the key value is found, and when the key value is not found.

Let's run the example above on the value 7 in order to illustrate the various recursive calls and the case where the value is found.

Here is the array *numbers*, sorted in ascending order.

Value	3	6	7	8	12	15	22	36	45	48	51	53	64	69	72	89	95
Index	0	1	2	3	4	5	6	7	8	9	10	11	12	13	14	15	16

Figure 13.12

Two Runs of Example 13.8

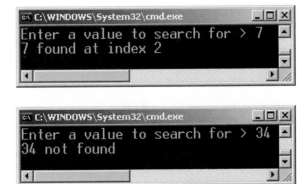

We calculate the index *middle* by adding the indexes *start* and *end*, then dividing by 2. Thus, when the *recursiveBinarySearch* method is first called, *middle* is 8.

The element at index 8 (45) is greater than 7, so we call the *recursiveBinary-Search* method, searching the left subarray, highlighted below.

Value	3	6	7	8	12	15	22	36	45	48	51	53	64	69	72	89	95
Index	0	1	2	3	4	5	6	7	8	9	10	11	12	13	14	15	16

The index *middle* is now calculated to be 3 ((0 + 7) / 2).

The element at index 3 (8) is greater than 7, so we call the *recursiveBinary-Search* method, searching the left subarray, highlighted below.

Value	3	6	7	8	12	15	22	36	45	48	51	53	64	69	72	89	95
Index	0	1	2	3	4	5	6	7	8	9	10	11	12	13	14	15	16

The index *middle* is now calculated to be 1 ((0 + 2) / 2).

The element at index 1 (6) is smaller than 7, so we call the *recursiveBinary-Search* method, searching the right subarray, highlighted below.

Value	3	6	7	8	12	15	22	36	45	48	51	53	64	69	72	89	95
Index	0	1	2	3	4	5	6	7	8	9	10	11	12	13	14	15	16

The index *middle* is now calculated to be 2 ((2 + 2) / 2).

The element at index 2 (7), is equal to 7. We have found the value and return its index, 2.

Let's now run the example above on the value 34 in order to illustrate the various recursive calls and the base case when the value is not found.

Here is the array *numbers* again:

Value	3	6	7	8	12	15	22	36	45	48	51	53	64	69	72	89	95
Index	0	1	2	3	4	5	6	7	8	9	10	11	12	13	14	15	16

The index *middle* when the *recursiveBinarySearch* method is first called is 8 ((0 + 16) / 2).

The element at index 8 (45) is greater than 34, so we call the *recursiveBinarySearch* method, searching the left subarray highlighted below.

Value	3	6	7	8	12	15	22	36	45	48	51	53	64	69	72	89	95
Index	0	1	2	3	4	5	6	7	8	9	10	11	12	13	14	15	16

The index *middle* is now calculated to be 3 ((0 + 7) / 2).

The element at index 3 (8) is smaller than 34, so we call the *recursiveBinarySearch* method, searching the right subarray, highlighted below.

Value	3	6	7	8	12	15	22	36	45	48	51	53	64	69	72	89	95
Index	0	1	2	3	4	5	6	7	8	9	10	11	12	13	14	15	16

The index *middle* is now calculated to be 5 ((4 + 7) / 2).

The element at index 5 (15) is smaller than 34, so we call the *recursiveBinarySearch* method, searching the right subarray, highlighted below.

Value	3	6	7	8	12	15	22	36	45	48	51	53	64	69	72	89	95
Index	0	1	2	3	4	5	6	7	8	9	10	11	12	13	14	15	16

The index *middle* is now calculated to be 6 ((6 + 7) / 2).

The element at index 6 (22) is smaller than 34, so we call the *recursiveBinarySearch* method, searching the right subarray, highlighted below.

Value	3	6	7	8	12	15	22	36	45	48	51	53	64	69	72	89	95
Index	0	1	2	3	4	5	6	7	8	9	10	11	12	13	14	15	16

The index *middle* is now calculated to be 7 ((7 + 7) / 2).

The element at index 7 (36) is larger than 34, so we call the *recursiveBinary-Search* method, searching the left subarray. However, that left subarray is empty. We have not found 34, so we return -1.

Skill Practice
with these end-of-chapter questions

13.10.1	Multiple Choice Exercises
	Questions 2, 6, 7, 8
13.10.2	Reading and Understanding Code
	Questions 9, 10, 11, 12, 13, 14, 15, 20, 21, 22, 23
13.10.3	Fill in the Code
	Questions 24, 25, 26, 27, 28
13.10.4	Identifying Errors in Code
	Questions 29, 30, 31, 32
13.10.5	Debugging Area
	Questions 33, 34, 35, 36, 37, 38
13.10.6	Write a Short Program
	Questions 42, 43, 45, 46, 47
13.10.8	Technical Writing
	Question 63

13.6   Programming Activity 2: The Towers of Hanoi

A well-known problem that lends itself to an elegant recursive formulation is the Towers of Hanoi. Here it is:

- There are three towers, which we can represent as the source tower, the temporary tower, and the destination tower.

- We have a stack of *n* disks piled on the source tower; all the disks have a different diameter. The largest disk is at the bottom and the smallest disk is at the top.

▪ The goal is to transfer all the disks, one at a time, to the destination tower using all three towers for help. No larger disk can be placed on top of a smaller one.

The recursive solution to the problem for the general case ($n >= 1$) is as follows:

1. Transfer the top ($n - 1$) disks from the source tower to the temporary tower.

2. Transfer the one remaining disk (the largest) from the source tower to the destination tower.

3. Transfer the ($n - 1$) disks from the the temporary tower to the destination tower.

The base case, when $n = 0$ (there are 0 disks to transfer), is to do nothing.

The first and third operations are simply recursive calls using a smaller number of disks ($n - 1$) than the original problem.

In the case of $n = 5$, Figures 13.13–13.16 illustrate the recursive solution and formulation. On the figure, the left, middle, and right towers represent the source, temporary, and destination towers, respectively.

In this activity, you will work with recursion to perform the following function:

Code a recursive method to solve the Towers of Hanoi problem

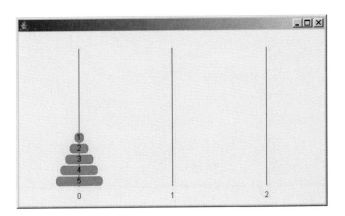

Figure 13.13
Starting Position With Five Disks

Figure 13.14
Position After Step 1

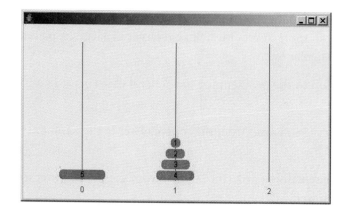

Figure 13.15
Position After Step 2

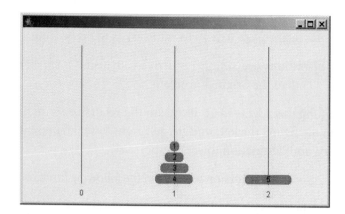

Figure 13.16
Position After Step 3

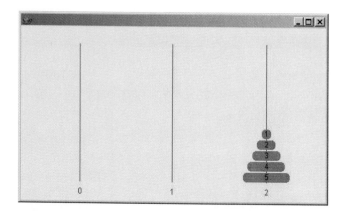

Instructions

In the Chapter 13 Programming Activity 2 directory on the CD-ROM accompanying this book, you will find the source files needed to complete this activity. Copy all of the files to a directory on your computer. Note that all files should be in the same directory.

Open the *HanoiClient.java* source file. Searching for five stars (*****) in the source code will position you to the code section where you will add your code. In this task, you will fill in the code inside the *recursiveTOfH* method to solve the Towers of Hanoi problem. Example 13.9 shows the section of the *HanoiClient* source code where you will add your code.

```java
public void recursiveTOfH( int numDisks, int fromTower,
                           int toTower, int useTower )
{
   // ***** Student writes the body of this method *****
   //
   // Using recursion, transfer numDisks disks from the tower
   // fromTower to the tower toTower using the tower
   // useTower

   // The disks are numbered as follows: if we started with n disks,
   //    the disk at the top is disk # 1
   //    and the disk at the bottom is disk # n

   // We call the moveDisk method inside the body of this method

   // The moveDisk method moves one disk and takes 3 arguments:
   //    an int, representing the disk number to be moved
   //    an int, representing the tower to move the disk from
   //    an int, representing the tower to move the disk to

   // So if these three variables are:
   //    diskNumber, fromTower, and toTower
   //    then the call to moveDisks will be:

   //    moveDisk( diskNumber, fromTower, toTower );

   if ( numDisks > 0 )
   {
```

```
// Student code starts here
// 1. Move ( numDisks - 1 ) disks from fromTower
//    to useTower using toTower

// 2. Move one disk from fromTower to toTower
//    Print a message to the screen, then
//    call moveDisk in order to animate.

// 3. Move ( numDisks - 1 ) disks from useTower to toTower
//    using fromTower

}

// Base case:  0 disks to move ==> do nothing

//
// end of student code
//
}
```

EXAMPLE 13.9   Location of Student Code in *HanoiClient*

The framework will animate your code so that you get some feedback on the correctness of your code. It will display the disks being moved from one tower to another until the whole set of disks has been moved from the left tower to the right tower. Code to enforce the rules has already been written.

To test your code, compile and run the application; when the program begins, a dialog box will prompt you for the number of disks as shown in Figure 13.17.

Click "Cancel" to exit the program; click "OK" to continue and animate your code.

If you enter an integer less than 1 or greater than 9, the program will use a default value of 4. If you enter 5, as shown in Figure 13.17, the first screen will be as shown in Figure 13.13. An intermediate position is shown in Figure 13.18.

Figure 13.17

Opening Dialog Box

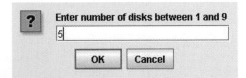

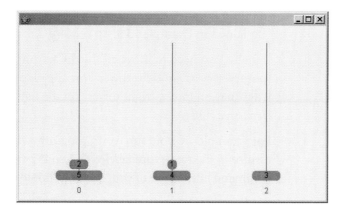

Figure 13.18
An Intermediate Position in the Animation

Task Instructions

- In the file *HanoiClient.java*, the *recursiveTOfH* method header is:

```
public void recursiveTOfH( int numDisks, int fromTower,
                      int toTower, int useTower )
```

This method takes four parameters: *numDisks*, representing the number of disks to be moved, and 3 *ints* representing the tower to move the disks from, the tower to move the disks to, and the tower to use to accomplish that task of moving *numDisks* disks from tower *fromTower* to tower *toTower*. For instance, with five disks, our method call in the *main* method is:

```
recursiveTOfH( 5, 0, 2, 1 );
```

The above method call is interpreted as: move 5 disks from tower 0 to tower 2, using tower 1 as a temporary holding tower.

- Your code goes in three places, all of them inside the *if* statement.

1. First, you need to move all the disks except the bottom one from the *fromTower* (source tower, "left tower" on the figures) to the *useTower* (temporary tower, "middle tower" on the figures) using the *toTower* ("destination tower, right tower" on the figures). You do this by calling *recursiveTOfH* with the appropriate arguments.

2. Then, you need to move the bottom disk from the *fromTower* (source tower, "left tower" on the figures) to the *toTower* (destination tower, "right tower" on the figures). To track your progress, output the move to the command line ("Move disk *x* from tower *y* to tower *z*"). You also need to call the *moveDisk*

method so that the code animates. The API of *moveDisk* is explained in Example 13.9.

3. Finally, you need to move all the disks from the *useTower* (temporary tower, "middle tower" on the figures) to the *toTower* (destination tower, "right tower" on the figures). Again, you call *recursiveTOfH*.

For example, if you run your program with three disks, and assuming the towers are labeled 0, 1, and 2 from left to right, the command line output of your method should read something like:

Move disk 1 from tower 0 to tower 2

Move disk 2 from tower 0 to tower 1

Move disk 1 from tower 2 to tower 1

Move disk 3 from tower 0 to tower 2

Move disk 1 from tower 1 to tower 0

Move disk 2 from tower 1 to tower 2

Move disk 1 from tower 0 to tower 2

Troubleshooting

If your method implementation does not animate or animates incorrectly, check these items:

- Check the feedback on the output to see if your code violates the rules.

- Verify that you coded the first recursive call correctly.

- Verify that you coded the second recursive call correctly.

DISCUSSION QUESTIONS ❓

1. What is the base case for the method?

2. As the number of disks increases, what happens to the time it takes for the method to run?

13.7   Animation Using Recursion

Sometimes, we want to animate an object on the screen by moving the object from one location to another. We could do this using a *for* loop by changing the starting *x* value of the object until we reach the destination location. A recursive solution to the same problem is to move the object one pixel, then move the object the rest of the distance.

Let's revisit the *Astronaut* class from Chapter 7. We will code one additional method in the *Astronaut* class: a recursive method that will move the astronaut from left to right a certain number of pixels. The number of pixels between the starting point and the end point, or distance to move, is a parameter of the method.

In the general case, when the distance is greater than or equal to 1, we draw the astronaut, move the *x* coordinate of the astronaut by 1 pixel to the right, and call the recursive method with the distance argument reduced by 1. Since the distance argument is reduced by 1, we are reducing the size of the problem.

As the distance argument decreases at every step, it will eventually reach 0. That is the base case. Thus, if the distance is negative or equal to 0, then we will not move the astronaut and the method does nothing.

The pseudocode for the general case, when the argument passed to the method is positive, is as follows:

```
draw the astronaut
erase the astronaut
increment sX, the starting x coordinate of the astronaut, by 1
call animateAstronautRecursive with the distance argument
    decreased by 1
```

Since the *draw* method is already coded, we use it to draw the astronaut each time our recursive method is called. Our recursive method is named *animateAstronautRecursive*. In Example 13.10, that method is coded at lines 17–35. The constructors and other methods of the *Astronaut* class are identical to those in Chapter 7.

Our *animateAstronautRecursive* method takes three parameters:

- *distance*, an *int*, the distance to move the astronaut
- *g*, a *Graphics* object reference, which represents the graphics context of the window
- *background*, a *Color* object reference, the background color of the window

At line 25, we test for the base case. If the distance is less than or equal to 0, we do nothing. Otherwise, we execute lines 27–32.

We first call the *draw* method to draw the astronaut, then pause for 100 milliseconds (1/10 of a second). At lines 29–30, we set the current color to the background color passed to the method, then erase the astronaut by filling a rectangle enclosing the astronaut with the background color. At line 31, we increment *sX* by 1. The next time we draw the astronaut—if we draw it—will be at a position one pixel to the right of the previous position. We make the recursive call to *animateAstronautRecursive* at line 32 with the distance decremented by 1.

```
1 /* An Astronaut Class
2    Anderson, Franceschi
3 */
4
5 import java.awt.Graphics;
6 import java.awt.Color;
7
8 public class Astronaut
9 {
10   // the starting (x,y) coordinate for the Astronaut
11   private int sX;
12   private int sY;
13   private double scale; // scaling factor, 1.0 is full size
14
15   // constructors and other methods, including draw, per Chapter 7
16
17   /** recursive horizontal animation method
18    *   @param    distance    the distance of the animation
19    *   @param    g           the Graphics context object
20    *   @param    background   the background color of the animation
21    */
22   public void animateAstronautRecursive
23              ( int distance, Graphics g, Color background )
24   {
25     if ( distance > 0 )
26     {
27       draw( g );
28       Pause.wait( 0.1 );
29       g.setColor( background );
30       g.fillRect( sX, sY, 270, 290 );
31       sX = sX + 1;
32       animateAstronautRecursive( distance - 1, g, background );
33     }
34     // if distance <= 0 do nothing
35   }
36 }
```

EXAMPLE 13.10 **The *Astronaut* Class**

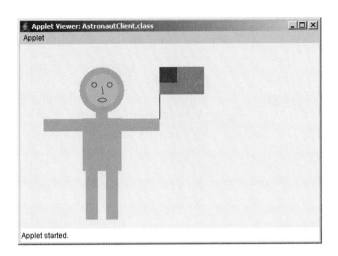

Figure 13.19
The Start of the Animation in Example 13.11

Now, we can create the applet class, which will be the *Astronaut* client. The applet has three instance variables: *contents*, a *Container* object reference; *astro*, an *Astronaut* object reference; and *width*, an *int*, which is the distance to move the astronaut. *Contents* represents the content pane of the applet. We will animate the astronaut horizontally over *width* number of pixels. To keep the example simple, we have initialized *width* to 100.

We call the *animateAstronautRecursive* method of the *Astronaut* class in the applet's *paint* method at lines 26–28. We want the background color of the animation to be the background color of the applet. Thus, the third argument passed to the *animateAstronautRecursive* method is the return value from *contents.getBackground( )*.

The method draws the astronaut, erases it, draws it again, erases it again, ... so the last step is to erase it. We call the *draw* method at line 29 so that the astronaut displays in the applet window after the animation finishes.

Example 13.11 shows the *AstronautClient* applet class. Its output is shown in Figures 13.19 and 13.20.

```
1 /* Astronaut client
2    Anderson, Franceschi
3 */
4
5 import javax.swing.JApplet;
6 import java.awt.Graphics;
7 import java.awt.Container;
8
9 public class AstronautClient extends JApplet
```

Figure 13.20

The End of the Animation from Example 13.11

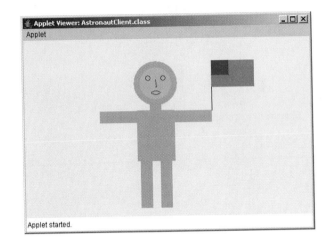

```
10 {
11   private Container contents;
12   private Astronaut astro;
13   private int width = 100; // width of the horizontal animation
14
15   public void init( )
16   {
17     // instantiate the Astronaut object
18     astro = new Astronaut( 0, 0, 1.0 );
19     contents = getContentPane( );
20     contents.setSize( 500, 300 );
21   }
22
23   public void paint( Graphics g )
24   {
25     super.paint( g );
26     // animate the astronaut over the current background
27     astro.animateAstronautRecursive
28             ( width, g, contents.getBackground( ) );
29     astro.draw( g );
30   }
31 }
```

EXAMPLE 13.11   The *AstronautClient* Applet

13.8   Recursion Versus Iteration

Recursion and iteration are different approaches to solving a problem.

- A recursive function is implemented using decision constructs (e.g., *if/else* statements) and repeatedly calls itself.

- An iterative function is implemented with looping constructs (e.g., *while* or *for* statements) and repeatedly executes the loop.

Most programmers would not use recursion to print "Hello World" *n* times; they would simply use the following *for* loop:

```
for ( int i = 0; i < n; i++ )
    System.out.println( "Hello World" );
```

Similarly, a factorial method can easily be coded using iteration.

However, other problems, such as the Towers of Hanoi and the binary search, are more easily coded using recursion rather than iteration.

Often, the recursive solution to a problem is more elegant and easier to understand than an equivalent iterative solution. The main difficulty in coding a recursive method is the problem-solving part. The implementation, using Java or any other programming language, is easier than the equivalent code that uses iteration.

Another consideration when deciding to use recursion or iteration is the efficiency of the method at execution time. This is called the running time of the method, and is often measured in order of magnitude as a function of the size of the input.

For instance, for the Hello World example, the input is *n*. Using iteration, we will execute the loop *n* times, and the test condition of the *for* statement will be executed $(n + 1)$ times. When the running time of a method can be expressed as *n* multiplied by a constant value $(n \times c)$, we say that the order of magnitude of its running time is *n*; we say it is "big-Oh" of *n* or *O(n)*.

Using recursion, and considering Example 13.1, the *printHelloWorld-NTimes* method will call itself *n* times before reaching the base case $(n = 0)$, for which the method does nothing. At each recursive call, the method performs a small and finite number of operations: it tests for *n* being greater than 0, and then prints "Hello World" once before calling itself; so it performs two operations before calling itself. Since it calls itself *n* times overall, the approximate running time of the method is $2 * n$, and therefore the order of magnitude of its running time is also *O(n)* (orders of magnitude ignore constant factors).

So in this case, the running times of iteration and recursion are of the same order of magnitude. However, the overhead associated with all the recursive method calls will add to the running time. That will make recursion slower than iteration, which is often the case.

 **SOFTWARE ENGINEERING TIP**

Readability and maintenance are important considerations when coding a method. If running times are equivalent and a recursion implementation is easier to understand than the equivalent iteration implementation, choose recursion over iteration, otherwise, iteration is generally preferred.

13.9   Chapter Summary

- The idea of recursion is to convert or reduce a bigger problem to a smaller, similar problem. The relationship between the bigger problem and the smaller problem is called the general case.

- By reducing the size of a problem to a smaller problem recursively, we eventually arrive at a small problem that is easy to solve. That small problem is called the base case.

- Solving a problem using recursion typically involves coding a recursive method.

- A recursive method
  - can be a *static* method or an instance method,
  - can take 0, 1, or more parameters,
  - and can be a *void* or a value-returning method.

- A recursive method calls itself.

- Problem solving using recursion involves two steps: generating a recursive formulation of the problem for the general case, and solving the base case(s).

- There can be one or more base cases.

- Most base cases are simple, but some can be more complex.

- Most general cases are simple, but some can be more complex.

- A recursive method calls itself repeatedly until a base case is reached.

- A recursive method typically includes an *if/else* statement that tests for the base case.

- If the recursive method does not test for the base case, calling the method will typically result in a stack overflow run-time error.

- Recursion is typically an alternative to iteration. The coding of a recursive method is typically compact and elegant. However, a recursive method may not be as efficient as its iterative equivalent.

13.10   Exercises, Problems, and Projects

13.10.1   Multiple Choice Exercises

1. A recursive method
   - ❏ is always a *static* method
   - ❏ is never a *static* method
   - ❏ may or may not be *static*

2. A recursive method
   - ❏ is always a method with a *void* return value
   - ❏ is always a value-returning method
   - ❏ can be either of the above

3. When formulating a recursive solution, what should you consider?
   - ❏ base cases and general case
   - ❏ base cases only
   - ❏ general case only

4. A recursive method
   - ❏ is a method containing a loop
   - ❏ calls itself
   - ❏ is part of the *java.recursion* package

5. When coding a class that includes a recursive method, we need to import the *java.recursion* package.
   - ❏ true
   - ❏ false

6. If the base case of a recursive method is not taken into account when coding the method, the likely outcome is
   - ❏ a compiler error
   - ❏ a run-time error
   - ❏ no error

7. If there are several base cases in a recursive method, omitting the code for one of them will result in

   ❏ a compiler error

   ❏ a run-time error

   ❏ no error

8. If a recursive method makes a recursive call with the same argument that it was passed, the likely outcome is

   ❏ a compiler error

   ❏ a run-time error

   ❏ no error

13.10.2 Reading and Understanding Code

For questions 9 to 11, consider the following method:

```
public static int foo1( int n )
{
  if ( n == 0 )
    return 0;
  else if ( n > 0 )
    return foo1( n - 1 );
  else
    return foo1( n + 1 );
}
```

9. What is the value of i after the following code is executed?

   ```
   int i = foo1( 0 );
   ```

10. What is the value of i after the following code is executed?

   ```
   int i = foo1( 4 );
   ```

11. What does the *foo1* method do?

   For questions 12 to 15, consider the following method:

   ```
   public static int foo2( int n )
   {
     // n is guaranteed to be >= 0
     if ( n < 10 )
       return n;
     else
       return foo2( n - 10 );
   }
   ```

12. What is the value of *i* after the following code is executed?

```
int i = foo2( 7 );
```

13. What is the value of *i* after the following code is executed?

```
int i = foo2( 13 );
```

14. What is the value of *i* after the following code is executed?

```
int i = foo2( 65 );
```

15. What does the *foo2* method return when the argument is a positive integer?

For questions 16 to 19, consider the following method:

```
public static void foo3( String s )
{
  if ( s.length( ) > 0 )
  {
    System.out.print( s.charAt( s.length( ) - 1 ) );
    foo3( s.substring( 0, s.length( ) - 1 ) );
  }
}
```

16. What is the output of the following code?

```
foo3( "" );
```

17. What is the output of the following code?

```
foo3( "Hi" );
```

18. What is the output of the following code?

```
foo3( "Hello" );
```

19. What does the *foo3* method do?

For questions 20 to 23, consider the following method:

```
public static int foo4( int n, int p )
{
  // p is guaranteed to be >= 0
  if ( p == 0 )
    return 1;
  else
    return ( n * foo4( n, p - 1 ) );
}
```

20. What is the value of *i* after the following code is executed?

```
int i = foo4( 6, 0 );
```

21. What is the value of *i* after the following code is executed?

```
int i = foo4( 5, 1 );
```

22. What is the value of *i* after the following code is executed?

```
int i = foo4( 4, 3 );
```

23. What does the *foo4* method return as a function of its two parameters, *n* and *p*?

13.10.3   Fill in the Code

24. This recursive method returns the number of times a given character is found in a *String*:

```
public static int foo( String s, char c )
{
   if ( s.length( ) == 0 )
      return 0;
   else
   {
      // your code goes here

   }
}
```

25. This recursive method returns "even" if the length of a given *String* is even, and "odd" if the length of the *String* is odd.

```
public static String foo( String s )
{
   if ( s.length( ) == 0 )
         return "even";
   else if ( s.length( ) == 1 )
         return "odd";
   else
         // your code goes here
}
```

26. This recursive method returns the sum of all the integers from 0 to a given number.

```
public static int foo( int n )
{
   // n is guaranteed to be >= 0
   if ( n == 0 )
         return 0;
   else
```

```
{
   // your code goes here

}
}
```

27. This recursive method returns *true* if its *String* parameter contains the characters *A* and *B* in consecutive locations; otherwise, it returns *false*.

```
public static boolean foo( String s )
{
   if (        )              // base case # 1

   else if (        )      // base case # 2

   else                     // general case
      return foo( s.substring( 1, s.length( ) ) );
}
```

28. This recursive method squares a number until the result is greater than or equal to 1000, then returns the result. For instance, *foo(10)* returns 10000, *foo(6)* returns 1296, and *foo(1233)* returns 1233.

```
public static int foo( int n )
{
   // n is guaranteed to be greater than 1
   if ( n >= 1000 )           // base case

   else                       // general case

}
```

13.10.4   Identifying Errors in Code

29. You coded the following in the file *Test.java*. Where is the error?

```
int p = foo( 4 );
System.out.println( foo( 5, p ) );
// more code here

public static int foo( int n )
{
   int p = foo( n - 1 );
   if ( n == 0 )
      return 1;
   else
      return ( n * p );
}
```

30. You coded the following method. Where is the error?

```
public static double foo( int n )
{
 if ( n == 0 )
   return 1.0;
 else if ( n < 0 )
   return foo( n - 1 );
 else
   return foo( n + 1 );
}
```

31. You coded the following method. Where is the error?

```
public static boolean foo( int n )
{
 // n is guaranteed to be >= 0
 if ( n == 0 )
   return true;
 else
   foo( n - 1 );
}
```

32. You coded the following method. Where is the error?

```
public static boolean foo( int n )
{
 // n is guaranteed to be >= 0
 if ( n == 0 )
   return true;
 else
   return foo( n );
}
```

13.10.5   Debugging Area

33. You coded the following in the file *Test.java*:

```
System.out.println( foo( 5 ) );
// more code here

public static int foo( int n )
{
 return ( n * foo( n - 1 ) );
}
```

The code compiles, but when it runs, you get the following message, repeated many times:

```
Exception in thread "main" java.lang.StackOverflowError
```

Explain what the problem is and how to fix it.

34. You coded the following in the file *Test.java*:

```
System.out.println( foo( 5 ) );
// more code here

public static int foo( int n )
{
  if ( n == 0 )
    return foo( 0 );
  else
    return ( n * foo( n - 1 ) );
}
```

The code compiles, but when it runs, you get the following message, repeated many times:

```
Exception in thread "main" java.lang.StackOverflowError
```

Explain what the problem is and how to fix it.

35. You coded the following in the file *Test.java*:

```
System.out.println( foo( 5 ) );
// more code here

public static int foo( int n )        // line 9
{
  if ( n == 0 )
    return 1;
  else
    System.out.println( n * foo( n - 1 ) );
}        // line 15
```

At compile time, you get the following error:

```
Test.java:15: missing return statement
}
^
1 error
```

Explain what the problem is and how to fix it.

36. You coded the following in the file *Test.java*:

```
System.out.println( foo( 5 ) );
// more code here

public static int foo( int n )
{
  if ( n == 0 )
    return 1;
  else
    return ( foo( n ) * ( n - 1 ) );
}
```

The code compiles, but when it runs, you get the following message, repeated many times, before finally stopping.

```
Exception in thread "main" java.lang.StackOverflowError
        at Test.foo(Test.java:15)
        at Test.foo(Test.java:15)
        at Test.foo(Test.java:15)
```

Explain what the problem is and how to fix it.

37. You coded the following in the file *Test.java*:

```
System.out.println( foo( "Hello" ) ); // line 6
// more code here

public static int foo( String s )     // line 9
{
  if ( s.length( ) == 0 )
    return 0;
  else
    return ( 1 +
      foo( s.substring( 0, s.length( ) - 2 ) ) ); // line 15
}
```

The code compiles, but when it runs, you get the following output:

```
Exception in thread "main" java.lang.StringIndexOutOfBoundsException:
String index out of range: -1
at java.lang.String.substring(String.java:1444)
        at Test.foo(Test.java:15)
        at Test.foo(Test.java:15)
        at Test.foo(Test.java:15)
        at Test.main(Test.java:6)
```

Explain what the problem is and how it happens.

38. You coded the following in the file *Test.java:*

```
System.out.println( foo( "Hello" ) ) ; // line 6
// more code here

public static int foo( String s )     // line 9
{
 if ( s.length( ) == 0 )              // line 11
   return 0;
 else
 {
   String temp = null;
   if ( s.length( ) > 1 )
       temp = s.substring( 0, s.length( ) – 1) ;
   return ( 1 + foo( temp ) ) ;       // line 18
 }
}
```

The code compiles, but when it runs, you get the following output:

```
Exception in thread "main" java.lang.NullPointerException
        at Test.foo(Test.java:11)
        at Test.foo(Test.java:18)
        at Test.foo(Test.java:18)
        at Test.foo(Test.java:18)
        at Test.foo(Test.java:18)
        at Test.foo(Test.java:18)
        at Test.main(Test.java:6)
```

Explain what the problem is and how to fix it.

13.10.6   Write a Short Program

39. Using recursion, write a program that takes a word as an input and outputs that word backwards.

40. Using recursion, write a program that keeps prompting the user for a word containing a $ character. As soon as the user inputs a word containing the $ character, you should output that word and your program will terminate.

41. Using recursion, write a program that takes a word as an input and outputs that word with all characters separated by a space.

42. Using recursion, write a program that takes a word as an input and outputs the number of times the letter *a* is found in that word.

43. Using recursion, write a program that takes an integer value as an input and outputs the Fibonacci value for that number. The Fibonacci value of a number is defined as follows:

```
Fib( 1 ) = 1
Fib( 2 ) = 1
Fib( n ) = Fib ( n – 1 ) + Fib( n – 2 ) for n >= 3
```

44. Using recursion, write a program that takes a positive number as an input and keeps dividing that number by 3 until the result is less than 1, at which time output that result.

45. Using recursion, write a program that takes 10 numbers as inputs and outputs the minimum of these numbers.

46. Using recursion, write a program that takes 10 words representing Internet addresses as inputs and outputs the number of words containing .edu.

47. Rewrite Example 13.8, *RecursiveBinarySearch*, using an array sorted in descending order.

13.10.7   Programming Projects

48. Write a class with just one instance variable, a *String* representing a binary number. Write a recursive method taking only one parameter that converts that binary number to its decimal equivalent. Your program should include a client class to test your class.

49. Write a class with just one instance variable, an *int*. Your constructor should take an *int* as its only parameter. Write a recursive method that checks if that *int* is a multiple of 5. Your program should include a client class to test your class.

50. Write a class with just one instance variable, a *String* representing some HTML code. Your constructor should take a file name as its only parameter (you will need to make up some sample HTML files to test your program). Write a recursive method returning the number of occurrences of a specified character in the HTML *String*. Your program should include a client class to test your class. In particular, call the recursive method to check whether the sample files contain an equal number of < and > characters.

51. Write a class with just one instance variable, a *String* representing a password. Write a recursive method to check if the password contains at least one character that is a digit (0 to 9). Your program should include a client class to test your class.

52. Write a class with two instance variables, representing the same password. Write a recursive method that checks if both passwords are equal. Your program should include a client class to test your class.

53. Write a class with two instance variables, representing an old password and a new password. Write a recursive method that returns the number of places where the two passwords have different characters. The passwords can have different lengths. Write another, non-recursive method returning whether the two passwords are sufficiently different. The method takes an *int* parameter indicating the minimum number of differences that qualify the passwords as being sufficiently different. Your program should include a client class to test your class.

54. Write a class with just one instance variable, an integer array. Your constructor should take an integer array as its only parameter. Write a recursive method that returns the sum of all elements in the array. Your program should include a client class to test your class.

55. Write a class with just one instance variable, an integer array. Your constructor should take an integer array as its only parameter. Write a recursive method that returns the maximum value of all the elements in the array. Your program should include a client class to test your class.

56. Write a class with the functionality of checking a list of names to determine whether the same name is present in two consecutive locations; you can assume that the list contains fewer than 100 names. The method solving that problem should be recursive. Your program should include a client class to test your class.

57. A professor has a policy to give at least one A in his or her class. Write a class that encapsulates that idea, including a recursive method checking for at least one A in a set of grades. You can assume that there are 30 students. Your program should include a client class to test your class.

58. Write a class with just one instance variable, an array representing grades between 0 and 100. You can assume that there are 15 grades.

Your constructor should take an array as its only parameter. Write a recursive method that returns the average of all grades. Your program should include a client class to test your class.

59. Write a class with just one instance variable, an *int*. Your constructor should take an *int* as its only parameter. Write a recursive method that converts that *int* to a *String* representing that number in binary. Your program should include a client class to test your class.

60. Write a class potentially representing a *String* of binary digits (0s and 1s). Your constructor should take a *String* as its only parameter (that *String* may contain only 0s and 1s, or it may not). Write a recursive method that checks whether that *String* contains 0s and 1s only. Write another recursive method that converts that *String* to its decimal equivalent. Your method should be different from the one in exercise 48: it should take two parameters, the *String* representing the binary number, and an *int* representing an exponent. Your program should include a client class to test your class.

61. Write a class with an *int* array as its only instance variable. Write a recursive method that uses the following recursive strategy in order to sort the array:

   ❏ Sort the left half of the array (this is a recursive call).

   ❏ Sort the right half of the array (this is another recursive call).

   ❏ Merge the two sorted halves of the array so that the array is sorted (there is no recursive call here).

62. Write an applet that shows a very small circle growing from small to large and then shrinking to its original size. Your applet should allow the user to input the minimum radius and the maximum radius (and also check that the minimum radius is smaller than the maximum radius). The expansion and contraction of the circle should be performed by two recursive methods.

13.10.8   Technical Writing

63. Think of an example of a problem, different from the chapter problems, which can be solved by an iterative formulation and a recursive formulation. Discuss which one you would prefer to code and why.

13.10.9   Group Project

64. Consider a rectangular grid of integers. We are interested in computing recursively the largest sum of any path from a top position to a bottom position. A valid path is defined as follows:

❑ It should start at a number in the top row and end at a number in the bottom row.

❑ It should include a number in every row.

❑ From row i to row ($i + 1$), a valid path can be created:

▪ down vertically (in the same column)

▪ down diagonally one column to the left (if possible)

▪ down diagonally one column to the right (if possible)

For instance, let's assume we have the following rectangle of numbers:

2	5	17	12	3
15	8	4	11	10
9	18	6	20	16
14	13	12	1	7

Note: In this example, we have selected numbers that are different in order to better illustrate the example; your program should accept any positive number at any spot within the rectangle.

Examples of valid paths are:

$2 \rightarrow 8 \rightarrow 18 \rightarrow 14$

$17 \rightarrow 4 \rightarrow 18 \rightarrow 14$

$5 \rightarrow 4 \rightarrow 20 \rightarrow 12$

In this example, the path generating the largest sum is:

$17 \rightarrow 11 \rightarrow 20 \rightarrow 12$ for a total of $17 + 11 + 20 + 12 = 60$

Your program should accept from the user a rectangle of integers; to keep it simple, you can limit the size of the rectangle to a maximum of 10 columns by 20 rows. Your program should, recursively, compute and output the path that generates the largest sum.

CHAPTER 14

An Introduction to Data Structures

CHAPTER CONTENTS

Introduction

As our programs execute, we often need a means to organize data in memory. In Chapters 8 and 9, we used arrays as a convenient method to store multiple variables of the same data type. In Chapter 9, we also introduced the *ArrayList* as an array that dynamically expands, as needed.

In fact, arrays and *ArrayLists* are just two examples of **data structures**, which are methodologies a program uses to store its data in memory.

An *ArrayList* dynamically adjusts its size by increasing its capacity by approximately 50% whenever it runs out of space. If an *ArrayList*'s current capacity is 640 objects, and it is full (that is, it holds 640 objects), adding one more object will cause its capacity to increase to 961 objects. If that 641st object is the last object added to the *ArrayList*, then memory space for 320 elements will have been allocated, but unused. Obviously, this is not an efficient use of memory space.

However, *ArrayLists* are useful in some situations, such as reading data from a file, where we don't know in advance how many items we will need to store in memory. Once the data is read, we know that the size of the *ArrayList* will not change further, so we can trim the capacity of the *ArrayList* to its current size using the *trimToSize* method, thus releasing the unused memory.

In other situations, however, the number of data items may dynamically increase or decrease as the program executes. For these cases, we need a data structure that efficiently grows and shrinks as items are added and removed.

A new data structure that we will illustrate in this chapter is the **linked list**, which can expand (or shrink) one object at a time, keeping the size of the list to a minimum at all times. An advantage, then, of linked lists is that they do not consume unnecessary memory.

14.1   Linked List

14.1.1   Linked-List Concepts and Structure

A **linked list** can be thought of as a chain of linked nodes.

A **node** is an object with two attributes:

- data—The data can be a primitive data type (for example, an *int*), or it can be a reference to an object of a specified class

- the location of the next node in the chain—We say that a node "**points to**," or "**refers to**" the next node.

Figure 14.1 shows how we can visualize a node containing the integer value 5. The arrow points to the next node in the list.

In the last node of the list, the location of the next node contains the value *null*, to indicate that there are no more nodes in the list.

Figure 14.1

A node

Figure 14.2 illustrates a linked list of four video game players. The object data stored at each node has the following attributes: the player's ID, the player's name, and the name of the player's favorite game.

From the standpoint of program design, this linked list can be implemented using three classes:

- a *Player* class, encapsulating a player
- a *PlayerNode* class, encapsulating a node
- a *List* class, encapsulating the linked list.

In the *Player* class, we will have three instance variables:

- an *int* storing the user ID of the player
- a *String* storing the name of the player
- a *String* storing the name of the player's favorite game.

Often, a node class is designed in a general manner to store a generic *Object*. Implementing a list of generic *Objects* has the advantage of reusability. Because every class inherits from the *Object* class, objects of any class could be stored in a node of this type. However, working with generic *Objects* makes the implementation more complex than working with objects of a specific class. Thus, we have chosen to implement a *PlayerNode* class, using a *Player* object, so that we can concentrate on the linked-list data structure.

In the *PlayerNode* class, we have two instance variables:

- a *Player* object reference
- a *PlayerNode* object reference, representing the next *PlayerNode*

Figure 14.2

A Linked List

Thus, the *PlayerNode* class is defined using an object reference of its own type. Indeed, one of its instance variables is a *PlayerNode* object reference.

We define our two instance variables using the following statements:

```
private Player player;
private PlayerNode next;
```

Based on this definition of the *PlayerNode* class, we need only one instance variable in the linked-list class, a reference to the first node, which we call the **head** of the linked list. Indeed, the first node will give us access to the second node, which in turn will give us access to the third node, and so on, until we reach the last node. We will know when we have reached the end of the linked list, because the reference to the next *PlayerNode* will have the value *null*.

Often, linked-list classes have another instance variable that holds the number of items in the linked list. Although the number of items can be calculated by looping through and counting all the nodes in the linked list, it is convenient to store the number of items as an instance variable. So our *PlayerLinkedList* class, encapsulating the linked list, will have two instance variables:

- a *PlayerNode* object reference, named *head*, representing the first node of the linked list

- an *int*, named *numberOfItems*, representing the number of items in the linked list

SOFTWARE ENGINEERING TIP

Include an instance variable in the linked-list class to store the number of items in the list for quick and direct access to that information as needed.

14.1.2   A Linked-List Shell

Since each node in our list will store a *Player*, we start by defining our *Player* class, shown in Example 14.1:

```
1 /* The Player Class
2    Anderson, Franceschi
3 */
4
5 public class Player
6 {
7    private int id;
8    private String name;
9    private String game;
10
11   public Player( int i, String n, String g )
```

```
12   {
13     id = i;
14     name = n;
15     game = g;
16   }
17
18   public int getID( )
19   {
20     return id;
21   }
22
23   public String getName( )
24   {
25     return name;
26   }
27
28   public String getGame( )
29   {
30     return game;
31   }
32
33   public void setID( int i )
34   {
35     id = i;
36   }
37
38   public void setName( String n )
39   {
40     name = n;
41   }
42
43   public void setGame( String g )
44   {
45     game = g;
46   }
47
48   public boolean equals( Player p )
49   {
50     return ( id == p.id && name.equals( p.name )
51              && game.equals( p.game ) );
52   }
53
54   public String toString( )
55   {
56     return ( "id: " + id + "\tname: "
```

```
57                    + name + "\tgame: " + game );
58    }
59 }
```

EXAMPLE 14.1   The *Player* class

The code for this class is straightforward. We declared the three instance variables, along with an overloaded constructor, accessors and mutators methods, and the standard *equals* and *toString* methods.

Example 14.2 shows our *PlayerNode* class:

```
 1 /* The PlayerNode class
 2    Anderson, Franceschi
 3 */
 4
 5 public class PlayerNode
 6 {
 7   private Player player;
 8   private PlayerNode next;
 9
10   public PlayerNode( )
11   {
12     player = null;
13     next = null;
14   }
15
16   public PlayerNode( Player p )
17   {
18     setPlayer( p );
19     next = null;
20   }
21
22   public Player getPlayer( )
23   {
24     return new Player
25         ( player.getID( ), player.getName( ), player.getGame( ) );
26   }
27
28   public PlayerNode getNext( )
29   {
30     return next;
31   }
32
33   public void setPlayer( Player p )
```

```
34  {
35    player = new Player( p.getID( ), p.getName( ), p.getGame( ) );
36  }
37
38  public void setNext( PlayerNode p )
39  {
40    next = p;
41  }
42 }
```

EXAMPLE 14.2   The *PlayerNode* class

The code for this class is also straightforward. We code two constructors at lines 10 to 20. The overloaded constructor allows the client to set the *Player* object, while the default constructor sets the reference for the *Player* object to *null*. Both of these constructors set the value of *next* to *null*. This will be the desired action when a node is created. However, to allow a client (which will be the linked-list class) to reset the value of *next* as the list expands and shrinks, we provide the *setNext* method.

For our class encapsulating a linked list, we need to consider the following issues:

- We anticipate having many linked-list classes. Therefore, it makes sense to set up a linked-list superclass from which our more specialized linked-list classes will inherit. We provide some basic utility methods, but we omit methods to insert or delete nodes in the list, because those methods will have different names and implementations, depending on the functionality of a given subclass. We do not intend to instantiate objects from our superclass; thus, we declare our superclass *abstract*.

- We also do not want client programs to change the head node of our list. Thus, we will not provide an accessor or a mutator for the head node.

- Client programs also should not be able to change the number of items in the list. Only the methods of the subclasses should update the number of items as we insert or delete items in the list. Thus, we provide an accessor for the number of items in the list so that the client can view the number of items, but no mutator.

Example 14.3 shows our *abstract ShellLinkedList* class. This class defines methods that will be common to all subclasses. For example, in addition to

TABLE 14.1   *ShellLinkedList* Methods

Constructor and Methods of the *Abstract ShellLinkedList* Class	
Class	**Constructor and argument list**
ShellLinkedList	ShellLinkedList( )
	constructs an empty list
Return value	**Method name and argument list**
int	getNumberOfItems( )
	returns the number of items in the list
boolean	isEmpty( )
	returns *true* if the list contains 0 items, *false* otherwise
String	toString( )
	returns the contents of every node in the list

the methods mentioned above, we provide a method to determine whether the list is empty and a *toString* method that can be used to print each node in the list. We declare both instance variables as *protected* so that our linked-list subclasses inherit the head and number of items in the list.

Table 14.1 shows the APIs of *ShellLinkedList* constructor and methods.

```
1 /* The ShellLinkedList class
2    Anderson, Franceschi
3 */
4
5 public abstract class ShellLinkedList
6 {
7    protected PlayerNode head;
8    protected int numberOfItems;
9
10    public ShellLinkedList( )
11    {
12       head = null;
13       numberOfItems = 0;
```

```
14   }
15
16   public int getNumberOfItems( )
17   {
18     return numberOfItems;
19   }
20
21   public boolean isEmpty( )
22   {
23     return ( numberOfItems == 0 );
24   }
25
26   public String toString( )
27   {
28     String listString = "";
29     PlayerNode current = head;
30     for ( int i = 0; i < numberOfItems; i++ )
31     {
32       listString += current.getPlayer( ).toString( ) + "\n";
33       current = current.getNext( );
34     }
35     return listString;
36   }
37 }
```

EXAMPLE 14.3   The *ShellLinkedList* class

We declare the object reference to the first node, *head*, and the count of the nodes, *numberOfItems* (lines 7–8). The default constructor, coded at lines 10 to 14, constructs an empty list, so we set the head node to *null* and the number of items to 0.

We coded the method *isEmpty* at lines 21 to 24. It returns *true* if the list is empty, *false* otherwise.

Finally, we coded the *toString* method at lines 26–36. Our *toString* method traverses the list and returns a *String* containing the contents of each object in the list. **Traversing** a list means looping through the nodes in the list, one after the other, starting at the first node. A *toString* method traversing the list is especially useful at the debugging stage, when we want to check if we properly added or deleted an element to the list. We can test our code by calling *toString* before and after such operations.

SOFTWARE ENGINEERING TIP

Do not include a mutator method for the number of items. Only the linked-list class should alter the number of items as items are inserted or deleted. Including a mutator method for the number of items could allow the client to corrupt its value.

SOFTWARE ENGINEERING TIP

Do not provide an accessor or mutator for the head node instance variable of the linked list. This will protect the head node from being accessed or changed outside the class.

SOFTWARE ENGINEERING TIP

Choose names for instance variables and methods that illustrate their function within the data structure. Your class will be easier for others and yourself to understand at maintenance time. Provide a *toString* method that traverses the list. This is helpful in testing the other methods of the class. In particular, traversing the list after calling the insert or delete methods can verify that an item was correctly added or removed.

14.1.3   Generating an Exception

Now that we have a shell class for a linked list, we want to add some methods to perform operations on the linked list, such as inserting or deleting elements.

An issue may arise with the return value of the *delete* method. When deleting a node, we want to return the item that we are deleting. Indeed, we want to be able to delete a node based on the value of one or more of the fields of the object stored at that node, that is, the value of one or more of the instance variables of the *Player* class. For example, if the client wants to delete the first *Player* on the list with an ID of 5, we would then return that *Player* object to the client. If the list is empty or we cannot find a *Player* with ID 5, we do not want to return *null* because the client likely will attempt to use the returned object reference. A solution to this problem is to *throw* an exception when we are unable to delete the requested node. To do this, we will create our own exception class, *DataStructureException*, which we will use throughout this chapter.

It is good practice to define your own exception class as a subclass of the *Exception* class. This way, your class inherits the existing functionality of the *Exception* class, which simplifies coding the new class: you need to code only the constructor.

Here is our *DataStructureException* class, which *extends* the *Exception* class.

```
 1 /* The DataStructureException Class
 2    Anderson, Franceschi
 3 */
 4
 5 public class DataStructureException extends Exception
 6 {
 7   public DataStructureException( String s )
 8   {
 9     super( s );
10   }
11 }
```

EXAMPLE 14.4   The *DataStructureException* class

The constructor for the class is coded at lines 7 to 10; it simply takes a *String* parameter and passes it to the superclass constructor. When one of our methods detects an error situation, such as an attempt to delete from an empty list, we will *throw* the exception using a statement like the following:

```
throw new DataStructureException( "Some error message here" );
```

The message we pass to the constructor will identify the type of error we detected.

The header of any method that *throws* the *DataStructureException* will look like

```
accessModifier dataType methodName( parameter list )
                    throws DataStructureException
```

Now we are ready to expand our shell linked-list class with more meaningful methods.

14.1.4   Other Methods of a Linked List

With a linked list, there is some basic functionality that we need to provide, such as

- insert an item

- delete an item

- retrieve, or **peek** at, the contents of a node

Table 14.2 shows the APIs of the *insert*, *delete*, and *peek* methods.

In our linked list of *Players*, we do not store the *Player* objects in any predetermined order. Thus, there are only two logical places to insert a node: at

REFERENCE POINT

Exceptions are discussed extensively in Chapter 11.

TABLE 14.2   *PlayerLinkedList* Methods

Methods of the *PlayerLinkedList* Class	
Return value	**Method name and argument list**
void	insert(Player p)
	inserts *Player p* at the beginning of the list
Player	delete(int searchID)
	returns and removes the first *Player* of the list with an ID equal to *searchID*. If there is no such Player on the list, the method *throws* a *DataStructureException*
Player	peek(int searchID)
	returns a copy of the first *Player* on the list whose ID is equal to *searchID*. If there is no such *Player* on the list, the method *throws* a *DataStructureException*

the beginning and at the end of the list. Inserting at the end will consume CPU time, since we will have to traverse the list to find the end. So we have decided to insert at the beginning of the linked list because it is easier and faster. Since it will always be possible to insert a new node at the beginning of a list, our *insert* method has a *void* return value.

Other options for implementing a linked list include providing methods to insert at the end of the list, or at a specified position in the list, or at a position before or after a node containing a specified object.

When inserting a new *Player*, our *insert* method performs the following steps:

1. Instantiate a new node containing the *Player* to be inserted.

2. Attach that node at the beginning of the list, that is, make that node point to the previous head node. If the list originally was empty and the previous head node has the value *null*, then the *next* field of the new node is given the value *null*.

3. Indicate that the new node is now the head of the list, that is, make *head* point to the new node.

4. Increase the number of items in the list by 1.

Figures 14.3a to 14.3d illustrate the first three steps above.

There are many alternatives for deleting an item from a linked list. We can delete the first element or the last item, or delete an item based on specified criteria. Such criteria can be the value of one (or several) instance variables of an item, or it can be the position of an item in the list. We will implement one *delete* method only: one that deletes an item based on a specified value of its *id* field. The implementation of a *delete* method that deletes an item based on a specified value of its *name* or *game* field is similar.

In order to delete an item, we will traverse the list searching for an item whose *id* matches a specified value passed as the argument of the *delete* method. If we find such an item, we will remove it from the list and return a reference to that item.

There are three possible outcomes when searching for such an item:

1. Such an item can be found and is located somewhere after the head node.

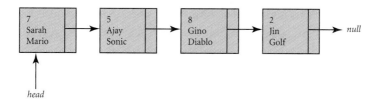

Figure 14.3a

Inserting: Our Original Linked List

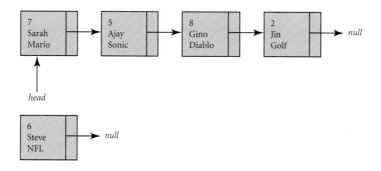

Figure 14.3b

Step 1: The New Node is Instantiated

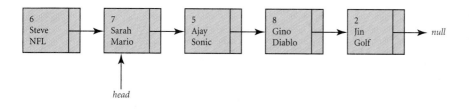

Figure 14.3c

Step 2: The New Node Has Been Attached to the Beginning of the List

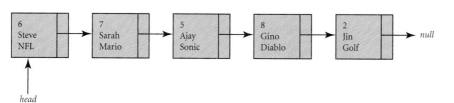

Figure 14.3d

Step 3: *head* Now Points to the New Node

2. Such an item can be found and is located at the head node. Special care must be taken here. There will be a change in the head node of the list and our code will need to reflect that.

3. Such an item cannot be found. In this case, no deletion can take place, so we will *throw* a *DataStructureException*.

In the first case, when the node to delete is located after the first node in the list, we need to connect the node before the deleted node (the "previous" node) to the node after the deleted node. To do this, we replace the previous node's *next* field with the *next* field of the deleted node. Thus, as we traverse the list, we need to keep track of the previous node, as well as the current node. To do this, we maintain two node references, *previous* and *current*.

Once we have located the node to delete (somewhere after the first node of the list), we perform the following steps:

1. Set the *next* field in the *previous* node to the *next* field in the node to be deleted (*current*).

2. Decrease the number of items in the list by 1.

The *current* node becomes unreachable and is therefore a candidate for garbage collection.

Figures 14.4a and 14.4b illustrate deleting a node with an *id* of 8, which is located somewhere in the middle of the list.

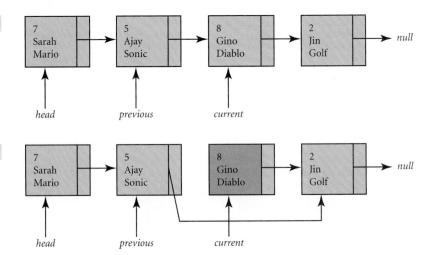

Figure 14.4a

The List Before Deleting the *Player* whose *id* is 8

Figure 14.4b

The *previous* Node is Connected to the Node After *current*, Deleting the *Player* whose *id* is 8

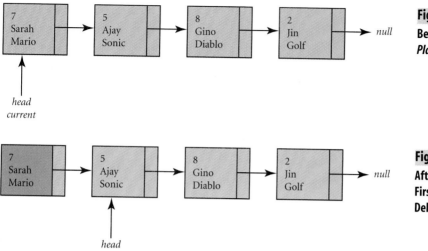

Figure 14.5a

Before Deleting the Player whose id is 7

Figure 14.5b

After Updating head, the First Node in the List is Deleted

When the node to delete is the head node, we need to make the node pointed to by the deleted node the new *head* of the list. Thus, we perform the following steps:

1. Assign the *next* field of the *current* node to *head*.

2. Decrease the number of items in the list by 1.

Figures 14.5a and 14.5b illustrate deleting the first node in the list.

Example 14.5 shows our *PlayerLinkedList* class. This class *extends* and inherits the functionality of our *ShellPlayerLinkedList* class.

 **REFERENCE POINT**

Inheritance is discussed extensively in Chapter 10.

```
 1 /* The PlayerLinkedList class
 2    Anderson, Franceschi
 3 */
 4
 5 public class PlayerLinkedList extends ShellLinkedList
 6 {
 7   // head and numberOfItems are inherited instance variables
 8
 9   public PlayerLinkedList( )
10   {
11     super( );
12   }
13
14   /** insert method
15    *   @param   p   Player object to insert
16    */
```

```
17   public void insert( Player p )
18   {
19     // insert as head
20     PlayerNode pn = new PlayerNode( p );
21     pn.setNext( head );
22     head = pn;
23     numberOfItems++;
24   }
25
26   /** delete method
27    *    @param    searchID    id of Player to delete
28    *    @return    the Player deleted
29    */
30   public Player delete( int searchID )
31                            throws DataStructureException
32   {
33     PlayerNode current = head;
34     PlayerNode previous = null;
35     while ( current != null
36            && current.getPlayer( ).getID( ) != searchID )
37     {
38       previous = current;
39       current = current.getNext( );
40     }
41
42     if ( current == null ) // not found
43         throw new DataStructureException( searchID
44                    + " not found: cannot be deleted" );
45     else
46     {
47       if ( current == head )
48         head = head.getNext( );   // delete head
49       else
50         previous.setNext( current.getNext( ) );
51
52       numberOfItems--;
53       return current.getPlayer( );
54     }
55   }
56
57   /** peek method
58    *    @param    searchID    id of Player to search for
59    *    @return    a copy of the Player found
60    */
61   public Player peek( int searchID )
```

```
62                   throws DataStructureException
63    {
64      PlayerNode current = head;
65      while ( current != null
66              && current.getPlayer( ).getID( ) != searchID )
67      {
68        current = current.getNext( );
69      }
70
71      if ( current == null ) // not found
72          throw new DataStructureException( searchID
73                      + " not found: cannot be deleted" );
74      else
75      {
76        return current.getPlayer( );
77      }
78    }
79 }
```

EXAMPLE 14.5   The *PlayerLinkedList* class

The default constructor (lines 9–12) calls the constructor of the superclass to initialize the *head* and *numberOfItems* instance variables. The *insert* method, coded from lines 14 to 24, inserts a node containing its *Player* parameter at the beginning of the list. At line 20, we create a new node *pn* with *Player* argument *p*. At line 21, we connect *pn* to the first node in the list by setting its *next* field to the current head of the list. At line 22, we assign the new node, *pn*, to *head*, making it the first node in the linked list. Figures 14.3a to 14.3d illustrate the impact on the list of lines 20–22. At line 23, we update *numberOfItems*, increasing its value by 1.

The *delete* method, coded from lines 26 to 55, returns the *Player* deleted if the deletion was successful and *throws* a *DataStructureException* if the deletion was not successful.

Using a *while* loop at lines 35–40, we first traverse the list searching for a node containing a *Player* object whose *id* has the same value as *searchID*, our *delete* method's parameter. At lines 33 and 34, we declare and initialize two *PlayerNode* references, which we will use to track the current and previous nodes as we traverse the list. A node points only to the next node in the list, so we can traverse the list in a forward direction only. Once we have reached a node, we do not have a way to backtrack to the previous node. Thus, as we traverse the list, we must remember the previous node by storing its reference in *previous*. We update *previous* and *current* at lines 38–39 by assigning *current* to *previous*, then moving *current* to the next node in the list by calling the *getNext* method.

Once we find a *Player* whose *id* field matches *searchID*, we will connect *previous* to the *PlayerNode* after *current*. If we have reached the end of the list, that is, *current* is *null* (line 35), or if we have found a *Player* whose *id* value is *searchID* (line 36), we are ready to either *throw* an exception or delete the node by updating the links in our list. At that point, we exit the *while* loop and skip to line 42.

As we step through the list, our *while* loop condition makes two checks. The first expression checks whether *current* is *null*, which indicates either that the list is empty or that we have reached the end of the list without finding a matching *id*. The second expression checks whether we have found the target *id*.

Note that the order of the expressions in the *while* loop condition is critical. Expressions in a compound condition are evaluated left to right, so (*current != null*) is evaluated first. If this expression is *false* (if *current* is *null*), then the whole *while* loop condition cannot evaluate to *true*, so the second expression is not evaluated. This is important because the second expression uses *current* to call the *getPlayer* method. If *current* is *null*, the evaluation of the second expression would generate a *NullPointerException*. In this way, we are taking advantage of short-circuit evaluation of logical AND operations.

COMMON ERROR TRAP

If a compound logical expression uses an object reference to call a method, check whether the object reference is *null* in the first expression

REFERENCE POINT

Short-circuit evaluation of logical expressions is discussed in Chapter 5.

If we reversed the order of the expressions in the *while* loop condition, as shown below,

```
// incorrect ordering of expressions!
while ( current.getPlayer( ).getID( ) != searchID
        && current != null )
```

reaching the end of the list would always generate a *NullPointerException*.

At line 42, we test whether *current* is *null*, because a *null* value indicates that we exited the *while* loop because the list is empty or we reached the end of the list (without finding a *Player* whose id is *searchID*). Either way, the deletion is unsuccessful and we *throw* a *DataStructureException* with an appropriate message at lines 43–44.

If *current* is not *null*, that means that we have found a *Player* whose id is *searchID*. We update the list and return the deleted *Player* at lines 47–53. If *current* is the head node, we found the *Player* at the beginning of the list, so we need to update the *head* instance variable. In this case, we assign the node after *head* to *head* at line 48. Note that if there was one element in the list before the deletion, *head* becomes null at that point (the list is empty then). Figures 14.5a and 14.5b show the impact of executing line 48 on the list (before and after).

If *current* is not the head node, we skip to line 50 where we set the node pointed to by *previous* to be the node after *current*. After line 50, *current* is no longer part of the linked list.

At line 52, we update *numberOfItems*, decreasing its value by 1. Finally, at line 53, we return the *Player* object reference stored in *current*, using the *getPlayer* method of the *PlayerNode* class. Figure 14.4a and 14.4b show the impact of executing line 50 on the list (before and after).

The *peek* method is coded at lines 57–78. We traverse the list in the same way as the *delete* method, except that because we will not delete a node, we do not need to mark the node before *current*.

If we do not find a node containing a *Player* whose id is *searchID*, we *throw* an exception at lines 72–73. If we find one, we return a copy of the *Player* object contained in that node at line 76.

14.1.5   Testing a Linked-List Class

Like any class that we design, we want to test the class before using it in a program. In particular, we should test two important methods: *insert* and *delete*. Furthermore, we want to test all possible scenarios.

Considering our *insert* method, which always inserts at the head of the list, we want to test a minimum of two situations:

- inserting into an empty list
- inserting into a nonempty list

As we will see later in the chapter, there are other types of linked lists and their *insert* methods may require more test cases than the ones mentioned above.

After each insertion, we can use the *toString* method to verify that the items were inserted correctly.

For the *delete* method, we should test the following scenarios:

- attempting to delete from an empty list
- deleting an item in the middle of the list
- deleting an item stored in the head node
- deleting an item stored in the last node in the list
- attempting to delete an item not in the list

COMMON ERROR TRAP

When traversing a list, always test if a node reference is *null* before calling a method using that reference. Failure to do so might result in a *NullPointerException* at run time. More generally, when coding a linked-list method, always pay attention to the possibility of an object reference being *null* before using that reference to call a method.

SOFTWARE ENGINEERING TIP

There are many ways to code the deletion of a node in the list. Try to write code that is easy to read and maintain.

SOFTWARE ENGINEERING TIP

Take care to avoid compromising the encapsulation of your linked list. Do not return an object reference to an item still on the list. Return a reference to a copy of that item.

After each deletion, we can use the *toString* method to check that the items were deleted correctly.

Example 14.6 shows a client program that tests the *PlayerLinkedList* class.

```java
1  /* The PlayerLinkedListTest class
2      Anderson, Franceschi
3  */
4
5  public class PlayerLinkedListTest
6  {
7    public static void main( String [ ] args )
8    {
9      Player p1 = new Player( 7,"Sarah","Mario" );
10     Player p2 = new Player( 2,"Jin","Golf" );
11     Player p3 = new Player( 5,"Ajay","Sonic" );
12
13     // construct empty PlayerLinkedList
14     PlayerLinkedList players = new PlayerLinkedList( );
15     System.out.println( "Number of items in the list: "
16       + players.getNumberOfItems( ) + "\n" + players.toString( ) );
17
18     players.insert( p1 );   // insert in empty list
19     System.out.println( "Number of items in the list: "
20       + players.getNumberOfItems( ) + "\n" + players.toString( ) );
21
22     players.insert( p2 );   // insert in list of one item
23     System.out.println( "Number of items in the list: "
24       + players.getNumberOfItems( ) + "\n" + players.toString( ) );
25
26     players.insert( p3 );   // insert in list of two items
27     System.out.println( "Number of items in the list: "
28       + players.getNumberOfItems( ) + "\n" + players.toString( ) );
29
30     Player temp;      // will be assigned the deleted item
31
32     try
33     {
34       temp = players.delete( 8 );      // unsuccessful
35       System.out.println( "Player deleted: " + temp );
36     }
37     catch ( DataStructureException dse1 )
38     {
39       System.out.println( dse1.getMessage( ) + "\n" );
40     }
41
```

```
42      try
43      {
44        temp = players.peek( 2 );        // test peek
45        System.out.println( "Player retrieved: " + temp );
46        System.out.println( "Number of items in the list: "
47         + players.getNumberOfItems( ) + "\n" + players.toString( ) );
48
49        temp = players.delete( 2 );      // delete in the middle
50        System.out.println( "Player deleted: " + temp );
51        System.out.println( "Number of items in the list: "
52         + players.getNumberOfItems( ) + "\n" + players.toString( ) );
53
54        temp = players.delete( 7 );      // delete the last item
55        System.out.println( "Player deleted: " + temp );
56        System.out.println( "Number of items in the list: "
57         + players.getNumberOfItems( ) + "\n" + players.toString( ) );
58
59        temp = players.delete( 5 );      // delete the first item
60        System.out.println( "Player deleted: " + temp );
61        System.out.println( "Number of items in the list: "
62         + players.getNumberOfItems( ) + "\n" + players.toString( ) );
63
64        temp = players.delete( 7 );      // delete from empty list
65        System.out.println( "Player deleted: " + temp );
66        System.out.println( "Number of items in the list: "
67         + players.getNumberOfItems( ) + "\n" + players.toString( ) );
68      }
69      catch ( DataStructureException dse2 )
70      {
71        System.out.println( dse2.getMessage( ) );
72      }
73    }
74 }
```

EXAMPLE 14.6   The *PlayerLinkedListTest* class

In this example, we instantiate three *Player* object references *p1*, *p2*, and *p3* at lines 9, 10, and 11. We instantiate the *PlayerLinkedList players* object reference at line 14, then traverse the empty list *players* at lines 15–16.

We successively insert *p1*, *p2*, and *p3* and traverse *players* after each insertion at lines 18–28.

After that, we test our *delete* method. Because our *delete* method *throws* a *DataStructureException*, we need to use *try* and *catch* blocks when calling that method.

Figure14.6
Output of Example 14.6

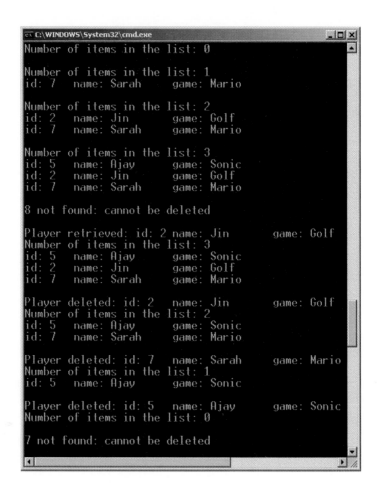

```
C:\WINDOWS\System32\cmd.exe

Number of items in the list: 0

Number of items in the list: 1
id: 7    name: Sarah      game: Mario

Number of items in the list: 2
id: 2    name: Jin        game: Golf
id: 7    name: Sarah      game: Mario

Number of items in the list: 3
id: 5    name: Ajay       game: Sonic
id: 2    name: Jin        game: Golf
id: 7    name: Sarah      game: Mario

8 not found: cannot be deleted

Player retrieved: id: 2 name: Jin          game: Golf
Number of items in the list: 3
id: 5    name: Ajay       game: Sonic
id: 2    name: Jin        game: Golf
id: 7    name: Sarah      game: Mario

Player deleted: id: 2    name: Jin          game: Golf
Number of items in the list: 2
id: 5    name: Ajay       game: Sonic
id: 7    name: Sarah      game: Mario

Player deleted: id: 7    name: Sarah       game: Mario
Number of items in the list: 1
id: 5    name: Ajay       game: Sonic

Player deleted: id: 5    name: Ajay        game: Sonic
Number of items in the list: 0

7 not found: cannot be deleted
```

At line 34, we attempt to delete an item in the list whose *id* is 8; we know this will fail, and as the output shows in Figure 14.6, we execute the *catch* block at line 37.

In the next *try* block, at line 44, we call the *peek* method to see if there is a *Player* whose *id* is 2. We traverse the list at lines 46–47 to verify that the list has not been modified by the call to *peek*.

 **SOFTWARE ENGINEERING TIP**

Testing all the methods in a linked list is critical to avoid errors at run time. Try to test all possible scenarios of all methods.

We then delete in the middle of the list at line 49, at the end of the list at line 54, and at the beginning of the list (actually the only item left at that point) at line 59. Another attempt to delete is made at line 64, but at that time the list is empty. This causes us to execute the second *catch* block at line 69, as shown in Figure 14.6.

CODE IN ACTION

To see a demonstration of linked-list methods, watch the Shockwave movie in the Chapter 14 directory of the CD-ROM accompanying this book. Double-click on the *LinkedLists.html* file to start the movie.

Skill Practice
with these end-of-chapter questions

14.12.2   Reading and Understanding Code

Questions 14, 15, 16, 17, 18, 19, 20, 21

14.12.3   Fill in the Code

Questions 22, 23, 24, 25, 26, 27, 28, 29, 30, 31, 32

14.12.4   Identifying Errors in Code

Questions 33, 34

14.12.5   Debugging Area

Questions 39, 40, 41, 42

14.12.6   Write a Short Program

Questions 43, 44, 45, 46, 47, 48, 49, 50, 51

14.12.8   Technical Writing

Question 70

14.2   Implementing a Stack Using a Linked List

Imagine a group of college students on a spring break, sharing an apartment. After they eat, they typically pile up the dirty dishes in the kitchen sink. Another meal is consumed, and more dirty dishes are piled on top of the existing ones. At the top of the pile is the dirty dish that was placed there last. Soon the students run out of clean dishes, and somebody will have to start cleaning them. He or she will start by cleaning the dish at the top of the pile, that is, the last dish placed on the pile. That approach is called **last in**, **first out**, or **LIFO**. With a last in, first out pattern, the object that was inserted last will be deleted first.

A **stack** is a linear data structure that organizes items in a last in, first out manner. Figure 14.7 shows a stack of trays. The tray at the top of the stack was put on the stack last, but will be taken off the stack first.

Figure 14.7
A Stack of Trays

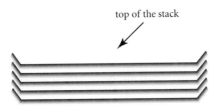

top of the stack

A stack can be represented by a linked list. In a linked list representing a stack:

- we insert, or **push**, at the beginning of the list
- we delete, or **pop**, the item at the beginning of the list

Since we insert and delete at the beginning of the list, the item deleted is the last one that was inserted, reflecting the LIFO pattern.

Table 14.3 shows the APIs of the *push*, *pop*, and *peek* methods.

The *push* method is identical to the insert method of the *PlayerLinkedList* class discussed earlier, and is illustrated in Figures 14.3a to 14.3d.

The *pop* method is different from the *delete* method we coded earlier in our *PlayerLinkedList* class. In a stack, we always delete the first item in the list. Therefore, in a linked list implementing a stack, we do not delete an item based on the value of one of its instance variables. The *pop* method for our stack returns a *Player* object, the one stored at the head of the linked list. If

TABLE 14.3   *PlayerStackLinkedList* Methods

Methods of the *PlayerStackLinkedList* Class	
Return value	**Method name and argument list**
void	push(Player p)
	inserts *Player p* at the top of the stack
Player	pop( )
	returns and removes the first *Player* of the list. If the list is empty, the method *throws* a *DataStructureException*.
Player	peek( )
	returns a copy of the first *Player* on the list without deleting it. If the list is empty, the method *throws* a *DataStructureException*.

A similar program to Example 14.6 can be coded to test all possible scenarios when using the methods of the *PlayerStackLinkedList* class. This is proposed in the short program section of the exercises.

14.3   Implementing a Queue Using a Linked List

Imagine a line of people at an automatic teller machine, or ATM, waiting to withdraw cash. The person at the front of the line is using the ATM. When a new customer arrives, the customer goes to the back of the line. As customers use the ATM, they exit the line, and the next customer moves to the front of the line. Thus, customers use the ATM in the order of their arrival times. We call this pattern "**first in**, **first out**," or **FIFO**.

A queue is a linear data structure that organizes items in a first in, first out manner.

Figure 14.8 shows a queue of people at an ATM. The person at the front of the queue arrived first and will use the ATM first. The person at the back arrived last and will use the ATM last. The next person to arrive will stand after the person currently at the back of the queue. That newly arrived person will become the new back of the line.

A queue can be represented by a linked list by providing the following operations:

- we insert, or **enqueue**, an item at the end of the list

- we delete, or **dequeue**, the item at the beginning of the list

- we *peek* at the item at the beginning of the list

Table 14.4 shows the APIs of the *enqueue*, *dequeue*, and *peek* methods.

back   front

Figure 14.8

A Queue of People Waiting at the ATM

TABLE 14.4 *PlayerQueueLinkedList* **Methods**

Methods of the *PlayerQueueLinkedList* Class	
Return value	**Method name and argument list**
void	enqueue(Player p)
	inserts *Player p* at the end of the list
Player	dequeue( )
	returns and removes the first *Player* from the list. If the list is empty, the method *throws a DataStructureException.*
Player	peek( )
	returns a copy of the first *Player* on the list, but does not delete the *Player*. If the list is empty, the method *throws a DataStructure-Exception.*

We can implement a queue using a linked list; however, we will make an important change. Because a queue inserts items at the end of the list, we will add an instance variable that represents the last node of the linked list. We call this the **tail reference**.

This way we will have direct access to the last node, without having to traverse the list. We will call that instance variable representing the last node in the list *tail*.

When inserting a new *Player*, our *insert* method will perform the following operations:

1. Instantiate a new node containing the *Player* to be inserted,

2. Attach that new node at the end of the list, i.e., make the last node in the list, *tail*, point to that new node,

3. Mark the new node so that it is the last node of the list, i.e., assign that node to *tail*,

4. Increase the number of items by 1.

Figures 14.9a to 14.9d illustrate the first three operations.

The *dequeue* method is identical to the *pop* method of a linked list implementing a stack.

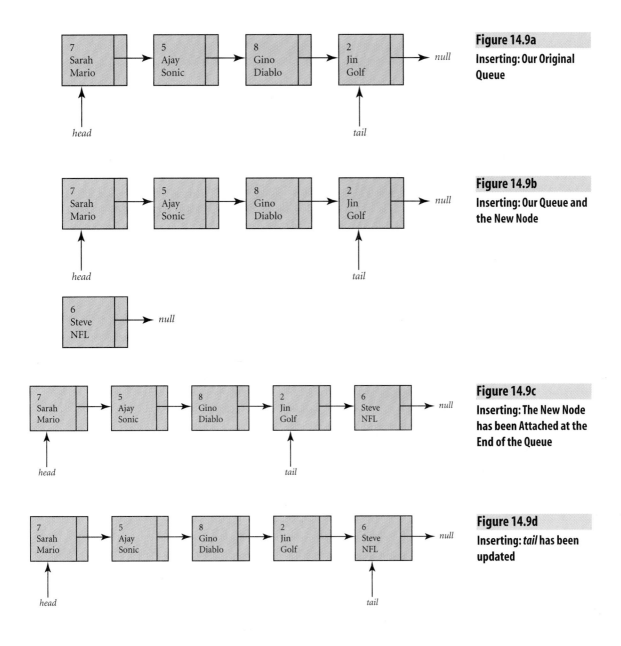

Figure 14.9a

Inserting: Our Original Queue

Figure 14.9b

Inserting: Our Queue and the New Node

Figure 14.9c

Inserting: The New Node has been Attached at the End of the Queue

Figure 14.9d

Inserting: *tail* has been updated

Example 14.8 shows our *PlayerQueueLinkedList* class. This class also *extends* and inherits the functionality of our *ShellPlayerLinkedList* class.

```
1 /* The PlayerQueueLinkedList class
2    Anderson, Franceschi
3 */
4
5 public class PlayerQueueLinkedList extends ShellLinkedList
6 {
7   // head and numberOfItems are inherited instance variables
8   private PlayerNode tail;  // last node
9
10   public PlayerQueueLinkedList( )
11   {
12     super( );
13     tail = null;
14   }
15
16   /** enqueue method
17    *   @param    p   Player object to insert
18    */
19   public void enqueue( Player p )
20   {
21     // insert as tail
22     PlayerNode pn = new PlayerNode( p );
23     if ( numberOfItems == 0 )
24     {
25       tail = pn;
26       head = pn;
27     }
28     else
29     {
30       tail.setNext( pn );
31       tail = pn;
32     }
33     numberOfItems++;
34   }
35
36   /** dequeue method
37    *   @return    p   the Player object deleted
38    */
39   public Player dequeue( ) throws DataStructureException
```

```
40    {
41      if ( numberOfItems == 0 )
42          throw new DataStructureException
43              ( "empty queue: cannot dequeue" );
44      else
45      {
46        Player deleted = head.getPlayer( );
47        head = head.getNext( );
48        numberOfItems--;
49        return deleted;
50      }
51    }
52
53    /** peek method
54    *    @return    p    the Player object retrieved
55    */
56    public Player peek( ) throws DataStructureException
57    {
58      if ( numberOfItems == 0 )
59          throw new DataStructureException
60              ( "empty queue: cannot peek" );
61      else
62      {
63        return head.getPlayer( );
64      }
65    }
66 }
```

EXAMPLE 14.8　The *PlayerQueueLinkedList* class

The constructor, from lines 10 to 14, calls the constructor of the superclass, and because it constructs an empty list, sets *tail* to *null*. The *dequeue* and *peek* methods are identical to the *pop* and *peek* methods of our *PlayerStack-LinkedList* class, except for the message passed to the *DataStructureException* constructor.

The *enqueue* method, which we coded at lines 16–34, inserts an item at the end of the list. We first instantiate a *PlayerNode* object reference named *pn* at line 22, using the parameter *Player p* of the *enqueue* method.

Because we insert at the end of the list, we must properly handle the case when the queue is empty, in which case *tail* is *null*. We test if the queue is empty at line 23. If it is, we assign *pn* to *head* and *tail* at lines 25 and 26. After we execute these two lines, the queue contains one element, and that element is both the first and last item in the queue.

If the list is not empty, control skips to line 30, where we attach *pn* at the end of the list by setting the *next* instance variable of *tail* to *pn*. We then assign *pn* to *tail* in order to reflect that *pn* is now the last node of the list. Finally, and in all cases (empty list or not), we increment *numberOfItems* by 1 at line 33.

Figures 14.9a to 14.9d show the impact on the list of executing lines 22, 30, and 31 step by step.

COMMON ERROR TRAP

Before inserting or deleting an item in a linked list representing a queue, always check if the linked list is empty. Not doing so results in a *NullPointerException* at run time.

It is important to test if a queue is empty when coding the *enqueue* method. Indeed, if the queue is empty, then both *head* and *tail* are *null*. The code

```
tail.setNext( pn )
```

at line 30 would, in this case, generate a *NullPointerException*.

A similar program to Example 14.6 can be coded to test all possible scenarios when using the methods of the *PlayerQueueLinkedList* class. This is proposed in the short program section of the exercises.

Skill Practice
with these end-of-chapter questions

14.12.1	Multiple Choice
	Questions 2, 3, 4, 5, 6, 7
14.12.6	Write a Short Program
	Questions 52, 53
14.12.8	Technical Writing
	Question 71

14.4   Array Representation of Stacks

Earlier in this chapter, we discussed how a stack can be represented by a linked list. Since a stack is a last in, first out data structure, we coded the *push* (insert) and *pop* (delete) methods of the linked list to insert or delete at the beginning of the list. Linked lists offer the advantage of being expandable one object at a time, so we do not have to worry about running out of capacity.

However, if we know in advance that the number of objects on a stack will always be less than some maximum number, we can represent the stack using an array, which is easier to implement.

Table 14.5 shows the APIs of the *push*, *pop*, and *peek* methods.

To match the LIFO functionality of a stack, we instantiate the array with the maximum number of elements. We add items to the stack starting at index 0, storing the items in adjacent locations in the array. To keep track of the array index of the last element inserted, we maintain an index **top**, short for "top of the stack." We always remove (*pop*) the item at the top of the stack.

To push an item onto the stack, we increment the value of *top* by 1 and store the element at the new *top* index. To pop an item from the stack, we return the item at index *top* and decrement the value of *top* by 1.

Figure 14.10a shows how we can visualize a stack of *Players*. Figure 14.10b and 14.10c show the stack after pushing a *Player* (6, *Steve*, *NFL*) and then

TABLE 14.5 *ArrayStack* Methods

Methods of the *ArrayStack* Class	
Return value	**Method name and argument list**
boolean	push(Player p)
	inserts *Player p* at the top of the stack, if the stack is not full. Returns *true* if the insertion was successful (that is, if the stack was not full before insertion); *false* otherwise.
Player	pop( )
	removes and returns the *Player* at the top of the stack, if the stack is not empty. If the stack is empty, the method *throws* a *DataStructureException*.
Player	peek( )
	returns a copy of the *Player* at the top of the stack if the stack is not empty. If the stack is empty, the method *throws* a *DataStructureException*.

Figure 14.10a

Our Original Stack

	index	*Player* object
top	2	(8, Gino, Diablo)
	1	(7, Sarah, Mario)
	0	(2, Jin, Golf)

Figure 14.10b

Our Stack After Inserting Player (6, Steve, NFL)

	index	*Player* object
top	3	(6, Steve, NFL)
	2	(8, Gino, Diablo)
	1	(7, Sarah, Mario)
	0	(2, Jin, Golf)

Figure 14.10c

Our Stack After Popping Once

	index	*Player* object
	3	(6, Steve, NFL)
top	2	(8, Gino, Diablo)
	1	(7, Sarah, Mario)
	0	(2, Jin, Golf)

popping one element. Figure 14.10c shows that the array element at index 3 is still *Player (6, Steve, NFL)*, but that is irrelevant. Since *top* has the value 2, the element at index 3 is not on the stack. When the next item is pushed onto the stack, we will reuse that element.

One disadvantage of implementing a stack with an array is that the array has a fixed size, and it is possible that the array can be filled completely with elements of the stack. Thus, our *push* method needs to test if the array is full before pushing an element onto the stack. Similarly, our *pop* method needs to test if the array is empty before popping an element from the stack.

Example 14.9 shows our *ArrayStack* class.

```
 1 /* The ArrayStack class
 2     Anderson, Franceschi
 3 */
 4
 5 public class ArrayStack
 6 {
 7   private static final int STACK_SIZE = 100; // maximum array size
 8   private Player [ ] stack;              // array of Player objects
 9   private int top;               // last used index; top of the stack
10
11   public ArrayStack( )
12   {
13     stack = new Player [STACK_SIZE];
14     top = -1; // stack is empty
15   }
16
17   /** push method
18    *   @param    p   Player object to insert
19    *   @return    true if insertion was successful false otherwise
20    */
21   public boolean push( Player p )
22   {
23     if ( !isFull( ) ) // is there room to insert?
24     {
25       stack[++top] = p;
26       return true;
27     }
28     else
29       return false;
30   }
31
32   /** pop method
33    *   @return    the Player deleted
34    */
35   public Player pop( ) throws DataStructureException
36   {
37     if ( !isEmpty( ) ) // is there an item to delete?
38       return ( stack[top--] );
39     else
40       throw new DataStructureException
41                   ( "Stack empty: cannot pop" );
42   }
```

```
43
44    /** peek method
45     *    @return   the Player at the top of the stack
46     */
47    public Player peek( ) throws DataStructureException
48    {
49      if ( !isEmpty( ) ) // stack is not empty
50        return new Player( stack[top].getID( ), stack[top].getName( ),
51                           stack[top].getGame( ) );
52      else
53        throw new DataStructureException
54                    ( "Stack empty: cannot peek" );
55    }
56
57    /** isEmpty method
58     *    @return   true if stack is empty, false otherwise
59     */
60    public boolean isEmpty( )
61    {
62      return ( top == -1 );
63    }
64
65    /** isFull method
66     *    @return   true if stack is full, false otherwise
67     */
68    public boolean isFull( )
69    {
70      return ( top == ( STACK_SIZE - 1 ) );
71    }
72
73    public String toString( )
74    {
75      String stackString = "";
76      for ( int i = top; i >= 0; i-- )
77        stackString += ( i + ": " + stack[i] + "\n" );
78      return stackString;
79    }
80  }
```

EXAMPLE 14.9   The *ArrayStack* class

We declare *STACK_SIZE*, *stack*, and *top*, our three fields at lines 7–9.

Stack is an array of *Players*. *STACK_SIZE* is the size of the array *stack*. *Top* represents the index of the element of the array *stack* that is at the top of the stack. The value of *top* will vary from *–1* (when the stack is empty) to *STACK_SIZE – 1* (when the stack is full).

In the default constructor, coded at lines 11–15, we instantiate *stack* and then set *top* to −1, which indicates that the stack is empty. When a client program pushes the first *Player* onto the stack, *top* will be incremented, so that the top of the stack will be the array element at index 0.

We coded the *push* method at lines 17–30. The *push* method returns *true* (line 26) if the stack is not full before we insert, and *false* (line 29) if it is, in which case we cannot insert. We test if the stack is not full at line 23. If it is not full, we use the prefix auto-increment operator to combine two operations at line 25: first increment *top* by 1, then assign *p*, the *Player* parameter of the *push* method, to the element at index *top*.

We coded the *pop* method at lines 32–42. The *pop* method attempts to delete and return a *Player* object from the top of the stack. The method *throws* a *DataStructureException* at lines 40–41 if the stack is empty, in which case we cannot pop. If it is not empty, we use the postfix auto-decrement operator to combine two operations at line 38: first return the *Player* stored at index *top* in the array *stack*, then decrement *top* by 1.

We have also coded a few other methods in this class. The *peek* method, at lines 44–55, is similar to *pop*, except that it does not delete from the stack and it returns a copy of the element at the top of the stack, rather than the element itself, preserving encapsulation. The *isEmpty* and *isFull* methods are coded at lines 57–63 and 65–71 respectively. And the *toString* method, coded at lines 73–79, returns a *String* representation of the contents of the stack. Note that in that method, we loop from *top* to 0, not from *STACK_SIZE – 1* to 0.

COMMON ERROR TRAP

Do not confuse the top of the stack with the last index in the array. Array elements with an index higher than *top* are not on the stack.

As before, a program similar to Example 14.6 can be coded to test all possible scenarios on the methods of the *ArrayStack* class. This is proposed in the short program section of the exercises.

14.5   Programming Activity 1: Writing Methods for a Stack Class

In this activity, you will work with a stack represented by an array, performing this activity:

> Code the *push* and *pop* methods to insert onto and delete from a stack represented by an array of *ints*.

The framework will animate your code to give you feedback on the correctness of your code. It will display the state of the stack at all times. The result of your operation will be displayed, reflecting the value returned by your *push* or *pop* method. The items in the stack will be displayed in black while the array elements that are not part of the stack will be displayed in red.

Instructions

Copy the contents of the Programming Activity 1 folder for this chapter on the CD-ROM accompanying this book onto a directory on your computer. Open the *StackArray.java* source file. Searching for five stars (*****) in the source code will position you to the code section where you will add your code.

In this task, you will fill in the code inside the methods *push* and *pop* to insert onto and delete from a stack. Example 14.10 shows the section of the *StackArray* source code where you will add your code. This example is different from the one in the chapter. The stack is an array of *ints*, not *Players*. The *isFull* and *isEmpty* methods have not been provided; you can code them or not, depending on how you want to implement the *push* and *pop* methods.

```
/** push method
 *    @param    value  value to be pushed onto the stack
 *    @return   true if successful, false if unsuccessful
 */
public boolean push( int value )
{
  // ***** 1. Student code starts here *****
  // stack is an int array instance variable representing
  // the array that stores our stack

  // top is an instance variable representing
  // the index of the top of the stack

  // CAPACITY is a static constant representing
  // the size of the array stack


  // The push method adds the argument value
  // to the top of the stack, if it is possible
  // code the push method here


  // end of student code, part 1
}
```

```
/** pop method
*    @return    the value of the top element of the stack, if
*               successful
*/
public int pop( ) throws DataStructureException
{
  // ***** 2. Student code restarts here *****
  // stack is an int array instance variable representing
  // the array that stores our stack

  // top is an instance variable representing
  // the index of the top of the stack

  // CAPACITY is a static constant representing
  // the size of the array stack

  // The pop method deletes the element
  // at the top of the stack, if it is possible
  // code the pop method here



  // end of student code, part 2
}
```

EXAMPLE 14.10   Location of Student Code in *StackArray*

To test your code, compile and run the application; the class *StackPractice* contains the *main* method. When the program begins, a window will display the state of the stack, along with two buttons labeled "push" and "pop," as shown in Figure 14.11.

Click on the "push" button to insert onto the stack. Click on the "pop" button to delete from the stack. Close the window to exit the program.

If you successively push 34, 56, 12, and 98 onto the stack, then pop once, the window will look like the one shown in Figure 14.12.

Troubleshooting

If your method implementation does not animate or animates incorrectly, check these items:

- Check the feedback in the window to see if your code gives the correct result.
- Verify that you updated the value of *top* correctly.

Figure 14.11

Opening Window

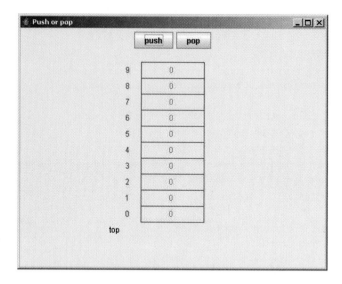

Figure 14.12

Sample Window After Performing Some Stack Operations

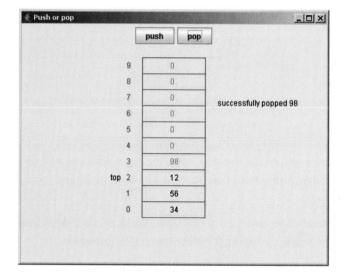

- Verify that you correctly coded the cases where the stack is full (*push* method) and the stack is empty (*pop* method).

1. Explain how the array elements above the index *top* can have assigned values, but are still irrelevant.

2. Explain what happens if you do not test whether the stack is empty in the *pop* method or full in the *push* method.

14.6   Array Representation of Queues

Earlier in this chapter, we also saw how a queue can be represented by a linked list. Again, if we know in advance that the number of objects in a queue will always be less than some maximum number, we can also use an array to represent the queue.

To match the FIFO functionality of a queue, we will need to keep track of two things:

1. the location of the back of the queue—This is the index of the last element added to the queue. We will call the index of that element *back*.

2. the location of the front of the queue—That is the index of the element that will be retrieved next. We will call the index of that element *front*.

The queue will be comprised of the elements whose indices are between *back* and *front*, inclusive.

To dequeue, or delete from the queue, we will return the item at index *front* and increase the value of *front* by one. To enqueue, or insert an element in the queue, we will increment the value of *back* by one, and insert the element at the array index *back*.

There is one important problem in representing a queue with a standard array: the number of available elements for the queue in the array will shrink over time as we enqueue and dequeue, since enqueueing and dequeueing both advance their indexes toward the end of the array.

To illustrate this point, let's consider a queue represented by an array of eight elements. We start by enqueueing five players in this order: (5, *Ajay, Sonic*), (2, *Jin, Golf*), (7, *Sarah, Mario*), (8, *Gino, Diablo*), and (6, *Steve, NFL*). Since (5, *Ajay, Sonic*) was the first to be inserted in the queue, that *Player* is now at the front of the queue. (6, *Steve, NFL*), inserted last, is at the back of the queue. Thus, (5, *Ajay, Sonic*) will be stored at index 0 and (6, *Steve, NFL*) will be stored at index 4, as shown in Figure 14.13a. Suppose now that we dequeue once. *Front* now has the value 1, as shown in Figure 14.13b. The array element at index 0 is no longer in the queue and its value is irrelevant. Since we insert at the back, the array element at index 0 can no longer be used for the queue. If we dequeue again, *front* will have the value 2, and we will no longer be able to use the array element at index 1. As we keep enqueueing and dequeueing, the values of *back* and *front* keep increasing and we have less and less usable space in the array. Indeed, when *back* reaches 7, we will no longer be able to enqueue at all.

Figure 14.13a

Our Queue After Enqueueing the First Five Elements

	index	*Player* object
	7	
	6	
	5	
back	4	(6, Steve, NFL)
	3	(8, Gino, Diablo)
	2	(7, Sarah, Mario)
	1	(2, Jin, Golf)
front	0	(5, Ajay, Sonic)

Figure 14.13b

Our Queue After Dequeueing Once

	index	*Player* object
	7	
	6	
	5	
back	4	(6, Steve, NFL)
	3	(8, Gino, Diablo)
	2	(7, Sarah, Mario)
front	1	(2, Jin, Golf)
	0	(5, Ajay, Sonic)

SOFTWARE ENGINEERING TIP

When implementing a queue as an array, think of it as a circular array.

There is a solution to this problem: it is to deal with the array as if it were circular. After *back* reaches the last index of the array, we start enqueueing again at index 0. Thus, in a circular array, the next index after the last array index is 0. Let's say that at one point the *back* marker reaches 7 and the *front* marker is at 5. When we enqueue a new object, we will store that object at index 0, which is the "next" index after 7 if we imagine that the array is circular. This way, our useful array capacity never shrinks and is always 8.

How do we know that we have reached the last array index and that the next index should be 0? We simply add 1 to the value of *back*, and then take that number modulo the size of the array, which we call QUEUE_SIZE.

Table 14.6 shows the APIs of the *enqueue* and *dequeue* methods.

Figure 14.14 illustrates a sequence of insertions and deletions in a queue of *Players* implemented as a circular array. When we begin, the queue is empty. The value of *front* is 0 and the value of *back* is *QUEUE_SIZE – 1*. When we enqueue the first item, that element is placed at index

```
( back + 1 ) % QUEUE_SIZE
```

TABLE 14.6 *ArrayQueue* Methods	
Methods of the *ArrayQueue* Class	
Return value	**Method name and argument list**
boolean	enqueue(Player p)
	inserts *Player p* at the back of the queue if the queue is not full. Returns *true* if the insertion was successful (queue was not full), *false* otherwise.
Player	dequeue( )
	returns and removes the *Player* at the front of the queue. If the queue is empty, the method *throws* a *DataStructureException*.
Player	peek( )
	returns a copy of the *Player* at the front of the queue. If the queue is empty, the method *throws* a *DataStructureException*.

which is now 0, and *back* will be given the value 0. If we enqueue again, the new element will be placed at index 1 and *back* will be given the value 1. If we enqueue two more items, they will be placed at indexes 2 and 3, respectively, and back will be given the value 3. If we then dequeue, we will return the item at index 0, and *front* will become 1. If we dequeue again, we will return the item at index 1, and *front* will become 2.

When we enqueue, we first need to check if the queue is full. When the queue is full, the relationship between *back* and *front* is:

```
( back + 1 - front ) % QUEUE_SIZE == 0
```

For example, in a full queue with 8 elements, the values of *front* and *back* could be 0 and 7, respectively, or they could be 5 and 4 or any other pair of values for which the expression above is *true*.

When we dequeue, we first need to check if the queue is empty. When the queue is empty, the relationship between *front* and *back* is the same as when the queue is full:

```
( back + 1 - front ) % QUEUE_SIZE == 0
```

Figure 14.14

Starting with an Empty Queue, Four Successive Insertions Followed by Two Deletions

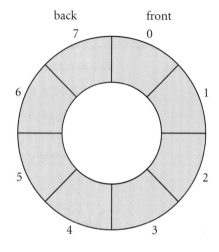

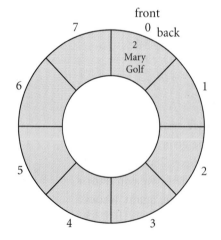

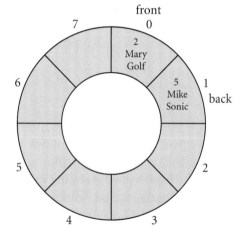

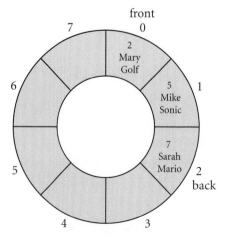

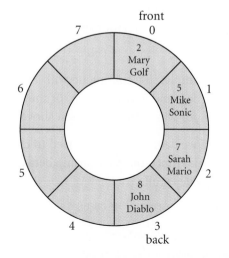

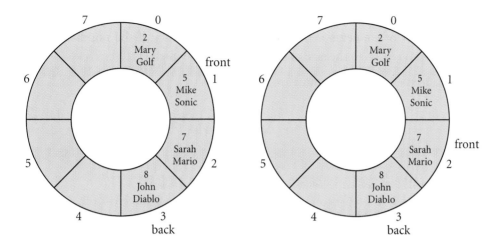

Figure 14.14
(continued)

Indeed, when there is only one item in the queue, *back* and *front* have the same index value. When we dequeue that last item from the queue, *front* will increase by 1 modulo *QUEUE_SIZE*, resulting in the above relationship between *front* and *back*. Figure 14.15 shows an example of an empty queue and a full queue.

So, how do we know if the queue is full or empty? In order to distinguish a full queue from an empty queue, we must add another instance variable to

COMMON ERROR TRAP

Do not confuse array indexes 0 and QUEUE_SIZE − 1 with *front* and *back*. In a queue represented by a circular array, the indexes 0 and QUEUE_SIZE − 1 are irrelevant.

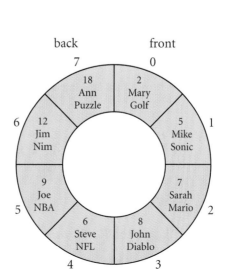

Figure 14.15

An Empty Queue and a Full Queue.

our class. We will keep track of the number of elements in the queue: if the number of elements is 0, then the queue is empty; if the number of elements is equal to the size of the array, then the queue is full.

Example 14.11 shows our *ArrayQueue* class.

```
1 /* The ArrayQueue class
2    Anderson, Franceschi
3 */
4
5 public class ArrayQueue
6 {
7    private static final int QUEUE_SIZE = 8;
8    private Player [ ] queue;
9    private int front;
10   private int back;
11   private int numberOfItems;
12
13   public ArrayQueue( )
14   {
15     queue = new Player[QUEUE_SIZE];
16     front = 0;
17     back = QUEUE_SIZE - 1;
18     numberOfItems = 0;
19   }
20
21   public boolean isFull( )
22   {
23     return ( numberOfItems == QUEUE_SIZE );
24   }
25
26   public boolean isEmpty( )
27   {
28     return ( numberOfItems == 0 );
29   }
30
31   /** enqueue method
32    *    @param    p    the Player to insert
33    *    @return   true if list is not full, false otherwise
34    */
35   public boolean enqueue( Player newPlayer )
36   {
37     if ( !isFull( ) )
38     {
```

```
39        queue[( back + 1 ) % QUEUE_SIZE] = newPlayer;
40        back = ( back + 1 ) % QUEUE_SIZE;
41        numberOfItems++;
42        return true;
43      }
44    else
45      return false;
46  }
47
48  /** dequeue method
49   *   @return      the Player deleted
50   */
51  public Player dequeue( ) throws DataStructureException
52  {
53    if ( !isEmpty( ) )
54    {
55      front = ( front + 1 ) % QUEUE_SIZE;
56      numberOfItems--;
57      return queue[( QUEUE_SIZE + front - 1 ) % QUEUE_SIZE];
58    }
59    else
60      throw new DataStructureException
61                  ( "Queue empty: cannot dequeue" );
62  }
63
64  /** toString method
65   *   @return    a front-to-back String representation of the queue
66   */
67  public String toString( )
68  {
69    String queueString = "";
70    if ( !isEmpty( ) )
71    {
72      if ( back >= front )
73      {
74        for ( int i = front; i <= back; i++ )
75          queueString += queue[i].toString( ) + "\n";
76      }
77      else
78      {
79        for ( int i = front; i < QUEUE_SIZE; i++ )
80          queueString += queue[i].toString( ) + "\n";
81        for ( int i = 0; i <= back; i++ )
82          queueString += queue[i].toString( ) + "\n";
83      }
```

```
84      }
85      return queueString;
86    }
87  }
```

EXAMPLE 14.11   The *ArrayQueue* class

In the constructor, coded at lines 13–19, we instantiate the array *queue*, set *front* to 0, *back* to *QUEUE_SIZE – 1*, and *numberOfItems* to 0. When the first element is inserted in the queue, *back* will be increased by 1 modulo *QUEUE_SIZE* and its value will become 0.

The *isFull* and *isEmpty* methods, coded at lines 21–24 and 26–29, enable a client program to check if the queue is full or empty before enqueueing or dequeueing a *Player*. Our *enqueue, dequeue,* and *toString* methods also call these methods.

In the *enqueue* method, coded at lines 31–46, we attempt to insert a *Player* into the queue. The *enqueue* method returns *false* if the queue is full (line 45) to indicate that we cannot insert. If the queue is not full, we place the *Player* at the back of the queue, update *back* accordingly, increment the number of items, and return *true* (lines 39–42).

In the *dequeue* method, coded at lines 48–62, we attempt to delete and return a *Player* from the front of the queue. The method *throws* a *DataStructureException* at lines 60–61 if the queue is empty, in which case there are no *Players* to delete. If the queue is not empty, we update *front*, decrement the number of items, and return the *Player* that was at the front of the queue (lines 55–57).

We could also code a *peek* method. It would be similar to the *peek* method we coded for the *StackArray* class, except that *top* would be replaced by *front*. Coding the *peek* method is included as an exercise at the end of the chapter.

The *toString* method, coded at lines 64–86, is more complex than the *toString* methods we have written so far. If the queue is not empty (line 70), we want to loop from *front* to *back* in order to build the *String* representation of the queue. With a circular queue, however, *back* is not always greater than *front*. Thus, we need to check where *back* is located in relation to *front*. If *back* is greater than or equal to *front*, we use a single *for* loop at lines 74–75 to loop from *front* to *back* as we build our *String* representation of

TABLE 14.7 Array Versus Linked List Implementation of a Stack or a Queue		
	Array	**Linked List**
Easily expanded	No	Yes
Direct access to every item	Yes	No
Easy to code	Yes	No

the queue. If *back* is less than *front*, however, we need to use two *for* loops: one to loop from *front* to the last array index, *QUEUE_SIZE − 1* (lines 79–80), and one to loop from 0 to *back* (lines 81–82).

As before, a very similar program to Example 14.6 can be coded to test all possible scenarios on the methods of the *ArrayQueue* class. This is proposed in the short program section of the exercises.

As we have demonstrated, a stack or queue can be implemented using either an array or a linked list. Each implementation has advantages and disadvantages. Arrays are easier to code and every item in the stack or queue can be accessed directly through its index. Linked lists are easily expanded one item at a time. To expand an array, we would need to instantiate a new, larger array and copy the elements of the existing stack or queue to the new array, which is quite tedious.

Table 14.7 summarizes these tradeoffs.

14.7   Sorted Linked Lists

Let's go back to our linked list of video game players. If we want to display that list on a Web site so that all the players can see it, we might want to display the list in ascending (or descending) order by *id* number, or in alphabetical order by name or game. If we store the items in the list in sorted order, we can display the list by simply calling the *toString* method.

The items can be sorted based on the values of one of their instance variables. Often, but not always, a class is designed so that one of the instance variables uniquely identifies an object: that instance variable is called a **key**. For the *Player* class, it is reasonable to assign a different *id* value to every *Player* object, and designate the *id* instance variable as the key.

A linked list that stores its nodes in ascending order (or descending order) according to a key value is called a **sorted linked list**. Without loss of generality, we will consider a linked list sorted in ascending order.

Table 14.8 shows the APIs of the *insert*, *delete*, and *peek* methods for a sorted linked list. The only difference in this API from that of our unsorted list is that the location for inserting an element is dependent on the key value, rather than always inserting at the beginning of the list.

By default, an empty list is sorted, so a newly instantiated list is sorted. As we add elements, we need to maintain the sorted order of the list. Thus, the *insert* method must locate the proper position for inserting each element so that the inserted element's *id* is greater than the *id* of the previous element (if any) and less than or equal to the *id* of the next element (if any). We will find that proper place by traversing the list, comparing the value of the *id* of the new *Player* with the values of the *ids* of the *Players* stored at the various nodes in the list.

If the value of the item to insert will place it at the beginning of the list, then we will insert it in the same manner as we did in our earlier examples.

TABLE 14.8   *PlayerSortedLinkedList* **Methods**

Methods of the *PlayerSortedLinkedList* Class	
Return value	**Method name and argument list**
void	insert(Player p)
	inserts *Player p* in a location that keeps the list sorted in ascending order
Player	delete(int searchID)
	returns and removes the first *Player* of the list with an *id* equal to *searchID*. If there is no such *Player* on the list, the method *throws* a *DataStructureException*.
Player	peek(int searchID)
	returns a copy of the first *Player* on the list whose *id* is equal to *searchID* without deleting the *Player*. If there is no such *Player* on the list, the method *throws* a *DataStructureException*.

When inserting a new *Player* in the middle or at the end of the list, our *insert* method will do the following:

1. Instantiate a new node containing the *Player* to be inserted.

2. Traverse the list to identify the location to insert the new node. We will call the node before the insertion point *previous*, and the node after the insertion point *current*.

3. Attach the new node to *current*, that is, make the new node point to *current*.

4. Attach *previous* to the new node, that is, make *previous* point to the new node.

5. Increase the number of items in the list by 1.

Figures 14.16a to 14.16d illustrate inserting a node somewhere in the middle of the sorted list.

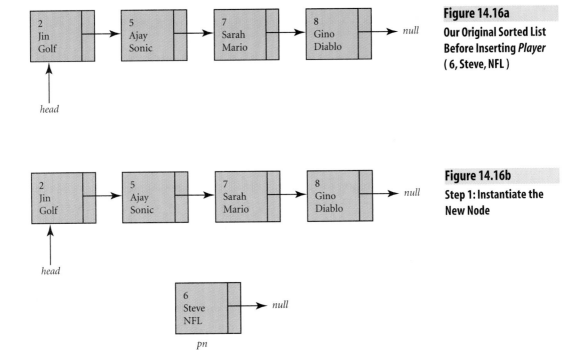

Figure 14.16a
Our Original Sorted List Before Inserting *Player* (6, Steve, NFL)

Figure 14.16b
Step 1: Instantiate the New Node

Figure 14.16c

Steps 2 and 3: Insert Occurs between _previous_ and _current_. Attach the New Node to _current_.

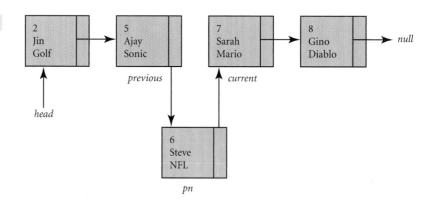

Figure 14.16d

Step 4: Attach _previous_ to the New Node.

The insertion code corresponding to Figures 14.16c and 14.16d is shown in Example 14.12 at lines 38–39.

Keeping the list in sorted order also impacts our _delete_ method. If the item we are looking for is not in the list, we may be able to determine that fact without traversing the entire list. As soon as we visit an item with a value greater than the key value, we know that the item we are looking for is not in the list. Because the list is sorted in ascending order, all the _Players_ stored after that node must have an _id_ value greater than the key. Thus, we will be able to exit our _delete_ method at this point, saving CPU time.

Example 14.12 shows our _PlayerSortedLinkedList_ class. This class also _extends_ and inherits the functionality of our _ShellPlayerLinkedList_ class.

The list is sorted in ascending order according to the value of each *Player*'s *id*.

```
 1 /* The PlayerSortedLinkedList class
 2    Anderson, Franceschi
 3 */
 4
 5 public class PlayerSortedLinkedList extends ShellLinkedList
 6 {
 7   // head and numberOfItems are inherited instance variables
 8
 9   public PlayerSortedLinkedList( )
10   {
11     super( );
12   }
13
14   /** insert method
15    *   @param    p   Player object to insert
16    */
17   public void insert( Player p )
18   {
19     PlayerNode pn = new PlayerNode( p );
20
21     // we will insert after previous and before current
22     PlayerNode current = head;
23     PlayerNode previous = null;
24     while ( current != null
25            && ( current.getPlayer( ) ).getID( ) < p.getID( ) )
26     {
27       previous = current;
28       current = current.getNext( );
29     }
30
31     if ( previous == null ) // insert as head
32     {
33       pn.setNext( head );
34       head = pn;
35     }
36     else
37     {
38       pn.setNext( current );
39       previous.setNext( pn );
40     }
```

```
41    numberOfItems++;
42  }
43
44  /** delete method
45   *   @param    searchID   id of Player to delete
46   *   @return   the Player deleted
47   */
48  public Player delete( int searchID )
49                      throws DataStructureException
50  {
51    PlayerNode current = head;
52    PlayerNode previous = null;
53    while ( current != null
54          && current.getPlayer( ).getID( ) != searchID )
55    {
56      if ( ( current.getPlayer( ) ).getID( ) > searchID )
57          throw new DataStructureException
58              ( searchID + " not found: cannot be deleted" );
59      previous = current;
60      current = current.getNext( );
61    }
62
63    if ( current == null ) // not found
64        throw new DataStructureException
65            ( searchID + " not found: cannot be deleted" );
66    else        // searchID found at Player at node current
67    {
68      if ( current == head )
69          head = head.getNext( );  // delete head
70      else
71          previous.setNext( current.getNext( ) );
72
73      numberOfItems--;
74      return current.getPlayer( );
75    }
76  }
77 }
```

EXAMPLE 14.12   The *PlayerSortedLinkedList* class

The *insert* method, which we coded at lines 14 to 42, inserts a node containing its *Player* parameter *p*. Line 19 declares and instantiates a *Play-*

erNode object, called *pn*, which we will insert in the linked list. To get ready to search for the insertion point for the new *Player*, we declare two *PlayerNode* object references, *current* and *previous*, at lines 22–23, and assign them *head* and *null*. We use *current* to traverse the list, going just past the point of insertion, and we use *previous* to track the node just before *current*. We will insert *pn* between *previous* and *current*. From lines 24 to 29, we use a *while* loop to traverse the list. We construct our *while* loop condition so that we will exit the loop if the list is empty or if we have reached the end of the list (we test if *current* is *null* at line 24), or if we are visiting a node containing a *Player* whose *id* is larger than or equal to the *id* value of *p*, the *Player* parameter of the *insert* method (line 25).

As mentioned earlier, there are two different cases for insertion: either we insert at the beginning of the list, or we insert in the middle or at the end of the list. At line 31 we test if *previous* is *null*, in which case we never entered the *while* loop because the list is empty or because the head node contains a *Player* whose *id* value is greater than *p*'s *id*. Either way, we insert at the beginning of the list at lines 33 and 34.

If *previous* is not *null*, we will insert in the middle of the list or at the end of the list. To insert the node *pn* between *previous* and *current*, we connect *pn* to *current* at line 38, and *previous* to *pn* at line 39. Figures 14.16a to 14.16d show the step-by-step impact of lines 19, 38, and 39 on the sorted linked list.

The *delete* method (lines 44–76) is very similar to the *delete* method of the *PlayerLinkedList* class. The only difference is at lines 56–58. We first test at line 56 if the *id* of the *Player* at *current* is greater than *searchID*. If that is *true*, we have no chance of finding a *Player* object with an *id* of *searchID* since the list is sorted in ascending order. Therefore, we *throw* a *DataStructureException* with an appropriate message, and we exit the method.

Let's test our *PlayerSortedLinkedList* class. In order to keep things simple, we will test the *insert* method only, because the *delete* method is, as discussed, almost identical to the *delete* method of the *PlayerLinkedList* class.

We want to test the following cases:

- insert in an empty list

- insert at the beginning of the list

- insert in the middle of the list

- insert at the end of the list.

We traverse the list after each insertion to check that the *Player* was inserted at the correct location in the sorted linked list.

Example 14.13 shows how to use the *PlayerSortedLinkedList* class and how to test its methods.

```
1 /* The PlayerSortedLinkedListTest class
2    Anderson, Franceschi
3 */
4
5 public class PlayerSortedLinkedListTest
6 {
7   public static void main( String [ ] args )
8   {
9     Player p1 = new Player( 7,"Sarah","Mario" );
10    Player p2 = new Player( 2,"Jin","Golf" );
11    Player p3 = new Player( 5,"Ajay","Sonic" );
12    Player p4 = new Player( 8,"Gino","Diablo" );
13
14    // construct empty PlayerSortedLinkedList
15    PlayerSortedLinkedList players =
16                  new PlayerSortedLinkedList( );
17
18    System.out.println( "Number of items in the list: "
19      + players.getNumberOfItems( ) + "\n" + players.toString( ) );
20
21    System.out.println( "inserting " + p1 );
22    players.insert( p1 );    // insert in empty list
23    System.out.println( "Number of items in the list: "
24      + players.getNumberOfItems( ) + "\n" + players.toString( ) );
25
26    System.out.println( "inserting " + p2 );
27    players.insert( p2 );    // insert at the beginning of the list
28    System.out.println( "Number of items in the list: "
29      + players.getNumberOfItems( ) + "\n" + players.toString( ) );
30
31    System.out.println( "inserting " + p3 );
```

```
32      players.insert( p3 );      // insert in the middle of the list
33      System.out.println( "Number of items in the list: "
34          + players.getNumberOfItems( ) + "\n" + players.toString( ) );
35
36      System.out.println( "inserting " + p4 );
37      players.insert( p4 );      // insert at the end of the list
38      System.out.println( "Number of items in the list: "
39          + players.getNumberOfItems( ) + "\n" + players.toString( ) );
40  }
41 }
```

EXAMPLE 14.13   The *PlayerSortedLinkedListTest* Class

In Example 14.13, we instantiate our usual four *Player* objects *p1*, *p2*, *p3*, and *p4* at lines 9–12. We chose the *id* values so that our four test cases will be covered when we successively insert the *Player* objects. We instantiate the *PlayerSortedLinkedList players* object at lines 14–16.

We first traverse the empty list at lines 18–19. Then, we successively insert *p1*, *p2*, *p3*, and *p4*, traversing the list after each insertion (lines 21–39). Figure 14.17 shows the output of Example 14.13. As we can see, *players* remains sorted in ascending order after each insertion.

Figure 14.17

Output of Example 14.13

CODE IN ACTION

To see the insertion and deletion process in a sorted linked list, watch the Shockwave movie in the Chapter 14 directory of the CD-ROM accompanying this book. Double-click on the *LinkedLists.html* file to start the movie.

14.8   Programming Activity 2: Writing *Insert* and *Delete* Methods for a Sorted Linked List

In this activity, you will work with a sorted linked list of integers, performing the following activity:

> Code the *insert* and *delete* methods to insert and delete nodes in a sorted linked list of *ints*.

The framework will animate your code to give you feedback on the correctness of your code. It will display the state of the sorted linked list at all times.

Instructions

Copy the contents of the Programming Activity 2 folder for this chapter on the CD-ROM accompanying this book onto a directory on your computer. Open the *LinkList.java* source file. Searching for five stars (*****) in the source code will position you to the code section where you will add your code.

In this task, you will fill in the code inside the *insert* and *delete* methods for a sorted linked list of integers. Example 14.14 shows the section of the *LinkList* source code where you will add your code. This example is different from the one presented earlier in the chapter. The linked list is an array of *ints*, not *Players*. The *delete* method returns a *boolean* value to indicate whether the deletion was successful. Since the client has already provided the *int* value to delete, there is no reason to return the value to the client.

You can first code the *insert* method and run the application. Once the *insert* method works properly, you can code the *delete* method and run the application again. We have provided a dummy *return* statement in the *delete* method so that the *LinkList.java* file will compile if only the *insert* method is coded. When you write the *delete* method, modify the dummy *return* statement to return the appropriate value.

```
public void insert( int i )
{
    // ***** Student writes the body of this method *****

    // code the insert method of a linked list of ints
    // the int to insert in the linked list is i

    // we call the animate method inside the body of this method
    // as you traverse the list looking for the place to insert,
    // call animate as follows:

    //    animate( head, current );
    // where    head is the instance variable head of the linked list
    //          current is the node that you are visiting

    // you can start coding now

    // in order to improve the animation (this is optional):
    // just before inserting, i.e., connecting the nodes,
    // make the call

    //    animate( head, previous, Visualizer.ACTION_INSERT_AFTER );

    // where    head is the instance variable head of the linked list
    //          previous is the node (not null) after which to insert

    // if you are inserting at the beginning of the list,
    // just before inserting, make the call

    //    animate( head, head, Visualizer.ACTION_INSERT_BEFORE );

    // where    head is the instance variable head of the linked list

    //
    // Student code starts here
    //

    //
    // End of student code, part 1
    //

    // call animate again with one argument, head,
    // to show the status of the list
    animate( head );
}
```

```
public boolean delete( int i )
{
  // ***** Student writes the body of this method *****

  // code the delete method of a linked list of ints
  // the int to delete in the linked list is i
  // if deletion is successful, return true
  // otherwise, return false

  // we call the animate method inside the body of this method
  // as you traverse the list looking for the node to delete,
  // call animate as follows:

  //    animate( head, current );

  // where    head is the instance variable head of the linked list
  //          current is the node that you are visiting

  // you can start coding now

  // in order to improve the animation (this is optional):
  // just before deleting, i.e., connecting the nodes,
  // make the call

  //    animate( head, current, Visualizer.ACTION_DELETE );

  // where    head is the instance variable head of the linked list
  //          current is the node that you are deleting

  //
  // Student code starts here
  //

  // call animate again to show the status of the list
  // if returning true
     animate( head ); //  draw the list

     return true;  //  replace this return statement
  //
  // End of student code, part 2
  //
}
```

EXAMPLE 14.14   Location of Student Code in *LinkList*

TABLE 14.9   API of the *Node* class

Constructors and Methods of the *Node* Class	
Constructors	
Class	**Constructor and argument list**
Node	Node(int i)
	constructs a new *Node* object whose *data* instance variable is *i*. The *Node* points to the value *null*.
Node	Node(int i, Node next)
	constructs a new *Node* object whose *data* instance variable is *i*. The *Node* points to *next*.
Methods	
Return value	**Method name and argument list**
void	setNext(Node next)
	sets the *Node* object reference pointed to by this *Node* to *next*.
void	setData(int i)
	sets the *data* instance variable to *i*.
Node	getNext( )
	returns an object reference to the *Node* pointed to by this *Node*.
int	getData( )
	returns the data stored in this *Node*.

When coding the *insert* and *delete* methods, you will need to use constructors and methods of the *Node* class. The API of the *Node* class is shown in Table 14.9.

To test your code, compile and run the *LinkedListPractice.java* file, which contains the *main* method. When the program begins, a window will display the state of the linked list (the list is empty when we start), along with various buttons labeled "insert," "delete," "traverse," "count," and "clear," as shown in Figure 14.18.

Figure 14.18

Opening Window

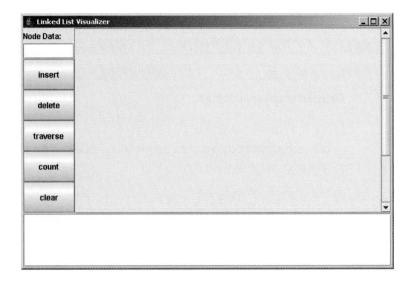

To insert or delete a value, type the integer into the text field labeled "Node Data," then click on the "insert" or "delete" button. The application only accepts integers greater than or equal to 0 and less than or equal to 9999; it will not let you enter characters that are not digits. The main panel will visually represent the sorted linked list. The text area at the bottom will give you feedback on your operations. Close the window to exit the program.

Figure 14.19 shows the application after successively inserting 45, 67, and 78, traversing the list, then deleting 67. The ground symbol on the second node indicates a *null* value for the *next* instance variable.

Figure 14.19

Sample Window after Performing Some Operations.

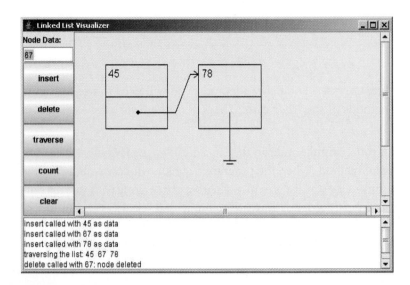

Troubleshooting

If your method implementation does not animate or animates incorrectly, check these items:

- Check the feedback in the window to see if your code gives the correct result.

- Verify that you correctly call *animate* inside the two methods (you may need to call *animate* more than once).

- Verify that you correctly coded both cases of the *insert* method: insert at the beginning and insert in the middle of the list.

- Verify that you correctly coded all the cases of the *delete* method: fail to delete, delete at the beginning, and delete in the middle or at the end of the list.

? DISCUSSION QUESTIONS

1. Explain why it is important to update *head* when inserting at the beginning of a list.

2. Explain the difference between deleting in a nonsorted list and deleting in a sorted list.

14.9   Doubly Linked Lists

So far, when traversing a linked list and looking for a node containing a particular value, we have used two nodes, which we called *previous* and *current*. We kept track of the *previous* node because we had no way to go backward in the list from the *current* node.

This problem can be solved by using a **doubly linked list**, which provides two links between nodes, one forward and one backward. Using the backward link, we can now backtrack from *current* if needed. The backward link is also represented by a node object reference.

Figure 14.20 shows how we can visualize such a node. The data in the node is 5, *Ajay*, and *Sonic*. The right arrow points to the next node and the left arrow points to the previous node.

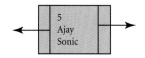

Figure 14.20
A Node with Two Links

In order to implement a doubly linked list, we need to modify our *Player-Node* class by adding a *previous* instance variable along with its accessor and mutator methods. Example 14.15 shows a summary of our revised *PlayerNode* class.

```
1  /* The PlayerNode class
2     Anderson, Franceschi
3  */
4
5  public class PlayerNode
6  {
7    private Player player;       // the player at that node
8    private PlayerNode next;     // the next PlayerNode
9    private PlayerNode previous; // the previous PlayerNode
10
11   // constructors
12   // accessors are getPlayer, getNext, getPrevious
13   // mutators are setPlayer, setNext, setPrevious
14 }
```

EXAMPLE 14.15   Summary of the *PlayerNode* Class for a Doubly Linked List

When inserting a node, we need to reset both forward and backward links, i.e., the *next* and *previous* instance variables. Suppose, for example, that we insert a node containing *Player p* before a node named *current*. We will illustrate only the general case, when *current* is in the middle or at the end of the doubly linked list, that is, *current* is neither *head* nor *null*.

The steps we need to perform are the following:

1. Instantiate the new node.

2. Attach the new node to *current* by setting its *next* field to *current*.

3. Attach the node before *current* to the new node by setting its *next* field to the new node.

4. Set *previous* in the new node to point to the node before *current*.

5. Set *previous* in *current* to point to the new node.

6. Add 1 to the number of items in the list.

Steps 2 and 3 set the forward links and Steps 4 and 5 set the backward links.

Figures 14.21a to 14.21f provide a step-by-step illustration of the steps for inserting a node in the middle of a doubly linked list. Note that we no longer need to keep a *previous* object reference, because we can get the location of the previous node from the *current* node.

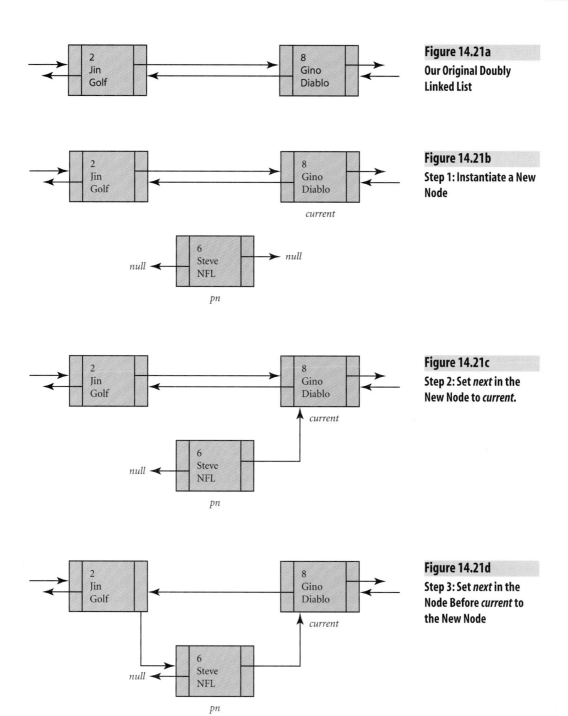

Figure 14.21a
Our Original Doubly Linked List

Figure 14.21b
Step 1: Instantiate a New Node

Figure 14.21c
Step 2: Set *next* in the New Node to *current*.

Figure 14.21d
Step 3: Set *next* in the Node Before *current* to the New Node

Figure 14.21e

Step 4: Set *previous* in the New Node to the Node Before *current*

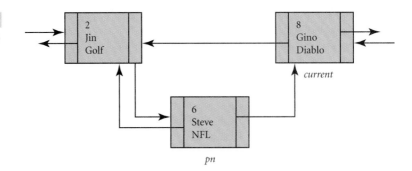

Figure 14.21f

Step 5. Set *previous* in *current* to the New Node

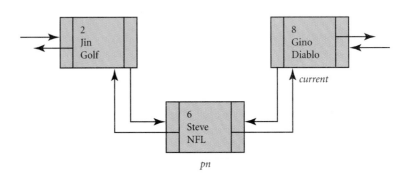

Our code updating the links inside the *insert* method of the doubly linked list class will be the following:

```
PlayerNode pn = new PlayerNode( p );              // Step 1
pn.setNext( current );                            // Step 2
( current.getPrevious( ) ).setNext( pn );         // Step 3
pn.setPrevious( current.getPrevious( ) );         // Step 4
current.setPrevious( pn );                        // Step 5
numberOfItems++;                                  // Step 6
```

The order in which these statements are executed is important. Indeed, if Step 5 were executed immediately after Step 1, we would overwrite the reference to the previous node. Then we could not access the node before *current*, and we would be unable to properly reset the links between the nodes.

Note that if *current* is either *head* (insert at the beginning) or *null* (insert at the end), the above code needs to be modified; that is proposed in the group project.

When deleting a node, we also need to reset all the appropriate forward and backward links. Suppose, for example, that we delete a node named *current*. We will illustrate only the general case, when *current* is in the middle of the

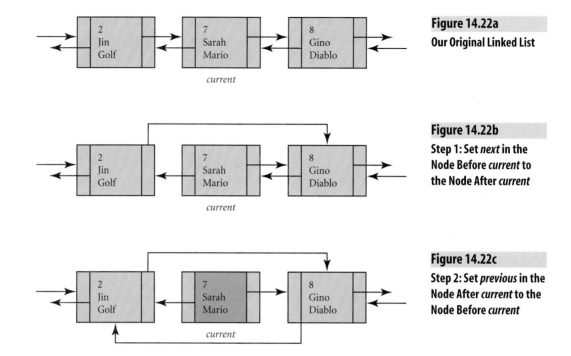

Figure 14.22a
Our Original Linked List

Figure 14.22b
Step 1: Set *next* in the Node Before *current* to the Node After *current*

Figure 14.22c
Step 2: Set *previous* in the Node After *current* to the Node Before *current*

doubly linked list. In this case, *current* is neither the *head* nor the last node in the list (since we are deleting *current*, we are assuming that *current* is not *null*), that is, there is a node after *current* in the list.

To delete a node, *current*, from the middle of a doubly linked list, we need to perform the following steps.

1. Set *next* in the node before *current* to the node after *current*.

2. Set *previous* in the node after *current* to the node before *current*.

3. Decrease the number of items by 1

Figures 14.22a to 14.22c give a step-by-step illustration of deleting a node.

Our code updating the links inside the *delete* method of the doubly linked list class is:

```
( current.getPrevious( ) ).setNext( current.getNext( ) );     // Step 1

( current.getNext( ) ).setPrevious( current.getPrevious( ) ); // Step 2

numberOfItems--;                                              // Step 3
```

Again, note that if *current* is either *head* or the last node in the list, the previous code would need to be modified; that is also proposed in the group project at the end of the chapter, which builds a sorted, doubly linked list.

14.10   Recursively Defined Linked Lists

REFERENCE POINT

Recursion is discussed extensively in Chapter 13.

A linked list can be defined recursively. A recursively defined linked list is made up of two items:

- *first*, an item, which is the first item in the linked list
- *rest*, a linked list, which consists of the rest of the linked list.

Figure 14.23 shows a representation of a recursively defined linked list.

In our recursively defined linked list, we have two instance variables: the item *first* and the linked list *rest*. Because we can access the rest of the list through the *rest* instance variable, we do not need the *PlayerNode* class.

In designing our class encapsulating a recursive linked list of *Player* objects, we will limit ourselves to an unsorted linked list. We will insert at the beginning of the list. When we delete, we will attempt to delete and return a *Player* object from the list based on the value of the *id* instance variable of that *Player* object. When we cannot delete, we will *throw* a *DataStructureException*.

Table 14.10 shows the APIs of the *insert* and *delete* methods.

After we insert, *first* will hold the item inserted, and *rest* will hold the original list. Figures 14.24a and 14.24b show a recursively defined linked list before and after inserting a *Player* named *p*. In the figures, *p1* represents the current first item, and *r1* represents the rest of the list before the insertion. The *insert* method is not recursive.

The *delete* method is recursive. We have three base cases:

- The list is empty.
- The element to delete is the first item of the list.
- The element to delete is not the first item of the list and the rest of the list is empty.

Figure 14.23

A Recursively Defined Linked List

first (an item)	rest (a linked list)

TABLE 14.10   *PlayerRecursiveLinkedList* Methods

Methods of the *PlayerRecursiveLinkedList* Class	
Return value	**Method name and argument list**
void	insert(Player p)
	inserts *Player p* at the beginning of the list.
Player	delete(int searchID)
	returns and removes the first *Player* of the list with an *id* equal to *searchID*. If there is no such *Player* in the list, the method *throws* a *DataStructureException*.

Figure 14.24a

The List Before Inserting Player p

Figure 14.24b

The List After Inserting Player p

In the general case, we try to delete the element from the rest of the list.

If the list is empty (the first base case), we will *throw* an exception. If the list is not empty, we will look at *first* and check to see if its *id* matches the parameter value. If it does (the second base case), we will delete *first*, and *rest* will become our list. If the *id* of *first* does not match the key value, then we will attempt to delete inside *rest*. If *rest* is *null*, we cannot delete (the third base case) and we will *throw* an exception. If *rest* is not *null*, we will make a recursive call to the *delete* method with *rest* (the general case).

More generally, we want to do the following:

- If the list is empty (base case #1), the method returns.
- Process *first*, that is, the first element in the list (base case #2); the method may or may not return at that point.

- If *rest* is *null*, that is, the list has only 1 item, (base case #3), the method returns.

- If *rest* is not *null*, make a recursive call on *rest*.

Example 14.16 shows our *PlayerRecursiveLinkedList* class. Because of its recursive design, the *PlayerRecursiveLinkedList* class does not extend the *ShellLinkedList* class.

```
1 /* The PlayerRecursiveLinkedList class
2     Anderson, Franceschi
3 */
4
5 public class PlayerRecursiveLinkedList
6 {
7   private Player first;
8   private PlayerRecursiveLinkedList rest;
9
10    public PlayerRecursiveLinkedList( )
11    {
12      first = null;
13      rest = null;
14    }
15
16    /** insert method
17     *   @param    p   Player object to insert at beginning of list
18     */
19    public void insert( Player p )
20    {
21      if ( isEmpty( ) )      // is list empty?
22        first = p;
23      else
24      {
25        PlayerRecursiveLinkedList tempList =
26                  new PlayerRecursiveLinkedList( );
27        tempList.first = first;
28        tempList.rest = rest;
29        first = p;
30        rest = tempList;
31      }
32    }
33
34    /** delete method
35     *   @param    searchID   id of Player to delete
```

```
36    *    @return    the Player deleted
37    */
38    public Player delete( int searchID ) throws DataStructureException
39    {
40      if ( isEmpty( ) )                        // is list empty?
41        throw new DataStructureException
42                  ( searchID + " not found: cannot delete" );
43      else if ( first.getID( ) == searchID )  // found it
44      {
45        Player temp = first;
46        if ( rest == null )
47          first = null;
48        else        // rest not null
49        {
50          first = rest.first;
51          rest = rest.rest;
52        }
53        return temp;
54      }
55      else if ( rest == null )
56        throw new DataStructureException
57                  ( searchID + " not found: cannot delete" );
58      else                                    // try to delete in rest
59        return rest.delete( searchID );
60    }
61
62    public boolean isEmpty( )
63    {
64      return ( first == null );
65    }
66
67    public String toString( )
68    {
69      String listString = "";
70      if ( first != null )
71      {
72        listString = first.toString( ) + "\n";
73        if ( rest != null )
74          listString += rest.toString( );
75      }
76      return listString;
77    }
78 }
```

EXAMPLE 14.16   The *PlayerRecursiveLinkedList* Class

We declare the two instance variables at lines 7–8: *first* represents the first *Player* in the list, and *rest* represents the rest of the list, which is a *PlayerRecursiveLinkedList* object reference itself. We coded the default constructor, which constructs an empty list, at lines 10–14.

We coded the *insert* method at lines 16–32. After insertion, *first* will be the method's *Player* parameter *p*, and *rest* will be the list before we inserted *p*. We begin by testing if the list is empty by calling the *isEmpty* method (defined at lines 62 to 65), which returns *true* if *first* is *null*. If the list is empty, we assign *p* to *first* at line 22. If *first* is not *null*, we copy the current list into a new list at lines 25–28. We instantiate a temporary list, *tempList*. We then assign *first* to the *first* instance variable of *tempList* and *rest* to the *rest* instance variable of *tempList*. At that point, we have copied the current list into *tempList*. Now we can insert the new item into the first position (line 29) and make *tempList* the rest of the list (line 30).

The recursive *delete* method (lines 34–60) takes the *int* parameter *searchID*. If the list is empty (line 40), we *throw* a *DataStructureException* with the appropriate message. If the list is not empty, then *first* is not *null*, and we can call the *getID* method on *first*. More generally, when processing a recursively designed list, not testing for all the base case conditions could result in a *NullPointerException*.

If the list is not empty and the *id* of *first* is equal to *searchID* (line 43), we do the necessary bookkeeping on the list to delete the first element at lines 45–52 before returning the first *Player* of the list at line 53. In order to delete the first element of the list, we need to update *first* and *rest*. First will be assigned the first element of *rest*. However, *rest* could be *null*, in which case *rest* does not have a first element. Thus, we test if *rest* is *null* at line 46. If it is, the list is now empty, so we assign *null* to *first* at line 47. If *rest* is not *null*, we assign the first element of *rest* to *first* at line 50, and we assign the rest of *rest* to *rest* at line 51.

Figures 14.25a to 14.25c show the list before deleting *Player p*, after line 50 is executed, and after line 51 is executed, when *Player p* has been deleted from the list.

Finally, if the list is not *null* and the *id* of *first* is not equal to *searchID*, we skip to line 55, where we test if *rest* is *null*. If it is, we cannot delete and *throw* a *DataStructureException*. If *rest* is not *null*, we make the recursive call to try to delete from *rest* at line 59.

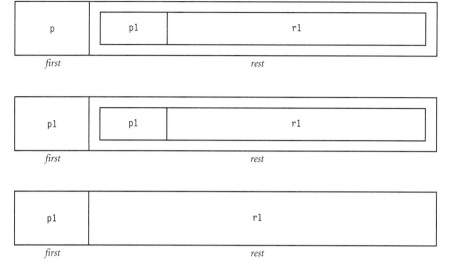

Figure 14.25a
The List Before Deleting *Player p*

Figure 14.25b
The List After *first* **is Assigned** *first* **of** *rest*

Figure 14.25c
The List After *rest* **of** *rest* **is Assigned to** *rest. Player p* **has Been Deleted.**

We coded our *toString* method at lines 67–77. This method is also recursive. If the list is empty, it returns the empty *String*. If the list is not empty, we assign the contents of *first* to the temporary variable *listString* at line 72. We then need to traverse *rest* in order to add its contents to *listString*. But *rest* could be *null*, in which case we are finished traversing the list. So if *rest* is not *null* (line 73), we traverse *rest* at line 74 by making the recursive call:

```
rest.toString( )
```

That recursive call returns a *String* representing the contents of *rest*; we concatenate that *String* to *listString* at line 74 before returning *listString* at line 76.

Example 14.17 shows how to use our *PlayerRecursiveLinkedList* class in a client program.

```
 1 /* The PlayerRecursiveLinkedListTest class
 2    Anderson, Franceschi
 3 */
 4
 5 public class PlayerRecursiveLinkedListTest
 6 {
 7   public static void main( String [ ] args )
 8   {
 9     Player p1 = new Player( 7,"Sarah","Mario" );
10     Player p2 = new Player( 2,"Jin","Golf" );
```

```
11     Player p3 = new Player( 5,"Ajay","Sonic" );
12
13     PlayerRecursiveLinkedList players =
14                 new PlayerRecursiveLinkedList( );
15     System.out.println( "The list is\n"
16        + ( players.isEmpty( ) ? "empty\n" : players.toString( ) ) );
17
18     players.insert( p1 );
19     System.out.println( "Inserting " + p1 );
20     System.out.println( "The list is\n"
21        + ( players.isEmpty( ) ? "empty\n" : players.toString( ) ) );
22
23     players.insert( p2 );
24     System.out.println( "Inserting " + p2);
25     System.out.println( "The list is\n"
26        + ( players.isEmpty( ) ? "empty\n" : players.toString( ) ) );
27
28     players.insert( p3 );
29     System.out.println( "Inserting " + p3 );
30     System.out.println( "The list is\n"
31        + ( players.isEmpty( ) ? "empty\n" : players.toString( ) ) );
32
33     Player p4;
34
35     try
36     {
37       p4 = players.delete( 2 );   // delete in middle of list
38       System.out.println( "Player deleted: " + p4 );
39       System.out.println( "The list is\n"
40         + ( players.isEmpty( ) ? "empty\n" : players.toString( ) ) );
41
42       p4 = players.delete( 7 );   // delete at end of list
43       System.out.println( "Player deleted: " + p4 );
44       System.out.println( "The list is\n"
45         + ( players.isEmpty( ) ? "empty\n" : players.toString( ) ) );
46
47       p4 = players.delete( 9 );   // attempt to delete will fail
48       System.out.println( "Player deleted: " + p4 );
49       System.out.println( "The list is\n"
50         + ( players.isEmpty( ) ? "empty\n" : players.toString( ) ) );
51     }
52     catch ( DataStructureException dse1 )
53     {
54       System.out.println( dse1.getMessage( ) );
```

```
55     }
56
57     try
58     {
59       p4 = players.delete( 5 );   // delete only Player in list
60       System.out.println( "\nPlayer deleted: " + p4 );
61       System.out.println( "The list is\n"
62         + ( players.isEmpty( ) ? "empty\n" : players.toString( ) ) );
63
64       p4 = players.delete( 9 );   // try to delete from empty list
65       System.out.println( "\nPlayer deleted: " + p4 );
66       System.out.println( "The list is\n"
67         + ( players.isEmpty( ) ? "empty\n" : players.toString( ) ) );
68     }
69     catch ( DataStructureException dse2 )
70     {
71       System.out.println( dse2.getMessage( ) );
72     }
73   }
74 }
```

EXAMPLE 14.17   The *PlayerRecursiveLinkedListTest* class

In Example 14.17, we again instantiate our usual three *Player* object references *p1*, *p2*, and *p3* at lines 9–11. We instantiate the *PlayerRecursiveLinkedList players* at lines 13–14. This example tests the following operations:

- inserting in an empty list (line 18)

- inserting in a list of one element (line 23)

- inserting in a list of two elements (line 28)

- deleting an element in the middle of the list (line 37)

- deleting an element at the end of the list (line 42)

- failing to delete from a non-empty list (line 47)

- deleting the only element in the list (line 59)

- failing to delete from an empty list (line 64)

COMMON ERROR TRAP

When processing a recursively defined list, not testing for all the base case conditions can eventually result in a *NullPointerException* at run time.

SOFTWARE ENGINEERING TIP

When a class is defined recursively, think in terms of implementing recursive methods.

Figure 14.26

Output of Example 14.17

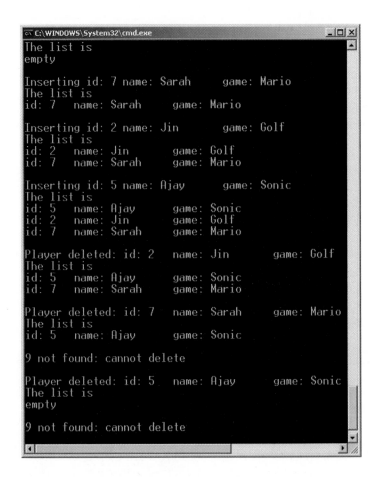

Figure 14.26 shows the output of Example 14.17.

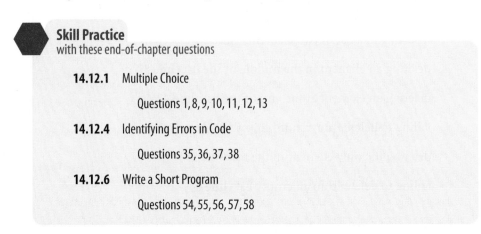

Skill Practice
with these end-of-chapter questions

14.12.1   Multiple Choice

Questions 1, 8, 9, 10, 11, 12, 13

14.12.4   Identifying Errors in Code

Questions 35, 36, 37, 38

14.12.6   Write a Short Program

Questions 54, 55, 56, 57, 58

14.11   Chapter Summary

- A data structure is a mechanism for organizing the data a program stores in memory.

- A linked list is a data structure consisting of nodes linked together like a chain.

- Typical instance variables for a node are an object reference to the data stored at the node, and a node reference, which points to the next node in the list.

- Because each node has a reference to the next node as an instance variable, a linked list needs only one instance variable, its first node, which is usually called *head*. Often, for convenience, we also include an instance variable representing the number of items in the list.

- A linked list can be expanded one node at a time, therefore optimizing memory use.

- A stack is a data structure organized as Last In, First Out.

- A queue is a data structure organized as First In, First Out.

- A linked list can be used to represent a stack. In that case, we push onto the stack by inserting an item at the beginning of the list. We pop by deleting the first item of the list.

- A linked list can also be used to represent a queue. In that case, we enqueue by inserting at the end of the list. We dequeue by deleting the first item of the list. Because we insert at the end of the list, it is useful to have an instance variable representing the last node in the list, often called *tail*.

- A stack can also be represented by an array, if we know in advance the maximum number of items that will be stored on the stack at one time. An instance variable called *top* represents the index of the last array element pushed onto the stack. We pop, or delete, that element, unless the stack is empty. We push, or insert, onto the stack a new element at index (*top + 1*), unless the stack is full.

- A queue can also be represented by an array, if we know in advance the maximum number of items that will be stored in the queue at one time. A circular array is usually implemented for the queue. Two instance variables called *front* and *back* represent the indexes of the first and last element inserted in the queue. We dequeue, or delete, the element at index *front* unless the queue is empty. We enqueue, or insert, a new element at index (*back + 1% QUEUE_SIZE*), unless the queue is full.

- In a class encapsulating a data structure, a method returning an object can *throw* an exception if we cannot return or cannot find the object. Indeed, when the object we are looking for is not found, it is preferable to *throw* an exception than to return *null*.

- A linked list can be sorted in ascending or descending order. One of the instance variables of the list objects is used as the key to sort the list elements. The *insert* method finds the appropriate location to insert an item so that the list remains sorted.

- A variation of the linked list includes a doubly linked list. In this case, each node contains three instance variables: an object representing the data, a node reference representing the next node, and another node reference representing the previous node. The latter enables us to backtrack in the list, if we need to, whereas in a singly linked list, we can traverse the list in a forward direction only. However, implementing such a list is more difficult; each method, in particular *insert* and *delete*, involves more operations to maintain these double links between nodes.

- Linked lists can also be recursively defined. A recursively defined linked list is made up of two elements: *first*, which is the first item in the linked list, and *rest*, a linked list that consists of the rest of the linked list.

14.12   Exercises, Problems, and Projects

14.12.1   Multiple Choice Exercises

1. What is an advantage of linked lists over arrays?

   ❏ Linked lists are easily expanded.

   ❏ Linked lists are limited in size.

   ❏ Linked lists can store objects, whereas arrays are limited to primitive data types.

2. How is a stack organized?

   ❏ FIFO

❑ LIFO

❑ Items are sorted in ascending order.

❑ Items are sorted in descending order.

3. How is a queue organized?

❑ FIFO

❑ LIFO

❑ Items are sorted in ascending order.

❑ Items are sorted in descending order.

4. The linked list below represents a stack. If we pop once from the stack, what item is popped?

(7, Ajay, NFL) → (3, Sarah, Mario) → (9, Jin, Golf) →
      head

(5, Joe, Sonic) → null

   ❑ (7, Ajay, NFL)

   ❑ (3, Sarah, Mario)

   ❑ (9, Jin, Golf)

   ❑ (5, Joe, Sonic)

5. The linked list below represents a stack. After we push the player (5, Joe, Sonic) onto the stack, what are the first and last items on the stack?

(7, Ajay, NFL) → (3, Sarah, Mario) → (9, Jin, Golf) → null
      head

   ❑ (7, Ajay, NFL) and (9, Jin, Golf)

   ❑ (5, Joe, Sonic) and (9, Jin, Golf)

   ❑ (3, Sarah, Mario) and (5, Joe, Sonic)

   ❑ (7, Ajay, NFL) and (5, Joe, Sonic)

6. The linked list below represents a queue. If we dequeue once, what item is dequeued?

(7, Ajay, NFL) → (3, Sarah, Mario) → (9, Jin, Golf) →
      head

(5, Joe, Sonic) → null
      tail

- ❑ (7, Ajay, NFL)
- ❑ (3, Sarah, Mario)
- ❑ (9, Jin, Golf)
- ❑ (5, Joe, Sonic)

7. The linked list below represents a queue. After we enqueue the player (5, Joe, Sonic), what are now the first and last items on the queue?

(7, Ajay, NFL) → (3, Sarah, Mario) → (9, Jin, Golf) → null
   head   tail

- ❑ (7, Ajay, NFL) and (9, Jin, Golf)
- ❑ (5, Joe, Sonic) and (9, Jin, Golf)
- ❑ (3, Sarah, Mario) and (5, Joe, Sonic)
- ❑ (7, Ajay, NFL) and (5, Joe, Sonic)

8. The diagram below shows the current state of a stack represented by an array of 50 integers. After pushing 36 and 62 onto the stack and then popping once, what will be the value of *top*, and what element will be stored at index *top*?

Index	Item stored
47 (*top*)	28
46	98
..	..
3	17
2	12
1	20
0	45

- ❑ *top* is 47 and the element at index *top* is 28
- ❑ *top* is 49 and the element at index *top* is 62
- ❑ *top* is 48 and the element at index *top* is 36
- ❑ *top* is 49 and the element at index *top* is 20

9. The diagram below shows the current state of a stack represented by an array of 50 integers. After pushing 36, 88, and 62 onto the stack and popping three times from the stack, what will be the value of *top* and what element will be stored at index *top*?

Index	Item stored
47 (*top*)	28
46	98
..	..
3	17
2	12
1	20
0	45

❑ *top* is 49 and the element at index *top* is 62

❑ *top* is 47 and the element at index *top* is 28

❑ *top* is 46 and the element at index *top* is 98

❑ *top* is 50 and the element at index *top* is 17

10. The diagram below shows the current state of a queue represented by a circular array of 8 integers. After enqueuing 36 and 62, and dequeuing once, what are the values of *front* and *back*, and what elements are stored at indexes *front* and *back*?

Index	Item stored
7	
6 (*back*)	28
5	97
4	25
3	54
2 (*front*)	12
1	
0	

❑ *front* = 0, stores 62; *back* = 5, stores 97

❑ *front* = 3, stores 54; *back* = 0, stores 62

❑ *front* = 3, stores 54; *back* = 8, stores 62

❑ *front* = 1, stores 36; *back* = 6, stores 28

11. The diagram below shows the current state of a queue represented by a circular array of 8 integers. After enqueuing 36, 100, 83, 77, and 62, what are the values of *front* and *back*, and what elements are stored at indexes *front* and *back*?

Index	Item stored
7	
6 (*back*)	28
5	97
4	25
3	54
2 (*front*)	12
1	
0	

❑ *front* = 2, stores 12; *back* = 11, stores 62

❑ *front* = 2, stores 12; *back* = 3, stores 62

❑ *front* = 3, stores 62; *back* = 6, stores 28

❑ *front* = 2, stores 12; *back* = 1, stores 83

12. The diagram below shows the current state of a queue represented by a circular array of 8 integers. After dequeuing 5 times, what are the values of *front* and *back*, and what elements are stored at indexes *front* and *back*?

Index	Item stored
7	
6 (*back*)	28
5	97
4	25
3	54
2 (*front*)	12
1	
0	

❑ *front* = 7; *back* = 6; the queue is empty

❑ *front* = 2; *back* = 1; the queue is empty

❑ *front* = 2; *back* = 6; the queue is empty

13. The diagram below shows the current state of a queue represented by a circular array of 8 integers. After dequeuing 8 times, what are the values of *front* and *back*, and what elements are stored at indexes *front* and *back*?

Index	Item stored
7	
6 (*back*)	28
5	97
4	25
3	54
2 (*front*)	12
1	
0	

❑ *front* = 7; *back* = 6; the queue is empty

❑ *front* = 2; *back* = 1; the queue is empty

❑ *front* = 2; *back* = 6; the queue is empty

❑ *front* = 6; *back* = 2; the queue is empty

14.12.2 Reading and Understanding Code

For questions 14 to 21, consider the following classes from this chapter: *Player*, *PlayerNode*, and *PlayerLinkedList*.

14. What does this method of the *PlayerLinkedList* class do?

```
public void foo1( Player p, Player q )
{
 insert( p );
 insert( q );
}
```

15. What does this method of the *PlayerLinkedList* class do?

```
public int foo2( )
{
 PlayerNode nd = head;
 int i = 0;
 while ( nd != null )
 {
  i++;
  nd = nd.getNext( );
 }
 return i;
}
```

16. What does this method of the *PlayerLinkedList* class do?

```
public boolean foo3( )
{
 if ( numberOfItems > 0 )
 {
   head = null;
   numberOfItems = 0;
   return true;
 }
 else
   return false;
}
```

17. What does this method of the *PlayerLinkedList* class do?

```
public int foo4( )
{
 PlayerNode nd = head;
 int i = 0;
 while ( nd != null )
 {
  if ( nd. getPlayer( ).getGame( ).equals( "Sonic" ) )
     i++;
  nd = nd.getNext( );
 }
 return i;
}
```

18. What does this method of the *PlayerLinkedList* class do?

```
public boolean foo5( int i )
{
 PlayerNode nd = head;
```

```
 while ( nd != null )
 {
  if ( nd.getPlayer( ).getID( ) == i )
     return true;
  nd = nd.getNext( );
 }
 return false;
}
```

19. What does this method of the *PlayerLinkedList* class do?

```
public void foo6( )
{
 PlayerNode nd = head;
 while ( nd != null )
 {
   if ( nd.getPlayer( ).getGame( ).equals( "Diablo" ) )
     System.out.println( nd.getPlayer( ).toString( ) );
   nd = nd.getNext( );
 }
}
```

20. What does this method of the *PlayerLinkedList* class do?

```
public void foo7( Player p )
{
 if ( numberOfItems == 0 )
   System.out.println( "Do nothing" );
 else
 {
   PlayerNode pn = new PlayerNode( p );
   pn.setNext( head.getNext( ) );
   head.setNext( pn );
   numberOfItems++;
 }
}
```

21. What does this method of the *PlayerLinkedList* class do?

```
public boolean foo8( )
{
 if ( numberOfItems <= 2 )
   return false;
 else
 {
   head.setNext( ( head.getNext( ) ).getNext( ) );
   numberOfItems--;
```

```
        return true;
      }
    }
```

14.12.3   Fill in the Code

22. Consider the following state of a linked list of *Player* items.

    → (7, Ajay, NFL) → (3, Sarah, Mario) → (9, Jin, Golf) →
        previous

    (5, Joe, Sonic) →

    As indicated, *previous* is the *PlayerNode* whose player is (7, Ajay, NFL)

    Write the code to modify the list so that (9, Jin, Golf) has been deleted (see below).

    → (7, Ajay, NFL) → (3, Sarah, Mario) → (5, Joe, Sonic) →

    ```
    // your code goes here
    ```

23. Consider the following state of a linked list of *Player* items.

    → (7, Ajay, NFL) → (3, Sarah, Mario) → (9, Jin, Golf) →
        previous

    (5, Joe, Sonic) →

    As indicated, *previous* is the *PlayerNode* whose player is (7, Ajay, NFL)

    Write the code to modify the list so that the two items in the middle have been deleted (see below).

    → (7, Ajay, NFL) → (5, Joe, Sonic) →

    ```
    // your code goes here
    ```

24. Consider the following state of a linked list of *Player* items.

    → (7, Ajay, NFL) → (3, Sarah, Mario) → (9, Jin, Golf) →
        previous   *current*

    (5, Joe, Sonic) →

    As indicated, *previous* is the *PlayerNode* whose player is (7, Ajay, NFL) and *current* is the *PlayerNode* whose player is (3, Sarah, Mario). Write the code to modify the list so that the two nodes in the middle have been swapped as shown below. (You need to swap the actual nodes, rather than modify their respective data.)

→ (7, Ajay, NFL) → (9, Jin, Golf) → (3, Sarah, Mario) → (5, Joe, Sonic) →

```
// your code goes here
```

For questions 25 to 28, consider the *LLNode* class below, representing a node with a *char* instance variable, representing a grade (A, B, C, D, or F):

```
public class LLNode
{
    private char grade;
    private LLNode next;

    // constructors and methods here
}
```

25. Code the overloaded constructor with one parameter, a *char*.

```
// your code goes here
```

26. Code the overloaded constructor with two parameters.

```
// your code goes here
```

27. Code the accessors for the class.

```
// your code goes here
```

28. Code the mutators for the class.

```
// your code goes here
```

For questions 29 to 31, consider the *DifferentLinkedList* class below, using the *LLNode* class from questions 25 to 28 (assume that the *LLNode* class has all appropriate accessors, mutators, and other methods).

```
public class DifferentLinkedList
{
    private LLNode head;
    // there is no instance variable for
    // the number of items in the list

    // constructors and methods here
}
```

29. Code a method that returns *true* if the list is empty; *false* otherwise.

```
// your code goes here
```

30. Code a method that returns *true* if the list contains at least one item; *false* otherwise.

```
// your code goes here
```

31. Code a method that returns the number of items in the list.

```
// your code goes here
```

32. Consider a method of class *PlayerLinkedList* with the following header:

```
public Player retrieveMe( int index )
```

Write a few statements showing how you would call that method from a client program.

```
// your code goes here
```

14.12.4   Identifying Errors in Code

33. What would happen if you execute the code below just before traversing a linked list?

```
head.setNext( head );
```

34. Suppose we have coded the following method in the *PlayerLinkedList* class. Where is the error?

```
public int getHeadID( )
{
   return head.getID( );
}
```

35. Suppose we modify the code of the *push* method in the *StackArray* class as follows (that is, without incrementing *top*). What type of problem could that method create?

```
public boolean push( Player p )
{
   if ( !isFull( ) ) // is there room to insert?
   {
     stack[top] = p;
     return true;
   }
   else
    return false;
}
```

36. Suppose we modify the code of the *pop* method in the *StackArray* class as follows (that is, without decrementing *top*). What type of problem could that method create?

```
public Player pop( ) throws DataStructureException
{
  if ( !isEmpty( ) ) // is there an item to delete?
    return ( stack[top] );
  else
    throw new DataStructureException
                   ( "Stack empty: cannot pop" );
}
```

37. Suppose we modify the code of the *enqueue* method in the *QueueArray* class as follows (that is, without incrementing the number of items). What type of problem could that method create?

```
public boolean enqueue( Player newPlayer )
{
  if ( !isFull( ) )
  {
    queue[( back + 1 ) % QUEUE_SIZE] = newPlayer;
    back = ( back + 1 ) % QUEUE_SIZE;
    return true;
  }
  else
    return false;
}
```

38. Suppose we modify the code of the *dequeue* method in the *QueueArray* class as follows (that is, with a change in the expression computing the index in the *return* statement). Where is the error?

```
public Player dequeue( ) throws DataStructureException
{
  if ( !isEmpty( ) )
  {
    front  = ( front + 1 ) % QUEUE_SIZE;
    numberOfItems--;
    return queue[(front - 1 ) % QUEUE_SIZE];
  }
  else
    throw new DataStructureException
                   ( "Queue empty: cannot dequeue" );
}
```

14.12.5   Debugging Area

39. You coded the following inside the *main* method of the *Test* class, using the *Player* and *PlayerNode* classes.

```
PlayerNode pn = new PlayerNode( );
Player p = pn.getPlayer( );
p.setID( 10 );            // line 10
```

The code compiles, but at run time you get a *NullPointerException* at line 10.

```
Exception in thread "main" java.lang.NullPointerException
    at TestLL.main(TestLL.java:10)
```

Explain what the problem is and how to fix it.

40. You coded the following in the *main* method of the *Test* class, using the *Player* and *PlayerLinkedList* classes.

```
Player p = new Player( 5,"Ajay","Mario" );
PlayerLinkedList pll = new PlayerLinkedList( );
pll.insert( p );
PlayerNode temp = pll.getHead( );         // line 10
System.out.println( " head is " + temp.toString( ) );
```

At compile time, you get the following error:

```
TestLL.java:10: cannot resolve symbol
symbol  : method getHead ()
location: class PlayerLinkedList
  PlayerNode temp = pll.getHead( );
                       ^

1 error
```

Explain what the problem is and how to fix it.

41. You coded the following in the *main* method of the *Test* class, using the *Player* and *PlayerLinkedList* classes.

```
Player p = new Player( 5,"Ajay","Mario" );
PlayerLinkedList pll = new PlayerLinkedList( );
pll.insert( p );
if ( pll.delete( 5 ) )      // line 10
    System.out.println( "Successful deletion" );
```

At compile time, you get the following error:

```
TestLL.java:10: incompatible types
found    : Player
required: boolean
  if ( pll.delete( 5 ) )
            ^
1 error
```

Explain what the problem is and how to fix it.

42. You coded the following inside the *foo* method of the *Player-LinkedList* class.

```
PlayerNode current = head;   // line 9
while ( current.getPlayer( ).getID( ) != 99 )
     current = current.getNext( );
// more code here but no problem
```

The code compiles, but at run time you get a *NullPointerException* at line 10.

```
Exception in thread "main" java.lang.NullPointerException
      at PlayerLinkedList.foo(PlayerLinkedList.java:10)
      at TestLL.main(TestLL.java:24)
```

What would be a possible scenario that may have caused this error? Explain how to fix this problem.

14.12.6   Write a Short Program

43. Modify the *PlayerLinkedList* class to include one more method: that method inserts a new player in the third position of the list, *head* being the first position. If the list is empty, the method will insert the new player as the head of the list. Be sure to test your method with the appropriate client code.

44. Modify the *PlayerLinkedList* class to include one more method: that method inserts a new player in the next-to-last position of the list. If the list is empty, the method will insert the new player as the head of the list. Be sure to test your method with the appropriate client code.

45. Modify the *PlayerLinkedList* class to include one more method: that method inserts a new player in the last position of the list. For this, you cannot use the *tail* instance variable. Be sure to test your method with the appropriate client code.

46. Modify the *PlayerLinkedList* class to include one more method: that method deletes the second node of the list, if there is one. Be sure to test your method with the appropriate client code.

47. Modify the *PlayerLinkedList* class to include one more method: that method inserts a new player at a given position (a parameter of the method). If the list is empty, the method will insert the new player as the head of the list. If the value of the parameter is greater than the number of items in the list, then the method inserts at the end of the list. You should consider that *head* is at position 1 in the list. Be sure to test your method with the appropriate client code.

48. Modify the *PlayerLinkedList* class to include one more method: that method deletes a *Player* at a given position (a parameter of the method). If the value of the parameter is greater than the number of elements in the list, then no item is deleted. Your method should return the *Player* deleted, if any. You should consider that the first node is at position 1 in the list. Be sure to test your method with the appropriate client code.

49. Modify the *PlayerLinkedList* class to include one more method: that method takes a parameter that represents a game. The method inserts a new player at a position just after the first *Player* of the list with a *game* instance variable equal to that game. If there is no such node, then your method should insert at the end of the list. Be sure to test your method with the appropriate client code.

50. Modify the *PlayerLinkedList* class to include one more method: a traversal that outputs the players in the list until we reach a player with a given id; that player's data should not be output. Be sure to test your method with the appropriate client code.

51. Modify the *PlayerLinkedList* class to include one more method: a method that returns the *n*th *Player* on the list (*n* is a parameter of the method). If there is no *n*th *Player* on the list, the method should *throw* an exception. Test your method with a client that traverses the list by requesting each *Player* in position order.

52. Modify the *PlayerStackLinkedList* class to include one more method: a method that returns the ID of the last player on the stack. Be sure to test your method with the appropriate client code.

53. Modify the *PlayerQueueLinkedList* class to include one more method: a method that outputs every other player in the queue, that is, it outputs the first player, skips the second, outputs the third player, skips the fourth, and so on. Be sure to test your method with the appropriate client code.

54. Modify the *PlayerRecursiveLinkedList* class to include one more method: one that inserts at the end of the list. Be sure to test your method with the appropriate client code.

55. Modify the *PlayerRecursiveLinkedList* class to include one more method: one that deletes at the end of the list. Be sure to test your method with the appropriate client code.

56. Modify the *PlayerRecursiveLinkedList* class to include one more method: one that deletes at the beginning of the list. Be sure to test your method with the appropriate client code.

57. Code a class encapsulating a stack of *doubles* using an array of 10 elements. Be sure to test your methods with the appropriate client code.

58. Code a class encapsulating a queue of *chars* using a circular array of 10 elements. Be sure to test your methods with the appropriate client code.

14.12.7   Programming Projects

59. Modify the *PlayerLinkedList* to include two more methods: one that returns the *Player* with the minimum *id*, and one that returns all the games played by players with a given *id*. You also need to include the appropriate client code to test your classes.

60. Modify the *PlayerLinkedList* to include two more methods: one that returns the *Player* with the first name in alphabetical order, and one that returns all of the *ids* of the players playing a given game. You also need to include the appropriate client code to test your classes.

61. Code a class encapsulating a singly linked list of Web site objects. A Web site has two attributes: a URL address (a *String*, you do not need to use the existing URL Java class) and ten or fewer keywords describing the topic of the Web site. In addition to *insert*, *delete*, *peek*, and

toString, add one more method: a method that, based on a keyword, returns all URL addresses in the list containing that keyword. Your *delete* method should delete an item based on the value of its URL. You also need to include the appropriate client code to test your classes.

62. Code a class encapsulating a singly linked list of football teams. A football team has three attributes: its nickname, its number of wins, and its number of losses (assume there are no ties). In addition to *insert, delete, peek,* and *toString,* add two more methods: a method that returns the nicknames of the teams with the most wins, and another method that returns the five best teams based on winning percentages (in case of a tie, you can return the first five such teams in the list). You also need to include the appropriate client code to test your classes.

63. Code a class encapsulating a singly linked list of HTML tags. We will define a valid HTML tag as a string of characters starting with < and ending with >. In addition to *insert, delete, peek,* and *toString,* add two more methods: a method that returns *true* or *false,* checking if the list contains valid HTML tags only (as defined above), and another that counts how many items in the list contain the slash (/) character in them. You also need to include the appropriate client code to test your classes.

64. Code a class encapsulating a singly linked list of stocks. A stock is defined by the following attributes: its ticker symbol (a short word, for instance AMD), its price (for example 54.35), and the company's earnings per share (for example 3.25). In addition to *insert, delete, peek,* and *toString,* add two more methods: a method that returns the list of all the tickers for the penny stocks (a penny stock is a stock whose price is $1.00 or less), and another method that, given a number representing a price earnings ratio (the price earnings ratio of a stock, also known as P/E ratio, is the price of the stock divided by the earnings per share), returns all the tickers with a price earnings ratio less than or equal to that number. You also need to include the appropriate client code to test your classes.

65. Code a class encapsulating a singly linked list of books. A book is defined by the following attributes: its title, its author, its price, and how many are in stock. In addition to *insert, delete, peek,* and *toString,* add two more methods: a method that, based on a word, returns all the

book titles in the list containing that word, and another returning the list of book titles that are out of stock, i.e., there are quantity 0 in stock. You also need to include the appropriate client code to test your classes.

66. Code a class encapsulating a stack of clothes using an array. A clothing item has the following attributes: its name, its color, and whether it can be washed at high temperature. We will limit our stack to 100 clothing items. In addition to *push*, *pop*, *peek*, and *toString*, add two more methods: a method that returns all the clothing items of a given color, and another method that returns how many clothing items in the stack can be washed at high temperature. You also need to include the appropriate client code to test your classes.

67. Code a class encapsulating a queue of foods using a circular array. A food has the following attributes: its name, the number of calories per serving, and the number of servings per container. We will limit our queue to 100 foods. In addition to *enqueue*, *dequeue*, *peek*, and *toString*, add two more methods: a method that returns the average calories per serving of all the foods in the queue, and another method that returns the food item with the highest "total calories" (i.e., calories per serving times number of servings). You also need to include the appropriate client code to test your classes.

68. Code a class encapsulating a sorted linked list of *Auto* objects (you can use the *Auto* class from Chapter 7). Your list should be sorted in ascending order using the model as the key. In addition to *insert*, *delete*, *peek*, and *toString*, add two more methods: a method that returns all the *Auto* objects in the list that have a number of miles greater than a given number, and another method that returns all the *Auto* objects in the list that are located after a given model name. You also need to include the appropriate client code to test your classes.

69. Code a class encapsulating a sorted linked list of *Auto* objects (you can use the Auto class from Chapter 7). Your list should be sorted in descending order using *gallonsOfGas* as the key. In addition to *insert*, *delete*, *peek*, and *toString*, add two more methods: a method that returns the average value of *gallonsOfGas* of all the *Autos* in the list, and another method that returns all the *Autos* in the list that have a *gallonsOfGas* value less than a certain number. You also need to include the appropriate client code to test your classes.

EXERCISES, PROBLEMS, AND PROJECTS

14.12.8   Technical Writing

70. In this chapter, we coded a linked list class with just two instance variables: the head node and the number of items in the list. We also said that we did not really need the number of items in the list. Explain how we can traverse the whole list if the class has only one instance variable, *head*.

71. Consider the *PlayerQueueLinkedList* class presented in this chapter, which includes an instance variable called *tail*, in addition to *head*. We want to make the list circular, that is, *tail* "points to" *head*. If you made the method call *tail.getNext( )*, it would return *head*. Describe why and how you would need to modify the *toString* method of the class (assume you do not know the number of items in the list).

14.12.9   Group Project (for a group of 1, 2, or 3 students)

72. Code a doubly linked, sorted list (in ascending order). Each item of the list will just store an *int*.

    You need to code three classes: *Node*, *SortedList*, and *GroupProject*

    The *Node* class has three instance variables, all *private*:

    ❑ an *int*, representing the value stored inside the *Node*

    ❑ a *Node* (*next*)

    ❑ another *Node* (*previous*)

    The methods to code are: constructor (at least one), accessors, mutators

    The *SortedList* class is a doubly linked list, sorted in ascending order.

    It has two instance variables, both private:

    ❑ an *int*, representing the number of items in the list

    ❑ a *Node*, representing the head node in the list

    The methods to code are:

    ❑ *insert*: this method takes one parameter, an *int*; it has a *void* return value.

    ❑ *delete*: this method takes one parameter, an *int*; it returns a *boolean* value. If we were successful in deleting the item (i.e., the value of the parameter was found in the list), then we return *true*; if we were not successful, then we want to output a message that the value was not found, and therefore, not deleted, and return *false*.

❑ *toString*: this method takes no parameters and returns a *String* representation of the list.

❑ constructor (at least one), and accessors and mutators as appropriate.

All methods should keep the list sorted in ascending order.

The *GroupProject* class contains the *main* method; it should do the following:

❑ create a *SortedList* object reference.

❑ insert successively the values 25, 17, 12, 21, 78, and 47 in the sorted list

❑ output the contents of the sorted list using the *toString* method

❑ delete from the sorted list the value 30, using the *delete* method (obviously, 30 will not be found)

❑ output the contents of the sorted list using the *toString* method

❑ delete from the sorted list the value 21, using the *delete* method

❑ output the contents of the sorted list using the *toString* method

Your *insert* and *delete* methods should work properly in all possible scenarios: inserting in an empty list, inserting at the beginning of a list, inserting in the middle of a list, inserting at the end of a list, deleting from an empty list (cannot delete), deleting an item not in the list (cannot delete), deleting the first item in a list, deleting in the middle of a list, deleting the last item in a list.

APPENDIX A

Java Reserved Words and Keywords

These words have contextual meaning for the Java language and cannot be used as identifiers.

abstract	default	goto	package	synchronized
boolean	do	if	private	this
break	double	implements	protected	throw
byte	else	import	public	throws
case	enum	instanceof	return	transient
catch	extends	int	short	true
char	false	interface	static	try
class	final	long	strictfp	void
const	finally	native	super	volatile
continue	float	new	switch	while
	for	null		

The words *true*, *false*, and *null* are literals. The remainder of the words are Java keywords, although *const* and *goto* are not currently used in the Java language.

APPENDIX B

Operator Precedence

These rules of operator precedence are followed when expressions are evaluated. Operators in a higher level in the hierarchy—defined by their row position in the table—are evaluated before operators in a lower level. Thus, an expression in parentheses is evaluated before a shortcut postincrement is performed, and so on with the operators in each level. When two or more operators on the same level appear in an expression, the evaluation of the expression follows the corresponding rule for same-statement evaluation shown in the second column.

Operators	Order of Same-Statement Evaluation	Operation
( )	left to right	parentheses for explicit grouping
++ −−	right to left	shortcut postincrement and postdecrement
++ −− !	right to left	shortcut preincrement and predecrement, logical unary NOT
* / %	left to right	multiplication, division, modulus
+ -	left to right	addition or *String* concatenation, subtraction
< <= > >=	left to right	relational operators: less than, less than or equal to, greater than, greater than or equal to
== !=	left to right	equality operators: equal to and not equal to
&&	left to right	logical AND
||	left to right	logical OR
?:	left to right	conditional operator
= += -= *= /= %=	right to left	assignment operator and shortcut assignment operators

APPENDIX C

The Unicode Character Set

Java characters are encoded using the Unicode Character Set, which is designed to support international alphabets, punctuation, and mathematical and technical symbols. Each character is stored as 16 bits, so as many as 65,536 characters are supported.

The American Standard Code for Information Interchange (ASCII) character set is supported by the first 128 Unicode characters from 0000 to 007F, which are called the Basic Latin characters. These characters can be found online at the address: *www.unicode.org/charts/PDF/U0000.pdf*

Any character from the Unicode set can be specified as a *char* literal in a Java program by using the following syntax: '\uNNNN' where NNNN are the four hexadecimal digits that specify the Unicode encoding for the character.

For more information on the Unicode character set, visit the Unicode Consortium's Web site: *www.unicode.org*.

APPENDIX D

Representing Negative Integers

The industry standard method for representing negative integers is called **two's complement**. Here is how it works:

For an integer represented using 16 bits, the leftmost bit is reserved for the sign bit. If the sign bit is 0, then the integer is positive; if the sign bit is 1, then the integer is negative.

For example, let's consider two numbers, one positive and one negative.

0000 0101 0111 1001 is a positive integer, which we call a.

1111 1111 1101 1010 is a negative integer, which we will call b.

Using the methodology presented in Chapter 1 for converting a binary number to a decimal number, we can convert the binary number, a, to its decimal equivalent. Hence, the value of a is calculated as follows:

$$a = 2^{10} + 2^8 + 2^6 + 2^5 + 2^4 + 2^3 + 2^0$$
$$= 1{,}024 + 256 + 64 + 32 + 16 + 8 + 1$$
$$= 1{,}401$$

In contrast, b, the negative number, is represented in binary using the two's complement method. The leftmost bit, which is the sign bit, is a 1, indicating that b is negative. To calculate the value of a negative number, we first calculate its two's complement. The two's complement of any binary number is another binary number, which when added to the original number, will yield a sum consisting of all 0s and a carry bit of 1 at the end.

To calculate the two's complement of a binary number, n, subtract n from 2^d, where d is the number of binary digits in n. The following formula summarizes that rule:

```
Two's complement of n = 2^d - n
```

Knowing that $2^d - 1$ is always a binary number containing all 1s, we can simplify our calculations by first subtracting 1 from 2^d, then adding a 1 at the end.

```
Two's complement of n = 2^d - 1 - n + 1
```

So to calculate the two's complement of b, which has 16 digits, we subtract b from a binary number consisting of 16 1s, then add 1, as shown below.

```
            2^d - 1   1111 1111 1111 1111
                - b   1111 1111 1101 1010
                      0000 0000 0010 0101
            + 1                          1
two's complement of b   0000 0000 0010 0110
```

Thus, the two's complement of b, which we will call c, is 0000 0000 0010 0110.

Another, simpler, way to calculate a two's complement is to invert each bit, then add 1. Inverting bits means to change all 0s to 1s and to change all 1s to 0s. Using this method, we get:

```
        b   1111 1111 1101 1010

b inverted  0000 0000 0010 0101
      + 1                      1
        c   0000 0000 0010 0110
```

We can verify that the two's complement of b is correct by calculating the sum of b and c.

```
      b   1111 1111 1101 1010
      c   0000 0000 0010 0110
  b + c   1 0000 0000 0000 0000
```

Converting c to decimal will give us the value of our original number b, which, as we remember, is negative. We have:

```
b =   - (    2^5 +  2^2 +  2^1 )
  =   - (   32 +   4  + 2  )
  =     -38
```

Because a leftmost bit of 0 indicates that the number is positive, using 16 bits, the largest positive number (we will call it *max*) that we can represent is:

0111 1111 1111 1111

$$\text{max} = (2^{14} + 2^{13} + 2^{12} + 2^{11} + 2^{10} + 2^9 + 2^8 + 2^7 + 2^6 + 2^5 + 2^4 + 2^3 + 2^2 + 2^1 + 2^0)$$

This is equivalent to $2^{15} - 1$, which is $32,768 - 1$, or $32,767$.

Using 16 bits, then, the smallest negative number (we will call it *min*) that we can represent is:

1000 0000 0000 0000

The two's complement of *min* is *min* itself. If we invert the bits and add 1, we get the same value we started with:

```
        min             1000 0000 0000 0000

  min inverted          0111 1111 1111 1111
          + 1                              1
                        _____
two's complement        1000 0000 0000 0000
```

and therefore *min* is -2^{15} or $-32,768$.

Thus, using 16 bits, we can represent integers between $-32,768$ and $32,767$.

APPENDIX E

Representing Floating-Point Numbers

IEEE 754, a specification accepted worldwide and used by the Java language, defines how to represent floating-point numbers in binary numbers. Single-precision floating-point numbers use 32 bits of memory, and double-precision floating-point numbers use 64 bits.

Here is how single- and double-precision floating-point numbers are represented:

Single precision (32 bits)

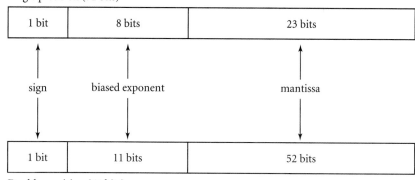

Double precision (64 bits)

The leftmost bit stores the sign of the floating-point number; a 0 indicates a positive number, while a 1 indicates a negative number.

To represent the exponent of the number, which can be positive or negative, each representation stores a positive, biased exponent, calculated by adding a fixed bias, or scaling factor, to the real exponent of the number.

The purpose of the bias is to be able to represent both extremely large and extremely small numbers. The bias is equal to

$$2^{(\# \text{ of bits of the biased exponent } - 1)} - 1.$$

Thus, for single precision, the bias is

$$2^{(8 - 1)} - 1 = 2^7 - 1 = 127.$$

In single-precision, the 8-bit biased exponent can store 256 positive values (0 to 255). Thus, with a bias of 127, we can represent floating-point numbers with real exponents from -127 to 128, as shown below:

```
Real exponent     -127   -126   ...     0    ...   127    128
      + Bias        127    127   ...   127    ...   127    127
Biased exponent       0      1   ...   127    ...   254    255
```

Conversely, to find the real exponent from the biased exponent, we subtract the bias. For example, if the biased exponent is 150, then the real exponent is $150 - 127$, which is 23. Similarly, if the biased exponent is 3, the actual exponent is $3 - 127$, which is -124.

For double precision, the bias is

$$2^{(11 - 1)} - 1 = 2^{10} - 1 = 1023.$$

A floating-point number is considered to be in the form:

$$(-1)^{\text{sign}} * (1 + \text{significand}) * 2^{(\text{biased exponent } - \text{ bias})}$$

By definition, the significand is of the form 0 followed by a dot followed by a string of 0s and 1s, for example, 0.1101. That string of 0s and 1s is known as the mantissa.

For example, if the significand is 0.1101, then the mantissa is 110100...0

As an example, let's convert a single-precision binary number to a decimal floating-point number. We will convert the following single-precision IEEE 754 floating-point number:

0	10000111	11010000....0

The leftmost digit, 0, tells us that the number is positive. The biased exponent is 10000111, which converted to decimal, is:

$$= 2^7 + 2^2 + 2^1 + 2^0$$
$$= 128 + 4 + 2 + 1$$
$$= 135$$

The bias for single-precision floating-point numbers is 127, so the number is

$$= (-1)^0 * (1 + .1101) * 2^{(135 - 127)}$$
$$= 1.1101 * 2^8$$
$$= 1\ 1101\ 0000$$

In decimal, the number is:

$$= 2^8 + 2^7 + 2^6 + 2^4$$
$$= 256 + 128 + 64 + 16$$
$$= 464$$

Given that .1 is $\frac{1}{2}^1$ or $\frac{1}{2}$ in decimal, and .01 is $\frac{1}{2}^2$ or $\frac{1}{4}$, and .0001 is $\frac{1}{2}^4$ or $\frac{1}{16}$ in decimal, we also could have calculated the number using this method:

$$= 1.1101 * 2^8$$
$$= (1 + 1 * \frac{1}{2}^1 + 1 * \frac{1}{2}^2 + 0 * \frac{1}{2}^3 + 1 * \frac{1}{2}^4) * 2^8$$
$$= (1 + \frac{1}{2} + \frac{1}{4} + \frac{1}{16}) * 2^8$$
$$= (1 + \frac{1}{2} + \frac{1}{4} + \frac{1}{16}) * 256$$
$$= 464$$

Now, let's convert a decimal floating-point number into single-precision, binary format. Here, we will convert the number -5.375, which we'll call y. First we convert the whole number portion (5) to binary, getting 101.

$$5 = 101$$

Then we convert the fractional part to binary:

$$.375 = .25 + .125$$
$$= \frac{1}{4} + \frac{1}{8}$$
$$= \frac{1}{2}^2 + \frac{1}{2}^3$$
$$= 0 * \frac{1}{2}^1 + 1 * \frac{1}{2}^2 + 1 * \frac{1}{2}^3$$

Thus, .375 as represented in binary is .011.

Therefore, y can be represented in binary as:

$$y = -101.011$$
$$= -1.01011 * 2^2$$

We now can deduce the sign, the biased exponent, and the mantissa. The sign is 1 because the number is negative. The significand is 1.01011, and therefore the mantissa is 01011000...00. The exponent is 2, so the biased exponent is 129 (2 plus the bias for single-precision numbers, which is 127).

Biased exponent = 2 + 127
= 129

Converting 129 to binary, we get:

129 = 1000 0001

Therefore, the IEEE 754 single-precision value of the number y is

1	10000001	010110000....0

APPENDIX F

Java Classes APIs

In this appendix, we have compiled the APIs for the Java classes and interfaces used in this book. There are more methods and constructors for the classes presented here, and there are many more classes in the Java class library. We invite you to explore the Java APIs at www.java.sun.com.

ActionEvent

Package: java.awt.event

Description: Contains information relating to the action event fired by a component. This event is passed to any *ActionListener* registered on the component.

A Useful Method of the *ActionEvent* Class

Return value	Method name and argument list
Object	getSource( )
	returns the object reference of the component that fired the event. This method is inherited from the *EventObject* class.

ActionListener Interface

Package: java.awt.event

Description: Interface implemented by a class that will handle *Action-Events* fired by a user interface component.

Interface Method to be Implemented

```
public void actionPerformed( ActionEvent event )
```

> An event handler that implements the *ActionListener* interface provides code in this method to respond to the *ActionEvent* fired by any registered components.

ArrayList

Package: java.util

Description: implements a dynamically resizable array of object references

Constructors

```
ArrayList<E>( )
```

> constructs an *ArrayList* object of data type *E* with an initial capacity of 10

```
ArrayList<E>( int initialCapacity )
```

> constructs an *ArrayList* object of data type *E* with the specified initial capacity. Throws an *IllegalArgumentException*

Useful Methods of the *ArrayList* Class
(<u>E</u> represents the data type of the *ArrayList*.)

Return value	Method name and argument list
boolean	add(E element)
	appends the specified *element* to the end of the list. Returns *true*.
void	clear( )
	removes all the elements from the list
E	get(int index)
	returns the element at the specified *index* position; the element is not removed from the list.

E	`remove( int index )`

returns and removes the element at the specified *index* position

E	`set( int index, E newElement )`

returns the element at the specified *index* position and replaces that element with *newElement.*

int	`size( )`

returns the number of elements in the list

void	`trimToSize( )`

sets the capacity to the list's current size

BorderLayout

Package: java.awt

Description: a layout manager that arranges user interface components into five areas: NORTH, SOUTH, EAST, WEST, and CENTER. Each area can hold, at most, one component.

Constructors

`BorderLayout( )`

creates a border layout with no gaps between components

`BorderLayout( int hGap, int vGap )`

creates a border layout with a horizontal gap of *hGap* pixels between components and a vertical gap of *vGap* pixels between components. Unlike *GridLayout*, horizontal gaps are not placed at the left and right edges, nor are vertical gaps placed at the top and bottom edges.

BufferedReader

Package: java.io

Description: reads text from a character input stream, using buffering for efficiency

Constructor

`BufferedReader( Reader r )`

constructs a *BufferedReader* object from a *Reader* object

Useful Methods of the *BufferedReader* Class	
Return value	**Method name and argument list**
void	close( )
	releases resources associated with an open input stream. Throws an *IOException*.
String	readLine( )
	reads a line of text from the current *InputStream* object, and returns the text as a *String*. Returns a *null String* when the end of the file is reached. Throws an *IOException*.

BufferedWriter

Package: java.io

Description: writes text to a character output stream, using buffering for efficiency

Constructor
BufferedWriter(Writer w)
constructs a *BufferedWriter* object from a *Writer* object

Useful Methods of the *BufferedWriter* Class	
Return value	**Method name and argument list**
void	close( )
	releases the resources associated with the *BufferedWriter* object. Throws an *IOException*.
void	newLine( )
	writes a line separator. Throws an *IOException*.
void	write(String s)
	writes a *String* to the current *OutputStream* object. This method is inherited from the *Writer class*. Throws an *IOException*.

ButtonGroup

Package: javax.swing

Description: creates a mutually exclusive group of buttons

Constructor

```
ButtonGroup( )
```

constructs a button group. Adding buttons to a *ButtonGroup* makes the buttons in the group mutually exclusive.

A Useful Method of the *ButtonGroup* Class

Return value	Method name and argument list
void	add(AbstractButton button)

adds the *button* to the button group. The argument can be an object of the *JButton*, *JRadioButton*, or *JCheckBox* class because these are subclasses of the *AbstractButton* class.

Color

Package: java.awt

Description: creates colors to be used in producing graphical output

Constructor

```
Color( int red, int green, int blue )
```

instantiates a *Color* object with the combined color intensities of *red*, *green*, and *blue*. Each color intensity can range from 0 to 255.

Predefined *Color* Constants

Color Constant	Red	Green	Blue
Color.black or Color.BLACK	0	0	0
Color.blue or Color.BLUE	0	0	255
Color.cyan or Color.CYAN	0	255	255
Color.darkGray or Color.DARK_GRAY	64	64	64
Color.gray or Color.GRAY	128	128	128
Color.green or Color.GREEN	0	255	0
Color.lightGray or Color.LIGHT_GRAY	192	192	192

Color Constant	Red	Green	Blue
Color.magenta or Color.MAGENTA	255	0	255
Color.orange or Color.ORANGE	255	200	0
Color.pink or Color.PINK	255	175	175
Color.red or Color.RED	255	0	0
Color.white or Color.WHITE	255	255	255
Color.yellow or Color.YELLOW	255	255	0

Container

Package: java.awt

Description: a user interface component that can contain other components. *JComponent* is a subclass of *Container*; thus, all *JComponents* inherit these methods.

Useful Methods of the *Container* Class

Return value	Method name and argument list
Component	add(Component component)
	adds the *component* to the container, using the rules of the layout manager. Returns *component*.
void	removeAll( )
	removes all components from the container
void	setLayout(LayoutManager mgr)
	sets the layout manager of the container to *mgr*

DecimalFormat

Package: java.text

Description: provides methods for formatting numbers for output

Constructor

DecimalFormat(String pattern)

instantiates a *DecimalFormat* object with the output *pattern* specified in the argument

A Useful Method of the *DecimalFormat* Class	
Return value	**Method name and argument list**
String	format(double number)
	returns a *String* representation of *number* formatted according to the *DecimalFormat* pattern used to instantiate the object. This method is inherited from the *NumberFormat* class.

Commonly Used Pattern Symbols For a *DecimalFormat* Object	
Symbol	**Meaning**
0	Required digit. If the value for the digit in this position is 0, print a zero.
#	Digit. Don't print anything if the digit is 0.
.	Decimal point
,	Comma separator
%	Multiply by 100 and display a percentage sign

Double

Package: java.lang

Description: wrapper class that creates an equivalent object from a *double* variable and provides methods for converting a *String* to a *double* primitive type and a *Double* object.

Constructor
Double(double d)
instantiates a *Double* object with a *double* instance variable having the same value as *d*.

Useful Methods of the *Double* Wrapper Class	
Return value	**Method name and argument list**
double	parseDouble(String s)
	static method that converts the *String s* to a *double* and returns that value. Throws a *NumberFormatException*.
Double	valueOf(String s)
	static method that converts the *String s* to a *Double* object and returns that object. Throws a *NumberFormatException*.

Enum

Package: java.lang

Description: provides for creation of enumerated types

Useful Methods for *enum* Objects	
Return value	**Method name and argument list**
int	compareTo(Enum eObj)
	compares two *enum* objects and returns a negative number if *this* object is less than the argument, a positive number if *this* object is greater than the argument, and 0 if the two objects are equal.
boolean	equals(Object eObj)
	returns *true* if *this* object is equal to the argument *eObj*; returns *false* otherwise.
int	ordinal( )
	returns the numeric value of the *enum* object. By default, the value of the first object in the list is 0, the value of the second object is 1, and so on.
String	toString( )
	returns the name of the *enum* constant
enum	valueOf(String enumName)
	static method that returns the *enum* object whose name is the same as the *String* argument *enumName*.

Exception

Package: java.lang

Description: the superclass for all predefined Java exceptions. All subclasses of the *Exception* class inherit these *public* methods.

Useful Methods of *Exception* Classes	
Return value	**Method name and argument list**
String	getMessage( )
	returns a message indicating the cause of the exception. This method is inherited from the *Throwable* class.

void	printStackTrace( )

prints the line number of the code that caused the exception, along with the sequence of method calls leading up to the exception

String	toString( )

returns a *String* containing the exception class name and a message indicating the cause of the exception

File

Package: java.io

Description: represents platform-independent file names

Constructor

File(String pathname)

constructs a *File* object with the *pathname* file name so that the file name is platform-independent.

FileInputStream

Package: java.io

Description: reads bytes from a file

Constructor

FileInputStream(String filename)

constructs a *FileInputStream* object from a *String* representing the name of a file. Throws a *FileNotFoundException*.

FileOutputStream

Package: java.io

Description: writes bytes to a file

Constructor

FileOutputStream(String filename, boolean mode)

constructs a *FileOutputStream* object from a *String* representing the name of a file; if mode is *false*, we will write to the file; if *mode* is *true*, we will append to the file. Throws a *FileNotFoundException*.

FileReader

Package: java.io

Description: reads characters from a text file

Constructor

```
FileReader( String filename )
```

constructs a *FileReader* object from a *String* representing the name of a file. Throws a *FileNotFoundException*.

FileWriter

Package: java.io

Description: writes characters to a text file

Constructor

```
FileWriter( String fileName, boolean mode )
```

constructs a *FileWriter* object from a *String* representing the name of a file; if *mode* is *false*, we will write to the file; if it is *true*, we will append to the file. Throws an *IOException*.

FlowLayout

Package: java.awt

Description: layout manager that arranges components left to right, starting a new row when a newly added component does not fit on the current row

Constructor

```
FlowLayout( )
```

creates a flow layout with components centered.

Graphics

Package: java.awt

Description: represents the current graphical context, including the component on which drawing will take place and the current color.

Useful Methods of the *Graphics* Class

Return value	Method name and argument list
void	`clearRect( int x, int y, int width, int height )`
	draws a solid rectangle in the current background color with its top left corner at (*x, y*), with the specified *width* and *height* in pixels.
void	`drawLine( int xStart, int yStart, int xEnd, int yEnd )`
	draws a line starting at (xStart, yStart) and ending at (xEnd, yEnd)
void	`drawOval( int x, int y, int width, int height )`
	draws the outline of an oval inside an invisible rectangle with the specified *width* and *height* in pixels. The top left corner of the rectangle is (*x, y*).
void	`drawRect( int x, int y, int width, int height )`
	draws the outline of a rectangle with its top left corner at (*x, y*), with the specified *width* and *height* in pixels.
void	`drawString( String s, int x, int y )`
	displays the *String s.* If you were to draw an invisible rectangle around the first letter of the *String*, (*x, y*) would be the lower left corner of that rectangle.
void	`fillOval( int x, int y, int width, int height )`
	draws a solid oval inside an invisible rectangle with the specified *width* and *height* in pixels. The top left corner of the rectangle is (*x, y*).
void	`fillRect( int x, int y, int width, int height )`
	draws a solid rectangle with its top left corner at (*x, y*), with the specified *width* and *height* in pixels.
void	`setColor( Color c )`
	sets the current foreground color to the *Color* specified by *c*.

GridLayout

Package: java.awt

Description: a layout manager that arranges components in a grid with a fixed number of rows and columns

Constructors

```
GridLayout( int numberOfRows, int numberOfColumns )
```

creates a grid layout with the number of rows and columns specified by the arguments.

```
GridLayout( int numberOfRows, int numberOfColumns,
                        int hGap, int vGap )
```

creates a grid layout with the specified number of rows and columns and with a horizontal gap of *hGap* pixels between columns and a vertical gap of *vGap* pixels between rows. Horizontal gaps are also placed at the left and right edges, and vertical gaps are placed at the top and bottom edges.

InputStreamReader

Package: java.io

Description: reads bytes from an input stream and converts them to characters

Constructor

```
InputStreamReader( InputStream is )
```

constructs an *InputStreamReader* object from an *InputStream* object. For console input, the *InputStream* object is *System.in*

Integer

Package: java.lang

Description: wrapper class that creates an equivalent object for an *int* variable and provides methods for converting a *String* to an *int* primitive type and an *Integer* object

Constructor	

`Integer( int i )`

> instantiates an *Integer* object with an *int* instance variable having the same value as *i*.

Useful Methods of the *Integer* Wrapper Class	
Return value	**Method name and argument list**
`int`	`parseInt( String s )`
	static method that converts the *String s* to an *int* and returns that value. Throws a *NumberFormatException*.
`Integer`	`valueOf( String s )`
	static method that converts the *String s* to an *Integer* object and returns that object. Throws a *NumberFormatException*.

ItemEvent

Package: java.awt.event

Description: contains information relating to the item event fired by a component. This event is passed to any *ItemListener* registered on the component.

Useful Methods of the *ItemEvent* Class	
Return value	**Method name and argument list**
`Object`	`getSource( )`
	returns the object reference of the component that fired the event. This method is inherited from the *EventObject* class.
`int`	`getStateChange( )`
	If the item is selected, the value *SELECTED* is returned; if the item is deselected, the value *DESELECTED* is returned, where *SELECTED* and *DESELECTED* are *static int* constants of the *ItemEvent* class.

ItemListener Interface

Package: java.awt.event

Description: interface implemented by a class that will handle *ItemEvents* fired by a user interface component

Interface Method to be Implemented

```
public void itemStateChanged( ItemEvent event )
```

> An event handler that implements the *ItemListener* interface writes code in this method to respond to the *ItemEvent* fired by any registered components.

JButton

Package: javax.swing

Description: a command button user interface component. When a user presses the button, an *ActionEvent* is fired.

Constructor

```
JButton( String buttonLabel )
```

> constructs a command button labeled *buttonLabel*

A Useful Method of the *JButton* Class

Return value	Method name and argument list
void	addActionListener(ActionListener handler)

> registers an event handler for *ActionEvents* on this button. This method is inherited from the *AbstractButton* class.

JCheckBox

Package: javax.swing

Description: a checkbox user interface component. When a user clicks the checkbox, its state alternates between selected and not selected. Each click fires an *ItemEvent*.

Constructors

```
JCheckBox( String checkBoxLabel )
```

> constructs a checkbox labeled *checkBoxLabel*. By default, the checkbox is initially deselected.

```
JCheckBox( String checkBoxLabel, boolean selected )
```

constructs a checkbox labeled *checkBoxLabel*. If *selected* is *true*, the
checkbox is initially selected; if *selected* is *false*, the checkbox is
initially deselected.

Useful Methods of the *JCheckBox* Class

Return value	Method name and argument list
void	`addItemListener( ItemListener handler )`
	registers an event handler for *ItemEvents* on this checkbox. This method is inherited from the *AbstractButton* class.
boolean	`isSelected( )`
	returns *true* if the checkbox is selected; *false* otherwise. This method is inherited from the *AbstractButton* class.
void	`setSelected( boolean state )`
	selects the checkbox if *state* is *true*; deselects the checkbox if *state* is *false*. This method is inherited from the *AbstractButton* class.

JComboBox

Package: javax.swing

Description: a drop-down list user interface component. When a user
selects an item from the list, an *ItemEvent* is fired.

Constructor

```
JComboBox( Object [ ] arrayName )
```

constructs a new *JComboBox* component initially filled with the
objects in *arrayName*. Often, the objects are *Strings*.

Useful Methods of the *JComboBox* Class

Return value	Method name and argument list
void	`addItemListener( ItemListener handler )`
	registers an event handler for *ItemEvents* on this combo box.
int	`getSelectedIndex( )`
	returns the index of the selected item. The index of the first item in the list is 0.

void	`setMaximumRowCount( int size )`
	sets the number of rows that will be visible at one time. If the list has more items than the maximum number visible at one time, scrollbars are added.
void	`setSelectedIndex( int index )`
	sets the item at *index* as selected. The index of the first item in the list is 0.

JComponent

Package: javax.swing

Description: The superclass for swing user interface components, except for top-level components, such as *JFrame* and *JApplet*. Subclasses include *JButton, JCheckBox, JRadioButton, JList, JTextField, JTextArea, JPasswordField, JComboBox, JPanel*, and others, which inherit these *public* methods.

Useful Methods of the *JComponent* Class

Return value	Method name and argument list
void	`addMouseListener( MouseListener handler )`
	registers a *MouseListener* object on the component. This method is inherited from the *Component* class.
void	`addMouseMotionListener( MouseMotionListener handler )`
	registers a *MouseMotionListener* object on the component. This method is inherited from the *Component* class.
void	`repaint( )`
	automatically forces a call to the *paint* method. This method is inherited from the *Component* class.
void	`setBackground( Color backColor )`
	sets the background color of the component to *backColor*.
void	`setEnabled( boolean mode )`
	enables the component if *mode* is *true*, disables the component if *mode* is *false*. An enabled component can respond to user interaction.
void	`setForeground( Color foreColor )`
	sets the foreground color of the component to *foreColor*.

void	`setOpaque( boolean mode )`

sets the component's background to opaque if *mode* is *true*; sets the component's background to transparent if *mode* is *false*. If opaque, the component's background is filled with the component's background color; if transparent, the component's background is filled with the background color of the container on which it is placed. The default is transparent.

void	`setToolTipText( String toolTip )`

sets the tool tip text to *toolTip*. When the mouse lingers over the component, the tool tip text will be displayed.

void	`setVisible( boolean mode )`

makes the component visible if *mode* is *true*; hides the component if mode is *false*. The default is visible.

JFrame

Package: javax.swing

Description: a window user interface component

Constructors

`JFrame( )`

constructs a *JFrame* object, initially invisible, with no text in the title bar.

`JFrame( String titleBarText )`

constructs a *JFrame* object, initially invisible, with *titleBarText* displayed on the window's title bar.

Useful Methods of the *JFrame* Class

Return value	Method name and argument list
Container	`getContentPane( )`

returns the content pane object for this window.

void	`setDefaultCloseOperation( int operation )`

sets the default operation when the user closes this window, that is, when the user clicks on the X icon in the top-right corner of the window.

void	setSize(int width, int height)

sizes the window to the specified *width* and *height* in pixels. This method is inherited from the *Component* class.

void	setVisible(boolean mode)

displays this window if *mode* is *true*; hides the window if *mode* is *false*. This method is inherited from the *Component* class.

JLabel

Package: javax.swing

Description: a user interface component that displays text or an image. A *JLabel* does not fire any events.

Constructors

```
JLabel( String text )
```

creates a *JLabel* object that displays the specified *text*.

```
JLabel( String text, int alignment )
```

creates a *JLabel* object that displays the specified *text*. The *alignment* argument specifies the alignment of the text within the label component. The *alignment* value can be any of the following *static int* constants of the *SwingConstants* interface: LEFT, CENTER, RIGHT, LEADING, or TRAILING. By default, the label text is left-adjusted.

```
JLabel( Icon image )
```

creates a *JLabel* object that displays the *image*.

Useful Methods of the *JLabel* Class

Return value	Method name and argument list
void	setIcon(Icon newIcon)

sets the *Icon* to be displayed in the label as *newIcon*.

void	setText(String newText)

sets the text to be displayed in the label as *newText*.

JList

Package: javax.swing

Description: A list user interface component. When a user selects one or more items from the list, an *ItemEvent* is fired.

Constructor

```
JList( Object [ ] arrayName )
```

constructs a new *JList* component initially filled with the objects in *arrayName*. Often, the objects are *Strings*.

Useful Methods of the *JList* Class

Return value	Method name and argument list
void	`addListSelectionListener( ListSelectionListener handler )`

registers an event handler for *ItemEvents* fired by this list.

int	`getSelectedIndex( )`

returns the index of the selected item. The index of the first item in the list is 0.

void	`setSelectedIndex( int index )`

selects the item at *index*. The index of the first item in the list is 0.

void	`setSelectionMode( int selectionMode )`

sets the number of selections that can be made at one time. The following *static int* constants of the *ListSelectionModel* interface can be used to set the selection mode:

SINGLE_SELECTION—one selection allowed

SINGLE_INTERVAL_SELECTION—multiple contiguous items can be selected

MULTIPLE_INTERVAL_SELECTION—multiple contiguous intervals can be selected (This is the default.)

JOptionPane

Package: javax.swing

Description: pops up an input or output dialog box

Useful Methods of the *JOptionPane* Class

Return value	Method name and argument list
String	showInputDialog(Component parent, Object prompt)
	static method that pops up an input dialog box, where *prompt* asks the user for input. Returns the characters typed by the user as a *String*.
void	showMessageDialog(Component parent, Object message)
	static method that pops up an output dialog box with *message* displayed. The *message* argument is usually a *String*.

JPasswordField

Package: javax.swing

Description: A single-line text field user interface component that allows users to enter text, such as a password, without the text being displayed. When a user presses the *Enter* key with the cursor in the field, an *Action-Event* is fired.

Constructor

JPasswordField(int numberColumns)

constructs an empty password field with the specified number of columns.

Useful Methods of the *JPasswordField* Class

Return value	Method name and argument list
void	addActionListener(ActionListener handler)
	registers an event handler for this password field. This method is inherited from the *JTextField* class.
char [ ]	getPassword( )
	returns the text entered in this password field as an array of *chars*.

void	setEchoChar(char c)

sets the echo character of the password field to *c*.

void	setEditable(boolean mode)

sets the properties of the password field as editable or non-editable, depending on whether *mode* is *true* or *false*. The default is editable. This method is inherited from the *JTextComponent* class.

void	setText(String newText)

sets the text of the password field to *newText*. This method is inherited from the *JTextComponent* class.

JRadioButton

Package: javax.swing

Description: a radio button user interface component. When a user presses the button, other radio buttons in the *ButtonGroup* are deselected and an *ItemEvent* is fired.

Constructors

JRadioButton(String buttonLabel)

constructs a radio button labeled *buttonLabel*. By default, the radio button is initially deselected.

JRadioButton(String buttonLabel, boolean selected)

constructs a radio button labeled *buttonLabel*. If *selected* is *true*, the button is initially selected; if *selected* is *false*, the button is deselected.

Useful Methods of the *JRadioButton* Class

Return value	Method name and argument list
void	addItemListener(ItemListener handler)

registers an event handler for *ItemEvents* for this radio button. This method is inherited from the *AbstractButton* class.

boolean	isSelected( )

returns *true* if the radio button is selected; *false* otherwise. This method is inherited from the *AbstractButton* class.

void	setSelected(boolean state)
	selects the radio button if *state* is *true*; deselects the radio button if *state* is *false*. This method is inherited from the *AbstractButton* class.

JTextArea

Package: javax.swing

Description: a multi-line text field user interface component. When a user presses the *Enter* key with the cursor in the field, an *ActionEvent* is fired.

Constructors

JTextArea(String text)

constructs a text area initially filled with *text*.

JTextArea(int numRows, int numColumns)

constructs an empty text area with the number of rows and columns specified by *numRows* and *numColumns*.

JTextArea(String text, int numRows, int numColumns)

constructs a text area initially filled with *text*, and with the number of rows and columns specified by *numRows* and *numColumns*.

Useful Methods of the *JTextArea* Class

Return value	Method name and argument list
String	getText( )
	returns the text contained in the text area. This method is inherited from the *JTextComponent* class.
void	setEditable(boolean mode)
	sets the properties of the text area as editable or non-editable, depending on whether *mode* is *true* or *false*. The default is editable. This method is inherited from the *JTextComponent* class.
void	setText(String newText)
	sets the text of the text area to *newText*. This method is inherited from the *JTextComponent* class.

JTextField

Package: javax.swing

Description: a single-line text field user interface component. When a user presses the *Enter* key with the cursor in the field, an *ActionEvent* is fired.

Constructors

`JTextField( String text, int numColumns )`

> constructs a new text field initially filled with *text*, with the specified number of columns

`JTextField( int numberColumns )`

> constructs an empty text field with the specified number of columns.

Useful Methods of the *JTextField* Class

Return value	Method name and argument list
void	`addActionListener( ActionListener handler )`
	registers an event handler for *ActionEvents* fired by this text field.
String	`getText( )`
	returns the text contained in the text field. This method is inherited from the *JTextComponent* class.
void	`setEditable( boolean mode )`
	sets the properties of the text field as editable or non-editable, depending on whether *mode* is *true* or *false*. The default is editable. This method is inherited from the *JTextComponent* class.
void	`setText( String newText )`
	sets the text of the text field to *newText*. This method is inherited from the *JTextComponent* class.

ListSelectionListener Interface

Package: javax.swing.event

Description: interface implemented by a class that will handle *ListSelectionEvents* fired by a user interface component, such as a *JList*.

Interface Method to be Implemented

```
public void valueChanged( ListSelectionEvent e )
```

> An event handler that implements the *ListSelectionListener* interface writes code in this method to respond to the *ListSelectionEvent* fired by any registered components.

Math

Package: java.lang

Description: provides methods for performing common mathematical computations. All methods are *static*.

Predefined *Static* Constants

	Data type	Description
E	double	the base of the natural logarithm. Approximate value is 2.78
PI	double	pi, the ratio of the circumference of a circle to its diameter. Approximate value is 3.14.

Math Class Method Summary
Note: All methods are *static*.

Return value	Method name and argument list
dataTypeOfArg	abs(arg)
	returns the absolute value of the argument *arg*, which can be a *double, float, int,* or *long*.
double	log(double a)
	returns the natural logarithm (in base e) of its argument. For example, log(1) returns 0 and log(*Math.E*) returns 1.
dataTypeOfArgs	max(argA, argB)
	returns the larger of the two arguments. The arguments can be *doubles, floats, ints,* or *longs*.

dataTypeOfArgs	min(argA, argB)
	returns the smaller of the two arguments. The arguments can be *doubles, floats, ints,* or *longs.*
double	pow(double base, double exp)
	returns the value of *base* raised to the *exp* power
double	random( )
	returns a random number greater than or equal to 0 and less than 1.
int	round(float a)
	returns the closest integer to its argument, *a.*
double	sqrt(double a)
	returns the positive square root of *a.*

MouseEvent

Package: java.awt.event

Description: object containing information relating to a mouse event generated by the user moving or dragging the mouse or clicking its buttons on a component. This event is passed to any *MouseListener* or *MouseMotionListener* registered on the component.

Useful Methods of the *MouseEvent* Class

Return value	Method name and argument list
int	getX( )
	returns the x value of the (x, y) coordinate of the mouse activity.
int	getY( )
	returns the y value of the (x, y) coordinate of the mouse activity.

MouseListener Interface

Package: java.awt.event

Description: interface implemented by a class that will handle *MouseEvents* (press, release, click, enter, exit).

Interface Methods to be Implemented

```
public void mouseClicked( MouseEvent e )
```

called when the mouse button is pressed and released on a registered component.

```
public void mouseEntered( MouseEvent e )
```

called when the mouse enters a registered component.

```
public void mouseExited( MouseEvent e )
```

called when the mouse exits a registered component.

```
public void mousePressed( MouseEvent e )
```

called when the mouse button is pressed on a registered component.

```
public void mouseReleased( MouseEvent e )
```

called when the mouse is released after being pressed on a registered component.

MouseMotionListener Interface

Package: java.awt.event

Description: Interface implemented by a class that will handle *MouseEvents* (move, drag).

Interface Methods to be Implemented

```
public void mouseDragged( MouseEvent e )
```

called when the mouse is dragged after its button is pressed on a registered component.

```
public void mouseMoved( MouseEvent e )
```

called when the mouse is moved onto a registered component.

NumberFormat

Package: java.text

Description: provides methods for formatting numbers in currency, percent, and other formats. There are no constructors for this class.

Useful Methods of the *NumberFormat* Class	
Return value	**Method name and argument list**
String	format(double number)
	returns a *String* representation of *number* formatted according to the *NumberFormat* object reference used to call the method.
NumberFormat	getCurrencyInstance( )
	static method that creates a format for printing money.
NumberFormat	getPercentInstance( )
	static method that creates a format for printing a percentage.

ObjectInputStream

Package: java.io

Description: Reads serialized objects from a file.

Constructor
ObjectInputStream(InputStream in)
constructs an *ObjectInputStream* from the I*nputStream in*. Throws an *IOException*.

A Useful Method of the *ObjectInputStream* Class	
Return value	**Method name and argument list**
Object	readObject( )
	reads the next object and returns it. The object read must be an instance of a class that implements the *Serializable* interface. When the end of the file is reached, an *EOFException* is thrown. Also throws an *IOException* and *ClassNotFoundException*.

ObjectOutputStream

Package: java.io

Description: writes objects in a serialized format to a file

Constructor
ObjectOutputStream(OutputStream out)
creates an *ObjectOutputStream* that writes to the *OutputStream out*. Throws an *IOException*.

A Useful Method of the *ObjectOutputStream* Class	
Return value	**Method name and argument list**
void	writeObject(Object obj)
	writes the object *obj* to a file. That object must be an instance of a class that implements the *Serializable* interface. Throws an *InvalidClassException*, *NotSerializableException*, and *IOException*.

PrintWriter

Package: java.io

Description: writes primitive data types and *Strings* to a text file

Constructor
PrintWriter(OutputStream os)
constructs a *PrintWriter* object from the *OutputStream* object.

Useful Methods of the *PrintWriter* class	
Return value	**Method name and argument list**
void	close( )
	releases the resources associated with the *PrintWriter* object.
void	print(boolean b)
	prints the *boolean b* to the *OutputStream*.
void	print(char c)
	prints the character *c* to the *OutputStream*.
void	print(double d)
	prints the *double d* to the *OutputStream*.
void	print(int i)
	prints the *int i* to the *OutputStream*.
void	print(String s)
	prints the *String s* to the *OutputStream*.
void	println(boolean b)
	prints the *boolean b* to the *OutputStream* and appends a newline.

void	`println( char c )`
	prints the character *c* to the *OutputStream* and appends a new-line.
void	`println( double  d )`
	prints the *double d* to the *OutputStream* and appends a newline.
void	`println( int i )`
	prints the *int i* to the *OutputStream* and appends a newline.
void	`println( String s )`
	prints the *String s* to the *OutputStream* and appends a newline.

Scanner

Package: java.util

Description: provides support for reading from an input stream or file

Constructors

`Scanner( InputStream source )`

> creates a *Scanner* object for reading from *source*. If *source* is *System.in*, this instantiates a *Scanner* object for reading from the Java console.

`Scanner( File source )`

> creates a *Scanner* object for reading from a file. (See the *File* class.)

Selected Methods of the *Scanner* Class

Return value	Method name and argument list
boolean	`hasNext( )`
	returns *true* if there is another token in the input stream; *false*, otherwise.
boolean	`hasNextBoolean( )`
	returns *true* if the next token in the input stream can be read as a *boolean; false*, otherwise.
boolean	`hasNextByte( )`
	returns *true* if the next token in the input stream can be read as a *byte; false*, otherwise.

boolean	hasNextDouble( )	
	returns *true* if the next token in the input stream can be read as a *double*; *false*, otherwise.	
boolean	hasNextFloat( )	
	returns *true* if the next token in the input stream can be read as a *float*; *false*, otherwise.	
boolean	hasNextInt( )	
	returns *true* if the next token in the input stream can be read as an *int*; *false*, otherwise.	
boolean	hasNextLong( )	
	returns *true* if the next token in the input stream can be read as a *long*; *false*, otherwise.	
boolean	hasNextShort( )	
	returns *true* if the next token can be read as a *short*; *false*, otherwise.	
String	next( )	
	returns the next token in the input stream as a *String*.	
boolean	nextBoolean( )	
	returns the next input token as a *boolean*. Throws an *InputMismatchException*.	
byte	nextByte( )	
	returns the next input token as a *byte*. Throws an *InputMismatchException*.	
double	nextDouble( )	
	returns the next input token as a *double*. Throws an *InputMismatchException*.	
float	nextFloat( )	
	returns the next input token as a *float*. Throws an *InputMismatchException*.	
int	nextInt( )	
	returns the next input token as an *int*. Throws an *InputMismatchException*.	

String	nextLine( )

returns the remainder of the input line as a *String*.

long	nextLong( )

returns the next input token as a *long*. Throws an *Input-MismatchException*.

short	nextShort( )

returns the next input token as a *short*. Throws an *Input-MismatchException*.

String

Package: java.lang

Description: provides support for storing, searching, and manipulating sequences of characters

Constructors

String(String str)

creates a *String* object with the value of *str*, which can be a *String* object or a *String* literal.

String( )

creates an empty *String* object.

String(char [ ] charArray)

creates a *String* object containing the characters in the *char* array *charArray*.

Methods

Return value	Method name and argument list
char	charAt(int index)

returns the character at the position specified by *index*. The first index is 0.

int	compareTo(String str)

compares the value of the two *Strings*. If the *String* object is less than the argument, a negative integer is returned. If the *String* object is greater than the *String* argument, a positive number is returned; if the two *Strings* are equal, a 0 is returned.

boolean	equals(Object str)
	compares the value of two *Strings*. Returns *true* if *str* is a *String,* is not *null,* and is equal to the *String* object; *false* otherwise.
boolean	equalsIgnoreCase(String str)
	compares the value of two *Strings,* treating upper- and lowercase characters as equal. Returns *true* if the *Strings* are equal; *false* otherwise.
int	indexOf(char searchChar)
	returns the index of the first occurrence of *searchChar* in the *String*
String	indexOf(String substring)
	returns the index of the first occurrence of *substring* in the *String*
String	substring(int startIndex, int endIndex)
	returns a substring of the *String* object beginning at the character at index *startIndex* and ending at the character at index (*endIndex – 1*)
String	toLowerCase( )
	converts all letters in the *String* to lowercase
String	toUpperCase( )
	converts all letters in the *String* to uppercase

StringTokenizer

Package: java.util

Description: parses a *String* into tokens using specified delimiters

Constructors

StringTokenizer(String str)

constructs a *StringTokenizer* object for the specified *String* using space, tab, carriage return, newline, and form feed as the default delimiters.

StringTokenizer(String str, String delim)

constructs a *StringTokenizer* object for the specified *String* using *delim* as the delimiters.

Useful Methods of the *StringTokenizer* Class

Return value	Method name and argument list
int	countTokens( ) returns the number of unretrieved tokens in this object; the count is decremented as tokens are retrieved.
boolean	hasMoreTokens( ) returns *true* if more tokens are available to be retrieved; returns *false* otherwise.
String	nextToken( ) returns the next token.

System

Package: java.lang

System.out

The *out* class constant of the *System* class is a *PrintStream* object, which represents the standard system output device. The following *PrintStream* methods can be called using the object reference **System.out** in order to print to the Java console.

Methods

Return value	Method name and argument list
void	print(argument) prints *argument* to the standard output device. The argument is usually any primitive data type or a *String* object.
void	println(argument) prints *argument* to the standard output device, then prints a new-line character. The argument is usually any primitive data type or a *String* object.

APPENDIX G

Solutions to Selected Exercises

1.7   Exercises, Problems, and Projects

1.7.1   Multiple Choice Exercises:

1. Java

4. servers

7. is a multiple of 4

10. C

13. *javac Hello.java*

1.7.2   Converting Numbers

16. 11000011100

19. 0x15

1.7.3   General Questions

22. 750 millions

25. red = 51; green = 171; blue = 18

28. *javac*

2.5 Exercises, Problems, and Projects

2.5.1 Multiple Choice Exercises

1. `int a;`

2.5.2 Reading and Understanding Code

4. 12.5

7. 2.0

10. 4

13. 5

16. 2.4

19. 5

22. 0

2.5.3 Fill in the Code

25. `boolean a;`
    `a = false;`

28. `float avg = (float) ( a + b ) / 2;`
    `System.out.println( "The average is " + avg );`

31. `a *= 3;`

2.5.4 Identifying Errors in Code

34. cannot assign a *double* to a *float* variable (possible loss of precision)

37. there should not be a space between – and =

2.5.5 Debugging Area

40. cannot assign a *double* to an *int* variable (possible loss of precision). Change to:

    `int a = 26;`

43. =+ is different from += (shortcut operator). Here, *a* is assigned the value + 3. To add 3 to *a*, change the second statement to:

    `a += 3;`

3.10   Exercises, Problems, and Projects

3.10.1   Multiple Choice Exercises

1. `import`

4. `new`

7. it is a class method

10. `double`

13. `Math.E;`

3.10.2   Reading and Understanding Code

16. hello

19. 3.141592653589793

22. 8

3.10.3   Fill in the Code

25. `System.out.println( s.length( ) );`

28.
```
System.out.print( "Welcome\n" );
System.out.print( "to\n" );
System.out.print( "Java\n" );
System.out.print( "Illuminated\n" );
```

31.
```
// code below assumes we have imported Scanner
Scanner scan = new Scanner( System.in );
System.out.print( "Enter two integers > " );
int i = scan.nextInt( );
int j = scan.nextInt( );
int min = Math.min( i, j );
System.out.println( "min of " + i + " and " + j + " is " + min );
```

34.
```
// code below assumes we have imported Scanner
Scanner scan = new Scanner( System.in );
System.out.print( "Enter a double > " );
double number = scan.nextDouble( );
double square = Math.pow( number, 2 );
System.out.println( number + " square = " + square );
```

3.10.4   Identifying Errors in Code

37. The Java compiler does not recognize system. It should be *System*, not system.

40. The *round* method of the *Math* class returns a *long*; a *long* cannot be assigned to a *short* variable due to a potential loss of precision.

43. The *char* 'H' cannot be assigned to the *String s*. The two data types are not compatible.

3.10.5   Debugging Area

46. Java is case sensitive. The *Math* class needs to be spelled with an upper case M.

49. In the output statement, we are just printing the value of *grade* without any formatting. To format *grade* as a percentage, the output statement should be:

```
System.out.println( "Your grade is " + percent.format( grade ) );
```

4.7   Exercises, Problems, and Projects

4.7.1   Multiple Choice Exercises

1. `java.awt`

4. true

7. the (x, y) coordinate of the upper-left corner of the rectangle we are drawing

10. 256

4.7.2   Reading and Understanding Code

13. 250 pixels

4.7.3   Fill in the Code

16. `g.setColor( Color.RED );`

19. `g.fillRect( 50, 30, 50, 270 );`

4.7.4   Identifying Errors in Code

22. There should be double quotes around the literal *Find a bug*, not single quotes. Single quotes are used for a *char*, not a *String*.

25. There is no *public color* instance variable in the *Graphics* class. The *set-Color* mutator method should be used to set the color of the *Graphics* object.

4.7.5   Debugging Area

28. We are trying to override the *paint* method, which is an instance method. The header of *paint* should therefore not include the keyword *static*.

5.14   Exercises, Problems, and Projects

5.14.1   Multiple Choice Exercises

1.

❑	`a < b`	true
❑	`a != b`	true
❑	`a == 4`	false
❑	`( b - a ) <= 1`	false
❑	`Math.abs( a - b ) >= 2`	true
❑	`( b % 2 == 1 )`	true
❑	`b <= 5`	true

4. yes

7.

❑	`a < b || b < 10`	no
❑	`a != b && b < 10`	yes
❑	`a == 4 || b < 10`	yes
❑	`a > b && b < 10`	no

5.14.2   Reading and Understanding Code

10. *true*

13. 27 is divisible by 3
    End of sequence

16. Hello
    Hello
    Done

19. Number 3
    Number 4
    Other number

5.14.3   Fill in the Code

22.
```
if ( a )
    a = false;
else
    a = true;
```

25.
```
if ( b % c == 0 )
    a = true;
else
    a = false;
```

28.
```
if ( a && b > 10 )
    c++;
```

5.14.4   Identifying Errors in Code

31. The *&&* operator cannot be applied to two *int* operands (*a1* and *a2*).

34. We need a set of parentheses around *b*.

37. There is no error.

5.14.5   Debugging Area

40. The expression `a = 31` evaluates to an *int*, 31. The *if* condition requires a *boolean* expression. To fix the problem, replace `a = 31` by `a == 31`.

6.14   Exercises, Problems, and Projects

6.14.1   Multiple Choice Exercises

1. the code runs forever

4. true

6.14.2   Reading and Understanding Code

7. Enter an int > 3
    Enter an int > 5
    Hello
    Enter an int > −1
    Hello

10. 8 and 42

13. 3

16. 40 and 60

19. 3
    3
    3
    3
    4

6.14.3   Fill in the Code

22.
```java
System.out.print( "Enter an integer > " );
int value = scan.nextInt( );
while ( value != 20 )
{
  if ( value >= start )
    System.out.println( value );
  System.out.print( "Enter an integer > " );
  value = scan.nextInt( );
}
```

25.
```java
Scanner scan = new Scanner( System.in );
word = scan.next( );
while ( ! word.equals( "end" ) )
{
  // and your code goes here
  sentence += word;
  word = scan.next( );
}
```

28.
```java
Scanner scan = new Scanner( System.in );
int sum = 0;
System.out.println( "Enter an integer > " );
int value = scan.nextInt( );
while ( value != 0 && value != 100 )
```

```
{
    sum += value;
    System.out.println( "Enter an integer > " );
    value = scan.nextInt( );
}
System.out.println( "sum is " + sum );
```

6.14.4   Identifying Errors in Code

31. The variable *num* needs to be initialized after it is declared.

34. The loop is infinite. *Number* is always different from 5 or different from 7. The logical OR (||) should be changed to a logical AND (&&).

6.14.5   Debugging Area

37. It is an infinite loop; *i* should be incremented, not decremented, inside the body of the *while* loop so that the loop eventually terminates.

40. In the *for* loop header, the loop initialization statement, the loop condition, and the loop update statement should be separated by semicolons (;), not commas(,).

7.18   Exercises, Problems, and Projects

7.18.1   Multiple Choice Exercises

1. The convention is to start with an uppercase letter.

4. true

7. can be basic data types, existing Java types, or user-defined types (from user-defined classes).

10. one parameter, of the same type as the corresponding field.

13. These fields do not need to be passed as parameters to the methods because the class methods have direct access to them.

16. All of the above.

7.18.2   Reading and Understanding Code

19. *double*

22. an instance method (keyword *static* not used)

25. `public static void foo3( double d );`

7.18.3 Fill in the Code

28.
```
private int grade;
private char letterGrade;
```

31.
```
public TelevisionChannel( String newName, int newNumber,
                          boolean newCable )
{
  name = newName;
  number = newNumber;
  cable = newCable;
}
```

34.
```
public String toString( )
{
  return ( "name: " + name + "\tnumber: "
          + number + "\tcable: " + cable );
}
```

37.
```
public String typeOfChannel( )
{
  if ( cable )
    return "cable";
  else
    return "network";
}
```

7.18.4 Identifying Errors in Code

40. The *toString* method needs to return a *String*, not output data.

43. The method header is incorrect; it should be

```
public double calcTax( )
```

46. There are two errors: The assignment operator = should not be used when declaring an *enum* set. And the *enum* constant objects should not be *String* literals but identifiers.

7.18.5 Debugging Area

49. The compiler understands that *Grade* is a method since its header says it returns a *char*. It looks as if it is intended to be a constructor so the keyword *char* should be deleted from the constructor header.

52. The constructor assigns *letterGrade* to the instance variable itself, therefore not changing its value, which by default is the empty *String*. The constructor could be recoded as follows:

```
public Grade( char newLetterGrade )
{
   letterGrade = newLetterGrade;
}
```

8.10   Exercises, Problems, and Projects

8.10.1   Multiple Choice Exercises:

1. `int [ ] a;` and `int a[ ];`

4. `0`

7. `a.length`

10. false

8.10.2   Reading and Understanding Code

13. 48.3

16. 12

    48

    65

19. 14

22. It counts how many elements in the argument array have the value 5.

25. It returns an array of *Strings* identical to the argument array except that the *Strings* are all in lower case.

8.10.3   Fill in the Code

28.
```
if ( a[i] > 20 )
   System.out.println( a[i] );
System.out.println( "the dot product is " + dotProduct );
```

31.
```
System.out.println( "a[" + i + "] = " + a[i] );
```

34.
```
if ( a.length < 2 )
   return false;
```

```
else if ( a[0].equals( a[1] ) )
    return true;
else
    return false;
```

8.10.4   Identifying Errors in Code

37. Index –1 is out of bounds; the statement `System.out.println( a[-1] );` will generate a run-time exception.

40. When declaring an array, the square brackets should be empty. Replace `a[3]` by `a[ ]`.

43. Although the code compiles, it outputs the hash code of the array *a*. To output the elements of the array, we need to loop through the array elements and output them one by one.

8.10.5   Debugging Area

46. Index `a.length` is out of bounds; when *i* is equal to `a.length`, the expression `a[i]` will generate a run-time exception. Replace <= with < in the loop condition.

9.10   Exercises, Problems, and Projects

9.10.1   Multiple Choice Exercises

1. `int[ ][ ] a;` and `int a[ ][ ];`

4. *false*

7. a[2].length

10. true

13. *java.util*

9.10.2   Reading and Understanding Code

16. 3

19. Munich
    Stuttgart
    Berlin
    Bonn

22. Munich
    Berlin
    Ottawa

25. It counts and returns the number of elements in the argument array *a*

28. It returns an *int* array of the same length as the length of the array argument *a*. Each element of the returned array stores the number of columns of the corresponding row in the array argument *a*.

31. 7 (at index 0) 45 (at index 1) 21 (at index 2)

9.10.3   Fill in the Code

34. ```
System.out.println(geo[0][5]);
```

37. ```
for ( int i = 0; i < geo.length; i++ )
{
    for ( int j = 0; j < geo[i].length; j++ )
        System.out.println( geo[i][j] );
}
```

40. ```
int count = 0;
for (int j = 0; j < a[1].length; j++)
{
    if (a[1][j] == 6)
        count++;
}
System.out.println("# of 6s in the 2nd row: " + count);
```

43. This method returns the product of all the elements in an array.
    ```
public int foo(int [ ][ ] a)
{
    int product = 1;
    for (int i = 0; i < a.length; i++)
    {
        for (int j = 0; j < a[i].length; j++)
        {
            product *= a[i][j];
        }
    }
    return product;
}
```

46. ```
System.out.println( languages.size( ) );
```

49.
```
for ( String s : languages )
  {
    if ( s.charAt( 0 ) == 'P' )
      System.out.println( s );
  }
```

9.10.4   Identifying Errors in Code

52. array dimension missing in `new double [ ][10]`

Example of correct code: `double [ ][ ] a = new double [4][10];`

55. Cannot declare an *ArrayList* of a basic data type; the type needs to be a class (for example: *Double*)

58. Correct syntax is `variable = expression;` Because `a.size( )` is not a variable, we cannot assign a value to it.

9.10.5   Debugging Area

61. Other than `a[0][0]`, the first row is not taken into account because *i* is initialized to 1 in the outer loop. It should be `int i = 0;` not `int i = 1;`

64. Index 3 is out of bounds. There are only 3 elements in *a*; the last index is 2.

10.10   Exercises, Problems, and Projects

10.10.1   Multiple Choice Exercises:

1. a class inheriting from another class.

4. *protected* and *public* instance variables and methods.

7. You cannot instantiate an object from an *abstract* class.

10. The class must be declared *abstract*.

10.10.2   Reading and Understanding Code

13. *B* inherits from *A: name, price, foo2, foo3*

   C inherits from *B: name, price, foo1, foo2, foo3*

16.
```
A( ) called
B( ) called
B version of foo1( ) called
```

19. ```
    A( ) called
    B( ) called
    C( ) called
    ```

10.10.3   Fill in the Code

22. ```
    private char middle;
    public G( String f, String n, char m )
    {
      super( f, n );
      middle = m;
    }
    ```

25. ```
    public class K extends F implements I
    ```

10.10.4   Identifying Errors in Code

28. There is no error. `new D( )` returns a *D* object reference. *D* inherits from *C*, therefore a *D* object reference "is a" *C* object reference. Thus, it can be assigned to *c2*.

31. The *foo* method does not have a method body; it must be declared *abstract*.

10.10.5   Debugging Area

34. The instance variable *n* of class *M* is private, and is not inherited by *P*. Therefore, it is not visible inside class *P*.

11.11   Exercises, Problems, and Projects

11.11.1   Multiple Choice Exercises

1. exceptions enable programmers to attempt to recover from illegal situations and continue running the program.

4. false

7. the contents of the file, if any, will be deleted.

10. *java.util*

11.11.2   Reading and Understanding Code

13. ABCD

16. result is ABCABA
    ```

19. Nice finish

22. 0
    1
    2
    3
    4

11.11.3   Fill in the Code

25.
```
    BufferedReader br = new BufferedReader( isr );
    String s1 = br.readLine( );
    String s2 = br.readLine( );
    String s = s1 + s2;
    System.out.println( s );
    br.close( );
}
catch ( IOException ioe )
{
  ioe.printStackTrace( );
}
```

28.
```
while ( st.hasMoreTokens( ) )
{
  s = st.nextToken( );

  if ( s.equals( "C" ) )
    break;
}
```

31.
```
String s = br.readLine( );
while ( s != null )
{
  result += s + " ";
  s = br.readLine( );
}
System.out.println( result );
```

34.
```
average += grades[i];
...
average /= grades.length;
...
pw.print( average );
pw.close( );
```

11.11.4   Identifying Errors in Code

37. the *nextToken* method returns a *String*; the return value cannot be assigned to an *int* variable.

11.11.5   Debugging Area

40. the *catch* block is missing; you need to add it after the *try* block as follows:

```
catch ( IOException ioe )
{
   ioe.printStackTrace( );
}
```

43. at each iteration, the number of tokens left in *st* is 1 less than at the previous iteration. Therefore, the *countTokens* method returns successively 6, 5, 4, 3 whereas the value of *i* is successively 0, 1, 2, and 3, at which time the *for* loop terminates. To fix the problem, assign the value of the number of tokens in *st* to a variable, and use that variable in your *for* loop header as follows:

```
int numberOfTokens = st.countTokens( );
for ( int i = 0; i < numberOfTokens; i++ )
```

12.18   Exercises, Problems, and Projects

12.18.1   Multiple Choice Exercises

1. *JTextField*

4. true

7. All three of them

10. false

13. the horizontal and vertical gaps between the 5 areas of the component

12.18.2   Reading and Understanding Code

16. 3

19. "Hello" is output to the console

22. 3

25. 5 is output to the console

12.18.3   Fill in the Code

28. ```java
b = new JButton("Button");
```

31. ```java
public void actionPerformed( ActionEvent ae )
{
  if ( ae.getSource( ) == b )
    tf.setText( "Button clicked" );
}
```

34. ```java
c.add(label1, BorderLayout.NORTH);
```

37. ```java
for ( int i = 0; i < buttons.length; i++ )
    p1.add( buttons[i] );
```

40. ```java
for (int i = 0; i < textfields.length; i++)
    p2.add(textfields[i]);
```

### 12.18.4   Identifying Errors in Code

43. *ActionListener* is an interface; it can be implemented but not extended

### 12.18.5   Debugging Area

46. We are trying to add the label *l* to the content pane before *l* has been instantiated. To fix the problem, instantiate *l* before line 15 as follows:

```java
l = new Jlabel( "Hello" );
```

49. *ActionListener* and *ActionEvent* need to be imported. To fix the problem, add the following *import* statement:

```java
import java.awt.event.*;
```

13.10   Exercises, Problems, and Projects

13.10.1   Multiple Choice Exercises

1. may or may not be *static*

4. calls itself

7. a run-time error

13.10.2   Reading and Understanding Code

10. 0

13. 3
```

16. There is no output

19. *foo3* outputs the argument *String* in reverse

22. 64

13.10.3   Fill in the Code

25. `return foo( s.substring( 2, s.length( ) ) );`

28.
```
if ( n >= 1000 )     // base case
   return n;
else                 // general case
   return foo( n * n );
```

13.10.4   Identifying Errors in Code

31. In the *else* clause, the *return* keyword is missing.

13.10.5   Debugging Area

34. The base case is not coded properly; it needs to return a value, not make another recursive call. Instead of *return foo(0);*, you can code *return 1;*

37. In the general case, the method makes the recursive call with the original *String* less the last two characters as the argument. Therefore, there should be two base cases: when the *String* has 0 characters (empty *String*) and when the *String* has one character. Assuming this method counts the number of characters in the *String* argument, we can add the following code after the first base case:

```
else if ( s.length( ) == 1 )
   return 1;
```

14.12   Exercises, Problems, and Projects

14.12.1   Multiple Choice Exercises

1. Linked lists are easily expanded.

4. (*7, Ajay, NFL*)

7. (*7, Ajay, NFL*) and (*5, Joe, Sonic*)

10. *front* = 3, stores 54; *back* = 0, stores 62

13. *front* = 7; *back* = 6; the list is empty

14.12.2   Reading and Understanding Code

16. If the list is not empty, it resets it to empty and returns *true*. Otherwise, it returns *false*.

19. It outputs all the *Player* objects in the list whose *game* field is *Diablo*.

14.12.3   Fill in the Code

22.
```
previous.getNext( ).setNext(
                    previous.getNext( ).getNext( ).getNext( ) );
```

25.
```
public LLNode( char newGrade )
{
  grade = newGrade;
  next = null;
}
```

28.
```
public void setGrade( char newGrade )
{
  grade = newGrade;
}
public void setNext( LLNode newNext )
{
  next = newNext;
}
```

31.
```
public int numberOfItems( )
{
  int count = 0;
  LLNode current = head;
  while ( current != null )
  {
    count++;
    current = current.getNext( );
  }
  return count;
}
```

14.12.4   Identifying Errors in Code

34. The *getID* method belongs to the *Player* class and cannot be called using *head*, a *PlayerNode* object reference.

37. The number of items in the queue would never increase and we would always be able to insert into that queue, eventually overwriting items that are in the queue. This is a logic error. Furthermore, the

queue would always be considered empty since the number of items always has the value 0. We would never be able to delete an item from the queue.

14.12.5   Debugging Area

40. There is no *getHead* method in the *PlayerLinkedList* class. In order to get a copy of the *Player* object stored at the first node of the list, we can code a method returning the *Player*.

Index

Outstanding New Titles:

Computer Science Illuminated, Second Edition
Nell Dale and John Lewis
ISBN: 0-7637-2626-5
©2004

Introduction to Programming with Visual Basic .NET
Gary J. Bronson and David Rosenthal
ISBN: 0-7637-2478-5
©2005

Information Security Illuminated
Michael G. Solomon and Mike Chapple
ISBN: 0-7637-2677-X
©2005

Calculus: The Language of Change
David W. Cohen and James Henle
ISBN: 0-7637-2947-7
©2005

Applied Calculus For Scientists & Engineers: A Journey in Dialogues
Frank Blume
ISBN: 0-7637-2877-2
©2005

The Tao of Computing
Henry Walker
ISBN: 0-7637-2552-8
©2005

Databases Illuminated
Catherine Ricardo
ISBN: 0-7637-3314-8
©2004

Foundations of Algorithms Using Java Pseudocode
Richard Neapolitan and Kumarss Naimipour
ISBN: 0-7637-2129-8
©2004

Artificial Intelligence Illuminated
Ben Coppin
ISBN: 0-7637-3230-3
©2004

Programming and Problem Solving with C++, Fourth Edition
Nell Dale and Chip Weems
ISBN: 0-7637-0798-8
©2004

Java 5 Illuminated: An Active Learning Approach
Julie Anderson and Hervé Franceschi
ISBN: 0-7637-1667-7
©2005

Programming in C++, Third Edition
Nell Dale and Chip Weems
ISBN: 0-7637-3234-6
©2005

Computer Networking Illuminated
Diane Barrett and Todd King
ISBN: 0-7637-2676-1
©2005

Computer Systems, Third Edition
J. Stanley Warford
ISBN: 0-7637-3239-7
©2005

A Gateway to Higher Mathematics
Jason Goodfriend
ISBN: 0-7637-2733-4
©2005

Linear Algebra with Applications, Fifth Edition
Gareth Williams
ISBN: 0-7637-3235-4
©2005

Readings in CyberEthics, Second Edition
Richard Spinello and Herman Tavani
ISBN: 0-7637-2410-6
©2004

C#.NET Illuminated
Art Gittleman
ISBN: 0-7637-2593-5
©2005

Take Your Courses to the Next Level

Turn the page to preview new and forthcoming titles in Computer Science and Math from Jones and Bartlett...

Providing solutions for students and educators in the following disciplines:

- Introductory Computer Science
- Java
- C++
- Databases
- C#
- Data Structures

- Algorithms
- Network Security
- Software Engineering
- Discrete Mathematics
- Engineering Mathematics
- Complex Analysis

Please visit http://computerscience.jbpub.com/ and http://math.jbpub.com/ to learn more about our exciting publishing programs in these disciplines.